COURAGE
AND
CONSEQUENCE

—◆—

My Life as a Conservative in the Fight

—◆—

KARL ROVE

THRESHOLD EDITIONS

NEW YORK   LONDON   TORONTO   SYDNEY

Threshold Editions
A Division of Simon & Schuster, Inc.
1230 Avenue of the Americas
New York, NY 10020

First Threshold Editions hardcover edition March 2010

THRESHOLD EDITIONS and colophon are trademarks of Simon & Schuster, Inc.

For information about special discounts for bulk purchases,
please contact Simon & Schuster Special Sales at
1-866-506-1949 or business@simonandschuster.com.

The Simon & Schuster Speakers Bureau can bring authors to your live event.
For more information or to book an event contact the Simon & Schuster Speakers Bureau
at 1-866-248-3049 or visit our website at www.simonspeakers.com.

Designed by Joy O'Meara

Manufactured in the United States of America

10   9   8   7   6   5   4   3   2   1

ISBN 978-1-4391-9105-7
ISBN 978-1-4391-6658-1 (ebook)

Insert photo credits: PAGES 1, 3: Photos courtesy of the Rove family; PAGE 2: Photo
courtesy of the Rove family (top), postcard courtesy of Dan Mintz (bottom); PAGES 4, 5, 7,
8, 9, 11, 14, 15, 16: Photos by Eric Draper, courtesy of the George W. Bush Presidential
Library; PAGE 6: Top photo by Eric Draper, courtesy of the George W. Bush Presidential
Library; bottom photo by Paul Morse, courtesy of the George W. Bush Presidential Library;
PAGE 10: Photo © Brooks Kraft/Corbis; PAGE 12: Top photo by Tina Hager, courtesy of the
George W. Bush Presidential Library; bottom photo by David Bohrer, courtesy of the George
W. Bush Presidential Library; PAGE 13: Top photo by Joyce N. Boghosian, courtesy of the
George W. Bush Presidential Library; bottom photo by Shealah Craighead, courtesy of the
George W. Bush Presidential Library

To Andrew and Darby,
Louis and Reba

CONTENTS

The Road to History

On September 11, 2001, I was the first person to tell President George W. Bush that a plane had slammed into an office tower in New York City and was aboard Air Force One as it crisscrossed the country in the hours that followed. I was caught in the sweep of history, in a moment much larger than someone who came from where I did could have expected to be in. It was a turning point for a presidency and the country. The courage and conviction I saw among those aboard Air Force One and in the White House in the years ahead gave me the confidence of having been on the right side of the fight.

Politics is often considered a contact sport, and it is. But the focus on its play by play can obscure why politics is important in the first place: it provides an arena where Americans determine whose ideas will lead the country and how these will change people's lives. Leaders with conviction often shape the outcomes in that arena.

Politics is high-pressure, high-stakes, and often frustrating. It's also flooded with moments of joy, excitement, and victory. One of those moments for me came on January 20, 2001—the day George W. Bush was sworn in as President of the United States. I had made my way to the White House with my wife, Darby, to see my new West Wing office. As I approached the building, I was momentarily taken aback when a Marine snapped to attention and opened a door for us. I hesitated for just a second. I thought, *Do we walk through that door?* And then, *When I do, I become a witness to history.*

It was the start of a presidency, and a milepost in my life in politics. Along the way, there were moments where I thought I had sidelined

myself—as when I quit George H. W. Bush's nascent presidential campaign in 1978. And there were moments of luck and even surprise—one
of them in my twenties, when I knocked on a door only to find Elizabeth
Taylor standing in front of me wearing a revealing nightgown and inviting me in.

There were also moments of peril, enormous stress, and danger. In
my desk at home, I keep a copy of a newspaper clipping—a picture of
I. Lewis "Scooter" Libby and his wife. Scooter was a friend and the chief
of staff to Vice President Dick Cheney. On October 28, 2005, his world
came undone when a federal grand jury indicted him for obstructing an
investigation and lying to federal agents and a grand jury.

I keep that clipping because it reminds me of how brutal politics can
be, and because it captures a moment that is well known but widely misunderstood. What led to Scooter's indictment was a policy disagreement
that devolved into a legal fight. For me, being a subject of a federal investigation was a harrowing experience. But it was a small piece of a much
larger debate about a central issue of the Bush presidency—whether it
was right to have gone to war against Iraq.

I worked fifteen steps from the Oval Office. From that vantage point,
this book will set the record straight. It will pull back the curtain on my
journey to the White House and my years there. I will acknowledge mistakes. And I will make the case—defiantly and unapologetically—for
many controversial decisions.

I have often wondered how it was that I had landed where I have in
life. Growing up, I had a nerdish fascination with our political system.
But that's true of lots of kids. There wasn't anything special about my
family that would lead naturally to a front-row seat to history. When I
was young, my family bumped around the Rocky Mountain West, living
on the shabby side of the middle class. As a geologist, my dad was often
gone for months at a time on work. For a time in college, I had nowhere
to live and was lucky to find a space to sleep in the unheated storage
space above the porch in a fraternity house. Not exactly a grand start in
life.

It was, however, an appropriate one. Everyone's early life shapes their
perspective. Mine grew out of Western values that emphasized limitless
opportunities, even when people's circumstances constrain their lives.
The experiences I had early in my life helped make me a conservative

and led me both to the Republican Party and to the belief that I could make a contribution to the political battles that are the lifeblood of a democracy.

What follows is my account of the arc of my life, why I bent it one way over another, and how a kid from a broken home could be called "the architect" by a conservative president whose courage and conviction led our nation through consequential times.

CHAPTER I

A Broken Family on the Western Front

———— • ◆ • ————

Have you heard the joke about the Norwegian farmer who loved his wife so much he almost told her? My father—Louis C. Rove, Jr.—was a Norwegian, one of those taciturn midwesterners who held back a lot. But in the last decades of life, Dad began to open up about himself, his marriage, and my childhood. He would meet me and my wife, Darby, in Santa Fe for the opera and the Chamber Music Festival each summer, and while exploring New Mexico, he would reveal secrets of our family life that were shocking because they were so intimate. But I disclose them here because my early years have been painted very differently. There is something to be said about setting the record straight, especially when it involves your kin.

So before I get to my career in politics, I want to tell the real story of my family, with all the love and heartbreak it contained. My father was a geologist. At about six feet tall, trim, with short-cropped blond hair and glasses, he had a kind but somber demeanor. Born in Wisconsin, he served briefly in the Navy at the end of World War II. Afterward, he spent a year at Hope College in Michigan. Inspired by his uncle Olaf Rove, a consulting geologist of some renown, my father then transferred to the Colorado School of Mines, in Golden, Colorado.

It was there that he met my mother, Reba Wood. There were many differences. Dad was college-educated, well-read, and had grown up in a sensibly middle-class home with books, classical music, and opera. My mother never went to college, never had been exposed to books or classical music, and wasn't interested in them. It may have been that she was the only girl in a family that prized boys, or else it was an early misfortune that was hidden from me, but regardless, while she appeared strong and in control, in reality she was fragile. Her brittleness, emotional pain, and suffering were out of most people's view. But she and Dad were drawn to each other: he to her beauty and passion, and she to his solid dependability and dashing good looks. For a very long time, they were very much in love.

Mom was the only daughter of Robert G. and Elsie Wood and had three younger brothers. My maternal grandfather never went to college, but he was full of drive, dreams, and integrity. During the Depression, he found work on a Colorado Highway Department crew. Later, from a wooden shelf on the backseat of his car, Grandpa started selling butcher knives he had bought on consignment, to out-of-the-way grocery stores in southern Colorado. He eventually built it into a business—Robert G. Wood & Company, "Quality Butcher Supplies." It was to provide a good livelihood for three generations of Woods. I was to spend many happy hours in his shop in Denver and around Grandfather Wood and my three uncles.

My grandparents lived in the same house for most of their adult lives, at 3045 Lowell Boulevard in Denver. The only luxury they allowed themselves was travel, recorded on a primitive motion picture camera by my grandfather. Over a twenty-year period, they went to Mexico, worked their way through South America; flew to Hawaii; traveled to Lebanon, Israel, and Egypt in simpler times in the region; visited Cambodia and Vietnam before they became dangerous; and went to Japan when it no longer was. It was a highlight after each trip to go to our grandparents' house to see my grandfather's movies, carefully narrated by him. My grandmother decorated their house with things brought home from their travels, whether trinkets, rubbings from the Angkor Wat temples, or Peruvian village retablos.

When my grandfather died of a heart attack on Labor Day 1974, my grandmother attempted suicide by shooting herself in the stomach. She lived another twenty-five years in pain and loneliness, mourning her husband and, I later was to discover, indirectly showing her loved ones that suicide was an acceptable way to deal with hardship.

I was born early on Christmas Day 1950, in a hospital elevator in Denver, Colorado. I guess I started out eager to get going. I grew up on the genteel fringes of the lower middle class, the second oldest in what became a family of five kids—three boys (an older brother and a younger one) and two sisters (both younger). We lived in Colorado until I was nine; in Sparks, Nevada, until I was fifteen; and then in Holladay, Utah, as my father followed opportunities in the mining business.

In the 1950s, being a young geologist specializing in uranium, lead, zinc, and copper was not a lucrative calling, but it was a demanding profession. Dad was often gone for months at a time on stints in Angola and Mozambique; in Aruba; in Manitoba, Alberta, and on the Queen Charlotte Islands of Canada; in Alaska; and all across the western part of the lower forty-eight states. His trips prompted a childish interest in vexillology: I used to draw pictures of the flags of the countries and states he worked in and treasured a small book of flags of nations and history he gave me.

I keep a picture of my father on a shelf near my desk. It was taken in a remote corner of Angola in the early 1950s. He is surrounded by bush children who probably had not seen many Westerners. When I was young, the picture seemed to me to be of a young, tanned demigod. In reality, he was a gangly young man fresh out of college, trying to chart his way in life.

We were brought up on tales of Africa, of his beloved monkey Chico, who later died in the Lisbon Zoo, and how my father had come to possess an eighteen-foot-long snakeskin, a zebra hide, and a rhinoceros horn—revered as sacred family totems in our home. We showed them to our friends with great ceremony.

In Colorado, our family first lived briefly in the company town of Kokomo, near the Climax mine north of Leadville. Then we moved to a house in a big field outside Arvada. There was a large pond in the southeast corner and a ditch meandered over the lower part of the property, providing welcome territory for games and exploring.

We had a chicken coop and a garden that provided us with much-needed eggs, carrots, tomatoes, and green beans. To this day, I think there's almost nothing better than a ripe strawberry plucked fresh from the garden and nothing worse than eggplant, especially when it's been fried the night before and served cold for breakfast because you left it on your dinner plate.

We never lacked for anything we really needed, but the family budget was always under pressure. My mother could spend more money to less effect than almost anyone I have ever known. To her credit, she tried earning money, but her ideas usually lasted only a season or two. One year, we collected pinecones and sold them to local nurseries. Then Mom became an Avon lady and my brother and I (and eventually all the kids) became experts at bagging orders. I knew by heart the code for almost every shade of Avon lipstick. We delivered newspapers, cut grass, babysat the neighbors' kids, sold lemonade, and helped out at Grandfather's store. As a teenager, I waited tables and washed dishes, ran a cash register at a hippie shop that sold patchouli oil, worked in a hospital kitchen, and held down the night shift at a convenience store. My parents made me quit the last job after I was robbed twice—once with a pistol and the second time with a sawed-off shotgun. I was stoic during the robberies, but shaken afterward and happy my parents insisted I quit.

Even with all these efforts, and especially when we were young, there didn't seem to be enough money. The Christmas I turned five, the bonus Dad had been promised turned out to be a pittance, leaving him with no money for presents, so he talked a buddy who flew a helicopter like the one in the *M*A*S*H* television show into landing his chopper in the dusty field surrounding our house and taking us up. Dad explained it was Santa's helicopter, so we had to take our ride the day before Christmas rather than on Christmas itself. It's still the best Christmas I ever had.

For my brothers and sisters and me, it seemed like an idyllic childhood, with Boy Scouts, Little League, playing "war" in the fields nearby, stamp and coin collections, trading baseball cards, and fried chicken dinners on Sunday at our grandparents' house, where we watched *Bonanza* and *The Wonderful World of Disney* on their color TV. I looked up to my older brother, Eric, even though he used to beat me up, as all older brothers do. I thought he was the smartest person I knew. He spent his life outdoors, working in highway construction after attending the University of Nevada. Alma, six years younger than me, looked the most like

Mom and, like her, had more than her share of misfortune in life. Olaf, eight years younger than me, was a happy and thoroughly content child who grew up to run computer systems. And the baby, Reba—nine years younger than me—was especially smart, disciplined, funny, prone to tricks, and, at least when it comes to her childhood memories, also prone to good-hearted exaggeration. We were an outgoing, active group.

We didn't have a television at home until we moved to Nevada. Dad said it was because he wanted us to read, exercise our minds, and do our homework. I suspect family finances had something to do with it, too. When he was home and read to us or made us listen to the opera sponsored by Texaco and explained the stories we were hearing, not having a television didn't matter so much.

During breaks from school, Dad would take his children with him when he had geological fieldwork nearby. It fostered a love of the open spaces of the West and of nature and its processes. Dad's frequent travels and our family's mobility made me a natural extrovert, with both the ability and the need to make friends and connect with others. And living in a tidy middle-class household with only a few, but nice, pieces of furniture and art never made me yearn for material things.

Mom ran the household in Dad's absence and she could alternately act like a Marine drill instructor or a soft, caring figure. She was not stable or predictable and had a penchant for melodrama. The family was always headed over a cliff tomorrow. She would be seized by some crisis and then share her fear with her children. The moment would eventually pass for her, but some anxiety and uncertainty would remain with us.

My father and my grandfather helped organize the First Presbyterian Church of Golden, Colorado, so there was also Sunday school and summer church camp. The young minister they called to the pulpit told me many years later that he and my dad attended a local Presbyterian meeting where the little daughter of one of the pastors played the piano to entertain the group. She was Condoleezza Rice, whose father, John, was an associate pastor at Montview Presbyterian Church in Denver. My parents were later active in helping form Westminster Presbyterian Church in Sparks, pressing me into service as a canvasser and then an usher.

We caught glimpses of life's casual cruelty, especially after we moved to Nevada when I was nine. Sometimes neighborhood kids would show up unannounced for dinner at our house, which was inevitably spaghetti or macaroni and cheese with hamburger meat. I learned that these kids were from families where the parents had gambled away their paychecks. The experience gave me a lifelong aversion to gambling.

Because my father was often gone and my mother prone to erratic behavior, I took refuge in books. They were dependable, solid, and an exciting escape to a better place. "There is no Frigate like a Book / To take us Lands away," Emily Dickinson once wrote. I wasn't good at sports, and my family couldn't afford entertainment, so books were my savior: you can blame them for my love of politics, and the career it produced.

I still have the first frigate I can remember reading: a gift from my second-grade teacher called *Great Moments in History*. Its pages on the Declaration of Independence, the Constitution, the Alamo, and the Civil War fascinated me. I read everything I could get my hands on, especially biographies and histories. The coming of the centennial of the Civil War in 1960 meant I was exposed at the age of seven to a flood of books on it.

To me, the Civil War was not just compelling and stirring, it was real. It was a true drama of real people with real lives whose decisions settled the question of whether the young democracy would remain Lincoln's "last, best hope of freedom." I pored over Civil War picture books and even copied the wartime drawings from *Frank Leslie's Illustrated Newspaper* and *Harper's Weekly*, which appeared in Fletcher Pratt's *Civil War in Pictures*. The maps in the *American Heritage Picture History of the Civil War* especially enthralled me. They were pictures of the battlefields with drawings of tiny armies, North and South, smashing into each other at Bull Run, Spotsylvania, Gettysburg, Vicksburg, Atlanta, Petersburg, and Appomattox.

But my bookishness doesn't entirely explain why I fell in love with politics and became a Republican. My parents never expressed an interest in politics. My mother voted Republican in 1970 because I was working for the GOP, but in 1972 she voted for the Peace and Freedom Party, headed by radical Eldridge Cleaver, because my brother was supporting it.

Republicanism fit with my childhood of growing up in the Rocky Mountain West, a place of big horizons, long vistas, and most important of all, a palpable sense of freedom. There is something about the West that encourages individualism and personal responsibility, values I thought best reflected by Republicans. In the West, people tend to be judged on their merits, not their pedigree. From there, Washington seems undependable and a long way away.

At the age of nine, I decided I was for Richard Nixon in the 1960 presidential election. I got my hands on a Nixon bumper sticker, slapped it on my bike's wire basket, and rode up and down the block, as if that alone would get him a vote. Instead it drew the attention of a little girl who lived in the neighborhood. She had a few years and about thirty pounds on me and was enthusiastically for John F. Kennedy. She pulled me from my bicycle and beat the heck out of me, leaving me with a bloody nose and a tattered ego. I've never liked losing a political fight since.

At the age of thirteen, I was wild for Barry Goldwater. I loved that his philosophy celebrated freedom and responsibility, the dignity and worth of every individual, the danger of intrusive government, and the importance of politics to protecting those ideals. I had Goldwater buttons, stickers, and posters, a ragged paperback copy of Goldwater's *The Conscience of a Conservative*, and even a bright gold aluminum can of "Au H_2O," a campaign artifact that played on the candidate's last name. I got ahold of a Goldwater sign, but it didn't last long in our front yard. I don't know whether my parents or a supporter of Lyndon Baines Johnson removed it. LBJ not only crushed the Arizona senator, he also crushed me. I was devastated. But for budding Republicans like me, there was nobility in Goldwater's loss. He went down with guns blazing and his ideology on full, unapologetic display. Goldwater was a "conviction politician," the kind who shaped a movement.

Economics came on my radar screen when I was twelve or thirteen, when someone gave me a copy of *Capitalism and Freedom*, by Milton Friedman, one of the greatest defenders and advocates of capitalism. "Government power must be dispersed. If government is to exercise power, better in the county than in the state, better in the state than in Washington," he wrote. Reading Friedman led me to next plow through Adam Smith's *Wealth of Nations*. The pin maker, the division of labor, and the "invisible hand"—all of it made sense to me.

Then there was William F. Buckley, Jr. The Sparks, Nevada, library had a subscription to Buckley's *National Review* magazine, with its unadorned cover and its bold credenda. I eagerly awaited its arrival each week, devouring articles using words I didn't know (such as *denouement*) but whose meaning I could often guess. I couldn't get my hands on Buckley's books quickly enough. At age fifteen I laughed out loud all the way through *The Unmaking of a Mayor*.

When I took my first civics course in the fourth or fifth grade, and classmates were doing their first term papers on "Our Constitution" or "The Congress," I was writing on the communist theory of dialectical materialism, since I had read Karl Marx. But I wanted a bridge from the world of ideas to the world of practical politics—and at fifteen, I received my first experience in government.

Between junior high and high school, I wrangled a summer internship in the Washoe County clerk's office in Reno, Nevada. At the beginning of that summer, my family moved from Sparks to Holladay, Utah, near Salt Lake City. I stayed behind, living with my scoutmaster and his wife and spending the summer riding the bus to and from the courthouse to work. Somehow, filing papers and making photocopies in the clerk's office seemed exciting and fresh. The process of government was thrilling. I spent most of my time filing crime and divorce papers, but I also watched trials and county commission meetings and even sat in on the Board of Equalization, though I couldn't figure out what they were talking about, other than that it had to do with money and taxes. I was fascinated by county government and read whatever I could find about the esoteric disputes of county government theory.

Summer ended on a thrilling social note. On the final day of my internship, the cute eighteen-year-old clerk asked me to walk her home. Outside her apartment she gave me a quick kiss (my first). But the last bus from downtown Reno home to Sparks was fast approaching its stop a block away, so I had to bid her good-bye and run to catch it.

As we settled into a modest house in Holladay in the fall of 1966, I entered Olympus High School in suburban Salt Lake City feeling lost. I didn't know anyone. I was a non-Mormon in a school where 90 percent or more of the students did follow that faith. I had no particular skill at sports or with girls. But I did have an ability: I could talk and argue. I was fortunate that at Olympus specifically, and in Utah generally, high school debate was a big deal, an activity where a bookish boy could find affirmation. I joined the debate team, found my tribe, and was off.

The coach, Diana Childs, paired me with Mark Dangerfield, who was a year ahead of me. Mark and I clicked right away. He had a great smile, a sharp mind, a competitive spirit, and the ability to scrape away some of my rough edges. We turned out to be alike in many ways.

For example, we were obsessive about preparation. We wanted better research and more of it than any of our competitors (a habit I still have to this day). We spent a small fortune on four-by-six-inch cards on which we wrote our information in precise block lettering or typed it with a small manual typewriter we had scored at a secondhand sale. We then meticulously arranged the cards in giant boxes behind dividers that made possible the quick recovery of facts, quotes, and authorities. I developed an elaborate color scheme to help us pluck just the right card at that special moment to confound the opposing pair of debaters.

In high school debate, you had to be ready to argue both sides of the question on a moment's notice. So we picked apart our own arguments, anticipated the counterarguments, and picked those apart, too. Gaming the debate out as many moves in advance as possible was great training for politics. Debate gave me the habit of examining the case of my candidate and that of his opponent. In a campaign, you need to think not just about what you want to say now, but how that train of arguments, and even events, will play out over time. It taught me that staying on offense was important and that once you were on defense, it was hard to regain control of the dialogue.

Being fanatical about research, Mark and I came up with a favorite tactic. We'd quote authorities the opposition had never heard of, and when they rose to dismiss our source, we'd roll out their impressive title such as the "Assistant Secretary of Defense for International Security Affairs" and express astonishment that our worthy opponents had never heard of that significant policy leader.

The debates were staged in high school classrooms, generally in front of speech, history, or world affairs classes. They were often tough audiences, uninterested in what we had to say but stuck in their seats and forced to listen to the scrawny guys in three-piece suits. If we got them to laugh or otherwise favorably respond, it was almost as good as getting the most points on a judge's score sheet. We became the only undefeated team in the statewide high school speech and debate competition, and won an important western regional meet as well.

Debate led to other activities. I became involved in Model U.N., which was big in Utah, and eventually became Model U.N. Club president. I took part in speech competitions such as the Veterans of Foreign Wars' "Voice of Democracy" and the American Legion's "Americanism" contests. Students delivered patriotic addresses on an assigned topic to veterans audiences. I won several competitions, even traveling to Merced, California, for a western regional contest.

Debate wasn't the only way my horizons were broadened in high school. My political vista was ready to be stretched as well. The man who would do that was a short, natty, bespectacled, bow-tie-wearing high school teacher named Eldon M. Tolman. He was a lot of things I wasn't and didn't like—including a Democrat, and not just any kind, but an LBJ Democrat. Tolman was also a union official, president of the local chapter of the Utah Education Association. If I learned anything from Goldwater, it was not to trust union bosses.

But those differences were far less important than the fact that Tolman loved politics and wanted his students to love it, too. To his credit, he didn't care what his students' views were. As luck would have it, he was my teacher in 1968, and he made sure I kept up with all that year's earth-shattering events. But he also took me aside and in his prim, proper manner told me that if I wanted an A, I had to get involved in a political campaign. At the time, I was a little over five feet tall, had glasses with thick frames, wore hush puppies, and carried a briefcase. A's mattered a lot to me.

The campaign I chose was that of Utah's senior United States senator, Wallace F. Bennett. Bennett was seventy years old, having been elected to the Senate the year I was born. A brash, charismatic young professor at the University of Utah named J. D. Williams was running for the Democratic nomination. Anger was rising at the Vietnam War and many young people across the country were flocking to support antiwar candidates like Williams. Bennett supported the war and, unbeknownst to me, was planning a big effort among young people to counter the Democrats' appeal.

Somehow I became the Salt Lake County high school chairman of Students for Bennett. I cajoled friends to volunteer, handed out stickers, worked at the headquarters, and recruited teams of similarly minded young political junkies to put out yard signs and attend campaign events.

There weren't that many of us, so I pressed my younger siblings into service frequently.

Tolman, meanwhile, decided that in the spring Olympus would have mock conventions in which students would nominate the presidential tickets. I threw myself into helping organize the GOP one. Hundreds of students played the roles of state delegations and party leaders. Like the real Republican National Convention, we nominated Richard Nixon—but not before we'd made the rounds of campaign headquarters, scoring buttons, banners, and baloney to decorate the school cafeteria for our convention.

Tolman's greatest contribution was to make certain that his students saw all the presidential candidates who came to town. It's hard today to think of Utah as a swing state, but in 1968 it was. The three major candidates—Nixon, Hubert Humphrey, and George Wallace—appeared at the Mormon Tabernacle in Salt Lake, and I saw them all.

Wallace was angry, belligerent, and nasty, and even to my untrained ears, a pure demagogue. A protester heckled and the Alabama governor taunted him back, saying that if the protester lay down in front of Wallace's limousine, it would be the last one he'd lie down for. The crowd screamed in agreement. As the Alabama bantam rooster strutted on the Tabernacle stage, I realized this was the first time I had seen a bigot, and the racial hatred he engendered, up close. I actually felt fear: his harangue was practiced and effective, and drew angry shrieks from the audience. These ordinary people were furious with their country and this man fed their frustration.

Nixon was polished and programmed, promising change "from top to bottom." He was an odd combination: one of the most effective politicians of that year, yet a man who was visibly uncomfortable as a campaigner. He drove himself by force of will to great heights. Vice President Humphrey struck me as nervous and old-fashioned. Nelson Rockefeller came across as a patrician with a nice, unforced backslapping folksiness when he came to open his Utah campaign headquarters. He also had the best campaign materials and plenty of them. Robert Kennedy stirred the crowd into a frenzy but he seemed cerebral, distant, and tired, yet inspiring and sad, all at the same time. I saw Ronald Reagan leave Republicans on their feet screaming and cheering in the loudest room I'd ever been in.

The antiwar Eugene McCarthy was aloof and cold at a rally in a downtown park.

I had, then, a front-row seat in a rare, memorable, and consequential
year in American politics, all courtesy of a liberal high school teacher who
loved politics and his students. I was permanently bitten. I even became a
candidate myself. In fact, for the first time I watched a savvy campaign
manager (my world history teacher) pick a neophyte candidate (me), run
a clever campaign, and produce a winner.

She insisted I run for second vice president of the student body, even
though my nerds weren't numerous enough to elect anyone. But she recruited the senior captain of the basketball team and the popular senior
girl with the brand-new yellow sports car to co-chair my campaign. I had
instant credibility with influential endorsements and the adroit behind-
the-scenes maneuvering of a powerful sponsor. The fix was in.

There were two activities by which Olympus students judged candidates for student body office. The first was the quality of the posters candidates hung in the hallways. A friend who was an art student helped me
and my debate team buddies manufacture dozens of posters using cut-
outs from magazines and then covered them with a shiny shellac to make
them stand out. Most of the posters were witty, risqué, and eye-catching.
Having the help of people who played with words for fun turned out to be
an unanticipated advantage. I recall only one poster: it echoed a popular car ad by encouraging students to "Support the Mini-Brute." I was
confident we had the best ad blitz—but would that be enough?

The second test of the candidates was skits and speeches. My opponent, John, had gotten elected sophomore and junior class president on
the strength of being rolled into the gym in a full-sized cardboard out-
house, from which he sprang to give a speech sprinkled with references to
his fake outdoor commode. (A john—get it?) It had worked for him
twice and we correctly anticipated he'd fall back on the tactic again. Students had seen it before, so its novelty had worn off. But we had a surprise: As my name was announced over the sound system, we fired up a
VW convertible, flung open the gym doors, and drove the bright Bug
into the packed arena with a basketball hero in the front seat behind the
wheel and me in the back waving to the crowd, flanked by two attractive
girls. Principal John Larsen, a tall, brooding hulk, reacted to the scene
with a scowl that would have scared the bejesus out of the toughest biker

gang. But a VW driving across the gym with the nerd in the back between two babes brought the students to their feet cheering and laughing and made my remarks almost unnecessary. I won.

Something else happened to me that fired up my love of politics: I went to Washington, D.C. I was chosen by my state for the Hearst Foundation's U.S. Senate Youth Program, a seminar in the nation's capital on American government. I met senators, congressmen, past and future presidential candidates (Barry Goldwater and Ted Kennedy), and a future president (Gerald Ford). But the week culminated in a visit to the White House to meet President Nixon. When it came time to shake the president's hand in the receiving line, he asked me where I was from. When I told him Utah, he said, "It's really something when the Mormon Tabernacle Choir begins to sing, 'This is my country!' " as he warbled the tune for a few notes. I was taken aback by the singing president, which seemed to me so out of character, and wasn't quite sure what to make of the whole thing.

But for a boy of my interests, the week could not have been more exciting. It wasn't just the history that permeated every street corner, the famous buildings, the museums and monuments. This was the center of politics for the world's most powerful nation, a place where high-minded ideas and less high-minded practical politics mingled. I left Washington with a raging, incurable case of Potomac fever. I didn't know how and I didn't know when, but I knew someday, some way, I'd be back.

But while I was finding my life's work, my family was falling apart. In late 1968, Dad had gotten a new job with Getty Oil's minerals division in Los Angeles. At first the plan was for the family to join him by moving to California after my graduation from high school the following spring. But as the winter turned to spring, my mother hinted that the plans were on hold, raising questions about whether the Getty job would last. So facing application deadlines, I sent my paperwork off to the University of Utah. If we were still going to be living in Salt Lake, it was the only place I could afford to go. Between the mortgage, my father's small apartment in Los Angeles, and my brother's expenses at the University of Nevada in Reno, the family's finances were tight. In the fall of 1969 I entered the University of Utah with high hopes and, I thought, a bright future. I found the College Republicans and a fraternity, Pi Kappa Alpha.

Then it all started to go bad. My brothers and sisters and I were all looking forward to Christmas. Dad was coming up from L.A. for an extended stay. He hadn't been home since the summer and, I believe, had been out of the country on geological work for part of the fall. There was tension simmering in the household about why the family hadn't moved to Los Angeles after I graduated from high school. Dad arrived home on the afternoon of Christmas Eve.

Shortly after Dad's appearance, he and Mom argued—angrily and heatedly. Things were smashed. And Dad left. Before he stormed out the door, he told me where he would be staying until he could get a flight back to California. I didn't know what had caused the argument, but I knew his decision to leave wouldn't be reversed. My mother provided no answers and withdrew to her bedroom. A little while after Dad left, I drove to the airport motel he mentioned and found him getting ready to catch a plane to L.A. He said he was sorry it had come to this, that he loved my mother and she him, and that they both loved all of us children, and he asked me never to forget that. He hugged me, I cried, and we parted—him for the airport and me for the worst Christmas of my life.

It wasn't just that my parents were splitting up. Shortly after New Year's Day, Mom told me I'd have to find somewhere else to live. She was selling the house and moving back to Sparks. She'd always felt uncomfortable in Utah and wanted to return to Nevada immediately. Whether I survived now depended on whether I let myself falter.

After minor negotiations over child support, my parents' marriage was dissolved in a Washoe County courtroom in May 1970. After Mom arrived in Nevada in January, she farmed out my three younger siblings for a month or two to neighbors and friends she knew from Westminster Presbyterian Church in Sparks. My young brother and sisters thought she had returned to Salt Lake to sell the house (whose sale closed days after she left town), and I thought she was in Sparks, but she wasn't in either place. To this day, her whereabouts during that time are a mystery.

My mother's hasty moves made life a lot more difficult. Being left to shift for myself could have been a shattering event. But when faced with adversity, my tendency is to break the problem down into its parts and tackle what I can. I couldn't shrug off that Mom had proved unreliable, but I could focus on keeping things from falling further apart. Recovery would start with finding a place to stay.

I had too little money for an apartment. It was too late to get into a dorm—and that was too much for my budget, anyway. Fortunately, the fraternity house had an empty storage closet under the eaves and I was allowed to stay there until a bunk became available. The price tag for the storage area was in my price range: free. I moved in the day Mom left town.

My "apartment" was cramped and the ceiling slanted downward; I couldn't stand up straight. The floor was the uninsulated ceiling of the outside porch, so the space was cold. I hung my shirts, pants, and coats on a nail and stored everything else in a battered clothes hamper. Like other students, I kept my books on wooden boards held up by cement blocks. Light came from an industrial lamp that was plugged into an outlet with a cord that snaked down the hall. But I had a roof over my head and was grateful for it.

There would be no more meals at home, no family washing machine or dryer, no parents to buy school clothes or provide gas money. I had a few dollars from my part-time job at a gift shop and $500 a semester in tuition and books from a scholarship. I'd have to get more hours at work and figure out how to make ends meet until Mom and Dad were able to send money.

Only it turned out, there wouldn't *be* any money. When Mom surfaced a month or two later by phone, she told me Dad wasn't sending support money even though she was desperately urging him to do so. I found out two years later that my father had religiously sent money to all his children, starting in January 1970, and, starting several months after that, had sent separate checks specifically for me.

My Mom had hidden this from me, as she hid so much from all of us. When it served her purpose and especially when it affected her survival, she had a problem telling the truth.

I asked for more hours and found other jobs, like waiting tables. I got an internship at the Utah Republican Party that came with a small stipend. I watched pennies, ate lots of macaroni and cheese, stopped using my antique light green station wagon—bought during a flush moment the summer after my graduation—and rode the bus or walked instead. A bunk opened up in the frat house that spring after about three months.

But the shocks kept coming. I learned by accident several months later that I had been adopted. My father, it turns out, wasn't really my father. While working in Illinois that summer for a U.S. Senate campaign, I would visit my aunt and uncle who lived in suburban Chicago. My father's sister, Louise, and her husband, Colonel William Ver Hey, often invited me over for a home-cooked meal. The colonel was career Army and a paratrooper with multiple tours in Vietnam. He was my childhood hero, and my aunt reminded me of my father. They were terrific.

On one visit for dinner, the colonel presented me with a grown-up drink (a weak gin and tonic, I think) and the three of us began talking about Dad. Then my aunt said something like "When you were adopted." I dropped my glass. The look on my face must have shaken her, for she worriedly asked if I hadn't known I was adopted. I hadn't.

She then told me the real story: Louis C. Rove, Jr., adopted my older brother, Eric, and me when he married our mother. Eric, two years older than me, apparently recalled our biological father. As a teenager, Eric had tried to contact him but was rebuffed. I was blissfully ignorant about the situation, or at least had driven whatever memories I might have had of my life as a very small child into a dark recess.

After Aunt Louise's revelation, it took me months to finally confront Louis about his failure to mention the fact that he was my adoptive father. After confirming from aunts and uncles on my mother's side that I'd been told the truth, my head was spinning with questions. Why hadn't I been told before? What were the circumstances? Who was my biological father? I just couldn't bring myself to ask Louis these questions over the phone or in a letter. And when we were next together the following summer and I blurted out my questions over dinner in his L.A. apartment, he offered a simple explanation to the first. He said, "It never mattered to me and I hope it never matters to you." I have often thought about his statement, which could be taken as dismissive or nonchalant. I don't think it was either. My dad gave all five of his children unconditional love, whether he had brought them into this world or not. He sacrificed to make certain we wanted for nothing important. He nurtured in us an appreciation of art, music, and books, all priceless gifts. What mattered to him was that he was our father and that he loved us and we loved him.

As to my other questions, he told me that my mother had been married before to a fellow Colorado School of Mines classmate. He gave me the man's whereabouts, but cautioned me not to have high expectations of a relationship. Everything he told me was offered calmly and economically.

It took me more than a dozen years to try to contact my biological father. The delay was partly out of anger that he hadn't tried contacting either Eric or me; in fact, he'd rejected Eric's attempts to contact him. But part of the delay was also because I didn't want anything to interfere with my relationship with Louis. Eventually I reached out to the man who had given me up. I wish I hadn't. Dad had been right to dampen my hopes. While cordial, my biological father made it clear he did not want a relationship. It could have been devastating, but by then I was at peace with the knowledge that the man who raised me was not the man who brought me into the world.

For a long time, Louis was reticent about discussing his life with my mother. It was clear the breakup of his marriage stung deeply. I raised the topic when I visited him in Los Angeles in the summer after my sophomore year, but he refused to say why or how their marriage had dissolved. He also refused to speak ill of my mother, even when we discovered that his child support checks for my college expenses had been rerouted. He encouraged me to think about my mother's sacrifices for me and my brothers and sisters and how much she loved and cared for us. It was apparent he still loved her, regardless of what kept them apart. As for my mother, she never offered an explanation.

Over the years, Dad grew closer to all his children, especially after he retired from Getty and moved from Los Angeles to Palm Springs, California, in 1986. He had a large house with two extra bedrooms that were often filled by his children and grandchildren. It was there that, approaching his seventies, he opened up more about Mom. In response to gentle questions from Darby, Dad emotionally explained she was the love of his life and that he had never stopped loving her. The conversation touched a deep regret, and he started weeping, which I'd seen him do only once before, when his stepmother died. It was shocking to hear a stoic Scandinavian like him talk about his and Mom's physical passion and how, when he returned home from weeks or even months away on geological fieldwork, the "naps" he took were really an excuse to exile the children from the house so the two of them could repair to their bedroom to make love. My parents even tried "dating" years after they divorced, once embarrassing my youngest sister, who found herself their chaperone as they played footsy under the table.

I also think he wept in those later years because he wished he could have saved her. Twelve years after she deserted the family, when I was thirty years old, she committed suicide. Her third, and by now very unhappy, marriage was in the process of ending. It had lasted just three months. She was approaching her fifty-first birthday with the expectation that much of what she had in life—her modest home, her marriage, and her life savings—would all soon be gone. Her house had three mortgages on it. Between her and her latest husband, the little she had of value, everything she had saved, was now gone for boats and gambling and God knows what else. Even my childhood stamp, coin, and baseball card collections were gone. Mom was never good with money, and so a spouse who shared that weakness was a recipe for disaster.

On September 10, she had breakfast with my youngest sister, Reba, and they discussed Mom's declining prospects. The two of them made arrangements for what Mom would do once she had split from her husband—including a place to live and a car to use. Reba thought she had left Mom in good spirits, but Mom failed to appear at home the next day. However, her husband did not call the police.

While on routine patrol, the Washoe County Sheriff's Department found my mother, Reba Wood Rove, slumped over in her small pickup truck. It was September 11, 1981. She had driven into the desert north of Reno, found a secluded but visible place to park, run a piece of hose from the tailpipe through the cracked-open rear window of her pickup, methodically taped the area around the point at which the hose entered the vehicle, gotten in the truck, and killed herself by carbon monoxide poisoning.

Like her mother before her in 1974, my mother had dealt with life's punishing blows by attempting suicide. But unlike my grandmother, Mom succeeded. I was stunned when I got the news but at some deep level I had always known she was capable of this. My mother had struggled, even in placid waters, to keep a grip on life.

Why did she do it? There aren't easy answers. Mom left two letters in the truck, one to whoever found her and the other to her children. The first was to make it clear to the police that she took her own life and was not a victim of foul play. In the letter to her children, she wrote of her love for each of us and her pride in how we'd "grown up and matured into fine adults." She expressed her disappointment that after the "great hope" for a life with her new husband, "things hadn't turned out that way." "Living alone and being so bossy and making all the decisions that had to be made—made me into a very hard person to share a life with," she wrote, before saying, "it has also made me very tired, deep inside tired. So I am taking my own life and I know this is a chicken way to do it. Please forgive me for failing all of you." She wrote a few lines for her granddaughters and then closed, "Love you all—please forgive me."

I suspect she killed herself because her third marriage failed. Life had been hard for her after she failed to follow my father to Los Angeles in 1969. If our family had moved to L.A. after my high school graduation, as my parents had planned, I believe there would have been no reason for her to drive into the desert, write such a wretched letter, and then so meticulously end her life.

I write about this in more detail than is comfortable for me because some journalists have used her divorce and her death to advance theories about me. One journalist alleged that my father was gay and that my parents separated that Christmas Eve because he "informed his wife that he was gay and that he was coming out of the closet and wanted a divorce." Another journalist suggested Dad's coming out meant my mother "suffered emotional damage from which she never fully healed."

A pair of journalists wrote that as "a man of almost startling intelligence," I was "not likely to have ignored the possibility that [my] father's homosexuality might have figured in [my] mother's choice to end her own life." Actually, it never occurred to me that this would be the reason she wanted to kill herself. None of the five Rove children heard such a thing or believe that was the cause of their divorce and her lifelong pain. If this was the issue she wrestled with and lost to, she would have talked about it with family or close friends. But to her children, family, and friends she mainly talked of too little money or her fear of being without a loving husband; she never spoke of Louis's alleged homosexuality. Just over a year after their separation, Mom wrote Dad to admit "I am sorry I caused you so many lonely hours . . . I made a mistake by not moving [the children] with you to L.A." She wrote again to deny she'd been having an affair at the time of the breakup. These suggest that other reasons were at the heart of their dispute and they are a reminder of playwright

Tom Stoppard's insight: "No one, no matter how well informed, can possibly know what goes on inside a marriage except the two principals themselves."

Some reporters—a relatively small percentage, it should be pointed out—speculate on things they know nothing about in order to attack those with whom they politically disagree. They are an example of the ugliness to which journalism and journalists can descend. They are driven by hatred, and hatred submerges everything, including journalistic standards and even basic decency. Some reporters are inclined to practice psychology without a license—one of the modern media's biggest shortcomings, especially in its political coverage. For these writers, the juxtaposition of my father's alleged sexual orientation and my personal support for the traditional definition of marriage as being between one man and one woman is just too delicious to pass up. Karl Rove, antigay crusader, had a gay father. Get it? The pair of journalists even used the timing of my father's death to write that after living as "a gay man" my Dad "passed away quietly at home on July 14, 2004. His son was in the midst of launching the antigay issues campaign that was to lead to the reelection of George W. Bush."

Could Dad have been gay? I didn't see it. I know he had gay friends and volunteered for years at the Desert AIDS Project in Palm Springs. But having gay friends or being concerned about whether someone who is sick gets driven to a clinic appointment or gets a delivery of groceries doesn't make you gay. To this day, I have no idea if my father was gay. And, frankly, I don't care. He was my father, with whom I had a wonderful relationship and whom I loved deeply.

The writers who are fascinated with whether my father was gay are really more interested in implying that all people who have gay relatives or friends must support same-sex marriage; otherwise they are bigots and hypocrites. And if one of these people happens to be Karl Rove, so much the better.

This mind-set has also led some writers to offer up inaccurate accounts about his death. That same pair of journalists wrote, "The seventy-six-year-old Rove was not buried in either of the two cemeteries in the Coachella River Valley on the southern edge of the Mojave Desert. A close friend said there was no funeral. The final disposition of his mortal remains is known only to Louis Rove's immediate family. The son, of whom Louis was so proud, has kept a photo of his smiling father in a star-shaped frame in his office in the West Wing of the White House, a few steps from the Oval Office. And Karl Rove is convinced his father was a happy, contented person."

Actually, there was a simple and moving funeral service, presided over by the pastor whom my father had helped call as the founding minister of the First Presbyterian Church of Golden, Colorado, in the 1950s. My father's mortal remains were handled precisely as he wanted. I know because as he came to life's end, worried and anxious, Dad asked me time and again as his executor if I understood his instructions. He wanted to be cremated and have his ashes scattered at his family's ancestral cabin in northern Wisconsin, at the big rock beside the lake where the ashes of his father, his mother, and his stepmother were all scattered. His instructions were followed to the letter two years after his death on a bright day under a summer sky with his children and grandchildren, his sister, and his best friend as witnesses. Also in accordance with his desires, the ashes of his wife were mingled with his. They lie together again, only now for eternity.

I wasn't very close to my mother in her final decade. She was erratic and undependable when I was growing up, left abruptly when it was convenient for her, and withheld the financial support my father provided. So I was wary of her. We saw each other infrequently, once in the mid-1970s in Washington, D.C., and every once in a while in Denver, where her mother lived, or on my rare trips to Nevada.

When Mom called, it was generally to ask for money, which I tried to provide within my limited means. Sometimes I would receive, unannounced, packages filled with childhood drawings or elementary school report cards or black-and-white snapshots with scalloped edges or other debris of my early years. It was as if she wanted to share parts of those years when we had been an intact family. There is a picture taken shortly after she and Dad married. She is a young, beautiful woman, but even then there's a tired quality to her eyes. Sadness never left her. Our relationship was at times shaky and always insecure, but I love her still. And I will miss her always.

Every life contains sorrow and regret, and my father and mother carried their share. But I know that my father, for his part, knew happiness and contentment. Near his end, as I sat in his hospital room, or as he lay on his couch at home, tethered to an oxygen bottle, he would tell me how grateful he was for his life. He would express his thankfulness for a career spent in geology and his gratitude for children and grandchildren whom he loved and who loved him. That was difficult for such an emotionally contained man. If that's not an expression of contentment and happiness, I don't know what a life richly and fully lived would be. I am proud he chose to call me his son. And I am proud to call him my father.

CHAPTER 2

King of the College Republicans

———•◆•———

O ne of the stupidest things I've ever done, I did as a College Republican.

My association with the CRs started in the fall of 1969, when as a
freshman at the University of Utah I joined the organization. By then I
was already enthralled with politics and unbeknownst to me was quietly
making a name for myself. The previous year I had taken my first real
role in politics—as a volunteer in the reelection campaign of Senator
Wallace F. Bennett. And I had loved it. Tom Korologos, Bennett's chief of
staff, took me on as part of a broader strategy to draw young people to
the GOP senator's campaign at a time when college students across the
country were flocking to anti–Vietnam War Democrats. I threw myself
into the job, I had a blast, and got noticed.

The spring after joining the CRs, I got a call from Morton Blackwell,
the executive director of the College Republican National Committee
(CRNC). He was looking for competent students to help organize campuses in critical U.S. Senate races in 1970, and he had heard about my
work on the Bennett campaign. I flew to Chicago, endured a brutal interview that felt more like a prison interrogation, and landed the job. I was to
organize college students for the campaign of Senator Ralph Smith, appointed to the seat left vacant by the death of GOP Senate Leader Everett
Dirksen. I trundled off to Illinois after the spring semester.

What brought out my stupidity was a remarkably attractive young co-ed who volunteered as a receptionist at the Smith campaign's headquarters in downtown Chicago.

Her parents were nominally active Democrats and one day she brought to work a fancy invitation they had received to the opening of the campaign headquarters of Alan J. Dixon, the Democrat running for state treasurer. To impress her, I led a few young Turks in preparing a faux invitation to the Dixon event with a summons that read "Free Beer, Free Food, Girls, and A Good Time for Nothing" in bold letters. We listed the date and time of the real opening of the Dixon headquarters and then handed out the fake invitation to vagrants, homeless, and drifters in bad parts of downtown Chicago and at a free rock concert in Grant Park.

The hungry and dispossessed were thrilled to receive such an invitation. The Dixon headquarters was swamped at its grand opening. Elite Democrats were horrified to see a virtual army of what Dixon later described as "derelicts and hippies, some with bed rolls." It was near bedlam. Thirsty vagrants came close to rioting, while the more well-to-do attendees were unsure of what to make of it all. The press lapped it up. But Dixon flipped it to his advantage by declaring that the crowd showed "the Democratic Party is the people's party . . . the party of everyone."

Back at the Smith headquarters all heck broke loose when the flyer became public. When one of the Smith campaign muckety-mucks said whoever did this would never work in politics again, my superiors told me to make myself scarce in far-flung corners of the state. I regret the prank. It was not only foolish and childish, it was unhelpful. Dixon won his race and the prank didn't even raise me in the eyes of the attractive receptionist at Smith headquarters. Over two decades later, when President George H. W. Bush nominated me to serve on the Board for International Broadcasting, Alan J. Dixon was then the junior U.S. senator from Illinois. The post was subject to Senate confirmation. If Dixon wanted to make a stink, he could have killed my nomination. It could have been payback time, but Dixon displayed more grace than I had shown and kindly excused the youthful prank.

I learned four vital lessons from Smith's unsuccessful campaign— beyond the dangers of acting stupidly. The first was that not everybody votes. On average over the past sixty years, 58 percent of eligible voters have turned out for presidential elections and just 42 percent in off-year contests. This means that there is usually a large pool of possible voters on the table who can tip an election, if only they can be enticed to go to the polls. Smart campaigns focus on building the organization necessary to expand the pool of their voters. In my experience, organization can make a 2- to 4-point difference.

The second thing I learned was that a good "brand" matters a lot in politics. Smith was an able state legislator and a competent, long-serving Speaker of the Illinois House, but few people knew him outside his district. The campaign tried to expand the power of his name by resurrecting his middle name—Tyler—after realizing he was related to the tenth president of the United States, John Tyler.

But he was running against Adlai Stevenson III, great-grandson of a vice president, grandson of an Illinois secretary of state, son of an Illinois governor and two-time presidential candidate, and a state treasurer himself. Voters thought they knew a lot about Adlai Stevenson III from the reputation of his father and family and voted for him based on that assumption. It was a lesson I would recall as I worked with candidates whose families were well known. George W. Bush would be the most prominent of these, but neither the first nor the only one.

Third, I came to understand there are years in which one party has a structural advantage. In 1966, conflict over the Vietnam War divided Democrats and caused many swing voters to cast ballots for Republicans. In 1970, with a Republican in the White House, the war was cutting against the GOP.

Finally, I realized how bitter defeat tasted regardless of why my candidate lost. I didn't feel particularly strongly about Ralph Smith. I grew to like him (sort of), but I hated to lose. Tennis great Jimmy Connors, one of the most competitive athletes of his generation, once said that he hated losing more than he enjoyed winning. I know what Connors was getting at.

I grappled with this loss while back at school after missing nearly two months of classes to finish the campaign. I didn't know it yet, but a drama was playing out inside the CRNC that would have a big impact on my life.

The chairman of the CRs had stepped down after the 1970 elections and set off a chain reaction of events. The CRs' vice chairman, Joe Abate, a law school graduate who was studying for the New Jersey bar, automatically became the new chairman and was intent on winning the post in his own right for a full term. The College Republicans were just getting over being divided between two camps: the Eastern, moderate Rockefellerites and the dominant Goldwater conservatives of the South and West.

To consolidate his position, Abate cut a deal with his principal opponent, George Gorton of California. Gorton agreed to deliver votes for Abate in June if Abate would immediately appoint a close friend of Gorton's to be the CRs' executive director. It was a deft political maneuver and well above what I as a lowly college sophomore could see.

It turned out that the new executive director, while intellectually bright, was a wholly inadequate manager. But a sloppily run national office could hurt Abate's election chances. In the era before the Internet, fax machines, FedEx, or even cheap long distance, someone needed to be in the CR office to make certain that mailings went out, correspondence was answered, and other things got done.

I was asked if I could fly standby to Washington, D.C., on a regular basis, work long hours for three or four days, and sleep on a mat on the floor of the apartment of the current executive director. And, oh, by the way, the executive director would probably take umbrage at my presence and I wouldn't get paid.

How could I pass up an offer like that?

I didn't, and shortly after winning his election in June 1971, Joe offered me the job of executive director.

The College Republicans were then housed at the Republican National Committee headquarters at 310 First Street, southeast of the Capitol. Befitting our status, the CRs were in the subbasement, under the parking garage and next to the print shop. You couldn't get lower than that. The staff consisted of a secretary and me and as many interns and volunteers as we could stuff into our workspace.

It wasn't glamorous, but there was lots of energy and a sense of mission. There was also a slightly subversive atmosphere. Our peers were in rebellion against bourgeois culture and, often, America itself. We were in rebellion against them and their campus dominance. And we got away with things that other people in the building couldn't, such as printing up a bright orange poster with a drawing of two dancing elephants with "Get It On! Join the College Republicans!" printed on it. We cribbed the drawing from a German artist's pornographic sketches done during the Weimar Republic. Most of his work consisted of animals in obscene situations. The dancing elephants were one of his tamest works. The posters were a hit, both on campus and in the offices and headquarters of amused party leaders and candidates. We went through dozens of printings.

By and large, however, we were viewed with wariness by our superiors on the building's fourth floor—including the chairman, Senator Bob Dole. Our bitter infighting had soured many in the RNC on the CRs. Shortly after my arrival, I was summoned for a direct and brusque lecture by Senator Dole. His message was this: We're glad to have you—but don't make trouble. He did, however, do me one huge favor. After our conversation, Dole directed me to the office of Anne Armstrong, the RNC's co-chairman. We would report to her and were not to bother him. I will always be grateful for this crisp order: it led to a lifelong friendship.

Anne was a Phi Beta Kappa graduate of Vassar College who married an outgoing rancher named Tobin Armstrong and moved in 1950 from her home in New Orleans to a ranch in the middle of Kenedy County, Texas. The county is six times the size of the five boroughs of New York City put together, and when Anne arrived it had exactly 632 residents. Today it has a more manageable 402.

Anne and Tobin became active in the Texas GOP when its membership could, as they say, meet in a phone booth. Republicans had last elected a statewide officeholder in 1869. There was not a single Republican in the Texas legislature and only a handful of Republican officeholders in small rural courthouses in the historically Republican (and German) Hill Country northwest of San Antonio and in an occasional cow county at the tip of the Texas Panhandle, where enough Kansans had drifted south to make a difference. Texas was a Democratic state because it had been a Confederate state. Its Democratic roots were also deepened by the attention President Franklin Delano Roosevelt had lavished on Texas and by the ascent of LBJ and other Texans to national power.

Not that this deterred Anne and Tobin. They threw themselves into politics and rose up the ranks. Tobin became a widely respected party leader with a statewide network among ranchers. At a time when women in politics were expected to make coffee, Anne became a powerful figure. First as vice chairman of the Texas Republican Party and then as national committeewoman, she played vital leadership roles in the election in

1961 of John Tower as the first Republican senator from Texas since Reconstruction, and in the presidential campaigns of Nixon in '60, Goldwater in '64, and Nixon again in '68. As Nixon geared up for reelection in '72, he installed Anne as RNC co-chairman. That day in 1971 she laid down the rules: No funny business, stay inside your budget, expect to get regular assignments and complete them, tell us what you plan to do before you do it, and report in regularly. Then she flashed an incredible smile. This is going to be fun, I thought.

My job as executive director was to help state College Republican organizations and individual chapters expand the GOP's voting and volunteer base on campus. I wanted to avoid being caught in the long-existing rivalry between the Rockefeller moderates and Goldwater conservatives. While Joe was a conservative (as was I), we decided that all CRs would be treated equally. Our great contribution was to expand the "Student Fieldman Schools" (as in a field man for a political operation). We would take our Fieldman Schools program to college campuses on weekends and teach young Republicans how to organize. We covered campus recruitment, student canvassing, communication, and straw polls. We dealt with rudimentary campaign strategy, messaging, planning, fund-raising, scheduling fieldwork, and press work. Each of the participants received a massive notebook of "how-to" materials and the sacred texts of CR organizers, such as Saul Alinsky's *Rules for Radicals,* Tony Schwartz's *The Responsive Chord,* David Ogilvy's *Confessions of an Advertising Man*, and Sun Tzu's *The Art of War*. These and other books contained nuggets about how to organize and win political campaigns. Alinsky's slim volume was especially helpful in showing how our political adversaries thought.

One advantage of having to fly across the country and spend three days on your feet is that you end up meeting some of the smartest people in politics and making them your lifelong friends.

Another advantage is getting to meet local Republican leaders and candidates and soak in a state's political scene. My Rolodex grew and so did my understanding of the patchwork nature of American politics. Starting in 1971, I was to lead over 150 Fieldman Schools over the next six years with more than five thousand participants.

These schools churned out young GOP activists by the score. And their mission had a special urgency: the Twenty-sixth Amendment, adopted in July 1971, lowered the age to vote to eighteen from twenty-one.

Because of student opposition to the Vietnam War, conventional wisdom was that younger voters were solidly in the Democratic camp. GOP leaders were concerned about making sure Republicans were not drowned in the 1972 presidential election by a tidal wave of first-time young voters.

But something else was a little more pressing than the election—the draft. I had to continue working on my bachelor's degree or lose my student deferment. I applied and was accepted to the University of Maryland for the fall of 1971. But even though I showed up on the Maryland campus, the paperwork to my draft board in Salt Lake from U.M. didn't. Partway through the semester, I was notified that I had lost my deferment. My draft number was 84 out of 365. I was then placed at the front of the line to be drafted during the first four months of 1972 and there was nothing I could say to my draft board that would change that.

My first reaction was to feel that it was unfair to lose my deferment over a paperwork glitch. Then I realized I was simply going through what many other young men had faced. Some 19 million men turned eighteen between 1964 and the end of the draft in 1973 and 1.86 million of them were inducted during the Vietnam War. Now I could be one of them. I thought about enlisting in hopes of applying for a military specialty that would keep me out of combat, but then I turned fatalistic. This was the way my country decided who would fight. I had supported the war (though not LBJ's mismanagement of it); maybe this was how I was meant to serve. I prepared myself to be drafted, withdrew from the University of Maryland, and put my affairs in order. Then, on January 31, 1972, Secretary of Defense Melvin Laird announced no one would be called up in the first four months of 1972. I would not be drafted after all.

Thirty years later, my draft status was inserted in the 2004 presidential campaign by John Kerry. At an April rally in Pittsburgh he personally attacked Vice President Dick Cheney and me as people "who went out of their way to avoid their chance to serve when they had the chance." Later that day, en route to another rally, Kerry admitted he didn't know the details of my draft record but refused to apologize, saying "I'm just not going to be accused by any of these people of not being strong on defense, period." His campaign returned to the attack in September, questioning my patriotism by issuing a release and unleashing three surrogates to carry its message, including former senator Max Cleland.

It was a real insight into John Kerry. He spoke without knowing the facts, and he sounded as if he were attacking as unpatriotic the 15.97 million men who received student deferments during the Vietnam War. And he was also making two terrible mistakes for a candidate: he let anger drive his decisions, and he concentrated his fire on an aide rather than on the other candidate. Any day Kerry spent attacking me was a day he wasted.

But of course back in 1972, we had a different election to win—one where Richard Nixon would eventually face off against Senator George McGovern, the most liberal and the most vociferous critic of the Vietnam War of all the Democratic candidates.

I was staying focused on increasing the membership of Republican campus chapters. There was tension between the RNC and Nixon's campaign, the Committee to Re-Elect the President, or CREEP (with all those former Disney employees at his disposal, you'd think the Nixon people would have had better brand sense). CREEP wanted to downplay the Republican label, especially when it came to students, so it set up a parallel Nixon student organization with a budget that dwarfed the CRs'.

We worked with it as well as we could and worked by ourselves when we had to. Somewhere along the way, I was interviewed by a young White House reporter from CBS named Dan Rather, who would emerge as a key figure in an important event almost thirty years later when he published a false report on President Bush that cost Rather his job. Looking back at the 1972 interview, though, I almost don't recognize his interview subject—an earnest, long-haired kid with sideburns and an artificially low voice sitting on the couch, telling Rather, "You can't get a thirty-five-year-old to teach the Republican party how to get the young people."

As the spring passed and summer came, work on the Republican National Convention in Miami consumed everyone at the RNC. And unbeknownst to me, there'd be a special reward for the CRs' grunt work at the convention. Tickets for Nixon's acceptance speech were hard to come by, but Miss Josephine Good, who had run every Republican National Convention since 1956, handed me forty-seven—more than the Kentucky delegate had gotten, she said. For a few days, my friend Jim Dyer and I were kings.

We divvied up the tickets, focusing on the CRs who had been gung-ho, and reserved the last four for ourselves and two volunteers, the attractive Colorado CR chairwoman and some nebbishy kid from a place I can't recall. On the night of Nixon's big speech, the four of us grabbed a cab to the Convention Center. But the cabbie drove out of the security zone, got lost, and found himself on Collins Avenue, which was swarming with tens of thousands of protesters. Some began rocking the taxi. The cabbie panicked, ordered us out, and hightailed it to safety. At first, the thousands of angry, screaming antiwar hippies didn't impede our progress toward the Convention Center a few hundred yards away. As we got closer to the gate, however, they grew more aggressive and began spitting at us and pounding the pavement with long bamboo sticks while chanting "guilty, guilty, guilty."

There was tear gas in the air, fired in response to protesters who had thrown animal blood at those manning the barricades. It was too much for the nebbishy kid, who freaked out and froze up. Thinking fast, Ms. Chairwoman slapped him. Hard. Then she yelled, "Snap out of it! Get moving!" and began dragging him. It was a remarkable performance. With help from riot police and National Guardsmen who ventured out with bayoneted rifles to gather us up, we made it inside the sally port. A few minutes later, we took our seats in an arena filled with delegates, many of whom were coughing or suffering watery eyes from tear gas. It was a surreal way to arrive at President Nixon's opening speech.

The fall campaign was a blur of activity. The office worked virtually around the clock. I was on the road a lot for debates and training seminars. We joined in hammering McGovern for his far-left views on national security, the war, and spending while heralding Nixon's efforts to conclude the war honorably and open the door to China and better relations with the Soviet Union. The 1972 campaign's final weeks saw McGovern drawing huge crowds of enthusiastic antiwar supporters. But Nixon swept forty-nine states on Election Day, leaving Massachusetts and the District of Columbia for McGovern.

Even among the young, Nixon fared well. Exit polls showed the eighteen- to twenty-four-year-old vote went 50 percent for McGovern and 48 percent for Nixon. Students were slightly better for McGovern (52 percent to 46 percent for Nixon) while nonstudents split evenly,

49 percent to 49 percent. While McGovern ran 12.5 points better among the young than he did among all voters, the results showed a latent conservatism among young people.

At the 1973 inaugural, we celebrated Nixon's victory by hosting a giant block party for the CRs the night of January 20 at a run-down apartment building on Second Street, Northeast. CRs like me had come to occupy most of the eight units in the building and we'd opened our apartments to visitors to crash on couches and floors. Each floor had a big trash can with plastic bag liners filled with grain alcohol punch. I had a blast, even though I didn't drink. It wasn't because of any religious precept. I just didn't like the taste and getting buzzed made me feel uncomfortable.

I learned a lot in those intense two years at the CRNC. For one thing, I learned that politics worked. It was not a crapshoot, an irrational contest in which the results were decided by the best ad and the cleverest sound bite. Sure, elections are colored by the emotions and often cock-eyed philosophy of the voters. But within those constraints, it's a logical process in which voters—with imperfect information and differing amounts of attention—try to do the right thing. It is a process that can be understood, managed, and bent toward a preferred outcome by a campaign that knows what it wants to say and how, to whom, and when to say it.

I also learned that ordinary Americans tend to be conservative. Maybe not conservative in the mold of Adam Smith and Whittaker Chambers, or Barry Goldwater and Bill Buckley with a well thought out and coherent philosophical framework, but center-right in their mind-set and inclinations. The elite who run the media, dominate popular culture, captain the publishing houses, and fill out the ranks of America's writers are not. A perfect embodiment of this was Pauline Kael, then a film critic for the *New Yorker,* who complained after the 1972 election, "I don't know anyone who voted for Nixon." No, Nixon's 61 percent, 23-point victory didn't draw many voters on the Upper East or West Sides of Manhattan. But then, the people who live there don't reflect the views and attitudes of much of the rest of America.

Being a College Republican gave me and other political junkies a sense of efficacy. We could do this. We learned the power of mastering new technologies to communicate our message. We saw that politics was not about power or status, but about ideas and ideals. To view it as about power was to treat it as a game, cynical and ultimately meaningless and cruel. But to understand that it was about great principles was to understand that politics could be a hopeful and important exercise at the center of our democratic experience. CRs connected me with the GOP's leadership, helped me realize I was good at this stuff, could do it as well as others much older than me, and gave me a sense that I could contribute.

With Joe Abate's term as national chairman ending in June, a surprising number of College Republicans thought I should succeed him. I decided I'd make a run for it—and that set off one of the lasting controversies that still swirl around me in some corners.

There were three groups vying to put their guy in the top CR spot in 1973. The first was Abate's inner circle, the CRs' "old guard." It was led by Bernie Robinson and dominated by midwesterners. This group had traditionally run College Republicans and one of its potential candidates was Bob Edgeworth of Michigan. The second was made up of conservative die-hards who had never reconciled themselves to Abate's "open-door" policy. This group was led by mostly D.C.-based College Republicans such as Terry Dolan (later the founder of the National Conservative Political Action Committee). This crowd was skilled in convention politics and, because of the generosity of Richard Viguerie, the right-wing direct mail company president, they were well funded.

The third group was everyone else, a motley crew that included mostly state chairmen who hadn't played an active role in CR national politics and weren't part of either clique. Many of these people supported me because they appreciated how I had run the Fieldman Schools and the CRNC operation as its executive director. But as numerous and enthusiastic as my well-meaning supporters were, I couldn't win with them alone. We'd be ground down by the superior resources and expert convention talents of the other groups. We needed to create a synthesis of the old guard and the disorganized new crowd.

Fortunately, Joe, Bernie, and a third old-guard figure, John Zemaitis, led an effort inside Abate's establishment to pull it behind me. It worked.

I soon had two campaigns going. One was focused on preparing a platform and building a team of supporters. The other—more undercover—involved trading favors. To get the establishment to back me, I was told I would have to pick a midwesterner as co-chairman and give another midwesterner the right of first refusal as executive director. These were prices worth paying; there wasn't any other way to meld the Abate establishment with the Rove ragamuffins.

I had to travel to meet the delegates and personally solicit their votes. This was not easy for me. I was fine at making a speech, but it was difficult to make small talk. If I wanted to win, I had to let the voters know me. One trip stands out. It started with an overnight train ride on March 19 and 20 from Washington, D.C., to Columbia, South Carolina, where I met the "godfather" of that state's College Republicans, a quintessential southern right-winger named John Carbaugh. He was later to be Senator Jesse Helms's foreign policy advisor. When I met him, though, he controlled the votes of the South Carolina Young Republicans and College Republicans.

Bernie had cut a deal with him for the support of the South Carolina CR chairman. It was simple: if I'd name the South Carolinian as my southern area campaign chairman and take him on a trip through the South, the state's vote was mine. It was an easy deal to make. The title was a nothing title. And while I hadn't met the South Carolina chairman, we'd become friends over the telephone for much of the past year. He struck me as smart and conservative in his politics but not in his approach to life. I thought it'd be fun to take a drive with this guy.

His name was Lee Atwater.

In a rented, ugly yellowish brown Ford Pinto, Lee and I spent six wild days driving through the South. Our first stop was in Atlanta, where Lee was smitten with the state CR chairwoman, Andi Poynter, a cute co-ed who promised to try to lock up her successor. In Gainesville, Florida, the state chairman let us crash at his apartment and promised to do what he could for me. The law student who controlled the Alabama vote couldn't meet us: he had an exam. His name was Jeff Sessions (now a U.S. senator) and he'd locked up the support of the incoming state chairman. On our way to meet the new chairman, we stopped for breakfast and Lee ordered cornflakes and then doused them in Tabasco sauce.

From there it was on to Mississippi, where we met with Roger Wicker and his buddy Lanny Griffith, who were being pressured by the state's GOP executive director (and now governor), Haley Barbour, not to vote for me. But after dinner with them, I knew they would stand firm.

Lee and I left Pontotoc, Mississippi, late and didn't notice that we were low on fuel. So deep into the night of March 23, 1973, somewhere on Highway 78 in the Mississippi piney woods between New Albany and Byhalia, with Lee behind the wheel and the radio tuned (loud) to a Memphis R&B station, we ran out of gas—dead-plumb-rolling-to-a-complete-stop out of gas, with no town or service station in sight.

There were lights in the woods indicating some kind of house or structure. Lee confidently told me he'd check it out and told me to get behind the wheel. He disappeared into the gloom. About fifteen minutes later, he reappeared, running at a full gait, carrying a gas can. He slammed the gas into the tank, threw the can into the ditch, and himself into the passenger seat. "Go!" he yelled. He took over behind the wheel when we got to Memphis and drove into Arkansas, where we caught a few hours of sleep at a motel near the site of next day's state CR convention. He slept easily. I kept wondering where he got the gas and why he had been running.

Saturday, the Arkansas CR convention went well as we picked up that state's vote. Lee and I made a late-morning flight out of Little Rock to D.C., arriving about two and a half hours later and grabbing a cab to the Bellevue Hotel on Capitol Hill for a regional CR convention.

There were several hundred students attending the convention from colleges in the District of Columbia, Maryland, Virginia, West Virginia, and Kentucky. Its winner would pick up the two votes of the regional director and co-director, which would provide critical momentum as the spring CR state convention season got under way. Dolan was from the region, so he was looking for the gathering to give him a strong boost.

He fell short, in part because we were able to deploy Lee to win over delegates from the then all-women Radford College in southwestern Virginia. The Dolan guys thought of Radford as "their" school.

Lee, ever the ladies' man, was set loose to lobby the Radford girls. I, on the other hand, never the ladies' man, was bustled off to back-room meetings, mostly to thank supporters. I was hustled from room to room. While moving from one to another, I rounded a corner to find Lee—his fingertips intertwined, rocking back and forth on his heels, surrounded by a group of the Radford girls, all dressed in their colorful formals. Radford was in the middle of nowhere and the girls didn't get many excuses to pull out their finery. They were all laughing and holding drinks. Lee had a big grin on his face. He winked at me. I got the message and moved on. Lee was fully in control of the situation.

The next day, the voting at first went as our opponents had forecast and Dolan was confident he'd win. That is, until Radford College was called for its vote. When its chairwoman stood and cast the delegation's votes for my side, the place went nuts. It was clear to everyone just who would prevail. I glanced at the back of the room: Dolan and his crowd were one angry bunch.

There were other battles to be fought that spring, but the Dolan candidacy had no chance. A few weeks before the CRs gathered in Lake of the Ozarks, Missouri, he quietly withdrew from the race. But that cleared the way for a curious convention fight. Bob Edgeworth, who had earlier promised not to run, broke his commitment and tossed his hat in the ring. We had an overwhelming majority of the vote, but we braced for what we were about to get—an old-fashioned convention fight.

People might think that at the convention I was the central figure, inspiring the troops, providing critical strategic insights, and directing operatives hither and yon to nail down every last vote. But these people would be wrong. In the days leading up to the convention, I was generally assigned the less glamorous job of picking up CRs at the airport or train station. Mostly I sat by myself and read or watched TV in the back room of our headquarters suite while my future was in the hands of others and the swirl of College Republican politics engulfed the little Ozark beach resort.

The convention opened Saturday morning with my name and Edgeworth's placed in nomination. As the roll call was being read, Edgeworth produced a bullhorn and began reading his own from the side of the room. His purpose was to dispute the outcome of the convention by having competing roll call votes. He knew he'd lose the official count, but wanted a reed, however thin, upon which to allege that he'd been cheated at the convention. It was almost comical. The final official tally was 54 for Rove, 25 for Edgeworth, and 2 dead-enders for Terry Dolan. Bob's Bullhorn Roll Call produced God-knows-what-margin and arrived at a different conclusion, to which little attention was paid.

The intrigue began almost immediately with a challenge by Edgeworth to the convention's outcome. He asked Republican National Committee chairman George H. W. Bush to seat him as the rightful College

Republican national chairman and sent a blizzard of paper to Bush's office at the Republican National Committee. Bush appointed a committee to investigate Edgeworth's claims. The group quickly discovered, by calling the Republican chairman in the contested states, that Edgeworth's votes were specious. Bush signaled he expected to wrap up the investigation quickly.

But early in the week of August 6, 1973, it became clear that the other side knew they were losing. They escalated the fight. Rich Evans, the CRNC vice chairman whose hopes to succeed Abate had been dashed, had recorded a Student Fieldman School session in Lexington, Kentucky, in August 1972. That was fairly common: many students who attended the sessions made recordings and everyone took voluminous notes. But Evans's tape made its way to the *Washington Post*. In the part of the tape provided the *Post*, Bernie Robinson and I were heard talking in a wrap-up session devoted to the dos and don'ts of politics. I described my embarrassing Dixon episode, and Bernie described going through a Democratic gubernatorial candidate's garbage in 1968 and finding evidence a major donor was making contributions to both the Republican and Democratic candidates. Bernie's injunction not to ape his exploits was in the transcript and tape; my similar injunction not to duplicate the stupid thing I'd done was not. The intention seemed clear: to make me too toxic of a figure to be made the new chairman of the CRs by making it appear that I taught dirty tricks. On Friday, August 10, the *Post* ran a story under the headline "GOP Probes Official as Teacher of 'Tricks.'" The controversy reached a new level and probably drew more attention than it should have because it was developing just as scandals around Nixon were heating up.

Bush immediately instructed the committee to look into these new charges. It was not difficult to collect evidence. A handful of Edgeworth supporters echoed the line that the schools were nothing more than "dirty tricks" seminars, but Bush's office received a flood of letters and testimonials from attendees, guest expert lecturers (some of whom were personally known to Bush or the investigating committee members), and candidates and party leaders who were grateful for the young operatives trained at the schools.

Chairman Bush and his committee spent the next three weeks reviewing the matter; on September 6, Bush sent Edgeworth and me a letter announcing his decision. I had been duly elected at the CRNC convention and would be recognized immediately as chairman by the RNC.

I had pledged to the midwesterners to make one of their crowd the executive director, but their choice took a pass because of health problems and the midwesterners let me know the pick was now up to me. I asked Lee Atwater if he'd come to Washington as my executive director. I gave him his first job in Washington.

A few days later, Lee and I went to meet with RNC chairman George H. W. Bush in his office. I expected a quick visit. Instead the new chairman invited us in for a long talk. He touched on the controversy and asked what we were going to do to heal rifts. He seemed genuinely interested in what our plans for the CRs were and encouraged us to think big. He talked plainly about the challenges the party faced as the Nixon White House's difficulties grew and public confidence in the administration shrank. He was generous with his time and supportive of our efforts.

I was struck by the gentility, calm, and evident integrity of this lanky Texan. There were flashes of toughness, too. For example, he dismissed Edgeworth and some of his followers as irretrievably lost to rational persuasion.

As we stood to leave, Atwater nervously buttoned his jacket and, in a state of agitation that became obvious as he grew more intense, jutted his head forward and asked Chairman Bush, "Do you have a boat on the Potomac?" When the chairman responded that he did, Lee spat out, "Can I borrow it this weekend?" He had the look of anxious concern that came on whenever he was dealing with something really important. Lee went on to explain that a really attractive girl was coming up from South Carolina that weekend and his being able to take her out on the boat would really impress her. He allowed that he was familiar with boats, mentioning the specific kind the chairman had, and pledged to return it fully fueled. He'd done his homework. The request was unexpected, out of left field, edgy and chancy. It impressed Bush. With a laugh, he agreed and told Lee to get the keys from his office before leaving the building that afternoon. Lee would ultimately marry the girl.

A couple of weeks later, Bush's chief of staff, Tom Lias, called. The chairman wanted to know if I would be interested in working as his special assistant. I was blown away. I moved my office to the fourth floor, six floors above my old digs in the CR subbasement. It was October 1973.

My association with people named Bush had started, and it would last a whole lot longer than I could have imagined then.

It wasn't a glam job—but on Wednesday, November 21, 1973, the day before Thanksgiving, I was asked to meet the chairman's son in the lobby and give him the keys to the family car. When the call came after lunch, I slipped down to the lobby and waited. George W. Bush walked through the front door, exuding more charm and charisma than is allowed by law. He had on his Air National Guard flight jacket, jeans, and boots. I introduced myself and we chatted about nothing for a few minutes. I gave him the keys to the family car, a purple AMC Gremlin with a Levi Strauss interior. Say what you will about the senior Bush, he has never been car proud. His son, used to driving a red sports car around Harvard Yard, was not impressed. I did not see much of the younger Bush for several more years.

There was another fateful meeting I'd have after entering the Bush orbit—Val Wainright. An attractive, blond, chain-smoking intern and the daughter of one of Bush's most loyal volunteers, Val was from an old Houston family. She had a great personality, was cute as hell, and had a funny way of crinkling her eyes when she broke into a joyful big smile. I was smitten, though initially I thought I was playing way out of my league. It turned out that I wasn't. Great and wonderful things were to come from it—and pain, too. But for now, it was fun and not serious, a perk of youth.

In the meantime, there was my job and my duties as CR chairman. Within six months, Lee left to run Senator Strom Thurmond's intern operation. Fortunately, I convinced Kelly Sinclair, an able and affable Kentuckian, to take his job. Lee was supposed to overlap with him by two weeks to show him the ropes, but on the day Kelly arrived, Lee left at lunch and never returned. That was Lee: you took him on his terms or not at all. And while we were friends for a long time, we were never closer than the first week we traveled southern highways in the ugly Pinto. I am not certain how many really close friends he had, but loneliness may be the normal state of genius. And Lee was a genius at politics—at understanding people and what would move them.

As Bush's special assistant, I saw the country moving against the president. I was tasked with efforts to generate support for the beleaguered Nixon White House as it was becoming increasingly clear that Nixon and key people around him had been involved in Watergate. It was dispiriting and unpleasant. I found it increasingly difficult to defend Nixon. Had he known about the break-in at the Democratic National Committee headquarters? Had he authorized or known about the hush payments and cover-up and deceptions? What good could have come from burglarizing the DNC? Nixon had been way ahead, the Democratic Party was in disarray, their candidate was on the way to an enormous defeat, so why?

I saw Chairman Bush, an enormously decent man, balance his loyalty to the president who appointed him with his love for the party he led. And as time went on, it became clearer that his loyalty—our loyalty—to Nixon was misplaced. My days began to take on a hellish quality as the latest event in the drama caused the once-fervent Nixon backers I talked to fall away—disenchanted, distressed, and angry at the president's betrayal of their trust. Out around the country, they knew this was to have an unhappy ending. I hoped for a miracle that would restore Nixon's credibility and pushed my growing doubts about the president into the far recesses of my conscience.

Then, on August 8, 1974, Nixon resigned. I was on an airplane, returning from a student conference in Europe with another CR, when the pilot came on the intercom to announce the gist of the president's televised address to the nation. The passengers applauded. I was shocked and sat in silence. The next day, I watched on a television in the chairman's office as Betty and Gerald Ford accompanied Pat and Dick Nixon to Marine One and the now former president waved to the South Lawn crowd before lifting off from the White House one last time. I saw West Wing staffers and Nixon's daughters and sons-in-law weeping. I remember feeling anger that he'd let this happen to my party and profound disappointment in someone I'd trusted and worked so hard for.

Less than a month later, President Ford announced the appointment of George H. W. Bush as envoy to the People's Republic of China. His successor, Mary Louise Smith, asked me to stay on as her assistant, and before long I was shipped out to help one of the many endangered Republicans as their prospects in the 1974 elections dimmed.

My assignment was to help Virginia Haven Smith in Nebraska's 3rd District. One of the country's most Republican districts, it was nonetheless an open seat and Mrs. Smith had what barely passed for a campaign.

Her manager lived in a little town in far northwest Nebraska, well away from any voters. Her headquarters was in Grand Island, at the other end of the district, and most days lacked someone in charge. She had no set schedule—she just decided each morning where she'd campaign that day. There was no plan for mail, phones, get-out-the-vote, or even what the television and radio messages should be. I plopped myself down in Grand Island and tried to put what I'd been teaching in Student Fieldman Schools to work.

We had one great advantage: the candidate. Long active in the Farm Bureau Auxiliary, she knew people all over the district. And she was knowledgeable about the federal budget, having read every one since the early 1950s. I called for reinforcements, putting one of the RNC secretaries to work as office manager and phone bank director. She'd never done it before.

With less than six weeks to go, we targeted voters, cranked up a phone canvass, organized a real schedule that put the candidate where we needed her, drafted mail pieces, bid out the work to local printer and mail shops, coordinated getting computer labels for the target households, fleshed out the TV and radio scripts, and put to work as many volunteers as we could find. NBC's Tom Brokaw showed up to cover the race on a day when we had nothing scheduled, so we quickly picked a small town where Mrs. Smith had friends, and then organized an impromptu "drop-by": supporters would spontaneously spring out of their shops and stores to greet their longtime friend in a display of prairie politics. It worked, leaving Brokaw with the impression this was one popular woman with a heck of a following. She won by 737 votes. In contrast, the GOP lost four Senate seats and forty-eight House seats.

The Virginia Smith race showed me that what I had been teaching at the Fieldman Schools actually worked. We had been saying that the most important decisions are about structuring the campaign. The candidate's authority should be limited: he or she is in charge of deciding what issues, strategy, and tactics will be employed, but not in charge of the campaign itself. Virginia Smith was trying to do both—and failing at both as a result.

Operating people need to have operating authority (as George W. Bush much later put it, "authority and accountability need to be aligned"). To be successful, a campaign needs someone who has the final say to do something—a shot caller. Even if some of those decisions turn out to be wrong, it's vital that they are made and that the campaign carries out its broader strategy. Ad hoc changes kill campaigns.

When it came to people, we taught in the Fieldman Schools that the gap between professionals and amateurs is not that large. Smart people like the RNC secretary could be dropped into an unfamiliar setting and, with some guidance and her own smarts, get the job done. And while our existing technology was crude, we used to say, "Machines should work so people can think"—a slogan we stole from IBM ads. It made us open to being on the technological cutting edge.

A good strategy, so we taught in Fieldman Schools, starts with understanding your strengths and weaknesses so you can match your strengths against your opponent's weaknesses. Smith knew where the waste and fat was in the budget and had testified to Congress about it; making that a strength highlighted her opponent's failure to frame himself as a fiscal conservative. Good strategy also focuses the efforts on voters who are really up for grabs. For Virginia Smith, we focused on precincts whose Republican percentage swung more widely from one election to another and, in those precincts, on women voters who might be more disposed to vote for another woman.

Choosing the right issues helped strengthen the Smith campaign for its last six weeks. We focused on those on which she was most passionate and credible. In politics, there are two-sided issues, such as abortion, which deeply divide people, and one-sided issues, such as deficits, which tend to draw most of them together. We picked one-sided issues that could draw more people into our candidate's pool while having crisp, clear answers to the two-sided issues for those concerned about them. It's better to be clear on two-sided issues than to equivocate; somebody will trust you if you do the former and nobody will trust you if you do the latter.

The Smith victory was a notch in my belt and thus I returned to the RNC to be rewarded with a new assignment: executive assistant to the co-chairman, a Virginia conservative named Dick Obenshain. There were also rewards on the personal front. Toward the end of 1975, Val and I decided that even though we were just twenty-four and had known each other less than two years, we were in love and wanted to get married. I made the pilgrimage to Houston to ask her father's permission. Bill Wainright gave his blessing and I was accepted into Val's family.

We set the date for July of the next year, 1976. America's bicentennial would also mark the beginning of our marriage.

But 1975 also ended on a note of confusion, and then change. I received a call from Bill Royall, a former RNC field operative and at this time executive director of the Republican Party of Virginia. He wanted me to become the Virginia GOP's finance director. I told him I hadn't raised money before and besides, I was happy working for Obenshain. He told me Dick had suggested he call me. That floored me. I told Bill I'd think about it and get back to him in a few days. I thought to myself, What is up with my boss?

A few days later, Dick came up from Richmond for a couple of days. I found an open time on his schedule and went in to tell him about Bill's offer. He glanced up from the papers he'd been scanning and said he knew about it and thought I should take it. I was shattered. I thought about it for a day and then called Bill back and accepted.

The next Monday, Dick Obenshain announced his resignation as co-chairman of the Republican National Committee. A Reagan supporter, he felt President Ford deserved to have someone of his choice as co-chairman. Dick had been planning to go back to Richmond full-time and wanted me nearby in the event he ran for the U.S. Senate in 1978. He'd engineered the job offer but felt he couldn't bring me in on his secret. He was trusting Bill's persuasiveness and my instincts. So when 1976 came I was off to Richmond and, while I didn't know it yet, points farther west and south.

CHAPTER 3

Planting Roots in Texas

———— ◆ ————

N ecessity is the mother of invention. I also found it to be the midwife of new skills: I learned fast how to raise money. The chairman of the Republican Party of Virginia, George McMath, found it easier to write checks to keep the party operating than to ask others to contribute. As the party's finance director, I'd have to raise my own salary or ask George to write more checks, which I wasn't keen on doing.

Looking around the office, I discovered printouts with names of nineteen thousand people who had previously donated to the state GOP or its candidates. I drafted a letter from Chairman McMath asking them for donations. It was printed, stuffed into envelopes, and mailed. And the money poured in. Well, not poured—but it was satisfying to see the bundle of envelopes delivered each day by the Postal Service and to know that most contained checks or the occasional wadded-up ten- or twenty-dollar bill. The party would have funds, and I'd continue getting a paycheck. My love affair with direct mail had begun.

Direct mail is simple: Collect the names of potential donors to a cause like yours and send them an easy-to-read letter that explains why they should send money. Include a reply form printed with their name and address, along with a return envelope. Make your package stand out in the day's stack of mail with an attention-grabbing format, colorful stamps, a provocative headline on the envelope, or a popular name above the reply address.

At the same time, test larger lists of nondonors who have a history of contributing to similar causes or buying items through the mail. This is called "prospecting." Randomly pick, say, five thousand names from a bigger list and split them into two or more slices. Send each slice a different letter and track the results. Mail the best-performing letter to the rest of the names available on the lists that made money or came close to it. Then every year, ask the donors to renew their memberships. Most of them will.

The letter itself is the most important element. On some level, readers know it's a form letter, no matter how many times their name is used in its text. But while they understand it is advertising, they still want to be persuaded. The more authentic the pitch, the better the response, and more important, the longer the relationship with the donor. There was nothing like writing a letter that hit just the right note at just the right time with just the right list.

As Democrats gathered to nominate Jimmy Carter for president, I stopped politicking long enough to get married. In early July 1976, Val and I walked down the aisle in Houston, surrounded by lots of her family and friends, my dad, and a smattering of my College Republican buddies. We honeymooned by driving back to Richmond the week of the Democratic National Convention. Val was a political junkie, too, and from our Nashville hotel room we watched Barbara Jordan, an African-American congresswoman from Texas, turn in a powerful performance delivering the keynote address.

Carter's nomination meant that southern states, which had drifted toward the Republican Party since 1964, were likely to slam back into the Democratic column. Virginia would be a battleground for Gerald Ford, Carter's opponent, and I'd be on its front lines as the state's Republican Party finance director.

Ford's campaign in Virginia was primitive in comparison to what happens in battleground states today. Our budget was peanuts, and our guidance from Ford's high command in Washington was negligible. There wasn't even a TV blitz. But our mission was straightforward: put the Commonwealth of Virginia in the GOP column, or die trying.

In addition to my day job as finance director, I did everything from draft speeches to ship campaign materials to the far corners of the state. It was a unique opportunity for a twenty-five-year-old, and it paid off sweetly: by just over 1 percent, the Commonwealth became the only southern state to go for Ford.

After the election, I was at a loss for what to do. John Warner, the former Navy secretary and new husband of Elizabeth Taylor, was courting me for his Senate campaign. Warner and I had hit it off when he'd barnstormed the state full-time for Ford, in preparation for his own race for the U.S. Senate. He now asked me to help draft a speech he'd give at the Virginia Military Institute. As a reward, Warner invited me to join him in Lexington for the speech and at a party that was being hosted the night before by the president of Washington and Lee University. At the party, I was completely out of my element. W&L alumni swarmed around the handsome and outgoing Warner and his movie-star wife. Warner never missed a beat, however, and continued our political courtship by asking me to breakfast the next morning to go over the speech one last time. I knew he'd mentally put the speech to bed already, but it was the kind of personal gesture that young guys on the make, as I was, appreciate.

Early the next morning, I arrived at the W&L president's guesthouse for breakfast. I knocked—and Elizabeth Taylor answered the door. Herself. Alone. In a revealing dressing gown and lingerie. I was agog. Her eyes really were violet. I suspect my jaw was slack and my eyes glazed. She graciously invited me in as Warner descended the stairs, attired again in his black tie, and offered a hearty greeting. She laughed at him and asked if he really intended to make his speech in black tie. He laughed, too, and retreated upstairs to change into a suit. So Elizabeth Taylor and I went into the kitchen, where I had breakfast with one of history's most beautiful women sitting across the table from me in her nightie, making small talk about her husband's appearance later that morning. She was thinking about politics; I was not.

Shortly after, I decided to make my way to Texas. It wasn't because I brilliantly saw the Lone Star State as ripe for Republicans. It was for love. Val missed her family. We packed up our AMC Pacer and drove to Houston in time for Christmas. That move to Texas set the arc of the rest of my life.

I needed a job. Fortunately, as CRNC chairman, I'd met Fred Agnich, Texas's GOP national committeeman and a senior Republican in the Texas House. I took a job as his legislative aide. So New Year's Day of 1977 found me in Austin, a city dominated by the University of Texas Tower and the Texas Capitol dome and nestled on two lakes at the edge of the Hill Country. The university and state government were about all there was to Austin at that time.

Republicans like me were quite an oddity. Democrats had occupied every statewide office, as they had since 1872, until the Republican John Tower was elected to the U.S. Senate on a fluke in 1961. There had been little improvement since: in 1977, there were just thirteen Republicans in the 150-member state House and only one Republican in the 31-member state Senate. But change was coming.

The first important change was demographic. Texas was a jobs magnet that drew people from across America. The state had 7,711,194 residents in 1950, but thanks to in-migration and growing families, its population nearly doubled by 1980. The coastal plains outside Houston, the Hill Country northwest of San Antonio and around Austin, and the rolling prairies between and around Dallas and Fort Worth exploded in subdivisions, shopping malls, and office parks. Wherever these new Texans came from was more Republican than Texas had been. Voting and volunteering for and contributing to Republicans came a lot easier to these newcomers.

Politically, there were other changes. The National Democrats became even more liberal, and so did Texas Democrats, with conservative and moderate Democratic officeholders losing more primary contests every election as the '70s wore on. The liberals who had been an embattled minority within the Democratic Party in the 1950s and '60s were becoming an emboldened majority that didn't think twice about driving their opponents out of the party. Most conservative Democrats parked themselves on Independent Street. Some drove on over to Republican Boulevard.

Meanwhile, population growth was pushing more legislative seats into the rapidly growing Republican suburbs. Districts were redrawn every ten years, making the legislature and the congressional delegation more Republican. Then, in 1973, Democrats lost a vital advantage when courts struck down countywide legislative elections. Previously, candidates in the larger urban counties ran countywide, rather than in a district. This had made it difficult for Republicans to avoid being submerged in populous—and Democratic—counties. Once state legislators were elected by district in the big counties, suburban Republicans began winning.

As the state's population mushroomed, Texas received more congressional seats. For incumbents, self-preservation is more important than maintaining their party's dominance. So Democratic congressmen were eager to shed Republican neighborhoods, and Texas went from zero GOP congressmen in 1960 to four in 1980, to eight in 1990.

The GOP was also aided by congressional retirements of old-line conservative Texas Democrats, some of them first elected when FDR, Truman, or Eisenhower was president and Texans ran Congress with Lyndon Johnson as Senate majority leader and Sam Rayburn as Speaker. This was especially true in 1978, when four senior Democrats, all conservative and all from rural districts, retired. They had been impossible to beat.

Most of these changes would play themselves out in the years still ahead. As I started my duties in the Capitol in 1977, Representative Agnich had a more immediate task for me: working to standardize baitfish laws. There were over 270 state laws on how many baitfish you could take from the streams and ponds of the state's 254 counties. Agnich wanted one standard for all the counties' waters, set by biologists at Parks and Wildlife. It was a small but vital step in his long fight to modernize Texas's game laws. It was also boring as hell.

I was barely scraping by on my modest salary and a little income from some freelance direct mail letter-writing. Politics didn't seem like a way I could support a family, especially as a Texas Republican, so I was glad that my father-in-law arranged an interview with a regional brokerage house.

Before going for the interview, though, I called my former boss, George H. W. Bush. After Carter's victory, he'd left his post as CIA director, returned to Houston, and reentered the business world. He was pleased I'd ended up in Texas and said he might have an idea or two about jobs for me and asked me to drop by.

"I'm thinking of running for President, Karl, and I'd like your help," he told me. I was stunned and flattered. Ford wasn't running in 1980, and the other potential candidates didn't deter Bush. He had come close to being named vice president by Ford in 1974 and his board seats and other business activities gave him the financial freedom to look at the race. Friends had convinced him the next step was to form a political action committee so he could move around the country and test the waters. "Would you like to run my PAC?" he asked.

After recovering from my initial shock, I immediately accepted his offer. What political junkie wouldn't? Here was a man I deeply admired offering me a job in politics—and not just any job, but the opportunity to be on the ground floor of a presidential campaign. I put my future as a stockbroker on hold.

In retrospect, the next eighteen months seem amateurish, low-budget, and unsophisticated, especially when compared to what candidates do now when they run for president. But it was also a period of valuable lessons. Our chairman was Mr. Bush's good friend James A. Baker III, a successful Houston lawyer who had seen big-time politics up close and had enjoyed the responsibilities of public service. He would chair the PAC, the Fund for Limited Government, but his eyes were set on running for attorney general of Texas in 1978, so he wouldn't run the Fund day to day. That's where I came in.

For half the Fund for Limited Government's existence—and perhaps in order to embody the smaller-is-better spirit—I was its only staff, handling political invitations, using my CR friends and Bush's party allies to prompt requests from states we wanted to visit, keeping up contacts with the huge network of Bush friends around the country, traveling with Mr. Bush, and doing whatever a twenty-six-year-old could do to lay a foundation for a presidential bid.

Bush hit the candidate fund-raiser circuit, lining up support among party leaders for a future White House run. He and I flew around the country, carrying our own bags on countless commercial flights and little prop planes. Our model was old-fashioned, perfected by Richard Nixon in 1966. We focused on states and districts with high-profile contests, where Bush's appearance at a party or candidate fund-raiser or rally could make a difference. We aimed to pick up chits with political leaders by helping them and their candidates.

Traveling with George H. W. Bush was an extraordinary experience. He displayed his essential decency to everyone he came in contact with. There was no elevator operator or busboy or complete stranger undeserving of his respect, nor any party leader or fat cat who merited slavish attention. Civility is something that can't be faked, though it is a frame of mind that can be cultivated with patience and discipline. I learned it speaks volumes about a person's character.

Bush had an enormous reservoir of goodwill among state party leaders, members of the Republican National Committee, and old colleagues from Congress. Everywhere we went there were old friends from Andover and Yale, the Navy, the oil business, government, and his days at the RNC, all eager to help their friend. He steadily firmed up old relations and made new friends, carefully cataloging their names and sending many of them handwritten notes—notes that are still proudly displayed in frames and shown as treasured relics.

I saw how Bush's mind worked, drawing on broad principles that were deeply engrained, and how he constantly collected and sifted information. This made him open to profound growth, such as on the day we were flying into Des Moines in a commuter plane to catch a prop plane into Dubuque. He read in the paper that the number of abortions in the District of Columbia had eclipsed the number of live births. This callousness toward life deeply disturbed him and he began moving more firmly into the pro-life camp. It wasn't as if he were at one point on the continuum one day and at the opposite point the next day. He had a thoughtful and constantly engaged mind, a habit he passed on to his children.

Working with Bush at that early stage of his candidacy, I saw how important it was that a candidate place people who care about him at the core of his effort. Loyalty matters most at the beginning because candidates can always hire seasoned professionals later, many of whom wait to join a campaign when the race has taken shape.

I saw that party leaders influenced opinion, as they still do now. Long before the polls matter, people who play active roles in the party, political campaigns, and fund-raising begin shaping the opinions of others. It is much better to have these opinion makers leaning toward your candidate earlier rather than later. The senior Bush was in the game in 1980 because so many members of the party's leadership, broadly defined, had warm feelings toward him. Without them, he would never have been a serious contender and, later, vice president and president.

Candidates also need to draw in people who normally aren't deeply involved in politics, people whose ties to the candidate may be personal, professional, demographic, or philosophical. The senior Bush had his Yale, oil, and Texas friends. Reagan drew in previously uninvolved conservatives who fondly remembered his movies, radio speeches, and 1964 television appearance for Goldwater, as well as close friends from the entertainment business. John McCain had Vietnam vets, while Barack Obama had young people and African-Americans heretofore uninvolved but inspired by his historic candidacy.

I was happy as Bush's traveling mate, but more changes were in store for me. It started innocuously enough. A few days after the 1978 election, I met with Jim Baker to discuss melding the Fund staff into the soon-to-be-launched presidential campaign. Baker had lost his bid for attorney general, and Bush's son had lost his congressional race in West Texas. The senior Bush now wanted Baker running his presidential effort.

When Baker asked me if anybody with the Fund or on Bush's personal staff would have problems working together, I told him I didn't think so. But a problem soon developed. Bush had brought a majordomo into his business office, Jennifer Fitzgerald, and she became a problem for me. I had heard her grouse, after a couple of election night cocktails, that "we have a candidate who's a loser, who's got a son who's a loser, and now we've got a campaign manager who's a loser." She wanted someone other than Baker to manage the emerging presidential campaign. I told Baker about her comment, and he told the senior Bush. This caused a rift between Jennifer and me. So did the fact that I ordered a door cut in the new HQ between Bush's and Baker's offices so the candidate could have direct access to his campaign manager without having to go through Fitzgerald's office.

I hate infighting and this was one of the major reasons I did the improbable thing and didn't join Bush's presidential bid. But there were other factors. After being so close to the candidate, I didn't relish being another smart kid on the campaign's fringes. I had been promised a job in Washington if Bush ultimately prevailed, but I had seen the wunderkinder of the Carter administration stumble badly because of immaturity and wasn't certain I would do any better.

Finally, I was a newlywed who had been home only parts of seventeen weekends in eighteen months, and Val and I had hinted around the edges at starting a family. She'd played a big role in Bill Clements's gubernatorial campaign, running phone banks in Houston, and was being offered many jobs in Austin after Clements had pulled off a miracle and become the first Republican elected Governor of Texas since 1869. So after a complicated deliberation, she and I joined the new Clements administration. Still, in quiet moments, I couldn't shake the sense that I had closed an inviting door and was unlikely to ever go to Washington.

Bill Clements was a crusty, tough-as-an-old-boot, self-made millionaire. He'd worked as a roughneck in the oilfields before starting the Southeastern Drilling Company, which he built into the world's largest such company, pioneering offshore drilling and expanding worldwide. He'd also served as deputy secretary of defense under Presidents Nixon and Ford. He was used to making big, expensive bets—and winning them. Now he had made another, gambling his own millions that he could get elected as a Republican. Clements won by 16,909 votes out of 2,369,689 cast. Real change was in the air.

Clements had loaned his campaign $4.5 million, and I was given the goal of raising $200,000 in two years through direct mail to retire some of the $7.2 million debt and fund political operations. The campaign had five thousand donors in 1978, and was dubious about direct mail. I was also in charge of coordinating his political travel and activities, communicating with his county leaders around the state, and helping vet potential appointees.

By the end of the first year, my team and I had increased those five thousand names nearly fivefold and raised $1 million; the entire $7.2 million campaign debt was retired in eighteen months. I was able to supplement my salary with an occasional freelance writing assignment, too. Things on the professional level were going well enough, but not at home. My marriage was on the rocks.

In December, Val's grandmother, Alzina Mather Oberwetter, died unexpectedly. Miss Obie was eighty-six, but seemed like she would endure forever. Then, the day after Val's parents, Bill and Jane Wainright, joined us in Austin for Governor Clements's inaugural, Bill left to attend a barge brokers convention in New Orleans. He was found in his hotel room a few days later, dead of a massive heart attack.

Jane and Val went to pieces, and who could fault them? A heart attack victim herself, Jane had long feared she would suffer a fatal one, but now it was Bill, the steady presence that gave his family a safe and comforting center, who had died. Val and I drove to Houston most Friday afternoons to meet Jane at the family's Galveston Bay beach house. It was hard for mother and daughter to absorb so much loss so suddenly; they needed to be close. By the summer, things appeared to be righting themselves. Our weekend trips to Houston were less frequent and less emotionally taxing, and Val seemed to be getting over the trauma of losing her father and grandmother.

By then, the interest in me from direct mail firms had turned into more than the occasional assignment; on a trip to Washington I was offered a steady stream of such work, which I could do in my off-hours. I was elated: we could buy a home and start a family.

When I shared the good news with Val, she was cool and distant. She then explained that she hadn't planned to tell me, but she was leaving the next morning to go home to Houston. She wasn't certain what she was going to do next or how this would affect our marriage, but she needed time away to think. The next morning, she got in her car and drove to her mother's town home—and straight out of my life. A month later, her uncle—her father's executor and next-door neighbor—died. She filed for divorce shortly thereafter.

There was nothing I could do to stop it, though I tried to slow it. Through her attorney, she agreed to a counseling session. I arrived before the appointed hour, nervous and almost overcome with anxiety at what I thought was my last, best shot at reconciliation. This was one discussion for which I could not prepare. Val arrived a few minutes late with a cigarette and an attitude. It turned out her expectations were a lot different. The assistant rector of Palmer Episcopal Church turned blandly to Val to ask if she would like to say anything. She said, "Yes." She then looked at me and blurted out, "I don't love you. I've never loved you. I never will love you. And I don't see any purpose in this." With that, she walked out. The room seemed frozen in silence. Then the assistant rector exhaled deeply, looked at me, and said, "Well, that about says it all," and closed the portfolio holding his pad and pen. And that was that. Val's world had clearly come apart, and so had mine.

I have seen her once since. I mourned the end of my marriage and for several years found myself at loose ends whenever I thought about it. I reacted like many people do, I suspect, and plunged into my work to shrink the time my mind would linger on the marriage, mistakes, and recrimination. And whatever the truth of her statements and whatever my failings in helping her cope with her avalanche of grief, I will always be grateful that our brief marriage brought me to Texas and set the course for my future.

By the summer of 1980, politics had swept me up again. That meant for me a role in the campaign to carry Texas for Ronald Reagan and his running mate, my former boss, George H. W. Bush. Clements was determined to put Texas in Reagan's column in 1980. State parties could organize committees to spend money on volunteer-intensive activities in support of federal candidates, as long as the money was raised under federal campaign limits. A victory committee could run phone banks, conduct registration drives, send mailings, hold rallies, send out surrogates, and do everything a presidential campaign could do, short of running television ads. The governor called me into his office and brusquely told me to move my posterior over to the Victory Committee. He was to be its chairman and I was to be its executive director. The outcome of the presidential election could turn on the results in Texas—and so, he made clear, could my future.

The Reagan high command didn't fully trust Clements, because the governor was close to Ford, his 1976 primary opponent, and had played an important role at the 1980 Detroit convention in pressuring Reagan to tap Ford as his running mate. So they sent two people to look over our shoulders. One was the Texas Republican national committeeman Ernie Angelo, former mayor of Midland. The other was the campaign's southwestern political director, Rick Shelby. Both were parked in Austin for the rest of the campaign, and we hit it off. Angelo proved an invaluable link to the Reagan grassroots people, smoothing hurt feelings and helping glue all Republican volunteers into one massive effort. Shelby kept assuring the Reagan folks at Washington headquarters that the crazy Texans really were intent on winning.

Our headquarters was a vacant mortuary and my office was the former body-viewing room. We built a robust, statewide, grassroots organization in every county. Every conceivable voter group had its own state and local leadership, from farmers and ranchers to Hispanics to women to students to small business owners to doctors to African-Americans to left-handed orthodontists who played golf on alternate Thursdays. Well, just about.

The county committees and coalition groups were then drawn into an elaborate voter identification and get-out-the-vote operation run from more than a hundred phone centers and many more local headquarters. We put special efforts into precincts where past election returns provided evidence of lots of swing voters and even focused on Democratic primary voters in precincts where conservative Democrats ran well.

My mentor during my stint with Clements was a remarkable figure named Peter O'Donnell, Jr., Clements's close friend and the father of the modern Republican Party in Texas. As treasurer of the Victory Committee, he taught me vital lessons. "Your budget is your plan reduced to numbers and spread over time," he'd say as we started each week by reviewing reports of the committee's expenditures and income. Every expenditure had to be approved in advance with a paper trail, so there were no surprises. Everything in the campaign had to be measured against goals, from the number of volunteers recruited for each phone in each phone center to the number of county steering committee members to the number of yard signs displayed in each target precinct. If you didn't measure an activity, it tended to remain undone. We set goals for everything, then set things right where we were falling short.

The Victory Committee was a huge success. We raised $3.1 million—more than all the Victory Committees in America combined. The Reagan national campaign supported our efforts with a modest TV buy and a more-than-adequate number of appearances by Reagan and his home state vice presidential running mate, George H. W. Bush. In Texas, Reagan-Bush walloped Carter-Mondale by nearly 14 points.

My reward was to be named Governor Clements's deputy chief of staff. As the governor turned his attention to his 1982 reelection, I learned he was going to ask me to run his campaign. I would likely be made chief of staff if he were reelected. But I was hesitant. I was thirty years old. Was this the right course?

I thought about Clements himself. He had started his company when he was about my age. And while I didn't aspire to build a multigazillion-dollar one of my own, the idea of starting something and making it grow attracted me. I also saw the political changes that were taking place in Texas and I wanted to be part of them. So when I was summoned by the governor to visit with him at the end of the legislative session that May to talk about the future, I went armed with a brash idea.

The governor did ask me to run his reelection campaign and hinted at future rewards when he was reelected. I responded that like him, at my age, I wanted to start a business—a direct mail firm—and I'd like him to be my first client. He thought about it a second and said yes, he would be. He offered some sage business advice—get enough capital and talk to friends who know the pitfalls of starting a business. Then he dismissed me with a smile and a gruff wave of the hand. I think he liked my audacity.

In October 1981, Rove + Company opened its doors on Brazos Street in Austin with a staff of three and a bank of computerized printers. Within a few days, we mailed nearly a million fund-raising appeals for Governor Clements's reelection. The letter itself came in twenty-six different versions, based on the information we had about the donor, where they lived, how much they gave, and how long they'd been part of Clements's team. The programmer who wrote the code to match each version to a specific donor said the permutations were impossible. I asked him to do it anyway. I was counting on cutting-edge technology to carve out my niche in the direct mail business. I was glad to be right: the letter brought in more than $2 million in contributions.

Before long we expanded and moved to a nondescript office building outside downtown Austin. A neighbor in the duplex next door was a young cyclist in training. He rode off on his bike early in the morning as I arrived. He seemed dedicated and talented, and I thought he had a shot at doing pretty well at the sport. His name was Lance Armstrong.

While I was building my company, I was also rebuilding my personal life. There was a smart and very creative freelance graphic designer who did work for my firm. Her name was Darby Hickson. She was a cute brunette with a really big heart, a free spirit, and a complete indifference to politics. We started going out because neither of us thought we were ready to be in a serious relationship. So of course, it turned serious. We were married in 1986 and our son Andrew came in 1989. Darby is a fantastic mother. And the shy, soft-spoken artist turned out to have a warrior spirit when she was twice diagnosed with breast cancer. Her sound advice and steadiness made it possible to weather all that came in the years ahead.

I started my business because I wanted to build something and to have an impact in politics. And for the next eighteen years, that's what I tried to do. We would handle over seventy-five campaigns for governor, senator, or congress—and even more campaigns for other offices, including presidential races and work for the Moderate Party of Sweden.

Rove + Company was hard work, with late nights and early mornings, even an overnight shift at times to feed the printers that churned out fund-raising and voter contact letters. It was fun, too, but the quality of our years depended on whether our clients won or lost. Losing not only meant sometimes waiting to get paid, it could also mean facing retribution. After Governor Clements was defeated for reelection in 1982 by Democratic attorney general Mark White, for example, White's people called my nonpolitical clients, such as the Museum of Fine Arts, Houston, and a recreational fishing group, the Gulf Coast Conservation Association, to suggest it would be better if they worked with someone else. Those clients stuck with Rove + Company, but it was a sobering reminder of the perilous field I had entered.

In the 1982 elections, we did direct mail exclusively, which was profitable but not always rewarding. Big decisions were being made in the Clements reelection campaign, for instance, and I didn't have a seat at the table. I couldn't veto dumb ideas as they came up. For example, Clements imported a specialist in political tabloids from California, David Janison, who designed a fake newspaper to be mailed to swing voters. That newspaper highlighted a college drinking incident involving White. It was a dumb thing to do and voters reacted negatively. It irked me that I knew something like that was a bad idea but I had no power to stop it.

In the end, it wasn't the fake tabloid that did Clements in: the national economy was in the tank and there was a Republican in the White House. Texan families were paying record-high utility bills. White blamed the economy on the GOP and wrapped those utility bills around Clements's neck just as Clements had wrapped Carter around his opponent in 1978. Clements's defeat forced some Republicans to wonder if the party's 1978 victory had been a fluke and to ask if GOP candidates could be competitive for governor and other statewide offices in Texas. I wanted to make certain that they would be.

So starting in 1984, I started handling general consulting for Texas candidates. My firm began working on direct mail outside of Texas, too, with clients including John Ashcroft in Missouri, Orrin Hatch in Utah, and Vice President Bush's presidential campaign. By 1988, most of Rove + Company's business was for out-of-state clients.

That year was big for Republicans in Texas. The first Republicans to win statewide seats in races other than for governor or for the Senate were both my clients. Kent Hance won a seat on the powerful Texas Railroad Commission, which regulates oil, gas, and trucking, and Tom Phillips was elected as the chief justice of the Texas Supreme Court.

Two years later, in 1990, two more Republicans (Rove clients as well) were elected to statewide office, and they would shape state politics for two decades. Kay Bailey Hutchison was elected treasurer, succeeding Ann Richards. Democrats then abolished the position, which made me wonder if political payback is about the only grounds on which Democrats abolish government posts. Hutchison later became a U.S. senator. The other winner, Democrat Rick Perry, had planned to retire from the legislature until his best friend, David Weeks, and I talked him into switching parties and running for the GOP nomination for agriculture commissioner. Perry swept rural counties because, as a rancher, he actually knew something about agriculture; he won the suburbs because of his marquee good looks and conservative values. He became governor in 2000.

By 1992 I had my hands full with the senior Bush's reelection campaign, where we handled a lot of the direct mail. It was painful to watch. The Bush campaign was not worthy of the forty-first president. After Bush lost, we became busy with the 1993 special election to fill the vacancy created by the elevation of Senator Lloyd Bentsen to secretary of the Treasury by President Bill Clinton. That special election produced a delightfully shocking result: my client, Kay Bailey Hutchison, led the first round by getting more votes than the rest of the GOP field combined and then, in the run-off, routed Governor Richards's appointee by more than two to one.

But as my success grew, so did the ranks of my critics, and they propagated many myths about my work in Texas. Some are true; most are not. Here's the true story behind a few of the Myths of Rove.

Let's start with the accusation that I destroyed the career of one of the Democratic Party's rising stars, Texas Railroad Commissioner Lena Guerrero, in order to clear the field for George W. Bush's ascent in Texas politics.

This myth is true, in part. I did, as two journalists noted, pass "along information that state Railroad Commissioner Lena Guerrero . . . had lied about graduating from college. The story hit the front pages of Texas newspapers and ended Ms. Guerrero's political career."

At the time, I was working on the campaign of Barry Williamson for Texas railroad commissioner. Guerrero, his opponent, was bright, outgoing, confident, and charismatic. She had lots of raw, impressive, natural talent and she also had an important patron, Governor Richards, who understood this young woman could rise very far in politics. That's why Richards had appointed her to the powerful Railroad Commission. In that job, she once met with a bunch of truckers she regulated. One of them asked, "What's your bra size?" She shot back, "Not big enough."

But Guerrero had a problem: she had embellished her past. She claimed to be an honors graduate of the University of Texas at Austin, but in fact had never earned a degree—a fact our campaign had been tipped to by Carole McClellan, whom Williamson had beaten in the Republican primary. We had sketchy information but couldn't get university records or official confirmation of her status. In late August or early September, I called a reporter and passed on our doubts about her academic record.

The Guerrero campaign began getting calls from journalists and realized it had a problem. That September 11, Lena Guerrero admitted she hadn't earned a degree. Williamson immediately called for her to resign as railroad commissioner, and our campaign pounded her for inconsistencies. Newspaper editorials began questioning her credibility. After two weeks of growing controversy, Guerrero resigned from her post but did not drop out of the race; Williamson won by 14 points. A brilliant political career had been cut short by a padded résumé.

Did I pass on to a reporter the information that pointed to our opponent's lie? Absolutely, you bet, and I have no regrets about it whatsoever. Why should I? The information, after all, was true. That should have some bearing on this issue.

In campaigns, the public makes judgments about the values, views, and character of the candidates. The press plays a vital role in that process. Campaigns routinely share with reporters disparaging information about their opponents; it's the responsibility of journalists to decide whether the charges are accurate and, if they are, whether they are worthy of being shared with the public.

Guerrero was an extraordinary political talent who led a remarkable life after leaving politics. She never blamed others for her defeat: she accepted responsibility for misleading voters and developed a reputation as a savvy, hardworking lobbyist. She died of brain cancer in the spring of 2008 at the age of fifty after a heroic struggle.

Another Myth of Rove is that in 1986, I bugged my own office in order to drum up a negative story against Governor Mark White, when my client Bill Clements was running to unseat him. My detractors say I got the idea from a Richard Gere movie, *Power*. The real story is that on the morning of October 1, 1986, I had a telephone conversation with George Bayoud, Clements's campaign manager, about bringing Lee Atwater in for the final weeks of the campaign and raising our television ad buy to 650 gross rating points.

Television gross rating point levels are one of those findable secrets you want to keep locked up as long as possible. Generally, 100 gross rating points means a viewer will see your ad one time in a week. The opposition always wants to know how much you're buying and where. Opponents can get information on your TV buys, but they should have to work for it by checking individual station logs.

That afternoon, the Clements campaign press secretary received a phone call from a *Dallas Morning News* reporter, Sam Attlesey, about the two items George and I discussed in our call. It rattled us. How could someone know about both sensitive topics? Since we had not yet placed the additional orders for our buy, it was troubling if the opposition knew what we were going to purchase before we did. What added to our concern was that after our talk that morning, I'd run into George and told him I'd given him the wrong number of gross rating points the buy was being increased to. It wasn't really 650. But that was Attlesey's number.

We were entering the campaign's final month and could leave nothing to chance. Bayoud decided to have the headquarters swept for electronic bugs and picked a Fort Worth firm to do it. The afternoon of the sweep, I was in Dallas attending a prep session for the following night's televised gubernatorial debate. George called me to say the security team had found nothing in the headquarters. They had finished early and he wanted to sweep my company office as well. I called Jamie Clements (no relation to Bill), who ran my firm's nonpolitical business, and asked him to let the security team in.

By the time I returned that evening, the security team had told Jamie they'd discovered a listening device in the frame of a small needlepoint elephant that hung on a wall near my desk. George and I agreed we had to let federal, state, and local law enforcement know. By the morning, FBI agents had brought in enough electronic equipment to launch a satellite. After another round of discussions, we decided we needed to say something to the press and so hastily called a news conference Monday. We did not say the White campaign had planted the bug, though I did say, "There is no doubt . . . the only ones who would benefit from this detailed, sensitive information would be the political opposition." The White campaign immediately denied having anything to do with it. The incident dropped off the front pages within a few days and, after a long investigation, the FBI never indicted anyone.

Journalists have pointed out that the security team removed the bug from the office and took it to their hotel room with them. But I didn't pick the firm or direct their work. One member of the security team that swept the office and the owner of Knight Diversified, Gary Morphew, refused to take a polygraph exam. Maybe he refused because being in the security business, he didn't trust lie detectors. In any case, not taking it was his right. But I didn't hire him and he certainly didn't have any reason to cover for me if he had any evidence that would implicate me. In the end, law enforcement officers were just as baffled as I was as to just how the bug got into my office.

The device had a regular six-volt battery with a ten-hour life span and the "juice" remaining on the battery pointed to its having been turned on that day. But I'd been in Dallas, and there had been no plan to sweep my office when I boarded my plane. To bug the office, I would have had to get an electronic listening device, hide it behind the frame early Sunday before departing for Dallas, and wait for Bayoud to decide—at the last minute—to sweep my company's suite. That's a pretty cheeky gamble.

Finally, it has been surmised that I got the idea of bugging my own office from the movie *Power*, in which Richard Gere stars as a rock-star political consultant. I admit I've seen the movie. On VCR. From the rental store. Long after the 1986 Clements campaign. I howled at the image of a political consultant who got paid vast sums every month by all his clients and got them elected through contrived ads that would last about five minutes in the real world.

Yet another myth about me calls into question the integrity of the FBI and the Justice Department. It claims that between 1988 and 1990 I directed the FBI to investigate statewide elected Democratic office-holders, including Treasurer Ann Richards, Comptroller Bob Bullock, Land Commissioner Garry Mauro, and Agriculture Commissioner Jim Hightower.

The FBI did investigate Texas officials during that span, but I had nothing to do with it. The investigation was called "Brilab" and was part of a broad anticorruption probe that looked at officials in Louisiana, Oklahoma, Los Angeles, and Washington, D.C., as well as Texas.

What got the most attention in Texas at the time was the agency's investigation of Agriculture Commissioner Jim Hightower's office. An official for the U.S. Department of Agriculture spotted expenses claimed by Hightower's shop that raised red flags. That official alerted the FBI, which dug deeper and discovered enough to indict some of Hightower's top aides; they were later found guilty and sent to prison. The story became a live political issue in the campaign because newspapers covering the story printed details that embarrassed Hightower.

The myth that I had something to do both with spurring the investigation and with airing all of this has stuck around because it is convenient for some to blame me rather than those aides who ran afoul of the law. Some of the dust kicked up by the investigation swirled around Hightower for a long time, giving him and others an incentive to find someone other than themselves to blame.

Ultimately, the "proof" behind the myth comes down to the claim that I controlled FBI agent Greg Rampton, who led the investigations in Texas. The truth is that I met Agent Rampton once or perhaps twice in person and talked to him on the phone at his request several times. We met because he had sought me out—as he had scores of others involved in Texas politics—to see if I had any information that might be useful in his investigation of corruption at the Texas Department of Agriculture. I didn't.

As much as I wish I could claim credit for discovering the illegal activity at the Texas Department of Agriculture, I did not. And while it would have been nice during the 1990 campaign to have known in advance how much bad stuff happened beneath the roof of that department under Hightower's stewardship, I didn't. I read about it in the newspaper along with everyone else.

Of course, these Myths of Rove that grew up in Texas in the 1980s had consequences for me. I felt those effects with particular force after I had been appointed to the Board of Regents of East Texas State University, now called Texas A&M University–Commerce, by Governor Clements. The appointment was subject to a vote of approval by the state Senate when the legislature next met. In the sixteen months between my appointment and the legislative session, Democrats won back the governor's office. It was payback time. I was sent word that Senate Democrats would "bust" me and it was in my interest to withdraw. I knew they had the votes to do it, but I get stubborn sometimes. If Democrats were going to "bust" me, they'd have to do it in public.

On the appointed day, I appeared before the Senate Nominations Committee, meeting on the floor of the Senate chamber. Three Democratic legislators, led by state senator Bobby Joe Glasgow, hammered me for what seemed like hours about getting the FBI to investigate statewide Democratic elected officials. Several other Democratic senators rushed in to push a few more lances into my hide before the committee voted five to one to send my name to the complete Senate without a recommendation, which was a death sentence for my nomination.

I was later told that following the contentious Nominations Committee hearing, the powerful Democratic lieutenant governor, Bob Bullock, who'd been watching the sordid little beating from the front of the chamber, sidled up to Glasgow. "Senator, I want you to think about what you've just said," Bullock began. "You have alleged this young man investigated me, Richards, Mauro, and Hightower. If what you've said is not true, then you've slandered his good Christian name and you owe him an apology." Bullock paused so his words could sink in before saying, "And if you believe what you said is true, then you're dumber than you look." This was a Democrat I could love.

CHAPTER 4

What Is à Rovian Campaign?

———— • ◆ • ————

Ihave become an adjective. There is something called a "Rovian" style of campaigning, and it's meant as an insult. President Barack Obama said many times during the campaign that he wanted to end "the Karl Rove era of politics." One columnist said it consists "mainly of throwing mud until it sticks." Another pair of journalists characterized my style as "episodes of dirty tricks, well-timed investigations, and electoral legerdemain." One prominent blogger described the elements of "a textbook Rovian race" as "fear-based, smear-based, anything goes." Yet another writer found it "remarkable . . . the way the media consistently respond to being lied to, pissed on and manipulated by Rove." And then comes this version: "Even the most hardened cynics find themselves continually surprised by the ability of Rove and his minions to always hit that evasive new low, coming up with things that would shock a 60-year-old Greyhound-station hooker."

Where should I begin to respond to that? These criticisms not only fail to capture what a Rovian campaign is, they are also grounded in a fundamentally negative, even absurd view of voters. These writers think the electorate is stupid, easily misled by smashmouth TV ads, dirty tricks, and fear-and-smear politics. These writers also believe the media are equally susceptible to being manipulated by political consultants—not just briefly, but over decades.

In reality, there are eight hallmarks of a "Rovian" campaign.

To be Rovian, a campaign must first be centered on big ideas that reflect the candidate's philosophy and views and that are perceived by voters as important and relevant.

Second, the campaign needs to be persistent in pursuing this strong, persuasive theme in a way that resonates with what voters know. This requires a campaign to have a clear awareness of the electorate's attitudes, and its candidate's strengths and weaknesses, as well as those of its opponent.

The third hallmark of a Rovian campaign is that it is driven by historical data. Past races can help you understand what might happen in the next. Democrats dominated Texas in the late 1980s. To find voters who might be drawn to a Republican candidate, I studied election patterns to find counties with strong support for Reagan in 1980 or 1984 but whose voters also chose Democrats in local races or for governor or senator. In 2000, hoping to pull some states away from the Democrats for George W. Bush's presidential race, I looked at places in Tennessee and Arkansas that had voted for GOP Senate and gubernatorial candidates in the 1990s while voting for Clinton-Gore in 1992 and '96.

The fourth hallmark of a Rovian campaign is the use of sophisticated modeling to identify potential supporters and match them with issues that will persuade and turn them out. All kinds of publicly available information about voters can be used to predict which party or candidate someone will support, what issues will win them over, and the likelihood they will actually vote. That information can include, for example, their age, what kind of car they have, whether they rent or own, the magazines they read, their TV viewing habits, whether they have a gun, where they shop and what they buy, if and where they go to church, their hobbies, their birthplace, and whether they own stock. There is no one piece of data that can predict the behavior of a voter: it's the relationship between all kinds of data points that can be revealing. So the modeling is complex and difficult to do, but it can make a huge impact by allowing a campaign to focus its energies on voters who are truly up for grabs and on those who need extra encouragement to turn out.

The fifth hallmark of a Rovian campaign is that it understands that there are right and wrong ways to criticize an opponent. Too many campaigns spend too much time going after their opponents in a scattershot way and on trivial issues. Bob Dole's 1996 campaign against Bill Clinton suffered from this problem. He attacked Clinton for, among other things, cheating at golf. And the campaign of George H. W. Bush in 1992 also made the mistake of attacking Clinton's running mate, Al Gore, as an environmental extremist by calling him "Ozone Man."

The sixth Rovian hallmark is that the campaign has a strategic plan, discipline, and a bias for action. It is structured to keep momentum. Second-guessing, or allowing warring factions to develop inside a campaign, is destructive. A Rovian campaign sets goals and repeatedly checks performance against those goals.

The seventh hallmark of a Rovian campaign is that it depends on the broadest possible use of volunteer-friendly technology. As one pair of journalists put it, "This may sound prosaic, but there is no way to overstate its relevance to Rove's success. His campaigns always had the most advanced gizmos." I have enormous respect for Net Nerds, Applications Junkies, Tech Heads, and Data Dudes.

Finally, a Rovian campaign is focused on collecting three vital resources: knowledge and information for the candidate; volunteers to persuade and get out the vote; and the money to make the other elements of the campaign possible.

Of these eight hallmarks, the first four are the most important, with the first being *primus inter pares*. A campaign needs to be centered on a big theme that is in turn made up of big ideas that will capture the support and the imagination of voters. The Bush 2000 campaign was centered on compassionate conservatism, which itself was based on four big foundations: education reform, the faith-based initiative, a generous middle-class tax cut, and Social Security and Medicare reform.

A campaign's essential argument must be easily understood, capable of being widely disseminated, backed by evidence, and authentic. The argument must be clearly laid out in the open; otherwise voters will miss it. Even if the theme is essentially negative ("throw the bums out"), it is better argued in a positive and optimistic way ("We are the change that we seek" or "Together we can have a new beginning, for ourselves and for our children"). And the candidate should play a large role in shaping the message—he will have to be comfortable delivering it.

This point can't be emphasized often enough: a campaign should be based on what the candidate believes, not simply on what the polls say.

Campaigns that search endlessly through surveys for "80/20" issues—propositions that 80 percent or more of voters favor—often end in failure or help elect a politician who will be frustrated in trying to enact the policies that got him into politics in the first place. Dole talked about how his campaign's focus group had pointed to certain attack lines against Clinton. At one presidential campaign rally, for example, he asked supporters whether they would feel more comfortable leaving their children with him or with Bill Clinton, because focus groups had told Dole that they would be more comfortable with him. Were voters supposed to be impressed with that? California governor Arnold Schwarzenegger has also zoomed from one side of the ideological spectrum to the other, chasing polls. He has opposed spending and taxes one month and then embraced them the next, often because that appeared popular in the latest poll.

In the 2000 election, we wanted voters to see George W. Bush as a different kind of Republican who would restore dignity and honor to a tarnished White House. In 2004, we wanted voters to see President Bush as a strong leader who, even if you didn't agree with him, was making decisions on what he thought would best protect America. The central question voters have for every campaign is: Why elect your guy? In both cases, we answered that with a clear, compelling, and true message that met an overarching political issue at the time—in the first it was a desire to erase the bitterness and scandal that then characterized Washington, and in the second it was the belief that America needed a leader who could protect the country from further terrorist attacks.

Issues are also ways for people to understand a candidate's character and values. For example, when Bush said education was the civil rights struggle of our time or that the absence of an accountability system in our schools meant black, brown, poor, and rural children were getting left behind, it gave listeners important information about his respect and concern for every family and deepened the impression that he was a different kind of Republican whom suburban voters (many of whom had defected in 1992 and 1996 to Clinton) could be proud to support.

Still, it isn't enough to have a big theme. That theme needs to be structured and delivered in a way that resonates with the information that voters carry around in their heads. Here's where the second element of campaigns I have been associated with comes into play. There's plenty of information in most people's brains, but it isn't well organized. Most voters pay little attention to the day-to-day of a campaign. They tend to tune in when it's convenient and tune out when work, family, or just plain life takes over. Campaigns make a mistake if they either underestimate the information available to a voter or overestimate the average voter's attention.

So how does a campaign convey information that will stick? The idea that elections are settled only by attack ads, nasty rumors, or unsupported personal assaults isn't (fortunately) the way politics works. A better way to think about a campaign is to remember the childhood tale "The Emperor's New Clothes." The higher a race's profile, the more likely it is that at its conclusion, voters see the candidates as they truly are. Most voters, even if they have partisan leanings, tend to see both the good and bad points of each candidate and then try to make a sensible judgment about who would do a better job. It's very difficult, if not impossible, for candidates to hide their true natures, especially after our long, grueling presidential campaigns. A strategist's goal is to help people see candidates as they really are—but as they really are on their better days.

In shaping a candidate's essential message, I have often drawn on the insights of Tony Schwartz, a reclusive Democratic media consultant who pioneered the use of sound in advertising. He's the creator of Lyndon Johnson's famous 1964 "Daisy" ad, which, as Schwartz explains it, "shows a little girl in a field counting petals on a daisy. As her count reaches ten, the visual motion is frozen and the viewer hears a countdown. When the countdown reaches zero we see a nuclear explosion. . . ." Most people think the ad then goes on to attack Barry Goldwater as trigger-happy. Yet Goldwater's name is never mentioned. The ad features the voice of President Johnson saying, "These are the stakes, to make a world in which all God's children can live, or to go into the darkness. Either we must love each other or we must die." The ad was shown only one time: during NBC's *Monday Night at the Movies* on September 7, 1964.

It was highly effective because it drew on an existing impression about Goldwater. As Schwartz put it in *The Responsive Chord,* "Political advertising involves tuning in on attitudes and beliefs of the voter and then affecting those attitudes with the proper auditory and visual stimuli." He goes on, "We are not concerned with getting things *across* to people as much as *out* of people." While Schwartz was writing about ads, I think his theory applies to the general message of a campaign: it has to be structured to evoke a reaction from voters that will cut through the clutter and focus attention on a central question. That means the important question is, What values and attitudes do voters already have in their minds about a candidate and what message will draw on that information to produce the response you want?

That's different from asking, What do I need to educate voters about? For example, in Bush's 2000 campaign, we targeted suburban couples with children. Many of these voters had defected to Clinton in 1992 or 1996; some had simply stayed home. Bush's focus on No Child Left Behind and education reform resonated with their natural desire to want the best for their children and the inclination of many of these voters to see a quality education for other children as a social good.

Another question that needs to be answered is, Which supporters of your opponent can you poach by emphasizing a certain aspect of your message? Senator Barack Obama did this in the 2008 campaign by emphasizing his Christian faith, pledging to continue President George W. Bush's faith-based office, and doing serious outreach to evangelical leaders. He was under no illusion he would win a majority of religiously observant voters, but he knew some were lukewarm toward Senator John McCain and he wanted to seem minimally acceptable to them. He did the same thing by dispatching his wife to campaign among military families, hoping at the very least to make his campaign appear friendly toward the military and perhaps even to diminish Senator McCain's strength among the broader veteran community.

Sometimes making a connection between a candidate and a voter means telling your candidate what he is doing right, and what he is doing wrong. I have had to be brutally frank with my candidates over the years. In 1985, Bill Clements was thinking of running again for Texas governor the following year after being defeated for reelection in 1982. So I wrote him a memo to tell him that in his losing 1982 campaign he "came across as too negative, too mean and without hope for a better future for Texas." He had to overcome weaknesses: there was "little enthusiasm" among Republican voters, "outright hostility" among party leaders, and an "attitude . . . of resignation" among supporters and donors. The press shared these views and was eager to write that Clements was running to get his job back "for revenge-inspired reasons." If not dealt with, these weaknesses could prove fatal to his candidacy. It was a hard memo to write, but it was necessary. He was smart enough to accept the diagnosis and act on it, even if I was essentially telling him that people saw him as a jerk.

Another myth about my campaign approach is that I preach to the already committed. My model, it is said, is to "sharpen the differences, energize the conservative base, and microtarget the faithful." Many pundits and experts said it was the model used to reelect Bush in 2004. Charlie Cook, an otherwise sharp-eyed student of American politics, was asked about our efforts to reach "the middle for independent and swing voters" in that contest. His answer: "The Bush campaign never tried."

This is silly. How do you win elections by only "talking to the base"? A party's base is, by definition, part of a larger whole, which itself is only part of an even larger electorate. The base is not enough to win any election, except in the deepest blue or red districts or states. It's certainly not enough to win two presidential races.

Elections are about addition, not subtraction, about combining those who are predisposed to be for a candidate because they are from the same party with enough other voters to win. So how do you get there?

First, you determine what the likely turnout is. This tells you how many voters you need to win. Candidates start with those who will vote for them almost no matter what—the hard-core "base" of a party. To figure that out, look at the number, take the number of votes the worst Republican or Democratic candidate on the ballot has received, and toss out any candidate who has been arrested or is dead: that's the base vote.

The next group to consider consists of those who are inclined to vote for your candidate and need to be motivated to turn out. In an average presidential election, 58 percent of eligible voters actually cast a ballot; in a midterm year, it's 42 percent. Registered voters who don't show up at the polls look like the voters who do. With a focused organization and strong message, they can often be convinced to turn out for the party to which they are naturally affiliated. But in the vast majority of contests, this is still not enough to win.

That puts the focus on swing voters. In recent decades, there has been a rise in "independent" voters who have not registered with one of the major parties, but the number of true swing voters has shrunk, declining from 16 percent of the electorate in 1988 to 7 percent in 2002. This has made swing voters more difficult to find and, paradoxically, more important to the outcome of an election.

These voters either move from one party to another between elections or, more commonly, split their tickets, voting for a candidate of one party for one office and then crossing over to vote for a candidate from the other party for another office. They can be found by looking at past county or precinct elections. The more widespread the pattern of swing in a precinct or county, the more important it is to focus on that area with volunteers, advertising, and the candidate. I've gone so far as to apportion a candidate's time based on each county's share of the swing-voter pool.

Another group to try to entice into supporting your candidate overlaps a bit with swing voters—it's the persuadable members of the opposition party. This is usually a small group, but it has double the impact of other swing blocs because for every one of these voters you move into your camp you also move one vote out of your opponent's camp. Databases compiled from the results of old campaign phone ID surveys are particularly helpful in identifying opposition party members who have previously bolted from their party's nominee and therefore might be willing to bolt again.

In 1999 and early 2000, I became convinced that George W. Bush could win West Virginia. To others it seemed like a dubious proposition. Bob Dole had lost the Mountain State by 14 points. But Clinton had won the state with only 51 percent of the vote and the growing number of ticket splitters was a sign of an electorate in transition. The state's coal industry was under attack from the Clinton administration, many Democratic voters were pro-life, pro-prayer, and pro-gun, even if they had voted Democratic for decades, and it seemed Bush would be a better fit than the elitist Al Gore. We made a concerted effort to win the state, and it paid off. Bush beat Gore by 6 points in West Virginia. That was a 15-point swing from four years earlier: more than one out of every ten voters who cast a ballot for Clinton-Gore in 1996 pulled the lever for Bush-Cheney in 2000. In the end, the presidential election was so close that without West Virginia's electoral votes, Bush would not have won the presidency. If Bush had focused only on the base of the Republican Party, he would not have swiped a tenth of those who had voted for

Clinton-Gore in 1996 in a state that last went for the GOP in an open race for president in 1928. West Virginia's results destroy the myth that Bush was interested only in his party's base.

So do the results of his 2004 reelection. How could President Bush have run a "base election" and won 62,040,610 votes—3 million more than any previous candidate for president? Bush received 23 percent more votes—11,580,500—than he won in 2000. One hundred fifty-six counties went from voting for Gore in 2000 to voting for Bush in 2004, while only sixty counties went the opposite direction. Bush nearly erased the gender gap, carried the highest percentage of Hispanic voters for a Republican since exit polls began measuring the group, and improved his record among African-Americans by 20 percent from four years before. He even increased his support by 4 points among union members.

None of this could have happened if Bush was just talking to hardcore Republicans, and many smart Democrats acknowledged this when it was over. Al Gore's campaign manager, Donna Brazile, said, "Karl Rove did not leave one state behind in putting together the president's reelection strategy. If you need proof, just look around Washington, D.C. They put up Bush-Cheney signs in areas as blue as the Pacific Ocean." Terry McAuliffe, then chairman of the Democratic National Committee and as partisan a Democrat as there is, said, "They were smart. They came into our neighborhoods . . . with very specific messages to take Democratic voters away from us."

Bush's success would have been impossible if he had ignored swing voters, persuadable Democrats, and the 40 percent of adults who don't bother to vote or even register in a presidential election.

So what is the secret to winning over that last group? At any given time, roughly 30 percent of eligible voters are unregistered. The consensus among political scientists is that the unregistered are different from registered voters attitudinally more than demographically. They are less interested in specific issues and more interested in character, less trusting of government, more cynical about politics, less partisan than those who are registered to vote, and busier in their personal lives. These voters are hard to find, especially in rapidly growing areas where they haven't become rooted in a community. But in a district or state that's closely balanced, a concerted registration effort can alter, over time, the underlying political landscape to the benefit of one party or the other. In 2004 in particular, the Bush campaign used new tools to pinpoint unregistered Republicans and beat the Democrats and their special interest allies at the registration game.

The question of addition comes down to this: Can you realistically hope to win by cobbling together a coalition of nearly predictable hard-core partisans; some newly energized supporters; a reasonable number of swing voters; modest defections from the opposition party; and some newly registered voters? If so, where are these people and what will it take to get them to cast a vote for your candidate? And if one slice of this group can't be reached, how do you make up the difference?

I saw all of this come together in a February 1991 special election runoff in Texas Senate District 9. It was the home seat of the Democratic governor and lieutenant governor. The district had never elected a Republican. Our candidate was a maxifacial oral surgeon from Waco named David Sibley, who had suffered a debilitating accident at the age of thirty-six that ended his medical practice. He went to law school and then, after graduating, rather than join a major law firm, he became a $19,000-a-year prosecutor in the district attorney's office. He had served on the city council and now was running for Senate against an eleven-term Democratic powerhouse named Betty Denton. The odds were long, but there were enough swing voters who, if matched with a big Republican turn-out in the Dallas suburbs on the far northern edge of the district, could help pull off an upset win for Sibley. We set county-by-county targets and developed a plan to reach them.

On election night, Sibley's backers rallied in the unused office of a local highway contractor to await the returns. Many of them thought that the night would mark another defeat for Republicans. Jeff Norwood, the campaign manager, and I huddled over a laptop that contained our election model. As the results rolled in, we entered them into the computer and cheered early returns that showed Sibley getting shellacked in rural counties. He lost Limestone County with Denton's 61 percent to his 39 percent, Falls County with her 53 percent to his 47 percent, and Navarro County with her 55 percent to his 45 percent. Sibley's backers couldn't understand our excitement. But we knew that we were running ahead of what our model required in those counties and were on course to win if the trend held.

As the more populous and suburban counties began coming in and

we inched closer and closer to Denton's total, we turned a group of skeptical donors and local luminaries into a cigar-chomping, jittery, almost-
ready-to-believe mob—one that exploded when Dallas County finally
came in and Sibley moved ahead. The scene was electric, like the locker
room after a high school football game where an underdog has upset the
state champs. Sibley won 54 percent to 47 percent. The little model on
the laptop had projected the outcome within a handful of ballots.

I also learned that victories beget resentments, which beget enemies,
which beget myths. The most tiresome one about me is that my modus
operandi is to "destroy the opponent at all costs," generally through an
onslaught of vicious attacks, most of them subterranean and all of them
unfair.

My critics would never accept the truth of the matter, which is that I
wouldn't employ such tactics regardless of their efficacy. It assumes there
are plenty of good candidates who'd hire an amoral bastard. There aren't,
and I'm not. But set those facts aside for a moment and look only at
whether this kind of campaign really works. Attacks are like nitroglycer-
ine: powerful and volatile, capable of inflicting great damage to an intended target and to those who deploy it. They are insufficient to win all
but the very rare election, especially those launched "at all costs."

To be successful, an attack must be perceived as both fair and relevant, backed with credible evidence, and launched at the right time. And
since every argument generates a counterargument, successful attacks
have to sway a significant number of people without causing a counter-
reaction among a larger number of voters.

"Fair" means that most voters will think the charge is instructive
about the candidate's character and ability to do the job. Tone matters:
angry, desperate, and undisciplined rhetoric undermines a perception of
fairness; a calm, somewhat reluctant but principled tone strengthens it.
The key element is credibility. The more voters see credible evidence for
the charge, the more likely they are to believe it. The more that evidence
comes from third parties or, most powerfully of all, from the actions and
words of the person being attacked, the stronger the argument.

I once had a candidate who criticized an incumbent Texas state senator for being in business with a corrupt land speculator—a fact the senator tried to hide even after the developer went to jail. Unfortunately for
him, we had copies of the developer's notes, telling his aide the make and

color of the car the senator wanted for having completed some politically sensitive legal work. It was hard to deny the connection when the request was in the developer's own handwriting and it matched the car in the senator's garage. My client, Florence Shapiro, won a tremendous upset and later became Republican leader of the Texas Senate.

In the era of broadband and cheap video cameras, there is no more powerful evidence to employ than a candidate's own words, particularly if they resonate with people's views about his true character. Eric Schmidt, Google's CEO, recently said that because of the Internet and tools like YouTube, "We are witnessing the end of Rovian politics." He's wrong. Mr. Schmidt's creation, Google, has helped many campaigns launch a smart bomb at an opponent by providing ready access to embarrassing, but often highly relevant, quotes or images.

Just ask former U.S. senator George Allen, a Republican from Virginia. He called a Democratic opposition researcher who had been assigned to follow his campaign "macaca." The racially insensitive gaffe was all over the Internet and contributed to his defeat; it added to an existing perception that Allen was not senatorial enough.

Timing also plays a key role. It's hard to attack someone if people don't know who you are. A candidate must build his own credibility before launching an attack. On the other hand, waiting too long gives voters a reason to decide that an attack is nothing but a last-minute smear. Too many campaigns not only wait too long, they exaggerate the charge once it's made. Democrats long ago wore out the effectiveness of their old attack that Republicans want to abolish Medicare and Social Security, as Gore discovered in 2000. Making the case against an opponent is best done in a positive way. This isn't always easy and it is best done when a candidate can describe what he would do, so that the contrast with the opponent is implied. This was Texas governor George W. Bush's approach in 2000.

Americans were repulsed by the knowledge that the president of the United States had had oral sex with an intern in the Oval Office. On the other hand, they were sick of the vicious, undignified way in which both parties had handled the scandal. Bush decided not to attack Bill Clinton's behavior, but to describe what he would do if entrusted with the responsibilities of the presidency. This was encapsulated in his pledge to "restore dignity and honor to the White House." The criticism was offered in an oblique way, but people knew perfectly well what he was talking about and accepted the message. A frontal assault would have backfired.

Another important thing to remember is that a counterpunch is often stronger than an initial punch. That may mean a candidate tries to maneuver his opponent into striking the first blow on a topic. It certainly means that when the truth is on a candidate's side, he can turn the attack to his advantage. The best example I've seen of that happening came in response to a television ad that CBS News labeled the worst of the 1996 campaign. It wasn't a Clinton or Dole commercial; it was a spot put on the air by Alabama Supreme Court justice Kenneth Ingram. The commercial attacked his Republican opponent, a University of Alabama Law School professor named Harold See, who was a client of mine.

Ostensibly sponsored by a previously unknown group called "Committee for Family Values," the spot featured a woman in a blue wingback chair who said:

A Supreme Court Justice should have integrity.

According to court documents, Harold See abandoned his wife and two children in Chicago, was accused of adultery and emotional abuse, and fought over child support.

He came to Alabama and started dating one of his college students.

Now he says he's for family values. Harold See's trying to hide his past—a past that makes him unfit for our Court.

We'd received advance warning from a friend at a TV station that the ad was coming, so when it appeared on Wednesday evening six days before the election, we were ready. The next day, Harold See and his wife, Brenda, along with his daughter from his first marriage, Mary See Tait, held four news conferences across the state to denounce the ad. Mary was a powerful presence, telling reporters that Ingram's "cruel personal attacks" were "very hurtful to me and my family" and calling her father "an honest and kind man . . . a devoted father, husband and good example for all his children." Mary read a statement from her mother and See's first wife, Judi See, denying the allegations and praising See as "a good man whom I believe will make a great Supreme Court justice for Alabama." She described how See had remained close to his children and met all his obligations following their divorce. She also revealed that the

Ingram campaign had tried to contact her "through a friend under false pretenses" in order to obtain negative information about her former husband.

The news conferences were riveting and emotional, especially as Brenda and Mary hugged each other. I arranged for Mary to cut a television ad drawing on her mother's words and decrying the Ingram ad.

The attack was tough and vicious; the problem for Ingram was that it was also late and untrue. So the counterpunch proved to be far more powerful than the punch. Each news conference was the kind of moment that producers call "great television" and that voters take as revealing and honest. See beat Ingram 53 percent to 47 percent.

Here's another rule to keep in mind: People are inclined to disregard attacks whose source is either unknown or suspect. To be effective, an attack must be launched by someone with credibility and defended when the candidate on the receiving end, the media, credible third parties, or some combination of the above launches a counterattack. A candidate must be willing to defend and stand behind his charge.

I can't think of any candidate who won a race because of anonymous smears circulated underground, though I'll later write about one candidate I worked with who came close to losing because of an attack launched at the last minute through the media. But in that instance, the charge was true, and I was one of the people who bungled an important decision that could have defused the attack in advance. My poor judgment nearly cost George W. Bush the White House.

But most elections are conducted among too many voters for an Internet smear or ugly flyer or whispered rumor to turn the contest. Of course, that doesn't keep writers from suggesting that it happens and that often, I am behind the ugliness.

One gullible magazine journalist has written that in the 1996 Harold See campaign I arranged to print flyers "viciously attacking" See and his family, hoping the over-the-top attacks would generate a backlash against See's opponent, Justice Ingram. The alleged flyers were never described in the story, and their content never revealed for a simple reason: they never existed. Such a tactic—printing flyers attacking my own client to create sympathy—makes absolutely no sense. First, it would have been impossible for a handful of staffers to distribute the "Hefty bags" full of smear sheets that the journalist claimed had been produced. Second, no amount

of under-the-radar flyers can turn a race when 2,470,766 registered voters are at stake. Had it existed, such a piece of paper would no doubt
have been splashed on the front pages of local newspapers. Yet no newspaper carried a single report in the entire 1996 campaign about the phan-
tom pamphlet. The magazine writer got snookered.

One of the persistent Rove myths is that I advise campaigns to attack
the strengths of their opponents. For example, it's been suggested that I
had a role in the attacks launched by the Swift Boat Veterans for Truth
against John Kerry in 2004. The Swift Boat Vets were Vietnam veterans,
many of whom had served with John Kerry and were highly critical of his
antiwar, antimilitary statements and actions. The most powerful attack
they launched was to run a tape of Kerry testifying before the Senate Foreign Relations Committee in 1971 criticizing the war in Vietnam. Kerry
said that his comrades in America's military had "raped, cut off ears, cut
off heads, cut off limbs, randomly shot at civilians, razed villages in a
fashion reminiscent of Genghis Khan . . ." I didn't have anything to do
with the ad (or the Swift Boat Veterans for Truth), but it was very effective because it used Kerry's own face and words to show him attacking
the U.S. military specifically and, by implication, our country. It damaged Kerry's campaign because it was true and because he was trying to
run for president on his war record.

Truth be told, I'm partly responsible for creating this myth about
punching the enemy where he is strong. I once told Texas reporters, "I
don't attack people on their weaknesses. That usually doesn't get the job
done. Voters already perceive weaknesses. You've got to go after the other
guy's strengths. That's how you win." What I should have said is: Never
go after someone's strength; go after what he *thinks* is his strength, but
what is, in reality, a weakness. Al Gore thinks he's strong because he's
smarter than most people. Fine; depict him as someone who looks down
on voters. John Kerry thinks he's strong on defense because he served in
Vietnam; go after his nearly thirty-year history of voting against a strong
military, including voting against funding the troops in combat in Iraq
and Afghanistan. Ann Richards thinks she's strong with the largely conservative Texas electorate because she has avoided issues that would alien-
ate them; go after her for not taking on school funding, welfare, juvenile
justice, and legal reform.

Some people believe that politics would be better if campaigns were without strife. I like the thought, but I also know that such campaigns have never existed. The founders—including Thomas Jefferson, James Madison, and John Adams—leveled attacks on their opponents that make modern campaigns look like meditation sessions. In the end, elections are about differences. They are how we channel disagreements on how to move this country forward. But I do think politics would be better off if campaigns drew on facts and real differences that matter to voters rather than trivial allegations.

As Rove + Company celebrated its twelfth anniversary in the fall of 1993, all these "Rovian" campaign theories were about to be tested on a big stage with consequences few could anticipate. The goal was the Texas governorship, held by an enormously charismatic, wisecracking Democrat named Ann Richards, whose job approval was at 67 percent and who had more than $4 million in her war chest. And on top of it, my client had a career won-lost record of 0 and 1 and said he'd never attack Richards personally. How on earth were we supposed to win?

CHAPTER 5

Conquering Texas

———•◆•———

A nn Richards burst onto the national scene in 1988 when, as Texas
state treasurer, she skewered George H. W. Bush at the Democratic
National Convention, saying, "Poor George, he was born with a silver
foot in his mouth." The country roared with laughter and the first President Bush later acknowledged the barb by giving Ms. Richards a silver
pin shaped like a foot after he won the election.

Texans had come to appreciate her outsize character and her ability to
thrive in a male-dominated political arena despite being a liberal in a
conservative state. She'd done so by deploying her big gray hair, crinkly
eyes, deep ambition, and wicked wit. She outmaneuvered her competitors and proved to be very tough.

Her Christmas cards were famous. There was one with a picture of
Richards and a friend in biblical costumes looking lovingly at a manger.
It read, "It's a girl!" She was also known for her collection of costumes,
including one of Dolly Parton, that she would bring out on the smallest
excuse. *Texas Monthly* once put on its cover a Photoshopped image of her
dressed in white leather with fringe, sitting astride a Harley. The headline: "White Hot Mama: Ann Richards Is Riding High. Can She Be the
First Woman President?" She was also a recovering alcoholic with a deeply
moving story of rehabilitation and redemption.

In the 1990 Democratic gubernatorial primary, she faced the "junkyard dog" of Texas politics, Attorney General Jim Mattox, beating back his false charges that she had abused drugs. Then she beat a rich Republican rancher named Clayton Williams, who tried to portray her as a liberal politician out of step with Texas.

She made herself into an advocate for building a "New Texas," a phrase that could mean all things to all people. Conservatives saw it as nationalistic praise for Texas greatness. Liberals viewed it as evidence that she was with them on the issues, but just couldn't say so publicly. To many voters, it struck just the right feel-good note.

Defeating Ann Richards in 1994 would be a daunting task. Yet George W. Bush did win, focusing on four big issues, spending months campaigning in small-town Texas, throwing counterpunches that were stronger than the punches he received, and delivering three just-right words in a debate.

Why did George W. Bush—whose only previous race for office ended in defeat—even try?

For one thing, he had long been interested in politics and felt he was good at it; also, running the Texas Rangers ball team gave him confidence that he was better suited for executive, rather than legislative, office. By the time his father was defeated in 1992, the son had developed his own reputation in Texas as the fan-friendly owner of the Rangers who had helped build a handsome new ballpark in Arlington. But even that was not enough to propel George W. Bush to run for governor. He needed an issue and an opening. He got both when Governor Richards failed to lead on education.

On May 1, 1993, voters rejected Richards's Proposition One, which would have allowed the state to redistribute property tax revenues from wealthier school districts to poorer districts in an attempt to close achievement gaps between different groups of students. The vote wasn't even close. Called "Robin Hood," the measure was thoroughly disliked because many districts with modest, middle-class neighborhoods believed their tax base would be targeted. In the end, 63 percent of the voters were against it. That put the governor into a tailspin. She simply didn't know what to do. She sent certified letters to opponents of her plan, summoning them to testify on their ideas before a meeting of the state Senate and House education committees four days after the election. It was a stunt, a desperate attempt to move past the rejection of her ideas.

To Bush, it illuminated a bigger problem. While Texans were inclined to give her a second term, their support was driven by her personal appeal, not confidence that she could address the state's pressing problems.

Bush and I talked shortly after the May 1 vote. I went into our discussions with one overriding impression: Richards's façade looked big and imposing, but the foundation was weak. This judgment wasn't based on polls or focus groups, but intuition and instinct.

Somewhat to my surprise, Bush shared my assessment. We both believed she was avoiding controversies—in part, I felt, because on some level she knew she would end up on the wrong side of an electorate more conservative than she was. Bush could oust the governor if he could show Texans how he would tackle big challenges facing the state. As it turns out, he had thought a lot about this.

He believed education is to a state government what defense is to the federal government: its first responsibility. Bush had watched as Texas grappled with raising money and setting standards in the 1980s and '90s and became concerned that too much of the focus was on inputs, not results. He wanted to free local school districts from state mandates so they could design their own curriculum, decide student-teacher ratios, and set teacher certification rules. He also wanted to expand charters and choice options and focus on improving reading, which he felt was the skill on which all else depended.

There was also the matter of juvenile justice. Bush was troubled by a system that gave up on young offenders by expelling them from school or warehousing them in prisons without regard to the long-term consequences. He also felt young people must understand there will be bad consequences for bad behavior, or else many will be lost forever to crime and drugs.

This dovetailed with his longtime interest in the challenges posed by poverty. As a young man, he had worked for an inner-city mentoring program in Houston called the Professional United Leadership League, or "Project PULL." His friend John White, a former Houston Oilers tight end, had recruited fellow professional athletes to become mentors and asked Bush, too. "My job gave me a glimpse of a world I had never seen," as Bush once put it. "It was tragic, heartbreaking, and uplifting, all at the same time. I saw a lot of poverty. I also saw bad choices: drugs, alcohol abuse, men who had fathered children and walked away, leaving single mothers struggling to raise children on their own. I saw children who could not read and were way behind in school." Perhaps the most heartbreaking moment of all happened years later when Bush discovered that Jimmy—a young charge of his from PULL who'd become "like a little brother" to him—was killed in a gangland shooting.

Bush's experience with Project PULL was one reason he became convinced that some of the values of the '60s—a rebellion against social and parental authority that emphasized moral relativism and a frontal assault on character-forming institutions—had undermined communities and families. This was not the sum total of the 1960s, of course; it was a decade of great strides in civil rights and in social awareness. But there was a downside to those years, and one that could be measured in human terms. The '60s resulted in growing dependence on government through a collapse of the family and, along with it, the habits of responsibility, initiative, and hard work that give people dignity and self-worth. Bush was also interested in the role of "mediating structures" such as church, neighborhood, and community groups in fostering a more responsible society. I loaded him up with books by such scholars as Michael Novak, Myron Magnet, and Marvin Olasky. Bush read them with gusto and was eager to discuss them.

With education, juvenile justice, and poverty, Bush had the makings of a robust agenda. I had only one suggestion: add tort reform. Texas was awash in junk lawsuits filed by personal injury trial lawyers. "Jackpot justice" was costing Texans jobs and economic growth as businesses picked up and moved to other states. Those that remained paid bigger lawyers' bills and larger insurance premiums instead of investing in plants, equipment, and jobs. The trial lawyers were battling to maintain control of the Texas Supreme Court in the face of a bipartisan reform effort. The small business community was wired up about junk lawsuits, and it gave Bush a natural opportunity to talk about jobs and economic growth. He agreed.

What struck me about each of these issues, especially the original three, was Bush's way of framing them. His approach was conservative yet broad and inclusive. He didn't sound like a run-of-the-mill Republican. For example, when he spoke on education, you could hear the first hints of why he felt it was important that no child be left behind. While conventional Republicans talked about juvenile crime by emphasizing locking up young thugs, Bush emphasized saving a generation of young people before they were lost. Where Republicans were comfortable talking about welfare cheats, Bush condemned not the recipients but the system that creates dependence on government and "saps the soul and drains the spirit" of people who had been designed by their Maker for something better.

The good news was Bush's policy interests could help create a political coalition that was broad enough to propel him into the Governor's Mansion. He had to start by winning back Republican defectors in the suburbs, particularly younger women, who'd gone for Richards in 1990 and stayed in her camp ever since. They liked her, even if they had doubts about her record as governor. But he couldn't win on Republican votes alone.

In addition to consolidating fractured Republicans, Bush needed to add a significant slug of independents to his column. My calculations showed he needed to come darn close to winning an absolute majority. Then there were Democrats. Bush had to pry away about one out of every eight self-identified Democrats. Many of these would have to be Hispanics, whom Richards had carried overwhelmingly four years earlier. Then Bush needed to do better among African-Americans than the last two Republican gubernatorial candidates had done. I felt then, and still do today, that the nominee of the party of Lincoln had a moral obligation to fight for black voters, regardless of whether it paid off in the short run. So did Bush.

My analysis showed that there was enough swing in the electorate to pull off an upset. It would take an almost flawless campaign, substantial resources, and a candidate with steady nerves and enormous discipline. Richards had been attacked in 1990 by Clayton Williams, who'd once said he'd "head her and hoof her and drag her through the dirt" as if she were a cow on his ranch. He later refused to shake her hand at a joint appearance and called her a liar. Because Richards predictably benefited from Williams's crass treatment of her, I knew she would try to goad Bush into attacking her in 1994 so she could be a victim a second time.

Bush spent the summer of 1993 boning up on issues and drawing experts into his orbit. He was a prodigious consumer of articles, memos, and books. He'd see an article or read a memo and use his ever-present Sharpie pen to scribble in the margins "we need to address this" or "how can we fix this?" or "get more on what this state is doing." Bush had a way of throwing people off balance by asking fundamental questions that focused on first principles, such as "what's the goal of our state education system?" or "how should success be measured at the Texas Youth Commission?" or "what should be the object of punishing juvenile offenders?" It was the mark of a mind concerned with game-changing, not tinkering. Because of that, one of our first hires was a brilliant young lawyer named T. Vance McMahan, whose job was to develop Bush's platform.

Vance quickly formed a Vulcan mind meld with Bush, providing the candidate with tons of materials. Bush wanted to be able to defend every difficult point and answer every critical question about his programs.

Part of this was just Bush. He was, by disposition, a person who enjoyed the process of mastering a subject. That not only gave him fluency on the issue but also passion and authority. He recognized that because he was a novice statewide candidate, the media would hold him to a higher standard than they would the incumbent governor. Behind the scenes, the Richards camp was already making an issue of Bush's lack of involvement in state government and Texas issues. He knew he had to be ready.

In the fall of 1993, Bush road-tested his message at two events intentionally closed to the press. Bush wasn't at his best delivering remarks from a prepared text. I helped write the speech, and after each appearance, he edited his remarks based on his interpretation of the audience's reactions.

On November 8, 1993, the forty-seven-year-old Dallas businessman announced he was running for governor. He then made speeches in twenty-seven cities in five days. "If you want someone to fine-tune or tinker with the present system, that's not me," he said. "If you're happy with the status quo, I'm not your candidate." I still have the text he used that day, with Sharpie notes and all.

He took a gentle swipe at Richards, telling the crowds, "Our leaders should be judged by results, not by entertaining personalities or clever sound bites." Richards had traveled to Washington and responded to reporters there. She cited rising SAT scores and a lower dropout rate and 350,000 new jobs during her tenure. This didn't jibe with voters' growing concern about the quality of public schools, increasingly violent juvenile crime, and uneven economic progress. It also made it clear she was running on the past, not her vision for the future. That mind-set is always dangerous, but especially so in a rapidly growing state like Texas, where officeholders must introduce themselves to a lot of new people every four years to convince them they know what to do in the years ahead.

The Bush campaign also kicked up its efforts to organize all 254 counties in the state and raise the millions of dollars that would be necessary for the contest. Staff could do the former, but a lot of the latter fell on Bush's shoulders. One of Bush's early visits was on October 7, 1993, with Don Carter, the owner of the Dallas Mavericks basketball team. Bush made an earnest pitch and asked for a major gift. The wealthy businessman reached in his desk drawer, pulled out a battered checkbook, and scribbled for a few moments before handing the check to Bush. Without looking at it, Bush put it in his pocket and thanked Carter for his generosity. He thought he'd received $10,000 or so. After he walked out, he pulled it out and glanced at it. Carter had given him ten times that amount. Bush wondered if it was a mistake. He thought about going back.

Shortly after the meeting, Carter told a mutual friend he admired the young candidate but didn't think he had much of a chance. I thought if Bush could get $100,000 from people who thought he couldn't win, we just might be able to pull this thing off.

By early 1994, Bush began laying out the four planks of his platform. His first move was to outline a juvenile justice reform program in January, including tougher sentences and sharing fingerprints and photographs of young offenders to better track them.

Richards was quick to volley back, saying she was going to form "a 1,100 member multiagency task force to monitor violent parolees and convicted sex offenders." For a moment it appeared that she and Bush were going to emphasize different facets of the same issue.

But Bush stayed on the issue, traveling to each of the state's twenty-two media markets to hold news conferences on juvenile justice, meet with local law enforcement officials, drop by rehab or antigang programs, or talk to local community groups about the issue. Bush had done his homework; he was knowledgeable, engaged, and passionate about it. Richards, on the other hand, touched on the issue of crime for a day, and went on to other things. There was a check-the-box quality to what she was doing.

After about six weeks on juvenile justice, Bush laid out his education reform program in mid-February—once again with a thick white paper, fact sheets, and a chorus of supportive voices from experts, teachers, and school district officials. He traveled a second time to all twenty-two media markets, drawing attention to this new issue and mixing up the kinds of events and appearances he made in each city. His welfare reform package was rolled out in April, and his nine-point tort reform package was rolled out in June. By the summer, opinion leaders and the press knew exactly what Bush thought the governor's race was about and what he would do if elected.

As Bush worked to establish his dominance on his four issues, the campaign faced a problem. More than 64 percent of the state's voters were concentrated in the six biggest metropolitan regions, but it was next to impossible to get press coverage in them. There was just too much local news and too many statewide candidate visits for the press, especially local television, to make a big deal out of an appearance by Bush. I used to joke that if Bush ran naked down Louisiana Street in Houston or Commerce Street in Dallas, we'd be lucky if one television camera showed up.

But as it turns out, a lot of swing voters lived in rural counties, and while it was difficult to get coverage in the six largest media markets, a television station in the sixteen smaller markets was likely to show up to cover him. Stations in Amarillo or Corpus Christi or Tyler simply had a lot less news on their plate than the stations in Dallas, Houston, Fort Worth, Austin, San Antonio, or El Paso. So we decided that during the winter, spring, and summer of 1994, George W. Bush would spend a lot of time in small towns.

One of these visits took place in the East Texas town of Palestine. The local state representative was a friend of mine, Elton Bomer. He was a hardworking, thoughtful Democrat. He was not fond of Ann Richards, because he thought that she was reluctant to get her hands dirty on tough issues. I called Bomer and told him Bush would like to visit Palestine, outlined the kind of day we'd like to have, and asked if he could suggest an influential community leader who might help put the day together. Bomer put his hand up for the job. Years later, Bomer told me he'd read for months how Bush would reform education, juvenile justice, welfare, and a favorite for Bomer, tort laws. Our jackhammer repetition was working.

Bush stopped by and met with guards from a large state penitentiary near town, swung by a local radio station for an on-air talk with the disc jockey, called on the publisher of the local paper, visited the largest employer in town (a repair shop for Union Pacific railroad cars), and made a pilgrimage through the courthouse, shaking hands, posing for pictures, chatting with the clerks behind the counters, and paying homage to county officials, all of whom were Democrats.

He had lunch in town and then met with local opinion leaders in a bank's conference room. Around the table were the sheriff, the district judge, business owners, some pastors, the mayor, council members, and a few local elected officials. Not a single one was a Republican. Elton introduced Bush, which gave him instant credibility. Bush made his pitch, answered questions until his listeners ran out of them, and left after shaking hands and posing for pictures. The group remained behind to talk about their impressions. Judge Bascom Bentley turned to the sheriff and said, "Well, I understand why Elton wanted us to meet this young man." Bush went on to carry Anderson County by 12 points, 56 percent to 44 percent—up from a nearly 3-point margin for the Republicans four years before.

This scene was repeated across Texas as Bush covered more than one hundred counties in the same intense way, with four or five events a day. The rural tour fed on itself: Bush was once accosted by a woman who complained that while he had spent a day in Stephenville, Bush had yet to make a similar visit to Brownwood—a town with a population of 19,465 that was located fifty-nine miles southwest of Stephenville. In rural Texas, word travels far and fast. Kent Hance, who'd beaten him in the 1978 congressional race, told me that while that had been Bush's "first rodeo," he didn't want to be around when Bush did his second.

The winter and spring of 1994 were the times of greatest vulnerability for George W. Bush. My fear was that Governor Richards would lay out a compelling—or even just a marginally interesting—vision for her second term and back it with substantive ads; we would have been in trouble. Instead she and her people took an increasingly petty, shrill tone toward Bush, referring to him as "shrub" or "that young Bush boy."

We knew she was vulnerable when the primary results came in. Richards took only 77.8 percent of the more than 1 million votes cast in the Democratic primary. Gary Espinosa of Bois d'Arc, a forty-nine-year-old retired graduate of an auto body repair school who listed his membership in the National Geographic Society as a credential, took nearly a quarter-million votes. It wasn't because he campaigned. Nor was his vote particularly concentrated in the Hispanic community. He ran stronger than Richards in small, rural, and conservative counties, especially in historically Democratic East Texas. The vote totals in these districts were a treasure map for us—each Espinosa voter was a potentially dissatisfied Democrat open to replacing Governor Richards.

Once I saw Richards's primary performance, I knew we had a real shot to win the race. But our operation was bogged down in its own bureaucracy and not primed for action. I felt responsible because I had recruited most of the hierarchy from Kay Bailey Hutchison's successful bid for a U.S. Senate seat in 1993.

The Bushes are famously loyal, but they can also be demanding and willing to make changes if success is threatened. So out went the campaign manager, the press secretary, and half a dozen other people. The rest of the staff buckled down and redoubled its efforts. We hired a tall, taciturn, mustachioed cowboy named Joe Allbaugh, then deputy highway commissioner in his home state of Oklahoma, to manage the campaign.

Allbaugh's hair is cut in a flattop that is roughly the size of a World War II carrier's landing deck, and when he draws up his 265 pounds and 6'4" frame and gets that I'm-going-to-pinch-your-head-off look on his face, he is an intimidating figure. He was exactly what we needed to shape up the campaign.

In the spring and summer, Governor Richards gave us three openings, and we used every one.

The first one popped up in March, when Republican primary voters overwhelmingly approved a referendum supporting the right of "concealed carry"—a law that made it much easier to get a permit to carry a concealed handgun after receiving appropriate training. Richards had vetoed the bill in 1993, saying, "We say no to amateur gunslingers who somehow think they're going to be braver and smarter with a gun in their hand." Her dismissive comment didn't play well in rural Texas. Bush supported concealed carry but he didn't intend to make it a big issue. But it became one anyway because Richards's comments had come off as a put-down to gun owners.

The next issue emerged in May, when the governor wanted to put five Texas waterways under federal, not state, protection. Done at the behest of environmentalists, the move would likely have shut down development in parts of Central Texas that were in the 354 square miles of watershed around Barton Springs. Richards's move angered Texas ranchers and farmers, who are naturally suspicious of Washington, especially when it involves water rights. We made a stink about the plans to hand the waterways over to the feds and so did a lot of people in rural Texas. By July, Richards flip-flopped on the issue.

In late June, Richards went before the American Legion Girls State gathering in Austin and stuck her foot in her mouth. She told the high school girls to be careful about men, saying, "Prince Charming may be driving a Honda and telling you you have no equal, but that's not going to do much good when you've got kids and a mortgage, and I could add he's got a beer gut and a wandering eye. Prince Charming, if he does ride up on a Honda, he's going to expect you to make the payments." The uproar was deafening, though some Democrats tried to spin their way out of it by describing Richards's bleak sentiments as honest, helpful, and "pro-family."

We didn't say much about her remarks because Bush didn't want us to. He sent a memo that he cranked out himself on his home computer, typos and all. He reminded us, "We have established broad themes of change" and that our issues "are our beach heads." When the other camp threw darts our way, "we should never debate on their terms nor should we fall into their traps by playing gotcha." Whenever we responded, we needed to "score on the need for change in areas that matter to people and their lives." He closed with "Fight fiercely / Yours in victory." A campaign's tone is set—and kept in place—from the top.

Governor Richards's life, already more difficult than she ever imagined, got measurably worse in July when a smart, energetic, and tall woman showed up in the Bush headquarters, booming orders left and right and raising the energy level about six gigawatts. Karen Parfitt Hughes had joined the campaign as communications chief.

As Vance explained, "We were creating bullets and needed someone to shoot them." Karen was our Annie Oakley. As the daughter of the last military governor of the Panama Canal Zone, she was disciplined and tough. She kept Richards off stride with a constant stream of hits from our research geeks.

Karen had a lot of important strengths, starting with a great feel for how reporters would react. That is indispensable in a campaign, since the press plays such a vital role in determining how candidates are seen. She not only picked up on things George W. Bush said that he needed to change, she was fearless in getting them changed. For example, at the start of Bush's gubernatorial campaign, he had a habit of referring to himself as a "capitalist." Polite suggestions that he drop the reference were ignored. So Karen badgered, hectored, and shamed him into finally finding a better way to describe himself. It was delicious to watch her ridicule him to his face. She had high standards: people who worked for her knew they'd be called upon to stretch themselves a lot. With a booming laugh and outbursts of infectious humor, she was also fun to be around.

There were differences between us, though never personal—which is fairly unusual for a campaign. Karen and I were more alike than we were different—and where we were different, most of the time those differences complemented one another. I felt at times that Karen was too focused on the press and she thought I was too focused on the politics. She would think about how something would impact the *Dallas Morning News*—and I would think about its effect on "East Texas small-town rural swing voters." I tended to be somewhat more conservative, and more willing to acknowledge and directly confront critics. Her constituency was the press, and it required cajoling. I was something of a policy wonk; she had more interest in how the policy would be perceived. But whatever differences we had, we could have them civilly—even if we both had a tendency to raise our voices a bit and keep pressing the point.

That summer, pressure from grassroots Republicans to attack Richards by tying her to Clinton grew from occasional suggestions into open demands. It's almost always true that a loyal volunteer base of activists wants to drag the contest in a meaner, uglier, more contentious direction. But we did not want to make the race seem like a vendetta by the Bush family against the woman who had belittled President George H. W. Bush at the 1988 Democratic convention. And we wanted to stay on track with the issues.

We were worried that Richards would outspend us on television. She had more money and easily could have, but for inexplicable reasons she waited until August 9 to start her ads. That's fairly late for a Texas campaign. We'd decided we didn't want to go up on television and then be forced by lack of money to come down. The first Bush television ad appeared a week later.

The Bush spots were focused and particularly effective. Developed by GOP ad maker Don Sipple, they had the same format: the candidate looked straight into the camera and described his plans for education, juvenile justice, welfare, and tort reform. They were broken up with "b-roll" footage appropriate to the topic, but Bush was on-air most of each spot and his voice the only narration. Around the headquarters, they were jokingly called the "Bush in a box" spots. But the thinking behind them was sound: focus group testing showed Bush was his own best spokesman and his presence strengthened the message. One particularly effective spot showed Bush promising to take away the hunting and fishing licenses of Texas men who failed to make child support payments. It struck a nerve.

As the ads started, Governor Richards caused a minor tempest by calling Bush "some jerk" in an August 16 speech in Texarkana. She and her staff had been launching similar verbal missiles all during the race, but this one drew more attention than the others. She said it on the record and then denied she'd said it before everyone went to the audiotapes. Bush laughed it off: "The last time I was called a jerk was at Sam Houston Elementary School in Midland, Texas. I'm not going to call the Governor names. I'm going to elevate this debate to a level where Texans want it."

We gained the upper hand for a couple of days—but then it was our turn to go into the barrel. A respected moderate Republican state senator and the honorary chairman of our East Texas campaign, Bill Ratliff, told a *Houston Post* reporter that Richards would lose votes in his area because she'd appointed self-identified gays to state boards and commissions. Ratliff then expanded on his comment to another reporter, saying, "I simply don't agree to appointing avowed homosexual activists . . . to positions of leadership. . . . It tends to elevate the lifestyle to the equivalent of the traditional family." The press demanded a response. Karen responded that Bush "has never asked anyone applying for a job about their sexual preference, and he doesn't intend to start now." But that didn't keep the Richards camp from attacking us.

Nor did it keep my critics years later from blaming me for Ratliff's remark. One suggests I did it so "Bush [could] step forward as a voice of understanding and reason" in disavowing Ratliff. The sole proof that I was behind Ratliff's comments was that he had once been a client of mine. But some of these same observers described Ratliff as a man "known for his principle and integrity." So the accusation that I was behind his comments breaks down to this: I maneuvered a man of integrity into making remarks that would hurt us with suburban voters at about the same time that suburbs were increasingly becoming the battleground of the campaign. Ludicrous.

Actually, the person who made it an issue in the race and created the damage was Ann Richards. Rather than emphasizing that she'd appointed highly qualified people, she went out of her way at the time of her appointments to emphasize that some of her nominations were the first homosexual or lesbian appointee to the Public Utility Commission or to the funeral board. By emphasizing sexual preference, Richards scored points in the gay community; at the same time, she had to know she was offending socially conservative people. That issue existed before Bill Ratliff ever said a word.

The controversy was brief, shortly drowned by another one, this time with Bush at the center. But his blunder—a hunting mistake—turned into a plus.

September 1 was the start of dove season. Richards was going to bond with every red-blooded Texas male by hunting on opening day, because, as she later said, "Man, after that [1990 trip], my numbers went straight up in East Texas. . . . So I thought I'd come back hunting last year—and I did—and this year because I want to keep my numbers up in East Texas." I am always amazed when politicians tell reporters they're doing something not because they enjoy it but because of crass political considerations. They speak as if no voters are listening or watching.

So the governor parked herself in a field east of Dallas and gathered the press around her, waiting for the chance to demonstrate her markswomanship. It never happened. No doves showed up. The press corps goaded her into shooting off a few shells for the cameras.

Being a bird hunter myself, I've always felt there's something alluring about an attractive woman who's proficient with a shotgun, especially a side-by-side. But the governor wasn't demonstrating proficiency—she was showing off.

Bush was also hitting the fields on opening day. He was east of Houston and there were birds. Unfortunately, they included some of the wrong kind. The hunting guide yelled "bird" and Bush took aim and pulled the trigger. A bird fell to the ground. Bush turned to reporters and asked, "Anybody say 'Nice shot?'" as the guide hustled over to pick it up. The guide immediately realized he'd called in fire on a killdeer, a protected nongame bird. He stuffed it in his kill bag and when Bush asked to see it, the guide pulled a dead dove from his pouch instead.

It's frankly amazing that George W. Bush shot the bird in the first place. Having hunted with him for a long time, I know of what I speak. He may be a fine fisherman and an outstanding mountain biker and he was once a strong runner—but he's never been considered a good shot. A local television sports reporter getting ready for the evening broadcast later that day looked at the footage and saw Bush had shot the wrong bird. The word got passed to the campaign as Bush changed out of his hunting gear at a motel on the east side of Houston before catching a flight to Dallas. His instincts kicked in.

On the way to the Houston airport, he called every reporter who'd been with him to fess up to his crime. It gave him a chance to tell them a lame joke: "I am glad I wasn't hunting deer, otherwise I would have shot a cow." Because a politician owning up to a mistake is novel, the reporters treated him more gently than they otherwise would have. As the car neared the airport, Bush handed Dan Bartlett, a young press assistant, a signed blank check and told him to find the guide and go pay the fine.

By the time Dan connected with the guide, the game warden had appeared. But neither had any experience with a hunter turning himself in for shooting a killdeer, so confusion ensued. They decided to troop downtown, where, after a lot of shuffling, consulting, and contemplation, Dan was told the fine would be $130, court costs included. He filled out the check and then posed for pictures, awkwardly surrounded by giggling clerks and amused game wardens. The story made every Texas newspaper and news program as well as the national *CBS Morning News,* and, of course, the *New York Times.* The chattering class initially thought this blunder would hurt Bush badly, but in fact it humanized him. Here was a candidate admitting he screwed up and, besides, how many Texas hunters had shot at the wrong bird?

By late September, the public polls showed the race deadlocked, with Richards leading with 43 percent to Bush's 41 percent.

With just six weeks until the election, we left rural Texas and focused on the suburbs and cities, driving home our four big issues. Richards continued on the defensive, spending most of her time attacking Bush and very little of her time laying out a positive agenda.

In mid-October, Richards unleashed an attack spot alleging that the companies on whose boards Bush sat had lost $371 million. Her ad also belittled his role as managing partner of the Texas Rangers by saying he owned only 2 percent of the team. Both charges were inaccurate or twisted and Karen led the communications team into the fray, answering the charges in a tone of disappointment, lamenting that Richards would stoop to these kinds of attacks. More importantly, however, it gave us the opening we needed to immediately put up a spot that had been readied weeks before.

The spot featured Bush talking into the camera, decrying Richards's "personal attacks" and saying they would not solve the problems Texas faced in educating our children, saving young people from lives of crime, ending welfare dependence on government, or creating jobs by ending junk lawsuits. The counterpunch was stronger than the punch.

This may have been the pivotal moment in the campaign, the instant when voters leaning Bush's way began to lock in and the undecideds started moving his way.

The last chance for either candidate to shake up the race was during its only debate, in late October. To minimize Bush's exposure, Richards wanted only one. We were grateful because Bush had been doing poorly in the prep sessions.

There were some private fireworks beforehand. Both campaigns were staying at the same large Dallas hotel before the debate, though on separate floors. The plan was they'd meet for the first time onstage. Then Bush, hotel security, and Bush's personal aide—his "body man" in political parlance—stepped into an elevator. As it descended, it stopped and the doors opened. There stood Governor Richards, her security detail, and a few aides. They all stepped aboard. Bush said "Governor" and tilted his head to greet her. She said nothing. Then, as the elevator reached the ground floor, Richards turned to Bush and said, sotto voce, "This is going to be tough on you, boy." Governor Richards had misread her sparring partner. The insult didn't intimidate Bush, it appealed to his competitive instincts.

Richards was on the attack almost from the beginning, raising questions about Bush's lack of experience and repeating her earlier claim that he had failed in his business dealings. He kept pounding away at his four issues and promising responsible change in Austin. The difference in strategy could not have been clearer. Afterward, Bush said to me, "It may not have been a home run, but I got some good wood on the ball." It may have been better than that. *Texas Monthly's* Paul Burka told me he thought Bush won with his opening three words. Richards had spoken first and complimented rescue efforts following terrible flooding in Houston that week. Bush followed her praise of the first responders by saying, "Well said, Governor." Burka's point was that Bush showed himself as confident. It was just what voters on the fence needed to envision him in the governor's office.

The election's frantic, final week opened on Tuesday, November 1, with Ross Perot endorsing Richards, calling her "the steel magnolia of Texas" and praising her as "one of the greatest governors in the history of Texas." The diminutive billionaire was just two years past his impressive third-party White House run and he still had a big following. Bush was at his parents' home in Houston exercising with Don Evans, a Midland oilman and his closest friend, when word came of Perot's endorsement. They joined Barbara Bush in the kitchen, where she perused her recently published book to see what she'd written about Perot. Mrs. Bush was momentarily taken aback with how tough she'd been on Perot and wondered if he had endorsed Richards in retaliation. Bush downplayed the endorsement's impact, saying, "She's got Ross Perot; I'll take Nolan Ryan and Barbara Bush."

In reality, the race was too developed for Perot's embrace of Richards to change much. For one thing, it was confusing for some: Perot had gone on *Larry King Live* the previous week to urge Americans to vote Republican and now he was backing a high-profile Democrat. More importantly, too many Texans had already decided to vote for Bush. There was nothing in Perot's endorsement that could change people's minds. Even his slap at Bush—"Never forget, the state of Texas is big business—not a sport"—rang hollow after the campaigns Bush and Richards had run.

My son, Andrew Rove, then five years old, insisted on attending the final campaign rally in Austin, just before the election. As the crowd waited for Bush's arrival, Andrew told me to hoist him onto my shoulders. I asked why and he said, "George wants to see me." I complied, and sure enough, Bush saw Andrew and waved.

On election eve, I found myself in an SUV traveling to the last rally in Dallas with George and Laura and Don Evans. The tension was thick. On a lark, I pretended to call Ross Perot to have a few words with him about his endorsement of Richards. It broke the ice. Others in the car began calling out names of people who'd defected to Richards or sat on the sidelines, often with lame excuses. I pretended to call them, too. By the time we got to the event, the nervous energy had been swamped by gales of adolescent laughter.

The next night was an evening to be savored. Almost from the first returns, it was clear Bush would win a stunning upset. He beat the incumbent governor by 53.5 percent to 45.9 percent, the widest margin of any candidate since 1974. He recaptured the suburbs, running 16 points better than the GOP had received in 1990. Rural Texas went from Richards in 1990 to Bush in 1994. Suburban women voted for Bush, as well as 37 percent of Hispanics, up from 33 percent for the Republican candidate four years before.

Bush ducked into a bathroom in his suite at the Four Seasons in Austin to take a call from his parents. They were so anguished over his brother Jeb's loss in the Florida governor's race, it was hard for it to sink in that their other son had pulled off an extraordinary upset. Like many parents, the pain experienced by one child overwhelmed the joy experienced by another. Bush listened to his father's distress over his brother's defeat; when the conversation finished, he shrugged his shoulders and went back into a room awash in joy and excitement. Soon he appeared before a wild mob at the Austin Convention Center to declare victory, saying, "I have heard the call of constructive change: change of our juvenile justice system to save a generation of our young, change of a welfare system to end dependency on government and change of our education system. . . ."

I have a picture from that night, inscribed by Bush to "the man with the plan." The photo shows Bush, then a young man in a dark suit, red tie, and a light blue shirt with a white collar, a wide grin, and a color other than gray in his hair. With one hand outstretched, he is waving to an unseen crowd. His other hand lies lightly on the shoulder of his attractive, shy wife, who had not made a single speech during the campaign. To their right are two pretty but uneasy-looking teenage girls. Behind and over the heads of all four hangs a banner with just one word, appearing from the campaign's logo: GOVERNOR. Now the title would be official.

CHAPTER 6

A New Kind of Governor

———•◆•———

The victory over Ann Richards changed my relationship with George W. Bush. I went from being a longtime friend to being a political partner. Most political relationships have the opposite trajectory—professional first, personal second.

I think he appreciated my independent streak. This was confirmed for me years later in the private quarters of the White House, the night of the disastrous 2006 elections that cost Republicans control of Congress. I was running around getting results from dozens of states and districts. A friend of Bush's, California investment guru Brad Freeman, asked Josh Bolten, then White House chief of staff, "How is it to be Karl's boss?" Josh hesitated for a while, then replied, "He comes when you call." As if on cue, Bush added: "But he doesn't fetch."

My relationship with Laura Bush is more complicated. It was distant at first, but it deepened and improved over that gubernatorial election. I have always thought she might have resented that I was pressuring her husband—first to run, and then to do certain things when he was running or serving. She never shared her feelings with me, so I never quite knew where I stood with her. She was comfortable with that and since I couldn't do anything about it, I became so, too. Her advice to him was sound and powerful. She would bring up hard things, the bad news, or the unpleasant truths. There is something about Bush men that makes them want to marry strong women, whether it is the brash and outspoken Barbara or the retiring yet keenly observant Laura.

After Bush was elected governor, I had to decide between going in with him or staying out. Texas law requires a governor's political activity to be run through a private committee and Bush asked me about heading up his. He broached the subject as if its outcome were already settled. Here was the niche that would keep me close but also allow me freedom to pursue other endeavors. It would be part-time, so I could keep running Rove + Company, he told me. The Governor Bush Committee would handle fund-raising; keep in touch with his political team in all 254 counties; mobilize support for his legislative agenda; vet potential appointees; recruit and back candidates for state and local office; and worry about upcoming elections, especially Bush's reelection in 1998.

As the head of the Bush Committee, I'd also be a member of the governor's senior staff, attend its regular Thursday lunch meetings, and have a hand in policy discussions as an all-purpose advisor. That was important. I wasn't in politics for the sport or the money. I knew his conservative reform ideas had the potential to significantly change Texas.

Bush's offer came with limitations. I couldn't cash in, he told me. In Texas, I could support only the campaigns of allies of the governor. I'd be seen as an extension of him, so no freelancing. He suggested making up for lost Texas business by getting more out of state work. He said I could keep a few long-standing corporate clients, but no new ones without his approval and no lobbying or associating with a lobbying firm.

To his credit, he continued to let me mock him even after we became a professional pair. After the inaugural, we went hunting at Anne and Tobin Armstrong's South Texas ranch with the new governor and First Lady. We flew into the ranch strip on a small prop airplane. I sat near the front, so I embarked last. I had arranged that when I appeared in the plane's hatch, the assembled hunting party would break into cheers as I assumed my best Nixon victory pose at the top of the plane's stairs. The governor was momentarily unsure why the group was cheering until he turned around. He was mildly amused.

I hunted with George W. Bush for years and I don't recommend it. The National Rifle Association's ironclad gun-safety rules include always treating a firearm as if it were loaded; always pointing a gun in a safe direction; and always keeping your finger away from the trigger until ready to shoot. One of our group, a superb outdoorsman and state senator from Amarillo named Teel Bivins, started the day politely suggesting that the new governor keep his barrel up. Bush decided to needle Bivins by making a show of occasionally letting his (unloaded) shotgun barrel go down. By day's end, an exasperated Teel was yelling profanely, "George, keep the goddamn barrel up." Neither approach worked well.

Bush knew his term would be unproductive and unpleasant unless he could gain the support of those who ran the Texas legislature, especially the powerful lieutenant governor, Bob Bullock, and Speaker Pete Laney. Instinctively, Bush called Laney and Bullock the morning after the election and asked to meet as soon as possible. He also began a conscious effort to reach out and smother whomever he could with his charm and his ideas—putting an emphasis on those who, while they might be of another party or philosophy, might be open to persuasion. He phoned legislative kingpins and set up visits. It became common to see dazzled legislators emerge from Bush's cramped quarters in the transition offices. I heard one longtime Democratic senator exit his meeting and remark that "I just spent more time with the governor-to-be than I did in four years with Richards, and she was a Democrat." By January, Bush had traveled to Austin nearly a dozen times and met most of the major players in the Texas House, as well as many younger and newer members, and twenty-nine of thirty-one state senators.

The governor-elect took time to attend the Republican Governors Association meeting in Williamsburg, Virginia. I went with him. The atmosphere was giddy, since the GOP had expanded its ranks from nineteen governors to thirty in 1994. Bush and other newly elected Republican governors sat in the back of the room, wisecracking like high school truants. More senior governors, such as Pete Wilson of California and John Engler of Michigan, sat in the front, warning of the challenges they'd face. I'm not certain the new governors took this advice too seriously, but I could see bonds developing between Bush and his fellow newly elected chief executives.

Those relationships would portend a future for Bush outside of Texas, but before that future could unfold, he would have to make allies out of Bullock and Laney. A fixture since being elected to the legislature in 1957 at twenty-seven, Bullock knew more about Texas government than dozens of legislators, bureaucrats, professors, and newspaper editors combined. As a state representative, assistant attorney general, Texas secretary of state, comptroller, and lieutenant governor, Bullock had been in the middle of every big controversy in Texas politics—and a hell of a lot of small ones—for almost forty years by the time Bush was elected. He was a man of big passions, big grudges, and big ambitions. At times it seemed that what he loved most was to hate and scrap. His political enemies had scars, missing appendages, or near-death experiences to show for their run-ins. His adversaries included the press: following hemorrhoid surgery, he sent a hated reporter what he claimed was the excised tissue. It was really canned oysters.

He lost part of his right lung to cancer at forty-three. He had heart bypass surgery at sixty-five and too many broken bones to enumerate. He was diagnosed as a manic-depressive. He had a Ph.D. in abuse, especially in his drunken years. He once woke up in a stranger's backseat going 60 miles per hour north out of Austin after trying to sleep off a bender. He sobered up at fifty-two. He was married five times, to four women. Once he demanded that an aide leave his own family on Thanksgiving to pick up a jar of sage from the grocery store and drive the spice over to Bullock's house. Bullock was juggling two Thanksgiving dinners—one with Amelia, his current, third wife, who had also been his first wife, and one with Kathryn, his second (and then former) wife. He finally settled down at fifty-five with the love of his life, Jan.

Bullock was so demanding that I saw senior aides break into a cold sweat when their beepers went off. I saw overweight lobbyists sprint across the Capitol when Bullock summoned them.

He had a fascination with weapons—rifles, shotguns, and pistols—which often happened to be lying nearby in full view when his current worst political enemy appeared. Bullock once said all drunks carried guns because they always thought somebody was after them.

He didn't like Republicans, particularly during the years when they were inconsequential in Texas. His sympathies were populist, rural, and slightly left of center. More importantly, he understood power, how to get it, how to use it, and how to deny it. He demanded aides give him regular "fornication reports" on who was sleeping with whom around the Capitol. Information like that often comes in handy. As Bush said at Bullock's funeral, "Everybody has a favorite Bob Bullock story. The problem is, you can't tell most of them in polite company." Yet people spoke with pride of having worked for him and boasted that once employed by Bullock, you always worked for him the rest of your days, no matter how many times he fired you and no matter where you got your paycheck. He inspired that kind of loyalty.

Bob Bullock had one standard: Is it good for Texas? As the years went on, he became less concerned with party or personality, as long as that person could help him achieve that goal. He even favored a state income tax, normally the kiss of death for a Texas politician, because he believed the state needed the revenue. But it did not hurt him: he won 61 percent in his next race for lieutenant governor.

But for all of Bullock's brashness, he was both intrigued and intimidated by bigwigs. Bush, the son of a president and a possible new governor, fit that category. So Bush made a point of meeting with him privately before the 1994 election. Both men seemed a little uptight. Bush thought he was meeting with a crazy man delivering a monologue, and Bullock assumed Bush was another one of those blue-blooded, country-club Republicans he detested. By the time it was over, both men were pleasantly surprised.

Bush saw Bullock as a shrewd, knowledgeable insider who, while a consummate politico, was interested in Texas's progress and open to the Bush agenda. Bullock appreciated Bush's authenticity and passion on issues such as education. And he realized Bush shared more of Bullock's small-town Texas values than he had thought. After the meeting, Bullock asked the Austin lobbyist who'd helped arrange the meeting to hang back a minute. The lieutenant governor said he was impressed and Bush knew his stuff. "Tell him to call me back," Bullock instructed. Then out of the blue, he grew a little wistful (an unusual emotion for Bullock) and said, "He seems like the kind of guy if something happened to you, you'd be comfortable with him raising your children."

Speaker Pete Laney was the opposite of Bullock in many ways: colorless, taciturn, and introverted. Laney was hard to read, held his views close, and quietly ran the House through a team of lieutenants who were mostly self-contained people like himself. As Speaker, he didn't weigh in often, but when he did, members paid attention. He was a cotton farmer from Hale Center, a farming town of about two thousand residents on the flat, dry prairies forty-seven miles north of Lubbock. He had learned long ago that nature is unpredictable and life is hard for no good reason except rain and market conditions. He knew the value of most things and drove a fair political bargain with no fireworks.

Like Bullock, Laney didn't like Republicans, having grown up in a Texas where they were little known, wore expensive Hickey Freeman suits, and had more than a glancing familiarity with the better New York hotels. He didn't like big business, either. As a cotton farmer, he believed that big banks and corporations wouldn't hesitate to break you.

Unlike Bullock, Laney didn't have an expansive policy agenda. He saw his principal responsibility as protecting his members by keeping them from getting cut up on votes hard to explain back home. He would often kill controversial bills.

Laney invoked "the will of the House" many times to Bush as the reason he could not be immediately forthcoming on issues such as tort and welfare reform. It wasn't because he didn't care. It was partly because he was a consummate poker player who wanted leverage. But it was mostly because he really wanted to divine the opinions of his members, limited by their own ideologies, constituent needs, and obligations to benefactors.

Bush got into the habit of dropping by the Speaker's office at the end of the day. Most of the time, there was no agenda. Bush would chew on an unlit cigar, and they soon discovered they shared a West Texas sensibility that comes from living in a place with flat, big horizons and sturdy people. They took to going to events such as Future Farmers of America and Boys State together. Bush loved to imitate Laney's flat, clipped, high-pitched West Texas accent, especially to his face. The Speaker didn't seem to care.

The three—governor, lieutenant governor, and Speaker—agreed to meet for breakfast each week during the legislative session. Bush hosted the first at the Mansion, but Bullock complained the food was too healthy. The rest of their breakfasts alternated between the Speaker's dining room at the west end of the Capitol and Bullock's on the east. They featured eggs cooked in grease, biscuits and gravy, and lots of bacon and sausage. The governor ordered pancakes.

In his early days in office, Bush would walk the long block and a half from the state Capitol to the Governor's Mansion for lunch. The press caught on to this routine and would ambush Bush for a question or two as he strolled out of the Capitol.

This seemingly innocuous habit nearly had disastrous results. One question was about an issue pinging around the Capitol that Bullock, Laney, and the governor had discussed. Bush answered, and word got back to Bullock that their internal decisions were being aired in public. Bullock was livid. He worried that the governor would prove to be a press hound. Soon everyone in the Capitol heard how angry Bullock was. Bush heard, too. He walked over to the lieutenant governor's office, told Bullock what had happened, and apologized. The governor was not going to allow a little misstep to develop into a bigger issue. He was focused on long-term results and that required a cordial relationship with Bullock. Bush also did something else—he stopped walking to the Mansion for lunch.

Bullock tested Bush early on. During the weekly breakfast, Bullock announced he was blocking part of a Bush initiative by saying, "Governor, on this I'm going to have to f*** you." With that, Bush got up, walked over to Bullock, hugged him, and made like he was going to kiss him full on the lips. Bush told him, "If you're gonna f*** me, you've at least gotta kiss me first." It's the only occasion I'm aware of Bush using the f-word. Taken aback, Bullock momentarily lost his composure and fled the room. Laney roared with laughter. It was one of the last times Bullock felt he needed to take the measure of the governor.

Bullock could be petty and nurse a grievance. Bush learned this when he appointed the wife of Bullock's 1990 GOP opponent to the Department of Human Services Board without giving the lieutenant governor a heads-up. Shortly after, Bush showed up on the Senate floor uninvited and wandered around visiting with members as the Senate conducted its business. Bullock left the dais, walked down to the floor, sidled up to the governor, and said grimly, "You're a cocky little motherf*****, aren't you?" The governor, used to Bullock's ways by now, smiled and moved on. The Senate confirmed Bush's nominee.

Bush cemented the relationship with Bullock in an inadvertent and poignant way. On March 30, 1995, Senate parliamentarian Bob Johnson died unexpectedly of a massive heart attack at sixty-six. Johnson had been like Bullock's brother, the one person capable of telling Bullock he was dumb as a post. Nicknamed "Big Daddy," Johnson had sheltered legislators and political players from Bullock's excesses and fiery personality and made the Senate operate. He was beloved around the Capitol.

No two men could be closer than Bullock and Johnson had been since they came to the legislature together in 1957. Shortly after his burial, the Senate met to memorialize him. When Betty King, the long-time secretary of the Senate, choked up while reading the resolution honoring Bullock's best friend, Bush came down from the dais to the podium where she stood weeping, put his arm around her, and finished reading the resolution for her. It was a gesture that cantankerous Bob Bullock never forgot.

The Texas legislature meets only every other year and then for only 140 days. (The joke is that Texans would prefer it if the legislature met for two days every 140 years.) Most bills get passed as the session comes to a close at the end of May, after being ground through committee hearings and the normal legislative back-and-forth for the previous four and a half months. A governor typically lays out his agenda in January, works as hard as he can to convince the powerful legislators who control the requisite committees to take his proposals seriously, then sees only a part of it enacted by May's end, and is grateful for that. Rookie governors tend to fare worse because they lack relationships with Austin's power brokers.

It was different with Bush. "The governor passed his entire legislative program without a hitch," reported *Texas Monthly* in its session wrap-up. His education package completely rewrote the state's education code, passing the legislature overwhelmingly. Bush's rewrite of the juvenile justice code passed by an equally large margin. Bush's welfare reform passed almost intact, but in a compromise worked out with Bullock, with the time limit watered down to between six months to five years. The passage of six legal reform bills clamping down on lawsuit abuse rounded out Bush's first session. After Ann Richards, it was almost as if the legislature had a pent-up desire to legislate.

But in truth it was Bush's corralling of legislative allies that produced his success: he enlisted them not only to help write the bills, but also to help sell them to the skeptics. Bush cultivated legislators by visiting them in their offices, and, almost as important, mingling with their staff, mostly twenty-somethings who'd never been so close to a governor. It's easier to do when all 181 legislators and their aides are in the same building, the Governor's Mansion is nearby, and you have willing partners on both sides of the aisle. He also went to their districts to sign bills they had helped write so he could share the credit.

Among the places where he did some of this informal coalition building was my back porch. A decade earlier, I had spotted the house—an 1884 clapboard farmhouse near New Braunfels, Texas. I bought it for $1,200, carted it in three pieces fifty-four miles to Austin, and slapped it on three acres on the side of a hill looking west. Starting in the spring of 1994, we'd had annual dinners to cook up all the wild game birds we'd shot that season and to blow off some steam. Laura liked wild dove and quail, so when the Bushes moved into the Governor's Mansion, Bush decreed we'd continue the game dinners. I'd shoot the birds and cook them. He'd decide on the guest list. In the odd-numbered years, when the legislature was in session, the guests would be House and Senate allies. In the even-numbered years, when the legislature was out of town, state Supreme Court justices would be invited for dinner. Each spring of Bush's years as governor, my role changed from political genius to wild game cook. We'd watch the sun set over the Hill Country as we ate salad, jalapeño quail, and cheese grits. Then we would linger over coffee and berry pies made without sugar. Bush complained about the pies, usually not long before asking for seconds. There would also be cigars. We would talk long after the sunlight faded.

During the early gubernatorial years, George W. Bush's personal style of leadership emerged. I had known him as friend, political operator, and candidate; watched him as baseball owner; and heard of his years hustling his next deal as an oil man and small independent producer. But none of that prepared me for his M.O. after he took office. I'd seen him operate in a world where the small and personal was sufficient. I had no idea how his personal skills would translate into a broader world of policy discussions, mind-numbing negotiations over legislative provisions, horse-trading, and running a government with an $80 billion biennial budget in a state of 18.7 million people.

Maybe the first thing that stood out—and in some senses surprised me, since he was a disciplined candidate—was that he had an aggressive governing streak. While Clinton talked about school uniforms in 1996, Bush talked about ending "social promotion," the practice of automatically passing children from grade to grade regardless of performance.

Bush's focus was on institutional reforms that would produce profound results over time. He was impatient: he knew he had a limited time in office and a finite amount of capital, and he wanted to spend both doing big things. It's also how he thinks. He was a history major at Yale and learned that game-changing moves are the ones that endure. He also knew swinging for the fences often meant striking out. But he would rather take the risk of failure if it gave him the chance of solving a problem.

This approach sometimes created the simplistic criticism that Bush was not concerned with details. But Bush understood there are different paths to the same goal. He wanted staff and legislative actors to buy into a proposal; having them sketch out details could aid that. Bush also had a strong sense of where he couldn't give and where he could, what would undermine the vision, and what would strengthen it. This caused him to emphasize results, not process. For example, his goal was to have every child read at grade level by the third grade, whereas others might have pursued the goal of doubling education funding.

Bush organized his people in a flat structure—no hierarchy for his top staff. Each had open access to him, providing him lots of insights and impressions. If he wanted something, he'd call them or go see them. His key aides became a "Team of Equals," which kept us from becoming a "Team of Rivals." This structure did require him to be very engaged with his advisors. It would have been easier to have everyone report through a chief of staff. But that would have made it harder for him to be hands-on when he needed to be. It also would have filtered out too many ideas and criticism.

Bush worked hard to set a tone of collaboration. If you went to him on a subject, he'd ask what others had to say. Once he asked an aide what Karen Hughes thought about an idea, and was told she was at her son's sports event. "That's what cell phones are for" was his retort.

It made him most comfortable to observe others debate, see how the arguments unfolded, and ask clarifying questions now and then. He welcomed opposing views, but you'd better have been prepared to back them up. He wanted dissent expressed in front of others to minimize "end runs" that could cause friction and mistakes. And he wanted candor to be the norm among his people because this brought uncomfortable issues to the fore quickly. He saw circumlocution as a sign of weakness.

If you demonstrated you could operate this way, you won Bush's trust.

And with that trust came his loyalty; he understood it ran both ways. But this was a weakness, too, for he was sometimes too trusting of people. He put up for too long with people who were no longer getting the job done, or who turned out to be disloyal. One person in this group was Rand Beers, a Democrat kept on the National Security Staff who bailed in time to become an advisor to John Kerry in the 2004 presidential campaign.

Bush also could get to the nub of an issue quickly. When state coffers were flush with cash going into the 1997 session, the higher education community showed up to plead for a $1 billion spending increase. The assembled university leaders made their pitch and then Bush asked, "Would you accept $500 million?" Hardly believing their good luck, the presidents and chancellors quickly said, "Yes!" Bush told them since he'd cut their request by 50 percent in five seconds, maybe they should go figure out what they really needed and come see him again.

Bush believed it was easy to criticize and carp; it was a lot harder to chart a course forward. He insisted people take responsibility for finding a solution to a problem, not just identifying it. This usually worked out very well; the downside, though, is that sometimes you needed one person to identify a problem and another person to solve it.

But occasionally I saw Bush react with jocularity and good humor to meetings that lacked value, were stuck, or lacked credible recommendations. His frat boy attitude was his way of concluding a bad meeting on a good note, to ease the end of a waste of his time by leaving 'em laughing. It sometimes left the impression he was bored by the whole process of governing, when the truth was that the meeting needed to end and this was the most graceful way to do it.

This fit his habit of downplaying his own intelligence, to accentuate his Sam Houston Elementary and San Jacinto Junior High background rather than Yale and Harvard Business School. This may have been effective populism that helped him bond with his staff and colleagues or with ordinary voters on the campaign trail, but it left some with the impression he was disengaged from the issues. Nothing could be further from the truth.

Bush also has formidable recall that allows him to dredge up a fact, sentence, argument, or viewpoint that you expressed months before and were now contradicting or discarding. He'd be interested in why. His recall on people was near miraculous. In 1997, we went hunting in

Wheeler, in the Texas Panhandle. No governor had ever visited Wheeler, population 1,378, so the town fathers asked the governor to attend a community pancake breakfast before hunting. I expected a few people to turn out, a quick round of handshakes, and some small talk before breakfast. But on the appointed Saturday morning, we showed up at the high school gym to find it packed. People had come in from Mobeetie and Old Mobeetie, twelve miles to the northwest, many on school buses. Others had driven up from Shamrock, seventeen miles south, including the Shamrock High band. I was pleasantly surprised, but I shouldn't have been. This was like little towns I had grown up in.

As Bush was shaking hands, up came a good old boy with about half his teeth missing. He said, "Governor, you remember me?" Without blinking an eye, Bush said "1978" and then referenced a house where he had met the man in Levelland. Bush was running for Congress then, and the house was one of his campaign stops. The meeting had occurred nearly twenty years earlier and some 259 miles away. And Bush had met the fellow just once. "You had three kids," Bush said. "Got five now, Governor, got five now!" was the man's response. These same powers of memory caused Bush's people to do their homework and keep track of what they had argued.

At the right point, Bush would decide, usually quickly, easily, and without agony, in large measure because he'd absorbed a lot of information, organized and analyzed it, and spun out the implications of different courses of action. And he ran a tight ship.

Bush made it clear that press leaks undermined the process he wanted, that they caused people to pull punches and trim their advice. He considered leaks to be an act of disrespect, and the leakers to be—well, almost—dishonorable.

Bush treated staff as good friends, knowing loyalty flows both ways and must be nurtured and fed. He took sports fans to University of Texas basketball games and invited runners to join him on his daily jog around Austin's Town Lake. There was barbecue at the Mansion and drop-bys at your office when you were meeting with outsiders. He got to know each of his top people personally, as well as their families. Eventually, everyone got a nickname.

Somewhere along the way, I got mine: "Turd Blossom," a Texas spring wildflower that pops up from a cow patty. Don't ask me to explain why I got this particular appellation. It must have been on a day when I was particularly exasperating. Once I received it, however, it stuck, though thank God most people are reluctant to say it publicly or privately. Margaret Spellings got labeled "la Margarita" and Karen Hughes "the High Prophet," a play off her maiden name, Parfitt, and her height. But they are not in the same league with Joe Allbaugh's "Pinkie," because of his sunburned face, or Vance McMahan's three nicknames: the predictable "Vancealot" and "Sir Vancealot," or when particularly geeky, "Sir Nerdalot."

Bush is not an angry person. He can be short or agitated at times; he wears his emotions on his sleeve, his lapel, and his pant legs. But anger was quite unusual for him. Unlike many people in politics, he doesn't manage by outburst, fury, or rage, which ultimately leads people to ignore the message. On the rare occasions when he does get angry, it leads to action. I recall two times when I saw the governor really mad, and both dealt with education.

One happened after a meeting with the Texas Education Agency staff, who'd come to report that thirty-three thousand children had failed the third-grade minimum reading skills exam. This test was at the "see Spot run" level. When he asked what happened to the children, the bureaucrats shuffled a few papers and told the governor that twenty-nine thousand of them had been passed to the fourth grade. It made Bush mad because he understood a child who doesn't learn to read by the third grade cannot possibly succeed. The meeting helped convince him to make a reading initiative a top priority.

As he later traveled the state to whip up support for it, an elderly teacher in East Texas lectured him that it would fail because, as she put it, "Governor, there are just some kids who can't learn to read." Her implication was that this was because their skin color was different. That just made Bush mad as hell. After that, nothing was going to stand in the way of getting this proposal done. The passage of a bill to retrain every Texas elementary school teacher in reading instruction would be one of Bush's big successes in the 1997 legislative session.

CHAPTER 7

Glimmers of the White House

———•◆•———

I can't remember the day when the idea of Bush's running for president first came up—though I was the one brash enough to bring it up. Our extended conversation began after Bob Dole became the presumptive Republican nominee for president in early March 1996. Dole is an admirable man, but it was already clear that he was unlikely to defeat Bill Clinton. That meant that come 2000, there would be new leaders scrapping for the GOP presidential nomination. That he could be one of those leaders had crossed Bush's mind, as it turns out.

And why not? He was the successful governor of the second-most-populous state. And he had a brand: he was a Bush. His father had been defeated in his bid for reelection as president in 1992, but remained popular and well respected. What's more, Republicans were on the ascendancy. In 1994, they had pulled off a stunning series of victories to capture control of both the House and Senate for the first time in forty years and picked up twelve governorships across the country.

We weren't the only ones thinking about Bush's running for president. By midsummer, he was receiving a regular stream of phone calls, letters, and visits from people asking about his plans. One person thinking ahead was Bullock. He had decided Bush should be president. At Bush's fiftieth birthday party, in July 1996, at the Governor's Mansion, Bullock toasted Bush as "the next president of the United States." Such heartfelt words from the usually gruff, hard-nosed lieutenant governor were a surprise to many in the room.

When Bullock decided what he wanted, he worked to get it, and he had seen an obstacle to his goal. He was worried a controversial tax reform Bush was pushing could paint the governor as a tax raiser, even though the reform was revenue-neutral and would be a boon for the state's economy.

I felt Bullock's passion on the issue firsthand on a searing hot day in August 1996 with no clouds in the sky, the temperature in the triple digits, and the humidity not far behind. I emerged from the Capitol's north side to drive back to Rove + Company. Bullock was standing next to a monument near the entrance, smoking a cigarette, and posing for a picture with tourists.

When he saw me, he motioned me over and, after the tourists wandered off, sat me down on a ledge and proceeded to say, in detail, why tax reform was a bad idea. Bullock feared it would hurt Bush in New Hampshire, where the antitax animus of Republicans was legendary. He went on for more than forty-five minutes, smoking cigarette after cigarette. I almost passed out from the heat and sweated through my shirt and sport coat. When an aide came to find Bullock, I thanked the lieutenant governor for his advice and stood to feel the sweat pouring down my legs. Bullock had never allowed a bead of sweat to appear on his forehead. I told Bush about Bullock's concerns, but he waved them off.

Meanwhile, the Dole campaign cratered. I had never seen a presidential campaign more badly run and less worthy of a candidate. But Texas gave him an outpouring of support when he visited Houston in late October. It was apparent something was up as Bush and I approached the rally site off Interstate 10, in a small shopping center outside Houston. People had abandoned their cars on the side of the freeway and on access roads and had walked the last mile or two to the rally. The energy of these frantic Republicans made it feel like a victory celebration.

Afterward, Dole invited Bush to ride with him back to the airport, and Bush waved me into the vehicle with him, the Doles, and one of Dole's Texas leaders. The local campaign leader told Dole about reports he'd just heard from Dole's traveling party that Dole was closing the gap, but none of the optimistic reports were backed up with public polling. The former U.S. senator from Kansas looked off into the distance as the limo sped down the freeway. He let the man's words pass. Then, sucking on a lozenge, he quietly said, referring to his traveling aides, "They don't need to lie to me. I'm a fighter." In that moment you couldn't help but love him. Eleven days later, Dole won Texas by 5 points while losing the country by 8. He did, however, hold Clinton to less than 50 percent of the vote. There would now be a wide-open race for the 2000 GOP presidential nomination.

Before he could do much about it, however, Bush had to win reelection in 1998. It never crossed his mind or mine that he could run for president without first winning reelection. It was a prerequisite for a presidential run. Besides, while I was now committed to a race for the White House, he wasn't. It was easy for me to commit: I wouldn't be the candidate.

And that's the way it would be for the next two years. I was constantly plotting, planning, and scheming about electing Bush president. On the other hand, he left open the possibility without binding himself. He didn't need to; there was plenty of time. He knew the price such a decision would entail. I also think he felt that my stirring things up was enough. As long as someone was lining up supporters, keeping a friendly buzz going, cataloging potential problems, and keeping in touch with potential rivals, he could put off a final decision.

In the meantime, it was important for Bush's future that he win reelection big—running well among groups Republicans traditionally didn't do well with. We especially wanted to show he could attract Hispanics, and so decided we would push hard to win El Paso County. It is Texas's sixth-most-populous county and over 70 percent Hispanic: of the seventy-eight statewide Republican candidates in Texas from 1972 to 1990, only ten carried El Paso. If Bush won it or came close, his appeal among Latinos would be clearly established.

We wanted to raise a lot of money from around the country. In the first gubernatorial election, we focused on Texas, in part because we couldn't afford the time away from his rural campaign. Now, raising money outside Texas would leave more political money in the state for down ballot candidates. We could build and road-test a national network that would help in a White House bid while allowing Bush to quietly impress elected officials and party opinion leaders around the country.

By campaign's end, we had held fifty-three fund-raisers in twelve states, raising over $11 million. We were pleasantly surprised that Bush 41's more senior fund-raisers, rather than being ready to hand off the chore to younger faces, were among our most eager and energetic supporters.

We also wanted to use Bush's popularity among the Republican grassroots to build an army of volunteers to run up his margins in the governor's race and to avoid a "lonely victory"—one where he won while the rest of the ticket was defeated. Republicans across America would appreciate someone who'd pulled out the stops to elect other GOP candidates down the ballot. This meant putting together the most extensive and best-organized campaign Texas had ever seen, with the most influential community and business leaders we could recruit to lead Bush's reelection effort in each county.

Karen Hughes wisely suggested that Bush handle the question of a possible presidential bid straight on. Texans were proud their governor was being mentioned for president, but they didn't want to be lied to. She advised that he give the same answer each time he was asked: he hadn't made a decision and understood why Texans would take that into consideration when they voted. It had the virtue of being honest.

By spring 1997, Bush's campaign preparations and fund-raising were so thorough that most Democrats decided to sit on the sidelines. The only one with any statewide presence who talked about running was Land Commissioner Garry Mauro, a close personal friend of President Clinton and one of the least impressive statewide candidates the Democrats had ever fielded.

On June 5, shortly after the end of the legislative session, Bob Bullock announced he was retiring. Increasingly ill, he'd decided to quit at the top. But before he left the stage, he had a few more acts to perform. One was to show up unexpectedly at a Bush fund-raiser in Austin that June with a $2,500 contribution. That stung Mauro, who was Bullock's driver in the 1974 campaign and later a deputy comptroller under Bullock.

I kept up my presidential scheming. Bush was familiar with state issues but would need a network of experts on national and international issues if he were to run for the White House. It would be better if these people were brought together well in advance of an election. I began to draw them together with the help of associates of Bush and friends of mine around the country.

Al Hubbard was an Indiana businessman and a Harvard Business School classmate and friend of Bush. He called in May 1997 to recommend that Indianapolis mayor Stephen Goldsmith advise Bush on domestic issues. I encouraged Bush to invite Hubbard and his wife, Kathy, to overnight at the Mansion in mid-July to talk more. Hubbard recommended Larry Lindsey as an economic advisor. I liked the idea, having just given Lindsey's book *The Growth Experiment: How the New Tax Policy Is Transforming the U.S. Economy* to Bush. In late October 1997, Lindsey came down to Austin with Hubbard and agreed to informally advise the governor and suggest other economic thinkers he could consult.

The same process took place with Myron Magnet, author of *The Dream and the Nightmare*, which Bush felt captured his concerns about the aftermath of the 1960s, and University of Texas professor Marvin Olasky, who'd done groundbreaking work on faith-based social entrepreneurship. Magnet came in July and met with Bush, Vance McMahan, and me. Out of the conversation came one of Bush's gubernatorial reelection planks—homes for unwed, pregnant teenagers. Other policy experts and idea people began making their way through Austin. The list of informal advisors grew, and we were inundated with papers, memos, and articles from them.

Some of my scheming got ahead of us. I let myself get talked into convincing Bush to speak in August to the midwestern GOP conference in Indianapolis. I thought accepting it would help keep the early buzz going, by providing a chance to show off Bush's talents. Bush thought it was premature and worried he was not ready. He was right. A *New York Times* reporter accurately criticized Bush's remarks as "stiffly delivered." But attending the event helped lasso key party leaders throughout the Midwest. They might have ended up in our camp eventually, but Bush's visit locked them in early. It also helped us identify chinks in his armor— the vagueness of his early speeches and the reserve that came over him when he had to deliver prepared remarks. Having learned our lesson, we went back to Texas and thereafter made our way around the country below the radar, raising money at events closed to the media.

In early October, I had one of the more surreal experiences I've ever had in politics. It showed me how some politicians can mislead themselves and misjudge other people. Democrat John Sharp was state comptroller and a candidate for Bullock's lieutenant governor post. Bush needed Republican Rick Perry to be elected lieutenant governor. The argument that sending Bush to the White House would leave Texas in Democratic hands would not keep Bush from the GOP presidential nod, but it would be a nuisance, giving people an excuse to back someone else. Electing Perry was a goal to which we devoted a lot of money, energy, and attention, including the only two Texas fund-raisers former president George H. W. Bush did in Texas that election.

Sharp was determined to undermine the Perry plan. On October 3, 1997, at the Wildlife Expo dinner—an event that attracts Texas politicos, outdoorsmen, and good old boys who sit in a big open-air shed, eat barbecue, and hear tall tales about hunting and fishing—he tried to hire me. The offer came through a mutual friend, a San Marcos car dealer named Chuck Nash. Nash sidled up to me during the predinner mob scene to talk politics. Sharp admired my talents, he said, and wanted my help in his campaign. He could pay me $1 million and it would be funneled through a media firm as part of the advertising buy so no one would know. It'd be a good piece of work for me, and had he mentioned Sharp really admired my brilliance?

I suspected Nash had spent too much time in the sun selling pickups, but he assured me Sharp wanted to talk that night. And sure enough, when I ran into Sharp he said he had a high regard for my talents, hoped we could find a way to work together, and implied Nash had authority to work out an arrangement. As dinner was served, we cordially parted.

I never followed up on it and they didn't pursue me further. My silence was sufficient. Not that I consider a million dollars to be ungenerous, but whatever my failings are, I am not as dumb or unprincipled as Sharp thought. His success was clearly not in Bush's interest and I was committed to Bush's victory.

The next month, Bullock unexpectedly dropped a bomb on Garry Mauro's headquarters with a statement that read, "I respect and admire Governor George Bush and feel he deserves reelection to a second term. During my public career, I've served under seven governors, and Governor Bush is the best I've served under." Bullock hadn't given Bush a heads-up. Bush was moved and responded that he was "deeply honored and touched." It was a bitter moment for Mauro. Bullock, after all, was the godfather to one of his children. Mauro's campaign had effectively ended before it began.

A poll showed Bush 50 points ahead of Mauro. We had $13 million in the campaign war chest. But rather than bank on that, Bush spent more time outlining an agenda for a second term than he did touting his success of the four big reforms from his last campaign. He promised to end social promotion and to cut taxes for small businesses.

Looking back, I am especially proud of our effort to win over Hispanic voters, which was best represented by what we did in El Paso. An art gallery owner named Adair Margo ran our campaign there. Having never been involved in politics, she refused to believe things couldn't be done. She opened our headquarters in a heavily Democratic and Latino neighborhood. The big warehouse was crowded with volunteers, many of them speaking Spanish as they manned the phone bank. There were always trays of Tex-Mex pastries, including cookies in colors that don't appear in nature. Adair's volunteers even did a CD of pro-Bush songs written and performed by local supporters. One volunteer put them on the jukeboxes in the Joker Club, a bar in a shady part of town. They were the only free songs on the jukeboxes in the booths, so the CD got a lot of play. The campaign cut special television and radio ads for El Paso, and the GOP held its state convention in the city. We organized a statewide Hispanic coalition called "Juntos Podemos," which translates roughly "Together, we can." Our local leaders thought the slogan was too vague and opted instead for the more conventional "Amigos de Bush" for its El Paso chapter. It became fun to visit the city just to see what wild things Adair and her crowd of political first-timers were up to. The Democratic mayor shook things up when he gave Bush an early endorsement.

Texas Democrats were flummoxed again in April when we announced that Mark McKinnon would handle Bush's advertising. McKinnon had sterling Democratic credentials, having been Governor Mark White's press secretary before becoming an ad guy, first in New York and then back in Texas, where Bullock had been his client. We had planned on using Bush's 1994 campaign ad consultant, Don Sipple, until stories broke in August 1997 that Sipple's former wives alleged he had abused them. It was a painful but necessary decision not to hire Sipple, and it left him embittered.

McKinnon first met Bush at a small dinner in early 1996, where McKinnon gave Bush a rough cut of a documentary he was preparing on a charter school in inner-city Houston. Bush liked what he saw, both in the film and in its creator. But it was Bullock who recommended McKinnon to Bush, who then asked me to sniff it out.

Mark and I first met at an off-the-record press briefing a few days before the 1986 election. I represented Governor Clements, and McKinnon was there for Governor Mark White, then locked in a bitter election battle. I accused the White camp of attempting to make Clements seem an angry curmudgeon (which he was, sort of). Mark, believing off-the-record really meant off-the-record, replied that of course the White campaign wanted to paint Clements as a "cold, heartless son of a bitch." A reporter burned him by running with it. McKinnon had also worked for Chet Edwards against Bullock in Bullock's 1990 primary for lieutenant governor. That was a perilous career move, since Bullock never forgot his adversaries and almost never forgave them. Bullock knew talent, however. He hired Mark for his 1990 general election, but only after confronting him by asking, "You remember all those goddamn lies you told about me?" Mark was so shocked he couldn't speak. Bullock then spat out, "Well, I hope you haven't forgot how to do that." Bullock was right to recommend Mark. Bush and McKinnon clicked from moment one. In a bow to McKinnon's cool image, Bush dubbed him "M-Kat."

Mark not only became a close friend of Bush but an even closer friend of mine. Besides being a really decent person, "M-Kat" has a keen mind, a readiness to listen, and a goofy eccentricity that keeps things entertaining. At times he wore black and white checked slip-on tennis shoes, affected a beret, and carried a man-purse. To this day, he keeps fit by biking long distances with his pal Lance Armstrong and a certain former president. The only time I've seen him wear a tie was in the Oval Office—and even then it was weird, narrow, and out of style. Mark and I both are fans of *Rocky and Bullwinkle*. I call him Rocky. He calls me Boris.

While Bush was nailing down new talent, he was also attracting the old kind. George Shultz, Ronald Reagan's secretary of state, called me to ask if Bush was interested in being hosted at Shultz's house in Palo Alto, California, during a fund-raising swing through the state.

In April 1998, Bush pulled together an eclectic group that included economists Michael Boskin and John Cogan, Reagan's domestic policy chief Marty Anderson and his wife, Annelise, and Stanford University provost Condoleezza Rice. The conversation was wide-ranging, moving from the economy to domestic policy to foreign affairs and back to the economy. Shultz and his crowd were taken with the governor's thirst for information and his give-and-take. Bush was comfortable saying what he didn't know. At one point, a lively debate erupted over the International Monetary Fund (IMF) and its mission. Bush listened intently.

When the time came to leave and Bush was saying his good-byes, Shultz took me aside and told me he was impressed. "He's presidential timber," he said, and the secretary would like to help if Bush ran. Shultz was standing by the front door and gestured back toward the living room. "Ronald Reagan had a meeting just like this in this room before he ran for president," he told me. I could only hope the good karma held.

The next day, Bush gave a speech to the Lincoln Club of Northern California. During the Q&A session, Bush was asked his views on the IMF. He repeated the arguments pro and con he'd heard the day before and endorsed reform, explaining the points that shaped his views. Boskin sat in the back of the room, slyly grinning. Word got back to Shultz that his pupil had actually paid attention. It made it easier to attract bright minds as advisors for a presidential bid.

Back in Texas, Bush, taking nothing for granted, barnstormed aggressively. Occasionally we hit small snags, most put in Bush's path by allies. We were trying to limit public discussion about a presidential bid, but some "friends" wanted to be heard from, such as Nebraska Republican U.S. senator Chuck Hagel. He insisted on coming to Austin for what we agreed would be a private visit. But he immediately trumpeted the meeting to the papers back home by endorsing Bush and saying, "There's only one person who is a giant among that crowd, and that's George Bush. I think George Bush is tougher than his dad . . . more conservative than his dad and more disciplined than his dad." Someone elevating the younger Bush by trashing the elder Bush just thrilled—thrilled!—the governor, who questioned my judgment in allowing Hagel anywhere near Austin during the gubernatorial campaign. Hagel later ended up endorsing McCain.

In August, Bush joined his parents in Kennebunkport, Maine, for a brief vacation. There he whiled away hours talking foreign affairs with the Stanford University provost and former National Security Council aide to his father who was also a guest of the senior Bushes. Condi Rice had sat in on the Shultz seminars that spring, but this was the first time George W. Bush spent a lot of time with her.

As the fall campaign opened, we decided it was best to have just one debate in mid-October, at 8 P.M. on a Friday night in El Paso. There'd be one moderator—Bob Moore from the *El Paso Times*—and both candidates would be seated on the same side of the table, looking at the camera, not at each other. This made personal assaults more difficult and ignoring the opponent easier.

In Texas, Friday night high school football is akin to a religious obligation, and since El Paso is the only city in Texas in the Mountain Time Zone—8 P.M. there is 9 P.M. in the rest of Texas—very few Texans would be watching the debate. That turned out to be a good thing because it was a low moment for both candidates. Bush didn't like Mauro and worked himself into a foul humor before arriving at the studio. As for Mauro, he was ham-handed in his attacks and nervous. But Bush's generally impatient performance showed he didn't want to be there, and he was panned by the political press.

In retrospect, it was a mistake to press for only one debate. I think Bush would have benefited from more experience, and debating Mauro more would certainly not have changed the outcome of the governor's race. And I learned a lesson: If your candidate really dislikes his opponent, do everything you can to push those thoughts out of his mind before the debate. If he dwells on his disdain for his opponent before the debate, it will usually come out.

As the election drew near, anxiety in our ranks grew. Not about winning, but about whether Bush would get a large enough margin of victory. The chattering class had declared that less than 60 percent would be embarrassing for Bush. And the Perry-Sharp battle for lieutenant governor was nip and tuck. The Texas Poll in mid-October showed their race tied at 37 percent. We stepped up phone bank efforts to identify households that supported Bush but were undecided in the lieutenant governor's race so the Perry campaign could focus on these persuadable voters. Households backing Bush and Perry got an all-out push to turn out via absentee or early voting or on Election Day, while voters backing Bush and Sharp got dropped from the turnout efforts.

Bush crushed Mauro 68 percent to 31 percent, carrying every region and 240 of 254 counties. Adair, the Democratic mayor, and their un-likely collection of amateur campaigners made Bush the first Republican gubernatorial candidate in history to carry El Paso. He also won the state by the largest margin in any gubernatorial race since 1966, when Texas was still a one-party, Democratic state.

The governor's coalition showed he was a different kind of Republi-can: he received 49 percent of the Latino vote, 27 percent of the African-American vote, and carried 65 percent of women and 70 percent of independents. His coattails were long: all fourteen statewide Republican candidates won.

At a packed news conference the next morning, the press treated Bush's victory as almost an afterthought, even though he was the first Texas governor in history to win back-to-back four-year terms. They bad-gered him to declare for president right then and there. He dashed their hopes, telling them, "I haven't made up my mind whether I will run for president or not."

During an earlier interview, Bush had described himself as a "conser-vative with a heart." Bush's words caught Karen's interest; she refined them into "compassionate conservative" and repeated the alliterative phrase in his draft victory speech—four or five times. He said it just once that night and then repeated it in response to a question at the news con-ference the next morning. Still, we had our mantra.

CHAPTER 8

The Grand Plan

..

———————•◆•———————

The trouble with being the front-runner so early in a presidential campaign is that everyone wants to shoot at you.

Although Bush had not yet declared, New Jersey governor Christie Whitman helpfully explained he should worry, because "when you're this far out in front, even the tiniest little slip, insignificant as it may be, is going to look very significant." It wasn't clear whether this was an observation or a hope.

It's easy to look back and conclude that Bush's indecision on whether to run was contrived. But I was there. He was genuinely unsure of what to do and reserved the right not to pull the trigger. And following the election, he simply would not be hurried in making up his mind. Everybody had a view about this, but only two people's opinions mattered, and they were married to each other. Laura and he talked a lot about it.

Being governor was a great job. He also knew, better than most, the impact a presidential race would have on his twin teenage daughters. He knew that if he did it, he'd never have any semblance of a private life again—including the ability to wander the sporting goods store to pick out fishing lures.

My sense was that Laura wanted him to run because of what he could do for the country, but she never revealed her thoughts openly. I knew, based on how he spoke about it, that Governor Bush leaned toward running. But I also knew Bush doesn't make a decision until he finally makes a decision. Some people mistakenly think he's an instinct or "gut" player. That's wrong. He has very good, if occasionally erring, instincts about people. But he never makes big decisions—and certainly not a decision as monumental as running for president—merely or mostly on instinct.

On occasion I had to fight back the impulse to grab him by the shoulders and yell, "Make the damned decision!" But I knew better. Or at least I knew there was always a burly, armed Texas Department of Public Safety trooper by his side.

But I could prod him on other things, such as settling on a foreign policy advisor. Harvard economist Larry Lindsey, former Indianapolis mayor Steve Goldsmith, and a growing army of others counseled him on domestic issues. But who could help him sort through foreign policy? He had not forgotten the meeting in George Shultz's living room or his time with Condi Rice at Kennebunkport. She struck him as smart, easy to talk to, good at explaining the often tortured language of the foreign policy crowd, and able to keep discussions focused. Besides, she was a fellow sports nut, he told me. I thought the last credential was odd, but then I was about the only non-sports nut in Bush's orbit, so what did I know?

What finally pushed Bush to run was a sermon by Pastor Mark Craig of Dallas at a service the morning of Bush's second gubernatorial inaugural on January 19, 1999. Craig delivered an extraordinary and extemporaneous homily about ethical and moral leadership. Barbara Bush later told her son, "He was talking to you." Bush was on the edge, prepared to jump into the fray, and Craig gave a little push. Within a day, Bush signaled full speed ahead for the preparations to join the race. He seemed relieved now that he'd made his decision.

Bush was still determined to have a good legislative session. It would bolster his case that he could be an effective president on education and it would shorten the campaign's public phase—the period during which primary opponents would most likely try to soften him up by taking shots at him.

First, though, there was the question of who would run the presidential campaign. Bush was happy with Allbaugh as his de facto gubernatorial chief of staff and me as resident rocket scientist and agent provocateur. In December, Bob Teeter—the senior Bush's pollster and respected Republican graybeard—suggested former congressman Tom Tauke be tapped as campaign manager. Tauke was then a high-ranking official at Verizon and was from the critical state of Iowa. He had a good reputation around Washington and would give Bush's effort some heft. Bush was intrigued, met with Tauke, and came to a tentative arrangement that Tauke would run the campaign, if there was one. It didn't last.

Allbaugh and I were dispatched to Washington to brief Tauke on the state of preparations and who on Bush's team was available to come to the campaign. Tauke reassured us that there would be a place for us on the campaign, which had the unintended effect of making us feel there wouldn't. He then discussed how he had tentatively cut a turn-key deal with a state legislator to run Bush's Iowa caucus efforts out of the legislator's eastern Iowa office.

We had been offered that deal in December and turned it down. It ran counter to Bush's way of operating. We didn't like its high price tag. We wanted our effort staffed by people working at reasonable wages. We wanted an emphasis on grassroots volunteers organized in county and town committees, not a plan that emphasized the consultant's staff. We thought the operation should be run out of Des Moines, the state's largest city and centrally located, not an eastern Iowa Mississippi River town, especially since most Republicans lived on the western side of the state. We wanted to carefully measure and monitor activities, not depend on reports from an independent contractor.

The people around Bush had a habit of talking to each other before making major decisions like this. After a few weeks, it became clear to Tauke and to us that this wasn't going to work. Bush reluctantly agreed. I think he had been initially concerned that I, Allbaugh, and others who had run his reelection campaign lacked the smarts and Washington connections to pull off a presidential one. But Allbaugh ultimately got the job.

We ran the campaign out of Austin, not Washington. That meant people who came to work for Bush were likely to be more loyal to him and not treat the campaign as just another job. We also realized that we would be insulated somewhat from D.C. and the habits of its permanent political class. D.C. lobbyists and insiders made a practice of floating into a presidential campaign, more with an eye to burnishing their credentials than actually doing hard work. And then they leaked to reporters, mostly to impress them with their importance. We suffered their indignation at being held at arm's length. Some of them were especially critical of our efforts in off-the-record comments to the press whenever we hit a rough patch.

With the campaign's management and headquarters settled, Bush told me to get rid of Rove + Company. I could sell it, shut it down, give it away—he didn't care. "I want you focused full-time on my business," he said. He was all-in for the race and wanted me all-in as well. I agreed without hesitation. A day or two later I realized I was lighting a match to eighteen years of hard work. I sold the company to two young politicos who would handle the presidential campaign's direct mail. As a result, the new owners had a better first year than any year I'd ever had. They paid off the note early.

We made another important decision that January, about how we would satisfy the Bush supporters who wanted to do more than give at the $1,000-per-head limit. Bush's friend James B. Francis, Jr., suggested we build a network of money raisers, not just money givers. The idea was simple: supporters had friends, family, business associates, college class-mates, and Rolodexes to tap. The group set a $100,000 goal for each fund-raiser, developed a rough outline of how to track their efforts, and decided to call them "Pioneers." They represented Bush's first such grass-roots bundling effort. And we liked the western-sounding name of the group. We plucked Jack Oliver from the wreckage of Missouri senator John Ashcroft's short-lived presidential campaign, made him finance di-rector, and told him to figure out how to make the "Pioneers" plan work.

In late February, Bush went to Washington for a National Governors Association meeting. I tagged along. The city was buried in snow and the streets shut down. Our hotel was nearly empty; Warren Buffett and a few of his associates were the only others in the dining room. But New Hampshire senator Judd Gregg was accustomed to snow and made his way to the hotel to meet the Texas governor. Their fathers—Hugh Gregg and George H. W. Bush—were close friends. Hugh Gregg had backed the senior Bush in 1980 and led his Granite State campaign. Now the sons hit it off and the taciturn, gloomy Judd Gregg would lead George W. Bush's campaign in this difficult and dangerous first primary state.

I believed that as the front-runner Bush had to win four "invisible" primaries before facing any of the real ones: Money, Establishment, Reas-surance, and Substance. The first was the easiest to understand: Would

Bush's fund-raising total be larger than everyone else's in the rest of the pack by a sizable amount? Steve Forbes was running and could always dip into his large personal pocket to finance his campaign. But by raising a ton of money, Bush would also demonstrate that he had a ton of support. Also, people who donate also tend to defend their investment. We also worked to keep costs low—raising money was useless if you also spent it all frivolously. We had a lean operation with a smaller than normal staff, lower salaries (of the ten highest-paid GOP presidential campaign staff that summer, none worked for Bush), and no consultants.

As for the second primary: the Establishment is not what it used to be. There's no small group of party elders, furiously smoking cigars in some poorly lit back room. Each party's Establishment is now tens of thousands of people. Some are members of Congress, statewide elected officials, or state legislators. Others are state or county party chairmen and committee members or local party officials. Still others are activists who recruit volunteers, man the phone banks, walk the doors, sit on the finance committees, and host fund-raisers. There is no list hidden away on a computer somewhere that has all their names. But go to any state, and people know who these leaders are and primary voters pay attention to their candidate choices. We set about winning them over with calls and visits. But we knew we had a big advantage: Bush was the epitome of Establishment, the son of a former president, the front-runner, and the candidate to whom most Republicans would naturally migrate.

Then came the third invisible contest: for that Reassurance Primary, we hired two people to build a national, grassroots Bush fan club and keep it constantly fired up. One of the leaders was Maria Cino, who was barely five feet tall but perceptive and full of energy. She'd been executive director of the National Republican Congressional Committee in 1994 when the GOP ended its forty years in the House wilderness. She took a serious pay cut when she left a D.C. law firm to head up our organization. She combined elements of General Patton and the stereotypical Italian mama, though in fact there may not be that much difference between the two.

Her principal deputy was a brainy, intense, methodical, workaholic Jewish political junkie named Ken Mehlman. A Harvard Law graduate and classmate of Barack Obama's, Mehlman was a rising lawyer on a fast track to partnership at Akin Gump. But he loved politics and left to work for two Texas congressmen before ending up in the Bush campaign. He was the first in the office and often the last to leave. He was disciplined enough to set aside time each day to work out, but he also knew how to have fun. When Mehlman went to Iowa to oversee our operation there, he never missed karaoke night on Saturday at the Rock Bottom Bar in West Des Moines.

.Maria and Ken's job was to find the right balance between selling Bush as his father's son and as his own man. Many people knew of Bush's record as governor, but they also needed to see he had the values and character of his parents, which so many Americans, especially Republicans, had come to admire. This meant that while Governor Bush could frequently talk about his parents and his family, public appearances by the senior Bushes needed to be rare. They were great resources in building our organization and raising funds, but it was best for them and their son that they keep a low profile. They knew that and were gracious in accepting their behind-the-scenes role. When we forgot that rule later in the campaign, we hurt ourselves needlessly.

Finally, there was the Substance Primary, which was the most important. Republicans needed to know that Bush had an optimistic, positive agenda for the country's future. Republicans wanted to end the Clinton-Gore years, but their enthusiasm depended on knowing what the next president was going to do. Did he have a concrete plan about big issues that made sense?

In laying out our ideas, we faced a "Press Paradox": We would be attacked for not being specific when we painted in broad brushstrokes. But if we spelled it all out, the media would attack us later for saying nothing new. It was a balancing act. We decided to highlight three things in particular—that Bush was the effective conservative governor of a big state; that he was a compassionate conservative who talked about issues in an attractive new way; and that he was a different kind of Republican who attracted support from women, Hispanics, young people, and others who were not typical Republicans. It's not a coincidence that these messages reinforced each other.

We didn't want there to be two Bushes—a primary / more conservative Bush; and a general election / more moderate Bush. We wanted to run from start to finish with the same candidate, emphasizing a consistent theme. Events and circumstances and the coverage itself would pull

us a few degrees this way or that, but where we started for the early primaries of 1999 is where we wanted to remain for the real primaries of
2000 and for the general election.

This was contrary to the counsel of a lot of people. Richard Nixon
popularized the theory that Republicans need to run to the right (and
Democrats to the left) to win their respective primaries and then move
back to the center for the general election. But that's a cynical approach.
It makes sense only if you believe voters aren't paying attention—and in
the information age, that is not a safe assumption. Candidates who follow Nixon's advice could come across as unreliable, unprincipled, and in-
authentic. The danger to us was that reporters could become bored by
hearing the same thing over and over.

We also recognized the strategic imperative of building a national
campaign rather than focusing on one or a handful of early states and
hoping to break through and create unstoppable momentum. A front-
runner can't choose the contests he'll compete in. Some front-runners
try, but they generally lose. That happened in 2008 when the leader of
the GOP pack (Rudy Giuliani) tried to bypass early contests and made
Florida the first real test of his appeal. And on the Democratic side, the
front-runner (Hillary Clinton) thought she could avoid making a strong
effort in any caucus states that followed Iowa. By June, her opponent's
lead among elected delegates came from his caucus, not primary, contest
victories.

We anticipated "sequential warfare" with different challengers in different states. No single candidate had the resources or standing to fight
Bush everywhere. So in Iowa, we expected Forbes and Elizabeth Dole to
be our competitors; in New Hampshire, McCain and Dole; and in South
Carolina, McCain and at least one other surviving candidate.

Winning every primary is nearly impossible, so we knew Bush would
lose somewhere and that the press would use that upset to write that an
insurgent candidate was breaking through. Ronald Reagan was upset in
the 1980 Iowa caucuses by George H. W. Bush. Reagan himself had
upset Gerald Ford in the North Carolina primary in 1976. Gary Hart
stunned Walter Mondale in New Hampshire in 1984, defeating him by a
double-digit margin. Somewhere, we thought, voters were going to give
Bush his comeuppance. It is important not to be shocked when it happens; having internalized the possibility in advance, you can keep morale

from collapsing. An upset victory gives a competitor positive press, quick money, and momentum. The only way to break that momentum is to have the resources, issues, and strong organization in the states that follow to bend the campaign's course back in your direction.

If Bush won the nomination—and at that point, I put the odds of that extremely high—Vice President Al Gore was the most likely general election opponent. I knew Gore brought impressive strengths to the race. For one thing, the country was prosperous. While stock markets began declining in March 2000 and growth would slow as the economy eventually fell into recession in the opening months of 2001, jobs remained plentiful through Election Day. The country was also at peace. Few candidates have ever had such a strong wind at their backs as Gore. Only twice in the twentieth century did the party in power during a time of peace and prosperity fail to win reelection. Nixon's loss in 1960 was extremely close; Taft's defeat in 1912 required the presence of a serious third-party candidate—former Republican president Theodore Roosevelt.

Gore was also an excellent debater who had wiped the floor with Ross Perot during a debate over NAFTA hosted by CNN's Larry King. He was smart and knowledgeable about national issues, having been in Congress before becoming vice president. He had weaknesses, too. But at the start of the race, his strengths were both visible and daunting.

We had another challenge. From January to the end of May 1999, the Texas legislature was in session and the demands placed on the governor over that period made it too difficult to travel—a reality confirmed when Bush made a quiet trip to Louisiana in February that almost ended in disaster when news of it leaked. Traveling for his campaign would diminish his chances of having a successful session. Critics could carp about his not attending to the business he had just been reelected to do. And front-runners generally don't want to extend the campaign's length; they want to shorten it.

So how to run a campaign when your candidate can't or won't travel? Actually, I'd thought about this a lot after stumbling onto the 1896 presidential campaign of William McKinley. For a number of years, I taught an undergraduate class at the University of Texas at Austin on press and politics. I'd also taught a graduate course in 1997 at the LBJ School on the "modern presidential campaign." I'd even been provisionally accepted to the Ph.D. program in government at UT with one caveat: I had to get my undergraduate degree first. All my years of politicking had left me a couple of dozen hours short of my baccalaureate degree. Over the course of the '90s, I finished off the science requirement and the upper-division political science courses I needed to have in residence at UT. I still had the math and dreaded foreign language requirements, and something called the "upper-division writing requirement," to complete. Despite my having run a public affairs firm for almost two decades and created a heck of a lot of political advertising, the university needed proof I could string two sentences together.

So in 1997, I did what any other forty-six-year-old with a family, business, and a busy work calendar would do: I looked for the easiest course I could take to fulfill that requirement. Flipping through the UT course catalog, I found "Seminar in Historical Source Writing." It looked attractive enough: research the original documents on a subject, write a paper, and, bingo, requirement fulfilled. I showed up in the history department, asked the secretary how to sign up, and was told I needed to find a professor to take me on. Brashly, I asked, "Who's here?" She directed me to the office of Dr. Lewis Gould, the only professor around at that moment. The gods of serendipity were protecting me.

The topic I wanted to write about was Theodore Roosevelt in the 1896 campaign. I'd long been interested in how the brash young TR backed the wrong candidate for president in the Republican convention, thought the nominee—William McKinley—was "a dolt," yet somehow wormed his way into McKinley's campaign and, after the election, into his subcabinet. TR's future as Rough Rider charging up San Juan Hill, as governor of the nation's most populous state, as vice president, and then as president upon the assassination of McKinley was possible only because he'd somehow become McKinley's assistant secretary of the Navy and was at his post when a crisis broke while his boss, the Navy secretary, was on a long vacation.

Gould, it turned out, was one of the nation's leading historians of the Gilded Age, and he rarely, if ever, agreed to a "Seminar in Historical Source Writing." But he was intrigued and took me on with the condition that I had to read the McKinley papers. He told me that almost all historians get McKinley wrong. If this was the price of admission, I was happy to pay it, not knowing the McKinley papers were completely disorganized and available only on microfilm.

While I almost went blind from sitting in front of a microfilm reader, I learned McKinley was a master politician who understood America's changing demography. He wanted to modernize the country and the Republican Party. Confined by tradition to his home in Canton, Ohio, while the campaign was fought out across the country by surrogates and advocates, McKinley hit on a brilliant idea. If he couldn't barnstorm among the people, then bring the people to him. Thus was born McKinley's famous "Front Porch" campaign, where supporters were brought by the trainload to northeastern Ohio and then paraded from the railroad station to McKinley's home, where he received them with a short speech of platitudes and appreciation. Delegations were organized to show the McKinley campaign's outreach to new immigrants and other voters not historically identified with the largely Anglo-Saxon Republican Party.

We began our own "Front Porch" campaign on June 8, 1998, with a small group assembled by former U.S. ambassador to Australia Mel Sembler. A past RNC finance chairman, Sembler brought dozens of fund-raisers to Austin over the course of the summer; Bush spoke to them at the Mansion. He became comfortable with the format, convinced of their utility, and ready to green-light more.

At first the emphasis was on encouraging Bush's finance network to bring other fund-raisers from their state or region. They'd get into Austin in the morning in time for an early lunch. Governor Bush would break away from the Capitol, come to the Mansion, and join his guests in the formal dining room. We could fit up to about thirty-six people at tables of six. The governor would be at a table at the room's southeast corner, generally surrounded by bigwigs and prospects needing a little extra personal attention. I'd also host a table.

While people ate, Bush stood at his table, held on to his chair, and held forth. He'd talk about the Mansion's history and, after loosening everyone up, dive into his vision, the campaign he'd run, and the country's challenges. He'd take questions until his guests had to leave for planes or were exhausted. Bush was in his element: the historic Governor's Mansion with its artifacts and tales of great Texas politicians like Sam Houston was the perfect backdrop for his charm offensive. And unlike McKinley's "Front Porch" events, these were private. Good press came from the positive comments of the attendees. It added to the sense of a draft, of a genuine grassroots movement for Bush because, well, it sorta was. The lunches also let Bush road-test messages, phrases, even words, without the press around. He'd say something, his sensors would collect the vibes in the room, and he'd file away all the information for future use.

We stumbled on another way to build support for Bush: recruiting state legislators. This began when our New Mexico organizer said he thought he could get most Republican legislators in his state to sign a letter encouraging Bush to run. All that he needed to do was find time to get to Santa Fe for a day. I encouraged him to go. Two days later, he called with a letter endorsing Bush that was signed by virtually every Republican state senator and representative. The same tactic was deployed all over the country.

By early February 1999, we'd received an important addition to our ranks with the arrival of Joshua Bolten as the campaign's policy director. Bolten, a Washington native and the son of a career CIA employee, had been Goldman Sachs's legal and government affairs guy in London. He was highly organized, thoughtful, and low-key. He listened more than he talked and when he spoke, it was with keen precision. His wit was very dry.

As a polite and brainy graduate of St. Albans, Princeton, and Stanford Law, he did not seem like a guy who owned two high-performance motorcycles or would later escort Bo Derek to a presidential inauguration, but he was. He was also a bowler who would sometimes relieve his staff's stress by arranging a trip to the lanes. His job was to win the Substance Primary, which would end by early fall 1999.

On March 2, the governor and Laura Bush announced he would soon form an exploratory committee to allow us to begin raising money. Since federal campaign laws limited contributions to $1,000 a person, time was money. We filed a committee in March because waiting until the legislature's end would cut by a third the time we had to raise money in 1999. And conventional wisdom said a serious presidential candidate needed $25 million by the end of 1999.

Five days later, Bush formally introduced his ten-member exploratory committee at a news conference in Austin: former secretary of state George P. Shultz; Condoleezza Rice; Senator Paul Coverdell; Representatives Henry Bonilla, Roy Blunt, J. C. Watts, Anne Northup, and Jennifer Dunn; Michigan governor John Engler; and former GOP national chairman Haley Barbour. "A good leader surrounds himself with smart, capable people. . . . That will be my hallmark as I explore a national campaign," Bush declared. I had recruited the group with phone calls and visits during February, and we believed its membership communicated seriousness. Shultz's presence was particularly comforting to Reaganites and the GOP's foreign policy establishment.

We could keep a low profile through the end of the Texas legislative session, but pressure would build quickly after it for Bush to throw himself into the race. And how he was seen in his first forays on the trail was important. Expectations were almost impossibly high.

Bush entered the campaign on a June 12 trip, lifting out of Austin at 7:30 A.M. en route to Iowa in a chartered plane packed with press and dubbed "Great Expectations." Bush played flight attendant, taking the microphone to tell passengers to "please stow your expectations securely in your overhead bin as they may shift during the trip and could fall and hurt someone, especially me." The staff laughed, but it was a nervous laugh. Some among the press chortled, as if they were looking forward to a smash-up and a chance to report on casualties. The campaign refused to say whether Bush was going to formally announce, only that he would attend fund-raisers for two of the state's GOP congressmen.

First stop was Cedar Rapids. The plane taxied into a big hangar so the governor and his party would disembark in front of a crowd. There's nothing like rolling the nose of a jet into a hangar packed with wild partisans. When the plane's door opened and Bush emerged at the top of the stairs, it was just the jolt of energy and passion we wanted the media to see.

Then he was off to nearby Amana Colonies for a fund-raising lunch for Congressman Jim Nussle. Bush walked into a barn and was greeted by more than one thousand enthusiastic Republicans. On a stage with hay bales and red International Harvester and green John Deere tractors, Bush surprised the press and delighted the crowd with a simple, straightforward statement: "I'm running for the president of the United States. There's no turning back. And I intend to be the next president of the United States." What followed was what for most Americans would constitute a polite show of enthusiasm; for Iowans, it was a roar of approval.

He said his goal was to help "usher in the responsibility era . . . that stands in stark contrast to the last few decades, when the culture has clearly said: If it feels good, do it." He talked about tax cuts, Social Security, and education reform, his faith-based initiative, and the need for increased defense spending. He was mildly criticized for being light on specifics. It didn't bother me; there was plenty of time for details later. He spent an hour and ten minutes shaking hands. Blaring over the loudspeakers was Stevie Wonder singing, "Here I am, baby! Signed, sealed, delivered, I'm yours!" That's what many in the crowd may have been thinking. Me, I was focused on another line Stevie repeats: "You got my future in your hands." Now that Bush had declared, the lyric made me nervous.

We ended the day seventeen hours after it started, arriving in Sanford, Maine, after one o'clock in the morning. I entertained my traveling companions—well, some of them—by singing nonsensical songs about the day's sights, sounds, and flavor during the drive there.

Sunday, we basked in good reviews from Iowa before Bush held a news conference at his parents' Walker's Point compound in Kennebunkport. While the press conference reminded people of the family's values, it also gave the senior Bush a chance to make clear that he and his wife would not be fixtures on the campaign trail. Bush 41 pointed to his son and said, "He doesn't need a voice from the past."

The next morning we began a jam-packed day of campaigning in New Hampshire, jolted into action when Senator Judd Gregg, Bush's campaign chairman there, opened a press conference by deploying an eight-foot-long piece of paper with the names of the 180-member Bush steering committee. A new poll showed Bush ahead of the GOP field in the state with 45 percent of the vote. We were flying high—and when you do that so early, there's generally only one place to go. In a taste of what was to come, the Manchester *Union Leader* wrote that Bush "may have flunked the first measure" of his conservative credentials by refusing to pledge a "litmus test" on abortion for any judicial appointments.

At June's end, we headed to California for a three-day swing before the end of the second-quarter fund-raising period. We didn't think we could put away the Money Primary by June 30, but we could build a strong lead. One of the events was a meet-and-greet at the Bel Air home of Hollywood powerhouse and nominal Democrat Terry Semel, then co-chairman of Warner Bros. Among his guests was Warren Beatty. Beatty, a committed liberal, watched Bush circulate through the room and answer questions. You could tell the star was impressed. Bush didn't reciprocate. Hollywood never impressed him.

At a Los Angeles news conference on the 30th, Bush was asked what his campaign would report by July 15 for the quarter's fund-raising. The reporter didn't expect Bush to answer and neither did we. Jack Oliver had insisted we keep the number quiet and make a big deal of it nearer to the Federal Election Commission's reporting deadline. But Bush couldn't keep from sharing it. When he said his campaign would report raising $35.5 million, the assembled press corps let out an audible gasp. This figure was twice as much as what Vice President Al Gore had raised and six times as much as Bush's nearest Republican fund-raising competitor. In fact, Bush's second-quarter fund-raising total was $7 million more than the entire GOP field raised in the first six months of the year. Asked by a reporter to explain his fund-raising prowess, Bush said that it must have been his "wonderful personality." Reporters called the figure "staggering," saying Bush had "dropped a bomb" on his competitors and "left [his] GOP opponents slack-jawed."

Not all the news was good in June, however. On June 18, Bob Bullock died. Bullock's lifelong interest in all things political remained strong to the end. Bush had been a frequent visitor in Bullock's final weeks and was one of the first to arrive at Bullock's house when he passed. At one point, Bullock had summoned me and Allbaugh to give him a report on the campaign's progress, the coming launch in Iowa and New Hampshire, and gossip about our competitors. Bullock machine-gunned us with questions as he lay in bed, catheterized, and smoking nonstop. He grew tired, the room became silent, and we said our good-byes. When we were standing on his porch and the front door closed behind us, Allbaugh started weeping. I followed right after him.

Bullock had asked Bush to give the eulogy, scripted the funeral service, and even oversaw his gravestone's preparation. Before he died, Bullock also wanted to deliver one last favor to Bush: he asked his wife to go to the Republican National Convention the following summer and endorse Bush in his name. She did.

CHAPTER 9

Stung by New Hampshire, Rescued by South Carolina

Before Bush made his first campaign stop in Iowa, we had to decide if he would participate in the "straw poll" to be held in Ames on August 14. Staged by the state's Republican Party, the "straw poll" is a weird political ceremony—a combination rally, PR stunt, and mating ritual. Grassroots activists wander through tents sponsored by candidates, drink their beverages, chow down on their barbecue, listen to their entertainment, and pay desultory attention to their speeches. And then they vote, often against the candidate who transported, feted, and fed them. It draws more than the normal number of cranks. It is demeaning to candidates as well as attendees.

But it is important because it raises money and attention for Iowa Republicans, who cloak the circus in high-minded phrases such as "citizen participation" and "grassroots decision-making" that make it irresistible for candidates who want to win the state. Still, it's a potential disaster for front-runners and an expensive proposition for everyone. So why does it matter? One veteran Iowa newsman, David Yepsen, explained that it has "meaning because the political community gave it meaning." If a candidate ignores it, he risks giving the appearance that he doesn't care about Iowa, which can have disastrous consequences for a candidate hoping to win its caucuses.

So we were in. And Bush let Iowans know it when he arrived in their state June 12. The spending began almost immediately. Ken Mehlman negotiated a bargain price for the second-best tent site: $43,500. Publisher Steve Forbes had already scooped up the best location. And we countered other candidates who were camping out in the state by moving Mehlman there full-time. He was paired with our state director, Luke Roth, a gregarious former football player for Princeton who had been involved in so many Iowa campaigns that he sometimes drew more cheers than Bush when they marched in small-town parades.

Every campaign's core group of straw poll supporters are organized by county or community. But the extra edge often comes from affinity groups—collections of people who have a common interest or background, such as veterans or Hispanics. My favorite was "Bikers for Bush," led by a grizzled hog driver with the charming handle of "Bitch." He was thrilled to know the campaign's policy director, Josh Bolten, would lead the group's ride into Ames after picking up a new Victory motorcycle from its plant in Spirit Lake, Iowa. There was only one thing. What would Bolten's handle be? "Rabbi" was too obvious—and it was already taken. After chewing on it for a while, I finally came up with the perfect handle for him: "Bad Mitzvah."

On the day of the poll, all of our organizing came together. We had a fleet of buses that could rival Greyhound and a tracking system that only FedEx or UPS could match. Mehlman, after realizing that in 1996 Bob Dole ended up feeding his competitors' voters, required supporters to show proof of voting before they touched a morsel of food. And he had worked out a system that leveraged Bush's celebrity by allowing volunteers who signed up more than ten other verified Bush voters to get a picture taken with the governor.

Meanwhile, Forbes's massive, three-story-high tent offered air-conditioning, gourmet food, chandeliers, and the best Nashville country music that money could hire, and drew sunbaked straw-poll-goers of all kinds. It was clear that the wealthy publisher was our biggest competitor. Brad Freeman, who'd grown up in Fargo, North Dakota, was tagging along dressed in farm-appropriate attire with a gimme hat and a fake pair of crooked dentures. With protruding bogus teeth, he sidled up to Forbes and in his best prairie accent, said "Hello." Don Evans was there with a disposable camera. The three posed for a photo. Forbes didn't seem to know he'd just been punked.

But when the results came out, it was clear he had been beaten. Bush had captured 31 percent of the vote, far outpacing Forbes (21 percent), Elizabeth Dole (14 percent), and Lamar Alexander (6 percent). Alexander dropped out of the race two days later. Bush had solidified his status as front-runner.

Encouraged by Iowa, we continued laying the groundwork for a general election campaign. The good news is that this set us up well for later on down the road. The bad news was that it meant that we weren't paying anywhere near enough attention to New Hampshire, where John McCain had practically set up camp. By the end of the primary, he had spent sixty-five days there compared to our thirty-six, and most of his events were town hall meetings where he roamed across a stage and took any and all questions with humor, barbs, and gusto. He moved between stops in the "Straight Talk Express" bus, surrounded by a fawning national press corps that loved his raps on the GOP. I thought McCain was crazy to spend so much time in one state, because he would leave himself vulnerable in other early contests, and believed that we had plenty of time to overpower his retail campaigning down the stretch. I was right on the first and in a few months we would find out that I was almost lethally wrong on the second.

When the first debate was scheduled in Manchester, New Hampshire, one reporter characterized it as "Get-the-Governor" night. Forbes attacked Bush for too small a tax cut and for supporting gradually increasing the age at which retirees could receive their maximum Social Security benefits. Bush responded by reading an editorial by Forbes endorsing such an increase. Other candidates took potshots at Bush, too. After the event, the press piled on, complaining that Bush "didn't dominate" and "often retreated to lines from his stump speeches." Unfortunately, they were right. Bush was ahead and confident, but also tense and formulaic. We were trying to avoid mistakes while forgetting that the best way to do that is to go on offense.

Two other debates followed. Both of them showed that McCain was betting the farm on New Hampshire. One of the debates was in Arizona, his home state. He beamed into it via satellite from Boston so he could stay close to New Hampshire. The other was in Iowa, a state he had written off long ago. He flew in for the event, spent less than a day in the state, and used the debate to attack ethanol subsidies, near blasphemy in corn-rich Iowa. His ethanol comments gave him a clear talking point for why he'd lose Iowa's caucuses and reinforced his reputation as a maverick. He was using the debate to talk to voters in New Hampshire.

But the Iowa debate did produce a defining moment for Bush. WHO-TV anchor John Bachman asked the candidates to name a "favorite philosopher." Bush answered, "Christ, because he changed my heart." Bachman asked how and Bush replied, "Well, if they don't know, it's going to be hard to explain. When you turn your heart and your life over to Christ, when you accept Christ as the savior, it changes your heart. It changes your life. And that's what happened to me."

It stunned the audience and made some in the press corps nearly apoplectic. Many in the media just didn't get it and saw it as a cynical and raw appeal to evangelical voters. But it struck lots of ordinary people who said grace before a meal, went to church on Sunday, and turned to their Maker in times of need as being sincere and revealing of who Bush really was. And that's what it really was. It was not the kind of answer you would draw up in advance.

In late January, we won the Iowa caucuses with 41 percent of the vote, while McCain took just 5 percent. But eight days later, he halted Bush's march to the nomination by taking New Hampshire, 49 percent to our 30 percent.

There are lots of reasons why. New Hampshire's primary voters are irascible, independent, and aware of the pivotal role they play in the selection of presidents. With Bush being the front-runner and the man who had won Iowa, New Hampshirites had a reason to vote against him. What fun is there in validating the choice of voters in Iowa—a state that everyone in New Hampshire believes doesn't represent "real" America? Bush also has Texas oil roots, which is not a plus in a northeastern state where a substantial number of homes are heated with pricey oil. And our ads were not as effective as they could have been. McCain had shot his with a New Hampshire backdrop: it was clear he was betting on the state—and New Hampshire voters like being bet on.

What's more, with our private tracking polls showing we were still ahead in most states, and the fact that we were building solid organizations in every one that followed New Hampshire, we were overconfident about winning the nomination. That made us cautious and unwilling to get into a wrestling match by responding to McCain's negative TV ads. McCain's spots called Bush's tax cuts "too big, too tilted to the wealthy, too little focused on debt reduction and blind to the challenges of shoring up Social Security and Medicare." They weren't, but our silence helped convince some voters they were and made them wonder if we had enough steel for a general election fight.

We let Bush be seen as if he felt entitled to the nomination. We didn't really engage New Hampshire voters intimately—the way they like to be engaged. We also should have copied McCain's town hall format starting in September; by the time we did, with "Fire Station Chats" in the remaining weeks, it was too late.

A *New York Times* reporter whacked us for projecting "an aura of willful levity." Other reporters criticized the governor for saying he missed sleeping in his own bed, as if that were a mortal sin. As a result, anyone left up for grabs moved away from us and even some of our supporters defected. Hell, no one wants to be with a loser except the true believers.

On the day of the vote, I was having Chinese food in a local restaurant with *Los Angeles Times* reporter Ron Brownstein, McKinnon, and two of our other ad guys, Stuart Stevens and Russ Schriefer, when a reporter called me with the early exit polls. He wanted to know our reaction at finding Bush 19 points behind McCain. That was easy: I felt like vomiting. I quietly signaled that we needed to wrap up, check out our fortune cookies, and get back to the hotel. I told my campaign partners the bad news when we'd ditched Brownstein. Stevens immediately went to pack his bag, saying we were all going to be fired.

I went to tell Bush, who was relaxing in his suite with Laura. "Governor," I said. "I've got some bad news. The exit polls say we're going to lose and it could be big—as much as 20 points." He clenched his jaw and ever so slightly narrowed his eyes as I told him, before letting out his breath with a "Well . . ." I had expected a strong reaction, perhaps anger, perhaps depression. Neither happened. In a matter of seconds, he was all business.

He told me to go inform Joe Allbaugh, Karen Hughes, Don Evans, and the rest of the high command and get them all into the suite after he had exercised. He wanted to call Senator Gregg and other New Hamp-

shire leaders who had helped run our ground campaign so they didn't
think it was their fault. He was going to accept blame for the defeat himself. Laura asked him, "Do you want to win? Then don't let them define
you." Her words, delivered in a quiet tone, had real power.

When we assembled in his room, most of the high command were
in shock. Bush had seen enough floundering campaigns—including his
father's in 1992—not to repeat their mistakes, one of which was to shoot
a wounded staff. So he told us we were a team, and we'd win as a team.
He took full responsibility for the New Hampshire loss. He wanted no
recriminations, no finger-pointing, and no looking back. We were to project confidence to our supporters. People would be looking to see how we
handled adversity. Put your game faces on. I was to call our political leadership; he didn't want them to find out we'd lost by turning on the television that night. Joe was to call governors, Don the finance team. Karen
was to draft a concession speech that was optimistic and upbeat—a tall
order after a walloping. That night, it looked like a Bush victory rally, not
a Bush concession speech. Voters don't like losers, but they dislike gloomy
and angry losers even worse. The moment had a tonic effect on us—and
on me perhaps more than anyone else. We left emboldened rather than
embarrassed, ready to storm any hill for the man: he took a devastating
loss onto his shoulders, and we wouldn't forget it. It was how a leader got
the best out of those around him.

As I stood outside our rally site that night, waiting for Bush's speech,
I got a frantic call from an aide to the governor. No one had bothered to
exchange phone numbers with the McCain camp and now Bush wanted
to call to congratulate him. Did I know how to get McCain's number?
Alexandra Pelosi, an ABC News producer and Nancy's daughter, was
nearby. She had a number where she thought I could get John Weaver of
the McCain campaign. She was willing to dial him on her phone, as long
as she could listen to my side of the conversation. Desperate, I agreed.
The exuberant McCain aide who answered took delight in my request
and finally coughed up a number at which Bush could call McCain. In a
small sign of pettiness that would later consume them, McCain operatives began telling the press I had attempted to concede on Bush's behalf.
It was a fabrication, but it probably felt good to them, especially when
gullible members of the media fell for it. It was a sign of the McCain
team's new cockiness.

As we headed to South Carolina, the press was about ready to write our obituary. Two weeks before the New Hampshire primary, Bush had led McCain in South Carolina by 24 points. A week after, he trailed by 8 points. Our national lead cratered, too, going from 50 points to 22 points in just four days. We had just eighteen days to turn things around. Bush himself made the stakes clear by telling me, "If I lose South Carolina, I will lose the nomination."

The good news was that we had solid grassroots organizations in all of South Carolina's forty-six counties. Carroll Campbell, a popular former governor, supported Bush, as did the immediate past governor, David Beasley, Lieutenant Governor Bob Peeler, and Attorney General Charlie Condon.

Others backed away from us, hoping to get something out of sticking with an underdog when no one else would. Congressmen Lindsey Graham and Mark Sanford threw in with McCain after seeing so many others line up with Bush. But in this fight, I was happier to have our crew. Our county leaders had been painstakingly cultivated for months and, having put their names on the line, they were determined to make sure Bush won. And our state leaders had insisted on a massive phone canvass of every Republican, plus any Independent or Democrat who had supported a Republican in a recent general election. This allowed us to focus on a large number of voters who'd initially said they were for Bush but fell away after New Hampshire.

We also had a secret weapon in a wily and able old friend of mine, Warren Tompkins, Campbell's former chief of staff. He not only knew the precise placement of every body buried in the state, but also the color of the shirt it had been buried in. He was our southeast regional Bush chairman and volunteered the better part of a year.

McCain had a very able team and the behind-the-scenes backing of state GOP chairman Henry McMaster. But more than that, McCain had momentum after New Hampshire. That meant plenty of money, lots of public interest, an army of traveling reporters, large crowds, rising poll numbers, and tons of eager volunteers. Those are the ingredients for an upset. I knew it, and so did Bush.

Our South Carolina leadership came to an event in Greenville the day after the New Hampshire primary with sixteen things they wanted money for, ranging from radio ads to additional mailers, phones, and organizers. We shocked them by approving almost every item on the list. But to really change the momentum, we needed to change the narrative being written about Bush. Voters will come back if they hear a theme that reminds them of why they liked the candidate in the first place, and if we could provide subtle contrasts with McCain, all the better.

In Greenville, some of our South Carolina leaders argued we needed to "drive up McCain's negatives." But our problem was not McCain's low negatives; it was that we had failed to strengthen Bush's positives to withstand McCain's assault, especially on Social Security and tax cuts. It was time to go back to what had put us in the lead in the first place.

But what had people found attractive about Bush? A lot of it was his record as governor. He had done big things in a big state. We returned to that theme and strengthened it with a new slogan, devised by Karen Hughes: "A Reformer with Results." In doing so we shamelessly laid claim to a word McCain wanted for himself—*reformer*—and gave it a twist that helped us and hurt him—"with results." Bush had reformed education, juvenile justice, welfare, and tort laws in Texas. McCain talked about reform incessantly, especially of campaign finance, but had few legislative achievements to back up his words.

By grabbing "his" label, we hoped to get a rise out of McCain. We did. He took the bait almost immediately, complaining that we were trying to steal his message. This in turn helped focus the argument on which candidate actually had gotten things done, which only helped us.

Next, we had to change what was not working about our campaign, starting with our events. Bush would do his best to mimic Oprah, microphone in hand, shirtsleeves rolled up, delivering a short new stump speech while roaming the stage, and taking questions. It was a knockoff of McCain's town hall format. We weren't even subtle about it. At the South Carolina Association of Home Builders in Columbia, for one, Bush answered every question, shook every hand, posed for every picture, and left almost an hour and a half behind schedule. For the next two weeks, we kept using this approach and stayed almost exclusively in South Carolina.

When losing candidates fall behind, the rhetoric gets hotter, unfair attacks are made, and more Hail Mary passes get thrown in the mistaken belief that no one will conclude the passer is desperate. Most of the time, these things simply accelerate a candidate's decline. In football games, and politics, most Hail Mary passes fail—with a lot of them picked off by the opposition and run to the opposite end zone for a touchdown. So Bush made sure to exude optimism and determination. He told the press at his first news conference in the state, "I want the people of South Carolina to know I'm fighting for every vote here. I'm in for the long pull. I believe I'm going to win here."

We disciplined ourselves to focus on the message that Bush had a record and a plan. The stump speech was retooled to emphasize Bush's executive experience; stress differences with McCain on education, tax cuts, and campaign finance reform; and draw contrasts with Bill Clinton. Bush gave three substantive, set-piece speeches—one on legal reform, one on agriculture, and a third on campaign finance reform.

McCain was running as a moderate, so we made clear to voters in this largely conservative state that he fit the profile. We adopted the line "Says one thing, does another" to show that what McCain was telling South Carolinians did not match what he had done in the Senate and what he'd said elsewhere on the campaign trail. For example, before the South Carolina primary, McCain decried Washington influence peddlers while staging a D.C. fund-raiser hosted by the capital's leading lobbyists, many of them with business before the Senate Commerce Committee that he chaired. This was a legitimate way to raise questions about him.

But before we could get traction, we were tripped up. On the morning after the New Hampshire defeat, Bush spoke to an enthusiastic crowd at Bob Jones University in Greenville, South Carolina. The Christian liberal arts institution's yellow-brick campus was home to five thousand mostly conservative students and had a history of controversial policies. The IRS had denied the university its tax-exempt status in the 1970s for refusing to admit black students. And while that policy had been changed decades ago, the university still banned interracial dating and marriage. Later that afternoon, Bush held a news conference at which he expressed his strong opposition to the school's policies, which we had told university officials before his morning speech we were going to do.

Democrats were quick to pounce, with the Florida Democratic Party and the Gore headquarters in Nashville issuing statements condemning Bush's visit. Some newspaper editorial writers chimed in. Seeing this, the McCain campaign stopped pressing for a date for its candidate to appear at the university. That McCain had wanted to speak there, that the other primary candidates planned appearances there, and that the university had long hosted political visitors from both parties did not save Bush from being the target of press criticism.

Was it a mistake to go to Bob Jones? Beforehand, it seemed like a close call. I came down on the side of going. Others in the campaign disagreed and suggested that by going Bush would diminish his "compassionate conservative" credentials and allow himself to be identified with the school's abhorrent policies. One local staffer even leaked his concerns to the press before Bush appeared at the university, a sure sign of rats getting ready to flee a ship taking on water. But Bush was not endorsing the university's controversial policies and, in fact, he distanced himself from them. It was a big venue, a major stop for GOP candidates, and a large and enthusiastic crowd the day after a bad defeat.

We suffered our second blow the next day. Bush was to be endorsed by three South Carolina Medal of Honor recipients and other prominent veterans, including Admiral Thomas Moorer, former chairman of the Joint Chiefs of Staff. Tom Burch, chairman of the National Vietnam and Gulf War Veterans Committee, was to introduce Bush. Introductions were usually reviewed in advance so they were short, accurate, and in tune with the message for the event. But something went wrong. The introduction didn't get reviewed and rather than a laudatory introduction of Bush, Burch delivered a blistering—and to us, unexpected—attack on John McCain for failing veterans. It was terribly off message and deeply unfair. No one in their right mind could actually believe that McCain would forget the men and women who had fought for our country. In response, McCain blasted Burch's remarks as a "joke," calling him "some whacko." Democratic senators Max Cleland, Bob Kerrey, John Kerry, and Charles S. Robb and Republican senator Chuck Hagel slammed Bush in a letter expressing "dismay at the misinformed accusations leveled by your surrogate." It threw our campaign off stride for several days as McCain rejected Bush's apology as inadequate.

During the rest of the South Carolina campaign, McCain repeatedly returned to Burch's insult in discussions with the press, town hall meetings, and even in a debate. A week before the election, McCain's fellow POW, Orson Swindle, and several Medal of Honor recipients stormed the Bush headquarters to protest Burch's comments. A staffer defused the situation by offering the protesters coffee.

We needed a break and it came in the form of a McCain TV ad. Mc-Cain was using the spot he had run in New Hampshire that suggested the Texas governor would "take every last dime of the surplus and spend it on tax cuts that mostly benefit the wealthy." Thursday, the same day as our disastrous veterans event, McCain stepped up the rhetoric by recycling another spot he had used in New Hampshire, accusing Bush of "political attacks after promising he wouldn't." It was a nice one-two slug, attacking us and then accusing us of attacking him.

We had not responded in New Hampshire. But this time we set the record straight by contrasting the two candidates' tax plans: McCain's was not only smaller than ours, but also smaller than one proposed by Bill Clinton. Then we put up two new ads. The first ad responded to the spot that accused us of "political attacks," with the voiceover saying "John McCain promised a clean campaign, then attacked Governor Bush with misleading ads." It blistered McCain over news reports that he "solicits money from lobbyists with interests before his committee." It replayed negative quotes published by the *Wall Street Journal* and the *Arizona Republic*. It was accurate but not very effective.

The second ad was completely positive. It talked about Bush's work on education, tort reform, health care, welfare, juvenile justice, and taxes. It wasn't splashy, but it helped remind voters why they'd been for Bush in the first place.

And then McCain made a fatal mistake. He put up an ad that asked, "Do we really want another politician in the White House America can't trust?" implying that Bush and Clinton were on the same spectrum. The next day, McCain made the comparison explicit with an ad that said of Bush: "His ad twists the truth like Clinton." This was the worst insult one Republican could hurl at another. Those seven words cost McCain the South Carolina primary and, with it, his chance at the presidency in 2000.

Not one in a hundred Republicans thought George W. Bush was the moral equivalent of Bill Clinton. South Carolinians liked both Bush and McCain, but McCain had crossed a bright red line. The reaction was negative and powerful. Even some in the press later understood how counterproductive the spot had been for McCain. One reporter wrote several weeks later, "The spot went too far. . . . Putting it on the air undermined McCain's claim that he was above politics as usual and freed

Bush to amplify his attack strategies while demonstrating that it was McCain—not Bush—who was hitting below the belt."

Bush saw McCain's spot late Tuesday evening after arriving in South Carolina. He called me to say he wanted to deliver a reply himself. He outlined his message and emphasized that he wanted a completely positive tone. We also talked about his victory in that day's Delaware primary. I told him the national press would give Delaware virtually no attention, even though twelve delegates were at stake—the same as in New Hampshire—and our margin was bigger than McCain's had been in the Granite State. Unfortunately, I was right.

I turned Bush's outline into a script and shared it and his instructions with the media team Wednesday morning at a working breakfast at Las Manitas Avenue Café in Austin. The new spot had to be up as soon as possible, Friday at the latest.

There was no time to put Bush into a studio, so Russ Schriefer would have to find some place between campaign appearances where Bush could stop Thursday afternoon to squeeze in the shoot. Mark McKinnon would fly to Charlotte, North Carolina, and drive into South Carolina early Thursday, hook up with the governor, do the shoot, edit it, and send the finished version to South Carolina stations Friday morning. Laura Crawford found an editing facility in Atlanta and talked an employee into keeping it open all Thursday night so the spot could be finalized. Russ located a state park near Bush's late morning venue that would be perfect for filming.

But then things fell apart. Thursday morning, there were schedule changes. Bush was now driving directly to Columbia, missing Russ's proposed venue by dozens of miles. McKinnon was about to land in Charlotte and needed to know where to go. The advance team scrounged up a new venue, but McKinnon and the cameraman (who was behind the wheel) began driving north out of Charlotte. Now, it's a well-known fact that South Carolina is *south* of North Carolina, something that Stuart Stevens, who was talking to McKinnon on a cell phone, pointed out. After a quick exit to spin the car around, the cameraman began barreling toward South Carolina at speeds that generally bring you a couple of days in jail.

Not long after that, a state trooper, complete with Smokey-the-Bear hat and aviator shades, appeared in the rearview mirror. He told our boys he'd observed more than a dozen infractions and was afraid that if he didn't intervene they'd end up committing vehicular homicide. The cameraman told the trooper in a hushed, confidential tone, "We are on a very important mission for George Bush." Mark blanched, thinking they'd just buried themselves under the jailhouse. But the trooper responded by letting them go with a caution to keep it under 70. Mark later discovered the cameraman was driving without a license at the time, having previously been charged with an alcohol-related traffic offense.

Mark and the cameraman arrived at the new venue to set up equipment just minutes before Bush arrived. Bush did a couple of run-throughs and then nailed the spot. Behind schedule, he rushed toward his car to race off as Mark realized there was dirt on the camera lens. The ad had to be reshot. Bush was anxious to get going and grumpy about having to redo the work. But reshoot he did, getting it in one take and leaving Mark and crew at the roadside park enveloped in a cloud of dust as he sped to his next event.

McKinnon ran into more trouble at the airport when, worried about damaging the film, he refused to carry it through a magnetometer. He broke into a cold sweat, thinking the spot would not get up, Bush would lose, and it would all be his fault. The airline offered to let Mark check his luggage with the film in it, which would allow him to avoid the magnetometer. There was only one problem: the plane was full and he didn't have a seat anymore. So while his film would make it to Atlanta right away, Mark wouldn't.

Fortunately, Laura Crawford was landing in Atlanta at exactly the same time as Mark's bag. She snagged it and hotfooted it to the editing facility. McKinnon was able to squeeze onto the last flight to Atlanta at midnight. He and Laura rendezvoused at the studio and edited the spot until 4 A.M. The new Bush spot was digitally distributed to South Carolina stations Friday morning and went up immediately.

Like McCain's ad, ours was simple. Bush looked into the camera and opened by saying, "Politics is tough. But when John McCain compared me to Bill Clinton and said I was untrustworthy, that's over the line. Disagree with me, fine. But do not challenge my integrity." He then talked about what he had accomplished on education, health care, welfare, and taxes as governor of Texas, repeating the themes of the positive ad we'd started earlier in the week and still had up.

A McCain spokesman, combining several hackneyed phrases in just a dozen words, referred to it as "a hatchet job du jour from the governor and his attack dogs." But McCain himself had begun feeling the blow-back from his attack ad. After our reply ad went up, he held a Friday afternoon news conference to say he would "run no attack or response or any other kind of negative advertising" and urged "Governor Bush to do the same thing."

The national press ate it up. They thought McCain was taking a great political risk to do the "right thing" and set a positive tone for the campaign. It didn't matter that McCain had delivered a reckless charge that boomeranged and was now calling for a truce. What mattered to many in the press was that he was the one calling for it. Reporters blamed Bush for the campaign's negative tone, with *Time* reporting that Bush "had unleashed the dogs of war" with "slashing tactics—ferocious even by South Carolina's down-and-dirty standards." It didn't matter to them that Mc-Cain continued running his attack ad over the weekend after promising to immediately pull it.

Bush said, "I'm going to make sure people understand exactly what I believe." So we left our counterpunch ad up, and it worked. McCain had been up by 8 points on Tuesday when the controversy erupted over his ad comparing Bush to Clinton. By the following Monday—when our response ad had been up for just three days—Bush had moved back into a 5-point lead, 41 percent to 36 percent, and continued to widen his margin for the rest of the primary. McCain's television ad and Bush's response to it were that powerful a combination. Rarely have I seen a campaign turn on one or two ads. But in politics, people want winners to be gracious, and when McCain was ahead, he wasn't. He was blinded instead by his distaste for Bush and came across as mean and unhappy.

While the campaigns were exchanging television blasts, the issue of "push polls" erupted. In a "push poll," a phone bank pretending to be a research firm calls tens or even hundreds of thousands of voters with incendiary questions that provide negative information about a candidate. Most of the time, the calls are made in the name of a nonexistent organization. The practice is inexpensive and underhanded, and like most cheap and sleazy tactics, it tends to blow back on its sponsor.

The push-poll front was opened on Monday, February 7, when the McCain campaign lacerated us over a call to a College of Charleston student from our polling firm. But it exploded into a big campaign event on Thursday, February 10, when a woman stood up at a McCain town hall meeting in Spartanburg and tearfully described how her teenage son had received a push-poll call the night before that described McCain as "a cheat and a liar and a fraud." She said, "I was so livid last night I couldn't sleep." McCain jumped on it, angrily denouncing Bush to reporters after the town hall and saying, "I'm calling on my good friend George Bush to stop this now."

McCain had no proof Bush was behind the call or that the call was accurately described to him or even whether more than just one fourteen-year-old Boy Scout had been called. McCain could have tempered his re-marks, saying he hoped Bush wasn't behind the call or denouncing the practice without assigning blame. That would have been fair.

But McCain didn't need proof. He wanted to be perceived as a victim of a dastardly deed, and being called "a cheat and a liar and a fraud" in this fashion was as good as it gets. The press, of course, gave the colorful story legs. Bush was asked about it on *Meet the Press* and the McCain campaign made charges of ugly Bush push-polling a constant drumbeat.

One staffer said the campaign had received "dozens and dozens of calls" complaining about push polling, and then escalated the number in his next sentence to "hundreds of calls." But these charges seemed fishy even to starstruck reporters. Press skepticism began growing when we re-leased the script of a poll the Bush campaign had fielded in which three hundred South Carolinians were asked, among many other things, their reaction to descriptions of McCain's stand on taxes and campaign finance reform and his involvement in the Keating Five scandal. It was standard stuff, testing possible angles for use in TV ads. We made our pollster available, Jan van Lohuizen of Voter/Consumer Research, and allowed reporters to visit and observe the survey firm's call center in Houston.

The McCain campaign was then asked for proof of its claim that a "push poll" had called a large number of voters. They coughed up the names of six people who'd complained about calls from the Bush side. When interviewed by the *Los Angeles Times,* "three described questions that, while negative, appear to have been part of a legitimate poll. An-other said she heard no negative information at all." Two of the six of-fered up by the McCain campaign refused to return press calls. On this controversy, we drew support from unusual quarters. Kathleen Frankovic, the director of surveys for CBS News, described the survey as "fairly common" and "not unusual." Gallup's Frank Newport told a disappointed Linda Wertheimer of National Public Radio "those kinds of questions would generally come under the purview of legitimate polling."

The larger question is this: Does it really work to have anonymous people make telephone calls to voters they have never met to say Senator John McCain is "a cheat and a liar and a fraud"? And how credible is a call made in the name of an organization that voters have never heard of or, more likely, in the name of no organization? During elections, people are skeptical of much of what they hear. Why add to their skepticism, waste money, and run the risk of having something blow up in your face? No one could pull that off without getting caught, which is why push polling is dangerous and counterproductive.

Despite the lack of evidence, the myth of the mysterious push poll has persisted. As one left-wing journalist explained in 2008, "Rove invented a uniquely injurious fiction for his operatives to circulate via a phony poll. Voters were asked, 'Would you be more or less likely to vote for John McCain . . . if you knew he had fathered an illegitimate black child?'" Of course, this was not what the woman's son was told. But why let facts get in the way of a good myth?

And it's not just the kooky left-wing blogosphere that takes it as fact that I "created the push poll specifically to smear McCain." Some prominent mainstream journalists have done the same. While admitting he couldn't prove I did the push poll, the former *Wall Street Journal* writer and bestselling author Ron Suskind wrote in *Esquire* three years later that I was "the prime suspect" for the stunt, even though he acknowledged he had no evidence for such a claim. The push poll was part of a broader assault, he asserted, in which "Bush loyalists . . . claimed in parking-lot handouts and telephone 'push polls' and whisper campaigns that McCain's wife, Cindy, was a drug addict, that McCain might be mentally unstable from his captivity in Vietnam, and that the senator had fathered a black child with a prostitute." That Suskind didn't have a single copy of any "parking-lot handout," couldn't document any "telephone 'push polls,'" and was unable to provide a single shred of evidence to link the Bush campaign to the tactics he described didn't matter. Suskind has a dusty Pulitzer in his closet somewhere and that gave him license to sling mud.

The truth is, I shut down the only push poll that one of our allies was planning. Friends inside the Christian Coalition passed on a warning that evangelical leader Pat Robertson, angered by McCain's frequent attacks on him in South Carolina, was about ready to unleash a robo-call that would take the bark off McCain. The calls would be an independent expenditure by the Christian Coalition or Robertson himself. I called Robertson and talked him out of it. Instead Robertson agreed to do a completely positive phone message on Bush's behalf if the campaign paid for it. Sending a positive message to twelve thousand South Carolina voters from the prominent social conservative leader, instead of having an angry attack message paid for by Christian Coalition dollars, was a trade we were happy to make.

But that wasn't the end of our troubles. Sometime before February 14, a nasty and malicious e-mail began to circulate throughout the state. Its author was a Bob Jones University professor named Richard Hand. Hand alleged that McCain at one point had chosen to focus his life on "partying, playing, drinking and womanizing." He said, "McCain chose to sire children without marriage," pointing out that one of McCain's children was not white. It was bigoted and nasty and sent to Hand's personal e-mail list.

It has since become an accepted myth that the Bush campaign was responsible for this e-mail attack. Some in the press blame Bush personally, saying he campaigned "by spreading lies about an eight-year-old child." Others blamed me for a "Rove-orchestrated whispering campaign." But they're wrong. The Bush campaign and I had nothing to do with Hand's racially charged e-mail.

To believe Hand's e-mail was effective, you would have to believe South Carolinians are easily swayed by racist gossip. Only a *New York Times* editorial page writer or card-carrying liberal could see the people of the Palmetto State through such a prism. Professor Hand's racist appeal might have worked decades ago, but those days are long gone.

To believe the e-mail had a big impact, you also have to assume that hundreds of thousands of voters in the South Carolina Republican primary that year could be affected by an e-mail that was probably circulated to no more than several hundred people. There is no evidence it was widely seen, let alone believed. And before you hold him responsible, you would also have to believe that George W. Bush, with his personal history of racial inclusion, would have sanctioned such an attack. Most South Carolina voters did not believe Bush would do such a thing. They were right.

CNN traced the e-mail to Professor Hand, and reporter Jonathan Karl confronted Hand for saying McCain had children out of wedlock. Hand responded, "Can you prove that there aren't any?" Karl reported that Hand "insists his letter was not coordinated" with either the Bush campaign or Bob Jones University. But the McCain campaign was convinced of it, and some reporters peddled the story.

In fact, after I got over the shock of reading Hand's e-mail, my fear was that the McCain campaign would see this as an opportunity to emphasize a positive aspect about the Arizona senator. I was worried that McCain would stop ranting about negative campaigning and start describing how he and his wife came to adopt their daughter Bridget. It is an extraordinary story of love and compassion. On a trip to Mother Teresa's orphanage in Bangladesh, Cindy McCain was shown an infant who was going to die because the orphanage couldn't provide lifesaving surgery and care. The nuns urged Cindy to take the child home. She did, arriving at the Los Angeles airport to meet her husband with an infant in her arms. It would have been a powerful, positive moment if McCain had chosen to explain who he was, rather than assert he was a victim. People would have gained insight into his character and that of his wife. But he didn't do it and, to this day, I don't know why.

The tone of the campaign became the focus of a ninety-minute debate held in the state before its primary. CNN's Larry King was the moderator. Fifteen minutes in, King turned to Bush and asked him, "What do you make of all these past two weeks, the charges and countercharges?"

The Texas governor replied, "I kind of smiled my way through the early primaries and got defined" by attacks. "I'm not going to let it happen again." He then challenged McCain over his TV ad, saying, "We'll debate issues, but whatever you do, don't equate my integrity and trustworthiness to Bill Clinton. That's about as low a blow as you can give in a Republican primary." The debate audience applauded. McCain responded by blaming Bush for the campaign's negative tone and bringing up Tom Burch's introduction. McCain used the word "ashamed" four times in less than a minute as he hung the disgruntled veteran around Bush's neck.

Bush responded by praising McCain's military service and dismissed Burch by saying "that man wasn't speaking for me." And then Bush turned the tables on McCain, asking him what he thought of his national co-chairman, former senator Warren Rudman, calling members of the Christian Coalition bigots. "I know you don't believe that," asked Bush, "do you?" McCain answered, "George, he's entitled to his opinion." It was illuminating. Bush was willing to distance himself from the outrageous comments of a supporter while McCain wasn't.

McCain recounted the story of the Spartanburg teenager at the center of the push-poll story, provoking King to ask, "Are you saying that Governor Bush was responsible for that call?" McCain admitted he didn't know who was responsible but complained that the attacks continued even after he stopped all his own negative ads. By accident, Bush had the evidence in his coat pocket to prove that McCain was still launching attacks. The day before, a distraught York County Bush volunteer had called about hundreds of leaflets being left on car windows in the Rock Hill Wal-Mart parking lot. The flyer attacked Bush on Social Security and taxes. One rain-soaked and rumpled copy had been retrieved and handed to us hours before the debate. I gave it to Bush and he put it in his jacket pocket. He thought it unlikely that the leaflet would come in handy.

But when McCain made his claim, Bush drew the leaflet from his coat pocket and said, "You didn't pull this ad"—waving the flyer at McCain across the small round table they shared with Alan Keyes, who was also vying for the nomination, and King. McCain replied, "That is not by my campaign," to which Bush said, "Well, it says, 'Paid for by John McCain.'" The audience laughed and so did I, heartily.

That Saturday, our massive get-out-the-vote operation helped generate the largest turnout in the state's history: 550,168 voters. Bush solidly beat McCain by 11.5 points, 53.4 percent to 41.9 percent, with Keyes getting most of the rest. Republicans voted for Bush by 3 to 1 while McCain carried Democrats and Independents by 2 to 1. A majority said Bush was the "real reformer" and even a third of those who said McCain was the "real reformer" voted for Bush. For the third time in a row, the

GOP front-runner lost New Hampshire only to bounce back in South Carolina.

With exit polls showing he would lose, McCain prepared by having a session with his advisors during which Congressman Lindsey Graham ran down a grievance list of the attacks the McCain camp blamed on Bush. Mrs. McCain "broke into tears." The gripe session produced what *Time*'s Eric Pooley called an "unforgiving concession speech," with McCain saying Bush's nomination would produce "Speaker Gephardt and President Gore" and accusing Bush of a "negative message of fear."

The following day, the McCain campaign began flooding Michigan with robo-calls accusing Bush of sanctioning "anti-Catholic bigotry," implying Bush believed the pope was "the antichrist" and that the Catholic Church was "a satanic cult." The calls were done in the name of a nonexistent group, the "Catholic Voter Alert." For the next three days—through the Michigan primary on Tuesday, February 22—McCain denied his campaign was behind the calls. Only after winning Michigan did the McCain campaign admit it had paid for them.

On *Meet the Press* the Sunday after South Carolina, I asked McCain's national co-chairman, former senator Rudman, why the man who had run a television ad that said "I will always tell you the truth" would lie about his campaign's involvement in a smear. We ended up losing Michigan, which Governor John Engler had promised would be our "firewall" in case we faltered in South Carolina. The McCain smear was part of the reason, but so was the fact that I had not taken into account a new twist in the state's primary rules: In 2000, Democrats and Independents were allowed to vote in the GOP primary for the first time. The Democrats' union allies came out in force just so they could hand the Michigan governor, whom they hated, a defeat. But Michigan was a small mishap in our rearview mirror. After South Carolina, we did the unthinkable: even before locking up the nomination, we began executing a detailed plan to win the White House.

CHAPTER 10

The Big Mo'

———•◆•———

Bush's South Carolina victory spelled the end of the nomination battle, even though the fighting sputtered on until Bush trounced McCain on Super Tuesday. If we had paused to recharge after locking up all the delegates, we would have missed a big opportunity. Consider how McCain squandered his spring in 2008 or how Barack Obama registered all those new voters during his spring fight with Hillary Clinton. A smart campaign will use the remaining primaries to set the field of battle for the general election on its own terms. Voters stay interested in the primary contest right after it is settled, then gradually tune out until the conventions.

I had begun sketching a postnomination plan long before Iowa and New Hampshire. In brainstorming sessions and late-night discussions in the late fall of 1999, I'd picked the brains of my colleagues on what to do. I scribbled, noodled, blue-skied, and questioned the people around me, all to develop a plan to execute once we secured the nomination.

Why? My study of previous campaigns had convinced me that too many presidential campaigns focused so much on the primaries, they found themselves ill positioned for the general election. Bob Dole had stumbled around in mid-1996, without clarity of message. Michael Dukakis had secured his party's nomination in 1988 and then basically gone to sleep. Walter Mondale got the nod in 1984 and through inaction nearly had America nod off on him. Bush in 2000 was, by all rights, the underdog. The nation was at peace. There was prosperity. The federal government had a surplus. Voters tend not to throw out an incumbent party when times are good. And in these circumstances underdogs don't win unless they are lucky. In politics, you make your own luck.

The 2000 Bush campaign had to be concerned with addressing weaknesses that needed shoring up, but we first needed to decide what we wanted the general election campaign to be about. We wanted people to see that Bush was a different kind of Republican, a reformer with a forward-looking and optimistic agenda, and someone who would bring honor and dignity back to the Oval Office. To achieve this, he would be talking about issues Republicans didn't generally talk about, go places Republicans typically didn't go, and let his passion and sincerity shine through.

All this required a label, which Bush had already introduced after being reelected governor of Texas in 1998, when he first uttered the phrase "compassionate conservative." We stepped up its use in the spring of 2000. President Bill Clinton later told Bush that when he heard the Texas governor first use the term, he knew Democrats were in trouble.

Some observers equate "compassionate conservatism" with "big-government conservatism," dismissing the phrase as a sop to liberalism or an excuse for increasing federal spending. But that wasn't how Bush meant it. "Compassionate conservatism" was a call for a new approach from the right to issues including poverty, education, health care, and a secure retirement. Ignoring these issues all but guarantees that they will be addressed in a way that runs counter to conservative values. And it's worth noting that many conservatives do not ignore them in their private lives. They contribute to charities, volunteer through their churches, and personally confront many of these problems in their own communities. By the time Bush used the label, it had had a solid track record, even occasionally winning Democrats' support. Welfare reform, for example, is "compassionate conservatism." So are school choice and a focus on educational results through an accountability system. Allowing people to save tax-free for their out-of-pocket medical expenses and leveling the playing field so families get a tax advantage for owning health insurance just as companies do are also facets of "compassionate conservatism." Bush wanted to take timeless conservative principles and apply them to the country's new circumstances.

As we thought about these themes in planning the 2000 general election, we kept returning to the issues on which Republicans lagged badly and could gain ground, especially among target voter groups. One issue stood out above the rest: education. It was a major concern with suburban independents, especially women, and soft Republicans. In 1996, the Dole-Kemp ticket had lost among those who considered education the number-one issue by 62 points to Clinton-Gore, 78 percent to 16 percent. But Governor Bush had a strong, credible record on education. And his passion about the issue made it even more important that he talk about it. It helped too that Democrats generally opposed reforms because teachers' unions were against them.

Beyond education, we identified issues below the national media's radar that would draw support in key states or regions. For example, mountaintop mining was an important issue in West Virginia. It was critical to keeping West Virginia coal competitive and West Virginians employed. We were for it; Gore wholeheartedly opposed it. Iowa and Missouri farmers, meanwhile, were concerned about efforts to withhold water flowing into the Missouri River. They depended on the water flows to ship their crops on barges. Gore, however, was held hostage to Democratic senator Tom Daschle of South Dakota, who preferred to keep the water penned up in reservoirs in his state. Gore said nothing; we spoke out in favor. New Mexicans were worried that environmentalists would shut down development in the state in order to save the Rio Grande minnow—a concern Bush shared and Gore seemed unaware of. And communities in the Pacific Northwest were all spun up by both the failure of Clinton's Northwest Timber Plan to help their towns and by calls from environmentalists to destroy the region's dams, a source of jobs and inexpensive green power. We wanted the Timber Plan carried out and dams preserved. Banging away on these issues was vital to our efforts, even though they were never picked up by the national media.

To lay out Bush's broad agenda, Josh Bolten and I plotted out a thematic calendar that stretched from March to July. We first wrote it with colored markers on butcher paper and taped it to Josh's office wall. It showed when we would talk about what and in which battleground state.

The preparation of these speeches and the materials that backed them up demanded a lot from Josh's policy operation. He brought in an "enforcer" to make certain the materials were accurate, ready on time, and as meaty as possible. The pressure reduced some of Josh's young team to tears: more than once I ran into a weeping researcher in a back hallway trying to pull himself together.

Preparing the education speeches was particularly challenging because, as the chief speechwriter, Mike Gerson, recalled, "the governor knew more about the issue than we did." Before a March speech, Mike and his scribblers spent thirty-two hours straight churning out drafts of the governor's remarks. Bush ended up speaking from notes he cobbled together himself.

The boldest move we made was to talk openly about reforming Social Security. Before 2000, it was an iron law of politics that even though Social Security was going broke, Republicans couldn't talk about reform and win. Bush wondered what the point was of being for reform if you couldn't talk about it. He had spent the 1990s boning up on the issue and had come to believe that voters were now much further along than elected officials. Voters knew Social Security was careening toward insolvency, and he believed they would reward candidates who confronted that.

Once we created our plan to emphasize Bush's strengths, we evaluated our weaknesses. How would Gore attack Bush and what could we do to shore up our defenses? Our vulnerability was foreign policy. By summer, we wanted respected commentators to see that Bush had a sure footing on this front. So he gave a speech on China and then one on the Middle East—both of which built up to a major address in Washington on May 23 on the issue of post–Cold War foreign policy. He called for missile defense to meet the threat of rogue nations, a reduction in America's nuclear arsenal, an end to the Anti-Ballistic Missile (ABM) Treaty now that the Soviet Union had collapsed, and a new relationship with Russia. This speech was well received by the Republican foreign policy establishment.

By June, the press felt Bush had grabbed the initiative, defined what the general election was about, and relegated Gore to the sidelines. The ultimate dispenser of conventional wisdom, David Gergen, declared: "There is a good reason why Governor Bush is forging ahead in this race: he is becoming the candidate of fresh ideas." The "change" mantle was crucial for us, and we had grabbed it. But how did we want to define Gore?

Fortunately, we had two walking, talking human computers who knew everything about Gore—RNC research director Barbara Comstock and her deputy, Tim Griffin. They'd never met the vice president but they knew him better than anyone except maybe his wife. Both had encyclopedic knowledge of his voting record, statements, mannerisms, strengths, and, most important for us, weaknesses. I'd read their research during the primaries and salivated at the thought of using it.

The funny thing was, both of them were worried they'd be unemployed once Bush won the nomination. They knew we had our own opposition researchers and, after being summoned to Austin for a meeting on two days' notice, they expected to be fired. Little did they know our headquarters was stuffed with people who considered them geniuses.

Barbara and Tim ran a staff of about thirty overly caffeinated geeks who'd work through the night and sleep under their desks for a few hours before charging back to their computers. Many of them were young, but this crowd included lawyers, accountants, budget analysts, and former Hill staffers. They also had savvy communicators among their ranks who could shape the material into bites the press could digest. Barbara and Tim had them work around the clock for forty-eight hours to prepare a notebook of several hundred pages detailing Al Gore's policy positions, quotes, and weaknesses and then carried this with them to Austin.

Their information was compelling. Gore had three weaknesses. He exaggerated, routinely made stuff up, and even lied; his convictions were not as strong as his political ambitions, so he had flip-flopped on critical issues such as abortion and gun control as he climbed the political ladder; and he was generally out of touch with most Americans on issues ranging from taxes to defense. The first two were the most important because they spoke to his character. If he lost voters because of these weaknesses, it wouldn't matter where he was on the issues.

As the campaign progressed, it was Gore's exaggerations that most damaged him. His proclivity to tell tall tales grew worse the closer we got to Election Day. Over the past few decades, Gore had said that he had created the Internet, been the model for *Love Story*, led a crusade against tobacco, discovered the Love Canal chemical disaster, lived on a farm while vice president, never grew tobacco on his farm, didn't know that his visit to a Buddhist temple was a fund-raiser, faced enemy fire in Vietnam, and sent people to jail as a reporter. It was a compelling life story; unfortunately, none of it was true.

On the issues, Gore said he had led the fight for a Nuclear Test Ban Treaty (though he'd been consistently against it), always been pro-choice (except when he'd been pro-life), co-sponsored McCain-Feingold campaign finance reform (except that he hadn't), always supported the death penalty (though he voted against it), wrote the Superfund and Earned Income Tax Credit legislation (though he really hadn't), and supported welfare reform (except for twice recommending Clinton veto it). No wonder his staff had written him a memo in 1988 warning him, in the gentlest language possible, "Your main pitfall is exaggeration."

After our meeting with Comstock and Griffin, we looked for every opportunity to draw attention to Gore's exaggerations and, to a lesser extent, his flip-flops. We swept his website for statements we could use. In Denver on May 30, for example, Bush went after the weak Clinton-Gore Pentagon record by saying, "My opponent—who's no stranger to exaggeration, I might add—boasts on his Web site that he has been intimately involved in the best-managed build-down in American military history." Bush then went on to describe how the Army was not combat-ready, how recruiting was falling short, and how thousands of soldiers' families were on food stamps.

By July, Gore was dealing with his past claims of being shot at in Vietnam when the record showed he never came under fire. The *New York Times* reporter covering the story tried to mitigate the damage for the vice president by suggesting it was "an exaggeration that may have been less an attempt to mislead than to make his experience more vivid." Only a *Times* reporter could excuse a politician's bald-faced lie as necessary literary license. Gore's exaggerations hurt him because they fit the impression ordinary people had acquired about him over the years as he defended Bill Clinton against charges of misconduct. As a result, they were impossible for Gore to disguise or defuse.

But how would Gore come at us? I asked Comstock and Griffin. Simple, they said, pulling out reams of paper. He would try to do to us what Republicans had tried to do to Bill Clinton in 1992: paint him as the failed governor of a backward southern state with big problems. That strategy hadn't worked very well for the GOP against Clinton and could be defeated by us this time if we pushed back with the facts. Besides, Bush had a brand name that protected him against jibes that he was a backwoods hick; and Texas is not, well, Arkansas.

Defining Bush and, when the opportunity arose, framing Gore were not our only challenges. First, we needed to raise $25 million to fund the Bush campaign from the end of the primaries up through the convention, while also raising $153 million for the RNC's voter identification, registration, and get-out-the-vote activities. After Super Tuesday, we had 118 days to do the first and 245 to complete the second. We focused on people who had backed another primary candidate or sat on the sidelines. As Lamar Alexander, Dan Quayle, and Elizabeth Dole fell by the wayside, we swept up their fund-raisers, and we ruthlessly recruited McCain's money people once he suspended his bid.

Immediately after securing the nomination, we also stepped up mail, Internet, and phone efforts to recruit more small donors. Republican enthusiasm made these efforts more successful than we had anticipated and gave us a large base of donors from which the national and state parties could draw. This was important because we were depending on battleground state parties to run larger voter ID and get-out-the-vote (GOTV) efforts than they'd ever done. Ken and I developed a model for each battleground state effort called "The Ideal Campaign." It set specific targets for registration, ID, and GOTV calls, doors to be knocked on, pieces mailed, yard signs, stickers, and numbers of headquarters. This information was stuck on a little laptop that was so password-protected I thought it would explode like something out of a *Mission: Impossible* movie if it fell into the wrong hands.

I'd hired a young University of Texas political scientist named Daron Shaw to help look at the Electoral College map. We started with Dole's 159 Electoral College votes. If we added Nevada, Arizona, Louisiana, Florida, Kentucky, Ohio, Missouri, and New Hampshire—states Republicans have historically been able to carry in winning races—then our total grew to 250. We needed 270. That meant we had to win Pennsylvania with 23 Electoral College votes or some combination of Iowa (7), Wisconsin (11), and Michigan (18). That was too risky a strategy. The more we studied the map, the more it looked like we'd have to expand our list of "target" states.

By late spring, we had added West Virginia, Tennessee, Arkansas, Illinois, Maine, Oregon, Washington State, and California to our list of targets. There was a clear case to be made for some of these, but others led most observers and plenty in the press to think we were nuts. For example, Dole had lost West Virginia by 14 points, Tennessee was Gore's home state, and Arkansas belonged to Clinton. But West Virginia was socially conservative (faith, guns, abortion) and dependent on coal for jobs and prosperity. Bush was right and Gore was wrong on all four. Polling there late in the spring of 2000 showed the state was up for grabs. There was some resistance inside the headquarters to targeting West Virginia, but my argument was that we would already be running television ads in Ohio and Pennsylvania stations that covered big parts of the state and buying the rest was relatively inexpensive. With fund-raising going well, we could afford the gamble. That, plus my simply being a pain in the keister about it, caused the campaign to add West Virginia to our target list.

Similarly, polling showed Gore much weaker than he should have been in his own home state. His ties to the state were frayed because he was far more liberal than its increasingly Republican voters. Then there was Arkansas, home to William Jefferson Clinton, the state's longest-serving governor and the only Arkansan ever to be president. While Clinton was personally popular, he wasn't on the ballot. Maine had two Republican senators and split its electoral vote by congressional district. Its senior senator, Olympia Snowe, was up for reelection and expected to win handily. We'd be making a strong bid for New Hampshire, which had Republican senators and a Republican governor, so we knew we would already be in the area.

Oregon looked like a possibility because of the Clinton administration's failure to deliver on the promise of the Northwest Timber Plan, which was meant to support blue-collar families. And if we were going to make a play for Oregon, why not Washington? Ads in Portland were seen in the neighboring state. Illinois had elected Republican governors since 1976 and the average of recent public polls showed Bush up by a point. Why not give it a shot, too?

California, on the other hand, was a special case. I knew the difficulty of a Republican presidential candidate winning the state. It had moved sharply left since the senior Bush captured it with 51 percent in 1988. But in mid-July, Bush was down only 2 points in the Golden State. This was 7 points below Bush's national standing, where he was up 5 points in our internal polling. If things broke our way and we had the infrastructure on the ground and an organized GOP, we just might be able to snake the state. I knew from Gerry Parsky, our Bush state chairman, that there would be ample money from within the state for all the necessary Victory Committee GOTV activity except advertising, in part because California donors were tired of seeing their dollars exported. We just had to keep ourselves from being suckered into dumping millions into what is essentially a bottomless advertising pit, if we had no real chance.

Only in West Virginia did some Republicans seem startled by our interest. We said we'd run months of television, have Bush visit the state at least three times, have his running mate stop at least twice, and spend a lot of money. All they had to do was knock on tens of thousands of doors, make hundreds of thousands of calls, put out scads of signs and stickers, organize key voter groups, and open four headquarters! Later, one long-time West Virginia Republican leader told me the last time a member of the GOP presidential ticket campaigned in the state was Nixon in 1956. They thought we were kidding. By the fall, we had eighteen offices and could generate massive crowds for events on less than forty-eight hours' notice. One rally even featured parachutists who formed a *W* with their bodies before pulling their ripcords.

In the end, we came very close but lost Maine, Oregon, and Washington state. But we took West Virginia, Tennessee, and Arkansas. The last time Republicans won West Virginia in an open race for the presidency was 1928. The only candidate to win the White House while losing his home state was another Tennessean, James K. Polk, in 1844. And the last time a home state turned against the party of a retiring president was in 1952, when Eisenhower won Harry Truman's Missouri. If we'd failed in any of the three states, Bush would have stayed in the Texas Governor's Mansion and Gore would have moved into 1600 Pennsylvania Avenue.

CHAPTER II

The Cheney Choice

———— •◆• ————

Every president makes his first presidential decision before getting elected: picking a running mate. It hasn't always been that way. The first vice presidents were the Electoral College runner-ups. That didn't work out so well. John Adams suffered through four years with an openly hostile Vice President Thomas Jefferson. In 1800, Jefferson saw the man who was supposed to become his vice president, Aaron Burr, tie him in the Electoral College and then press to be made president. The deadlock threw the election to the House of Representatives, which itself deadlocked before finally settling on Jefferson. That near crisis gave us the Twelfth Amendment, which established that the president and vice president would run as a ticket. Vice presidents used to be chosen by party elders to balance the ticket geographically or to unite disparate factions. Only since FDR have presidential candidates picked their own running mates.

In the last several decades, that decision has become more about governing and less about politics. Reagan chose George H. W. Bush in part to unite the party but principally because of Bush's foreign policy experience. Clinton picked Gore to make a New South, baby-boomer New Democrat ticket, but also because Gore had national security, environmental, and Washington credentials the Arkansas governor lacked. Bush's 2000 selection involved fewer political considerations than any choice in history. Both the decision and how it was made say something about what he considers important and how he decides.

Bush wanted an intensive, but invisible, process that would produce no surprises, no drama, no high-profile interviews, and no rushed decision. Fortunately, he had someone he felt could manage the process this way. Dick Cheney, the defense secretary from his dad's administration and a Wyoming congressman before that, had moved to Dallas to run Halliburton, a big oil services company, after leaving government. Bush had gotten to know him better through Cheney's participation on the campaign's foreign policy advisory group, a group that became known as "the Vulcans." Condi Rice was the inspiration for the nickname. She grew up in Birmingham, Alabama, where a fifty-six-foot statue of Vulcan—the Roman god of fire and the forge—stands at the top of Red Mountain overlooking the city. The world's largest cast-iron statue, it pays tribute to Birmingham's iron and steel industry. The name had started out as an inside joke among the foreign policy wonks, but I thought they were on to something. It was the perfect label to convey a sense of strength and resilience, and the campaign began using it in public.

There came to be over thirty people on the list of vice presidential possibilities, some suggested by campaign staff, some on Bush's personal list, and some that emerged from the ether. Cheney visited each prospect discreetly, and those who were willing to be considered received a questionnaire modeled on the forms that all White House staff must fill out for security checks. Prospects were then interviewed and asked unpleasant questions. They submitted tax returns and any writings, books, and speeches, all of which arrived by the boxload in Dallas. A tax attorney reviewed the former and Cheney's team consumed and distilled the latter. All of this was summarized in voluminous binders, which Cheney took to Bush's ranch in Crawford, Texas, to review with the governor. Then the tax returns and other sensitive material were returned to the prospect: no copies were kept.

Not everyone who was approached wanted to be considered. Former Florida senator Connie Mack jokingly told Cheney he would never speak to him again if he were considered. But most other prospects agreed to the political equivalent of a proctology exam. By summer, the governor was focused on nine candidates: former senator John Danforth of Missouri; former governor Lamar Alexander of Tennessee; Governors Tom Ridge of Pennsylvania, Frank Keating of Oklahoma, and John Engler of Michigan; and Senators Jon Kyl of Arizona, Chuck Hagel of Nebraska, and Bill Frist and Fred Thompson, both of Tennessee.

Although each prospect had strong points to commend him, by late June the governor was starting to feel that Cheney was as good as any. Bush had refused to rule Cheney out as a prospect at the search's start, more to keep all his options open than because he felt Cheney was a likely pick. As the calendar turned to July, though, Bush found himself increasingly certain he should select Cheney, a thought he shared with a small group of aides after threatening us with a painful, slow death if we leaked.

Bush had become impressed with Cheney's thoroughness as head of the VP search and the intelligence and insights he offered in meetings of the Vulcans. He had seen Cheney's command presence, including how people paid careful attention to what he said in policy discussions. He respected his record as secretary of defense and as Ford's chief of staff. He knew of Cheney's wide contacts on Capitol Hill and, more important, of his knowledge about how Congress operates. Bush liked Cheney's straightforward manner and his ability to question the fundamental premise of an argument. They shared a love of history and reading. In addition, Governor Bush warmed to the idea of a vice president without ambitions of his own, since he'd seen how that leads (often inadvertently) to staff conflict and internecine warfare inside the White House. Vice presidents with ambitions breed staffs whose principal interest is the elevation of the VP at the expense of the president. Dan Quayle's staff had been viewed with suspicion inside the Bush 41 White House. Gore's presidential ambitions increasingly put him at odds with Clinton in the latter's second term. And Hubert Humphrey was painfully restrained from breaking with LBJ over the Vietnam War until weeks before the 1968 presidential election.

Cheney arrived at Bush's Crawford ranch in early July with a stack of binders on other prospects. After they had worked their way through the pile, Bush took Cheney out to the backyard. I'm sure Cheney wondered what was up: Crawford in July is hot. Bush surprised Cheney by asking him to think about becoming his running mate. Cheney said he'd consider it but wasn't certain it was a good idea for Bush or for him.

The group privy to Bush's thinking was small—Laura, Joe Allbaugh, Don Evans, Karen Hughes, and me. Bush knew I leaned toward Danforth. Danforth was from a battleground state (Missouri), pro-life, and respected by Democrats and Republicans alike. While conservative, he had a moderate demeanor and was a person of deep faith. And the press liked him. Bush knew I had real doubts about Cheney, so he summoned me to the Governor's Mansion to discuss my opposition.

We met in a room called the Austin Library, named after the land speculator who founded Texas, Stephen F. Austin. The room is only about nineteen feet by eighteen feet, with space for four chairs and a few side tables. Glass-fronted bookshelves line the walls. A picture of Austin hangs over the mantel. To its right is the only portrait of Davy Crockett in his western duds done from life, painted by John Gadsby Chapman. Crockett doesn't look like John Wayne or Fess Parker. In fact, he has curls and appears a dandy, despite his coonskin cap, deerskin leggings, long rifle, and hunting dog.

The governor sat in front of the fireplace. I sat opposite him, about six feet away. He said, "Tell me why you think I shouldn't pick Dick Cheney." For more than half an hour I held forth, occasionally interrupted by the governor, who asked questions and prodded with opposing lines of argument. It was like an oral exam by a genial but tough professor.

"We don't need to worry about Wyoming in the general election," I said. The three electoral votes of the state Cheney had represented in Congress had been solidly in the Republican column for decades. The vice presidential pick could have an impact in a battleground state. And in a close election like this one, that could make all the difference. Bush was not so sure and parried with questions on what battleground state another VP pick might help guarantee. I was ready: I'd led with this point so I could make an early plug for Senator Danforth, who could help put Missouri in our column.

I said Cheney's health would be an issue. Cheney had suffered three heart attacks. While he was an active outdoorsman, the press would make a stink about his heart disease, chewing up valuable time and diverting attention from the issues we wanted to dominate the news. Bush disagreed.

I also said that Cheney had a strongly conservative voting record in Congress in the 1970s and '80s, on which the press and our opponents would seize. For example, I cautioned the governor we would spend time on the defensive explaining Cheney voting against, say, the resolution urging Nelson Mandela's release from prison. Bush was dismissive, asking me if I really believed the press would waste time on Cheney's congressional record, now more than a decade in the past. I did. He didn't.

I also knew we had worked hard to establish the governor of Texas as ready in his own right to be president and not dependent on the crowd who had populated his father's administration. Picking the senior Bush's defense secretary for VP would send the message, I feared, that the young governor was falling back on his father's administration for help. This was one place where I sensed Bush accepted my argument, but I couldn't tell how much weight he attached to it.

There was Cheney's residency. He had been born and raised in Wyoming and was its congressman for six terms. But since leaving the first Bush administration, he had lived in Texas. He was registered to vote in Dallas, though he had a home in Jackson Hole. The press would badger us for having two Texans on the ticket even if Cheney changed his registration to Wyoming. And while changing the registration could be done legally, someone could file a frivolous lawsuit, holding that the Twelfth Amendment's Habitation Clause meant the Texas electoral votes could not be cast for Bush and Cheney, just for Bush. Bush was openly skeptical.

Finally, picking Cheney would add to the perception that the GOP ticket was dominated by Big Oil, hurting us in the Midwest and the Northeast. Bush came out of the oil patch and Cheney was running a big oil services company. Why, I asked, make our perception problem worse?

At the end of thirty minutes or so, the conversation drew to a close. The governor seemed satisfied we'd exhausted the subject and asked me if I had anything more to say. I told him no. He turned to the man sitting in the chair next to him and said, "Dick, do you have anything you want to ask Karl?"

Cheney shook his head no. The entire time, he had sat motionless as I made a systematic case against him, highlighting every weakness I could think of. He'd looked at me impassively the entire time, with a poker face that betrayed not a hint of emotion. If he was amused, dismissive, angry, or impressed, I couldn't tell. And he could tell I couldn't tell. I had glanced at him occasionally—but since his stoicism made me a little nervous, I focused on the governor. Now, at last, Cheney raised one eyebrow and flashed that funny half smile of his. I thought, "Great, I've made an enemy for life—and he's going to be vice president." As we walked out of the room, Cheney turned to me and mumbled under his breath, "I agreed with some of what you had to say." I wasn't comforted.

It turned out that Bush was meeting with another opponent of the Cheney nomination: Cheney himself. Cheney had told his family that he was going to Austin to dissuade the governor from asking him.

Some people have suggested that Cheney engineered his own selection. This is far-fetched. I saw the man squirm as Bush pressed him to accept. Cheney had a clear understanding of what John Nance Garner, FDR's first vice president, had said about the office—that it was "not worth a bucket of warm piss." Cheney was too much of a patriot to act on that knowledge.

That conversation taught me some important lessons and reinforced others. Contrary to the myth that grew up around Bush, he wanted candid advice. He encouraged people to make their case in front of others who might disagree. I'd seen him nurture this kind of atmosphere over the years—as candidate, governor, and then president. This practice made everyone comfortable that everything was out in the open, and that there weren't secret conversations going on to undermine one person or another. He wanted people around him who would not back down or wilt under cross-examination. Some political leaders test their staff and associates by badgering or hectoring. Bush tested by asking a question or raising a point that would get to "the nub of a thing," as Lincoln's law partner, Billy Herndon, said in describing Lincoln's great talent. And Bush raised the big central questions often with humor and always with respect. This style of management was one of the reasons people enjoyed working for him.

The meeting was also an object lesson that the governor wasn't going to allow political considerations to trump other factors in his decision making—on this matter and many other important ones to come. At this stage in the campaign, almost all my concerns about decisions were political—their impact on the pace and tone of the campaign, their influence on a key electoral state, the reaction of the press. But Bush was primarily concerned with who would be a good White House partner. Who could provide insights and abilities that would complement his?

And if the unimaginable happened, whom could the nation have confidence in to succeed him as president?

It wasn't that the governor dismissed my arguments. He later told me that, like Cheney, he agreed with a lot of what I said—which I found marginally encouraging. But he felt the political downsides were more than offset by the advantages of having Cheney as vice president. The campaign could handle the problems of Cheney's health, voting record, and the Twelfth Amendment, he said. And he, Bush, would have the confidence he had picked the right person. He told me the day after our meeting, "If things go well, it doesn't matter who the vice president is. But if the unknown happens, the country will need Cheney's steadiness."

Bush was right. This decision was about governing. And I was wrong to view this decision as all about politics. Selecting a VP from a battleground state might have brought us one state we would not otherwise have won. But we won Missouri without Senator Danforth on the ticket and it's hard to see what other running mates could have contributed to winning the states we lost.

I learned something, too, about the laconic political science Ph.D. candidate from Wyoming who got tossed out of Yale not once, but twice. Cheney never held my brash judgments about him against me. In fact we established a good relationship during the campaign and kept it during our White House years. He became a good friend and, as strange as it sounds to say this about any vice president, a valued colleague. I grew to have great respect for his discretion, insight, thoughtfulness, and lack of pretense. He rarely offered an opinion in big meetings unless pointedly asked by the president. A former White House chief of staff himself, Cheney understood that if he expressed an opinion too early, it might retard robust argument and straightforward counsel.

Often, we found ourselves on the same side of policy disputes being argued out in the Roosevelt Room or the Oval Office. But even if we were on opposite sides, he never took disagreements personally. And my experience with him, a sharp contrast to the media portrayal of him, is that he always kept an open mind. Like a lot of westerners, he has a practical bent and an eye for facts and reality. He has an encyclopedic knowledge of the Hill, even having written with Lynne, his wife, a good little volume on past House Speakers. Sometimes, I found myself changing my view on how to handle an issue with Congress because Cheney had made a quiet, short, powerful observation about how things really moved in the House or Senate. All that and we hunted together, too.

Cheney and I never again spoke of the Austin Library meeting. I'm not sure I'd have set aside that conversation if I were him.

Cheney took a few days to think over Bush's offer. He and Bush talked again by phone on July 12. Cheney was in Minneapolis, accompanying his wife to a board meeting. Bush passed on that heart surgeon Dr. Denton Cooley had said Cheney's heart condition wouldn't keep him from doing the job. Cheney told Bush he'd be his running mate, but even then he asked that Bush meet secretly with Senator Danforth in Chicago on the 18th before making his final decision. It was clear it would take a lot to change Bush's mind, and the Chicago meeting didn't.

The campaign then moved carefully to make an announcement, now scheduled for July 25. We had more than a week to keep Bush's choice secret, and in a presidential campaign that's an eternity.

Most in the press are more fascinated by the process of politics than by the substance of policies. In the summer's dog days, there are few processes that compare to that of picking a vice president, and getting real news on Bush's pick was a top priority for every news organization on the planet.

As it happens, there was one way that reporters could get an early tip-off. Cheney needed to reregister to vote in Wyoming by no later than Friday, July 21, if he was to be able to vote in the August state primaries. Voting in the Wyoming primaries gave us a greater defense against a Twelfth Amendment challenge, so the Cheneys arranged to be in Jackson Hole on the 21st so they could stroll over to the courthouse. NBC's Pete Williams had a source in the Teton County clerk's office that alerted him minutes after Dick and Lynne Cheney's visit. The news immediately went out on the wires.

This put the press speculation too close to the truth for comfort. By Friday afternoon, it was reaching the point where all the steam might be taken out of the announcement, and our hopes for a big surprise were dwindling by the hour. We needed the press to be less certain about Bush's running mate. It was time for a little misdirection. We needed a selective leak.

The question was how to do it. It happened that there was one person in the campaign who could be counted on to share sensitive, unauthorized information with the press. So that Saturday, July 22, I made sure to run into this staff member in a hallway of the Austin headquarters. I told this staffer, in a conspiratorial tone, "Don't tell anybody—but it's going to be Danforth. The governor met with him secretly last Tuesday in Chicago. The Cheney thing was a feint. Danforth's on his way back into town now."

That evening, ABC, CBS, and CNN all announced on their news broadcasts that Senator John Danforth of Missouri had emerged as a top candidate for the number-two spot on the GOP ticket. ABC teased it with Elizabeth Vargas saying "a new name has emerged as a strong possibility," while CBS's Russ Mitchell said, "speculation is swirling faster than ever tonight" about Bush's pick, with "word of another name still in the running," before he tossed it to Gloria Borger and Bill Whitaker to discuss Danforth's emergence. Many in the press followed. We'd gotten what we needed: a little breathing room for Cheney's announcement.

Looking back, I feel bad that Danforth's name got splashed around, and maybe it didn't do much good to keep the press guessing a few days longer. In any case, the unauthorized leak confirmed suspicions that our colleague would use privileged information to appear to reporters as informed and important. And even though Bush got what he wanted—a story that took the media off the VP trail—my colleague had shown why it's important to know the strengths and weaknesses of those with whom you work. You want to call on the staffers' abilities, but you also want to be realistic about their frailties, too. I kept that in mind when my campaign colleague came into the administration.

Governor Bush called Cheney at his Dallas home the morning of July 25, and the two held a news conference at 3 P.M. in Austin to make the big announcement. Cheney flew the next day to Casper, Wyoming, for his first event as a vice presidential candidate. He and Lynne had a warm welcome at Natrona County High School, where they'd become sweethearts. To this day, Cheney views the call that morning as the official offer, inexplicably thinking that there was always the chance Bush could go with someone else. It shows even friends could "misunderestimate" Bush. The question was settled in Bush's mind July 12; that was clear to anyone with whom he shared the secret.

It didn't take long for the attacks to begin. By Thursday, Democratic consultant David Axelrod attacked Cheney as an oil company executive and ideal foil for Gore's populist economic views. TV host David Letterman joked that Cheney "had more heart attacks than I have. . . . This guy is just a heartbeat away from being dead." A *Rocky Mountain News* columnist was trolling an Internet discussion group of law professors for posts questioning whether the Twelfth Amendment precluded Texas's electoral votes being cast for both Bush and Cheney. And Reverend Jesse Jackson brought up Cheney's congressional voting record, hitting him for his "extreme views" and quoting Matthew 7:15 that "Jesus warned us to beware wolves in sheep's clothing." Not a single *New York Times* editorial condemned Jackson's dangerous mixing of religion and politics or the use of Holy Scripture for a political attack. But Bush was right that the tempest over Cheney would pass, and it did by the time the GOP convention opened in Philadelphia.

VOTERS KNOW THAT CONVENTIONS are Broadway productions, and that's the kind of smooth, high-quality spectacle they are looking for. Screw up the convention and people will wonder how well you will run the government. Thankfully, ours ran smoothly. Bush appeared by satellite each night as he made his way through battleground states, and then on Thursday gave his acceptance speech. It was his first prime-time, nationally televised address. McKinnon went over to Bush's hotel to help him pick out a tie and get ready and then ride with him to the convention. McKinnon took care not to say anything, so the governor would have a few minutes of quiet time before his speech. But McKinnon was startled to hear someone whistling the tune "Go Tell It on the Mountain." It was Bush. When they got to a room backstage, Mark couldn't contain himself any longer and said, "I was really surprised you were whistling. You seem at ease, not strung out." Bush replied he was "totally calm." McKinnon couldn't believe it. So he blurted out, "How can that be?" He was thinking of the arena and the bank of cameras Bush would face in minutes. "I am so confident this speech reflects who I am as a human being and where I want to take the country that people will know who I am," Bush explained. "After that, if they reject me, fine, I can accept that. But they will know my heart. My only fear was they wouldn't know me."

Bush went out and, in front of twenty thousand people at the First Union Center, knocked it out of the park with a speech praised by *Washington Post* columnist David Broder as "an acceptance speech of exceptional elegance." The liberal doyenne of the commenting class, Mary McGrory, agreed with her fellow *Washington Post* columnist when she wrote that Bush "proved he has first-class wordsmiths, but he showed Gore something more ominous. He was not inhaling. He's in touch with the world outside his party, the focus groups that warn him that the issue Republicans think is paramount—the bad behavior of Bill Clinton—must be handled with care."

The first Gallup poll after the convention showed Bush up 54 percent to Gore's 37 percent, a swing of six points from the preconvention poll eleven days earlier. That was normal—since 1964, the average convention bounce for all candidates has been 5 points and, for the party meeting first, 6.3 points. We'd gone into Philly 11 points ahead and came out 17 up.

We'd taken advantage of the window available in the spring to strengthen ourselves for a battle that was still an uphill climb, and we had capped the effort with a solid convention. If we had fumbled those months as Gore did, we could have gone into Philadelphia tied or behind and never recovered. The country was at peace and in apparent prosperity, a recipe for victory by the incumbent White House party. It was a good thing we had solidified our position: events outside our control, a little underhandedness from our opposition, and some crucial mistakes on our part were about to turn this race into one of the closest presidential elections in history.

CHAPTER 12

Derailed by a DUI

———— • ◆ • ————

A ugust was defined by Al Gore's recovery, and I was surprised at how he did it: by picking a Jew and kissing his wife.

Down by 17 points after the Republican convention at the start of the month, Gore was ahead by 1 point in a poll taken after his convention ended on August 17.

Gore's climb out of his big, dark hole began Monday, August 7, when he announced Senator Joseph Lieberman as his running mate. When I learned of the pick, I was worried. Lieberman was a shrewd choice. The Connecticut Democrat was a thoughtful, respected centrist who had famously criticized President Clinton for his dalliance with Monica Lewinsky. He had broken with his party by supporting school choice and the privatizing of Social Security, and by condemning Hollywood's low moral standards, which added to his significant crossover appeal. William F. Buckley, Jr., had endorsed him in 1988 in his Senate race against the liberal Republican Lowell Weicker. Former Education Secretary Bill Bennett had worked with him on curbing the excesses of popular culture. Lieberman was also the first Jewish candidate on a major party ticket, which was bound to generate excitement.

A running mate rarely influences a contest's outcome. When it happens, it's generally for the worse. But Gore's VP pick boosted his campaign. Picking Clinton's most prominent Democratic critic separated

Gore from the president, and choosing a strong running mate gave Gore an aura of confidence. Lieberman's selection was so well received by the press that many Americans took a second look at Gore.

And Gore gave voters a lot to look at, especially during his convention. As he made his way to the podium for his acceptance speech, he turned the obligatory brief spousal pat and peck with his wife Tipper into a deep kiss and full-body hug, followed by a second, shorter kiss. It was corny and contrived and I dismissed it as such. But it undercut the public perception of Gore as a stiff and unlikable know-it-all.

His speech's best lines shined brightly. "I stand here tonight as my own man, and I want you to know me for who I truly am," he said a third of the way in. As he turned toward his conclusion, he said, "if you entrust me with the presidency, I will fight for you." He turned himself into Populist Gore, taking on the rich and powerful. Among those he attacked were polluters, drug and insurance companies, special interest groups, private schools (which he had attended), the wealthy, tobacco (which he'd grown), and oil.

Ironically, the speech that relaunched Gore would undo him in the end. It gave voters yet another version of Al Gore and later left them wondering who the real one was. Gore had remade himself so many times over the course of the campaign that Beth Campbell, chairwoman of the Democratic Committee in Concord, New Hampshire, had joked that "Al Gore has gone through more reinventions than Madonna." He had been Bill Clinton's equal partner, then the man "disappointed" in Clinton; the "attack dog," then the optimist and intellectual; the new Democrat, then the angry populist. He had even been Earth Tone Al after writer Naomi Wolf advised him to dress differently to look like an "Alpha Male."

Watching the speech convinced us we had to make an issue out of Gore's chameleon character. Our narrative was that Gore would provide four more years of rancorous politics and that he was too flexible in his views to be trusted. For his part, Gore tried to portray himself as an independent populist who had none of Clinton's moral flaws. We put two competing narratives before voters; the narrative that prevailed would determine who would be president.

But then experts weighed in. Seven prominent election forecasters announced at a special American Political Science Association conference in late August in Washington that Gore would win—they disagreed only about his margin. Gore was awarded an average of 56.2 percent to Bush's 43.8 percent, more than a 12-point landslide. They argued the country was at peace, the economy seemed to be humming along, and the president remained personally popular. They assumed voters would line up behind the vice president, who had a more admirable private life than Bill Clinton. The political scientists were assuming that leaders can't shape opinions and voters won't form them based on ongoing events. The prognosticators' conclusions colored the opinions of important journalists: Bush was destined to lose.

Harold Macmillan, a conservative British prime minister in the late 1950s and early '60s, was once asked what a statesman's greatest challenge was. He replied, "Events, dear boy, events." And at that point in the campaign, events were about to inflict a series of terrible blows. One was primarily my fault. I wanted to get away from the format set by the Commission on Presidential Debates and instead put the candidates in a more informal, less regulated setting where reporters could try to rough them up. Doing so would make us look confident and would also likely win some support from the media.

Unfortunately, Bush and my colleagues were swayed by my arguments to get out of the commission debates and instead debate Gore on NBC's *Meet the Press* and at a forum organized by CNN. Gore had a smart comeback: he'd do *Meet the Press*, CNN, and any other debate— but only if Bush agreed first to the commission schedule. Gore looked magnanimous. We protested, which only put us into a debate about debates, almost always a waste of time. Bush came off looking weak and manipulative. After a few days, we cut our losses and promised to work out an agreement with the Gore campaign for the commission debates.

In the meantime, a private exchange that became public turned into a major pain in the butt. At a Monday rally just before the Naperville, Illinois, Labor Day parade, Bush was standing next to Cheney on the podium when he leaned over, pointed to a reporter and said, "There's Adam Clymer—major-league asshole from the *New York Times*." Cheney responded, "Oh, yeah. He is, big time." The crowd didn't hear Bush's remarks, but press tape recorders picked them up. A reporter asked Karen Hughes for a comment.

I am confident worse has been said by journalists about candidates, but in this line of work, turnabout is not fair play. Karen knew it was a problem right away and went to find Bush. Karen could tell that he knew that he had blundered because he looked sheepish when she asked him about it. He also was bothered and distracted as he walked a parade route that day. At a stop in Allentown, Pennsylvania, Bush said, "I regret that a private comment I made to the vice presidential candidate made it to the public airwaves." Bush resorts to profanity less than anyone I've worked with in politics, except maybe his father. It didn't matter. The Gore campaign had fun accusing Bush of "using expletives . . . in front of a crowd of families."

Now the Nervous Nellies were in full flutter. CBS's Bill Whitaker captured the moment when he reported that Bush was "facing sniper fire from worried Washington Republicans." Among the least helpful was Senator Arlen Specter, who advised us to abandon our tax cut and to stop attacking Gore for appearing at a fund-raiser at a Buddhist temple. Bush dismissed the criticism by saying, "Well, that's Washington. That's the place where you find people getting ready to jump out of the foxhole before the first shell is fired."

We got a little help. After months of negotiations, Colin Powell had agreed in August to appear with Bush. The date he was available—September 7—was one we had set aside for a long-planned endorsement in suburban Detroit by the state's largest Teamster local. Afraid Powell might back out if we tried for another date, we asked the local Teamster president to introduce the general, who would then introduce and endorse Bush. It all went great, except the union president said he was honored to welcome "Adam Clayton Powell," a former Democratic congressman from Harlem. At least that congressman couldn't complain. He'd died in 1972.

Starting in August, an RNC ad about creating a Medicare prescription drug benefit attacked Gore for "a big government plan that lets Washington bureaucrats interfere with what your doctors prescribe." On September 12, the *New York Times* broke a page-one, above-the-fold story saying an eagle-eyed Seattle retiree had examined the ad frame by frame and found the word "RATS" in one of the spot's nine hundred frames "in huge white capital letters, larger than any other word on the commercial" just as the announcer said "bureaucrats." All hell broke loose.

Our defense was the truth—we thought it was an accident. But advertising experts and both Democratic and Republican political ad consultants pronounced it "virtually impossible for a producer not to know the word was there." It didn't help when McCain's ad guy trashed it and our own outside advertising advisor said it was "pretty bad." The ad's creator added to our difficulties by claiming it was an accident and then saying, "That's all I want to say," leaving the impression there was more to be said. The offending frame got played over and over, Gore acted indignant, and Senators Ron Wyden and John Breaux called for a Federal Communications Commission investigation. As it happens, Fox's Tony Snow had actually broken the story on Fox's *Special Report with Brit Hume* as early as August 28, but no one on his pundit panel, including Juan Williams and Jeff Birnbaum, got exercised about it and the rest of the media ignored the story. The ad maker was forced to admit the spot wasn't changed after Fox discovered "RATS" in August; that made us seem calculating and insensitive. Bush was so upset that he refused to look at McKinnon's laptop when Mark attempted to explain the kerfuffle by showing Bush a downloaded copy of the ad.

It took five days for the media to move on, which is an eternity in the fall of a presidential campaign. There were only fifty-five days left until Election Day. We were being accused of dirty tricks and playing defense instead of talking about what we wanted.

Something had to be done to reverse our downward spiral. We started by introducing a new slogan suggested by Karen: "Real Plans for Real People." It wasn't the most inspired slogan I've ever heard, but it reinforced Bush as the change candidate and it signaled to the press that we were changing tactics, a process story that crowd would be interested in. Bush also started meeting with people who would benefit from his reforms, such as middle-class families who would get a tax cut, and we rolled out a new stump speech that drew sharp contrasts with Gore over taxes, Social Security reform, and other issues. We returned to unscripted town hall meetings we used in the South Carolina primary and, late in the month, introduced another new stump speech on the economy while in Green Bay, Wisconsin.

The campaign also received valuable advice from a normally quiet source—Laura Bush. She had been watching the news and was worried that the daily picture of her husband was too often of a man surrounded by reporters at the back of the campaign plane. Gore was always pictured smiling in front of big crowds. The subtle message there was that Gore was connecting with people, while Bush was fending off questions from the press. Our rallies were wild and well attended, but you'd never know it from the coverage because the press used the photos of themselves with Bush, rather than shots of him at his rallies. Karen immediately ratcheted down the candidate's visits to the back of the plane. Our pictures improved. Karen also booked interviews on *Oprah* and *Live with Regis* and with Diane Sawyer, Brian Williams, and Paula Zahn. The move earned us some good press.

We finally got our break in mid-September. Over the course of five days, it was revealed that Al Gore had told five whoppers. And I mean double-patty-with-cheese, supersize whoppers that even the media couldn't ignore. By then my young aides had developed a ritual for celebrating our winning moments. They lived outside my office door in a space we called the Lincoln Lounge because of the presence of a battered plaster bust of the Great Emancipator. They had taken to playing the movie *Gladiator* on DVD, especially the opening battle scene: because of it, they took to greeting each other by saying "strength and honor." They also had a tape of the Baha Men's "Who Let the Dogs Out?" that they played when a clean blow was struck against Gore or when we parried an assault. We heard the song a lot that week.

Gore's problems started with "Shilohgate." While attacking Bush in Florida over the issue of a prescription drug benefit for seniors on Medicare, Gore claimed his mother-in-law paid nearly three times as much for the same arthritis medicine given to his ailing dog, Shiloh. On September 18, the *Boston Globe* reported that wasn't true.

Two days later, Gore stepped in it again with a pair of exaggerations. First, he told a Teamsters rally, "I still remember the lullabies I heard as a child," then warbled the old union anthem, "Look for the union label!" The idea that Gore's mother, Pauline LaFon Gore, would sing her little boy to sleep in the family's apartment—Suite 809 of Washington's Fairfax Hotel—with a union song was laughable. But what a reporter noticed was that the jingle was launched by the Garment Workers Union in 1975, when Gore was twenty-seven.

The same day, Gore claimed that the Bush tax cut meant just 62¢ a day for the average working American. Even the director of the liberal think tank on whose work Gore based his attack said the attack was "a stretch I wouldn't make." When allies distance themselves from your ex-aggerations, you're in trouble.

The next day, Gore gave us what we needed to put this all in just the right context when he said that oil should be released from the Strategic Petroleum Reserve in an attempt to stabilize rising oil prices. Our opposition researchers had discovered that Gore had opposed such a move when oil prices spiked in the winter of 1999, having said then, "All they [oil-producing countries] would have to do is to cut back a little bit on the supply, and they'd wipe out any impact from releasing oil from that reserve." President Clinton's Treasury secretary, Larry Summers, had similarly trashed the idea.

Four comments from Gore in ninety-six hours—if connected in the right way—might metastasize into an enduring impression about his untrustworthy character. Bush immediately whacked Gore's flip-flop on the oil reserve as "bad policy" that sought "short-term political gain at the cost of long-term national security." The next day, Clinton released 30 million barrels of oil from the reserve and we stepped up the attack.

Responding to the media frenzy over his switch, Gore held his first news conference in sixty-seven days, but stumbled again by saying that "I've been a part of the discussions on the strategic reserve since the days when it was first established." The Strategic Petroleum Reserve was established in 1975, two years before Gore entered Congress. He just couldn't stop himself from embellishing.

This week was the general election's turning point. Gore was back to looking weird and untrustworthy. But we had to be well ahead of Gore to win; undecided voters were not necessarily going to break to us at the end if they felt times were good and Gore was acceptable.

On September 13 a package containing a videotape and a half-inch stack of documents was delivered to the Washington office of former congressman Tom Downey, a Democrat on Gore's debate team. He looked at the material long enough to ascertain that someone had sent him the Bush campaign debate briefing book and a tape of a practice session with Bush and Judd Gregg, our Al Gore stand-in. Downey called the FBI without reviewing the material any further.

The story broke in the press the next day. Initially, both campaigns handled it gingerly, making no accusations and seeking no advantage.

But it shook the confidence of people inside the Bush campaign—including me. We thought someone might have gained access at night to the offices of our in-house ad firm, Maverick Media, and copied the documents. But who?

Within two weeks, the investigation was leaking all over the front page. On September 24, it broke that a young Gore aide had bragged to ABC that he had a mole inside our camp. The next day, Jake Tapper wrote a long piece for Salon.com alleging—based on no evidence—that I had sent the debate materials to entrap the Gore camp. The idea was that the Bush campaign could cry foul play if it were discovered that Gore's team had gained illicit access to our debate preparation. The Texas Democratic chairwoman, Molly Beth Malcolm, helpfully gave him a quote making the charge explicit: "I have some idea of how both [Bush media consultant Mark] McKinnon and Karl Rove work on campaigns. . . . When I first heard about this, my immediate reaction was to turn to my husband and say, 'This thing has Karl Rove's fingerprints all over it.'"

But by Wednesday, the FBI was focused on Yvette Lozano, a young aide to Mark McKinnon, as the person most likely to have stolen the materials. Mark was aghast: the young woman had been with him for years, had babysat his daughters, and was almost like family. Like Mark, she was a former Democrat who came with him when he switched parties. At first he didn't believe it possible—and neither did I. But her story unraveled quickly, and it looked like the Gore campaign had scored a clean hit. The FBI interviewed me on Saturday. It was a short visit: there was nothing useful I could add. The following March the incident ended sadly when Lozano was indicted on federal charges of mail fraud, perjury, and false statements. She pleaded guilty in May 2001 to mail fraud and perjury, and was sentenced to a year in jail and fined $3,000. To this day, I don't know or understand what motivated her to do it.

In the meantime, we were about to move on to territory where Gore was strong: the debates. Gore was skilled and liked doing them: in his final Senate race, though he was at no risk of losing, he brutalized his GOP opponent in five encounters. We had organized two small debate prep teams, one for Bush and one for Cheney. I was on the Bush squad. We recruited Senator Judd Gregg to play Gore and Congressman Rob Portman to play Lieberman. Gregg got Gore dead right. While driving around New Hampshire, he listened to tapes of Gore and read transcripts of what wasn't available on tape. He studied video of Gore until he had Gore's hand gestures and voice inflection down cold. It was scary. But Portman, who stood in for Gregg at one session, nailed Gore particularly well in one critical respect: he invaded Bush's space while Bush was speaking. Everyone at the session criticized him for doing so, but Portman bet anyone $5 that Gore would try it: he'd seen him do it in an earlier debate. No one took Portman up on the dare.

Bush seemed ambivalent about the prep sessions. He knew he needed to practice—tough competitors always do. And he appreciated good advice from his people. But there was something about these sessions that seemed to grate on him, and after a while, I could sense he'd had enough. In my experience, the debate squad always wants to focus more on policy minutiae than is possible for one person to hold in his mind. My view is that it's more important for a candidate to be comfortable and have at the ready several ways to flip a question or an attack onto favorable territory. Reagan did this effectively in his reelection campaign in 1984 after stumbling in his first debate. Facing questions about his age (he was then seventy-three and running against the fifty-six-year-old Walter Mondale), Reagan shot back by saying, "I want you to know that also I will not make age an issue of this campaign. I am not going to exploit, for political purposes, my opponent's youth and inexperience."

Not all debate sessions went well. We wanted the dress rehearsal for the first debate to resemble the physical makeup of the real thing as much as possible. So we held it at Canaan Baptist Church, near Bush's ranch. I was driving Don Evans in from Waco and got lost on the back roads of Central Texas. It took a few terse calls from Bush to get us through the right series of turns. When we arrived, the candidate was steamed that we had arrived late, having been unable to follow simple directions. As a result, Bush did poorly. We were left concerned and depressed; I think he was left wondering why his people couldn't follow a map and arrive on time.

When it came to the real thing, I nearly screwed things up worse than a late arrival. Candidates normally arrive in a debate city the night before the event so they can relax and be well rested for the main event. But I was worried about demonstrators in Boston, the scene of the coming debate, keeping Bush up all night. So I pushed to stay over in West Virginia the night before. We could have a stop in a battleground state and still get into Boston in plenty of time for Bush to prepare. But things started to come apart when Bush and his traveling party adjourned to the Radisson Hotel for the night: they found the hotel dining room virtually abandoned. A bedraggled waitress greeted them with the news that the only thing the kitchen had on hand was chicken. After a considerable wait, nothing appeared except water and bread, so Don Evans went into the kitchen and started spreading some cash, along with polite but urgent pleas to get cracking. The $20 bills worked. Eventually, the chicken appeared and the tired but satiated campaigners made their way back to their rooms.

I'm not sure when everyone noticed it, but it turned out that the hotel was bracketed by train tracks on one side and the Ohio River on the other. Trains blew their whistles at crossings near the hotel all night long. Barge traffic on the Ohio replied by blasting their horns. Bush didn't sleep a wink and was unhappy about it. I was back at headquarters in Austin, but I heard all about it.

The next day, in Boston, union protesters lining Bush's route welcomed him with a less than polite hand gesture, and when he arrived at the auditorium, it was very cold. Gore had insisted it be 65 degrees for the debate and the commission had lowered the temperature even more because of the heat the cameras and lights would give off once the show started. I had flown in from Texas and could almost see my breath when we did our walk-through.

Gore's fibbing started with his first answer. He denied ever having questioned whether the governor had the experience to be president. Then he talked about a fifteen-year-old student at Sarasota High School named Kailey Ellis, who he claimed "has to stand during class" because of overcrowding. That wasn't true. The principal explained there were "more than enough desks" for every student, and Ellis's science classroom was overcrowded temporarily—only because $100,000 worth of lab equipment was being uncrated. She was without a desk that one day.

But Gore's most troublesome fib was his claim he had "accompanied [FEMA director] James Lee Witt down to Texas" to help oversee the taming of fires in Parker County. Dan Bartlett and oppo researcher Tim Morrison were sitting at their computer in our backstage lair with Karen looming over them when Gore said he had made the trip. Karen immediately spat out, "That's not true." She had been with Bush and Witt touring the fires—Gore wasn't there. Karen was sure of it. At debate's end, we made hay with his fabricated story. Gore's statement was so easily refuted that reporters explored the other untruths we gave them.

I was stuck backstage watching the debate directly from a limited camera feed. I had missed the debate's most important message: Gore's sighing, huffing-and-puffing performance, caught on camera for ordinary viewers. He looked as if he were auditioning for the role of the Big Bad Wolf from "The Three Little Pigs." He went from unlikable for some swing voters to intensely unlikable.

But as surprised as I was by Gore's strange behavior, I was even more surprised when Cheney won his debate two days later with his very dry and pointed sense of humor. About two-thirds through that showdown, as Lieberman extolled the economic record of the Clinton years, he went after Cheney with what was obviously a prepared jibe. He drew on recent reports on Cheney's personal wealth, accumulated while running Halliburton, to say, "I'm pleased to see, Dick, from the newspapers that you're better off than you were eight years ago, too." Cheney quickly shot back, "I can tell you, Joe, the government had absolutely nothing to do with it." The crowd broke into laughter and applause. Lieberman tried to rescue himself by saying, "I can see my wife and I think she's saying, 'I think he should go out into the private sector.'" Cheney volleyed back, "I'll help you do that, Joe." Cheney came across as well informed, calm, and reassuring, which reinforced in the minds of many voters that Bush had good judgment. This was exactly what we needed Cheney to do.

The second presidential debate was October 11, at Wake Forest University in Winston-Salem, North Carolina, and was devoted mostly to foreign affairs. Here, Gore the Agreeable showed up. He was almost compulsive in the way he agreed with Bush on a variety of topics—from same-sex marriage to education accountability. When Bush argued that people should look at America as a freedom-loving yet humble nation, Gore said, "I agree with that, I agree with that," then echoed Bush's answer. It was an inexplicable and startling change in demeanor.

While Gore disappeared into the background by being so meek and agreeable, Bush shined. It was his best debate performance ever: he was relaxed, funny, fluid, and (to the press) surprisingly conversant in foreign policy. It always helps to beat expectations.

Gore also appeared to have hired a makeup artist who thought he was getting paid by the pound. When I checked in with the Lincoln Lounge

crowd after the debate, they complained their television was broken because Gore looked orange. I assured them he looked even more unnatu-
rally orange in person, as if he were from another planet.

By the third debate, October 17, at Washington University in St.
Louis, Bush and everyone around him were sick of the encounters. We
had a three-hour debate prep session scheduled for that morning at Steve
and Kimmie Brauer's farm in suburban St. Louis, where Bush's traveling
party was camped out. Bush took about half an hour of being peppered
with suggestions and advice before he declared the session over. He knew
a better way to get his mind in the right place for the evening. So while
Al Gore was probably stuck in a hotel room thumbing through index
cards of "spontaneous" quips, Bush was fishing on the Brauers' pond with
Don Evans. If Bush hadn't shut down the prep session when he did, he
could have been tired and cranky at the debate. When he picked up his
fishing pole, I was delighted.

At the third debate, Menacing Al Gore showed up. At one point, he
got up from his stool and walked over to invade Bush's space while Bush
was speaking, grimly approaching him and trying to use his height and
bulk to overshadow the Texas governor just as Portman had predicted.
Bush glanced toward Gore and then paused, smiled, and nodded his head
in a dismissive and mocking gesture. Gore looked foolish. It was the
debate's defining moment, replayed over and over again on TV.

The complete series worked to our advantage. The next Gallup head-
to-head poll put Bush ahead of Gore by 10 points. If things went according to plan, Bush would win by a comfortable margin. But things didn't
go according to plan. Just before the final debate, on Sunday, October
15, the NAACP National Voter Fund ran full-page ads in the *New York
Times* and in African-American newspapers featuring Renee Mullins, the
daughter of James Byrd, Jr., the black man from Jasper, Texas, who in
June 1998 was dragged naked to his death by three white men in a pickup
truck, from whom he'd hitched a ride.

In the ad, Mullins declared: "I went to Governor George W. Bush
and begged him to help pass a Hate Crimes Bill in Texas. He just told me
no." The print ad was followed by radio spots and TV ads in many
battleground states. The television version featured Ms. Mullins saying:
"I'm Renee Mullins, James Byrd's daughter. On June 7, 1998, in Texas,
my father was killed. He was beaten, chained and then dragged three

miles to his death all because he was black. So when Governor George W. Bush refused to support hate crimes legislation, it was like my father was killed all over again. Call George W. Bush and tell him to support hate crimes legislation. We won't be dragged away from our future."

Accusing Bush of complacency in a murder drew criticism, and not just from Republicans and conservatives. The left-leaning National Public Radio's Mara Liasson said it was "unclear what hate crimes legislation would do . . . to prevent this horrific thing from happening." The ad was particularly cynical, because of the three whites convicted of James Byrd's brutal murder, two were given the death penalty. The third was sentenced to life in prison; he was spared the needle because of a lack of compelling evidence that he was a racist. How was a "hate crime" law going to provide even harsher punishment?

But Gore couldn't restrain himself. At a Spokane rally the day before the TV ad began running, he suggested Bush was responsible for Byrd's death because the murder took place in Texas. NPR's Liasson called Gore's comment "incendiary." There was little we could do except point to the convictions, decry the NAACP ads, and focus on where we wanted to drive the campaign.

We never got a chance. On Thursday, November 2, Fox News called Dan Bartlett, asking for confirmation that George W. Bush had been arrested in 1976 in Maine for driving under the influence of alcohol. He paged Karen (his message read: "911"). I got the call while sitting in my office in Austin with Don Evans. We sat there for half a minute or so, saying nothing. It felt like hours before anyone moved. Then I walked across the headquarters to tell Joe Allbaugh, who remained calm. Both of us had known for years this issue could emerge, but we hoped against hope that it wouldn't. Just before 6 P.M. Eastern, Dan spoke to Fox News's Carl Cameron, who was ready to go on air as soon as Dan confirmed Bush's arrest nearly a quarter of a century ago.

On Labor Day weekend in Kennebunkport in 1976, Bush, who was then thirty, had a few too many beers in an evening out on the town with friends. He then drove back to his parents' house with Australian tennis star John Newcombe and Newcombe's wife; an aide to George H. W. Bush, Pete Roussel; and Bush's younger sister Doro. Kennebunkport police officer Calvin Bridges observed Bush creeping along Ocean Avenue at less than ten miles an hour, slipping on and off the curb, and pulled him over. After administering a field sobriety test, he took Bush to the Biddeford Courthouse, administered a second sobriety test, booked him on a misdemeanor—driving under the influence—and released him ninety minutes later. Bush's blood-alcohol level was 0.10, the legal limit at the time. Bridges later recalled, "The man was . . . a picture of integrity. He gave no resistance. He was very cooperative." Bush paid a $150 fine and had his Maine driving privileges rescinded for thirty days. The story now had been developed by WPXT, the Fox affiliate in Portland, Maine. Dan confirmed it, and the news soon filled the airwaves.

It was critical that Bush respond rapidly and personally. People would form a quick judgment, and he was the best voice to explain the arrest. At a hastily called news conference following a raucous campaign rally in suburban Milwaukee, Bush admitted everything, saying, "It's an accurate story. I'm not proud of that. I've often times said that years ago I made some mistakes; I occasionally drank too much. I did on that night. I was pulled over. I admitted to the policeman that I had been drinking. I paid the fine. I regretted that it happened. I learned my lesson." Because their eighteen-year-old daughters didn't know of their father's long-ago arrest, Laura called Jenna at the University of Texas and Barbara at Yale. For the girls, who had their own run-ins with underage drinking, it must have been a strange moment.

Over the years, Bush had told a few confidants about the arrest— Karen, Joe, his gubernatorial legal counsel Al Gonzales, and I all knew, but Bush was adamant he didn't want it public. Even our own opposition researcher failed to find the arrest when we had an every-cavity search of Bush's life done in 1997 before the gubernatorial reelection to see what weaknesses a presidential bid would reveal. Despite our mild encouragement to make it public, Bush said no.

At the time, I thought most Americans would decide this was no big deal. Bush had been thirty, gave up drinking entirely ten years later, and the incident was far in the past. Nevertheless, we should have brought it up at a time and place of our choosing. I should have made a more convincing case for doing so. Instead I helped George W. Bush keep a secret that almost cost him the White House.

So why did Bush not talk about it publicly? As he explained to the press after the arrest was revealed, "I made the decision that as a dad I didn't want my girls doing the kinds of things I did and I told them not to drink and drive." His comment that Thursday was familiar to me: it's what he'd told Karen and me years before.

How did the story surface? The afternoon of November 2, Erin Fehlau, twenty-seven, a reporter for WPXT, the Fox affiliate in Portland, Maine, was at the Cumberland County Courthouse in Portland waiting for the verdict in an arson case when a policewoman told her that she had overheard a judge telling a lawyer about Bush's arrest for driving under the influence. Fehlau got confirmation of the arrest and its case number from the lawyer, Tom Connolly. Fehlau called the courthouse in Biddeford, Maine, and verified the arrest. She then got a copy of Bush's driving record faxed from the secretary of state's office in Augusta. WPXT news director Kevin Kelly then called Fox News Channel in New York "to see if we were flogging a dead horse." Fox checked with the Bush campaign before running the story, and WPXT followed an hour later. The Portland NBC affiliate, WCSH, and the *Portland Press Herald* also heard from Connolly and went with the story.

Connolly was a Democratic gadfly in Maine who was known for his irrepressible mouth and the long-billed fishing cap he wore everywhere. He'd been the Democratic gubernatorial candidate in 1998, receiving just 12 percent in a three-way general election. A Gore delegate at the Democratic convention, Connolly hated Bush, even showing up at a rally to yell "You wiener" at the Texas governor. He compared Bush's DUI arrest to Clinton's affair with Monica Lewinsky, saying that Bush could have a drinking relapse under the pressure of the White House just as Clinton had "acted out with Monica on his addiction under pressure." Connolly told reporters: "DUI may be considered by many to be a crime of moral turpitude" and disclosure "may help people evaluate who should be the next president." If people didn't consider Bush's DUI to be important, Connolly suggested, then that's simply another sign of "our dysfunctional alcoholic society." Connolly was a loudmouthed buffoon enjoying his moment, but he was effective at keeping the story alive, especially in Maine.

He was probably not the story's source, however. I believe he had received the information from Billy Childs, a lawyer, part-time probate judge, and son of the former Democratic speaker of the Maine House of Representatives. Connolly tried to hide Childs's role in pushing the story, claiming to have called the secretary of state's office himself to verify the arrest. That office later said it was Childs who called. And where did Judge Childs get the news about Bush's arrest? He said it had come from a chiropractor who'd heard it that Thursday morning from a patient who had been in the Biddeford Courthouse in 1976. Neither the chiropractor nor his patient ever surfaced, and that part sounded fishy. Fox's Carl Cameron reported that Judge Childs had four months earlier "requisitioned a document about the Bush arrest. The documents were in cold storage . . . and the judge used his influence as a member of the court to get the papers pulled."

The timing of the DUI disclosure—four days before Election Day, with the candidates tied in the polls—was suspicious. On Friday, Karen called it "gotcha politics" and a "last-minute dirty trick" and said "Democrats owe the American people an explanation." Later that day, Bush called it "dirty politics" and said, "I don't know if my opponent's campaign was involved, but I do know that the person who admitted doing it at the last minute was a Democrat and partisan in Maine."

On Thursday, Gore spokesman Chris Lehane first said, "We're not commenting on it. It literally is something that is still developing." Later that evening, Lehane distanced the Democratic campaign from it, saying, "This is just not something the Gore campaign is involved with in any shape, way or form. It's not something we would engage in."

That may be true, but we had our suspicions and they centered on Lehane. He had been raised in Kennebunk, was one of the Democratic Party's best opposition researchers, had run the Maine campaign for Clinton-Gore, worked on the White House rapid-response team handling scandals during the Clinton years, played around in Maine Democratic politics, knew Connolly, and had a sister who practiced law in Portland. While she said she'd never met Connolly, she didn't similarly disavow Childs.

Did this last-minute revelation of Bush's decades-old DUI hurt? Yes, a lot. First, it knocked us off message at a critical time. The campaign was swamped with questions about the incident, Bush's past drinking, if there had been other arrests, whether he had been truthful with reporters before, even if he had slipped off the wagon and was drinking again now. This was not a good note on which to close a nearly two-year bid for the presidency.

Second, we had made a big issue of Gore's credibility and now we had a problem with Bush's. He had never claimed to have a spotless youth. He talked openly about how as a young man he drank too much, and how he stopped drinking at the age of forty. But it was jarring for people to hear him admit he'd been arrested. Many Americans had been drawn by his pledge to restore integrity to the Oval Office and now he had surprised them with a DUI.

The revelation caused two things to happen. First, a number of people who supported Bush flipped and went for Gore. This took one vote away from Bush and gave it to Gore. Second, a larger number of voters—especially evangelicals and social conservatives—decided not to vote, taking votes away from Bush.

It's impossible to know what those numbers were, but we know that before the news broke, we were up 40 percent to Gore's 35 percent in Maine. After just one night's coverage of the DUI story, Gore pushed ahead, 44 percent to 40 percent. Bush went on to lose Maine and its four electoral votes by 5 percent.

Consider the national impact if just 2 percent of voters changed their minds because of the DUI arrest. That translates into 2,109,020 votes. That is nearly four times the 543,895 votes that represented Gore's lead in the popular vote. After the election, pollster John McLaughlin pointed to an exit poll in which 28 percent said Bush's DUI was important, and that group voted for Gore by three-to-one. If Bush did drop 2 percent nationally in the vote because of the DUI revelation, then it probably cost him four additional states that he lost by less than 1 percent—New Mexico, Iowa, Wisconsin, and Oregon. Had he won them, this would have added a total of thirty electoral votes to Bush's column, which would have allowed him to win the White House without Florida. Receiving a majority of the popular vote and winning the Electoral College by a margin of 305 to 232 would have given Bush a much better start. Of the things I would redo in the 2000 election, making a timely announcement about Bush's DUI would top the list.

After four and a half years of working toward the White House, I just had to be on Bush's plane on the last day of the campaign. Our penultimate stop was Bentonville, Arkansas. On our approach, daylight was fading and night coming on. I looked out of the plane and saw a river of lights. There were miles of cars moving toward the rally at an airport hangar. I got a lump in my throat. I knew better—big crowds in the closing days are never a guarantee of victory. But this was Clinton's home state. We might yet pull Arkansas away from Clinton's vice president.

The hangar was overflowing. Despite our exhaustion, the traveling party was giddy. Don Evans and I took to wearing a borrowed straw cowboy hat and snapping pictures of each other in it. There was new music as Bush worked the rope line. First was Clinton's 1992 theme song, "Don't Stop (Thinking About Tomorrow)." The crowd roared when it came on. We all laughed again when The Who's "Won't Get Fooled Again" followed.

After boarding the plane for home, exhaustion set in and many slept on the final leg. As we taxied after landing in Austin, I rose to disembark and found myself standing next to Bush. He quietly told me "thanks" and grabbed the back of my head to pull me closer. Then he thought the better of it. The press aboard would have loved to see us bawl. Bush was met by a spontaneous mass of well wishers, family, and campaign staff who'd shown up on their own. He got a little choked up as they cheered their welcome home.

My Election Day ritual is to stay busy by calling people around the country. What I am listening for is tone. Are they optimistic? Are they edgy? Depressed? It's not scientific, but it works. People in Ohio, Tennessee, Arkansas, West Virginia, New Mexico, and Nevada were giddy. There was both anxiety and hope in Pennsylvania, Wisconsin, New Hampshire, Missouri, Oregon, and, ominously, Florida. But people in Maine, Michigan, and Minnesota sounded downbeat. The rest of the country split predictably red and blue.

Early in the afternoon, we started getting the first exit poll numbers. They were dreadful, almost beyond belief. Actually, they were beyond belief. We were behind in Florida by 3, Michigan by 4. We were tied in Mississippi, Vermont, Colorado, Arizona, Alaska, and Delaware. We were up in Iowa by 3, up by nearly 4 in Missouri, 10 in Ohio, 9 in West Virginia, and over 3 in Wisconsin. New York went from down 21 points at 10 A.M. to dead even at noon. Go figure. We could win without Florida, Pennsylvania, or Michigan, but only by running the table and taking every state that was close, including Wisconsin, Iowa, New Mexico, Oregon, and Washington. That would be nearly impossible.

Exit polls are always unreliable, especially during a close election. As it turned out, these exit polls were screwed up even beyond historic standards. The Florida number just didn't feel right, as did a bunch of other states. But we started to hear the exit polls color the TV commentary. We also heard plainly irresponsible mistakes from the commentators themselves. Just after 5:30 P.M. Eastern, CNN's Bill Schneider said Florida was the big prize among the nine states whose polls closed at 7 P.M. Eastern. But Florida was in two time zones. Polls from Panama City west to Pensacola and the Florida-Alabama border closed at 8 P.M. Eastern. The Panhandle was Republican territory, where we'd win big. Matt Dowd and I wondered aloud what the heck CNN was saying.

At 6 P.M. Eastern, Indiana and Kentucky were the first states to report. Both were strong for Bush, so we began the evening with a lead in the Electoral College. By 7 P.M., the flawed exit polls were fueling near-lethal reporting: CNN anchor Bernie Shaw intimated Georgia was "a war" (Bush won it by 12 points) and in Virginia "again, the race is too close to call" (Bush won it by 8 points).

I was glued to the TV set when CNN's Al Hunt said, "We now go to our election headquarters in Atlanta, where it is 7 P.M. in the East. Polls have just closed in Florida, New Hampshire, and Virginia." I yelled at the TV. Hadn't CNN figured out their mistake?

Dowd, our dour Irishman, and I seethed at CNN's readiness to write off hundreds of thousands of Panhandle voters. An old friend, Randy Enwright, had quarterbacked our Florida effort and was in Tallahassee. It took him just a few minutes to draft a new script and crank up the phone banks to fire another frantic round of tens of thousands of calls into Republican households in the Panhandle, urging them to vote. The press shop called Panhandle television and radio stations, pleading for a public service announcement telling voters they still had time.

Bernie Shaw suggested that his inability to call Ohio and West Virginia at 7:32 P.M. Eastern—two minutes after polls closed!—was bad news for Republicans. He called the inability to put West Virginia into the GOP column "a marvel," notwithstanding the fact that Clinton carried the state by 14 points four years earlier. Bush went on to win Ohio by 3.5 points and West Virginia by 6.3 points.

CNN was not alone. The shoddy exit polls and competitive pressures pushed all the networks to call states early and wrong. At 7:48 P.M., and with polls *still* open in Florida's Panhandle, NBC became the first network to project that Gore had won Florida. If true, this meant Gore had probably won the presidential election. But this made no sense to Dowd or me. The Florida county returns we were looking at pointed to a Bush victory. I checked with Enwright, who was monitoring the county returns in Tallahassee and checking them against our targets. It didn't make sense to him, either. No one was in a position to call Florida.

I noticed staffers were congregated in the corridor outside the plate-glass window that formed the southern wall of my office, standing and watching us, as if our expressions would tell them what was going to happen. When I realized it, it made me even more tense. It was uncomfortable, but I couldn't close the blinds without doing even more damage to morale.

At 7:50 P.M. Eastern, just two minutes after NBC made its call, CNN anchor Judy Woodruff came on the air after a commercial to proclaim, "A big call to make. CNN announces that we call Florida in the Al Gore column." Jeff Greenfield, Candy Crowley in Austin, and John King with the Gore campaign in Nashville paraded across the screen, proclaiming their surprise at Gore winning Florida. Shaw came back, asking "Can you think of the agony and the anguish unfurling in the Bush camp and the Bush family?" Former Clinton press secretary Mike McCurry suggested a GOP victory might now sound "like a little bit of wishful thinking." And all across America, millions of people had hours yet to vote. I talked with Enwright. We were up by 75,000 votes in Florida in the AP and Florida secretary of state tallies.

CBS followed CNN's declaration almost immediately. And at 7:52 P.M. Eastern, the consortium running the exit polls for the networks and the AP—Voter News Service (VNS)—called Florida for Gore. Because of that, all five networks and the AP had projected Gore the winner in Florida by 8:02 P.M. To compound our morale problems, just before 9 P.M. Eastern, we lost the Electoral College lead we'd enjoyed all night when Pennsylvania fell into the Democratic column. They'd already called Michigan at 8 P.M. Eastern, while voters in parts of the Upper Peninsula still had an hour to vote.

We were all talking to people inside the networks, pushing back on the idea that the race was over and Florida comfortably in Gore's column. We not only pointed to the actual Florida numbers, we also pointed to the wide discrepancy between the exit polls and the actual results in states where most of the vote had been counted. I could tell from the tone of my conversations that network anchors like Tom Brokaw, Bob Schieffer, and Tim Russert were nervous about their networks' being out on a limb. CNN seemed oblivious. NBC invited me on. I criticized their early Florida call.

The networks calling Florida for Gore turned the media from observers to participants in the presidential race. Gerry Parsky, our California chairman, called fifteen minutes after the Florida announcement to say he was getting reports that volunteers were walking out of California phone banks and voters were getting out of lines at the polls. And California was not the only state where voters and volunteers cut short their effort. Similar calls came in from Nevada, New Mexico, Arizona, and other states where the polls would be open for hours.

There were twenty-four states where the polls closed after 8:30 P.M. Eastern time. In those twenty-four states, turnout increased 2.3 points between 1996 and 2000. But in the twenty-seven states and Washington, D.C., where the polls closed before 8:30, turnout increased 2.9 points. If the twenty-four late-closing states had seen the same turnout increase as the twenty-seven early-closing ones, there would have been 401,504 more votes cast. Since Bush supporters were more likely to stay home than Gore backers, the early call probably affected the outcome in New Mexico and Oregon (where Gore won by 6,765) and certainly the popular vote margin.

At 9:17 P.M., the national picture began swinging our way. Tennessee and Ohio went for Bush. Applause rippled through the HQ. At 9:54 P.M., the number crunchers in the back rooms at both CNN and CBS reconciled the exit poll results with the actual vote totals and advised their networks to move Florida back into the "too close to call" column. By 10:18, all the networks had retracted their Florida call. Cheers rang out throughout the office.

The cheers were still resounding when CNN called New Mexico for Gore around 10:21 P.M. Eastern. While its five electoral votes wouldn't swing the election back to Gore, consider this: CNN hesitated for hours to award West Virginia to Bush when he won it by 40,000, or Ohio, which he won by 165,000. But it put New Mexico in the Democratic column thirty minutes after the polls closed. It was a sign of gross bias: Gore won the state, but twenty-three days later and by 366 votes.

Shortly after calling New Mexico for Gore, CNN asked for a Bush representative to go on air with Bernie Shaw, and I used the occasion to attack CNN for having "called Florida before the polls had even closed" in the Panhandle. Shaw admitted "some difficulty with the VNS data" and said CNN called races when "75 percent of the precincts in a state have closed." I jumped on him: "[T]hat's one criteria you might want to think about changing." Shaw looked dumbstruck.

Meanwhile, winning Clinton's home state of Arkansas caused another round of cheers. The seesaw back and forth was making me sick. I had to force myself to remember that all of this didn't matter. We had enough electoral votes to win as long as Florida was in our column. But our lead there was dwindling. My office was a constant, churning mass of people stopping in for the latest numbers, the most up-to-date interpretation, and reassurance we were going to be all right. I did the best I could.

By 2 A.M., the networks reported Bush's Florida lead was 29,000 with 96 percent of the precincts reporting. At 2:08 A.M., Volusia County on Florida's central east coast and home to Daytona Beach reported almost all its precincts and we jumped to a 51,000-vote lead in the VNS tally being shared with the networks. VNS calculated 180,000 votes remained to be counted and Gore would need 63 percent of those to win. Their number crunchers now expected a 30,000-vote Bush victory and alerted the networks.

Out of nowhere, at 2:15 A.M., a swirling graphic appeared on Fox that materialized in Bush's face as Fox called Florida and the election for Bush. My son Andrew and Darby were standing in my office when the roar of hundreds of voices in the headquarters shook the glass wall that was one side of my office. If Florida was Bush's, then so was the White House. People stood on desks and waved wildly. Others jumped up and down hugging co-workers. McKinnon was so excited he grabbed the closest woman to him and kissed her. Then he sheepishly realized it was Dan Bartlett's wife. Andrew's face was pure joy and when he hugged me, I was nearly overwhelmed with emotion. What father wouldn't be?

A phone on my desk rang. It was jokingly labeled "The Bat Phone" because only Bush called it. I grabbed it and shouted into the receiver, "Mr. President!" I waved for the unruly mass of people in my office to settle down. Bush was ebullient; his brother Jeb had told him that the numbers coming out of precincts in Broward and Dade counties were good for us. Nervous, but expectant, he hung up and went to join his family.

I immediately talked with Enwright. He'd heard the same report that Jeb had shared. But Randy had checked it out and the Broward and Dade precincts didn't look that good to him. He said it would get tighter. My stomach immediately did the same. Darby was confused and shocked. She had never seen an election when I had not called the result before the networks. This time, I was as dumbfounded as everyone else. I exchanged a quiet word with Dowd. He was mystified, too. We didn't have access to VNS's data, but we were looking at AP and Florida secretary of state numbers. The race appeared much closer than the networks portrayed it. Earlier in the evening, Dowd and I knew Florida wasn't Gore's. Now we weren't certain it was ours.

Colleagues and friends, delirious that we'd won, jammed into my office and then, almost as one, began moving toward the stairs to the lobby and swarmed out the doors and began marching up Congress Avenue toward the stage and the inevitable victory speech. I found myself being pulled and dragged along by the ecstatic mob. I almost became separated from Darby and Andrew when friends and strangers tried to hoist me on their shoulders to parade up toward the Capitol. It was raining and cold. Part of me was elated, but part was wary, apprehensive, and sick to my stomach.

We stood there waiting for Governor Bush to appear. I called the Mansion, but Bush was on the phone with Al Gore. Then Enwright called. This was going to get even closer: he discovered that Volusia County had made a 20,000-vote error in Bush's favor in the numbers it reported to the Voter News Service. We'd have a lead of less than 40,000 when it was corrected, he predicted. At 2:48 A.M., Volusia corrected the mistake. Our lead dropped to 39,600. I called the Mansion back and Bush told me Gore had just called to retract his concession. I explained what had happened in Volusia. He was flabbergasted by both Gore and the Florida muddle. I turned, ashen-faced, and took Andrew and Darby back to the office.

At 3 A.M., the last of Palm Beach County, a Democratic stronghold, came crashing in. Our lead narrowed to 11,000. By 3:10 A.M. it was down to 10,000. Half an hour later, it was 6,060, and by 3:47 A.M., less than 2,000. By now, Enwright and others were at the Florida secretary of state's office, trying to resolve why their numbers showed Bush's margin at 1,000, while the AP's data put it at 1,800. It turned out that the supervisors in two counties hadn't turned in their reports to the courthouse. The secretary of state ordered them to deliver their counts. By 4:10 A.M., Bush's margin settled at just around 1,800 votes.

By 4:15 A.M., every network had Florida back as too close to call. It was 246 for Bush to 259 for Gore in the Electoral College and our lead for Florida's twenty-five electoral votes was 1,784 out of over 5.8 million cast in the state.

That's where it remained until lawyers entered the fray in just a few short hours. Thirty-six days of political hell were ahead. I felt I was going to collapse.

CHAPTER 13

Thirty-six Days in Hell

———•◆•———

The former secretary of state James A. Baker III hung up on me. He was running our fight in Florida and he wanted something, so he called the Austin headquarters and put Don Evans and me on a conference call. I can't now remember what he wanted, but Don and I pushed back. Baker's response was swift and brusque: hell, if we weren't going to agree, we could get our butts to Tallahassee and run the recount battle ourselves. Next came a click.

For more than two years, I had worked tirelessly to elect George W. Bush president. There was little within the campaign that I hadn't touched. Now it was clear I was a bystander, forced to endure the anguish of being on the sidelines and to accept that there were larger forces at play. It was an important lesson.

There has been a lot written and said about the thirty-six days that followed Election Day in 2000. Not all of it is true. Cut through all the clutter and it comes down to this: we insisted that Florida law as it stood on the day of the election be followed to the letter, while the Gore camp tried to overturn Bush's lead by arguing that the law should be ignored.

The morning after the election, around 4 A.M., Wednesday, November 8, Florida governor Jeb Bush left the Texas Governor's Mansion and boarded a private plane for Florida with his wife, Columba. His state was descending into controversy, and he needed to be there. Shortly after

that, Evans talked with the campaign's legal counsel, Ben Ginsberg from
the D.C. law firm of Patton Boggs. They agreed that Ben should get to
Tallahassee as quickly as possible. Don also roused Florida secretary of
state Katherine Harris out of bed to tell her she had a disaster on her
hands.

Ginsberg was in his Austin hotel room packing when the *Today* program came on TV. As the anchors talked about a recount, Ginsberg
thought, "Shit, this isn't supposed to happen in a presidential election!"
At about that time Ken Mehlman and a planeload of lawyers and political staff were dispatched from Austin to Miami. Gore would make a
stand in the big Democratic strongholds of Miami-Dade, Palm Beach,
and Broward counties, and we had no one on the ground there.

Jeb was on the ground at the small Tallahassee airport around 8:30
A.M. He immediately knew something was up. The only other plane on
the tarmac was a big DC-9 passenger jet emblazoned with the Gore-
Lieberman campaign logo. It had flown in from Nashville before 6 A.M.
loaded with fifty or more lawyers and Gore campaign aides. Jeb called
me. "We've been invaded," he said. An election for president was transforming into an epic legal battle.

To their credit, the Gore people had prepared for this moment, boning up on Florida election law and organizing a legal hit squad. We had
not. For the next few days, our Florida campaign team felt like freedom
fighters whose homeland had been occupied as they grappled with a
blitzkrieg of lawsuits filed by Gore's attorneys and street protests led by
Jesse Jackson.

In Austin, we gathered at the headquarters well before 7:30 A.M. on
that first day for a senior staff meeting. Don Evans presided. We learned
that Gore was tapping former secretary of state Warren Christopher to
run his recount campaign. We needed a marquee leader, too. So Don
called our own former secretary of state. Baker agreed. By 10:30 A.M.,
Evans, Allbaugh, Karen Hughes, and I were at the Mansion to review the
situation with the Bushes and the Cheneys.

By 2:30 P.M., Allbaugh, Baker, and Margaret Tutwiler, Baker's longtime aide, were on their way to Florida's capital. They met with Jeb at the
Governor's Mansion and then headed over to the state GOP headquarters for a meeting with the local legal team. It was depressing. Our Florida lawyers were earnest and well-meaning but they lacked the firepower

to go up against Gore. Ginsberg quickly realized we needed reinforcements. He and Baker got on the phone and began rounding up more experienced attorneys. We were late, but under Baker's direction, we caught up quickly.

The U.S. Constitution and federal law required that Florida's election laws in effect on Election Day be followed. If they were, Bush would narrowly win the election. The only way Gore could overturn our victory was to get state and local officials to change the rules after the election had ended and recount votes in precincts where Gore was strong. Their aim was to find enough votes to put Gore into the lead, but not open up a statewide recount that would likely turn up more votes for Bush. David Boies, one of Gore's top lawyers, later referred to this as "harvesting" and "trolling for votes." It was a brutally candid admission that Gore's goal was not to count every vote, but rather to create enough new votes to win.

Gore confidant Ron Klain ignited the first firestorm with an odd suggestion. He said that it wouldn't hurt if the dispute went past December 18, when the Electoral College was scheduled to meet. In essence, he was saying that Florida could be excluded from the presidential election and that Gore could be declared the winner because he had amassed more Electoral College votes than Bush outside of Florida (he had 262 votes; Bush had 246 if Florida's 24 votes were left uncounted). I don't think Gore's people ever seriously considered trying to push for this outcome. It's more likely that Klain's remark was meant to distract attention from what they'd already decided to do.

The actual Gore strategy was to get a manual recount of the "undervotes" in just four counties, all of which happened to be Democratic. ("Undervotes" are ballots where the machine registers a vote in another race—such as for Congress—but doesn't register a vote in the presidential race.) There were 6,000 undervotes in Broward County, 10,000 in Miami-Dade County, 10,000 in Palm Beach County, and 155 in Volusia County. Albert Gore, Jr., needed just 2 percent of these "undervotes" to be converted into votes for him to become the forty-third president.

On Election Day, these instructions were printed for voters to see:

AFTER VOTING, CHECK YOUR BALLOT CARD TO BE SURE YOUR VOTING SELECTIONS ARE CLEARLY AND CLEANLY PUNCHED AND THERE ARE NO CHIPS LEFT HANGING ON THE BACK OF THE CARD.

That seemed pretty clear to me. The law said that any ballot with a hanging chip, or "chad," to use the media's favorite term, was not a legal vote. The question was if that law would be followed or if election boards would throw it out and use different standards at different times—or different standards at the same time in the same room—to determine voter intent.

On Friday, November 10, the Gore campaign worked to keep us off balance by alleging that the "butterfly ballot" design in Palm Beach County confused voters there into voting for Reform candidate Pat Buchanan. Gore's people argued that this confusion required that a new election be held in that one county. We struck back later that morning in an Austin press conference. "Our democratic process calls for a vote on Election Day; it does not call for us to continue voting until someone likes the outcome," said Evans.

I followed by saying it was "ironic" that Gore campaign chairman Bill Daley, brother and son of Chicago mayors, had criticized the butterfly ballot as "confusing and undemocratic" when the design had historically been used in Cook County, Illinois, his home. Besides, I said, Democratic election authorities prepared the Palm Beach County butterfly ballot. Democrats ran the Election Day activities. And Democrats supervised the machines that counted the ballots. How could Democrats now say something was amiss?

Later that day, the statewide machine recount of all ballots was completed and Bush's Florida lead stood at 327. The military and overseas absentee ballots due by November 17 remained to be counted. Dole had carried the military absentee ballots by 15 points in 1996, so we expected Bush's lead to grow when they were included.

The Friday news conference was one of the last few useful things I did for the recount. The action was in Florida, and I was eight hundred miles to the west. To downplay the seriousness of the situation, I was barred from going there. That stopped making sense within a few days after the election, but for more than a month, I was stuck away from the battlefield. So I piddled around with some of the other states still outstanding. By Friday of the first week, Oregon was still counting ballots and we were behind there by around 5,183 votes. Our hope was that the results from two GOP strongholds in the southern part of the state could put us ahead. They didn't. We were also behind in Wisconsin and Iowa by a couple of thousand votes in each state. And there was evidence of fraud in the Badger State, especially in Milwaukee, where some city wards had more votes than registered voters. There were also reports of Marquette University students voting more than once and out-of-state Gore workers taking advantage of Wisconsin's same-day registration and voting law by bribing derelicts with cigarettes—and God knows what else— to vote.

Then there was New Mexico. The morning after the election, Gore led by 10,000 votes. But the county clerk in Bernalillo County (where Albuquerque is located) had not counted 27,000 absentee ballots. When she did, Gore's lead fell to 6,825. It dwindled more as counties certified their final results.

In the weeks ahead, Mickey Barnett, head of New Mexico Lawyers for Bush as well as an election expert, found there was a glitch in the computer software used to count the optical scan ballots in five counties, all of which Bush had carried, mostly by big margins. The voting software allowed voters to press a button for a straight party vote, but then modify their vote selection by picking candidates in specific races from different parties. This was critical for us because we hoped to win over conservative Democrats who would vote the party line in local or state elections but be open to a Republican presidential candidate. The problem was that in order for these votes to be counted, a switch embedded in the software must be turned on. A lot of votes had not been counted.

We pushed to repair the software and recount the ballots in Roosevelt County in the eastern part of the state. That one county's recount cut Gore's statewide lead from 481 to 366. Bush had carried most of the remaining counties we suspected had the software problem. The partisan-Democratic secretary of state had vehemently denied the possibility of an error and, when confronted with the Roosevelt County correction, continued her efforts to keep from correcting the other counties. We ran out of time to get them to fix their software and do recounts. My calculations showed that if we'd gotten a statewide recount, Bush would likely have carried New Mexico. But waging a protracted legal campaign to do that would have been a distraction and would not have determined who the next president would be. We needed Florida's twenty-four electoral votes, not just New Mexico's five.

I wanted to be in Florida, but Bush had other plans. He had put the right people in place, agreed on a strategy with Baker, and then stepped back to let his team go at it. Bush received daily briefings from Baker and was on top of every step. He also encouraged me to stay close to our political people on the ground about what was happening in the individual counties. I got the sense he wanted multiple channels of information open to him to ensure that he had an accurate read of all developments. What I saw during this period was a man who rebuilt his energy, prepared himself for the major decisions that had to be made in the recount, and turned his attention quietly to what would come after his victory was confirmed—building a Cabinet, assembling his staff, and governing. He was taking affirmative steps forward even while bogged down in a tough fight.

Bush and I talked every day. More and more, the conversations were about possible Cabinet picks or other decisions he would have to make if he became president. This kind of forward-looking attitude turned my energies toward governing, too. I let the Lincoln Lounge crew loose on studying the actions of all presidents back to FDR during their first hundred days. And I worked with Josh Bolten (who'd been detailed to Florida along with most of his staff) to get what was left of the policy shop in Austin to quietly start crafting an initial agenda.

I also saw Bush rebuild the morale of his people. His team had come through a brutal election and many of its members were stranded in the Austin HQ, feeling helpless to protect what they had won. A well-placed phone call, a few minutes spent bucking up spirits at a meeting at the Mansion or the ranch, or word that the president-elect had green-lighted a project did wonders for everyone's spirits.

What also did wonders for everyone's morale was the appearance of supporters at the Governor's Mansion. Immediately after the election, a few Gore backers protested outside the residence. Austin's Republican activists retaliated by showing up with pro-Bush signs and banners and American flags. Pretty soon, the Mansion was surrounded every day with Bush enthusiasts. They ranged from college students to senior citizens in wheelchairs. On weekends, their numbers were bolstered by families who had driven up to a hundred miles. The Texas Young Republicans paraded around the Mansion grounds in a heavy downpour, many wearing black garbage bags for raincoats. I took to going over to the Mansion whenever

I had a few minutes, so I could thank the rally brigades. Republicans tend not to be the protesting type, so during those trying Florida recount days, there were few things as uplifting as approaching the corner of Tenth and Lavaca and seeing a ragtag army of Republicans yell when they recognized me.

Meanwhile, America was being treated to the spectacle of election officials holding ballots up to the light to see if the chad was dimpled, dangling by one corner, or hanging by two. By November 15, Secretary of State Katherine Harris announced she would not accept further hand recounts and asked the Florida Supreme Court to halt them. The Associated Press estimated that the count of undervotes so far had reduced Bush's lead to 286 votes. But two days later, the Florida Supreme Court blocked Harris from certifying vote totals until it could rule on the Democrats' motion to allow the manual recounts.

The next day, November 18, the military and overseas absentee ballots were counted. Bush won 64 percent of them, gaining 1,380 votes to Gore's 750. I sat at my desk, entering the data into a computer as votes trickled in. We had people at each of the state's sixty-seven county courthouses call with their numbers. When all were in, Bush's lead had grown to 930 votes. I was never so happy about such a small change out of 6 million votes cast. But it could have been better. The Gore campaign succeeded in suppressing at least 1,400 military and overseas ballots, which could have added another 400 votes to our margin. In counties Gore carried, the mostly Democratic election boards rejected 60 percent of the military/overseas ballots they received. In counties Bush carried, 29 percent of the military/overseas ballots were kicked out. On Saturday, we released an instruction sheet that the Gore high command had drafted outlining how to challenge military ballots. Their tactic was too much for even Senator Joe Lieberman, who said on *Meet the Press* that he would urge local election boards "to go back and take another look" at the discarded ballots. It was too late.

On November 21, the Florida Supreme Court dealt us a harsh blow with a 4–3 vote to allow the Gore-requested manual hand counts to continue, and giving counties five days to complete them. We faced an important decision: Should we appeal the Florida Supreme Court decision to the U.S. Supreme Court? Baker asked Bush, whose instinct was yes.

My view was that it was an easy call. The Florida court had demonstrated faulty reasoning and a pro-Gore tilt throughout and had now, through a slim majority, contorted its logic in order to hand Gore one last chance to troll for votes. We needed the steady hand of the U.S. Supreme Court.

It was a troubled Thanksgiving Day in Texas while we waited for the U.S. Supreme Court to decide whether to take the case. We had thunderstorms in Austin that rattled the tin roof of my house and provided half an inch of rain. Cheney had just had a minor heart attack followed up by minor surgery. He phoned in to a turkey dinner arranged for several hundred people of our recount team at the Hyatt Regency in Fort Lauderdale. To great laughter, he told the crowd that he had been watching CNN and saw his press advance director Sean Miles at a protest dressed as a pilgrim standing next to a seven-foot turkey and holding a sign that said "Hey, Al—stuff the turkey not the ballot box!" when he felt a tightness in his chest and got rushed to the hospital. Everyone in the Bush camp was cheered the next day when the U.S. Supreme Court agreed to hear our appeal. Two days later, Harris certified the Florida results after a state Supreme Court deadline expired. Bush had a 537-vote lead over Gore.

The week of December 4 started with a big victory for the good guys. That Monday, Leon County district judge N. Sanders Sauls rejected every argument of Gore's contest of the Florida results. Gore immediately appealed to the Florida Supreme Court. The same day, by a 9–0 vote, the U.S. Supreme Court asked the Florida Supreme Court to explain why it had extended the manual recounts past the state's statutory limits. Even a nonlawyer like me understood what the high court had just done: the justices in Washington were saying the Florida Supreme Court had been dead wrong in allowing this fiasco to go on and had to stop it—or the U.S. Supreme Court would.

Democrats got desperate, discarding their mantra of "count all the votes" by moving two days later to throw out 25,000 absentee ballots in Seminole and Martin counties, both heavily Republican. The next day, Baker and his team faced off against the Gore election law squad in the Florida Supreme Court over the Leon County judge's rejection of Gore's case. If Gore lost, the election was over.

The Florida high court's decision came like a thunderbolt on a quiet afternoon. At 4 p.m. Eastern on Friday, December 8, by a 4–3 vote, the

Florida Supreme Court ordered a manual recount of all undervotes in the state. What I didn't know at the time is that some in the Gore campaign were not so sure Florida's highest court had done them a favor. Gore's chief lawyer, David Boies, was worried that the order to count undervotes in all counties—rather than just in the Democratically rich areas of Broward, Miami-Dade, and Palm Beach, as they'd wanted—would not be to Gore's advantage. Boies later wrote that the Gore high command was concerned it would be looking for votes "in Republican waters" and was unable to "predict how this recount would turn out." He acknowledged that Bush had carried the remaining sixty-three counties "by substantial margins" and that Michael Whouley, Gore's political chief for the Florida operation, had "expressed doubt as to whether a recount beyond the four counties selected would provide any additional votes for Gore." If all of the counties in the state were recounted under a uniform standard, Gore likely couldn't win. But even that—at this late hour—would violate the state law in effect on Election Day and, therefore, federal law.

But the immediate impact of the Florida high court's decision was that our lead would shrink. The court ordered a recount of all votes in Miami-Dade County, not just undervotes, and on its own authority added 215 votes in Palm Beach County and 168 more in Miami-Dade to Gore's total. The dissents by the court's three senior justices were strong. Chief Justice C. J. Wells said the majority decision "cannot withstand" constitutional scrutiny and there was no authority under Florida law to order a count of undervotes—especially "on the basis of unknown or, at best, ambiguous standards." This was "unprecedented and unnecessary," since the trial court had "found no dishonesty, gross negligence, improper influence, coercion or fraud in the balloting and counting," he wrote. The decision made no effort to comply with the U.S. Supreme Court's December 4 ruling. It was an act of extraordinary arrogance. We appealed immediately to the U.S. Supreme Court.

Immediately following the Florida Supreme Court's decision, Don Evans and I went to the Governor's Mansion in Austin. Bush was nervous but unflustered; he had confidence in Baker and his team and had the discipline to not waste energy on things beyond his control. Don and I asked to go to Florida. Bush agreed to allow us to fly to Tallahassee.

As we talked, hundreds of calls and e-mails were going out of Bush's Austin and Washington headquarters to enlist election lawyers and volunteers with experience in election contests in Florida. We had meticulously cataloged people around the country who could augment the thousands already on the ground in Florida. Each out-of-state lawyer or expert was assigned to a county in the event the recount started again. When the Florida Supreme Court's decision came down, these lawyers were immediately given an all-hands-on-deck call or e-mail from Maria Cino and her staff. It was a logistics nightmare to deploy six hundred people from around the country to the battlefront by Saturday morning.

Don and I boarded a small jet bound for Tallahassee early Saturday morning and landed just before 8:30 A.M. local time. I called the Washington office and no one answered, so I dialed the Austin headquarters. Karen Johnson, Maria Cino's deputy and a former colleague in my political firm, answered. I asked how the deployment was going. There was a catch in her voice, a long pause, and then she began to weep. This is a very bad sign, I thought, as my mind raced through the possibilities of what disaster might have befallen our recount efforts. Finally, Karen blurted out, "Everyone said yes." All six hundred people—and then some—were either in Florida or on their way there. People dropped everything they were doing to rush to the airport. "The sky is black with Learjets," Karen joked. Maria and her team had worked through the night to get everyone to their battle stations.

Sunday afternoon, I received a phone call from the Austin headquarters. Would I please call Karen to tell her to let someone drive her home? She was still at her post after three straight days. And while everyone had plane reservations, hotel rooms, rental cars, and had recovered their temporarily lost baggage, Karen refused to leave, in case another emergency arose. She was incoherent with exhaustion and sheets of icy rain were blowing through Austin. No one trusted her to drive herself home safely. I made the call, as gently as I could.

On Saturday afternoon, at 2:15 P.M. Eastern, the U.S. Supreme Court accepted our campaign's appeal of the Florida Supreme Court decision that had started the counting again. We were back in a good place: the chaos of standardless recounts had been halted and arguments were set for Monday, December 11, at 11 A.M.

I called Bush with the news and caught him driving Walter Isaacson, then the managing editor of *Time*, and his wife, Cathy, around the Crawford ranch. Walter was interviewing him for a possible "Man of the Year" cover. They were surprised by Bush's calmness in receiving the news. Both assured Bush it meant he would now be president. But he showed his guests the flora and fauna for half an hour longer, before returning to the house and calling Baker.

Our legal brief argued that the Florida Supreme Court's decision violated two constitutional provisions and a federal law. The first constitutional provision was Article II, which says, "Each state shall appoint, in such Manner as the Legislature thereof may direct, a Number of Electors . . . ." The campaign argued that the Florida Supreme Court, by throwing out the legislature's timetable and rules and imposing its own after the election, had usurped the Constitution's grant of authority to the Florida legislature to set the rules for the selection of electors.

Article II was reinforced by a federal law, contained in section 5 of Title III of the U.S. Code, that said any state laws about presidential electors had to settle all election contests at least six days before December 18, the federal deadline for a state submitting its slate of electors, and under state law as it existed on Election Day. Our lawyers argued the Florida Supreme Court was violating this statute by making wholesale changes to Florida's election law after the election, making it impossible to submit Florida's electors on December 12.

The final issue was the Fourteenth Amendment's Equal Protection Clause. The recount was being conducted without standards at all. Different counties set different rules, and some counties allowed different counters in the same room to evaluate similar ballots differently. And the Gore camp was pressing for a third count of some—but not all—ballots, though no third count was allowed under state laws, and the election had been certified.

Bush was ahead when the votes were first counted. Bush was ahead when, as required by law, the votes were recounted by machine. Bush was ahead when the overseas absentee ballots were counted. Bush was ahead when the election was duly certified under the laws in effect on Election Day. Bush was ahead during the entire process. And now, we hoped, we'd finally be able to settle the election once and for all.

Monday morning, Don and I entered the north side of the imposing U.S. Supreme Court building in Washington. We were taken through its bowels and ushered by a marshal upstairs, into the chamber and to our seats. It was going to be packed. The marshal sat Don and me several

rows apart. Montana governor Marc Racicot and Bush campaign counsel
Ben Ginsberg were put next to me. Columnist George Will was placed
two seats away. But most of the room was crowded with people I did not
know. All I could do was sit in this historic chamber and wait.

Jesse Jackson, drawn to controversy, was in the courtroom. His assigned seat was near the entrance, and he didn't like that one bit. Every
few minutes, he would stand and wander toward the front in hopes of
snagging a better seat. And every time he made the attempt, the Court's
deputy marshal, Paul McAdoo, an imposing retired military officer,
would intercept Jackson and guide him back to where he was meant to
be. Finally Jackson got the message and stayed put. In a setting of enormous tension, it was a bit of comic relief.

From my right, a small group was ushered into the row ahead of me.
A strikingly attractive young woman sat down directly in front of me.
After a few moments, she turned to scope out the room and I was face-
to-face with Karenna Gore Schiff, the vice president's daughter. When
she recognized me, she winced.

At exactly 11 A.M., the nine justices made their way into the chamber
and Chief Justice William Rehnquist called the court into session and
recognized Theodore B. Olson, our lead counsel.

Ted Olson is one of the nation's most accomplished Supreme Court
litigators. If you have an issue before the Supreme Court, you want him
as counsel: he has won more cases there than any other lawyer in history,
appearing nearly fifty times before the high court. He was so relaxed in
that chamber that he made other accomplished attorneys look like amateurs, nervous and easily thrown by questions from the bench. He'd
grown up in California, graduated from law school at Berkeley, where
he'd been one of a few conservatives, and then had a successful career
with Gibson, Dunn & Crutcher before joining the Reagan administration as an assistant attorney general. He stayed on in Washington to become one of the legal world's principal conservative figures as well as
Reagan's personal lawyer. Brilliant and personable, he is tall, with light
brown hair, large aviator glasses, and a penchant for sports cars.

As a nonlawyer, I was surprised to see that Supreme Court arguments
were not structured, linear explorations of issues. Instead the session came
across like the World Wrestling Federation of legal battles. Each side's attorney began laying out his argument but was immediately interrupted,

and often battered, by the justices. The lawyer had to answer their questions while struggling to find ways to return to the points he wanted to make.

I also assumed the nation's highest court would always be a solemn, emotionless venue. But there was humor along the way. When Olson sidestepped a question, saying he hadn't raised a point in his brief because "it may not be the most powerful argument," Justice Kennedy quickly interjected "I think that's right," provoking laughter in the courtroom.

Olson played off a question by Justice Antonin Scalia to focus the Court's attention on his principal point: that the case centered on "wholesale revisions" of the state election code by the Florida Supreme Court. Olson argued that the Florida legislature did not "turn over to the judiciary the power to completely reverse, revise, and change the election code in all of the major respects," or to undertake "a major overhaul" of the election code "in almost every conceivable way" after the election was over. Justice John Paul Stevens wasn't buying the argument, and neither was Justice David Souter. Both expressed skepticism.

Olson then turned to the question of standards, arguing that the Florida Supreme Court had not required a uniform way of evaluating ballots. How could voters be treated differently depending on which county they voted in, let alone treated differently in the same county, without violating the Fourteenth Amendment's Equal Protection Clause? Olson's time drew to a close.

Joseph Klock was next. A Democratic lawyer from Miami, he represented Florida secretary of state Katherine Harris. It was Klock's first time before the Court, and it showed. He kept addressing justices by the wrong name, provoking corrections from the bench and laughter in the chamber.

But Klock also drew the Court's attention to the question of "what constitutes a legal vote," saying the Gore campaign "presumes that it's a legal vote no matter what you do" with the ballot. Klock argued a legal punch card ballot was one where the card was punched through— no hanging chads, no dimples. This seemed to me to add weight to the equal-protection claim. Were not all votes, and voters, meant to be treated equally under the law?

Next up was David Boies. He had a reputation for brilliance and eccentricity; both were on display. He was not only good on his feet, he was wearing tennis shoes. Boies made his name famously defending IBM against the Justice Department and then later helping the Justice Department prosecute Microsoft. He didn't read until the third grade because of dyslexia and even today he refuses to use a computer. He compensates for his learning difference by committing everything to memory. Boies's recall and command of the material in his cases are legendary.

He drew fire almost immediately from what I thought was an unlikely source: Justice Kennedy, who was concerned the rambunctious Florida Supreme Court's decisions had changed the state's election laws after the election. Boies insisted the Florida Supreme Court was interpreting the Florida law, not creating it.

But Kennedy pounded away, asking if the Florida legislature could have convened after the election and changed the rules as the court's decision had. Boies made what sounded like a critical admission, saying, "It would be unusual." To my ears, Boies had admitted the Florida legislature could not do what the Florida Supreme Court had done. Didn't that mean the Florida court had created new law? Justice Sandra Day O'Connor, for her part, sounded reproachful. She said, "I did not find really a response by the Florida Supreme Court to this court's remand" of December 4. In other words, the Florida Supreme Court had simply ignored her bench's not-so-subtle directive to provide a cogent rationale for its November 21 decision. The Florida Supreme Court had deliberately told the U.S. Supreme Court to take a hike. Boies had no good answer. Scalia came in behind O'Connor, castigating the Florida court for counting 383 newly discovered Palm Beach County and Broward County ballots after being told not to do so by the U.S. Supreme Court.

Kennedy also hammered Boies. "Could each county," he asked, "give their own interpretation to what intent means, so long as they are in good faith and with some reasonable basis [of] finding intent?" From my vantage point, Boies made a second key admission, conceding "it can vary from individual to individual" county. Kennedy pointed out that the manual recount was even less standardized: "You say it can vary from table to table within the same county."

Souter echoed Kennedy's concern, asking, ". . . is it a violation of the Constitution . . . to say, 'I don't care if there are different standards, as long as they purported to follow intent of the voter, that's good enough?' " Boies replied directly: "Yes, I do not believe that that would violate the equal protection of due process clause." It sounded wrong to me to say different standards could be used to count ballots in different counties. We conservatives have often been unhappy with Justice Souter's decisions, but Boies later wrote that Souter's questions were the hardest he faced.

The chief justice struck a skeptical note, asking how an open-ended contest without rules could be completed by the December 12 deadline set in the federal law, written under the constitutional structure spelled out in Article II for the selection of electors. O'Connor reinforced Rehnquist. It was not an auspicious end for the Gore camp, I thought. Justice Rehnquist gaveled the hearing to a close at 12:27 P.M.

I was staying at the Hilton in McLean, Virginia, Tuesday night. At 10 P.M., with the television on and a discarded room service tray and a half-eaten meal sitting on the desk, I was in my pajamas and trying to read when the moment that I and most of America had been waiting for arrived. A television news alert said the Supreme Court was about to announce its decision in *Bush v. Gore*. In the enormity of the moment, time for me suddenly suspended itself.

I had the TV tuned to NBC, where legal affairs experts Pete Williams and Dan Abrams were delivering confused and uncertain reports on the decision, but I understood its essential element: seven members of the United States Supreme Court—Chief Justice Rehnquist and Justices Kennedy, O'Connor, Scalia, Thomas, Souter, and Breyer—found that the Florida Supreme Court had violated the Equal Protection Clause of the Fourteenth Amendment. They rejected the Florida court's willingness to allow varying counting standards to be used. These seven justices also objected to the Florida court's decision to add hundreds of "undervotes" to the tally. The Gore campaign's strategy was held unconstitutional by seven of the Supreme Court's nine members. Only Stevens and Ginsburg dissented.

By 5 to 4, the U.S. Supreme Court also said it was finished with giving the Florida Supreme Court gentle guidance. The election must end, the Court decided, and Florida's law must be obeyed. George W. Bush was going to be the forty-third president of the United States.

I dialed Governor Bush at the Mansion in Austin. He answered, in his pajamas and in bed reading, as I had been. I told him, "Congratulations, Mr. President!" But his television was off. He hadn't yet heard the

news. He turned on his television, which was set to CNN, to hear correspondent Charles Bierbauer reading the decision, starting with the dissents on the back page, not the majority opinion. Bierbauer had no idea
where it was going. The president-elect was listening to both CNN and
me. I continued to insist it was good news—but he still wasn't convinced
even after he switched to NBC. After several impatient minutes, he said,
"I'm calling Baker," and hung up.

It wasn't the moment I had envisioned for Election Night with Bush
in front of the Texas Capitol with tens of thousands of cheering supporters. Instead I was standing in my pajamas, looking out a hotel window
into a dark, deserted office park, having been hung up on by the man
who would now be president. But then it hit me: nearly four years of
dreaming and planning and bone-aching hard work had ended in victory.
The emotion and excitement of the moment rushed through me, but
mostly I was overwhelmed by a sense of relief. I stood at the window and
thought about all that had transpired. I was going to take in this moment, with or without the participation of America's new president-elect.
Then I was going to call my wife and son.

CHAPTER 14

The Real West Wing

————— •◆• —————

W e didn't have much time. If George W. Bush had been declared the winner on Election Night, we would have had seventy-three days to help him recruit a Cabinet, assemble a staff, and lay a foundation for his governing agenda. Now we had just thirty-seven. And what's more, Bush needed to rally the country after the acrimonious recount—a demand made of few other presidents-elect.

Bush delivered his victory remarks during prime time from Austin, thanking Gore for a gracious concession phone call and saying, "Tonight I chose to speak from the chamber of the Texas House of Representatives because it has been a home to bipartisan cooperation. . . . It is an experience I will always carry with me, an example I will always follow." He delivered these words in good faith and with optimism about how he would be treated in Washington. But we would quickly see that others were not willing to reciprocate. The next day, for example, Bush took a cordial call from the Reverend Jesse Jackson, but Jackson's cordiality lasted only a few days. "We want Bush to understand that while he may occupy the White House, he will be there illegitimately. He is there only because the Supreme Court prevented an accurate count of the ballots," he told the press later. It was a preview of the bitterness to come.

After the victory speech, Bush and I connected for a minute and he squeezed my shoulder. We both looked away to keep our feelings in check. I was full of swirling thoughts and emotions, at least in part because I had barely made it to the speech. On our way to Dulles airport for the last-minute flight, a car had suddenly turned in front us. I saw us headed for a fiery crash, but our young driver swerved and saved us from what was nearly a fatal accident. Then, once our group touched down in Texas, we were whisked to a van where I met up with Darby and Andrew, then we raced to the Capitol. We fell into our seats just seconds before Bush emerged to rousing applause. It had been a long journey to this moment, and like the short one to Dulles airport, it had taken sharp, unexpected turns.

But there was one more surprise left. The day after Bush's speech, Darby dragged me out for dinner at the home of our friends Julie and Pat Oles. An unusually large number of cars were parked on the streets near the Oleses' home. My suspicions rose when I spied men with earpieces; large black SUVs; and the black presidential Cadillac limousine parked in the Oleses' driveway. It was an early surprise party marking my fiftieth birthday.

The Oleses' house was jammed with friends and campaign colleagues talking, laughing, drinking, faces bright and voices elevated and joyous. Against the wall in the kitchen stood an exhausted-looking yet ebullient man holding a nonalcoholic beer, chatting with a small group around him: the president-elect of the United States. He and Laura had taken their first ride in the presidential limo to get there.

During the party, we were jolted into understanding what our new lives would entail when Bush asked if there was a phone with a little privacy; Japanese prime minister Yoshiro Mori was on the line. Bush mangled Mori's name as he explained the reason he needed to step away. "I've got to go talk to that Japanese guy," he joked.

The capstone of the evening was Bush's toast. He used the moment to deliver a generous description of our friendship, which meant a great deal to me. For many people, a fiftieth birthday is bittersweet. There's a feeling of being deep into midlife, with the best days in the rearview mirror, when ambition gives way to a mundane, day-to-day existence. I had the exact opposite feeling, facing a new summit to scale. The transition from campaign to the White House was one of them, and despite its brevity it showed me how hard some of the climbs ahead would be.

One night I had taken Darby out for dinner at a little café called Barbara Ellen's in Austin. Shortly before, Bush had tapped Paul O'Neill to be the new Treasury secretary. It fell to me to work out travel arrangements for O'Neill's nomination announcement and to tell him about a meeting to be held with business leaders the first week in January so the president-elect could get firsthand intelligence on what looked like a souring economy. O'Neill called back shortly after Darby and I had ordered, so I stepped out into a blustery night to speak with him. How long could it take?

O'Neill looked great on paper—chairman of Alcoa, former president of International Paper, and a Ford administration budget official. He had the mix of business and public service the president-elect was looking for. His friend Dick Cheney had pushed hard for him to get the post. But on the phone he was grumpy. When I asked if he could keep his calendar clear for the January meeting, he turned angry. "Why would the president meet with business leaders?" he demanded. That was his job as Treasury secretary. He, not the president-elect, should hold such meetings. The meeting Bush wanted, he said, would be a useless PR exercise, much like one O'Neill had attended for Bill Clinton in 1992.

"I don't intend to be part of a giant photo op," O'Neill told me. "Maybe I should call Governor Bush and tell him I can't accept the job. If this is how it's going to be, maybe I don't want to be part of it."

I tried to remain cordial and keep O'Neill from turning down the job. After a little gutless backpedaling on my part, O'Neill stopped threatening to be a no-show at his own nomination announcement.

I thought many times after that day that the best service I could have rendered the new president would have been to tell O'Neill he was correct, the job might not be a good fit after all. But that was not my right.

O'Neill came to his announcement but skipped the meeting with business leaders—which was a bad sign. Bush did win praise in the press for the meeting, and the news he heard behind closed doors was sobering and valuable. Business leaders from all parts of the country and all parts of the economy said sales were dropping and profits weakening. The Dow Jones was down 9 percent from its January 2000 high and the NASDAQ down over 48 percent since its March peak. The country was headed into a recession and the Treasury secretary designate had missed an important session on what to do about it.

Not long after my exchange with O'Neill, Bush was off to Washington, where, after meeting with congressional leaders, he met with the outgoing president in the private quarters of the White House. Clinton was relaxed, even funny, as he treated his successor to a steak and his wide-ranging views on the world and life in the Oval. This contrasted with a tense and cold meeting at the vice president's residence. Gore was still terribly bitter and grimly said little before appearing before the cameras. However, their joint appearance was symbolically important for the country.

Behind the scenes, Bush had been putting together his Cabinet for weeks. During the Florida recount, he worked on his list of prospects, occasionally visiting with Cheney and people like me as he organized his thoughts. One of the toughest choices was for secretary of defense. Bush wanted to transform the military to meet the strategic challenges of the twenty-first century and therefore needed a strong leader to confront entrenched interests within the Pentagon. An early favorite was Fred Smith, CEO of FedEx, but he withdrew after suffering a heart attack. Another top prospect was former Indiana senator Dan Coats. But after a couple of face-to-face meetings, the president-elect was concerned whether Coats had the management skill and toughness to do the job, despite his many congressional friendships and outstanding character. Bush had also been visiting with former secretary of defense Donald Rumsfeld about heading the CIA. Rumsfeld gave an impressive interview, and Condi, who'd sat in on the meeting, suggested Bush consider the crafty and seasoned Washington hand for the Pentagon.

I liked Rumsfeld but told Bush that tapping him would feed the story line that Cheney was in charge. Bush dismissed the fear and told me that the old hands—Cheney, Powell, and Rumsfeld—would come to understand who was in charge if they didn't already know.

I weighed in on all his Cabinet prospects, but I played a more active role in filling two posts. The first was attorney general. Bush's initial pick was Marc Racicot—a former Montana attorney general and two-term governor. He was also one of the most prominent and reassuring voices we had on television during the Florida recount; his calm, even-tempered approach contrasted well with some of the more hysterical Gore supporters.

There was only one problem: after being paid $83,000 a year as governor, Racicot needed to make money. He had five kids, a mother in a nursing home suffering Alzheimer's, and other family responsibilities. After a painful consideration, he called me. "Karl, I've thought long and hard about it. Part of me wishes I could, but I can't accept the offer," he said. His disappointment was obvious, but so was the firmness of his decision.

The president-elect pressed me for another choice. I suggested former Missouri senator John Ashcroft, who had been both a governor and state attorney general. I'd gotten to know Ashcroft during his gubernatorial races and first senatorial campaign, when he was a client of Rove + Company. After reading a thick briefing book on him, Bush wanted to see him in person. I smuggled Ashcroft and his wife, Janet, into Austin. The two men clicked. They shared the same conservative philosophy, both liked to get to the bottom line, and both cared about the integrity of the law. It was a done deal. Ashcroft's experience as Missouri's attorney general and his personal faith were to give him a calm steadiness and toughness that was needed in the days after 9/11, though his staff sometimes made him look weird—like when they draped the naked breasts of Justice Department statues for a news conference and insisted he go out in the middle of the night on a trip to Moscow to announce the arrest of José Padilla, the al-Qaeda "dirty bomber."

The second post I played an active role in filling was interior secretary. Bush wanted a westerner for the post, someone who understood the region's concerns about intrusive federal policies, since so much land in the West is the government's. I suggested Colorado attorney general Gale Norton, who I knew shared Bush's desire to find a way out of the sterile showdown between growth-at-any-cost Republicans and environmentally obsessed Democrats. I'd been involved in her 1996 failed bid for the GOP nomination for the U.S. Senate. She was smart, well-versed in environmental law, an outdoorswoman, and unflappable. Again, Bush devoured a thick briefing book and interviewed her. He offered her the post after they talked. I admit I coached her a little bit on how to handle the interview. Bush needed to see she had opinions and a willingness to speak her mind. She was to do the country an enormous service in erasing the backlog of repairs at our national parks. And she was fearless in working to open public lands to environmentally sound energy production, an essential step to reducing America's dependence on Middle East oil.

Bush assembled his Cabinet in twenty days. There was only one misstep: Labor Secretary–designate Linda Chavez, who had headed the U.S. Commission on Civil Rights during the Reagan administration. She had to withdraw when it surfaced she had given haven to an illegal immigrant from Guatemala in the early 1990s. In her place, Bush named Elaine Chao, a former Peace Corps director and the wife of Senator Mitch McConnell. She won confirmation and remained in the post for Bush's entire eight years in office. It's a thankless post for a Republican: the unions hate any GOP labor secretary and they were personally rude and crude to Chao. It didn't dissuade her from protecting American workers, however, by making unions live up to the law by revealing how they spent their members' dues.

As Bush's inauguration approached I had a huge decision to make. Should I go with him to Washington or stay in Texas and rebuild my business? Bush assumed I was in for the whole deal, but I wasn't so sure. Over the years, friends who had worked for Democratic and Republican presidents had told me that working in the White House would be the greatest job I'd ever have. They said I could help shape history, but on many days it would be the worst job of my life. I would deal with big egos, and our internal battles would play out on the front pages of the *Washington Post* and the *New York Times,* making my colleagues look brilliant and me an idiot.

So when the president-elect asked me, "Isn't it going to be great we will be in the White House?" I shared my reservations. He was surprised but quickly grew serious. He told me he had seen how infighting had undermined his father's administration, as well as Reagan's. "Trust me," he said. "It won't happen in my White House." What swayed me to make the leap to Washington and become the senior advisor to the president was the thought that the things we regret most in life are the chances we don't take. Darby said it would be an experience our family would never forget. She was right. But we faced a historic challenge: my colleagues and I were coming to a city full of people embittered by the election and determined to undermine our ability to govern. This group quickly settled on a dangerous story line: Bush was an "illegitimate" president because the Supreme Court had delivered the White House to him on a narrow 5–4 vote.

But the facts showed Bush still would have won Florida and the presidency if a thorough statewide recount had been completed. That was the conclusion of two studies—one by *USA Today,* the *Miami Herald,* and Knight Ridder, and another by a large media consortium composed of the Associated Press, CNN, and nine newspapers. Both ballot studies revealed Bush would have won under almost all standards and scenarios and, in many instances, by a much wider margin.

I was a bit shocked when, on December 17, Democratic House leader Dick Gephardt went on *Meet the Press* and twice refused to answer Tim Russert's question about whether Bush "is the legitimate 43rd president of the United States." There was no question that he spoke for a huge number of Democrats.

Their assault failed. Bush won reelection four years later, which would never have happened if he had been seen as illegitimate in the first place. But by refusing to accept the outcome of the 2000 election, Bush's critics did succeed in further poisoning the atmosphere of American politics. I cannot recall liberal historians like Arthur Schlesinger, Jr., or Robert Dallek writing that JFK had a special obligation to discard his agenda and govern in a different manner after the close and hotly contested 1960 election, in which vote fraud and ballot-box stuffing in Chicago gave the election to the Democrats. You will search in vain for liberal columnists like E. J. Dionne and Jonathan Alter or Democratic Party leaders or elected officials saying after Bill Clinton's 1992 election with only 43 percent of the vote that he must therefore "exercise democratic humility" and pursue only policies his Republican opposition agreed with.

Clinton was right not to see himself as less than a president. The American political system requires an effective chief executive. The first man to become president upon the death of his predecessor was John Tyler, in 1841, when William Henry Harrison died a few weeks after giving his inaugural address. Tyler had been put on the Whig ticket for political reasons, but faced the legitimacy question head-on. Many Whigs thought he should be a caretaker president and cede the policy initiative to others. But he insisted that he govern as a full president. He served only one term but set an important precedent. Either you are president or you are not: someone has to make the tough decisions, serve as a check on the other coequal branches of government, and unite the country behind solutions to pressing problems.

It is important to remember that Bush had run and won on an agenda that included providing tax relief, reforming Social Security and education, strengthening our military, and modernizing Medicare. For the president-elect to cast aside his governing ideas to curry favor with Democrats would have been wrong and foolish. Democrats never understood this. They were surprised that he didn't come to them on bended knee. He was, as they discovered, a "conviction politician," which drove them around the bend. Those of us who worked closely with Bush can take comfort in the fact that many of the nation's most accomplished presidents—Lincoln, FDR, Reagan—were polarizing figures during their times in office.

We were coming to town, whether we were welcomed by the political class or not. Darby and Andrew flew to the capital a few days before the inaugural. I was already there working. We'd looked at houses online and hired a Realtor. We knew where we wanted to live because Darby had settled on the school she wanted Andrew to attend. About to turn twelve, Andrew was a very smart sixth-grader with learning differences. He was in advanced math and science classes and had a large vocabulary, but he was in remedial reading. His challenges were described as "sensory integration, fine motor skill difficulties, and written language." Darby was his ferocious advocate and had hired a consultant to pick out what school could meet his needs. She found the right place in the Lab School of Washington, which turned out to be one of the blessings of our time in D.C. It gave Andrew the tools to prepare for college, to which he earned an academic scholarship.

I entered the White House surreptitiously on Inauguration Day 2001—slipping away to spy my new office after watching the parade with Darby from the presidential reviewing stand on Pennsylvania Avenue. The skinny kid from Utah—with thick glasses, lots of hair, and a love for politics, who had visited the White House in February 1969 as a U.S. Senate Youth Program delegate—was back. I was later startled to learn I'd been assigned a call sign by the Secret Service: "Pilgrim." I never found out if the service had discovered my affection for John Wayne, but I never got used to hearing a guy with an earpiece say into a wrist microphone "Pilgrim departs" when I got into a White House car.

Chief of Staff Andy Card often said it was normal to feel a touch of awe when arriving each day at 1600 Pennsylvania Avenue, and if you later realized the feeling was missing, it was time to go. I never lost that touch of awe, not just because of the building I was entering, but also because of the view it gave me on history.

I covered my office walls with Texas landscapes and a big painting of the Rocky Mountains, a large print of Lincoln reading the Emancipation Proclamation to his Cabinet, military commissions signed by Theodore Roosevelt, letters signed by James Madison, memorabilia from President William McKinley and TR, and three framed passport documents from my great-grandfather, Olaf Rove. I also hung an 1860 Lincoln photograph in a hand-carved frame that I had bought at an estate sale in Kerr County, Texas. Kerr was a tiny part of the Lone Star State that sided with the Union in the Civil War and has voted reliably Republican ever since. I wanted things on the wall that reminded me of where I came from and whom I admired.

The next day was my first full day of work. I arrived well before the 7:30 A.M. senior staff meeting and spent the day in a swirl. An ancient custodian, wearing a beat-up ball cap and missing several teeth, appeared at my office door at about 9:30 P.M., asking if he could clean up and empty my trash basket. We introduced ourselves and he went about his chores. When he'd finished, he turned and quietly said "good night," adding, "I hope you will honor the House." He left without waiting for a reply. It was a simple, powerful statement.

It also had a special poignancy because some of our predecessors had not "honored the House." Members of the Clinton staff had trashed offices in the Eisenhower Executive Office Building, ripped the W's off keyboards, left obscene messages on walls and furniture, scribbled profane graffiti in restrooms, poured glue or something sticky on furnishings, broke glass tops on desks, burned furniture with cigars, and left vulgar greetings on the voice-mail system.

The most disruptive thing they did was to remove phones from one office and put them in another. At the White House, each phone is programmed to work at a specific outlet. Plug it in elsewhere and it won't work. Departing Clinton staffers moved about one hundred phones to the wrong outlets and there was no simple way to figure out where each one belonged. Some of my colleagues were without phone service for almost a week as technicians sorted out the mess.

Every president since John Adams has lived in the White House. Jefferson was the first president to spend his entire term there and designed two long colonnades stretching to the east and west. Jackson planted a magnolia on the South Lawn that still stands there. Theodore Roosevelt ordered the West Wing built. Lincoln asked Ulysses Grant to stand on a couch in the East Room so guests could see the victor of Vicksburg. In a now seldom-used room on the first floor, FDR spent many hours looking at the latest maps and intelligence during World War II. Hanging above the fireplace is the last map he saw of the European front before he died.

Everyone's West Wing office had a story behind it. Mine involved the former First Lady and then junior senator from New York, Hillary Clinton. She had occupied the office in the previous administration and, upon moving into it, I noticed that there was a full-length mirror on the side of a bookshelf. It was the only such mirror I could find in a private office in the West Wing.

Early in 2001, I was speaking to constituents for an upstate New York Republican congressman when I mentioned the mirror in Mrs. Clinton's old office space. My comment drew a laugh, and also got back to Mrs. Clinton. A few days later she was at the White House for a meeting, after which she sought me out. She was blunt: "I heard what you said," she said. "I did not put that mirror in that office." I smiled. It was amusing to know that she was so sensitive about the mirror.

The Oval Office itself has a way of intimidating visitors. Before heading into the room, members of Congress and others would bluster that they were about to give the president a piece of their mind. Once inside, however, they somehow forgot their grievance and would compliment the president instead. Even hardened former KGB chief Vladimir Putin was stunned by the office: "Oh, my God!" is what he said when he laid eyes on it.

Now that I was in the White House, I saw that my long relationship with the president was both an advantage and a challenge. I was on the ground floor for this whole enterprise but could easily end up being resented by new members of the team for that reason. I had to figure out this new venue quickly to be effective and accepted.

I would have to do my homework on every issue that came up, as there was always someone more knowledgeable than me around. And I couldn't afford to take policy disagreements personally. I have strong opinions, but so do others. I had to operate on the assumption that everyone shared the same goal—crafting the best policy.

In those early months I defined my role. I pressed to have views laid on the table when colleagues were playing their cards close to the vest—I thought it was much better to have an open look at all points. And I pushed for consensus or at least a decision. If we didn't make decisions, then other policy actors in Washington would, or worse yet, we would be at the mercy of events.

I often reminded people to put political considerations out of their mind and instead focus on making good policy. I agree with the saying that "good policy makes good politics." I let people know that I would take care of the politics down the road, or let the politics take care of itself.

Then there was the tension between loyalty and ability. Both matter a great deal. But if you can't have both, I learned it was important to go with ability and work to foster loyalty. In a firefight, I'd rather have an able soldier next to me than an ineffective friend.

And because days were long and the pressures unrelenting, I went out of my way to develop cordial relations with as many people as possible. There is a long list of people who were indispensable in making the Bush White House run who will never see their name in print or even know that the full impact of their contributions was known or appreciated. Cultivating connections up and down the ranks is both right and smart to do if you want to get things done.

But I came up short in some ways. Andy Card once told a reporter I was a "formidable adversary." That comment stung. I didn't think of my immediate boss as an adversary, but apparently he saw me as one because he feared that my close relationship with Bush would allow me to do end runs around him. As much as I loved Andy, there wasn't anything I could do to alter his mind-set, so I looked for ways to be deferential without trimming my opinions to him or the president.

My day usually began at 6:15 A.M. with paperwork and newspapers, then a stop in the Oval when the president arrived around 6:40 A.M. That was followed by a visit with the chief of staff at 7:00 A.M. Those brief meetings were invaluable. They were a chance to gauge the president's mood and his thoughts on the day ahead, as well as find out what was on the mind of the chief of staff. It also allowed me to weigh in on overnight developments, the morning press, brewing controversies, or political gossip. After America went to war, the moment would also allow the president to unburden himself a little about the toll on the battlefield or the latest terrorist threats.

Andy Card, a veteran of the Reagan and Bush 41 administrations, knew that the urgency of events made it difficult to think beyond the day's headlines. So he created the Office of Strategic Initiatives (OSI), an in-house think tank to focus on long-term plans, and asked me to oversee it. Its meetings included all the senior staff and came to be called "Strategery" sessions, named after a *Saturday Night Live* skit that featured Will Ferrell as a Bush look-alike mangling the word *strategy*.

To augment the "Strategery" group, OSI's director, Barry Jackson, and I also organized the "Conspiracy of Deputies." This group consisted of the principal assistants to the members of "Strategery" and a few others. Barry drew them together almost every week to generate ideas. The group was critical to the smooth functioning of the West Wing because it gave more junior staffers a powerful way to influence West Wing policy priorities.

As I settled into my new office and Darby and I settled into our new life in Washington, we faced a problem: books. We came from Texas with 158 boxes of them, but the shelves in our new home could hold a mere three or four boxes' worth. So we brought in Tom Baumgartner, an excellent carpenter from Austin and a family friend. He stayed with us for five months while he built shelves and cabinets and made other minor repairs to our home and provided us with one funny, lasting memory of working for the Bush White House. Tom, ever the consummate professional, has one unbreakable rule: no visitors if the homeowners aren't home. Period.

One day, Laura Bush unintentionally tested that rule. She stopped by unannounced to check out the remodeling. One of Tom's subcontractors answered the door and told an aide to the First Lady, "Sorry, no visitors." The shocked aide pressed, saying that the First Lady was good friends with the Roves and was certain that they wouldn't mind her stopping in. Mrs. Bush was waiting in her car and very interested in seeing the shelves. He repeated "no visitors" and went back to work. The First Lady had only one option. She stood in the side yard and jumped up and down to catch a glimpse of the bookshelf project through the windows. Fortunately, she has a sense of humor and a tolerance for eccentric carpenters.

At the White House one of my first tasks was to help execute a plan for the first 180 days of the Bush administration. The belief that the pivotal period in a president's first term is his first hundred days dates back to FDR, who used his first hundred days to carry out frantic legislating amid the Great Depression. But it's an arbitrary time frame. What really matters is the first 180 days, because voters look for real achievements by the middle of a president's first summer, when Congress breaks for its August recess. Major pieces of legislation need to be well along by then if they are to pass in the president's first year.

To occupy time during the Florida recounts, my staff had pulled together briefing books on the start of each modern president's term in office. What we found was that to be successful, a president has to push for ideas he campaigned on, treat the other party with respect, and avoid getting roped into unnecessary fights, especially on issues that were not addressed in the campaign.

Bush's instinct was to do all of these things. In his first hundred days, he met with 301 members of Congress and was the first president to attend a congressional retreat of the opposition party, accepting invitations to both the Senate and House Democratic getaway sessions. But the outreach didn't succeed at dispelling the animosity against him.

Coming into office in January 2001, we knew that we would have a steep hill to climb. A CBS poll found that only 51 percent saw the president as legitimately elected; just 19 percent of Democrats and 12 percent of African-Americans agreed he was. His first postinaugural Gallup poll job approval rating was a respectable 57 percent, 6 points better than Ronald Reagan received and only a point below Clinton's number and 2 points below Nixon's. But Bush's disapproval rating was 25 percent, the highest of any modern president when he came into office (George H. W. Bush came in with a 12 percent disapproval rating, and Ronald Reagan with 13 percent). A *Wall Street Journal*/NBC News poll found that 40 percent of voters were uncertain or pessimistic about Bush's doing a good job and only 41 percent in a *Washington Post*/ABC News poll said he had a mandate. Getting off to a strong start could make or break Bush's presidency.

So with Andy Card's approval, Josh Bolten, Karen Hughes, I, and others fleshed out a clear 180-day plan focused on tax cuts, education reform, Bush's faith-based initiative, and energy policy. Senate majority leader Trent Lott privately advised us not to shove too much into the congressional pipeline or it would complicate things in the Senate. Following the 2000 elections, the Senate was evenly divided—fifty Republicans and fifty Democrats. We had the edge because the Constitution gave the vice president a vote to break tie votes, a power the GOP used in order to give itself the chairmanship of each committee. It was a slim margin to move legislation, and one that could be upset if we pushed for too much too quickly. To make sure we heard him, Lott repeated his advice to the press.

But things in the Senate were about to grow a lot more complicated. On May 24, 2001, Vermont senator Jim Jeffords, who had just won reelection as a Republican, defected to the Democrats, swinging control to the opposition party. Why did he do it? Publicly, one reason Jeffords gave in the spring of 2001 was that he wanted Bush to remove $200 billion from his tax cut and divert it to special education funding under the Individuals with Disabilities Education Act (IDEA) and to make the increase automatic in future federal budgets. He told the White House that he wouldn't vote for our tax cut unless we gave him his special education money.

The White House balked at the request. Too much of the budget was already on autopilot and a 300 percent increase in IDEA funding was huge, especially for a program that lacked accountability and was known for waste and fraud. If special education received more money, we wanted it matched with reforms that would focus on results. White House staff, including Margaret Spellings, made these points to Jeffords. He wasn't going to budge.

In truth, special education funding was only one thing on his mind. Personal rivalry and pique also seemed to be part of his motivation. He didn't like that Bush had developed a close relationship with New Hampshire senator Judd Gregg, a member of the Health, Education, Labor and Pensions (HELP) Committee, and was working with him on the No Child Left Behind (NCLB) reforms. It didn't seem to matter that Gregg was far better informed than Jeffords on education policy.

Jeffords made his displeasure known as early as January 25, when

Bush kicked off the push for education reform with an event at Merritt Elementary School in Washington, D.C. Jeffords rode to the event in a White House van with Congressman George Miller and Senator Ted Kennedy, the top Democrats on the House and Senate committees that would consider the NCLB bill. Jeffords complained about being used as a prop and expressed his disappointment in Gregg's involvement. He was also grumpy that Congressman John Boehner, the Republican chairman of the House Education Committee, somehow ended up in the limousine with Bush.

Apparently, whatever it was just kept eating away at Jeffords and he met with Tom Daschle, the Democratic Senate leader, to talk about it. Shortly after the 2000 election, Daschle had gone looking for a Republican to switch parties and flip control of the Senate. His targets were Jeffords, Lincoln Chafee of Rhode Island, and John McCain of Arizona.

On Tuesday, May 15, Jeffords met with Daschle and Senate Democratic whip Harry Reid in Jeffords's office in the Capitol. As Daschle reported it, "Jim got right down to business. He had three primary concerns, and they could be summarized as cows, committees, and co-workers."

"Cows" was the Northeast Dairy Compact, a price-fixing scheme that benefited northeastern milk producers but drove up the price of milk for consumers. Bush opposed it. Jeffords wanted assurances that Democrats would protect it.

Since Jeffords would lose his Republican committee assignments if he switched, Democrats offered him a plum assignment, chairmanship of the Environmental and Public Works Committee, which Reid was entitled to if Democrats became the majority. "Jim was blown away by the generosity of Harry's offer," Daschle wrote. Jeffords later wrote that I tried to "smear" him by "suggesting that [his] motivation was for a better committee assignment." But it was clear Jeffords was uncomfortable with Senate Republican term limits that would force him to relinquish his chairmanship of the HELP Committee at the end of 2002.

On Jeffords's third point—co-workers—Democratic leaders assured him that all his office and committee staffers would have jobs. "With that we shook hands, and the deal was done," Daschle wrote with obvious pride. Nine days later, Jeffords announced his switch.

Just before the announcement, Jeffords told Republican senator Olympia Snowe that he "was seriously thinking of switching." She alerted Andy Card, who invited Jeffords to visit with the president.

While sitting with Jeffords in the Oval Office, it quickly became clear to President Bush that nothing constructive could be said. Jeffords was withdrawn and unresponsive to arguments to stay in the GOP. The president made a low-key case for what a change in the Senate control would mean and Jeffords mumbled in reply. Jeffords did make clear that if he did switch, he wouldn't jeopardize the Bush tax cut and then offered the president some gratuitous and lame advice—that if Bush didn't increase IDEA funding, he'd be defeated for reelection.

Bush wasn't overjoyed by the meeting's outcome. But he wasn't angry, either—certainly not as upset as I was. He accepted Jeffords's defection, knew it had little to do with him, and understood it would have far-reaching implications for his agenda. But one of Bush's best qualities is that when bad news hits, he absorbs it, with a touch of fatalism but also with renewed determination to focus on what he can do constructively to accomplish what needs to be done. Bush gets calmer as times get harder.

Jeffords later offered conflicting explanations for his switch. He claimed to be uncomfortable with the Republican agenda, saying at his May 24 news conference that he did "disagree with the president on very fundamental issues: the issues of choice, the direction of the judiciary, tax and spending decisions, missile defense, energy and the environment, and a host of other issues, large and small." But Bush had spent two years making his ideas and proposals clear. For Jeffords to say he was shocked at Bush's positions in 2001 was disingenuous, especially after our campaign worked to help him win reelection and after he'd insisted he be made chairman of Bush's Vermont delegation to the Republican National Convention.

Our concern during this episode was what would happen if we caved to the senator's demands. Rewarding him with $200 billion would be giving in to blackmail and would give every other senator license to make outlandish spending demands. That would make it difficult to pass the rest of our agenda, let alone enforce any level of spending discipline.

In the end, Tom Daschle and Senate Democrats didn't attempt to increase special education funding 300 percent or make it mandatory. Democrats declined to push for it even after Obama was elected.

Senator Jeffords did live up to one promise. He didn't allow his switch to block the president's tax cuts. And it was a good thing for our economy he didn't. Our economy and our country were about to be tested in a way that would make Jeffords's defection seem almost inconsequential, irrelevant.

CHAPTER 15

Thinking Big

———•◆•———

Bush's presidency was and is largely defined by war. But it began with ambitious, transformative ideas about domestic policy—and to this day, many Americans are unaware of his achievements, or get them wrong.

Bush critics believed he was both against science and saving the environment; that his tax cuts were too costly, favored the rich, and hurt the economy; and that his education reform was underfunded and ineffective. But these criticisms are not based on the facts, or real outcomes.

And Bush didn't have critics only on the left. He was also sniped at by some on the right who bought into the false story line that he didn't control federal spending, that he didn't take a stronger hand with Congress by vetoing more legislation, and that two of his central domestic policy efforts (education reform and adding a prescription drug benefit to Medicare) expanded rather than contracted the scope of the federal government. Critics on the right say Bush's compassionate conservatism made the GOP lose touch with its small-government principles. But these criticisms also stem from a misreading of the facts, of the man, and of the reforms he enacted that ingrained conservative principles into lasting policies in Washington.

All of these Bush myths deserve to be exposed and blown up.

Let's start with taxes. When Bush was sworn in on January 20, 2001, the economy was lurching into recession and the federal government was taking a bigger share of the U.S. economy in taxes than in any year since 1944. Adjusting for inflation, Washington collected twice as much income tax revenue in 2001 as it did in 1981. Bush summed up his view this way: "Enough is enough. The American people deserve tax relief."

In response, on June 7, 2001, Congress approved a tax relief package that was shaped to win bipartisan support in Congress. In the end, a quarter of Senate Democrats voted for the tax cut. But with this support came a few revisions to Bush's proposals. The total tax cut was slimmed to $1.3 trillion from a proposed $1.6 trillion. The bill that Bush signed into law also let the tax cuts expire at the end of 2010, lowered the top rate to 35 percent (not 33 percent, as Bush wanted), and included a $300 rebate sent directly to taxpayers—all concessions to Democrats. But the tax relief followed Bush's blueprint. It reduced federal income tax rates for everyone who paid income taxes. The child tax credit was doubled from $500 to $1,000 a year per child. The penalty on working married couples was reduced. The death tax was to be phased out in 2010. And tax-favored retirement savings plans were expanded.

Bush's support for tax cuts was grounded in three premises. First, he understood that money collected from the people belonged to them, not the government. Many Democrats believe paying higher taxes is a virtue, a proxy for "compassion" for the poor. They would rather have high taxes and a lower standard of living than low taxes and a higher standard of living. To them, apparently, equality is more important than prosperity.

Second, Bush knew that while government cannot create wealth, it can affect the environment in which entrepreneurs flourish and jobs are created.

Third, Bush saw that tax cuts would create new jobs and ease the financial burdens of average Americans. That is exactly what his tax cuts did. Yet the myth has persisted that Bush tax cuts favored the rich, that they were "like Robin Hood in reverse," and were "skewed to the wealthiest."

In fact, 31.2 percent of the income tax cuts in the first year went to families making $40,000 per year or less and 56.5 percent to families making $75,000 per year or less. Wealthy individuals received a larger per capita tax cut because they paid more to begin with, but they received a smaller-percentage reduction in their tax burden. Families earning $40,000 per year or less received an average 96 percent income tax cut, while those earning $200,000 per year or more got an average 9 percent cut.

Wealthier taxpayers paid a bigger share of the income tax burden after Bush's tax cuts and less affluent families a smaller share. The top 20 percent of earners paid 81.2 percent of the income tax burden before the Bush tax cuts and an average of 84.3 percent afterward. The bottom 20 percent of income tax filers paid less than they had before because the new law removed 7.8 million families from the tax rolls.

Bush matched his 2001 tax cuts with additional cuts in 2003 that ended double taxation of dividends, reduced capital gains taxes, and cut small business taxes. These tax cuts—along with spending restraint—produced 52 straight months of job creation, and more than 8 million new jobs. The Bush years witnessed the longest period of economic growth since President Reagan. From 2000 to 2008, real gross domestic product (GDP) grew by more than 18.5 percent. Labor productivity increased an average of 1.5 percent annually, faster than in the 1970s, '80s, and '90s. Real after-tax income per capita increased by more than 11 percent. The American economy grew from $9.7 trillion in 2000 to $14.2 trillion at the end of 2008, even while suffering a financial crisis late in the Bush presidency. That $4.5 trillion in growth alone is bigger than the entire Japanese economy. Such things do not happen by accident.

Bush's tax cuts are often criticized for having returned us to "deficit spending." In fact, the main causes for deficits during Bush's time in the White House were the recession that greeted him when he took office and the economic fallout of the terrorist attacks on 9/11. The result was three straight years of falling federal tax revenues. When revenues fall, deficits balloon. When revenues fall three consecutive years, deficits balloon a lot. The way to eliminate deficits is not by raising taxes; it is to pursue pro-growth policies, to which tax cuts are central.

Tax cuts don't fully pay for themselves by increasing revenues, but history shows that the cost of tax cuts and their effects on the deficit are considerably offset by an expanding economy.

In fact, Bush focused on creating the conditions to jump-start the economy (which produced a record 20 percent increase in tax revenues over his eight years in office) and restraining nonsecurity discretionary federal spending. In Clinton's last budget, that category of spending grew 16 percent. By Bush's final years, it was held below inflation. Bush's veto threats over spending worked: in terms of a percentage of GDP, economic growth and spending restraint hemmed the government into spending far below the average over the last three decades. This also meant that federal deficits under Bush ran an average of 2 percent, close to the 1.7 percent average since World War II and significantly less than President Barack Obama's plan to run deficits to 5 percent of GDP over the next decade.

For the record, every alternative budget offered by Democrats during the Bush years called for more spending and higher taxes than the president's budget. For example, the proposed fiscal 2002 alternative Democratic budget called for $694.3 billion in discretionary outlays, compared to $660.6 billion in Bush's budget. Democratic critics were wrong about Bush economics and many were hypocrites.

ON EDUCATION, BUSH'S CORE insight was to use the federal government as a lever for reform while respecting that education is a state and local responsibility. Three days after his inauguration, Bush sent Congress No Child Left Behind, which required states to set academic standards for each grade. Students in grades three through eight would be tested annually and their schools held accountable for results. Parents would have the power of more information and more choices. States and school districts would have flexibility to craft programs to meet local needs. This preserved local control—while also demanding results. In exchange for accepting these federal policies, NCLB made sure states would receive federal money to help failing students catch up through tutoring, afterschool programs, or whatever else it took.

Bush was committed to improving education for everyone, but he was most animated by the gap in achievement between white and minority students. He repeatedly decried "the soft bigotry of low expectations" and thought shuffling children from grade to grade when they weren't ready bordered on criminal neglect.

For helping to redress that problem and others, NCLB is one of the great modern domestic policy successes. Because of NCLB, reading scores for nine-year-olds have improved more in the last nine years than in the previous twenty-eight years combined, and math scores have reached record highs. Improvements were greatest among African-American and Hispanic children and students with disabilities.

NCLB also changed the conversation about education. There's less talk now about money and more about how children are doing; less talk about feel-good pedagogy and more about what works, such as phonics. That's what happens when parents have the tools they need to find out if their child's school is doing its job.

But the education establishment continues to look down on NCLB. Many complain that the law forces educators to "teach to the test." Well, if it is a sound test that measures knowledge of the basics, that is a good thing. But let's get this straight: NCLB requires an annual reading and math test in grades three through eight and then once in high school. One test a year is too much? And, after all, it allows parents to know if their children are learning. Some critics also insist NCLB has focused too much on failing students at the expense of average and gifted ones. But since the law was carried out, test scores have risen for every category of learner.

Other critics say NCLB elevates reading and math to the exclusion of social studies, science, art, and music. But the facts tell a different story. NCLB's improvements in reading have led to improving performance in all other subjects—in 2006, for example, NCLB produced the best history scores ever for all groups and all grades. Mastering reading helps children master other core subjects.

Another line of attack on NCLB is that it is "desperately underfunded," in the words of Obama's secretary of education, Arne Duncan. This is nonsense. Despite slowing the overall growth of discretionary nonsecurity spending, Bush increased federal outlays on elementary and secondary education by 34 percent. States have complained that the federal government imposed new unfunded costs on them. Connecticut even sued the federal government over this issue. But in the end, it lost. The reason is simple: the federal government pays the cost of testing. What critics really want is for Washington to pay for the job that states should already be doing—making certain every student learns.

No Child Left Behind, then, has been a great success by the standard that matters: what children learn. But I'm not embarrassed to say that the law has also brought political benefits to the GOP. In 1996, only 16 percent of voters for whom education was the top issue voted for Bob Dole over Bill Clinton. After Bush talked about education endlessly during his 2000 presidential campaign, he received 44 percent of the vote from those for whom education was their top issue. In March 2001, Gallup reported that for the first time in its sixty-six years of polling, Americans trusted Republicans more on education than Democrats. That's because Republicans have better ideas.

IF BUSH'S IDEAS ABOUT education were radical, so was his belief that faith-based groups should be allowed to compete for government grants without having to jettison what made them effective or change their missions. They couldn't use taxpayer dollars to preach or refuse to serve someone because of religion, but Bush said, "The days of discriminating against religious institutions, simply because they are religious, must come to an end."

He set up a White House office to promote these efforts and issued an executive order providing religious charities equal access to government grant monies. No longer could only secular nonprofits apply for the roughly $20 billion available in competitive grants each year from eleven federal agencies to confront addiction, homelessness, and domestic violence. By 2007, roughly 10.8 percent of these funds were going to faith-based charities. Bush's focus was not whether you were a sacred or secular organization, but whether your program changed lives.

The White House Office of Faith-Based and Community Initiatives organized conferences that gave tens of thousands of social entrepreneurs in religious and community charities advice on how to run their organizations better, raise funds, and apply for grants. It also sought to increase the number of volunteer mentors for children of prisoners, provided the first-ever voucher program for drug treatment with pilot projects in fourteen states, and organized efforts to help prisoners reenter society. The Faith-Based Office also battled discrimination against religious organizations that had been denied FEMA disaster recovery aid and historic preservation funds or found their housing aid jeopardized.

But no good deed goes unpunished. We were accused of using the Faith-Based Initiative to channel money to evangelical groups as "patronage for its friends on the Christian right" and "one of the largest patronage programs in American history," as one hyperventilating Democrat put it. This was lunacy. The Associated Press investigated the charge in 2003 and found no such pattern.

The criticism always struck me as odd because the first two directors of the initiative were Democrats: University of Pennsylvania professor John DiIulio, Jr., and Jim Towey, who had been former Florida governor Lawton Chiles's director of human services and Mother Teresa's lawyer. They, and their successor Jay Hein, regularly held events with Democrats and they helped more than thirty governors and more than one hundred mayors—mostly Democrats—open their own faith-based offices to mobilize what Bush called "the armies of compassion."

Others attacked the program because it "punched a dangerous hole in the wall between church and state," and they backed up their charges with lawsuits. But the courts disagreed: the Bush administration prevailed in every major legal challenge.

Still, critics saw evidence that the initiative allowed "religious organizations . . . to discriminate against people they hire." But the right of faith-based groups to consider religion in their hiring decisions is protected by Title VII of the Civil Rights Act of 1964 and was upheld in 1987 by the Supreme Court. How can a religious organization maintain its identity if it is forced to hire people who don't share its faith? The law was silent on whether such groups can hire on a religious basis while receiving public money. The Bush administration tried to clarify that they could but repeatedly faced threats of a Democratic filibuster in the Senate if we tried to push legislation that would resolve this question.

In the end, President Barack Obama chose to preserve the faith-based initiative and the White House office that runs it and spoke glowingly of the efforts of governors and mayors to encourage the groups. But unlike Bush, Obama tapped a political operative to head his Faith-Based Office—Joshua DuBois, Obama's presidential campaign's religious outreach director. No one in the press has raised a peep. Mixing politics and religion is a problem only if Republicans can be accused of it.

BUSH LEFT OFFICE WITH the reputation that he was hostile to the environment and uninterested in solving the pressing issue of global warming. Much of the criticism of his administration is focused on its approach to the Kyoto Protocol, named for the Japanese city where it was written in 1997. But here again, the record shows quite the opposite: he was aggressive and smart on this front from the moment he took office.

An international agreement to limit greenhouse gas emissions, Kyoto had a laudable but wholly impractical goal that was impossible to achieve. For one thing, Kyoto left out the developing world, including China (now the world's largest emitter), India, and Brazil. To limit greenhouse gas emissions by some countries while ignoring the world's worst violators made no sense. For one thing, nations could evade Kyoto by moving energy-intensive jobs to developing countries not subject to its limits. As it was, most countries that joined Kyoto failed to meet their emission reduction targets.

The estimates were that Kyoto could have cost America up to $400 billion and almost 5 million jobs, while nations like China got off scot-free. The *Washington Post* editorialized that complying with Kyoto would have required a 35 percent emission reduction, a move it described as "radical" and one "that would be politically untenable because of the unpopular taxes it would require and the disruption it would cause in the daily lives of most Americans."

Many Americans believed this was unfair and unwise—and so, overwhelmingly, did the U.S. Senate. In 1997, it unanimously passed a resolution saying that America should not participate in any climate agreement that would harm our economy or failed to include developing countries. Kyoto did both and President Clinton never submitted it to the Senate for ratification.

To decide what to do, Bush formed a Cabinet-level working group that met for ten weeks. The group heard from scientists offering a wide spectrum of views and asked the highly respected National Academy of Sciences to provide the most up-to-date information about what was known and unknown about climate change science. Following those deliberations, Bush said that Kyoto "was fatally flawed" and that the United States would not participate.

You'd have thought the president had thrown a brick through a cathedral's stained-glass windows. Critics who never criticized Clinton for refusing to move forward with Kyoto went ballistic against Bush. "When President Bush trashed the Kyoto treaty on climate change, the message the world got was that the Bushies will do whatever they please, on a range of issues, and if the world doesn't like it—tough," wrote *New York*

Times columnist Thomas Friedman. Representative Dick Gephardt thundered, "it must not stand."

In truth, Kyoto was pure political symbolism—an empty, hypocritical way for nations to pretend they were doing something when they weren't.

Bush wanted a dramatically different approach: he wanted to focus on cost-efficient ways to produce the biggest energy savings which, in turn, would restrain and then reduce greenhouse gas emissions. He also believed that the emerging technologies that made efficiency gains possible would keep good-paying environment-related jobs at home. His record shows that this approach proved to be environmentally savvy and successful.

Here are facts not one person in a hundred knows. By 2006, the last year for which numbers are available, only one industrialized economy grew its GDP *and at the same time* reduced its absolute level of greenhouse gas emissions: the United States. After rejecting Kyoto, Bush committed $22 billion to climate change technology, research, and deployment—more than any president in history and more than the rest of the world combined.

This patient diplomacy paid off at the July 2008 G-8 meeting when major industrialized nations adopted Bush's approach and scrapped Kyoto's scheme of arbitrary, mandatory reductions for only developed economies. The G-8 instead agreed that climate efforts must include developing nations such as China, India, and Brazil and that progress depends on "affordable, new, more advanced, and innovative technologies." It took years, but Bush's persistent leadership had committed the world to a new approach, and put America on the path to exceed his 2012 goals. This, in turn, provided President Obama a substantial portion of what's needed to reach his goal of a 14 percent emissions reduction by 2020.

Under President Bush, the nation's air, water, and land got cleaner, as they have for nearly forty years under Republican and Democratic presidents. The only difference is that on many measures, environmental improvement under Bush moved at a faster pace than under President Clinton.

Between 2001 and 2007, for example, air pollution fell 12 percent. The administration put in place the most stringent air quality standards in history, cutting sulfur dioxide and nitrogen oxide emissions from diesel engines by 90 percent and from coal-fired power plants by nearly 70 percent. It also imposed the first national rule on mercury emissions from power plants, saying they must be cut by 70 percent.

The Clinton/Gore administration talked about doing some of this, but never carried it out. And the Obama administration and environmentalists have held hostage Bush's rules that would have required utilities to spend tens of billions of dollars to upgrade older, less efficient coal-fired plants with the latest pollution controls—which would have an immediate effect on greenhouses gases—in favor of pushing climate change legislation that will produce no tangible benefits for decades. Go figure.

Bush's strong environmental record goes on and on: it includes his "Healthy Forest" initiative, which improved more than 27 million acres of federal forest, the $6.5 billion he spent to erase the national parks' maintenance and repairs backlog, his initiative to restore 3 million acres of wetlands, his brownfields legislation that in just two years doubled the number of grants to clean up environmentally damaged industrial sites, and his creation of the world's largest marine preserve. When historians look at facts, they will conclude he was forceful and innovative about protecting the environment.

EVERY PRESIDENT HAS AN issue that the frontier of science thrusts upon him, and Bush not only reckoned with his, but also helped change the course of an important branch of science. President Bush was not looking for a fight on embryonic stem cell research; the fight came to him. When he took office, commercial start-ups and disease advocacy groups were looking for large-scale funding from the federal government, hoping it would lead to cures for terrible diseases. As a parting "gift," the Clinton administration left a legal opinion that might allow this kind of federal funding—despite a 1995 law (called the Dickey Amendment) that banned federal funding of research in which human embryos are destroyed. The Clinton administration took the novel approach that if private money were used to destroy embryos and to produce stem cells derived from them, then public money could pay for research on those same stem cells.

In early February 2001, eighty Nobel laureates wrote Bush supporting federal funding and opposing the Dickey Amendment. Congressional leaders mobilized in favor of funding, too. A month later, Health and Human Services secretary Tommy Thompson testified that he opposed restricting federal funds for this purpose. We were in danger of having this issue decided for us. Bush needed to decide where he stood on the issue. Scientists believe embryonic stem cells have remarkable healing abilities because of their potential to be transformed into any type of cells or tissues. If true, they could help replace diseased or defective organs and body tissue and help those afflicted with illnesses ranging from spinal injuries to juvenile diabetes to Parkinson's.

The problem in 2001 was that research into unlocking the mysteries of embryonic stem cells involved collecting these stem cells from living human embryos by destroying the embryos. Looking ahead, it was also clear that large-scale embryo destruction might be necessary before stem-cell-derived tissues could be effectively used to treat disease. To minimize a patient's body's rejecting the foreign cells, researchers envisioned eventually creating personalized therapies, harvesting embryonic stem cells from a cloned embryonic copy of the patient. That would require creating human life and then destroying it to acquire the personalized embryonic stem cells needed for a cure. Researchers didn't talk much about cloning people or creating human embryos on a mass scale to kill them for research or medical use. But these were the gruesome realities involved.

Deputy White House Chief of Staff for Policy Josh Bolten pulled in the Domestic Policy Council deputy director, a brainy lawyer named Jay Lefkowitz, to lead a review of the issue, on which he and I worked closely. For the better part of five months, Bush met with leading advocates and opponents of stem cell research as bioethicists, molecular biologists, moral philosophers, and other experts made treks to the West Wing. On the same day, for example, he heard from the National Right to Life Committee and the Juvenile Diabetes Research Foundation, groups about as far apart as possible on this issue. He visited with Democratic and Republican members of Congress on both sides of the issue and sought out friends who were physicians, as well as friends whose families had been touched by illnesses like diabetes, and raised the issue in a Cabinet meeting. More than a few White House staffers were surprised when they answered their phones and found it was the president asking their opinions. He read voluminous briefing papers, articles from scientific journals, summaries of bioethical issues, and passages from Aldous Huxley's *Brave New World*. This issue had an intensely personal dimension for Bush: he has a deep reverence for human life, but he also had lost his four-year-old sister, Robin, to leukemia and watched Laura cope with her father's Alzheimer's.

In the course of exploring the issue, Jay and I had met University of Chicago physician-scientist turned humanist Leon Kass. In June, I asked his opinion of an idea Jay was tossing around: Was it morally permissible to spend taxpayer dollars on the existing embryonic stem cell lines that had been derived using private funds? We didn't resolve the issue that day, but it turned out to be the beginning of a solution.

Meanwhile, the lobbying was intense, particularly by the Juvenile Diabetes Research Foundation. John Brady had succeeded me in 1977 as College Republican national chairman. I hadn't heard from him in years, until he asked to see me about his preteen son, who was stricken with the disease. He brought me a survey from the foundation that showed strong support for embryonic stem cell research. I did Brady a favor and didn't carry the giant notebook into the Oval Office; the last thing Bush wanted to see was a poll.

On May 16, 2001, while I was in Atlanta for a GOP fund-raiser, an attendee asked for a word with me after the event. He had a child with diabetes and had been recruited by the foundation to lobby me. With anguish in his voice, he said, "They tell me if the president will only allow this research, my son will be made healthy." I understood his pain, but I was also angry: every scientist I'd heard from said that any potential diabetes therapy drawn from embryonic stem cells was, at best, years away. The man weeping uncontrollably in front of me had been given false hope by the foundation. All I could do was listen and commiserate. I didn't have the courage to tell him he'd been misled.

By late June, Bush wanted a final session to help put the bioethical issues facing him in sharp relief. I called Leon Kass and asked if he would bring an articulate proponent of embryonic stem cell research to debate the issues with him in front of the president. He suggested Daniel Callahan of the Hastings Center for Bioethics. On July 10, as Jay and I listened, Kass and Callahan met with the president for an hour and fifteen minutes. It was an extraordinary meeting. Callahan turned out—to Kass's surprise and ours—to have views similar to Kass's, though both ably laid out the pros and cons of the research being considered.

During the discussion, Bush asked Kass about the ethics of using embryonic stem cells that had been created before any decision about government funding. In that case, Kass responded, the federal government would not be complicit in their destruction, provided that the principle that had been violated was affirmed again and that no encouragement was given to future violations. If tax dollars were confined to supporting research using existing embryonic stem cell lines, the money could not be seen as an incentive to destroy future embryos, but could still advance science.

A few weeks later, Bush made up his mind: he would support federal funding for research using embryonic stem cells that had already been harvested but not for research on new lines of stem cells created after his announcement. Bush also decided he would expand research into ethically acceptable alternatives and create a Bioethics Council to monitor the progress. He became the first president to give a speech on a bioethical issue, trying his best to ensure that science did not get ahead of the humanity making it. It was not a political compromise, it was a moral solution to a difficult dilemma.

But Democrats saw in his decision a great opportunity to help them regain power. During the 2004 campaign, for example, John Kerry and John Edwards routinely demagogued the issue, with Edwards saying that if only Bush's ban were removed, actor Christopher Reeve, paralyzed by a horse riding accident, would "get up out of that wheelchair and walk again." Edwards's words were a cruel hoax—and perfectly in keeping with the kind of man he turned out to be. Bush twice vetoed legislation overturning his policy and twice it was sustained.

But the criticism—fierce and unrelenting—also came from prominent Republicans such as Nancy Reagan and Senators Orrin Hatch and John McCain. Other Republicans supported Bush—but reluctantly, tepidly, and through gritted teeth. The overwhelming consensus was that Bush's compromise position on embryonic stem cell research was politically unpopular. And it may well have been. But it was also vindicated in the end.

In November 2007, in articles in *Cell* and *Science*, researchers reported it was possible to create stem cells functionally identical to those taken from human embryos without using or destroying human embryos. Moreover, these cells could be obtained from adult individuals, avoiding any need for cloning to obtain personalized, rejection-proof therapies. This was an extraordinary breakthrough, precisely the kind of alternative Bush encouraged and hoped would occur. He helped steer scientific research in the direction of discovering exciting new frontiers while avoiding the morally troubling burden that industrial cloning and wholesale destruction of human embryos would carry.

SOME ON THE RIGHT argue that by putting the word *compassionate* in front of *conservatism*, George W. Bush somehow diminished the principles that have animated the conservative movement since at least the rise of Barry Goldwater in 1964. That wasn't my sense of it at all. Bush is among the more conservative presidents of the modern age. Just look at his tax cuts, pro-life and pro-family stands; his support of free trade and reducing regulation; his belief that competition improves health care, the environment, and Social Security; and his insistence on education results. In fact, his willingness to stake the first half of his second term on pushing for private accounts for Social Security alone should be enough to prove his conservative bona fides.

But the myth persists that he was a moderate Republican who went wobbly on conservative ideas. It likely persists for two reasons.

First, Bush lacks the harsh and judgmental edge of some other conservative political leaders. One aspect of his governing style was a concerted effort to calm inflamed passions. He tried to bring along members of the other party when he could. His aim as president was to steady the nation and not to tug at strings that would unravel the fabric of our society or politics. Like others who looked at the America of the 1960s and '70s, he understood what could follow when that fabric was pulled apart in either space.

Second, he did alter the course of the conservative movement that he came to lead. And the direction he steered it in was productive, principled, and healthy for the country.

Consider for a minute his policy goals of building an ownership society with health savings accounts, school vouchers, expanded access to private retirement accounts (including new hybrid systems that combine aspects of old-style pensions with 401[k]-type systems). His reforms struck at fundamental assumptions about the role of government, were built on the premise of creating individual control, and were aimed at transforming public policy. On education, it was to give parents a choice by giving them the information they needed about whether their children were really learning. On health care, it was to bring market forces to bear (both with health savings accounts and with a market-based prescription drug benefit) on a system dominated by government spending. On retirement, it was to let workers take personal responsibility for their golden years by setting aside and managing their money responsibly.

Where was conservatism headed before George W. Bush? Bill Clinton had won two presidential elections, even as the GOP won control of Congress in 1994, when the American people seemingly rejected his left-leaning policies. If that was the entire story, it would be easier to argue that conservatism was doing just fine before Bush came along. The story, however, has a few more turns to it. It's true Clinton signed welfare reform to win a second term. But politics in Washington also grew acrimonious during his last few years in office—capped by his impeachment—and the tone of the fighting was turning many voters against Republicans. The loss of House seats is one reason why Newt Gingrich stepped aside after the 1998 midterm elections. By 2000, Republicans were slowly being edged off the stage as the party lost support in suburban areas and ran out of big ideas its congressional majorities could push into law.

What the GOP specifically and the conservative movement in general needed were fresh ways to apply their ideas to emerging issues that would appeal to a broad cross-section of voters. They needed to provide solutions to problems Americans faced every day and talked about around the kitchen table. From the quality of their local schools, to the ability of a faith-based organization to help solve vexing social problems, to tax cuts that would help create jobs, to health-care reforms that put the patient and their doctor in charge, compassionate conservatism provided a framework for carrying conservative principles into a new era and made them relevant to a vast number of Americans. And it should be noted that Bush did use them to win two presidential elections and also to bolster Republican seats in Congress in 2002 and in 2004. One wonders what would have happened if Congress had followed Bush's lead and enacted other big reforms before the 2006 congressional elections.

CHAPTER 16

9/11

——— • ◆ • ———

September 11, 2001, began bright and clear on the East Coast, especially in southwest Florida. We had come in the night before and had dinner with Jeb Bush and friends at the Colony Beach Resort on Longboat Key. Conversation touched lightly on the next day's schedule and dwelled mostly on a book on the Civil War the president was reading. No one was thinking that wartime leadership would become a pressing topic.

That morning, the president got up well before the sun and ran three miles. As Bush neared the end of his run and was going by the press pool, Richard Keil of Bloomberg News yelled out his interest in running with the president. Bush invited Keil to join him and, together, they ran another two miles or so. Bush then received his national security briefing from 8:10 to 8:25 A.M., and immediately left for Emma E. Booker Elementary School in nearby Sarasota. The event was aimed at promoting the No Child Left Behind legislation then pending before Congress.

At 8:46 A.M. Eastern time, American Airlines Flight 11 flew into the North Tower of the World Trade Center in New York City.

Within a minute or two, my assistant Susan Ralston called about the incident. It wasn't clear whether it was a commercial or private plane. No details on loss of life or damage. I walked over to the president, who was a few feet away with Secretary of Education Rod Paige, shaking hands with staff and teachers outside the school, and passed on the information. I was the first to tell him the news. He nodded, shot me a quizzical look, and said, "Get more details." We both thought it an odd, tragic accident. I assumed at some point the president would say something about it.

Wherever a president has an event, there's a nearby room called the "staff hold." White House Communications installs special phones for the president and his staff. Pick one up and someone with a quiet military voice answers; you make a request and a moment or two later, you're talking to anybody you want, anywhere in the world. That morning, Bush stepped into the hold to take a call from Condi Rice, who had the same sketchy information I'd given him. He then went into the second-grade classroom for a reading demonstration.

Chief of Staff Andy Card, Staff Secretary Harriet Miers, Press Secretary Ari Fleischer, Communications aide Dan Bartlett, other traveling staff, and I remained behind in the hold. I wanted to check the TV for an update on the World Trade Center "accident," but there wasn't a TV in the room. We rounded one up, and I unceremoniously crawled under the television stand and found the wall jack for the cable. With the TV on, it was apparent this wasn't an accident. A few minutes later, at 9:03 A.M., we received horrifying proof when United Airlines Flight 175 flew into the South Tower. In a last malevolent gesture, the hijacker-pilot wagged his wings to take out as many floors as possible when the plane slammed into the Trade Center.

As chief of staff, Andy Card sat in on the president's intelligence briefings, and because terrorists had attacked the World Trade Center in 1993, Andy immediately thought al-Qaeda was behind this latest assault. He quickly went into the adjoining classroom to tell the president. Aware that cameras were trained on him and that reporters were watching, President Bush waited for a few minutes after Andy whispered the news of the second plane. When the students finished reading, he excused himself and quietly walked out of the classroom and into the staff hold. The president wanted to project calm.

As Bush came into the hold, the television was replaying footage of the second plane smashing into the Trade Center. The president said simply, quietly, and in a clear voice, "We're at war. Get me the director of the

FBI and the vice president." He then talked with Condi Rice and reached New York governor George Pataki, who was in Manhattan that morning. Details were hazy, but it was clear that unknown assailants were executing a well-planned attack, of unknown dimensions, against America. The room was a swirl of activity and filled with a staccato of phone conversations. The steadiness of Marine Corps Major Paul Montanus, the military aide who patched through our calls, was reassuring.

After whispering the news of the second plane to the president, Andy told Eddie Marinzel, the head of the Secret Service detail. Eddie immediately began making arrangements to beef up the motorcade and get it ready to move. He was eager to get the president out of the school, to Air Force One, and airborne. But before the president left, Bush wanted to speak to the media. Ari, Dan, the president, and I collaborated on a brief statement, with Bush scribbling on a pad at a short table meant for elementary school students.

The president described "a national tragedy" in the "apparent terrorist attack on our country." He spoke for less than a minute. Just over half an hour after American Flight 11 struck the Trade Center, it was still not clear whether it had been an act of domestic or international terrorism. So Bush announced he had ordered "a full-scale investigation to hunt down and to find those folks who committed this act." He proclaimed, "Terrorism against our nation will not stand," and closed by asking for a moment of silence. We left the school at 9:35 A.M. Less than three minutes later, American Airlines Flight 77 smashed into the western side of the Pentagon.

I rode with Bush in the limo to the airport. The president was quiet, but his face revealed his intense focus. The Secret Service agents seemed unusually cool, too, as the motorcade barreled north from the school.

We moved much faster than normal: it took a little over five minutes to make the four-and-a-half-mile trip to the airport. Eddie had arranged for the Sarasota Police Department to mobilize every available patrol car, so the motorcade was surrounded by a flood of them. The Secret Service was clearly anxious to get the president into a space they had complete control over—Air Force One.

During the car ride, the president received word of the Pentagon strike. Not only had terrorists attacked a symbol of America's financial strength in New York City, they also wanted to destroy the headquarters of America's military might. Bush's jawline firmed. I was aghast at the news and probably seemed anxious; he seemed preternaturally calm.

When any president arrives at an airport to board Air Force One, there's a certain amount of ritual. The presidential limo pulls up to the plane's front stairs, followed by a long motorcade of vans, SUVs, an ambulance, and other vehicles. The president emerges from the limo, waves to the crowd behind barricades, thanks hosts who have accompanied him, and shakes hands with the airport personnel and guests who've come to see him off. Then he walks alone up the steps to Air Force One at a leisurely pace, stopping to wave again to the people on the tarmac. All this is carefully filmed by the press, whose members have rushed forward to get a good picture. Only after the president has boarded do staff members and the press, guests, and other straphangers enter the plane. It usually takes another fifteen minutes before passengers get seated, the motorcade leaves, the doors are closed and the stairs withdrawn, and the engines power up.

Not this day. At the Sarasota airport, the Secret Service shoved everyone onto the plane as rapidly as possible. The agents made the press drop all their equipment before boarding so it could be quickly swept for explosives a second time, even though it had been swept earlier at the school.

The president beckoned me into his office after we boarded. As I sat in the swivel chair across the desk from him, I could see an Air Force crewman hanging out the still-open door as the engines throttled up. There was only empty air between him and concrete about twenty-four feet below. The crewman pulled the door shut as the plane moved down the taxiway.

I quickly dialed Darby on my cell and told her I was okay. She asked what was wrong. I repeated that I was okay and then realized she might not know what was happening. Darby doesn't leave the TV on as background noise and was getting ready for an event that morning. She hadn't seen what was unfolding in New York and at the Pentagon. "Turn on the television," I told her. "I'm okay, but I have to go."

The 747 shot down the runway with a force I had never experienced. Once in the air, Air Force One then stood on its tail to get as high as possible, as rapidly as possible. I had not been in a jet at such a steep incline.

The Secret Service was concerned about the possibility of terrorists with shoulder-launched ground-to-air missiles, and wanted AF-1 out of range quickly. It had taken less than ten minutes from the limo's arrival at the bottom of Air Force One's steps to get airborne. The plane flew first northeast across the Florida peninsula and then, once over the Atlantic, turned north.

Andy Card huddled with Eddie Marinzel, Air Force Major Tom Gould, and Air Force One pilot Colonel Mark Tillman in the president's bedroom cabin at the front of the plane. Marinzel had been in touch with Secret Service headquarters in Washington and told Card that Air Force One could not go to D.C. because it was an unknown security environment. Tillman was told to circle until a decision on Air Force One's flight path was made. In an earlier conversation with Bush, Card had delivered the same message and had seen Bush's negative reaction. He wanted company delivering the bad news a second time. He and Marinzel came into the president's office to deliver it.

The Secret Service agent insisted Bush stay away from Washington. But Bush had a responsibility as well, and that was to lead the nation. He acquiesced—for now—but was clearly not happy about the delay. He had an immediate and instinctive sense that he belonged back in the capital. Whenever the subject came up, his jaw clenched and I could see anger welling up, which he contained. He understood the Secret Service had their obligation to protect him, but he knew that his duties were different than theirs. At one point, he even barked at Card, "I am the president!" when Andy tried to importune him to listen to the Secret Service's concerns. Later that day Bush would override the Service's concerns and those of others, after being about as angry as I'd ever seen him.

Almost immediately after we were airborne, Vice President Cheney phoned with a tough decision for Bush to make. The Air Force had scrambled to put up a combat jet patrol over Washington but needed rules of engagement. What should happen if another plane were hijacked and could not be controlled? Could it be shot down? The president uttered a forceful "Yes." Cheney asked again and Bush said, "You have my authorization."

After he explained to Andy and me what he'd just done—he had just agreed that a plane loaded with innocent civilians could be shot down if it were considered a threat—I was a bit taken aback at the evenness of his voice. Still, I could see the enormity of the decision weighing on him in the hardness of his eyes and the tightness around his mouth. Bush then quietly showed his concern for any young pilot who was ordered to shoot down an airliner. He'd been a jet fighter pilot and knew the emotions this would bring. He left the thought dangling.

Information was now coming to the plane fast and continuously. Two planes had smashed into the World Trade Center and one had gone into the Pentagon; we knew what the terrorists had in mind. No hijacked plane was going to be brought safely to ground with the passengers alive unless the hijackers were overcome. At 9:45 A.M., Secretary of Transportation Norm Mineta ordered all civilian aircraft out of the sky immediately.

By now, too many people were coming into the cabin to listen in, to ask for information, or just to be there. Andy sent a blocking guard, Blake Gottesman—a twenty-one-year-old White House aide who was standing in that day for the president's personal aide, Logan Walters—to intercept anyone venturing up the hallway and to inquire what they needed. The number of unwanted visitors to the president's cabin dropped.

Vice President Cheney called back shortly and asked for reconfirmation of the shoot-down authorization. Ari then stuck his head in and the president told him of his decision. The difference between that morning's Sarasota visit and the decisions Bush had just made was jarring. We were no longer talking about reading scores, phonemic awareness, and education reform. Now the topic was life and death, and war and peace.

At 9:58 A.M., the South Tower of the World Trade Center collapsed. Millions of tons of steel, concrete, glass, and human beings hit the ground at more than 120 miles per hour. A cloud of dust then obscured what soon came to be known simply as Ground Zero and much of the rest of lower Manhattan. Five minutes later, United Airlines Flight 93 barreled into an open field near Shanksville, Pennsylvania, a fact we would not know for hours.

Air Force One didn't have a satellite TV feed, so we could watch television only when passing over a city with local broadcasting. This spotty coverage meant we came in and out of touch with what America was seeing and often saw the events only when footage of a moment was rerun. It added to the morning's surreal and chaotic feeling.

Since departing Sarasota, Andy Card and the Secret Service had been working out Air Force One's flight path. At one point, Andy and the president went forward to his bedroom cabin to talk about it. Bush again emphatically said he wanted to return to the nation's capital. Andy patiently explained how security officials on the plane and in D.C. felt the uncontrolled airspace over Washington was not safe.

Major Gould and others recommended flying to Barksdale Air Force Base in Shreveport, Louisiana, headquarters of the Eighth Air Force. By coincidence, Barksdale was engaged in a nuclear training exercise and was already at the highest alert level. Unlike other bases within range of Air Force One, it had already been secured. At Barksdale, the plane could be refueled and the president would have access to ground communications links with officials in Washington and elsewhere, such as Secretary of State Colin Powell, who was in South America. There were facilities that would allow him to speak directly to the nation. The president agreed. Soon after, Air Force One rose higher and banked to the west. The press aboard the plane were told we were at 40,000 or 45,000 feet.

The president was still not happy about our flight path. He expressed his anger bluntly and forcefully at me, telling me how important it was for him to get back to Washington and how fears about his security were overblown. He knew there was nothing I could do about it, but he didn't want to say something ugly to Eddie or others whose duty was to protect him. They were doing their jobs. I was useful because he could vent at me. The president's security was someone else's responsibility, and no one was asking my opinion. But I agreed with the president. The nation needed to see him in Washington, and I told him so.

Andy was busy making certain the Cabinet was being protected by Secret Service and their own department security details; he was also tracking down a contingent of White House staffers in New York City that morning. He was so busy he didn't talk to his wife, a Methodist minister in training, until that evening.

At some point, a picture of Barbara Olson, a passenger on the plane that crashed into the Pentagon, flashed on the cabin's television screen. I felt sick. I had met her through her husband, Solicitor General Ted Olson, who'd argued our recount case before the Supreme Court. I had found her smart, outgoing, and energetic, and thought briefly about trying to find a spot for her in the White House, but nothing came of it.

She had called her husband one last time before her plane crashed. At Barbara's funeral the following Saturday, the unflappable Karen Hughes broke down in tears and I did my best to comfort her. It was a horrible moment.

The deaths of that morning had been on a large scale, but with Barbara's death, it was suddenly personal. I felt helpless. I sat in the president's cabin on Air Force One and watched as people leapt from the North Tower of the World Trade Center, rather than be burned to death. At 10:28 A.M., it too collapsed. Just one hundred and two minutes had passed since the first plane flew into the World Trade Center.

In the course of those one hundred and two minutes, it seemed to me that, while the atmosphere on Air Force One was calm, time was flowing faster than normal. That may have been in part because I was trying to piece together what was happening and might yet happen. Who were our attackers? Were the assaults in New York and Washington the first of others to come? From where did they come? In what form and when would America respond?

I also felt extraneous. What was expected of me? What could I do? There were statements to draft, phone calls to make, information to collect, presidential requests to be answered, but sometimes a sharp pang would come with the thought I would be better employed pulling at rubble, not sitting in a cabin aboard a large airship rocketing across America at 45,000 feet.

As we made our way toward Louisiana, we occasionally caught sight of fighter escorts out the window. These were the early signs that America was now a nation at war. The conversation in Air Force One was stilted—at times I had the sense people were talking just to talk, hoping they might have something useful to say—but it all revolved around a new fact: America was at war.

If we didn't have all the information we wanted, I knew that when we did, these acts would be answered with all the might of the U.S. government. From the president's first words when he came into the staff hold, he knew the day was a turning point in America's history and he understood the special nature of the conflict ahead. I wasn't the only one struck by Bush's tone. Summoned with a group to the president's office, Eddie Marinzel later remembered Bush's first words when he entered the cabin were "Gentlemen, we're at war." I knew we were before Bush uttered those words; but hearing those words said by the president of the United States was still chilling. The president then went on to say he hoped the American people understood it would be a different kind of war against an enemy unlike any other we'd faced. It was likely to be a long struggle with years before victory, he said. As he later recalled, he realized on Air Force One this was a "defining moment in the history of the United States. I didn't need any legal briefs. I didn't need any consultations. I knew we were at war."

On the plane that day, there was no stirring speech, no outpouring of excitement, and no dramatic pronouncements. Those hoping to hear Henry V's rallying cry before Agincourt had to look elsewhere. We made an effort to dial down emotions. Yes, there was a lot of determination in the president's cabin, tempered by grief and some anger. Bush wanted the attacks met by calm and clarity.

Questions that seemed important before the hinge point of 9/11 seemed mundane after. For example, on September 10, we were preparing to announce a "Communities of Character" initiative to encourage character education efforts. In the blink of an eye, this and many other plans were replaced by the overwhelming necessity of defending the nation.

Over the coming years, the nation's attention would sometimes be diverted to other, less essential matters. For some Americans, the horror and terror of that day would fade, almost as if the events themselves never happened. But not for President Bush. He locked in on the struggle against terrorism with resolute focus. He never looked away from it. The immediacy of that day never left him as he occupied the Oval Office.

THE DAY'S EVENTS CAUSED all of us to think about our families and about getting word to them that we were fine. All the phones on Air Force One, though, were understandably occupied. I had the only BlackBerry in the White House. I had kept it from the campaign in order to be able to send and receive political messages without violating the Hatch Act. At the same time, the White House Communications Office had nixed BlackBerries for official business because they were still trying to figure out how to keep the White House's e-mail traffic secure. So Dan Bartlett and other staff members took turns using my BlackBerry to queue up e-mails to their families that would be sent when we passed over a cell

network. I've wondered since that day why the Federal Aviation Admin-
istration and airlines force passengers to turn off their wireless devices.
My BlackBerry didn't interfere with the operation of Air Force One on
September 11.

The president was concerned about his family, too, but fortunately,
Eddie had confirmed that Mrs. Bush and their daughters had been secured. The news reassured the president and allowed him to put off calling Laura until later in the morning, when events provided a brief
window to do so. I heard only one side of some of his brief conversations
and tried not to hear even that, but the tone was quiet and calm. She told
him the girls were safe and that she had been meeting with Senators Ted
Kennedy and Judd Gregg about education reform up on Capitol Hill
when the attacks began, and had been taken with them to a secure location. It was oddly reassuring to hear him talk to Laura about the whereabouts of their girls as if she were calling to ask him to pick up milk on
the way home.

The president's whereabouts were a closely guarded secret, or at least
we thought so. Watching local Shreveport television on the final approach
to Barksdale, we saw our plane appear, preparing to touch down with
fighter escorts covering us. An enterprising local TV news director had
stationed a camera just off the base on the flight path. Everyone now
knew where the president was. The Secret Service was alarmed, but it
didn't seem likely there was a terrorist cell operating in northwest Louisiana and armed with surface-to-air missiles.

When Bush came down the stairs of Air Force One, the command
staff of the Eighth Air Force met him at the bottom in combat dress,
with each officer wearing a sidearm. Enlisted personnel wore flak jackets
and helmets. Most carried weapons. And while the Shreveport Secret Service office had been mobilized to oversee security arrangements, there
was no presidential limousine. Instead, Bush entered a dark blue Dodge
Caravan with Lieutenant General Thomas Keck, commander of the
Eighth Air Force. An armed Humvee with a .50-caliber machine gun on
top guarded it. As the Humvee pulled out behind the Caravan, the airman manning the machine gun cocked his weapon and put a live round
in the chamber. I could almost feel in my bones the sharp metallic click
of the weapon being loaded.

The staff scrambled onto a small bus and followed the president to the base conference center. Some press piled in, so it took a few moments after the lead vehicles had sped off for us to get going. While the tone in the front of Air Force One had been grim and yet strangely calm and businesslike, the press cabin in the back was different. All the reporters were jumpy and nervous. Jay Carney of *Time* became hysterical when the rest of the motorcade passed from our sight behind some buildings. Carney settled down when we sped up, turned a corner, and caught sight of the motorcade ahead.

After a few minutes of shuttling between various offices at the base headquarters because of inadequate communications, the president camped out in General Keck's office and talked to the vice president and Defense Secretary Donald Rumsfeld. Cheney argued against Bush's returning to Washington. We still didn't know the extent of the attacks. There was a real fear the terrorists wanted to decapitate the government by killing its leaders, starting with President Bush. Besides, the critical issue was communication: the president needed to have video communications with dispersed members of the government's leadership. Cheney pointed out that the nearest place to do that was Offutt Air Force Base, near Omaha, Nebraska.

Reluctantly, Bush gave in to the objections to a return to Washington, but it was the last time he would give in to that argument. Bush then talked to staff in the White House bunker about speaking to the nation from Barksdale and what the shape of his remarks would be.

At Barksdale, Andy made the decision to off-load—how to put it?—extraneous passengers such as Florida congressman Dan Miller, who was cadging a flight back to Washington, and White House education policy advisor Sandy Kress. There was no need for guests or additional staff. The press was a different question, but Andy caucused with Ari and—over hearty objections and loud complaining—the media herd was slimmed down to just five that would continue with the president. Andy and Ari probably made permanent enemies among those they kicked off. Blake Gottesman was given the task of getting the stranded—and probably angry, disgruntled, and scared—passengers back to Washington. He got them there with extraordinary skill by commandeering a 757 from the Air Force's special missions fleet. It lifted off forty-five minutes later.

As this was being arranged, President Bush made remarks from the nearby Eighth Air Force headquarters, prosaically named "Building 245."

The remarks showed the emerging tension of the day. On the one hand, the president reassured Americans frightened by the attack. "The full resources of the federal government" were being used to save lives and help victims. The president was in "regular contact" with other officials in the executive and legislative branches and with world leaders. "All appropriate security precautions to protect the American people" had been taken. On the other hand, the nation was in an armed conflict. "The United States will hunt down and punish those responsible for these cowardly acts," the president promised. "We will do whatever is necessary to protect America and Americans."

The tension between these two competing presidential responsibilities—reassurance and war leadership—had already played out in Washington between the speechwriters and Karen Hughes. Both camps acknowledged the two responsibilities, but Mike Gerson and the speechwriters emphasized war; Karen emphasized reassurance.

I knew from the president's first words when he came into the staff hold that he saw this day as the first in an armed struggle. But he was also open to Karen's arguments that the American people now wanted to be comforted. There was plenty of time for talk of war in the hours and days to come. Besides, as the president said to me on Air Force One after leaving Barksdale, to declare war you have to know who your enemy is, and as of then, we didn't know who was behind the assault on America. It seemed to me Bush had a point. He did not use the word *war* at Barksdale. That changed with information he received at our next stop.

Bush's remarks at Barksdale came across as flat. Part of it was the setting—a conference room in an unknown military office building in Shreveport, Louisiana, not the stirring venue of the White House or Congress. Part of it was the haste with which his remarks were prepared. Few people are as fluid and convincing as they can be when operating under the pressure and speed that Bush faced that day. And part of it was his words. The president had vital matters on his mind, and his best wordsmiths, who would have helped him shape more reassuring and stronger messages for use in Florida and Louisiana, were stuck on Washington bridges, huddled in D.C. office buildings, or hunkered down in a bunker under the South Lawn.

Just before 1:30 P.M., we boarded the motorcade to return to the plane. The president grumbled about being stuffed into the cramped quarters of an armed Humvee for the return drive. At 1:37 P.M., we were off on the second leg of our day's journey. An hour and a half later, we landed at Offutt Air Force Base in Bellevue, Nebraska, headquarters of the U.S. Strategic Command. Once on the ground, Bush told Card and me that he would return to Washington after the videoconference. It was not a suggestion or question. From the tone of his voice, it was also not subject to appeal.

This time, agents from the Secret Service office in Omaha had organized a more traditional motorcade. The vehicles took us to a small, unassuming concrete box. After entering, we went down flight after flight of stairs to a subterranean command center. Offutt had been the site of the Strategic Air Command during the Cold War, so its facilities were built deep underground to withstand a nuclear blast.

The president and Andy went into a special room for a videoconference of the National Security Council with Powell in South America and other members at the White House and undisclosed locations.

Bush opened the meeting by declaring, "We are at war against terror, and from this day forward, this is the new priority of our administration." For about an hour, Bush and Card talked with Cheney, Rice, Rumsfeld, Richard Armitage (Powell's number two at State), Mineta, CIA director George Tenet, and others. From the information the FBI, CIA, and others had collected, it was clear a Muslim terrorist group was behind the attack, and Tenet raised the possibility the attacks had likely been launched by al-Qaeda.

Cheney, Bolten, and others in the White House bunker counseled the president to remain in Nebraska and speak to the country from Offutt. The president's instinct was it would be terrible to address Americans from a Cold War–era fallout bunker in the middle of the country. He was testy on the point and told the conferees he would speak from the Oval Office.

During the meeting, Harriet, Ari, Dan, and I found ourselves in a control room filled with computer terminals that looked out over a large room with huge screens displaying radar plots and maps of the globe. As it had been at each new stop and with each new development, that the world had changed dramatically was driven home with jackhammer force. When the conference broke up, we gathered our bags and went back up the flights of stairs to the motorcade and Washington.

As our long line of vehicles drove back to the plane, I glanced to the right and saw a fuel truck barreling toward us. For an instant, I found myself wondering if a terrorist was behind the wheel. It was probably just an airman running behind schedule and trying to make up time. Still, for a fraction of a second, I saw headlines proclaiming, "Presidential aides killed by runaway fuel truck at Nebraska Air Base." But the driver stopped. Air Force One left Offutt at about 4:30 P.M.

I now came to understand that there is something to the phrase "fog of war." It comes from the strategic theorist Carl von Clausewitz, who said, "War is the realm of uncertainty; three quarters of the factors on which action is based are wrapped in a fog of greater or lesser uncertainty." On this opening day of what came to be the Global War on Terror, there was confusion and misinformation. At 10:26 A.M., for example, news reports said there was a car bomb outside the State Department. Just after 10:30 A.M., word came to the plane that there was a specific threat against Air Force One with a call to the White House that used Air Force One's secret code name, "Angel." There were reports of hijacked planes being crashed into Camp David and the president's ranch in Crawford. In fact, Logan Walters, the president's personal aide, called Ken Engelbrecht, the president's ranch manager, and told him to get as far away from the ranch as quickly as possible. The last thing Logan heard before hanging up the phone was Ken telling his wife, "Mama, get into the car. We're going!" At Offutt, we were told there was a hijacked plane on the ground in Yellowknife, Canada, and as many as seven planes inbound over the Atlantic without transponders or radio contact, one apparently destined for Philadelphia. Reports throughout the day indicated the death toll in New York could be in the tens of thousands.

Much of this was presented as fact; none of it was true.

Most of the "fog" was simply the result of it being the first day of a war. Part of the misinformation came because of poor communications to and from Air Force One, a problem that caught the military's attention and was largely solved over the next few months with a major upgrade of the aircraft's communications systems. A by-product of these efforts was that we could watch cable news and baseball games while in flight.

Throughout the day, I had talked with Governor Pataki, first at his Manhattan office and then in the afternoon at the Police Academy, where he and Mayor Rudy Giuliani had located their command centers. I was struck by Pataki's calm, focused manner, but at certain moments I could hear the anger and sadness in his voice at the strike on his state's people. Most of all, he didn't know what could be next. Even after the fourth plane went down, neither Pataki nor anyone else knew the day's assaults were over. He, too, was engulfed in a swirl of conflicting rumors.

But even in that day's fog, there were moments of intense clarity. As we passed from fighter protection from airbases in the Midwest into the airspace around Washington, F-16 fighters took position on the wingtips of Air Force One. They were so close you could almost make out the pilots' faces. I broke out my camera and took some photos. Then it dawned on me. This was no ceremonial escort, no staged event for a memorable picture. There had been fighters near Air Force One almost all day, most of the time out of sight. But as we neared Washington, these F-16s had been placed there for one purpose: to act as the last, desperate defense for Air Force One. If something or someone got through the other air defenses, it was their job to put themselves between that threat and the president. The realization was sobering. We touched down at Andrews Air Force Base at 6:30 P.M. and boarded Marine One, the president's helicopter, for the White House.

Before September 11, Marine One would rise off the tarmac at Andrews Air Force Base to a respectable height from which you could see much of D.C. It would then move leisurely to the Washington Monument, make a slight jog to the right, and land on the South Lawn of the White House. Not this evening. Marine One's pilots kept zigging and zagging to stay close to the earth's contour, moving the aircraft quickly over the countryside at treetop level, dipping into valleys and climbing just over the crest of hills, before coming up over the last ridgeline before the Potomac River. As we turned north, we could see smoke coming from the Pentagon. The airship was quiet; no one talked until the president broke the silence by pointing out the window toward the black plume and saying quietly, "You're looking at the face of war in the twenty-first century." We landed on the South Lawn at 6:55 P.M.

Karen and Mike's team had prepared several different drafts for the president's speech to the country. Bush had talked with Karen several times, especially on the flight out of Offutt, and given specific direction as to what he wanted to say and how. He decided to be clear that America was at war and its opponents were terrorists. By the time we arrived at the Oval Office, the drafts had been blended but the speech needed a little tweaking by Bush, who huddled with his speechwriters and some of us from the day's traveling party in the president's private dining room. The Oval was filled with technicians, cameras, and equipment in preparation for the broadcast.

There was one outstanding question. How many people had died? Was it hundreds, thousands, or tens of thousands? Again, the fog of war descended. I called Tony Carbonetti, Mayor Giuliani's aide, and asked the death toll. I oddly felt relieved when he said that thousands—not tens of thousands—of people were believed dead. As terrible a number as that is, more than fifty thousand people worked in the World Trade Center and I had expected many more to have died. As America learned in the days ahead, countless heroes—firemen, police officers, rescuers, and just ordinary people—had saved the lives of thousands of people through their actions that day, too often at the cost of their own. The third sentence of the president's remarks was finalized with the phrase "thousands of lives" just a few minutes before he was to go on television.

At 8:30 P.M., Bush sat down at his desk in the Oval Office, looked into a camera lens, and told Americans, "Our way of life, our very freedom came under attack in a series of deliberate and deadly terrorist acts" and "thousands of lives were suddenly ended by evil, despicable acts of terror." The images Americans had watched all day "of airplanes flying into buildings filled us with disbelief, terrible sadness, and a quiet, unyielding anger," he said. Terrorists "intended to frighten our nation into chaos and retreat. But they have failed," he went on. "Terrorist attacks can shake the foundations of our biggest buildings, but they cannot touch the foundation of America."

The president answered the question many Americans were asking: Why us, why our country? "America was targeted for attack," he said, "because we're the brightest beacon for freedom and opportunity in the world." It was enemies of the American ideal who had struck us.

He reassured Americans, saying the "first priority is to get help to those who have been injured, and to take every precaution to protect our citizens at home and around the world from further attacks." Federal agencies were back up and running that night and would be open for business the next day, as would be the nation's financial institutions.

Americans wanted to hear from Bush that more was being done, and he knew it. "The search," he declared, "is under way for those who are behind these evil acts." He had directed intelligence and law enforcement "to find those responsible and to bring them to justice." And in a foreshadowing of the key new policy, Bush said, "We will make no distinction between the terrorists who committed these acts and those who harbor them." Bush had added those seventeen words himself in the last editing session, minutes before going on air.

He thanked "the many world leaders" who had called with "condolences and assistance" and put this new struggle in its global context by saying, "We stand together to win the war against terrorism."

Bush asked for prayers to "those who grieve" and "children whose worlds have been shattered." And he gave hope and confidence by declaring, "America has stood down enemies before, and we will do so this time." He closed: "We go forward to defend freedom and all that is good and just in our world."

While brief, his remarks that night were far better than either of his earlier public utterances. He was resolute, concerned, calm, yet full of a coiled energy just beneath the surface. While acknowledging the horror all had seen, Bush described what was being done and what would be done, preparing the country for a response far different than it had seen after previous terrorist attacks.

I looked recently at footage of President Bush that night. His face is largely unlined and his hair has color. He was so young. We all seemed to follow him in going gray in the years ahead.

With his speech, Bush signaled two dramatic changes in American policy. First, terrorist strikes were no longer simply a law enforcement matter, to be turned over to the U.S. Attorney for the Southern District of New York and the FBI and the justice system, which would work its course. Terror attacks were now a question of national security, and all the force and power of the United States—diplomatic, economic, and, if need be, military—would be used to defeat those who carried them out.

Second, Bush was telling state sponsors of terror that they would be held accountable. Afghanistan and other countries that supported or tolerated terrorists within their borders were now on notice that the United States would no longer tolerate their support of those who attacked the West.

The first charge was so logical that no policy process was needed. But the second came from Bush, the product of a day of rapid phone conversations with key security and intelligence advisors, a longer conference call from Barksdale, a videoconference conducted from Offutt, and then quiet thought on the last leg of the day's journey. Bush had sorted all he had heard, organized it in his mind, studied it, considered its ramifications, and arrived at the nub of the thing. Policy makers and even presidents have to react to an untidy and often chaotic world. Bush's response was to hold the hosts of terrorists responsible for the actions of those they harbored.

Bush did not blame radical Islamists or Muslim extremists for the attacks, though there was evidence that such a terrorist group was behind them. He wanted to be precise when he described exactly who was responsible, and the intelligence community had not yet finished its work. Coincidentally, the president was to have met at 3:05 P.M. with American Muslim leaders after his planned return from the Florida education event. He had been scheduled to spend forty minutes, first with a small group in the Oval Office and then with a larger one in the Roosevelt Room. He would meet with many of them in the days ahead, but in a much different—and highly charged—environment.

After the address, President Bush left the Oval Office to attend a lengthy meeting of the National Security Council in the bunker and then returned to the private quarters on the second floor of the White House. The Secret Service tried to get him to spend the night in the bunker, but he refused. He told them if there was a problem, they knew where to find him, and went to bed. Hours later, Marinzel and others were meeting in the Secret Service director's office when alarms went off. An unknown aircraft was headed toward the White House. The president and First Lady were grabbed from their bedroom and "relocated" to the shelter. Marinzel arrived just in time to hear the "all clear" as the plane was identified and rerouted. The president jokingly asked him, "You did that on purpose, didn't you?" They laughed nervously before the Bushes returned to the private quarters and the rest of a busted night's sleep.

As for me, after the speech I visited my office briefly, then left the West Wing and got into my car on West Executive Drive for the short drive home. The city was eerily quiet, its streets occupied by armies of uniformed Secret Service, military, and Metro police, camped around government buildings and blocking major roads. I was utterly, completely exhausted. It wasn't physical exhaustion; my only strenuous exercise had been climbing up and down stairs in a Nebraska bunker. But I was emotionally and mentally spent. Like many Americans, I had heard and seen things that day I have never been able to escape.

Susan Ralston stayed in contact via BlackBerry that day. Her husband, Troy, didn't want her to go to work the next day, but after the president's speech that night, she e-mailed me as I was driving home. "See you in the morning?" she wrote. I replied, "Yes, see you in the morning."

I trudged up the staircase to Darby at home. The day had had a surreal quality for her, too. She recounted her day with fear and relief in her voice. She had wanted to pick up Andrew from school immediately, but school officials wanted parents to wait. She had paced the floor, eyes glued to the television, trying to make sense of what had happened. Eventually, Andrew called to say everyone was leaving and he wanted to come home. Relieved, a few minutes later she picked him up. Amid chaotic streets, she noticed neighbors had already begun to display American flags. Later, she recalled what an extraordinarily beautiful, crystal-clear day September 11 had started out to be.

CHAPTER 17

Ground Zero

I awoke the next morning before dawn, not yet able to fully process the previous day's events. In the space of one hundred and two minutes and four attacks, the country and therefore the Bush presidency had dramatically changed. We had witnessed a hinge moment in history. The Bush presidency would now be defined by 9/11.

The day after the attacks was going to be long and intense, emotional and surreal. Not knowing how long it would take to get into the White House, I left home even earlier than normal, just after 5 A.M. The surreal part started right away. In a city of 570,000 people, the streets were deserted. I had to pass through several military cordons and perimeters manned by the Secret Service before driving into the White House. At every checkpoint, my credentials were given extra scrutiny and K-9 units sniffed my car for explosives.

The senior White House staff that day was a group of people—me included—compensating for the previous day's trauma by pressing a bit too hard for normalcy. Everyone wanted to project a sense of calm. It was an important thing to aim for—we had a huge number of things to decide.

At the 7:30 A.M. senior staff meeting, the first thing Andy announced was that the president's schedule for the coming week was canceled. This triggered a discussion on what the president's public events should be.

Understandably, Bush wanted to go to New York City as soon as possible. But no one knew yet how many people were still trapped in the rubble. My strong view was that we should not go so early, because it would detract from the recovery efforts. Laura was to be dispatched to Walter Reed Army Medical Center, where the wounded from the Pentagon were being treated, that day. And the president wanted to go to the Pentagon as soon as possible. He wound up going that afternoon and visiting the building's wounded the next day.

We debated whether it was appropriate for the president to participate in a religious observance. The consensus was yes, perhaps as early as Friday. And we also debated whether he should speak to a joint session of Congress. My thought was that Bush should give the speech as soon as he could offer a comprehensive policy, but no later than early the following week. There was no staff agreement on a speech to Congress, but later that day Bush told the speechwriters to start working on both remarks for a religious observance and an address to Congress. He assured them that there would be plenty of substance for the speech to Congress.

We also talked about the economy. Wall Street had suspended trading in the aftermath of the attacks, so we talked about how to get America's financial markets going again. Reopening Wall Street was important for the economy, but it was also vital to demonstrate that our resolve had not been broken. Our enemies had targeted the World Trade Center and not, say, a train station in Brooklyn, in order to strike at our economic foundations that supported the free flow of goods and that tied the nation to global commerce.

After the meeting, I met with staffers who reported to me. I soon realized I had a lot of work to do in settling their fears. After the second plane hit the World Trade Center, Secret Service agents went through the West Wing, telling Susan Ralston, my other deputy, Israel Hernandez, and others to go to the Wardroom next to the White House Mess on the basement floor. Susan and Izzy waited in the small room with fifteen or twenty other staff for a few minutes before armed Secret Service officers dressed in black combat uniforms came and told them they had thirty seconds to walk to the West Basement exit. Women should take off their shoes if they were wearing heels and everyone should remove their White House badges. Once the doors were opened, they should run toward the north White House gates and out of the complex, tell no one they worked at the White House, and make their way home as best they could.

Susan and Izzy made their way with others, some of them in tears, to the West Basement doors. A heavily armed Secret Service officer opened the doors and pushed people out while urging them to "move, move, move!" People streamed down the steps of the Eisenhower Executive Office Building, which was also being evacuated. The crowds merged, turned north toward the gates, and picked up speed as Secret Service hustled them off the grounds.

To get to her home south of Washington in the distant Virginia exurbs, Susan tried to walk to Reagan National Airport, where she thought she could get onto the Metro. But she was blocked at the Fourteenth Street Bridge: police were turning away pedestrians. So she hitchhiked a ride to get over the bridge and made her way to a place south of the city where her husband, Troy, could pick her up hours later.

Izzy ran into the president's secretary, Ashley Estes, and his personal aide, Logan Walters, in Lafayette Park, and they threw in with Ken Mehlman, a deputy of mine and director of political affairs, and Brad Blakeman, director of presidential scheduling. They all made their way to the nearby Chrysler offices. There, Chrysler's D.C. director and former Bush 41 aide Tim McBride turned space over to the group as Mehlman established a command post and gathered White House stragglers. The group remained in Chrysler's offices until the president returned to Andrews that evening and Secret Service decided it was safe for them to return to the complex. They escorted the group back to the White House. Izzy was stunned: the streets were empty, except for armed military vehicles. The group walked in the middle of normally busy city streets amid an eerie quiet.

Others among the nearly sixty people who worked for me had simply kept walking that morning and made their way home on foot or in the cars of strangers. One woman started running and kept running until she realized she was in Georgetown, over a mile from the White House, and unable to run anymore.

Needless to say, the idea that your workplace could be the target of a terrorist attack unsettled a lot of White House staff. Nerves were jangled, emotions high, and safety concerns real. One young staffer was so traumatized by the experience, she never returned to work. I understood how frightened people were and did my best to calm and reassure them. I was inspired by how resolute and determined many were, even though many remained shaken. But I had to turn my attention from the staff to the outside world. A huge number of important matters had to be settled, and there was no precedent for us to rely on. We had to make it up as we went along.

At 9:30 A.M., the president started a National Security Council meeting in the Cabinet Room for the latest intelligence and discussion of a proposed congressional resolution authorizing the use of force against terrorists and their sponsors.

After a brief break, Bush met at 11:30 A.M. with congressional leaders, again in the Cabinet Room. He made clear that American policy had changed in fundamental ways. The United States would no longer be content with long-distance strikes on suspected terror camps, he told them. America would now do whatever was necessary to capture or kill terrorist leaders, obliterate training camps, and destroy their ability to wage war. Nations that harbored terrorists would be held accountable, he went on. "We are at war," Bush said, and there would be no half measures.

The president got unexpected pushback from Senate minority leader Tom Daschle, who cautioned him, "*War* is a very powerful word." He encouraged Bush to tone down his rhetoric and avoid any talk of war. I was taken aback. We had just been attacked on our soil and thousands had died.

Fortunately, Daschle was alone in these sentiments. Senator Robert Byrd of West Virginia closed the meeting by reminding the president, "There is still an army who believe in this country, believe in the divine guidance that has always led our nation," and telling Bush "mighty forces will come to your aid."

The National Security Council met again that afternoon for an hour and a half before Bush left for an early evening tour of the Pentagon with Rumsfeld. As much as I wanted to go, I had plenty on my plate that kept me at the White House.

I had talked several times with Governor Pataki, who urged President Bush to come to New York as soon as possible. Calm and steady, the governor had seen the prodigious energy of rescue workers and was looking ahead: he worried how anyone could keep at this work without breaking emotionally and physically. He was especially concerned about the effect on morale of so few people being found alive. He pressed for a Thursday visit, Friday at the latest, as essential to keeping spirits high. He was right.

We arranged for a telephone call with Pataki, Giuliani, and the president to be televised the next morning. A deputy of mine, Tim Goeglein, lined up the National Cathedral and Billy Graham as a participant for a religious service on Friday.

I spent the tail end of this long day in meetings on the status of arrangements for each event, discussing the minutiae involved in anything the president would do. We worked to numb ourselves to the fact of an attack on American soil that involved the deaths of thousands. That September, numbness was the only way to avoid paralysis.

I left the White House just before midnight and drove home through an armed camp. The surreal feeling I had that morning returned. It was like a scene out of a bad movie in which an alien spacecraft has landed on the Mall.

Thursday began with calls to world leaders. Bush was already on the phone when I stopped in the Oval Office just after 7 A.M. Our conversation didn't last long. He was not his normal cheery self. He wasn't interested in small talk, and certainly not forced small talk. He was more impatient and certainly more preoccupied than I had seen him before. A presidency that had been predicated on domestic issues was now, overwhelmingly, a national security one. If that wasn't your specialty, what you had to say to him was of less interest, at least for now. There was a new determination, and even a slight grimness to him I had not seen before.

Just after 11 A.M., Bush got on a conference call from the Oval Office with Governor Pataki and Mayor Giuliani. Audio and video feeds were sent to the networks so the country could see and hear the three leaders' conversation. Bush immediately settled the question of when he'd go to New York: it would be after the Friday morning service at the National Cathedral. He praised the efforts of first responders, pledged the federal government's complete support for rescue and recovery efforts, and joined the two New Yorkers in reminding the country that Arab Americans "love their flag just as much as the three of us do."

Bush took reporters' questions after the call ended. He refused to accuse Osama bin Laden just yet, warned Americans it would be a different kind of war, and thanked world leaders for their support. One question provided for the grace note the country wanted. "Could you give us a sense as to what kind of prayers you are thinking and where your heart is for yourself?" Francine Kiefer of the *Christian Science Monitor* asked.

Bush, leaning over the desk that Franklin Roosevelt once used, turned his head toward the Rose Garden and South Lawn, his palms still planted firmly on the desktop. He turned back a few moments later, his eyes watering. "Well, I don't think about myself right now. I think about the families, the children. I am a loving guy, and I am also someone, however, who has got a job to do—and I intend to do it. And this is a terrible moment." He then ended the news conference.

This was one of those times in which a president, even in a crowded room, seems almost alone, and in which his words have the power to move a nation. Almost more than his words of grief and resolution, however, were the gestures and sense that his face and movements conveyed. Even cynical, jaded reporters were moved: everyone—all his aides, all the reporters—had tears in their eyes. Bush moved to leave the Oval Office and head for his private study next door. He glanced at me, and then hurriedly looked away.

I tried to discreetly wipe away my tears and followed the president into his private study. His eyes were red; he was nearly overcome with emotion. I, on the other hand, was completely overcome. Nothing could stop my tears. We briefly hugged as I mumbled a few words about how powerful the scene had been in the Oval Office, and we each did our best to pull ourselves together. There was a lot more work to be done and grieving had to be set aside. He was embarrassed when he returned to the Oval. He didn't need to be.

Bush left a few minutes later to visit victims from the Pentagon. I went back to my office to handle any issues that came up from the visits. I need not have worried; my people had it under control.

When President Bush returned, he held a two-hour National Security Council meeting before we convened in the Oval Office to go over the text of the National Cathedral speech and to discuss the outline for his congressional address. Mike Gerson and his shop had done a splendid job on the National Cathedral draft, though it wasn't clear just how magnificent until the next day.

It was raining hard in Washington on Friday morning, September 14, as the presidential motorcade sped up Rock Creek Parkway and then Massachusetts Avenue. The support van that Darby and I were in was crowded but quiet, as were the sidewalks. The sky was filled with dark gunmetal blue clouds, and streets around the National Cathedral were wet and slippery as we rushed into the building for the "National Day of Prayer and Remembrance" service at noon.

As we made our way in, I saw Al and Tipper Gore walking under an umbrella toward the cathedral doors. During the previous year, I had spent most of my waking hours working to defeat him. It was a sign of how much things had changed in the hours since 9/11 that when I saw the Gores, there were none of those intense, sometimes bitter feelings everyone in a presidential campaign experiences in the heat of the contest and then later regrets.

Darby and I took our seats on the left-hand side of the cathedral, near one of the massive pillars that held up the vaulted ceiling 102 feet above our heads. In front of us was an extraordinary sight: five presidents and their wives—Gerald and Betty Ford, Jimmy and Rosalynn Carter, George H. W. and Barbara Bush, Bill and Hillary Clinton, and George W. and Laura Bush. Nearby were Nancy Reagan and virtually all the members of the Cabinet. Across the aisle sat the leaders of Congress, Republicans and Democrats together. The cathedral was also filled with hundreds of uniformed military. I imagined their minds must be filled with thoughts of the sacrifice and courage they would be called upon to render in the dangerous days ahead.

I had read the president's speech and attended the editing sessions with him, so I should have been braced for what was coming. I wasn't. Bush had known what he wanted to say and had played a larger than normal role in drafting and polishing the remarks. I hoped that process would dampen some of the emotion he would certainly feel when he took the pulpit at the National Cathedral. And mine, too.

President Bush had to define and direct the feelings of a grieving and angry nation. We wanted the language brief, elevated, and moving, but it also had to summon the country to a vital and dangerous task.

The president began with ten simple but very moving words: "We are here in the middle hour of our grief." Now, Bush said, "come the names of people who faced death, and in their last moments called home to say, be brave, and I love you." I was almost overwhelmed by how powerful it was to hear these words in the cathedral. The names were of "passengers who defied their murderers . . . men and women who wore the uniform of the United States, and died at their posts" and rescuers "whom death found running up the stairs and into the fires to help others." I was watching him closely and knew he was fighting against his own grief. His voice faltered slightly, and his eyes watered just a bit. But his voice stayed steady and conveyed resolve, especially when he pledged a fierce reaction and promised the conflict would "end in a way and at an hour of our choosing."

This was one of the finest speeches Bush would ever give, and one of the finest presidential speeches I could recall. It combined beautiful, elevated rhetoric; a simple, calm delivery; and a powerful moment. The president would later recall the National Cathedral service as among his presidency's "most dramatic" moments.

Darby and I sat feeling both sadness at the loss of life and fear that our nation had been attacked and could be attacked again. Yet I also felt pride in the man whose words not only rallied the country but encouraged determination and patience for the tough days and stern actions ahead. When the president finished his remarks and returned to his seat, his father reached over and squeezed his hand. It was a simple gesture of love from father to son, but also something more: the affirmation offered by one man who had ordered men and women into harm's way to another who shortly would. The ceremony ended with "The Battle Hymn of the Republic." I felt anger as we sang of a "terrible swift sword."

When we came out of the cathedral, the rain had ended, clouds were drifting off, and the sun was bright. We often associate words like "promise" and "hope" with skies that open like they did that day, but it's hard to do so when the ritual you have just experienced is about marking death and destruction.

The motorcade took us to a landing zone on the Mall, where we boarded helicopters to Andrews Air Force Base. There were missile batteries near the Washington Monument, and the Mall swarmed with military officers. The missile batteries were to become a fixture. For months, there was one barely disguised next to the Georgetown Reservoir that I passed on my way to work. It covered the approach to Reagan National Airport from the west so any hijacked aircraft could be shot down before hurtling into the White House or the Capitol.

There were still grave concerns about the safety of Air Force One and the president, so the plane flew to McGuire Air Force Base in New Jersey rather than to JFK or Newark, arriving at 2:45 P.M. There, New York governor George Pataki and New York City mayor Rudy Giuliani greeted President Bush; the three men boarded Marine One, which would take them to New York City.

When a president flies in Marine One, there are two or three other identical helicopters that fly with him. They engage in an aerial ballet, constantly shifting back and forth, slowing down or speeding up according to an elaborate choreography. The aim is to make it impossible for an observer to know which chopper is the real Marine One. It is like a shell game operated by a street-corner carny: you eventually lose track of where the marble is. I was in "Night Hawk Two."

Our flight path took us in and out of the smoke plume from Ground Zero. We were nearly forty miles south of the city when the acidic and pungent odor of destruction first filled the cabin. Though the Trade Center had come down three days earlier, the stench lingered and would do so for a long time. We looked to the west into the plume; it was so dark, it blotted out the view of the New Jersey coastline behind it.

Staten Island, the Statue of Liberty, and Manhattan itself were on our left as we flew up the East River and circled around the north side of Ground Zero before landing at the Wall Street Heliport at 3:50 P.M. Little was said during this twenty-minute aerial tour. The television footage had been clear and sharp, but it did not do justice to the enormity of the disaster. The destruction's scale was mind-boggling. How had anyone survived? At the landing zone, we piled into SUVs and went to view Ground Zero from the north side, where the World Trade Center's Building Seven had collapsed. FEMA director Joe Allbaugh joined us; he was doing an extraordinary job in coordinating Washington's assistance. Senator Hillary Clinton and Congressmen Charlie Rangel and Jerry Nadler were among those waiting to greet us. Rangel told Bush "an attack on one of us is an attack on all of us."

The remnants of Tuesday's violence were hard to comprehend. I kept thinking that the piles of debris and rubble and dust must be what the

My older brother, Eric, and me with our mother, Reba Wood Rove, and father, Louis C. Rove, Jr.

My dad in the early 1950s in Angola.

On Air Force One with my then eighteen-year-old son, Andrew, and my wife, Darby. It's August 13, 2007—the day I announce my resignation from the White House.

Republican National Chairman George H. W. Bush visits with Vice President Gerald R. Ford at the Republican National Committee's 1973 winter meeting. I was chairman of the College Republicans and Special Assistant to Bush.

He's Done a LOT
He'll Do MORE!

Campaign Slogan
Karl Rove College Republican Chairman,
1973-1977

This postcard for a reunion of College Republicans in 2000 featured a photo of me and my 1973 campaign slogan.

On November 7, 2000—election night—my office hosted a stream of anxious staffers. Dan Bartlett is on the far right. Immediately to Bartlett's left, with his back to the camera, is Ari Fleischer.

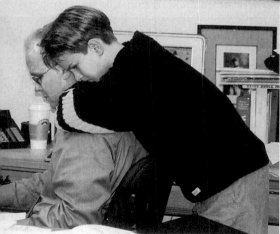

LEFT: As I check out returns on election night 2000, one especially interested observer is my son, Andrew.

RIGHT: Andrew hugs me at 2:15 A.M. when Fox News calls Florida for Bush. Two hours later, both Florida and the election are "too close to call." Thirty-six days of a high-stakes legal battle would follow.

As Air Force One makes its way from the Midwest into the Washington, D.C., area, F-16 fighters become our escorts. I could almost make out the pilots' faces.

Back in the Oval Office on the evening of 9/11, White House technicians and counselor Karen Hughes set up before Bush's address to the nation.

FROM LEFT TO RIGHT: Andy Card; Ari Fleischer; Blake Gottesman, the president's personal aide; me; Captain Deborah Loewer, director of the Situation Room; President Bush; and Dan Bartlett. We look out the window of Air Force One on 9/11 as the F-16s take up position on our wingtips.

Enjoying the "other white meat" at the World Pork Expo in Iowa on June 7, 2002.

Campaigning in Iowa on August 14, 2002, I take a nap. Bush's participation in the midterm elections after 9/11 was hotly debated inside the White House. In the end, Bush's efforts led the GOP to gains in both the Senate and House.

Ken Mehlman, President Bush, me, Ari Fleischer, and Blake Gottesman. We look at the returns from the midterm elections on November 5, 2002, in the private quarters of the White House.

President Bush and I walk through the colonnade between the West Wing and the White House on January 27, 2003.

The president shows me his best game face on March 4, 2004, as we play gin rummy on Air Force One. President Bush is the most competitive person I know.

On September 2, 2004, backstage at Madison Square Garden in New York City, I give President Bush a fist bump before he goes out to deliver his acceptance speech to the Republican National Convention. Bush's college friend Roland Betts is on the right.

In the war room on election night 2004, I cheer as Fox awards Bush New Mexico's five electoral votes. New Mexico was one of our target states because Bush had lost it in 2000 by 366 votes.

Always up for
friendly competition,
Bush compares height with
Andrew on May 26, 2003.
At six feet one, Andrew had
just overtaken Bush.

BELOW: Hunting with Vice
President Dick Cheney and
good friend Don Evans in south
Georgia on November 29, 2005.

Secretary of State Colin Powell would call me "Private Rove" and ask me to "drop and give him twenty." On May 27, 2004, I finally did so in the anteroom of the Oval Office—much to the delight of Press Secretary Scott McClellan, Chief of Staff Andy Card, Dan Bartlett, and National Security Advisor Condi Rice.

The most embarrassing moment of my life: putting on a show as "M.C. Rove" at the March 28, 2007, Radio and Television Correspondents' Dinner. NBC News's David Gregory and Ken Strickland served as my backup dancers, while Colin Mochrie (far right) and Brad Sherwood (far left)—from ABC's *Whose Line Is It Anyway?*—rap away.

Karen Hughes, the president's personal aide; Andy Card; Logan Walters; the president; and I go over an upcoming event in the Oval Office on January 17, 2002. The president always had an open-door policy for his senior staff.

Bush always made even the longest, most exhausting days on the campaign trail fun. The First Lady ignores her husband as he mugs for the camera backstage at a September 4, 2004, campaign appearance in Broadview Heights, Ohio.

I chat with former CIA chief Robert Gates, Chief of Staff Josh Bolten, and Secretary of Defense Donald Rumsfeld at the entrance the Oval Office on November 8, 2006—the day Rumsfeld resigned and Bush announced Gates as our new defense secretary.

On January 19, 2007, I make a comment as President Bush rehearses for his upcoming State of the Union address in the White House movie theater. Bush is open to suggestions, but becomes more resistant closer to the event.

aftermath of a nuclear blast looks like, only without radioactivity. A huge sheet of the South Tower's façade—which had fallen from the seventy-seventh floor—jutted from the ground. It looked like Zeus had smashed his trident into the earth in anger, trying to split Manhattan open. We walked down streets caked in the filth of the collapse. We then drove along West Street, which was clogged with rescue workers lining both sides, and turned right. The president's SUV rolled to a stop a few dozen yards down Murray Street.

We tumbled out of the vehicles into an ocean of noise. The president's arrival set the crowd off. Standing on rescue equipment and piles of debris, these huge and powerful ironworkers, steelworkers, and rescue personnel were screaming "U.S.A.! U.S.A.!" The president made his way around a horseshoe of chanting workers to shake hands and thank them. Some congressmen wanted to be in every photograph, so they pushed their way to his side. Representative Nadler was particularly insistent about the photo opportunity, getting mad first at a White House staffer and then making the near-fatal mistake of trying to push a Secret Service agent aside. The agent expertly parried the congressman's efforts to attach himself to the president's rib cage.

Bush was hearing and seeing the rescue workers up close. They were not shy about sharing their feelings. These men were working on adrenaline and passion and, after three days and increasingly less frequent good news about survivors, they were nearly spent. Pataki was right; the presidential visit was energizing for many of the people we met. Bush later told me what he felt from the workers was deep, almost overwhelming anger, even hatred.

I watched this from a short distance off. Behind me a few yards to the east were about twenty religious leaders, led by Cardinal Edward Egan. They too had joined in the chanting, many waving small American flags. Most were weeping. I could not glance at them for more than an instant: I felt I too would succumb if I looked too closely or too long at them.

There was a tug on my sleeve. It was Nina Bishop, a White House advance woman working the event. She pointed to the chanting workers and said, "They want to hear from their president." No one had prepared remarks, but she was exactly right. Nina later explained that she approached me to urge that the president speak because she had made a similar appeal to the advance team the night before but was turned down.

She thought I "would at least consider the idea." I didn't know my reputation was as an easy mark for an end run, but I asked her if there was a microphone available. She shook her head no. Could she get a bullhorn? She scurried off to grab one from some of the workers milling around. I looked for a place the president could speak from. The SUVs in the motorcade had wide running boards, but if he stood on one, he would still not be seen by all the people who had clambered up on piles of rubble and vehicles all around us.

Right next to me was a giant wrecked fire truck. The pumper had been smashed by falling debris. Its crumpled door read 76 ENGINE COMPANY. Its tires had blown out, and its body was crushed, but three men were standing on top of it and the entire crowd could see the president if he joined them. I looked up at the workers, and as I did one jumped off the truck. I got the attention of the remaining two and asked them if it was safe. The younger of the two replied it was, while the older man, wearing a fireman's hat from New York Fire Department Company 154, nodded in agreement. I was unconvinced, so I asked them to jump up and down. They looked quizzically at the strange guy in a suit and tie, and I repeated my request. They hesitantly jumped up and down; the truck looked steady enough for Bush to clamber up. I told the two men, "Stay there—someone might need your help to get up." Before going to look for Andy, I reached for a piece of paving block that had jiggled when the rescue workers jumped up and down. A policeman grabbed my wrist and stopped me, saying there might be a body part underneath. I felt sick.

I found Andy Card and shared Nina's suggestion; he immediately agreed that it was a good idea and asked where the president could speak. I pointed at the battered fire truck. Andy made a beeline to the president. Nina had commandeered a bullhorn from a man who worked for Con Ed and met me at the fire truck with it. The bullhorn's batteries weren't that good, but it was all we had. Nina gave it to Logan Walters. As she turned away, I grabbed a small American flag sticking out of Nina's courier bag and handed it up to the thin, older rescue worker who was now the last man standing on the truck. His companion had disappeared off the back of the pumper and out of history.

The president took the bullhorn and reached his hand up to the rescue worker, a retired sixty-nine-year-old New York firefighter named Bob Beckwith. Beckwith looked down into the scrum below him, saw the outstretched hand, grasped, and pulled. In an instant, Bush was sharing the top of the truck with Beckwith, who suddenly realized he'd helped up the president of the United States. Beckwith tried to crawl down but the president asked, "Where are you going?" Bob said he was getting down. Bush said, "No, no, you stay right here."

The cheers and chanting subsided and the president started to speak into the bullhorn. With the National Cathedral prayer service still fresh on his mind, Bush began by saying, "I want you all to know that America today is on bended knee in prayer for the people whose lives were lost here, for the workers who work here, for the families who mourn. This nation stands with the good people of New York City and New Jersey and Connecticut as we mourn the loss of thousands of our citizens." Someone yelled, "Go get 'em, George!" Someone else yelled, "George, we can't hear you!" and others echoed this complaint. Bush paused and then responded in a voice now fully magnified by the bullhorn, "I can hear *you.*" The crowd went nuts—and he knew what to do from there. "The rest of the world hears you," he went on, "and the people who knocked these buildings down will hear *all* of us soon." The crowd broke into defiant, even bitter, chants of "U.S.A.! U.S.A.!" Bush handed the bullhorn off and he climbed down.

In an iconic moment, George W. Bush was very much alone with an enormous responsibility. The nation wanted reassurance; it wanted to know it had a leader who understood the mission America now faced. No speechwriters, no aides, no advisors were involved in Bush's response. It was an authentic moment that connected with the public in a strong, deep way. Without assistance and in an instant, George W. Bush gave voice to America's desires.

Seeing President Bush hop up on that busted truck and stand shoulder to shoulder with a weary firefighter is a sight forever etched in my mind, and for many it remains one of the most inspiring scenes from the terrible events of 9/11. Presidential historian Douglas Brinkley's assessment of Bush's visit to Ground Zero was prophetic: "We can't just judge him as President Bush anymore, but we're going to soon be judging him as commander in chief."

By now, it was 4:45 P.M. and we were twenty minutes behind schedule. The next stop was the Jacob Javits Convention Center, which had been converted into a staging area and dormitory for rescue workers. The president was to greet them and then meet with family members of miss-ing first responders. Virtually every member of Congress from New York, New Jersey, and Connecticut had found their way into the motorcade. To keep on schedule and to make certain no senator or congressman got lost, I pulled random members into the support van, including Senator Joe Lieberman. It was an odd way to meet someone I'd spent much of the fall of 2000 trying to defeat. He and I chatted about the crowds, the Javits Center event, people still missing or whose fates were unknown. But unless you were one of the folks digging through rubble or manhan-dling twisted metal to look for survivors, near Ground Zero that day you felt totally useless.

As we drove north from Ground Zero, there were trucks and equip-ment parked along the West Side Highway that showed how Americans rushed to serve following September 11—including Humane Society ve-hicles from up and down the East Coast to take care of lost pets or the rescue dogs injured while searching for survivors. There were fire trucks and Red Cross vehicles from states and communities too numerous to count. And tens of thousands of New Yorkers lined every step on both sides of the road eight or ten deep, applauding the motorcade with wav-ing flags or homemade signs of encouragement for the rescue workers and the president. Many were in tears. It was easier to look inside the support van than out; the emotions on the curb were powerful and full of pain.

At the Javits Center we were greeted by hundreds of tired, exhausted, but strangely exhilarated rescue workers, most of them FEMA Urban Search and Rescue teams from around the country. The president shook every hand, posed for every picture taken with a disposable camera, squeezed every shoulder, and exchanged a word with anyone who wanted to say hello. We got further behind schedule—something that was almost unheard-of in Bush World—but it didn't matter to him. Not on this day, not in this city, not in this place.

Finally, it was time for a shift change. Off-duty workers headed for the showers, food, and brief sleep. Those going on duty piled into buses to head south to Ground Zero. Bush walked into the Javits parking ga-rage, where silver pipes and blue drapes were arranged to create a make-shift waiting room for the families of killed or missing first responders.

The president told Deputy Chief of Staff Joe Hagin he didn't want any press following him, saying, "We're not going to turn this into a circus."

Inside the enclosure were hundreds of family members of police, fire, rescue, Port Authority, or other first responders who were missing or dead at Ground Zero. The schedule said simply that the president would "visit" with them.

It wasn't that simple. He stood, surrounded by a swirl of people, not moving more than ten or twenty feet from the entrance to the room, as the families spontaneously organized themselves into a gigantic receiving line. These were moms and dads, husbands and wives, sons and daughters who wanted the president to know they suffered a loss almost beyond imagination. They wanted Bush to comfort them, to assure them their loved ones would be honored by action against those who had struck America.

Some—more than a few—wanted revenge. Emotions were understandably angry and bitter at killers who had taken someone so precious. Though it had been more than three days since the towers fell, some told the president their son or daughter, husband or wife, would somehow be miraculously found alive and pulled from the debris. I knew their prayers were not likely to be answered.

I watched President Bush patiently comfort each family, giving them his full attention. The conversations were often earnest and occasionally filled with laughter as they remembered the person taken from them. And there were tears, lots of tears, from the families, Bush, and those of us with him. I lasted for about ten or fifteen minutes before I realized I couldn't stop weeping. I was of no use and left the room.

Five or ten minutes later, Reverend Kirbyjon Caldwell, pastor of Windsor Village United Methodist Church in Houston, came out of the makeshift room. Windsor Village is a congregation of about fifteen thousand people and Reverend Caldwell had bonded with the then-governor Bush years before on faith-based initiatives. When I spotted him, Reverend Caldwell was weeping as well. It gave me a little satisfaction that a man of such great faith found himself in the same place as I was. He said of Bush that in his years as a pastor, "I have never seen someone ministering to the bereaved better." Feeling guilty, I would occasionally compose myself to make a foray into the room, again prove to be of no use, and find myself leaving again. The president stayed. So did Joe Hagin, who somehow steeled himself for the trial, and Governor Pataki, who displayed an admirable stoicism.

For most Americans, 9/11 was horrifying pictures on a television screen or a newspaper's front page. For George W. Bush, the most vivid memories are the families of those who died. These were faces and lives racked by grief; in their company, hearing their stories in a simple, makeshift room located in a New York City parking garage, he could not remain distant from the power of their grief.

A nine- or ten-year-old blond boy was hesitant to approach the president, but his mother pushed him and his sister forward. The boy wordlessly held up a photo of his father in his police uniform. The president took the photo and wrote on it that he had met the policeman's son and gave it back to the boy saying that he should give it to his father when he was found. The boy tearfully wrapped his arm around the president's waist and buried his head against him. Bush held the child close for a very long time. The child never said a thing.

One woman, waiting patiently to speak to the president, stood for a considerable time before someone finally found her a chair. As the informal receiving line thinned out, the president approached Arlene Howard and bent down to hear the story of her son, Port Authority police officer* George Howard. September 11 was his day off, but he rushed to the World Trade Center after it was hit. His body was found in the rubble. Ms. Howard wanted the president to have her son's badge to remind him of that day's cost. He carried George Howard's badge to the end of his presidency.

While Bush continued his visits, I waited with other staff near the Javits Center entrance through which rescue workers came and went to their makeshift lodgings. Senator Hillary Clinton was sitting to one side of the door. A group of rescue workers glanced behind as they entered and spotted her. They dug out a disposable camera and asked for a picture. She said yes but pleaded exhaustion and announced she would remain sitting. I took the camera, they clustered around her, and I took the shot. I found myself irritated she did not rise in the presence of such men.

Finally, at 7:58 P.M., an hour and forty minutes behind schedule, Bush had visited with the last family. He was completely sapped of energy. The motorcade left the Javits Center for the Wall Street landing zone, but on its way it was surrounded by thousands of people holding candles, crowding onto the street. As the limo inched slowly through the crowd, people began to applaud. I looked out the support van window at faces of strangers filled with loss and hope and tears, three feet on the other side of the glass, and found myself nearly overwhelmed.

At the heliport, choppers stood ready to take us back to McGuire. Richard Keil of Bloomberg wrote that as the press chopper banked over Ground Zero one last time, he "saw two rescue workers, looking skyward. They were saluting."

Bush later told me his time with the families in the Javits Center parking garage was a moment "when the comforter became the comforted." He was clearly moved by the experience, and I knew the people he had met were comforted by the time he spent with them.

At McGuire, we separated. In the decades I had known George W. Bush, I had never seen him as drained as he was when we wordlessly shook hands. The president flew to western Maryland and Camp David and the rest of us returned to Washington. As our motorcade moved up Fifteenth Street to the White House, I looked west to the Lincoln Memorial. Thousands of people stood quietly with candles that flickered like fireflies in a vast meadow.

That night, I sat in my darkened study at home. As I thought about the day's events, I realized there was no noise from passenger planes passing over the house in or out of Reagan National Airport, nor any racket from cars on nearby Arizona Avenue. All I could hear was the distant growl of the combat air patrol fighter jets that now prowled high above the capital. In coming months, it was to become a nocturnal reminder of our changed lives.

It was the last night I drove myself home for several weeks. At the suggestion of the Secret Service, Joe Hagin gave the president's senior staff "carpet" privileges. I and a few others were picked up by military drivers in the morning and delivered home at night until the city returned to a semblance of normality, and security concerns abated.

Back in New York, an exhausted retired firefighter drove home from Ground Zero to his Long Island home. Bob Beckwith had with him the small flag Bush and he had carried on the truck. Bob didn't know if his wife, Barbara, would believe that he had met the president of the United

States. But Barbara already knew. Earlier that afternoon, her then nine-year-old granddaughter, Megan Carney, had called from the living room to say, "Grandpa is on television." When Barbara came in to see what her granddaughter could be talking about, there was Bob on top of a crushed truck, standing next to President Bush, who had one hand on Bob's shoulder and the other holding a bullhorn.

As Bob pulled up in front of his modest Baldwin, New York, home that night, neighbors streamed out of their homes, many bearing lighted candles of remembrance. Some had waited hours for his arrival. As Bob got out of his car, his friend Mike, a retired New York cop, asked, "Beck, do you know you were on TV?" A quiet man, Bob characteristically nodded as if that fact were of no consequence and went into his house.

It was Friday night. The next morning at Camp David, George W. Bush was to convene his first war council.

CHAPTER 18

Striking Back

———— • ◆ • ————

The ground campaign began inauspiciously enough. On October 19, 2001, the Pentagon announced that a handful of American Special Forces soldiers had slipped into Afghanistan. A photo released later would show some of them riding horses along treeless mountains heading into the fight. They were the tip of a very long and lethal spear being driven into the heart of the Taliban regime and the network of al-Qaeda hideouts that pockmarked the country.

Afghanistan is a remote, tribal, and often violent place. It chewed up Soviet soldiers for nearly a decade after the Russians invaded in 1979. It repelled the British military in the nineteenth century. And by 2001, it was controlled by the Taliban, which was in a civil war with the Northern Alliance. Two days before 9/11, the Taliban had just scored a big victory with the assassination of Alliance leader Ahmad Shah Massoud. From its history, it was clear Afghanistan would not be subdued simply by America's uncoiling its military machine.

American war strategists developed an audacious plan that would tip the scales against the Taliban. In essence, the Pentagon and CIA decided to use the Northern Alliance's insurgency against Mullah Mohammad Omar—the elusive, hard-bitten leader of the Taliban who had lost an eye fighting the Soviets. Quickly, a few hundred Special Forces soldiers linked up with the Alliance's guerrilla fighters. They called in air strikes that included massive fifteen-thousand-pound "daisy cutter" bombs and smart bombs capable of decimating the enemy.

It was a new kind of war, the dimensions of which were hard to grasp at the outset. At a press briefing in November, Secretary of Defense Donald Rumsfeld was asked if we were air-dropping horses for our soldiers to use. Noting that such airdrops would likely break a horse's legs, Rumsfeld replied no: "Not that I'm that politically correct—but I love horses."

The defense secretary also deflected speculation that we would suffer the same fate as the Soviets—a long, losing campaign—pointing out that there was a critical difference between us and communist invaders: "[W]e don't covet their land," he said. Americans were there to crush two sets of Islamic extremists. One had attacked the United States and the other was oppressing the Afghan people. Each depended on the other for survival.

Many Taliban failed to grasp our intentions and capabilities in the war. Omar reportedly covered the roof of his house in Kandahar with layers of old tires under the assumption that this would shield him from an American air assault. He was half right. The tires didn't save him from having to flee, but they did save his house from an American bomb. Nancy deWolf Smith, an editorial board member of the *Wall Street Journal,* visited Omar's compound after it was captured and found the house still intact. She reported what locals had told her—that a bomb had bounced off the roof of the house and crashed into a nearby barn, killing several cows.

But even as the house stood, the Taliban regime run by the man who owned it was obliterated. Within six weeks of the start of Operation Enduring Freedom, the military offensive into Afghanistan, key cities had fallen. Kunduz was the scene of especially hard fighting. But it fell under the weight of American military power, as did Mazar-i-Sharif and Kabul, the capital. By the end of November, twenty-seven out of thirty provinces were no longer under Taliban control. Most of the Taliban had fled to Pakistan and much of al-Qaeda had been demolished. Muhammad Atef, a top lieutenant to Osama bin Laden and one of the operatives who planned the September 11 attacks, was reportedly killed in a November air strike.

Today many people consider it to have been a foregone conclusion that we could quickly topple the Taliban and inflict an early blow against the ideology of Islamic extremism. But on the morning of September 11, as smoke rising from the World Trade Center trailed past the Statue of Liberty and filled the previously clear blue skies of New York, it was far from certain what America's response would be. Clearly, there would be one, but how far-reaching and successful it would be turned on the decisions of one man, who at the time of the attacks was reading to school-children in a Florida classroom.

From the outset, Bush understood that we were at war. That understanding, however, was only a broad framework for how the country would meet the challenge of Islamic extremism. The hard work was in figuring out precisely what type of war this would be, what the strategy would be, what tactics would be most effective for winning. That work began immediately.

I was not part of the national security apparatus that would now dominate Bush's agenda. So even though I continued counseling the president on whatever he asked me and helped him gauge how the public would react to his decisions (along with explaining his policies to the public), I was not in the War Cabinet as he made his war decisions.

It was, however, clear to everyone in the White House that our principal responsibility was to prevent a second wave of attacks. It was al-Qaeda's style to deliver a second punch after a devastating first. So intelligence, law enforcement, military, and diplomatic resources were mobilized to forestall another blow. If a large one came quickly, it could cripple the country economically and psychologically.

We also knew that the country was grieving, angry, and would soon be impatient for a response. Going after al-Qaeda and by extension the Taliban was what the American people expected of us, though a few on the political left argued against the use of force.

Bush also knew instinctively this was a different kind of war—a conflict waged against a set of ideas and a stateless terrorist group that did not have a capital to defend and didn't worry about protecting its people. Indeed, it reveled in the carnage of war. These terrorists would hide among civilians and benefit from our unwillingness to be as ruthless as they were. The terrorists believed that when their fighters were killed, they went to heaven and that the killing of innocents would chip away at the civilized world's resolve to resist.

We were entering a global and often clandestine conflict that would take years and tremendous effort to win. But we did have advantages, and Bush immediately made a decision that would be the most significant shift in foreign policy since the Cold War and gave us an opportunity to shift the contest in our direction. He decided that the nations that harbored terror groups would be held as responsible as the terrorists. His critical insight was this: terrorists were most dangerous when they received state support, because that assistance could provide them with weapons of mass destruction as well as places to train and hide.

In the days right after 9/11, George W. Bush formulated the core of what would later become known as the Bush Doctrine. On September 20, 2001, he put forward the elements of that doctrine in his speech to a joint session of Congress.

He opened by making plain that the United States would not hesitate in its new task: "Tonight, we are a country awakened to danger and called to defend freedom. Our grief has turned to anger and anger to resolution. Whether we bring our enemies to justice or bring justice to our enemies, justice will be done."

He used the speech to spell out what we as a country would do to drive a wedge between other states and terrorist networks: "We will starve terrorists of funding, turn them one against another, drive them from place to place until there is no refuge or no rest. And we will pursue nations that provide aid or safe haven to terrorism. Every nation in every region now has a decision to make," he said. "Either you are with us or you are with the terrorists. From this day forward, any nation that continues to harbor or support terrorism will be regarded by the United States as a hostile regime."

The president's point was it didn't matter why terrorists were able to operate within your borders. If terrorists were active in your country, you either had to help crush them or we would do so, even if it required treating you as a hostile regime.

Bush went on to describe the nature of al-Qaeda and its ideology. He demanded that the Taliban hand over Osama bin Laden and other terrorists living in Afghanistan as well as open the country up to American forces. This was more than a perfunctory demand. It was one of the first steps to war.

The president also tried to prepare the American people for a long struggle. He said that what the terrorists hated most was our freedom, that they had attacked our very way of life. He warned that in the years ahead we couldn't afford to allow memories to fade and our resolve to waver. To make sure that he always remembered what we were fighting for, he said, "I will carry this," and held up the police shield of George Howard, who had died at the World Trade Center. "It was given to me by his mom, Arlene, as a proud memorial to her son," he said. "It is my reminder of lives that ended and a task that does not end."

He closed by saying:

> I will not forget the wound to our country and those who inflicted it. I will not yield, I will not rest, I will not relent in waging this struggle for freedom and security for the American people. The course of this conflict is not known, yet its outcome is certain. Freedom and fear, justice and cruelty, have always been at war, and we know that God is not neutral between them. . . .

I heard these words as I stood in the well of the House of Representatives. I had a lump in my throat. Congress responded with a standing ovation. On the way back to the White House, Bush called me from the presidential limo (I was trailing a few cars behind him). He was concerned about how the members of Congress had sat quiet for much of the speech, exploding with applause only periodically. I reassured him they were rapt, not bored.

It was an extraordinary night. The country, and virtually the entire Congress, were now behind him. We had reached a moment of national unity unlike any in my lifetime.

The moment needed to be handled properly, for the tasks before the nation were monumental and the stakes were as high as they come. The president was about to direct our soldiers to wage war in a far-off country, and we faced a foe that intended to kill as many innocent people as it could. "Full warning has been given," Bush said in a radio address on October 6 devoted to his demand that the Taliban turn over terrorists hiding in Afghanistan, "and time is running out."

The following day, the sand had run out of the hourglass. At 1 P.M. in the Treaty Room at the White House, the president began his third major address to the nation since the attacks: "Good afternoon. On my orders, the United States military has begun strikes against al-Qaeda terrorist training camps and military installations of the Taliban regime in Afghanistan."

I stood just inside the Treaty Room door, looking through its south window at the Washington Monument and its base surrounded by a circle of American flags. I thought about the first shot of the first war of the twenty-first century, fired at our country on September 11, and about the reality that the president was explaining on the other side of the room. The United States was now shooting back.

Some of those shots would be delivered by men who made their way into Afghanistan on horseback. Others came from airmen flying combat missions to deliver lethal payloads from the sky. And still others developed target lists, hammered out tactics, and painstakingly collected intelligence to locate and destroy enemy redoubts. Thanks to their efforts, as we entered the first winter of the war, things were going much better than we had expected. American military forces had succeeded in ousting the Taliban, and the scenes of liberation pulled at America's heartstrings.

Within these scenes we saw outlines of why this fight would be different than other wars. Women being freed from Taliban brutality and subjugation offered a glimpse at one of the most potent weapons we had—one powerful enough to drive millions of people to our side, yet misunderstood by many in the United States who would come to oppose the Bush administration's war efforts. That weapon was the idea that all people desired to live in freedom, and that by helping them achieve that goal, we could turn them into allies with a direct stake in the fight against Islamic extremists. Freedom itself was attacked on 9/11, and it was freedom itself in Muslim lands that could undermine the ideology that had spawned the nineteen hijackers and led them to attack us. We were now in a war of ideas.

Bush needed to prepare the nation for the fact that winning this war required a different kind of mobilization than had won World War II. Al-Qaeda's aim was to frighten us into ceding large sections of the world to their ideology. To resist that fear and to uproot the extremist ideology where it had already been seeded, Americans needed to do two seemingly contradictory things: return to their normal routines, and steel themselves for the moments when toughness would be required to press our war aims. Doing both of these things would create a foundation of support for our soldiers fighting abroad, strengthen our country from within, and give us the ability to spread freedom to peoples across the world who would otherwise be dominated by terrorists.

Striking back against terrorism required hardening America's resolve from the white-hot anger of September 11, 2001, into the deep-seated determination to wage a prolonged global war on terrorism. The country needed to be measured while also resolute.

Unlike World War II, there would be no military conscription, scrap drives, or victory gardens. We needed new ways to mobilize the compassionate spirit of Americans who wanted to serve their country after 9/11.

Some critics used Bush's call for a measured mobilization to attack him for supposedly telling Americans to "go shopping." Among those who later hurled this charge were *New York Times* columnists Thomas Friedman and Paul Krugman and the *Times* editorial board itself. Prominent politicians echoed the criticism. While running for president in 2008, both John McCain and Barack Obama blasted Bush for urging Americans to "go shopping" rather than sacrifice for the common good. *Time's* managing editor, Richard Stengel, repeated the charge, writing, "After 9/11, Americans were hungry to be asked to do something, to make some kind of sacrifice, and what they mostly remember is being asked to go shopping."

This last criticism is particularly rich, since it was not Bush but Frank Pellegrini, a *Time* writer, who said "go shopping" as he praised Bush's September 20 speech to Congress as "the finest, strongest, clearest, several-times-chill-giving speech of his life." When Bush said, "I ask your continued participation and confidence in the American economy," Pellegrini wrote that what the president meant was: "And for God's sake keep shopping."

But Bush never actually said to "go shopping." The closest he ever came was in a November 8 speech at the Georgia World Congress Center in Atlanta, in which he said, "This great nation will never be intimidated. People are going about their daily lives, working and shopping and playing, worshipping at churches and synagogues and mosques, going to movies and to baseball games." To take this one brief reference and then pretend Bush's words can be reduced to simply urging people to shop is intellectually dishonest.

Bush did exactly what his critics later said they wanted—he sought to calm passions and called for Americans to make sacrifices by volunteering.

He publicly reached out to America's Muslim community to set an example of tolerance toward Muslims and their faith. Less than a week after the 9/11 attacks, Bush went to the Islamic Center in Washington for a wide-ranging discussion at the mosque. The president told the press that terrorists represent "evil and war," not Islam, and called for Muslim Americans to be treated with respect.

Throughout the fall of 2001, Bush was also determined to channel the spontaneous outpouring of patriotism and public-spiritedness into a lasting and organized approach to solving problems. The American people's generosity and willingness to help others had deep resonance with Bush's compassionate conservatism.

He started on September 18 with a Rose Garden ceremony urging Americans to donate money, time, and even blood to charities in New York City, Pennsylvania, and Virginia. He reiterated this call in his September 20 joint-session speech, directing Americans to a website where they could find groups helping recovery efforts. In early October, Bush announced "America's Fund for Afghan Children." And on October 25 the president announced a broader partnership called "Friendship Through Education." Thousands of teachers in the United States and in Muslim nations were trained to use the Internet and school-to-school partnerships to promote understanding among tens of thousands of students across the globe. But to Bush, these efforts seemed ad hoc and small. In October, he tapped John Bridgeland, then deputy director of the Domestic Policy Council, to develop a more ambitious volunteer initiative.

The result was announced in the 2002 State of the Union address: "We want to be a nation that serves goals larger than self," the president said, explaining that 9/11 had caused Americans to begin "to think less of the goods we can accumulate, and more about the good we can do." Then he asked every American to commit two years—four thousand hours—of service over their lifetimes and outlined his community and national service agenda.

The national service agenda had three priorities: responding to emergencies such as 9/11, strengthening communities, and extending America's compassion abroad. The president also announced that a new White House council, reporting directly to him, would coordinate these service efforts throughout the federal government. It was called the USA Freedom Corps and it helped direct an extraordinary amount of good works to productive endeavors and ranks as one of the most successful service campaigns in our country's history. The results are there for all to see.

ON THE DAY BEFORE Thanksgiving the president decided to have lunch with troops soon to be deployed to Afghanistan. I accompanied Bush to Fort Campbell, Kentucky, home of the 101st Airborne and the "Screaming Eagles," a storied unit that played a vital role on D-Day. I was assigned to a table of helicopter mechanics who had been specially trained to repair choppers downed on the battlefield. The outfit's "old man" could not have been more than twenty-five years old. He was worried that the fight in Afghanistan would be over before his team got there. I asked the young woman sitting next to me to tell me about herself. "The Army saved my life," she said simply. In between mouthfuls of turkey, she explained she'd grown up in a poor home in a bad New Orleans neighborhood where her future held drugs and dependency. Now she had a skill, the promise of an education, and a career she cherished that allowed her to serve the country she loved.

This was the first of many occasions when I was to break bread with members of the military. Each time, I found myself in awe, wondering how it is that our nation develops such people to stand as sentries at the gate. I suspect providence has something to do with inspiring those young men and women to fight for our nation's ideals.

IN THE WAKE OF 9/11, Bush was determined to put America on a war footing by reforming its war-fighting institutions, including the military, intelligence community, and agencies tasked with dealing with terrorists inside the country. He was not the first president to have this instinct. Harry Truman had merged the War and Navy departments into the Defense Department, created the National Security Council, transformed the Office of Strategic Services into the CIA, and begun Radio Free Europe because he knew that these things needed to be done if the United States was to stand down the Soviet Union.

Bush insisted four days after the attack, "Our response must be sweeping, sustained, and effective." And it was. His administration undertook the broadest reorganization of the federal government since the mid-twentieth century.

Much of the work had to do with updating badly outdated institutions and practices. For example, because of a misreading of the 1978 Foreign Intelligence Surveillance Act (FISA) and a series of bureaucratic decisions, a "wall" had been erected that prevented law enforcement and counterintelligence officials from sharing information. This was insanity—and it had deadly consequences: two of the terrorists who crashed Flight 77 into the Pentagon on 9/11 managed to escape FBI detection the previous month because an agent on the West Coast was denied help from the criminal-investigative side of his own agency. This wall was torn down.

Another area ripe for reform was the surveillance of potential terrorists. We wanted to give intelligence agencies and law enforcement the tools to combat terrorism that they already used to fight conventional crime. Before 9/11, law enforcement could get a "roving wiretap" to listen to a drug dealer who constantly switched cell phones, but not a suspected terrorist. Law enforcement could get a "sneak and peek" warrant to search the house of an organized crime figure without his immediate knowledge, but not that of a suspected terrorist. An "administrative subpoena" could be used to obtain the business records of a doctor suspected of Medicare fraud, but could not be deployed against a suspected terrorist.

The Patriot Act, passed by huge bipartisan majorities in October 2001, gave law enforcement these necessary tools. The act was a major reason why America was not attacked again while George W. Bush was president.

We also needed to crack the financial foundations of the global terrorism network. Less than two weeks after 9/11, Bush signed an executive order to freeze the financial assets of dozens of terrorist organizations, individual terrorist leaders, and corporations that serve as front groups. He announced an international financial "most wanted" list and ordered the relevant agencies to work closely with allies to cut off terrorist financing. "Money is the lifeblood of terrorist operations," Bush said. "Today, we're asking the world to stop payment."

Above all, he made investigating terrorist activity the top priority for both intelligence and law enforcement agencies. He created a Cabinet-level position reporting directly to the president, and later formed the Department of Homeland Security out of twenty-two different organizations from across the government. He established the position of Director of National Intelligence and instructed our nation's intelligence agencies to create a layered system that could nab terrorists overseas, at the border, and within the country. Bush set up a National Counterterrorism Center where federal, state, and local department and agency personnel would work side by side to track terrorist threats. And he expanded the stockpile of drugs and vaccines that would be needed if there were a bioterrorist attack. None of this was easy, all of it took time, much of it needed to be refined and improved and tested—and all of it had the strong support of congressional Democrats.

Of all the steps the Bush administration took, though, no issue became as controversial as when the president—unbeknownst to me at the time—authorized the use of enhanced interrogation techniques (EITs) on high-value terrorist detainees. These tough, coercive techniques included stress positions, cramped confinement, "insult slaps," dietary manipulation, wall standing, water dousing, sleep deprivation, and waterboarding. They were used selectively against some thirty hard-core terrorist detainees who had successfully resisted other forms of interrogation. Only three were waterboarded.

The practices were authorized by the Department of Justice in August 2002 and done only with the explicit authorization of the CIA director. They were carefully monitored and conducted by professionally trained intelligence experts.

These procedures have become controversial because they have been called torture. So, are EITs torture? It's a ferocious debate that can be broken into two parts.

The first is political. Regardless of whether you support Bush's approach to the war on terror, it is clear that some Democrats opposed EITs retroactively to score points. That is both reprehensible and dangerous. When these techniques were first authorized, Democratic leaders had been briefed about them. Their silence made them complicit in their use.

Nonetheless, when political winds shifted and memories of 9/11 faded, some Democratic leaders claimed that they had never been told about the techniques and that the Bush administration used EITs only in secret. One Democrat who deserves to be singled out by name is Nancy Pelosi, now Speaker of the House. She claims to have been left in the dark—which the CIA has vigorously disputed and the record has proven false. The CIA conducted more than thirty briefings for congressional members on the practices. One summary released by the CIA of a September 4, 2002, briefing, for example, said, "Briefing on EITs including use of EITs on Abu Zubaydah [a high-level al-Qaeda operative], background on authorities, and a description of the particular EITs that had been employed." Pelosi was in attendance.

That Democrats claim to have been kept in the dark about EITs is dangerous because the United States is in a hotly contested war against terrorism. It is destructive for leaders of one party to deny their involvement in developing war policies. Doing so undermines the ability of everyone from the president on down to the CIA agent and soldier on the ground to carry out national security policies. Can we really expect CIA agents to carry out war policies if they fear that leaders of one of the two major political parties will punish them for good-faith efforts to protect America?

The second part of the debate is the more central one: Do these techniques cross the line into torture? Some critics of Bush dismiss the question altogether and simply assume that they are torture. After all, they say, many of these techniques, waterboarding in particular, are violations of the Geneva Conventions. But there is a problem with that assumption: They weren't. In fact, until the flawed 2006 Supreme Court decision *Hamdan v. Rumsfeld*, the Geneva Conventions' "Common Article III" protections were intended to cover civil wars, not international terrorist attacks.

Broader Geneva protections were meant to apply only to signatory nations, which means they don't apply to al-Qaeda. They were designed to create an incentive for soldiers to fight in a way that upholds the basic rules of war, including sparing innocent civilians and minimizing suffering even among combatants.

"When the Bush administration decided in early 2002 to deny al Qaeda and Taliban forces legal protections under the Geneva Conventions," Jack Goldsmith, who served as head of the Office of Legal Counsel in the Bush Justice Department in 2003–2004, has written, "it was acting in step with this long-held U.S. position that terrorists and other enemy fighters who did not wear uniforms or carry their arms openly would be denied POW status."

For some this misses the point. A detainee's status isn't what they worry about. Their concern is whether waterboarding itself is torture and whether it is therefore illegal to use on anyone for any reason at any time. But in fact, this wasn't a settled issue of law when President Bush put us on a war footing and still isn't today. Beginning in 2002, the Department of Justice's Office of Legal Counsel (OLC) carefully examined how the United States defined torture and whether each of the practices was legal under that definition. At the CIA's request, OLC carefully spelled out the limits to each EIT and what standards and procedures were required precisely to ensure it was *not* torture. Both the CIA and Justice wanted to make clear what interrogators could and could not do.

I can see that there are reasonable voices who believe that our use of EITs was wrong and unnecessary, that it alienated world opinion, and that it created more problems than it solved. Some, like Jack Goldsmith, believe the OLC memos that gave the green light to waterboarding were legally flawed, even if the technique was legal. I take these concerns seriously.

To those who have good-faith concerns, I say this: For those of us serving in government at the time—in the aftermath of 9/11 and when intelligence was collecting "chatter" from terrorist operatives that indicated another attack was imminent—this debate was not academic. We knew very little about the enemy who attacked us, not even the name of the operations chief who planned the attack: Khalid Sheikh Mohammed. Thousands—and perhaps many more than thousands—of American lives hung in the balance.

The weight of these circumstances is something that Democratic U.S. senator Charles Schumer of New York, of all people, understood in 2004. He said:

> Take the hypothetical: if we knew that there was a nuclear bomb hidden in an American city and we believe that some kind of torture, fairly severe maybe, would give us a chance of finding that bomb before it went off, my guess is most Americans and most Senators, maybe all, would do what you have to do. So it's easy to sit back in the armchair and say that torture can never be used. But when you're in the foxhole, it's a very

different deal. And I respect, I think we all respect the fact that the President's in the foxhole every day.

But the president never authorized torture. He did just the opposite by making sure the EITs did not cross the legal line into torture. What's more, EITs did help our intelligence agents gather critical information to thwart future attacks. Within months after the 9/11 attacks, the United States captured Abu Zubaydah, a top lieutenant of Osama bin Laden. Zubaydah provided some useful information when he was interrogated, but then clammed up, having been trained to resist interrogation.

After enhanced interrogation techniques were applied, including waterboarding, Zubaydah spoke voluminously. He provided information on key al-Qaeda operatives, including information that led to the capture of the terrorist Ramzi bin al-Shibh, before he could follow through on his plot to conduct an encore to 9/11 by flying planes into Heathrow Airport and London. Together, Zubaydah and bin al-Shibh provided information that led to the capture of other terrorist leaders, most prominently Khalid Sheikh Mohammed, the 9/11 mastermind who boasted of having personally beheaded journalist Daniel Pearl in 2002.

After Khalid Sheikh Mohammed was subjected to waterboarding, intelligence officers say he led what they called "terrorist tutorials." KSM "seemed to relish the opportunity to discuss, sometimes for hours on end, the inner workings of al-Qaeda and the group's plans, ideology, and operatives," said a source describing the sessions to the *Washington Post*. "He'd even use a chalkboard at times." KSM disclosed vital information on al-Qaeda's efforts to obtain biological weapons and plots to kill innocent people in London, Karachi, and Djibouti. He also provided information that led to the capture of the terrorist Hambali, which led to the discovery of an East Asian terrorist cell that had planned attacks, including one using planes to fly into the Library Tower in Los Angeles. It was a much different KSM than the one who, when captured, refused to cooperate, saying, "I'll talk to you guys after I get to New York and see my lawyer."

George Tenet, who served as director of the CIA under both President Clinton and President Bush, has said, "I know that this program saved lives. I know we've disrupted plots. I know this program alone is worth more than [what] the FBI, the [CIA], and the National Security

Agency put together have been able to tell us." Michael Hayden, director of the CIA from 2006 to 2009, and Michael Mukasey, attorney general from 2007 to 2009, have written, "As late as 2006 . . . fully half of the government's knowledge about the structure and activities of al Qaeda came from those interrogations." And former national intelligence director Mike McConnell put it this way: "We have people walking around in this country that are alive today because this process happened."

WHILE ALL THESE ACTIONS were taking place, our administration began looking toward Iraq in the early part of 2002. The question many people have is why.

Bush critics had a range of theories: that Bush was determined to finish what his dad started in the first Gulf War; that he was doing the bidding of Israel; or that he wanted to teach the Arab world a lesson.

None of these theories is true. The reason we turned our attention to Iraq was much more straightforward: we believed Saddam Hussein posed a threat to America's national security. This view reflected a significant shift in the president's thinking after 9/11, and it was a view he repeatedly laid out in public speeches. On June 1, 2002, for example, Bush delivered the commencement address at West Point. His key point was this: "We cannot defend America and our friends by hoping for the best. We cannot put our faith in the word of tyrants, who solemnly sign nonproliferation treaties, and then systematically break them. If we wait for threats to fully materialize, we will have waited too long. . . . The war on terror will not be won on the defensive."

We knew that Saddam Hussein had never fully accounted for his chemical, biological, and nuclear weapons programs. He repeatedly showed hostile intentions toward his neighbors, by invading Kuwait and attacking Iran. He maintained a brutal regime that held on to power by carrying out sadistic atrocities against its own people, killing three hundred thousand Iraqi civilians. He had supported terrorists, attempted to assassinate the first President Bush in the 1990s (after he had left office), continued to threaten American pilots overseeing a no-fly zone over Iraq, evaded the sanctions put on his country, and flouted sixteen United Nations resolutions demanding that he live up to the terms of the cease-fire agreement that ended the Persian Gulf War in 1991.

In the wake of 9/11, these actions made Saddam Hussein a unique threat. He thumbed his nose at the international community's demands, had unleashed unprovoked attacks in the past (including using weapons of mass destruction on his own people), and acted as if there were a state of military hostilities between his country and the United States. He gave all the signs of being a nightmare scenario for us: a state sponsor of terror willing to put the most deadly weapons into the hands of those who would use them against American cities.

This dangerous combination of factors—a post-9/11 world, Saddam Hussein in violation of a slew of U.N. resolutions, and the evil nature of his regime—made Iraq a unique threat in our eyes and, it cannot be said often enough, in the eyes of most of the leading figures in the Democratic Party. There was a bipartisan consensus—formed in the 1990s—that held Saddam was dangerous and that regime change in Iraq was U.S. policy.

Democrats would like people to forget this. Indeed, they have perpetrated the fiction that the Bush administration jammed Democrats by forcing Congress to vote before the 2002 election on a resolution authorizing force against Iraq. The Bush White House—read: Karl C. Rove—supposedly felt this would force Democrats to back war out of a fear that voters would otherwise see them as weak. This claim is not true and, as is so often the case, does not reflect a more complicated reality.

During July and August 2002, congressional Democrats peppered the president with demands to come to Congress before taking action against Iraq. In response, on August 29, unnamed senior administration officials told the press "they expected President Bush eventually to seek some new explicit approval from Congress—but not necessarily a formal vote—before launching any military campaign against Iraq." In fact, the president wanted congressional support. He believed it would give cover to coalition allies such as British prime minister Tony Blair and strengthen our hand at the United Nations.

Senate Foreign Affairs Committee chairman Joseph Biden and the ranking Republican on the committee, Richard Lugar of Indiana, wrote the president on September 10 cautioning against a vote on any war resolution until after the elections. Both men made it clear that leaving Saddam with weapons of mass destruction wasn't acceptable: "Simply put, either these weapons must be dislodged from Iraq, or Saddam Hussein must be dislodged from power."

Four Democrats—House minority whip Nancy Pelosi, Senate majority whip Harry Reid, Senator Richard J. Durbin, and Congressman Tom
Lantos (the ranking Democrat on House Foreign Affairs)—chimed in
that day to say Congress should take up a resolution after the election. At
his weekly briefing with reporters, Senate majority leader Tom Daschle
said his staff was researching why then–minority leader Bob Dole had
objected to a vote before the 1990 elections to authorize the use of force
to eject Iraq from Kuwait. Dole had delayed the congressional vote authorizing the Persian Gulf War until January 12, 1991. "We just want to
know what the parallel circumstances may be," Daschle said. This suggested he leaned toward a postelection vote. Daschle went on to warn,
"Any 2002 resolution authorizing force against Iraq should not be used
as an election issue."

For once, I agreed with Biden, Pelosi, Lantos, Reid, Durbin, and
Daschle. It wasn't helpful to the country if a use-of-force vote took place
in the midterm's closing weeks. If diplomacy failed and military action
was necessary, better that Congress had voted after an election, not before, to authorize force. I told Bush this in early September, but I knew
there were dissenting opinions: National Security Advisor Condi Rice
and her deputy, Stephen J. Hadley, thought an earlier vote would
strengthen America's hand at getting a U.N. resolution that might convince Saddam he would lose power unless he complied with the agreements. Most White House officials considered the question academic:
until Congress decided it wanted a vote, there wasn't going to be one.
Bush, for his part, wasn't focused on the vote's timing: he was working on
more immediate tasks, which included a speech he planned to give at the
United Nations and a massive effort to reach out to allies.

The president's speech was aimed at laying the foundation for another
U.N. resolution demanding that Saddam comply or face consequences.
On September 12, Bush laid out an argument intended to win U.N. support for confronting Saddam Hussein. He made it plain to the U.N.
General Assembly that Saddam's defiance not only was dangerous, it also
undercut the U.N.'s credibility: "The conduct of the Iraqi regime is a
threat to the authority of the United Nations, and a threat to peace. Iraq
has answered a decade of U.N. demands with a decade of defiance. All
the world now faces a test and the United Nations a difficult and defining moment. Are Security Council resolutions to be honored and en-

forced or cast aside without consequence? Will the United Nations serve the purpose of its founding or will it be irrelevant?"

Five days later, Senator Daschle changed his mind about a congressional vote. At his regular session with reporters on September 17, the South Dakota senator said, "I think there will be a vote well before the elections. I think that it's important to work together to achieve that." When I heard the news, I thought Daschle had settled the issue of the vote's timing.

Five years later, Daschle would dispute that he had set the vote for before the election, accusing me of having "a very faulty memory" or "not telling the truth" about his decision on when to hold the vote. He blamed the pre-election vote on Bush, saying he "asked Bush during a breakfast to delay the vote until after the election" but that Bush felt "time was of the essence and they needed the vote and they were going to move forward." This revisionist history is itself dangerous: it suggests Bush had politicized the vote to win approval for invading Iraq. It is a not-so-subtle attempt to take Democrats off the hook for having voted for going to war, while also undermining the legitimacy of the president's decision to remove Saddam Hussein.

And as a matter of fact, Daschle and Bush didn't have breakfast between September 10, when Daschle said he was looking into the 1990 precedent, and September 17, when Daschle said there should be a vote on Iraq. Their breakfast was September 18, the day *after* Daschle called for a pre-election congressional vote. I can't find a shred of evidence that Daschle asked Bush to delay the vote in any of the encounters he had with him that summer. Their previous breakfast was July 24, a month before the administration even said it would go to Congress. If Bush had asked Daschle for a pre-election vote before September 18, I suspect the majority leader would have revealed it in his September 10 or 17 press briefing. Daschle was not one to miss a chance to jab a political opponent.

The administration did not urge a pre-election vote before Daschle's September 17 statement and did not control the Senate calendar. If we could control the timing of congressional action, particularly in an unruly Democratic Senate, then we would be miracle workers. The truth is that Tom Daschle set the pre-election congressional vote on the use-of-force resolution. And so in early October—by a vote of 296–133 in the

House and 77–23 in the Senate—Congress authorized war with Iraq. The margin was much larger than the one that authorized the Persian Gulf War.

On November 8, the U.N. Security Council passed Resolution 1441 by a 15–0 vote, finding Iraq in material breach of its obligations and vowing "serious consequences"—which everyone took to be war—if Iraq did not fully and immediately disarm.

By now it was clear to everyone—except perhaps Saddam Hussein—that unless he acted, we were on the course toward war. Whether we ended up there or not rested entirely with the Iraqi dictator.

In January 2003, Hans Blix, who was head of the U.N. Monitoring, Verification and Inspection Commission (UNMOVIC), reported to the Security Council, "Iraq appears not to have come to a genuine acceptance, not even today, of the disarmament which was demanded of it." Mohammed ElBaradei, director general of the International Atomic Energy Agency (IAEA), reported that Iraq, in responding to Resolution 1441, "did not provide any new information relevant to certain questions that have been outstanding since 1998." The leaders of eight European countries—Spain, Portugal, Italy, the United Kingdom, Hungary, Poland, Denmark, and the Czech Republic—published an article saying they stood as one with President Bush on Iraq. Many Democrats expressed support. Time was running out for Saddam.

On February 6, Secretary of State Powell presented to the U.N. Security Council the comprehensive U.S. case against Iraq. This speech was viewed within the White House as extremely significant. Powell, after all, had wide bipartisan respect and, while he supported the war (and has never backed away from that fact), he was not viewed as a "hawk." He had enormous credibility from having personally reviewed the evidence exhaustively. Powell concluded his presentation with a call for resolve: "We must not shrink from whatever is ahead of us. We must not fail in our duty and our responsibility to the citizens of the countries that are represented by this body."

Powell's speech perfectly captured our thinking. We wanted to increase pressure on Saddam Hussein, which would, we hoped, cause him to change his ways, to comply with U.N. demands and live up to his obligations. On the eve of war, Bush made one last effort to avoid conflict, with Middle Eastern nations delivering public and private messages urging Saddam Hussein to leave Iraq. He refused. President Bush then said that Saddam Hussein and his sons had forty-eight hours to leave Iraq; their refusal to do so, he said, would result in military conflict. Once again, Saddam Hussein refused. And so on March 19, at 10:16 P.M., President Bush announced his fateful decision. "My fellow citizens," the president began in an Oval Office address, "at this hour, American and coalition forces are in the early stages of military operations to disarm Iraq, to free its people and to defend the world from grave danger."

Bush's hope, our hope, was that Iraq would comply with the world's just demands; that Saddam would scrap his country's programs to develop weapons of mass destruction and allow international inspectors to verify and oversee the process as Libya's Gaddafi was to do in December 2003 after seeing what happened to Saddam. But from the beginning, Bush made it clear that in a post-9/11 world he would not allow delay, indecision, and inaction to threaten the security of the United States. He was a man of his word.

CHAPTER 19

What Bipartisanship?

In the aftermath of 9/11, we expected any lingering questions about Bush's "legitimacy" to be set aside. Americans yearned to be brought together, and Bush recognized this. One of his first meetings as president-elect was with a powerful Democratic congressman, and shortly after his inauguration he held another that included Democratic graybeards and senior statesmen such as former senator John Glenn.

But within weeks of 9/11 the hyperpartisanship that had characterized Washington in the 1990s returned and the conviction among some Democrats that Bush had unfairly won the presidency reemerged. Democrats used their slim control of the Senate to go on the offensive, supported all the while by partisan Democrats in the House.

On September 27, 2001, I traveled with the president to Chicago's O'Hare Airport, where he delivered a rousing speech to airline workers in which he promised to put the federal government in charge of airport security as part of a long-term plan to protect the nation's airliners from terrorist attacks.

Emotions were high throughout the industry, but especially for American and United workers who had lost colleagues in hijacked planes on September 11. House Democratic leader Dick Gephardt graciously came to the event and caught a ride back to Washington on Air Force One. The president was eager to talk with him about three priorities:

responding to the terrorist threat, helping New York and the Pentagon rebuild, and pulling the nation's economy back from the edge of a cliff.

Gephardt wasn't so sure that action was needed on the economy. The week before our event in Chicago, he had said "the jury is still out" on whether the government should do anything and wondered, "Do we need a stimulus package?"

I watched Bush engage with Gephardt for ninety minutes in the president's private cabin on Air Force One. Unlike so many politicians, Bush is not evasive and does not make cryptic comments or subtle asides. Henry Kissinger once said that for Richard Nixon, words were like billiard balls; what mattered wasn't the initial impact, but the carom. Bush lays his cards on the table, faceup, and explains how he intends to play them.

The president had asked for proposals to stimulate the economy from Larry Lindsey, director of the National Economic Council, and Mark Weinberger, assistant Treasury secretary for tax policy. They recommended we cut the corporate tax rate by 20 percent; change tax laws to allow small businesses to take better advantage of tax write-offs for buying equipment or opening new plants; repeal the corporate minimum tax; and allow companies to write off current losses against past profits for a longer period. Lindsey and the administration's entire economic team believed the corporate tax cut would do the most good. Companies would quickly figure how much they would save and respond by hiring more workers and expanding their businesses.

Bush shared these ideas with Gephardt, who now agreed that something needed to be done. I took his response as evidence the president's personal diplomacy was paying off. But then the Democrat delivered his punch. He said the corporate tax cut was a nonstarter with his caucus. He suggested instead sending out rebate checks to low- and moderate-income households, something Democrats had pushed for earlier in the year.

Our team had considered rebates, but decided they would be saved or used to pay down credit card debt, and not stimulate the economy.

Still, the president wanted to reach across the aisle. He called Lindsey immediately upon getting back to the White House, and against his better judgment, told him to replace the corporate rate cut with Gephardt's rebates. We'd get less economic bang for our money and fewer jobs would be created, but the president wanted to signal to Gephardt he was willing to drop one of his priorities in order to pick up one of Gephardt's. I thought Bush was being overly generous.

Reporters were soon briefed on the president's plan, including a provision that would spend between $16 billion and $20 billion out of the $75 billion package on tax rebates for low-income workers. The following day, the *Washington Post* reported that Democrats had "swiftly rejected" Bush's plan after Gephardt, Senate Democratic leader Tom Daschle, and House Democratic whip David Bonior huddled for two hours with labor leaders. Gephardt said "much, much more" needed to be done, including offering health and unemployment benefits to part-time and seasonal workers. By early October, Gephardt was complaining about "failures of bipartisanship." It was then that I knew the Democrat had little interest in working with Bush. Gephardt not only did not reciprocate Bush's gesture, but had actually turned it against the president.

A few weeks later, the same kind of Democratic ill will surfaced again, this time over Trade Promotion Authority (TPA). TPA is also known as "fast-track" authority because it gives the president the ability to hash out the fine details of a trade agreement and then submit it to Congress for an up-or-down vote. Outside of "fast-track," it is virtually impossible to work out a trade deal without getting bogged down in Congress over side disputes. No country is eager to engage in trade talks with the United States unless the president has TPA. First passed in 1974, TPA had expired in 1994. It became important to pass in 2001 as a sign that the United States was taking a leadership role in shoring up a global economy shaken by 9/11.

As the House vote drew near, the president invited Democratic fence-sitters to a meeting in the Cabinet Room of the White House. Twenty-two representatives showed up. Each had cast tough pro-trade votes during the 1990s under Clinton, including votes for the North American Free Trade Agreement (NAFTA) and China's admission into the World Trade Organization (WTO). The president made his case and then asked Congressman Jim Moran of Virginia to speak. Moran complimented the president but said he was probably the only person in the room who had been persuaded to support TPA. He was right: when called on by the president, each member mumbled excuses, ill-defined concerns, and obscure reasons for not supporting it.

Congresswoman Ellen Tauscher of California, a member of the powerful Ways and Means Committee, said in her characteristically blunt way that trade was vital for the high-tech and manufacturing companies in her district, but that she had a problem. "You need to know something, Mr. President," she said. "[House Ways and Means chairman] Bill Thomas has been mean to us," meaning that the notoriously difficult Republican was running roughshod over his committee. Hell, I thought to myself, Thomas is mean to us, too. This was a reason to oppose free trade and the interests of her district? But it was just an excuse. Democrats who voted for trade under Clinton were looking for a way not to vote for it under Bush.

We all knew Congressman Adam Smith of Washington, but when Bush asked him to comment, he started out by saying, "My name is Adam Smith. And like my famous namesake, I support free trade." He then lectured us on the many benefits of trade, both to the country as well as to his district. "But I have concerns," he said. He stopped talking like Adam Smith the eighteenth-century Enlightenment thinker and father of modern free-market economics, and started talking like Adam Smith the politician. I could not make heads or tails of what he was saying. I passed Larry Lindsey a note, asking if he could follow the ramblings. He couldn't, either.

Only three of the Democrats in the room that day voted for TPA. The measure passed by a single vote, cast by North Carolina Republican Robin Hayes, whose district was full of textile mills and voters who feared losing their jobs if trade barriers were lowered. A textile mill owner himself, Hayes voted on principle: he believed TPA was a power any president should have. But it was not an easy vote for him to make. After casting it, he sat down on the House floor and wept, believing he had ended his political career.

I made it a personal crusade to see him reelected. Everyone, including the president and both his parents, campaigned for Hayes. He won.

THE WAY DEMOCRATS APPROACHED trade was unprincipled, but their treatment of judicial nominees was appalling. A year after the president sent eleven appellate nominations to the Senate, eight still waited to have a hearing. Only one had been confirmed—a Clinton pick Bush had renominated as a peace offering. One of five federal appeals courts slots and one of ten federal district bench seats were vacant. Democrats were so slow to move that Republicans had to use a filibuster on a foreign aid bill less than a month after 9/11 to extract promises for hearings, most of which never materialized.

Democrats had perfected the art of smearing a judicial nominee in the 1980s and 1990s, when Robert Bork and Clarence Thomas were nominated to the Supreme Court. And Democrats hadn't lost their touch. Senate Judiciary Committee chairman Patrick Leahy led Judiciary Democrats in voting against seating Judge Charles Pickering on the Fifth Circuit Court of Appeals by claiming he was a bigot.

It chapped me that Democrats were smearing Pickering as racially prejudiced. Pickering had taken on the Ku Klux Klan in the 1960s as a county attorney in Mississippi and was voted out of office for it. He had also joined with respected former governor William Winter, a Democrat, to take the lead on racial reconciliation efforts in the state. Local NAACP chapters also supported his nomination.

I hadn't been enthusiastic about Pickering's nomination, because at sixty-four years old, he wouldn't spend as long on the bench as a younger judge, and we'd have to work just as hard to get him confirmed. My preference was to find highly qualified individuals who could serve for decades. But Senate Republican leader Trent Lott insisted on him, and Pickering deserved better than to be smeared.

In September, Judiciary Democrats blocked Texas Supreme Court justice Priscilla Owen's nomination to the Fifth Circuit by a vote of 10–9. I knew Owen as a top-flight appellate specialist who displayed the cool temperament of a federal judge. I'd helped her win a seat on the Texas Supreme Court, to which she was reelected with 84 percent of the vote and with the endorsement of every Texas newspaper, from the most conservative to the most liberal. But Senator Patrick Leahy and his chums, including Senator Chuck Schumer, slammed her as a right-wing lunatic, saying, "I'd urge Karl Rove, [White House Counsel] Judge [Alberto] Gonzales, and Attorney General Ashcroft to take heed from today's votes. . . . Activists and ideologues like Judge Owen are going to have a much more difficult voyage."

Then came the case of Miguel Estrada, one of America's great young legal minds. Born in Honduras, Estrada had emigrated to the United States when he was seventeen, with limited command of the English language. He graduated magna cum laude from Harvard Law School, where he was an editor of the *Harvard Law Review*. He clerked for Justice Anthony Kennedy of the Supreme Court and served with distinction at the Justice Department. Judiciary Committee Democrats, fearful that Estrada might become the first Hispanic nominated to the Supreme Court, tried to paint him as a legal extremist even as the American Bar Association rated him "well-qualified" for his nomination to the U.S. Court of Appeals for the D.C. Circuit, the nation's second-highest court. The League of United Latin American Citizens also lauded Estrada for his "experience and strong bi-partisan support from those who have worked with him." When years later Schumer cautioned Republicans about offending Hispanics during the confirmation of Sonia Sotomayor to the Supreme Court, I laughed at his hypocrisy.

By August 2002, Democrats on the Judiciary Committee had compiled such a record of obstructionism that even the *Washington Post* rapped their knuckles. In an editorial, the *Post* said that under Leahy's chairmanship, his committee had confirmed a smaller percentage of Bush's nominees than the committee had confirmed for any of the last three presidents at a similar point and urged Leahy to show "fidelity to his own insistence . . . that all nominees get hearings and votes within reasonable periods of time." He never did.

PERHAPS THE MOST CRASS example of partisanship on the part of the Democrats was their behavior surrounding the creation of the Department of Homeland Security. Homeland Security Advisor Tom Ridge had persuaded skeptics like me that it would be more effective to have one Cabinet secretary and one agency in charge of all homeland security responsibilities, instead of spreading those responsibilities throughout the government.

Ridge received fresh evidence that a single agency was necessary when his efforts to merge border security agencies were stopped by interdepartmental turf battles. Congress was also demanding to be briefed on the administration's homeland preparations by a single person, not a succession of bureaucrats. Joel Kaplan, an aide to Deputy Chief of Staff Josh Bolten, Deputy Chief of Staff Joe Hagin, and Richard Falkenrath, an aide to Ridge, suggested that Bolten order a review of the federal government's homeland security organization. Josh went to Andy Card, who authorized it, but insisted it be closely held so it wasn't impeded by agency turf battles.

News of the review didn't leak, so it was something of a surprise when the president announced to the nation on June 6, 2002, that he wanted to create a new federal department and had ready-made plans to do so. His proposal was generally well received by the public, but drew hostility from congressional committee chairmen fearful of relinquishing their agency oversight to a different committee. But before those chairmen could build resistance to the idea, we sent up proposed legislation and Congress started hammering out a bill based on our suggestions.

There was one issue on which Democrats dug in, however—collective bargaining. The federal government has unionized employees, but in 1962 President John F. Kennedy issued an executive order that excluded the FBI and the CIA from collective bargaining for national security reasons and allowed Cabinet secretaries to exclude other units for the same reason. In 1978, Congress wrote that declaration into legislation, which President Jimmy Carter signed into law. Now Democrats were insisting that every part of the new Department of Homeland Security be subject to collective bargaining.

It made no sense to insist on collective bargaining for a department being organized to protect the homeland when units of Agriculture, Commerce, and other departments were off-limits for unionization for national security reasons. But congressional Democrats were catering to their union allies, who saw the creation of the new department as an opportunity to offset declining memberships with fresh recruits.

The issue tied up the bill for the latter half of 2002 as the Senate voted on it twenty different times. When the bill was finally approved without the pro-union provision, the Democrats insisted the Bush White House had "politicized" national security and destroyed the post-9/11 bipartisan goodwill by cynically making an election issue of Democrats' union concerns. The truth is that Democrats in Congress turned a proposal to improve America's security into an attempt to gain unprecedented protections for unions. In the end, that's how voters saw it, too: it became an issue that hurt Democrats in key House and Senate races.

One of those campaign debates about homeland security pulled me into a controversy I had no role in creating, but in which I became the central figure. The "Myth of Rove" was about to gain a new chapter. The claim was that I smeared incumbent senator Max Cleland of Georgia with a vicious ad that questioned his patriotism, compared him to Osama bin Laden, and caused him to lose his bid for reelection to Republican congressman Saxby Chambliss.

Some observers said I did the ad; others credited it to "Karl Rove and his minions," "the Rove machine," and "surrogates, led by Rove." Garry Trudeau, writer of the *Doonesbury* comic strip, got into the act, too, running comics devoted to how I'd concocted it. Cleland personally blamed me for the ad, saying I was guilty of "character assassination" and responsible for "the biggest lie in America."

I did not conceive, create, craft, prepare, or have anything to do with the Chambliss television ad. But I thought it was effective because it was factual.

This is how the ad came about: Cleland ran a spot associating himself with President Bush by suggesting Cleland had supported creating the Homeland Security department. It was a clever tactic, since Bush was very popular in Georgia. The problem was that it was false. Cleland had worked against Bush on creation of the new department by siding with the unions on the collective bargaining issue. Chambliss consultant Tom Perdue drafted a reply ad while driving home to Tennessee in his pickup.

The images of Osama bin Laden and Saddam Hussein appeared only briefly at the beginning of the ad, while the words "As America faces terrorists and extremist dictators" were read. The spot didn't morph either of these figures into Cleland or say he supported them. Only later in the ad did images of Cleland appear, followed by a scrolling list of the times he had voted against the homeland security bill. As Perdue later explained, his attack on Cleland was "not questioning his patriotism. What kind of fools would we be? We were questioning his integrity. The man couldn't tell the truth."

Nonetheless, Cleland insisted on being offended by the ad, hoping that he could hide behind the claim that his patriotism was being questioned. A columnist for the *Atlanta Journal-Constitution* suggested as much by writing that "this 'how-dare-you-attack-my-patriotism' ploy, replete with feigned outrage . . . is a device to put Cleland's voting records off-limits."

In the years since, Cleland has worked to portray himself as a victim, and in the 2004 presidential election, he tried to make an issue out of his defeat by misleading audiences about the content of his own ad and of the ad Chambliss ran against him. It is a key part of his book *Heart of a Patriot: How I Found the Courage to Survive Vietnam, Walter Reed and Karl Rove.*

In reality, Cleland lost because his voting record was more liberal than his conservative home-state voters were and he had the bad luck to run against a hardworking Republican in a year that tilted toward the GOP. Others have also pointed out that he did poorly in the debates, didn't win the endorsement of the Veterans of Foreign Wars, and failed to put out a coherent reason for why he had opposed Bush's homeland security bill.

For the record, there is one charge made against me by Senator Cleland to which I proudly plead guilty. When Saxby Chambliss asked for White House support, I told him we would be all in. "The White House wanted to take me out," Cleland said later. Think of the impertinence: a Republican White House helping a Republican challenge a Democrat in an open election.

Bush himself campaigned for Chambliss, but his participation in any midterm election after 9/11 was a subject that was hotly debated inside the White House. One group, led by Karen Hughes, the president's counselor, argued it would send a powerful, unifying signal if the president said he would not engage in any politics in 2002. I argued that any short-term goodwill from this above-the-fray behavior would be overwhelmed by the disadvantage of his party's losing ground in Congress. It would also undermine support within the GOP if he stayed cooped up at the White House. My argument, and mounting evidence that Democrats in Washington were obstructing Bush, carried the day.

I devised an aggressive campaign to find the candidates with the best shot at winning. That meant, for example, that the vice president and I had to call Tim Pawlenty, the Republican Speaker of the Minnesota House, to tell him that if he ran for the U.S. Senate, the White House would be supporting Norm Coleman, the mayor of St. Paul. With my encouragement, Pawlenty went on to win the governor's race. And I spent months pushing Congressman John Thune to get in the South Dakota senatorial race against incumbent Tim Johnson.

Those were the rewarding moments of being White House political chief. But the job also had its unpleasant ones. One involved the chairman of the National Republican Congressional Committee, Tom Davis. He is a political junkie with an encyclopedic knowledge of districts, returns, and issues. He had recruited a great staff and was a proficient fundraiser. He was initially easy to work with, though high-strung, emotional, and opinionated. But the relationship soured in late 2001.

Almost since we arrived at the White House, Davis had been pushing for the appointment of Virginia state senator Jeannemarie Devolites to the board of directors for the Student Loan Marketing Association (better known as Sallie Mae). Though a publicly traded company, Sallie Mae was chartered by Congress as a "government-sponsored enterprise," or GSE. Other GSEs included Fannie Mae and Freddie Mac. The majority of a GSE's board of directors are elected by shareholders and a small minority are appointed by the president. These appointees give GSEs the appearance that the federal government will bail them out if they run into trouble. The presidentially appointed slots are highly coveted—they pay well and come with group life insurance and favorable stock purchase rights.

Devolites represented a state Senate district that overlapped with a lot of Davis's Northern Virginia congressional district, and Davis had served as her mentor as she rose in politics during the 1990s. Davis argued she was qualified for the job because she worked on student loan issues in the Virginia Senate and because Sallie Mae's headquarters was in her district. He was persistent, and I finally recommended she be appointed. However, questions arose about whether Davis and Devolites were romantically involved. Davis was married; Devolites had filed for divorce the previous September. After some handwringing, I decided I needed to ask Davis directly about it.

Davis's answer was blunt, angry, and dismissive about the allegations. I told him I took him at his word. To this day, I have no idea whether Davis and Devolites were romantically involved at the time he proposed her for appointment to the Sallie Mae board. On October 9, the president nominated Devolites. From then on, my relationship with Davis was frosty and difficult, and I used intermediaries to do our political business. Davis and his wife later divorced. He and Devolites were married in June 2004.

But our efforts paid off on election night 2002. Republicans regained their majority in the U.S. Senate and added six seats in the House. It was only the second election in American history in which a president's party gained seats in both the House and Senate in the first midterm election. The only other time was 1934, when FDR's Democrats gained seats in the Senate and House in the midst of the Great Depression.

But the afterglow of our success evaporated fast after Mississippi senator Trent Lott, who was poised to become Senate majority leader, opened his mouth on Thursday, December 5, and firmly planted his foot in it. Lott is an old-fashioned southern orator who came of age in the 1950s South and for whom hyperbole is second nature. At the hundredth birthday party for Strom Thurmond, the senator from South Carolina and the oldest person to ever serve in Congress, Lott couldn't miss a chance to brag on Mississippi. He said, "I want to say this about my state: When Strom Thurmond ran for president, we voted for him. We're proud of it. And if the rest of the country had followed our lead, we wouldn't have had all these problems over all these years, either."

What? Lott had just said he was proud Mississippi had voted for a white supremacist for president and America would be better off if it had elected that man president. And what problems, specifically, was Lott referring to? His comments were vague enough to allow everyone to read the worst into it, and they did.

By the following Sunday morning, Lott was the target on the morning talk shows and he could no longer ignore the issue. He issued a written statement Monday that read, "A poor choice of words conveyed to some the impression that I embraced the discarded policies of the past. Nothing could be further from the truth, and I apologize to anyone who was offended by my statement." But dancing around the issue of racism made things worse. Not only did civil rights leaders, historians, and Democrats condemn him, but so did Lott's fellow conservatives. Remarkably, Lott received support that day from Senate majority leader Tom Daschle. He accepted Lott's explanation, saying, "there are a lot of times when he and I go to the microphone and would like to say things we meant to say differently, and I'm sure this was one of those cases for him, as well."

Reporters delved into Lott's past and dug out his defense of Bob Jones University's prohibition on interracial dating in the 1980s and a comment he had made at a 1980 Reagan rally in Jackson, Mississippi, using words very similar to his at Thurmond's party: that if we had elected

Thurmond to the presidency "thirty years ago, we wouldn't be in the mess we are today."

The senator mounted his first public defense in a telephone interview on *Larry King Live* Wednesday night. "Look, you put your foot in your mouth, you're getting carried away at a ceremony honoring a guy like this, you go too far," Lott explained. But Lott also said that he would not step aside as Senate leader and that neither the Bush White House nor Republican colleagues had asked him to. This put the pressure on the president to weigh in on the issue.

His senior aides—including me—felt that Bush needed to make clear that sympathy for segregation was unacceptable. Two paragraphs referring to the controversy were inserted into a speech the president would give in Philadelphia on Thursday, and Lott was given a heads-up. He was furious when the president distanced himself from Lott's remarks while accepting Lott's apology.

On Friday the 13th, Lott headed home to Pascagoula, Mississippi, for a news conference. In front of a bank of cameras, he apologized "for opening old wounds and hurting many Americans who feel so deeply in this area." He asked Americans to "find it in their heart" to forgive him, saying, "Segregation is a stain on our nation's soul. There's no other way to describe it." But the previous week, the country had seen an uninterested and out-of-touch politician, not a contrite and apologetic statesman. His colleagues had decided he had to go.

Now Daschle also flip-flopped, lashing out at Lott and saying the Mississippian "did not provide an adequate explanation." He later explained his readiness to excuse Lott on Monday but then assault him on Friday by saying he "took Trent's call just minutes" before a news conference, leaving the Democratic leader without "time to gauge my thoughts and feelings more fully." It was classic Daschle deviousness.

Lott then went on Black Entertainment Television and made his situation worse. He rightly denounced his own comments as "insensitive," "repugnant," and "inexcusable" and came across as heartfelt. But under further questioning by BET anchor Ed Gordon, Lott disavowed his longtime opposition to affirmative action. The next morning, Republican senators told the White House that if Lott would abandon his principles to save his leadership post, he was no longer able to lead. On December 20, Lott resigned and Bill Frist was later elected majority leader.

In the years since, Lott has nursed a grudge against Bush and the White House for what happened. In his memoir, he describes the president's two paragraphs in Philadelphia as "blunt" and "angry" and Bush's tone as "booming and nasty," while conceding he "couldn't argue with the words [the president] chose." Lott blamed "powerful White House staffers"—that is, me—for "stirring the pot, priming the media, and feeding the discord." Lott also took his shots on cable talk and news programs, questioning whether I was "good for American politics" and saying he'd "had problems" with me.

I must admit that when I arranged for Lott to be invited on a hunting trip with Vice President Cheney, some Republican senators, and me four years later, I wondered if the wounds from his terrible Christmas of 2002 would lead to an "accidental wound" for me. But Senator Lott and I had a pleasant time shooting quail and pheasant, though he constantly questioned my skills with a shotgun.

In retrospect, there was a moment where I might have been able to help save Lott. It was Tuesday, December 10, and Lott was at the White House for a meeting on Medicare, along with Republican senators Don Nickles of Oklahoma and Chuck Grassley of Iowa. As the meeting broke up, I stood with Lott. He said the entire hullabaloo about his Thurmond comments would peter out.

I thought it would get much worse and started to suggest that his only hope was an immediate news conference in which he admitted he had been boneheaded. He needed to acknowledge he understood how damaging a segregationist presidency would have been for the country, apologize profusely, and say he had learned from the incident and hoped Americans would forgive him. Most people would have accepted those heartfelt words if said at that early point. I'm not shy about sharing my views, but on that day, standing so close to Lott, I kept my thoughts to myself. I don't know why. I regret remaining silent: such advice might have worked and kept Lott as leader.

CHAPTER 20

Joe Wilson's Attack

———— • ◆ • ————

On Sunday, July 6, 2003, for no reason I awoke particularly early. And as on most Sundays, I headed outside in pajamas and an old T-shirt to retrieve the newspapers. I didn't know it, but it was to be a momentous day.

Once back inside, I skimmed the front page of the *New York Times* and then thumbed, as I always did, to the "Week in Review" section. I enjoy reading what the opposition is saying.

One op-ed grabbed my attention. It was titled "What I Didn't Find in Africa" and was written by someone I'd never heard of: Joseph C. Wilson IV, a career foreign service officer who had served as ambassador to Gabon and São Tomé and Príncipe under President George H. W. Bush.

Wilson alleged that a statement in President Bush's 2003 State of the Union address was false. He challenged the claim that Iraq had tried to buy uranium from Africa to facilitate creating a nuclear bomb, and singled out as wrong these sixteen words in the speech: "The British government has learned that Saddam Hussein recently sought significant quantities of uranium in Africa." Wilson's most explosive charge was to suggest that the White House had known this claim was untrue.

Wilson claimed he knew these sixteen words were "inaccurate" because he had been sent to Africa by the CIA in March 2002 to "provide a response to the vice president's office" on whether Iraq had attempted to acquire uranium from Niger. Based on what he learned from "eight days drinking sweet mint tea and meeting with dozens of people," Wilson wrote, "it was highly doubtful that any such transaction had ever taken place." He also claimed that "at least four documents" based on his report would confirm his mission and that his findings had been "circulated to the appropriate officials within our government," presumably including Vice President Cheney's office.

Now, fully awake after reading the op-ed, my sluggishness dissipated quickly. I made two calls right away: one to our communications shop and the other to the National Security Council, asking what to make of Wilson's charges. I was told that at that point, no one knew exactly what to think. Wilson's op-ed hit them like it hit me, a lightning bolt out of a clear blue sky. It had been available on the *Times* website Saturday night, but had not raised any alarms in the communications shop.

The situation quickly went from bad to worse. Wilson appeared on NBC's *Meet the Press* later that morning to trumpet his charge. He appeared pompous and more than a little sanctimonious, but it was clear to me he meant to do the president grave harm. His charges came at a critical moment: no weapons of mass destruction had been found in Iraq, and now a former ambassador was saying he advised the vice president's office—nine months before the State of the Union and a year before the United States invaded—that Saddam had not tried to acquire African uranium. It was just mid-morning and already this story had triggered an earthquake. We needed answers immediately.

After *Meet the Press,* I spoke to Dan Bartlett and learned that the vice president's office—which Wilson said had asked the uranium questions that subsequently led to his Niger trip and which he suggested had been briefed on his findings—said that the ambassador's account was inaccurate. Cheney had neither asked for the mission nor been briefed on Wilson's return.

That was reassuring. At the same time, I had a sick feeling in my stomach. Damaging misinformation had made its way halfway around the country, and we had not yet gotten our boots on.

On Monday, Wilson escalated his rhetoric on CNN, claiming that he had checked with "very senior officials in the vice president's office" and knew the VP's office had "received a very specific response" that showed Bush's State of the Union "was inaccurate." And later, he declared that "somebody from [the president's] own staff," perhaps even someone in Condi Rice's "circle," had kept Wilson's Niger report from the president and "allow[ed] this lie to get into the State of the Union address."

The White House press corps was ready to pounce on the story. Its members were on a long-scheduled trip to Africa with the president and had little to do but get worked up over Wilson. In the "hothouse environment of Air Force One," as CIA director George Tenet put it, they were "hungry for any tidbits or insider bickering to report." As for us, we were caught not knowing all the facts right away, were slow off the mark in sorting through the charges, and didn't do a good job of correcting the record.

Inside the White House, we were concerned with two interconnected sets of questions. First, had Wilson been sent at the request of the vice president, had he reported conclusively to the CIA what he found, and had his report circulated through the national security apparatus, including the White House? Second, what about the sixteen words? Did President Bush make a mistake by relying on British intelligence in asserting Saddam had sought uranium in Africa?

During the 7:30 A.M. White House senior staff meetings on Monday and Tuesday, we received key rebuttal points. Wilson had not been sent to Africa at the request of the vice president or his office. No report had been sent to the White House upon Wilson's return. The CIA was dubious about the quality of Wilson's information-gathering and his conclusions. In fact, he had apparently returned with information of an attempt by the Iraqis in June 1999 to get uranium from Niger, a fact Wilson conveniently omitted from his *New York Times* op-ed.

And someone—I can't remember if it was Steve Hadley or Cheney's chief of staff, Scooter Libby, or someone else—in a side conversation remarked that Wilson's wife worked at the CIA and had suggested her husband for the mission. This was almost an afterthought. Everyone's focus was on the substance of Wilson's charges, not the sponsor for his African junket.

Hadley was deputized to talk to George Tenet about who should say what in response to Wilson's claims. By Tuesday, it was my impression Tenet would soon set the record straight with a statement. In reality, it was more difficult than that. Tenet was in Sun Valley, Idaho, on a working vacation. Hadley's boss, Condi Rice, was on the other side of the globe with Bush on his six-day, five-country swing through Africa. More important, Tenet's reluctance to issue a statement was bound up in an intra-CIA fight over the sixteen words.

The discussion of the sixteen words during the senior staff meetings and with colleagues baffled me. British intelligence stood by their finding, but the CIA had been of two minds. Some elements inside the CIA were dubious of the British conclusion and thought the sixteen words unworthy of the State of the Union. These people apparently also briefed Tenet for his congressional testimony and meetings. But this group was not in charge of clearing the State of the Union address. The CIA personnel who cleared the president's speech did so with the British intelligence reference intact. Tenet later told me he never read the speech.

We vacillated and made the problem worse. On Monday morning, White House press secretary Ari Fleischer seemed to stand behind the sixteen words but gave confusing answers to confusing questions. Ari tried to put the sixteen words in a bigger context, saying, "We see nothing that would dissuade us from the president's broader statement." It wasn't clear what that meant. The press wanted more specifics.

By Monday's end, with questions now being raised in London by Parliament's Foreign Affairs Committee about the reliability of the British intelligence, the administration dramatically changed its position. Ari walked National Security Advisor Condi Rice back to the press compartment on Air Force One en route to Africa to answer the latest round of questions. As the voice of an unnamed "senior Administration official," Condi appeared to blame the CIA, saying, "Knowing all that we know now, the reference to Iraq's attempt to acquire uranium from Africa should not have been included in the State of the Union speech. There is other reporting to suggest that Iraq tried to obtain uranium from Africa. However, the information is not detailed or specific enough for us to be certain that attempts were in fact made."

Rather than defend the sixteen words, the White House was trying to distance the president from them. There were two messages being conveyed: first, we were not saying the sixteen words were untruthful and were not taking issue with British intelligence; but second, the sixteen words had not met the threshold necessary to appear in a State of the Union address (meaning we had learned, after the speech, that the CIA was not of one mind on the claim). This was felt by some people within the administration to be prudent and reasonable. But to the press and the public, the message was that the sixteen words were themselves false. And it created serious problems with the CIA, because Hadley had agreed that Tenet would put out a statement on the Wilson charges, with both the White House and CIA assuming joint responsibility for the sixteen words. Now it looked like the White House was blaming the CIA for not catching the sixteen words. Tenet was furious and later complained of White House officials "sniping" at him from Air Force One.

It took until Wednesday morning for Hadley's patient diplomacy with Tenet to pay off. Tenet had Bill Harlow, the CIA's public information chief, draft a statement. I was told to expect it Thursday. Instead Tenet, McLaughlin, and Harlow worked over the statement from Wednesday through Friday, as the agency continued to feel piqued by what Tenet called "incoming flak from the traveling White House in Africa." The CIA director was a prickly personality, now spun up by calls to the CIA press shop from reporters "with accounts from 'senior administration officials' on Air Force One who continued to insist that the CIA's share of the fault was 100 percent."

Tenet was losing sight of the goal, which was to set the record straight on Wilson's charges, and instead focused on covering the CIA's bureaucratic posterior over one part of his agency's having cleared the sixteen words after he had been counseled by others in the agency to distance himself from them. The CIA finally issued the statement about 6:15 P.M. on a Friday evening in July, hardly an auspicious time to maximize coverage. Tenet knew this was, as he put it, "a technique usually reserved in Washington for statements that officials want to bury," but said he was "anxious to get the statement out," and I accept him at his word. But ensconced in Sun Valley and preoccupied with real or imagined slights of the CIA, Tenet had not paid attention to the clock. The statement didn't get much coverage.

It was, however, a strong statement, because it made clear that Joe Wilson was wrong.

Joe Wilson was wrong when he implied in his Sunday op-ed that he had been sent to Africa at Vice President Cheney's behest to answer questions about Iraqi attempts to acquire uranium from Niger. The vice president never asked someone to be sent to Africa and was not briefed upon Wilson's return. Rather, as Tenet revealed in his statement, "CIA's counter-proliferation experts, on their own initiative" had recruited Wilson for the trip.

Joe Wilson's op-ed was wrong in implying he found no evidence Iraq had tried to acquire uranium. Wilson had collected information that showed Saddam Hussein attempted to do just that. During his trip, Wilson met with former Niger prime minister Ibrahim Assane Mayaki. Mayaki told Wilson that back in June 1999, Iraq, working through a third party, encouraged him to receive an Iraqi delegation to discuss "expanding commercial relations." Mayaki had interpreted this as meaning the Iraqis wanted to talk about purchasing uranium, Niger's only commercially attractive export. Wilson included this incident in his verbal report to the CIA but left it out of his op-ed. It didn't fit his claim.

Joe Wilson's op-ed was wrong to the extent it suggested he had disproved the British intelligence report that Saddam Hussein had attempted to purchase uranium from an African country. Wilson didn't know the basis on which British intelligence had made its September 2002 report, so he couldn't disprove it. Following Wilson's op-ed, the British government carried out a careful investigation, after which it reaffirmed the truth of the sixteen words. Their report, which came out a year after Wilson's op-ed, said, "We conclude that, on the basis of the intelligence assessments at the time, covering both Niger and the Democratic Republic of Congo, the statements on Iraqi attempts to buy uranium from Africa in the Government's dossier, and by the Prime Minister in the House of Commons, were well-founded." The investigation also reaffirmed the foundation of the sixteen words in Bush's State of the Union address, but there was little coverage of these findings in the United States.

Joe Wilson was wrong when he twisted the Bush administration's statement that Iraq had *attempted* to acquire uranium in Africa into a claim that Iraq had *obtained* uranium. Our argument was based on intent: we never suggested the Iraqi dictator succeeded in purchasing more than the 550 metric tons he already possessed.

Joe Wilson was wrong when he said the information he collected was conclusive. Wilson seemed to feel that a few days with past and current Niger government officials and his charm were all that were needed. The CIA felt Wilson's methods left something to be desired and that his information was inconclusive. Tenet said the CIA considered "that the former Nigerien officials knew what they were saying would reach the

U.S. government and that this might have influenced what they said," so Wilson "did not resolve whether Iraq was or was not seeking uranium from abroad."

Joe Wilson was also wrong when he speculated that Vice President Cheney had received his report, even suggesting the office of the vice president was likely to have had it "delivered orally." Wilson became indignant on CNN the morning after his op-ed when questioned by Bill Hemmer about the claim. Wilson said that from his experience on the Clinton National Security Council, he knew "the standard operating procedure" was that when the vice president's office "asked the question," that office "received a very specific response." Yet Tenet's statement said that because Wilson's report was not conclusive, "we did not brief it to the President, Vice-President or other senior Administration officials" upon Wilson's return from Africa.

Wilson was wrong when he later said that he had talked to "very senior officials" in Cheney's office and when he accused the president's "own staff" of personally withholding Wilson's report from Bush.

And Joe Wilson was wrong when he said he debunked forged documents sold to Italian intelligence and passed on to the French that appeared to document Iraqi attempts to buy uranium for nuclear weapons. He later claimed he told the CIA "that the dates were wrong and the names were wrong." On *Meet the Press* he boasted, "When I came back from Niger and debriefed, I had not, of course, seen the documents, but one of the points that I made was if these documents did not contain certain signatures—specifically, the signature of the minister of energy and mines and the prime minister—then they could not be authentic." The problem is that the documents didn't surface until October 7, 2002, eight months after his mission to Africa. So he was claiming that he had raised a red flag about forged documents that had not even surfaced at the time of his supposed warning. Tenet's statement pointed this out, saying, "there was no mention in the report [by Wilson] of forged documents— or any suggestion of the existence of documents at all."

A year later, the Senate Intelligence Committee chairman, Republican Pat Roberts, was even tougher on Wilson's claims. In a statement where Roberts was joined by Republican senators Christopher S. Bond and Orrin G. Hatch, he wrote:

In an interview with Committee staff, Mr. Wilson was asked how he knew some things he was stating publicly with such confidence. On at least two occasions he admitted that he had no direct knowledge to support some of his claims and that he was drawing on either unrelated past experiences or no information at all. For example, when asked how he "knew" that the Intelligence Community had rejected the possibility of a Niger-Iraq uranium deal, as he wrote in his book [*The Politics of Truth*], he told Committee staff that his assertion may have involved "a little literary flair." The former Ambassador, either by design or through ignorance, gave the American people and, for that matter, the world a version of events that was inaccurate, unsubstantiated, and misleading.

Wilson later admitted himself that he had nothing to do with disproving the so-called Italian forgeries and had "misspoken."

Joe Wilson was also wrong when he said his wife "had nothing to do" with sending him to Niger. The Senate Intelligence Committee was told by the CIA that Wilson's wife, Valerie Plame, "offered up" Wilson's name for the Niger trip and sent an e-mail on February 12, 2002, to a deputy chief in the CIA's Directorate of Operations saying Wilson "has good relations [in Niger] with both the PM [prime minister] and the former Minister of Mines (not to mention lots of French contacts), both of whom could possibly shed light on this sort of activity." Plame later denied this was a recommendation. But Wilson apparently didn't know about her "offering up" his name and seemed upset when he learned of it by reading a July 2004 Senate Intelligence Committee report. Ms. Plame later wrote that after reading that report, "Joe abruptly got up, dumped his unfinished plate in the sink, and left the room in a wordless rage." Later that evening, when Ms. Plame tried to describe what she'd written, he was "too upset" to listen to her explanation, "just glared" at her, and "left the room" again. Wilson was to tell his wife "that for him, reading this report and learning that I had written that e-mail were his lowest points in this entire ordeal."

But those revelations came later. In the meantime, we had to deal with the sixteen words. Five days after the op-ed appeared, the White House and the CIA accepted joint responsibility for the State of the Union address, with Tenet's statement saying, "These 16 words should never have been included in the text written for the President." But the withdrawal of the sixteen words didn't end the controversy; rather, it seemed to validate Wilson's claims.

The press drumbeat continued over the next week and tensions between the White House and the CIA grew. Tenet fretted and stewed over perceived White House slights. He took "comfort" from a *New York Times* piece where the White House appeared to "admit some error, too," as he later put it in his book. But that comfort was apparently short-lived. Secretary of State Colin Powell went to visit Tenet shortly afterward and told him that while Bush had personally backed Tenet up and expressed confidence in him during the trip to Africa, the vice president "had quite another view." That was just like Powell.

Finally, on Monday, July 21, chief White House speechwriter Mike Gerson called Steve Hadley. Mike had found memos from the CIA about a speech the president had given in Cincinnati, Ohio, on October 7, 2002, that objected to language similar to that used in the State of the Union speech. Both Gerson and Hadley had forgotten the memos.

What I found interesting about the memos was that the CIA's reservations about the president's speech were focused on whether Iraq could have gotten Niger to sell uranium, not with whether they tried to acquire it. But Hadley saw the memos as a way to end the controversy. The president, Hadley thought, was bleeding politically and the White House's relationship with the CIA was being strained. Hadley wanted to stanch the bleeding and restore harmony with Langley.

Hadley drafted a statement that acknowledged the earlier cautions from CIA, assumed full personal responsibility for allowing the sixteen words into the State of the Union, and then tendered his resignation. Showing the statement to President Bush, he argued that good relations with the CIA were at risk and that an act of accountability was necessary. He thought Tenet felt vulnerable because, while some in the CIA had cleared the British intelligence finding, others at the agency had not, and those were the officials who had prepared Tenet for his periodic briefings on Capitol Hill where he'd expressed skepticism about the British claim. Hadley felt that unless he, Hadley, took responsibility and resigned, Tenet might come under congressional pressure to go, and Hadley wanted to avoid this. So Hadley prepared to throw himself on his sword. That was, I thought, far too high a price to pay. And further distancing ourselves from the sixteen words when we still felt them to be true seemed intellectually dishonest.

Bush agreed to Hadley's making a statement taking some responsibility for the sixteen words, but rejected his resignation. The president didn't think the facts justified it and saw Steve as too valuable to lose. Bush also wasn't comfortable with the idea of accepting a resignation aimed at making him look good at the expense of Hadley's reputation.

To get the maximum attention for his statement and perhaps end the controversy, Hadley read it to the press in the Roosevelt Room. Hadley said, "I should have recalled at the time of the State of the Union speech that there was controversy associated with the uranium issue. I should have either asked that the sixteen words dealing with that subject be stricken or I should have alerted DCI [Director of Central Intelligence George] Tenet. And had I done so this would have avoided the whole current controversy. It is now clear to me that I failed in that responsibility." He then answered questions for forty-five minutes.

It was a selfless, even noble, gesture on Hadley's part. But it was also a mistake. The sixteen words were, to the best of our knowledge, accurate and their source, British intelligence, later reaffirmed them. Our explanation, that we believed the sixteen words were true but didn't rise to the level of the president's State of the Union address, was taken by the public and especially the press as a halfhearted admission that the words weren't true. Trying to look reasonable strengthened our adversaries' new line of attack: Bush took the nation to war based on lies and exaggerations.

If Hadley thought impaling himself in front of cameras and journalists would placate Tenet, he was kidding himself. It didn't. Tenet later wrote that the sixteen words, Wilson's op-ed, and Hadley's attempt at hara-kiri taken together meant his "relationship with the administration was forever changed." Tenet felt betrayed and began moving to leave the post as CIA director he had held under two presidents.

Meanwhile, I was being drawn into a swirl of controversy around Wilson that was to have enormous personal consequences for me. It started with a call I didn't need to return.

On Monday, July 7, the day after Wilson's op-ed, columnist Robert Novak phoned. I was in a meeting, so he left a message that he wanted to talk about Fran Townsend, whom the president had just named homeland security advisor. Some conservatives were suspicious of her service during the Clinton administration as chief of staff to Jo Ann Harris, assistant attorney general in charge of the Justice Department's Criminal Division. My "Spider-Man" senses tingling that Novak might want to trash Townsend, I asked Matt Schlapp in the Office of Political Affairs for talking points before I got back to Novak. Matt promised to get them to me the next day.

But before I could return Novak's call Tuesday, he had a 3 P.M. meeting with a high-ranking administration official and longtime source, Deputy Secretary of State Richard Armitage, Colin Powell's right-hand man. During their hour-long gossip session, Novak brought up the sixteen-words controversy and Armitage "generally confirmed" what Novak had already learned from calls Monday: administration officials thought it had been a mistake to include them in the State of the Union address. One thing still bothered Novak: Why would the CIA send someone with no intelligence or counterproliferation experience to Niger? "Well," Armitage replied, "you know his wife works at CIA, and she suggested that he be sent to Niger." Armitage went on to say she worked in counterproliferation, mentioned her first name, Valerie, and said of this nugget of inside information he'd just handed over, "That's real Evans and Novak, isn't it?" Novak later wrote that he interpreted that as meaning his source expected to see Novak use the information.

When I did call Novak back later Tuesday, I made no headway with him on Townsend. He'd been told she was unreliable and was flabbergasted about her appointment. That Thursday, his column blasted Townsend as "an intimate adviser of Janet Reno," Clinton's attorney general, and cited her appointment as evidence of a breakdown in the White House screening process. Not a single argument I made to him in her defense appeared in his column. Years later, I discovered Novak had already put the column to bed before I returned his call, making my effort useless and the call totally unnecessary.

But Novak had turned our conversation to Joe Wilson's op-ed after discussing Townsend. He'd met Wilson in the green room at *Meet the Press* the previous Sunday morning and said he found Wilson pompous, self-centered, egotistical, and "an asshole." Having watched Wilson on *Meet the Press*, I agreed with Novak's assessment.

We talked about Wilson's claims that he'd been sent at the request of the vice president's office, that his report conclusively refuted the sixteen words, that Vice President Cheney and others in the White House had received his report—all of which was untrue.

I told Novak the CIA was going to be issuing a statement shortly setting the record straight on these points and others (though I didn't think it would take until Friday). Off the record, I told him the CIA statement was also likely to say Wilson had actually uncovered an attempt by the Iraqis to get a trade delegation into Niger and that the Niger government had rebuffed it since the nation's only significant export was uranium, whose sale to Iraq was prohibited by the U.N. We agreed that Wilson's failure to include this information in his op-ed was revealing.

Novak brought up Wilson's wife and told me she worked at the CIA in counterproliferation and that she—not Vice President Cheney—had suggested Wilson be sent to Niger. Novak recalled I then said, "Oh, you know that, too." I remember saying, "I've heard that, too." There's not much difference, in length or meaning, between his words and mine. Novak went on to talk about her in a way that led me to believe he'd already been in touch with the CIA. The conversation drew to a close.

How was I able to say that I had "heard that, too"? I can't remember who might have mentioned it offhand in the White House in the two days since Wilson's op-ed, but someone did. I may also have heard it earlier in the spring from a journalist. I have a vague recollection of being accosted at a social event by an unfamiliar reporter who asked me about a CIA spouse disproving U.S. claims about Iraqi WMD. The reporter moved off when I drew a complete blank on what he said.

Novak said he received the confirmation he needed Wednesday afternoon from Bill Harlow at the CIA that Wilson's wife worked at the agency's Counter-Proliferation Division. But unlike Armitage, Harlow denied Wilson's wife had suggested her husband for the trip, saying she had instead been asked by colleagues to approach her husband about the assignment. As it turns out, Novak wasn't the only journalist who knew about this. Ari Fleischer pulled aside both David Gregory of NBC News and John Dickerson, then of *Time,* during the presidential trip to Africa to tell them that Wilson had been sent to Niger not by Cheney, but by his own wife, who worked for the CIA. Both reporters were unimpressed and didn't report it.

I was aiming to take advantage of the president's absence abroad to leave the White House late on Friday morning and drive my family to Mississippi to spend time with relatives. Darby and Andrew would go on to the beach in the Florida Panhandle after a few days and I'd return to Washington Monday by train—recent sinus surgery made air travel impossible for several weeks. Early Friday morning, I returned overdue phone calls, dislodged paperwork from my desk, and filled my briefcase and an extra bag with correspondence and reading I could do on the train.

That morning I received details of Novak's upcoming column from Rick Hohlt, a mutual friend of mine and Novak's, and later that day a truncated text of it. I knew the column would be critical of Wilson and told my West Wing colleagues about it. There was clearly no reason for me to disseminate the story about Plame to anyone, and certainly to no one in the media, since I knew that Novak was going to do that in his column—based, we now know, on his conversation with an administration source other than me.

In the midst of this whirlwind of activity, I apparently got a phone call from Matt Cooper of *Time*. I say "apparently" because to this day, I have no recollection of it. When you get dozens of calls a day steadily for years, individual conversations tend to get lost. But I wrote an e-mail after the call confirming it, and Cooper wrote a longer e-mail a few days later to his colleagues about the same call.

Cooper had first phoned at the start of the week, saying he wanted to talk about welfare, which was up for reauthorization. Apparently that Friday, we talked briefly about welfare before he tried to slide into the topic of Wilson. As I explained to Hadley a few minutes later in a terse e-mail, "Matt Cooper called to give me a heads-up that he's got a welfare reform story coming. When he finished his brief heads-up he immediately launched into Niger. Isn't this damaging? Hasn't the president been hurt? I didn't take the bait, but I said if I were him I wouldn't get *Time* far out in front of this." Cooper's e-mail to *Time* colleagues reporting on our conversation also makes clear I was discouraging him from writing about Wilson.

There was no need to rev Cooper up on the subject and every incentive to cool him down. The White House wanted the controversy to die down, not flare up with a story in *Time*. Tenet was about to respond to Wilson, and I presumed that move would help set the record straight.

Perhaps frustrated by Cooper's attempt at bait-and-switch—calling about welfare and then changing the subject to the obnoxious Wilson—and eager to get on the road to Mississippi (I was already late), I apparently steered the conversation to a rapid conclusion. Shortly thereafter, I climbed into my car and pointed it south toward a long weekend drive through places with spotty cell coverage.

On Monday, Robert Novak's column appeared. He wrote that the CIA's decision to send Wilson to Niger "was made routinely at a low level without Director George Tenet's knowledge" and Wilson's report "was regarded by the CIA as less than definitive, and it is doubtful Tenet ever saw it." It drew attention to Wilson's "oral report," saying Wilson had "mentioned in passing that a [1999] Iraqi delegation had tried to establish commercial contacts." Novak opined the controversy would be settled only by "scrutinizing the CIA's summary of what its envoy reported" and called for its release. Almost in passing, Novak reported, "Two senior administration officials told me that Wilson's wife suggested sending him to Niger."

Richard Armitage was the first senior administration official. Apparently, Novak considered me the second, based on five or four words. But I didn't know or think I was his second source. After all, he hadn't asked for confirmation. If he had, I would have said that I couldn't do so. All I had done was offer up the tentative "I've heard that, too."

I thought the column was good for us because it had emphasized that Wilson had found support for the sixteen words. But because it was one bad story for Wilson in a sea of uncritical comment about him, I concluded that Novak's column would not matter much. I was dead wrong, but would not realize it for several months.

For now, there was a more immediate threat. Powerful figures were to take up the essence of Wilson's charge, refine it, change it, enrich it, enlarge it, and then deploy it as a weapon aimed at the heart of the Bush presidency.

CHAPTER 21

Bush Was Right on Iraq

———◆·———

N ine days after Wilson's *Times* op-ed, the high command of the Democratic Party launched a full-scale assault on the president. The first salvo came on Tuesday, July 15, when Senator Ted Kennedy charged in a speech that Bush misled Americans. Senate minority leader Tom Daschle followed by challenging the administration in a press conference "to be forthcoming." The next day, Senator John Edwards raised the issue of Bush's truthfulness in a congressional hearing, and Senator John Kerry echoed Edwards's attacks with a speech accusing the Bush White House of giving "presidential sanction to misleading information." Congresswoman Jane Harman chimed in with questions about whether intelligence leading up to the Iraq War had been mishandled.

Five Democrats had opened up on us on the same front in two days. A well-coordinated attack was unfolding. The Democrats hoped to turn the American people against the president with a simple charge that was meant to be politically lethal: Bush had lied about the existence of weapons of mass destruction in Iraq and the threat posed by Saddam Hussein to win congressional approval of a use-of-force resolution against Iraq (also known as the Iraq War resolution). But those who accused Bush of sending America's military into harm's way on a bald-faced lie knew that their accusation was not true.

I don't know whether prominent Democrats planned their attacks with foreknowledge of Joe Wilson's *New York Times* piece, or whether its appearance was simply fortuitous. I have no doubt, however, that Democrats were emboldened by Wilson's op-ed and its largely uncritical reception by the media. It helped convince Democratic strategists to unleash the big lie.

The comments of key Democrats show what a disgraceful game they were playing. Take Senator Jay Rockefeller. Given his spot as one of the most prominent Democrats on the Senate Intelligence Committee, Rockefeller had special credibility among his colleagues. After voting for the use-of-force resolution, Senator Rockefeller later charged that Bush "bent, stretched and massaged" the intelligence. But if this is what he *really* thought, why didn't he say so in the resolution debate? Very much to the contrary, during the congressional debate five months before the liberation of Iraq, Senator Rockefeller made alarmist statements about the threat from Iraq, describing one even more imminent than what the administration was presenting, and making the same case as Bush did for toppling Saddam Hussein.

How extensive was the threat of Iraq's WMD? Rockefeller spoke in specific, gripping terms: "Saddam's existing biological and chemical weapons capabilities pose real threats to America today, tomorrow." Rockefeller even tied Saddam to Osama bin Laden. In a February 5, 2003, interview with Wolf Blitzer, he cited the October 2002 death of a U.S. foreign service officer at the hands of Abu Musab al-Zarqawi, a known al-Qaeda associate who had fled to Iraq from Afghanistan after the Taliban was overthrown. Zarqawi had been linked to a biological weapons "poison factory" in northeast Iraq that launched attacks in Europe. Rockefeller told Blitzer, "The fact that Zarqawi certainly is related to the death of the U.S. aid officer and that he is very close to bin Laden puts at rest, in fairly dramatic terms, that there is at least a substantial connection between Saddam and al Qaeda." Rockefeller's words were not random or uninformed; he was in a position to be highly conversant with the intelligence.

Representative Jane Harman was in a similar position as the highest-ranking Democrat on the House Intelligence Committee. In July 2003, she said her "tentative conclusion" was the "administration consistently omitted the caveats and qualifiers that the intelligence community generally try to attach to its assessments." Nine months earlier she had insisted—without caveats or qualifiers—that "Saddam Hussein's belligerent intentions and his possession and ongoing development of weapons of mass destruction to fulfill those intentions make him a clear and present danger to the United States and the world."

Some detractors, including Senator Bob Graham, went so far as to say that President Bush's statements that Saddam Hussein had WMD were themselves grounds for impeachment. But Graham had earlier echoed the Bush administration's views. In the aftermath of 9/11, Graham, who was then Senate Intelligence Committee chairman, organized a letter from four Democrats and six Republicans warning President Bush, "There is no doubt that . . . Saddam Hussein has invigorated his weapons programs. Reports indicate that biological, chemical and nuclear programs continue apace and may be back to pre–Gulf War status. In addition, Saddam continues to redefine delivery systems and is doubtless using the cover of a licit missile program to develop longer-range missiles that will threaten the United States and our allies." Just a year later, Graham would say, "We are in possession of what I think to be compelling evidence that Saddam Hussein has, and has had for a number of years, a developing capacity for the production and storage of weapons of mass destruction."

Perhaps the most pathetic display of hypocrisy came from one of America's most embittered politicians: former vice president Al Gore. He used Iraq to vent all his rage over losing in 2000. Just over fifteen months after the war began, he attacked Bush for "intentionally misleading the American people," "spreading purposeful confusion," and spending "prodigious amounts of energy convincing people of lies" that led to "a reckless, discretionary war against a nation that posed no immediate threat to us whatsoever." Asking if Bush was "too dishonest or too gullible," Gore went on to answer himself, saying, "if he is not lying, if they [sic] genuinely believe that, that makes them unfit in battle with al-Qaeda." And that was all in just one speech. At a later rally of Tennessee Democrats, Gore screamed, "He betrayed this country." No one chastened Gore for questioning Bush's patriotism and loyalty to his country.

But in September 2002, during the congressional debate on the Iraq War resolution, Gore had told a San Francisco audience, "Iraq's search for weapons of mass destruction has proven impossible to completely deter, and we should assume that it will continue for as long as Saddam is in power. . . . We know that [Saddam] has stored away secret supplies of biological weapons and chemical weapons throughout his country."

Rockefeller, Harman, Graham, and Gore were not alone in saying Saddam had WMD. Leading Democrat after leading Democrat on both sides of the Iraq War resolution said Saddam Hussein had weapons of mass destruction, including Hillary Clinton, John Kerry, Harry Reid, Ted Kennedy, Carl Levin, Robert Byrd, Barbara Boxer, Dick Gephardt, Henry Waxman, and others. Their language was at least as serious and explicit as the words of President Bush and, in some instances, tougher and even frantic.

These Democrats were echoing the statements of other Clinton-era leaders as varied as Secretary of State Madeleine Albright and Secretary of Defense William Cohen, who had argued as the 1990s came to a close that Saddam Hussein possessed weapons of mass destruction and was poised, as President Bill Clinton put it, "to threaten his neighbors or the world with nuclear arms, poison gas or biological weapons."

Antiwar critics such as the *New York Times* ignored statements from the Clinton era and excused Democrats, especially Bush's critics on Capitol Hill, saying, "Congress had nothing close to the president's access to intelligence."

But according to the *Silberman-Robb Report,* released by the bipartisan commission led by retired federal appeals Judge Laurence Silberman, a Republican, and former senator Chuck Robb, a Democrat, the intelligence in the President's Daily Brief was not "markedly different" from the intelligence given to Congress in the National Intelligence Estimate.

Let's step back. Leading Democrats looked at the same intelligence President Bush relied on and became at least as concerned as Bush about the threat posed by Saddam and his WMD. This domestic consensus produced a strong bipartisan vote on October 11, 2002, on the use-of-force resolution, with 110 Democrats and 263 Republicans in the House and Senate voting for it and only 149 Democrats and 7 Republicans opposing it. The vote in the House was 296–133 in favor and in the Senate 77–23. Of the 110 Democrats who voted for the use-of-force resolution in the House and Senate, sixty-seven asserted in statements delivered before the vote that Saddam Hussein had weapons of mass destruction.

How did this consensus emerge? The principal reason the world believed Saddam possessed WMD was that he had them before the Persian Gulf War in 1990 and 1991. Following Iraq's expulsion from Kuwait and defeat, Saddam produced an extensive report on his stocks of chemical and biological weapons. He also revealed "an extensive nuclear program" that was actually more advanced than Western intelligence had thought.

The United Nations and the international community then spent more than a decade trying to account for these deadly weapons and confirm their destruction, to little avail. The U.N. Special Commission on Iraq (UNSCOM) was charged with making certain Iraq complied with its surrender terms. It was first led by a Swede, Ambassador Rolf Ekéus, and then by an Australian, Ambassador Richard Butler. In January 2000, UNSCOM was replaced by the U.N. Monitoring, Verification and Inspection Commission (UNMOVIC), mentioned earlier, headed by another Swede, Hans Blix (France and Russia had vetoed Ekéus's reappointment since he had been too tough on Iraq). Yet as late as early 2003, even Blix reported "no convincing evidence" that Iraq's stocks of deadly anthrax were ever destroyed, while there was "strong evidence" that Iraq produced more anthrax than it had admitted "and that at least some of this was retained." Blix also said that Iraq possessed 650 kilograms of "bacterial growth media," enough "to produce . . . 5,000 liters of concentrated anthrax," and there were 6,500 "chemical bombs" that Iraq admitted producing but whose whereabouts were unknown.

After tracking Saddam's weapons programs, Richard Butler wrote in 2002 that it "would be foolish in the extreme not to assume that [Saddam] is developing long-range missile capability, at work again on building nuclear weapons, and adding to the chemical and biological warfare weapons he concealed during the UNSCOM inspection period."

It was not only that Saddam possessed these weapons in the past. He had used chemical weapons against the Iranian military during the 1980–88 Iran-Iraq War, against the Iraqi Kurds between 1987 and 1988, and then against the Shia and the Marsh Arabs in southern Iraq before and after the 1991 Gulf War. And in the hours just before the fall of Baghdad in March 2003, our forces intercepted communications between top Iraqi commanders asking when they would receive permission to unleash chemical and biological weapons on coalition forces.

There was a robust debate in the intelligence community over Saddam's priorities. What weapons was he focusing on? Which ones were ready for deployment? How close was he to a nuclear weapon? For example, the head of German intelligence warned in 2002 that Iraq would have nuclear weapons in three years and the missiles to target Berlin. The United States' view was that Hussein was five years or even further away from a nuclear bomb. Whatever the disagreements, however, there was a unified international view that Saddam had WMD.

Saddam also took active steps to create the impression he had them. He wanted Iraqis to think he had WMD; his ruthlessness, after all, helped keep him in power. He also wanted neighboring countries such as Iran and Saudi Arabia to think he had them. Charles Duelfer made this point in what's commonly called the *Duelfer Report*—the findings of the Iraq Survey Group (ISG). "In Saddam's view, WMD helped to save the Regime multiple times," the report said. "He believed that during the Iran-Iraq war chemical weapons had halted Iranian ground offensives and that ballistic missile attacks on Tehran had broken its political will." David Kay, who preceded Duelfer as head of the ISG, pointed to how Saddam "explained that he purposely gave an ambiguous impression about possession as a deterrent to Iran."

Above all, Saddam wanted the West to think he had WMD; it made him feared and discouraged Western attempts at regime change. It was a lesson, Duelfer wrote, the Iraqi dictator took from the Gulf War where "Saddam believed WMD had deterred Coalition Forces from pressing their attack beyond the goal of freeing Kuwait."

Those who insist that because Saddam did not have stockpiles of WMD he was not a threat should keep in mind that he wanted to reconstitute his WMD programs as soon as sanctions collapsed. Indeed, weapons inspector Kay said in his report that Saddam "had not given up his aspirations and intentions to continue to acquire weapons of mass destruction. . . . Saddam intended to resume these programs whenever the external restrictions were removed," even inquiring of his weapons scientists "how long it would take to either restart CW [chemical weapons] production or make available chemical weapons."

The problem was that he could have chemical and biological weapons in a matter of weeks, for he had the scientists, engineers, and technicians who knew how to make them and the dual-use facilities that could be turned into weapons factories almost overnight, once the U.N. inspections regime was ended. As the *Duelfer Report* concluded, "Saddam wanted to re-create Iraq's WMD capability—which was essentially destroyed in 1991—after sanctions were removed and Iraq's economy stabilized, but probably with a different mix of capabilities to that which previously existed."

For example, after 1991, Saddam demonstrated his "intent to retain the intellectual capital developed during the Iraqi Nuclear Program." The ISG found "Saddam directed a large budget increase for IAEC [Iraqi Atomic Energy Commission] and increased salaries tenfold from 2001 to 2003. He also directed the head of the IAEC to keep nuclear scientists together, instituted new laws and regulations to increase privileges for IAEC scientists and invested in numerous new projects."

Saddam went to great lengths to hide preparations for reactivating his WMD efforts. As Kay reported, "We have discovered dozens of WMD-related program activities and significant amounts of equipment that Iraq concealed from the United Nations during the inspections that began in late 2002." These "deliberate concealment efforts" were found after interviews with Iraqi scientists and in evidence uncovered after Saddam's defeat. The ISG also "uncovered information that the Iraqi Intelligence Service (IIS) maintained throughout 1991 to 2003 a set of undeclared covert laboratories to research and test various chemicals and poisons," primarily for assassinations and other covert operations.

Saddam Hussein also diverted millions of dollars from the U.N. "Oil for Food" (OFF) program to keep together his WMD knowledge base of scientists, engineers, and technicians and the dual-use facilities so he could rapidly reconstitute his WMD programs, especially the chemical and biological operations. Duelfer identified OFF's start in 1996 as a "key turning point" when Saddam "quickly came to see that OFF could be corrupted to acquire foreign exchange both to further undermine sanctions and to provide the means to enhance dual-use infrastructure and potential WMD-related development." As Duelfer found, Saddam wanted "to re-create Iraq's WMD capability," seek "a nuclear capability," but "focus on ballistic missile and tactical chemical warfare (CW) capabilities."

So what happened to the chemical and biological weapons Saddam had at the end of the Persian Gulf War? Iraq claimed to have 10,000 chemical weapons after the Gulf War. Inspectors disputed that figure, saying it was ten times that. Between 1991 and 1998, U.N. weapons inspectors methodically destroyed 40,000 chemical munitions, 690 tons of chemical warfare agents, 3,000 tons of precursor chemicals, 48 SCUD missiles, a "super gun," and biological-warfare-related factories and equipment. This was more weapons than were captured during the whole of the Gulf War. Secretary of State Colin Powell also reminded the U.N. Security Council, "As we all know, in 1991, the IAEA was just days away from determining that Iraq did not have a nuclear program. We soon found out otherwise." Indeed, the International Atomic Energy Agency discovered and dismantled a developing Iraqi nuclear weapons program after the Gulf War.

Saddam may also have destroyed most of his stockpiles. The ISG explained the possibility: "[I]n 1991 and 1992, Iraq appears to have destroyed its undeclared stocks of BW [biological weapons] weapons and probably destroyed remaining holdings of bulk BW agent. However ISG lacks evidence to document complete destruction. Iraq retained some BW-related seed stocks until their discovery after Operation Iraqi Freedom (OIF)." Saddam may not have understood how much had been discarded.

Another possibility is that some weapons may have been dispersed to other countries, such as Syria, before the war. That was the assessment of General James R. Clapper, Jr., then the director of the National Imagery and Mapping Agency (now called the National Geospatial-Intelligence Agency). He told the *New York Times:* "I think people below the Saddam Hussein-and-his-sons level saw what was coming and decided the best thing to do was to destroy and disperse." Clapper said satellite imagery showing "a heavy flow of traffic from Iraq into Syria, just before the American invasion in March, led him to believe that illicit weapons material 'unquestionably' had been moved out of Iraq." In January 2006, Georges Sada, who had been deputy chief of Saddam Hussein's air force, claimed Iraq moved weapons of mass destruction into Syria before the war. Later that month, Moshe Yaalon, Israel's top general at the time, said the same thing.

Would the Iraq War have occurred without WMD? I doubt it: Congress was very unlikely to have supported the use-of-force resolution without the threat of WMD. The Bush administration itself would probably have sought other ways to constrain Saddam, bring about regime change, and deal with Iraq's horrendous human rights violations. But that's a hypothetical. What America's leaders faced in 2002 and 2003 was an overwhelming international and domestic consensus that Saddam had WMD and represented, as President Clinton had said in 1998, "[a threat] to the well-being of his people, the peace of his region, the security of the world." And after 9/11 changed the risk assessment for the United States, President George W. Bush would echo Clinton's assessment, saying, "The dictator of Iraq and his weapons of mass destruction are a threat to the security of free nations."

So, then, did Bush lie us into war? Absolutely not.

In his book *Plan of Attack,* Bob Woodward recounts an Oval Office meeting on the morning of Saturday, December 21, 2002. The purpose of the meeting was to present the case on WMD. It was attended by CIA director George Tenet; his deputy, John McLaughlin; White House Chief of Staff Card; NSC advisor Rice; Vice President Cheney; and President Bush. After the CIA briefing, according to Woodward's account, Bush asked Tenet about the quality of the intelligence:

> From the end of one of the couches in the Oval Office, Tenet rose up, threw his arms in the air. "It's a slam dunk case!" the DCI [director of central intelligence] said.
>
> Bush pressed. "George, how confident are you?"
>
> Tenet, a basketball fan who attended as many home games of his alma mater Georgetown as possible, leaned forward and threw his arms up again. "Don't worry, it's a slam dunk!" . . .
>
> The president told Tenet several times, "Make sure no one stretches to make our case."

From my perch inside the West Wing—but outside the frantic activity in the Situation Room—I could see the care everyone was taking to not overstate the case or exaggerate the danger. The president emphasized this when we reviewed his speeches, and this care was reflected everywhere else in the administration. For example, before his February 2003 presentation to the U.N. outlining the case for going to war with Iraq, Colin Powell spent the better part of a week at the CIA with Tenet, McLaughlin, and Robert Walpole, the national intelligence officer for strategic programs. Powell carefully reviewed the intelligence and challenged each of the agency's findings in often-contentious meetings. Questions would be raised later, such as in a lengthy *Washington Post Magazine* article in 2006, about whether Powell felt he was forced into making the presentation to the U.N. and whether he believed the case against Iraq was strong enough. But Powell's chief of staff and caustic critic of the Bush White House, retired Army Colonel Larry Wilkerson, later admitted that the meetings at the CIA had tipped the scales for the secretary of state. "It is safe to say that he [Powell] changed his mind. He was convinced by what the agency and members of the IC [intelligence community] were able to present to him," Wilkerson said.

And what about Bush's claims about Saddam Hussein's ties to terrorism? Statements that Iraq provided safe haven for Abu Musab al-Zarqawi and other terrorists with ties to al-Qaeda and about Iraq's support for terrorist groups other than al-Qaeda "were substantiated by intelligence information," according to the Senate Intelligence Committee 2004 report.

So why did President Bush choose to go after Saddam Hussein in the first place? Wasn't it a diversion from what should have been the real goal, which was to defeat al-Qaeda and the Taliban in Afghanistan?

Part of the reason why the president felt strongly about Iraq has to do with how the attacks on 9/11 affected his mind-set and that of the administration, Congress, and the country. Having seen how much carnage four airplanes could cause, Bush was determined to do all he could to prevent the most powerful weapons from falling into the hands of the world's most dangerous dictators. He understood that conventional deterrence, which had worked with the Soviet Union, was far less useful in the situation in which we found ourselves after 9/11.

After 9/11, he believed Iraq represented a deeply dangerous threat— a rogue regime with WMD, no constraints on using them, and a record of support for terrorists. This all raised the possibility of Saddam slipping terror surrogates weapons that would bring death on an unimaginable scale.

In addition to all that, Bush believed overthrowing Saddam would provide the opportunity to transform the political culture of the Middle East, which had been fenced off from democracy and much of the progress of modernity. What's more, he saw democracy as a bulwark against Islamic extremism, which spawned terrorist networks. Encouraging the expansion of democracy and freedom in Iraq and the Middle East would serve our national security interests by creating civil institutions that would have a stake in defeating Islamic extremists.

Taken together, these considerations justified the decision to remove Saddam Hussein.

Still, the Iraq War became unpopular, in part because the claim that Bush lied was corrosive and harmful to the Bush presidency and made it harder for us to prosecute the war. At the beginning of June 2003, Gallup asked, "do you think the Bush administration deliberately misled the American people about whether Iraq has weapons of mass destruction, or not?" The response was 2-to-1 "no," with 31 percent saying the Bush administration had misled Americans and 67 percent saying no. Several months later, after Democratic presidential hopefuls hammered Bush on the issue, the percentage of Americans who believed the president had deliberately misled them had risen to 43 percent while 54 percent still rejected the claim. By July 2005, a majority of Americans—51 percent—believed Bush had deliberately misled them.

The acidic effect of the Democratic assault was felt more broadly as a decline in the president's approval ratings and other measures of trust. Left unanswered, the charge allowed Democratic critics to claim a moral high ground they did not deserve, since many of them had supported the decision to go to war.

But I am under no illusions; the failure to find stockpiles of WMD did great damage to the administration's credibility. Our weak response in defense of the president and in setting the record straight, is, I believe, one of the biggest mistakes of the Bush years. When the pattern of the Democratic attacks became apparent in July 2003, we should have countered in a forceful and overwhelming way. This assault was worthy of significant attention by the entire White House, including a rebuttal delivered in a presidential address. We should have seen this for what it was: a poison-tipped dagger aimed at the heart of the Bush presidency.

By not engaging, we let more of the public come to believe dangerous falsehoods about the war: that Bush lied, that Saddam Hussein never had and never wanted WMD, that we claimed Iraq had been behind 9/11. These attacks undermined support for the war and public confidence in the president.

So who was responsible for the failure to respond? I was. I should have stepped forward, rung the warning bell, and pressed for full-scale response. I didn't. Preoccupied with the coming campaign and the pressure of the daily schedule in the West Wing, I did not see how damaging this assault was. There were others who could have sounded the alarm, but regardless, I should have.

It is not as if we didn't respond here and there. Those of us in the West Wing read the charges on an almost daily basis. But there was not an intense, all-hands-on-deck attitude.

I have reflected on why this was the case in the years since. As I look back, there were a number of reasons for our inaction. One was that we felt it was beneath the dignity of the president to refute such outlandish charges. If you wrestle with pigs, the old line goes, you get muddy.

Another reason offered at the time was that it would appear to be too "defensive." It's a mistake, some people in the White House said, to "re-litigate the past." Our task was to focus on winning the war, not on the reasons it began.

And a third explanation was that many people in the Bush White House were simply worn down by the Iraq debate. The fact that stockpiles of WMD had not been found was a terrible blow to all of us. Some White House aides simply wanted to avoid the topic. And responding to the critics wouldn't help us, but would re-entangle us in the WMD debate. The hope was that the charges would evaporate.

The opposite happened. Our critics pounded us relentlessly. And the public saw our silence as a plea of nolo contendere. With a complicit media that refused to subject the Democratic attacks to even the most mild fact-checking, many Americans eventually came to side with the administration's adversaries on this important question.

The charge that Bush lied was itself a lie. Some who leveled the charge—Al Gore, Senators Harry Reid, John Kerry, and Ted Kennedy—were hypocrites who had earlier said much the same as, or more than, what they later criticized Bush for.

The charge did what its critics had hoped. It weakened the Bush presidency. And those who led the charge did grave damage to their country's ability to win a war it was hotly engaged in. They must have known at the start this would happen, but it was a price they were willing, even eager, to have their nation pay.

CHAPTER 22

The Special Prosecutor and Me

———— • ◆ • ————

I have been in plenty of political firestorms and I feel comfortable at their red-hot center. One observer has even said that I "appear to lack nerve endings.". But now I was entering a battlefield far more dangerous and draining than any I'd been on. It was a terrain dominated by a relentless special prosecutor and swarming with world-class lawyers, determined FBI agents, and dirt-hungry journalists. The last group was salivating at the chance to write my political obituary—and they came within a whisker of being able to do so.

I could have avoided an opening skirmish in this war if I hadn't healed up so damn quickly.

I had been invited by Dr. Martin Anderson—a former advisor to President Ronald Reagan—to be his guest at the Bohemian Club's summer retreat in northern California. I wasn't sure I could make it, because surgery on my sinuses in early July 2003 prevented me from flying. But at the eleventh hour, my otolaryngologist gave me permission to get on an airplane. On Thursday, July 17, I arrived in San Francisco and drove north to Bohemian Grove, the club's rustic 2,700-acre camp in the Redwoods near Monte Rio.

The Bohemian Club was founded in 1872 by the railroad barons, shipping magnates, land speculators, and cattle kings of Gilded Age California. Its members gather during the summer and are organized into camps where they and their guests take meals and gather for drink, entertainment, talk, and more drink. Bohemians are an unusual mix of leaders in business, finance, technology, and politics, with literary, musical, artistic, and entertainment types thrown in, which produces some surreal encounters. In a past visit to the Grove, I found myself sitting with the librarian of Congress and the drummer from the Grateful Dead, critiquing the lunch hosted by Henry Kissinger and the entertainment provided by George Shultz.

On Saturday afternoon, as my friend Michael Boskin, a professor at Stanford University and renowned economist, and I were out walking, we ran into MSNBC host Chris Matthews. Matthews brought up Joe Wilson's op-ed and Robert Novak's column. It was clear the cable TV host hadn't noticed the CIA's July 11 statement that said the White House had not sent Wilson on the mission to Niger. Nor did he know that the information Wilson returned with actually bolstered the case that Iraq had attempted to acquire uranium from Niger. Nor did Matthews seem aware that the CIA had concerns about how Wilson collected his information and therefore considered his conclusions uncertain. In short, Matthews appeared to know squat. Our conversation went on to other topics and, after a few minutes, Boskin and I parted from Matthews.

Back in Washington on Monday, I called Matthews to correct a statistic I had given him on a different subject, but Matthews didn't seem interested. Agitated, he brought up Joe Wilson again, asking if it was "fair game" to go after Wilson's wife. It was an unusual phrase. I parried. What was fair, I said, was to assess Wilson's claim that he was sent to Africa at the request of Vice President Cheney's office. What was fair was to inquire about why the CIA didn't think Wilson's claims were dispositive.

We now know that Matthews hung up the phone with me and called Wilson, who later recounted their exchange. "Matthews was blunt," Wilson later said, recalling Matthews saying, "I just got off the phone with Karl Rove. He says, and I quote, 'Wilson's wife is fair game.' " But "fair game" is not something I said, or would say. However, it is part of Matthews's lexicon—and not just in our conversation that Monday. The previous Wednesday, July 16, he used the phrase "fair game" on his program, *Hardball,* while asking Senator Trent Lott, "Is it a feeding frenzy or is it fair game to try to find out" if the vice president sent Wilson to Niger?

Wilson and his wife attribute the comment about "fair game" to me, not its real author—their friend Chris Matthews. Ms. Plame even used it as the title of her book. They were wrong to say it was my phrase, but their use of it shows how Chris Matthews became an agent provocateur in the Wilson affair.

Wilson also ludicrously argued that even my talking about Novak's column a week after it was published was "unethical behavior." He suggested that because I had talked with Matthews that Monday about a subject Matthews broached, the conversation constituted "a good place" to begin a criminal investigation. His call for an investigation was an attempt to criminalize political differences, a troubling proposition in a democracy. Should everyone else who talked about Novak's column around an office cooler or kitchen table have been investigated?

By the end of July, House Democrats were promising to look into the matter, New York Democratic senator Chuck Schumer was calling for an investigation, and an FBI spokeswoman told *Newsday* the agency would "look at the issue and make determinations about whether [an investigation] is warranted."

On July 28, rumors that I'd outed Valerie Plame as an undercover CIA agent prompted the press to show up at my house. A neighbor on the way to an early appointment called me just after 6 A.M. to say a cameraman, soundman, and reporter were crouched on the street behind my car, waiting to spring out of hiding when I left for work. I traded car keys with Darby, and the young ABC reporter was reduced to yelling at me for a comment as I drove out of the driveway. Media stakeouts of my house became routine for the next four years.

By early August 10, Wilson said on a lecture tour that White House political operatives gave his wife's name to Novak. While he knew who they were, he was "not ready, yet" to name them, and hoped for an FBI or congressional investigation. By the end of August, Wilson got more specific and, for me, personal, saying at a political forum hosted by Democratic congressman Jay Inslee of Washington State, "At the end of the day it's of keen interest to me to see whether or not we can get Karl Rove frog-marched out of the White House in handcuffs. And trust me when

I use that name. I measure my words." Actually, Wilson rarely measured his words. Less than a month later, he told *Slate* he didn't really mean me: my name was a metonym—a substitute—for "senior administration officials."

Calls for an investigation increased, and in late August and September, I visited with White House Counsel Alberto Gonzales about my call with Novak. I also mentioned it to Chief of Staff Andy Card. And I told President Bush. He called me from the Oval Office, where he was meeting with Card and Gonzales, and I explained to Bush that I'd talked to Novak and said "I've heard that, too" when the reporter told me about Wilson's wife, whose name and role I didn't know. Novak hadn't asked me to confirm anything; it sounded to me like he had his story and was running with it, and had even talked with the CIA. Bush sounded a little annoyed but took my word. Afterward, Gonzales cautioned me about talking with colleagues or outsiders about my contact with Novak. I took his advice to heart.

On Sunday, September 28, 2003, the *Washington Post* reported that at the CIA's request, "the Justice Department is looking into an allegation that administration officials leaked the name of an undercover CIA officer to a journalist, government sources said yesterday." What began as a damaging political story was quickly morphing into a dangerous criminal investigation. While the story quoted an unnamed intelligence official saying CIA director George Tenet "doesn't like leaks," the news of the investigation was probably leaked by the CIA or Justice Department. If it was, that leak itself could have been a violation of a 1982 federal law, the Intelligence Identities Protection Act, which carries a maximum sentence of ten years in prison and a fine of $50,000.

Almost as interesting as the news of the Justice investigation were quotes from an unnamed "senior administration official" asserting that two "top White House officials called at least six Washington journalists and disclosed the identity and occupation of Wilson's wife." This theory, which came to be known as "Two by Six," was never corroborated and didn't fit the White House MO—Bush administration officials, especially those in the White House, didn't operate that way. But the theory was simply too juicy for much of the media to worry about verifying. The *Post*'s source even spiced it up, saying of "Two by Six" that "clearly, it was meant purely and simply for revenge" and the leaks were "wrong and a huge miscalculation, because they were irrelevant and did nothing to diminish Wilson's credibility."

I wondered who Novak's sources were. He said in his column "senior administration officials." That seemed to rule out the CIA, though other White House colleagues disagreed. I couldn't accept the idea it was someone in the West Wing; I thought Novak's sources were more likely in the State Department. But then Secretary of State Colin Powell said on ABC's *This Week* the morning the *Post* story broke that "the CIA has an obligation, when they believe somebody who is undercover was outed . . . to ask the Justice Department to look into it. But other than that, I don't know anything about the matter." I assumed this meant Powell had looked into whether someone at State was involved and found nothing. I discovered years later that was not the case.

The next day, White House Press Secretary Scott McClellan said the president considered the allegations "a very serious matter" and would fire anyone who'd leaked Plame's name. The *Post*'s story on McClellan's briefing also quoted Wilson as saying he had "no evidence Rove was the original leaker," with Wilson then explaining, "My knowledge is based on a reporter who called me right after he had spoken to Rove and said that Rove had said my wife was fair game." Chris Matthews's phone call had made me Wilson's prime target.

On October 1, Robert Novak offered a little relief and a lot of indigestion. The leak investigation and the intense coverage of it provoked Novak to explain how his July column came about. He wrote:

> During a long conversation with a senior administration official, I asked why Wilson was assigned the mission to Niger. He said Wilson had been sent by the CIA's counterproliferation section at the suggestion of one of its employees, his wife. It was an offhand revelation from this official, who is no partisan gunslinger. When I called another official for confirmation, he said: "Oh, you know about it."

Novak was telegraphing to the world that I wasn't the original source for his story; that individual was "no partisan gunslinger." That was the good news. The not-so-good news—in fact, the flat-out bad news—was that Novak treated my offhanded "I've heard that, too" as a confirmation. And while it had sounded to me in our conversation that Novak had been in touch with the CIA, that's not the impression his column left. I was sick to my stomach.

Around this time, I was notified the FBI wanted to interview me the second week of October. Alberto Gonzales suggested that White House aides receiving such requests hire private counsel and he directed that all relevant documents be preserved. I was now in search of a lawyer.

The first lawyer I called was unavailable. The second lawyer I called came to the White House the next day to deliver his terms. He wouldn't take me on unless I agreed not to cooperate with the investigation and refused to testify before the grand jury. I was stunned. If I did what he said, I'd have to resign from the White House. But he was insistent: no client of his ever voluntarily put himself into jeopardy and that was what I'd be doing if I met with the FBI and later testified before the grand jury. Following that course and resigning from the White House would be taken as an admission of guilt. When I refused to do it, he expressed disappointment, offered me his best wishes, and left.

I was supposed to meet with the FBI in two days but I still didn't have a lawyer. So Darby called David Herndon, my personal attorney in Texas, and he called Ben Ginsberg, who'd been the Bush campaign counsel. Ben suggested Bob Luskin, a partner of his at the D.C. powerhouse law firm Patton Boggs. That evening I met Luskin at his office and began one of the most consequential relationships of my life.

The first thing that struck me about Robert D. Luskin was his appearance: at five-feet-eleven he looks boyish though he sports a shaved head, his pointy-topped ears are occasionally adorned with a gold hoop, and he has a habit of scratching his head with his left hand as if this could stir his brain cells into even more prodigious acts of analysis and recall.

He has a calming manner, never gets ruffled, never loses sight of the goal, remembers all, and explains everything in a clear, persuasive manner. At his Martha's Vineyard home, he drives an ancient pickup and a Ducati motorcycle, and in D.C., a rented Zipcar. He has a great smile, an even better laugh, a wonderful sense of humor, and endearing habits like his love of his cat, Charlotte. It's said you can judge someone by their friends. Bob Luskin's are legion, loyal, interesting, and eclectic, from Harvard-trained lawyers to the waitress at the coffee shop near his office. He's also a prostate cancer survivor.

As a 1972 graduate of Harvard, a Rhodes scholar at Oxford, a 1979 graduate of Harvard Law School, and a former chief counsel of the Justice Department's Organized Crime and Racketeering Section, Bob has the pedigrees. But he's also smart: I got confirmation of this when U.S. Trade Representative Robert Zoellick called me to say Luskin was the smartest person in their Harvard Law class. Coming from someone with a healthy appreciation for his own intelligence, that was quite a compliment.

The FBI was scheduled to interview me the next day, October 10. Luskin thought we needed more time to prepare and tried convincing me to put it off. I was adamant about not wanting to reschedule. I didn't have a good reason; I simply thought the sooner I was interviewed, the sooner this whole thing would be over.

That Friday at 9:30 A.M., FBI Inspector John C. Eckenrode and two special agents, Jeffrey Stetler and Kirk Armfield, came to the White House to interview me. Eckenrode had the ultimate poker face; he and Luskin had known each other for years.

After exchanging business cards, Eckenrode asked my full name, addresses, and security clearance. All three agents wrote the information on their pads and Eckenrode remarked, "It sounds like there's stuff you want to tell us." I did. I told him everything about my call with Novak. In detail. That he'd called July 7 about Fran Townsend. That I'd returned Novak's call the next day after being armed with background material on Fran Townsend. That I'd defended her appointment, citing among other things endorsements from the Coast Guard commandant and the FBI director; Novak had then changed the subject to Wilson. I went through it all, point by point. When Novak brought up Wilson's wife, I had been momentarily confused because he used the name Valerie Plame. It was only from the context that I came to understand Novak was referring to Wilson's wife. And I'd told Novak, "I've heard that, too."

Eckenrode wanted to know about other contacts with Novak during the balance of the year. I went through them as they appeared in my phone log, one by one. They focused on a September 29 call at 11:30 A.M. that I'd returned about 3 P.M. During that call, Novak told me I was not the source for his Wilson column in July and that he protected his sources. I inferred that he was letting me know that he hoped I would not be blamed for being the source of the leak.

Eckenrode was interested in why Wilson identified me as the source of the leak. I told him I assumed it was Chris Matthews and shared the details of our Bohemian Club encounter and the phone call that followed.

As the interview drew to a close, Eckenrode asked whether I would take a polygraph test: I said I would. Finally, he asked if I would give a waiver of confidentiality to Novak or any other journalist to overcome any resistance on their part to discussing any conversation. Luskin replied "of course" and offered to work up such a waiver. The trio of agents gathered up their pads and departed, their faces as expressionless as when they arrived.

It was the strangest sensation when they left; I had told them the truth, and I knew I hadn't committed any crime. Yet I was still being drawn into a story that I knew, even then, was going to weigh on me. Darby reminded me that at a party in Austin before the 2000 election, Bullock had told her, "Bush will win, you guys will to go Washington, and then they'll put you in the penitentiary."

In the days after the FBI's interview, I decided I needed to toughen up. I was letting the press chatter and Wilson's comments eat away at me. I felt my concerns and stress were becoming visible to colleagues and affecting my work. I talked with Darby, who said I needed to give this all over to a Higher Power. It was good advice—but hard to do. I obsessed about all the Wilson stuff, but out of everyone's view. I was determined not to let White House colleagues, the press, the public, or anyone else—up to and including Darby—see me suffer. Stiff upper lip, soldier on, all that. *Illegitimis non carborundum:* Don't let the bastards grind you down. But behind the mask, the whole thing was scaring the hell out of me.

November 17, Eckenrode called Luskin to ask for a second visit in early December to clarify a few points. In the first of a number of statements that created false hope, he told Luskin he did not anticipate any further need to speak to me; this would be the final interview. I didn't know enough at that point not to relax, so I let out a deep breath.

Eckenrode showed me a memo from the State Department Bureau of Intelligence and Research (INR). Its subject was Wilson's trip and his wife's involvement in it. He asked if I had seen or discussed it. I said, "No." I generally didn't see INR's work and I certainly hadn't seen this particular memo. He seemed satisfied; it felt to me like Eckenrode knew exactly who had seen this memo.

A new and ominous phase in the investigation opened December 30. "Attorney General John Ashcroft disqualified himself . . . from any involvement" in it. The reason was "his close ties to the White House." Well, I thought to myself, didn't that also apply to the deputy attorney general James B. Comey, Jr., another Bush appointee, who stepped into Ashcroft's place to assume oversight of the investigation? Comey held a news conference to applaud Ashcroft's "abundance of caution" in recusing himself, saying, "I agree with that judgment. And I also agree that he made it at the appropriate time." I thought Comey's tone odd for a subordinate.

Comey then named a special prosecutor to oversee the Justice Department's investigation: Patrick J. Fitzgerald, the U.S. attorney for the Northern District of Illinois, located in Chicago. Comey pledged a free hand for Fitzgerald, saying he needed to consult with Justice Department officials only if he needs more "money, chairs or sticky pads." Fitzgerald and Comey had been colleagues in the U.S. attorney's office in Manhattan. Comey described his friend as "Eliot Ness with a Harvard law degree and a sense of humor." In the years ahead, I saw the Ness side of Fitzgerald. Only much later did I see any of his much-vaunted humor.

I knew Fitzgerald's name. In 2001, the Republican senator from Illinois, Peter Fitzgerald (no relation to Patrick), had decided he would not approve any U.S. attorney nominee for Chicago who practiced in Illinois. Since the senator was a former client of mine, it fell to me to see if he could be talked out of it. The White House thought appointing out-of-state U.S. attorneys was a bad practice. One way to encourage more civic involvement by the local legal community was to appoint the U.S. attorney from lawyers within a district. If we reached outside a state or district for U.S. attorneys, we'd end up appointing more career Justice Department people and fewer lawyers who knew something about the community. But Senator Fitzgerald would have none of it. Anyone from Chicago would feel beholden to "the big law firms, the Chicago machine, the power brokers and influence peddlers," he said. "There's not a lawyer in Chicago they can't buy off."

I told him that was an extreme statement, but he didn't back down. And because the Senate generally deferred to home-state senators in confirming such appointments, Senator Fitzgerald's word carried a lot of weight. He went a step further: rather than waiting for the White House to agree, he announced that Patrick Fitzgerald would be the new U.S. attorney for the Northern District.

Talk about a power grab! The Constitution says the president appoints U.S. attorneys, while the Senate exercises the power of advise and consent. Not this time. In the name of comity, the White House went along with the headstrong senator. Nearly three years later, the man I'd failed to dissuade Senator Fitzgerald from supporting was now in charge of an investigation that would shortly focus on me.

Patrick Fitzgerald was born of Irish immigrant working-class parents in New York and rose by persistent ambition and hard work to a prestigious Catholic high school, Amherst College, and Harvard Law School. After a couple of years in private practice, he became a deputy U.S. attorney in the Southern District of New York in Manhattan, where he handled high-profile terrorism and organized-crime cases.

He is tall, earnest, and polite. Because of the nature of our interactions, I also came to see him as cold, calculating, and relentless. He is curiously deceptive in his approach, creating a lack of clarity about where he is going with his questions until you realize he is like a bird of prey, circling his victim and driving him to open ground. He struck me as someone who would rarely say he was wrong. Not because he wasn't, but because he formulated his views as working hypotheses to be carefully tested and honed through rigorous inquiry. But I couldn't shake the thought—the fear—that he was subtly driven to prove his original thesis.

I was reassured by the thought that while there was intense pressure to indict, he did not appear to be a man who bends. He would not do what he thought was wrong or unnecessary. But I did fear his hunter instincts: if he locked in on you, he had the need to destroy you.

One of Fitzgerald's first actions was to ask for an even more expansive waiver releasing any journalist that any witness might have talked to from any promise of confidentiality. I quickly signed the new waiver in early January 2004.

Shortly afterward, I was subpoenaed to appear before the grand jury convened to hear testimony about the possible violation of law in the revelation of Valerie Plame's name to Robert Novak. I was summoned for February 13, 2004. I had one advantage: I didn't know what I was about to go through.

My grand jury appearance was not public and didn't leak. Luskin and

I were picked up at Patton Boggs by the FBI and driven into the federal courthouse garage. We then made our way up to the grand jury room in an elevator closed to the public.

The Prettyman Federal Courthouse is one of those massive, classical postwar buildings grand in their day and scruffy and worn in this one. It is on Pennsylvania Avenue about halfway between the Capitol and the White House. The small room the grand jury gathered in resembled a college classroom, with desks with writing tables fixed to them in which the grand jury members sat and took notes. It was dingy, lit by fluorescent lights, and vaguely Third World. I entered through a small outer office with locked metal file cabinets. The office was occupied by a clerk who looked comfortable in her deserted corner of the building.

The grand jury was composed of people who were either in their twenties or quite elderly. For all but one of the times I came before them, they appeared listless and bored. I sat in a chair close to the door as you enter the room. Fitzgerald stood as far away from me as possible at the end of a pair of L-shaped tables that ran along the other wall.

In the windowless room, I was there under oath and by myself, with Luskin waiting in a long empty hallway outside. I could refuse to answer a question by invoking my Fifth Amendment right against self-incrimination (which I never did) or I could ask for a break whenever I wanted (which I periodically did) to use the restroom or confer with Luskin. But otherwise, it was Rove v. Fitzgerald, with lots of questions, some exhibits, and bored grand jury members looking on.

Each session (except my last) was filled with wildly different lines of inquiry and a mishmash of subjects. It seemed to me that Fitzgerald organized his inquiries in blocks that made sense to him, but he could discard one issue and take up a much different one in an instant. I assumed this was to keep me off balance. The only way I could keep track of what he was exploring was to occasionally take a five- or ten-minute break when my mind was ready to explode. I would step out to give Luskin a quick lowdown before returning to the fray.

The prosecutor asked me to review the events of the week of Wilson's op-ed. We went over every conversation, meeting, and discussion I could remember, and, of course, my phone call with Novak. He explored each day of the week at length, asking who inside and outside the White House I talked to, what communications I had with Air Force One and the presidential traveling party in Africa, what other reporters I might have talked to then and later. What had the White House said and done in response to Wilson? Did I know Plame's status? Her name? What she did? Whether she was covert?

He also asked about my relationship with Novak. I explained I had known him for several decades because Novak's mother-in-law happened to live in Hillsboro, Texas, and Novak had made it a habit to get a meal or cup of coffee with me when he and his wife spent the Christmas holidays with her. We talked Texas politics at length and stayed in touch by phone in between. Did I consider him a friend? Yes.

Fitzgerald asked whether I had had contact with reporters other than Robert Novak, running through a string of them. One name was Matt Cooper of *Time*. I said I didn't recall talking to him.

Fitzgerald had such a wide range of questions, he couldn't get them all into one day and told Luskin he wanted me for a second day. At some point, I stopped being able to remember what questions I got that first day and which the second. Fitzgerald went into my understanding of the terms "off the record" and "background." Then he brought up "Two by Six," the theory postulated by an anonymous source to the *Washington Post* that two White House staffers had been tasked with calling six reporters to trash Wilson by saying his wife had sent him to Africa. I hadn't heard of such an operation and dismissed the *Post* story.

Then the prosecutor spent a lot of time, of all things, on an incident that took place in 1992. Novak had written a column back then quoting an unnamed Texas Republican critical of the leadership of Rob Mosbacher, the chairman of the GOP's Texas Victory Committee effort. I heard Mosbacher blamed me for the piece.

So I had picked up the phone and called him. Mosbacher didn't accept my denial but also didn't have the courtesy to fire me as the Texas Victory Committee's direct-mail vendor himself. He had an underling call me a day later.

Amazingly and without being asked, Novak backed me up. He told the *San Antonio Express-News* that Mosbacher had the wrong guy. I hadn't been Novak's source. It was unusual for a reporter to go on the record to say someone was not a source. It didn't change Mosbacher's mind, but I appreciated Novak's setting the record straight.

I was astonished that Fitzgerald was reaching back to 1992. What did this have to do with anything? Only much later did it dawn on me that he was trying to suggest Novak had a pattern of covering up for his sources by concocting phony stories. I couldn't believe it when I figured it out. Luskin was amused.

It was a grueling pair of days. At times I could be crystal clear, especially about how the White House responded to Wilson, what points we emphasized, what our goal was. Other times I couldn't recall when I'd gotten what call and from whom or the names of every person who'd sat in on a discussion and what they said. By the session's end, I was mentally beaten to a pulp. Fitzgerald, on the other hand, seemed as crisp and fresh as he'd been when he looked at the first page of his pad on which he'd written his plan for the day's inquiries. He turned to the grand jury and asked its members if they had any questions. It's strange now, but I can't remember when any of them asked questions or what they were. It felt to me as if they were just the scenery. The real work was done by Fitzgerald and the platoon of lawyers and agents who pulled pieces of paper from files, put up transparencies, shared knowing glances, or huddled in quiet conversation at odd intervals. I was excused. The FBI agents drove us back to Luskin's office and he debriefed me as well as one can debrief a mindless noodle.

In April, Fitzgerald subpoenaed my home computers—and Darby's as well. They had already copied my office hard drives and the backups in the White House computer system. But grabbing our home computers was penetrating a zone of privacy. Our entire lives—e-mail, finances, electronic checkbook, photos, letters, and personal documents—were on our home computers, and now strangers in a town prone to leaking had copies of our hard drives. Darby especially felt invaded.

There was one bit of good news before my appearance. The Wilsons inexplicably agreed to an article—complete with photo spread—in *Vanity Fair*. Even in publicity-crazy Washington, the piece was thought by the Wilsons' friends and critics alike to be a mistake. It made both Wilsons seem like vain, arrogant celebrity wannabes.

The spring and summer of 2004 were quiet on the investigation front. There were no leaks from Fitzgerald's office, the Justice Department, or the grand jury. But it was wearing and expensive. I was paying for Luskin out of my own pocket. And because I had to report in my "Form 278" annual ethics report any debts outstanding at year's end, I made certain I stayed current on my bill. This required selling stock and juggling home equity lines. Luckily, these transactions are reported in ranges and not exact amounts, so no one could figure out precisely how much this was costing me. I didn't want the press or political opponents to know that this was bleeding me financially.

For Darby, the events of late 2003 and 2004 were a constant drain on her emotional reserves. She didn't have the advantage of burying herself in the reelection or West Wing issues. Late in the year, she slipped me a note I began carrying in my wallet that said, "Don't take the bait." She tried to talk every day with friends or family to keep her spirits up, including a longtime mentor who lived in a little town in central Texas. Her women's Bible study group gave her incredible support. The women involved called it their "Grace Group" and focused on the things in life over which we have no control and on how to find God in these challenges. I could relate to the lack of control, but I was having a bit harder time discovering the presence of God in this particular challenge, even as I believed on a deep level that He was in control of my life and events. But it was a distant knowledge, more head than heart, more rote than real, and not as strong a source of comfort to me as it was to Darby.

In early August 2004, it was reported that Fitzgerald had earlier issued a flurry of subpoenas to a number of reporters, including *Time's* Matt Cooper, the *Washington Post's* Walter Pincus, Robert Novak, and NBC's Tim Russert. Russert had avoided a contempt citation by answering "a limited number of questions" from Fitzgerald, as had the *Post's* Glenn Kessler, but Cooper was cited for contempt and faced a "confinement" order unless he talked. Two weeks later, Cooper talked with Fitzgerald's prosecutors about his conversation with Scooter Libby. The contempt citation against Cooper was dropped.

I didn't think any of this had anything to do with me. I hadn't talked to any of those reporters, except maybe Russert, and that would have been after the publication of Novak's column. Cooper was saying I was one of the White House officials who talked to him, but I was damned if I could remember our contact. Remembering any particular White House phone call is like grabbing one drop out of a rain shower.

I was summoned back to the grand jury for a third session on October 15, 2004. Sometime before, Luskin was told I was a subject, not a target. It was a routine notification, but still slightly ominous. Luskin told me I should be relieved: under federal rules, they had to tell me if I had become a target of the investigation. So the call simply meant my status had not changed. I tried to be happy. I wasn't.

Before my third appearance, Luskin undertook a herculean task. He had already gone through all my e-mails from April through September 2003. That may sound like a manageable chore, but the period covered 183 days and on any given day, I could have easily received several hundred e-mails. The e-mails had all been printed out and put into boxes. Luskin decided it was time for a redo. He went back through every e-mail. He didn't know what he was looking for, but he knew he'd know it when he found it. And he did. On July 11 at 11:55 A.M., I had written Deputy National Security Director Steve Hadley to report:

> Matt Cooper called to give me a heads-up that he's got a welfare reform story coming.
>
> When he finished his brief heads-up, he immediately launched into Niger/isn't this damaging/hasn't the President been hurt? I didn't take the bait but said, if I were him, I wouldn't get TIME far out in front on this.

I had told the grand jury in February that I didn't remember any contact with Matt Cooper. Finding the e-mail didn't jog any better recollection of the call—but finding the e-mail meant I needed to set the record straight. Fitzgerald hadn't shown me the e-mail during my earlier appearances at the grand jury, but Luskin surmised he had it. I had to let them know Luskin had found it.

I did so right after being sworn in before the grand jury, telling Fitzgerald I wanted to correct a statement I had made in my previous appearance. While I still had no recollection of talking to Matt Cooper, I told Fitzgerald, I had written Steve Hadley the morning of July 11 to say I had talked to the *Time* reporter. I also drew attention to Cooper's September 2003 *Time* article on welfare reform.

It was as if I'd detonated a bomb in the shabby little room. Fitzgerald was flustered—the only time I ever saw him in that condition. After I handed him the copy of the e-mail, his aides clustered around him as he examined it. Fitzgerald immediately recessed the grand jury and he and his staff rushed out to meet Luskin, who was waiting in a nearby corridor. Fitzgerald was uncertain of the provenance of the printed e-mail I'd offered him and wanted to know how Luskin had come to have it. Fitzgerald was "so upset he missed it," Luskin later recalled, he was almost "quivering."

When we went back into the grand jury room, Fitzgerald went over old territory, but some of his questions seemed petty and disconnected from the bigger issue. He was particularly interested in why White House records showed me logging in at one of the checkpoints on September 27, 2003, but not logging out. I don't have complete recall of every day of my life, but this one answer was easy: I had been traveling and came back to the White House to get my car. So I used my badge to check in (which was captured by the White House records system) and then drove out in my car (which wasn't similarly caught). Some of his questions seemed as if he were checking a box. For example, had I met *New York Times* reporter Judith Miller (maybe but didn't know her) or *Washington Post* reporter Walter Pincus (no).

One line of questioning was vaguely ominous: White House Political Director Matt Schlapp prepared a document summarizing the conservative criticism of Fran Townsend. Fitzgerald wanted to know how I could have defended her to Novak using such a document. I replied it was useful to know what the criticisms were. I wondered if Novak said something that caused Fitzgerald to think I was lying to him. I couldn't imagine Novak had gotten any impression other than that I was Fran's advocate. Looking back now, I see Fitzgerald was probing for places to assert I was misleading him.

Luskin had a more nuanced view. By now, Fitzgerald knew Novak had misled me when he pretended he was calling about Townsend: Novak had already put his Townsend column to bed when I returned his call. This led the prosecutor to wonder if the conversation between Novak and me was actually all about Wilson and whether we had concocted the story about Townsend as a smoke screen.

Excused after eight and a half hours, I left the grand jury room exhausted, yet elated. Exhausted because Fitzgerald quickly recovered from the bombshell I started with and went on to pummel me mercilessly. Elated because I had been able to set the record straight on Cooper. I did not understand then that by doing so I had painted a target on my back.

The Hadley e-mail may have been Fitzgerald's first evidence that I had had a call with Cooper about Wilson, though the prosecutor had already known Cooper said he had talked with me. Sharing that e-mail suggested that in my previous appearance I did not deliberately conceal the Cooper conversation. This removed the possibility of being charged with misleading the grand jury because of my February testimony. It certainly helped to cement Luskin's credibility with Fitzgerald, since Luskin found the Hadley e-mail, which we thought exculpatory.

But the production of that e-mail added weight to a concern Fitzgerald had not yet revealed in his questioning of me—namely, that I'd misled him about Matt Cooper. This concern would nag the special prosecutor for another twelve months and five days, and lead him to within inches of indicting me. For now, though, I was in blissful ignorance of the special prosecutor's unasked and almost obsessive concern.

CHAPTER 23

Getting Ready for Kerry

———— •◆• ————

I sat in the living room of Bush's Crawford ranch just after New Year's Day 2003. Laura was on the couch reading, pretending not to pay attention. But she was, which was a good thing. Bush had just come in from chainsawing some mountain juniper. Before I could boot up the laptop with the outline of the 2004 reelection, he told me two things: It would be a tough election because he might have to do unpopular things that would galvanize the Democrats. And he didn't want a lonely victory in which he won reelection and turned around to find no Republican army behind him. I took his advice to heart: it was to be prophetic in the months ahead.

To prepare for the reelection, I called every Republican who had been responsible for trying to give a president a second term, including James Baker III (who was there in 1976, 1984, and 1992), Michael Deaver (a longtime Reagan hand), and Bob Teeter, Sam Skinner, and Fred Malek (who worked for George H. W. Bush's reelection effort in 1992). They all had the same advice: if White House and campaign staffs are allowed to do what comes naturally to them—get in each other's way and even work at cross purposes—the campaign will be a disaster.

Damn, I thought. I am not a diplomat and I like being in control. And for all my reputation as a campaign street fighter, I am not particularly talented at backstabbing or gut cutting. But Chief of Staff Andy

Card, himself a veteran of many White Houses and campaigns, had a solution to minimize infighting. There would be one person at the White House through whom all information to and from the campaign must pass, and that person would be me.

Card also said I needed to make sure that key White House staff had a seat at the table and were involved in decision-making. To me, it sounded like I was being sentenced to perpetual meetings. But he was right. It was the only way to reduce end runs and ensure people would put all their issues out in the open.

I recommended Ken Mehlman be made campaign manager, and on January 27, 2003, we met to start planning the reelection campaign in earnest. It took four months and twenty-three meetings to finalize our strategy and gain consensus. It was adopted at a meeting of top White House and campaign aides that would later be known as the Breakfast Club, because we got into the habit of meeting for breakfast at my house on Saturday mornings or early Sunday afternoons. Its first meeting was February 2, 2003, and it met for the rest of the campaign.

I made certain the Breakfast Club attendees had "eggies," a scrambled egg concoction made with cheese and cream. There were also pastries, fruit, bacon, and other meats, including venison, wild boar, and nilgai sausage. The last is an antelope-like animal from India that was imported into south Texas and now runs wild there.

Ken Mehlman, Mark McKinnon, Matthew Dowd, and I developed an electoral strategy to share with the Breakfast Club. We divided the country into four tiers. The first consisted of the solid Bush states we didn't need to worry about. The second was the Bush states that had been close in 2000 (such as Florida, Nevada, and New Hampshire) that would be back in play in 2004. Also in this tier were states we'd won but needed to monitor. We gave these the sophisticated title of "Something Bad Could Happen" states. North Carolina and Arizona were among them. The third tier was states that were near misses for us in 2000 (such as New Mexico, Iowa, Wisconsin, Minnesota, and Oregon) and what we called "Something Else" states—ones we'd lost in 2000 but that polling showed now might be within reach. I jokingly said we wanted to "find another West Virginia," a 2000 surprise takeaway state; New Jersey, Connecticut, and Illinois were in this group. We kept California on the list because early polling suggested Bush had a chance, and I wanted to see

Democrats sweat to keep a state they took for granted. The fourth and final tier was the states Gore carried solidly, such as Massachusetts and the District of Columbia, that we had no chance to carry without the kind of sweep seen in 1964 and 1984.

We called in a group of Republican political scientists, led by Professor Daron Shaw of the University of Texas at Austin, to review our target state tiers. In a bow to the CIA's Cold War practice of commissioning independent analysis, we called this group of academic propeller heads "Team B." It was good to have number-crunching professors give us an independent look. Their analysis helped us understand why states belonged in each tier and led us to move states around in the rankings as conditions changed.

I believed the 2004 campaign would mirror the one in 1864, when Abraham Lincoln won reelection in the middle of the Civil War. Voters then asked themselves if they should, in the words of Lincoln, "swap horses when crossing streams." I thought that if we showed Bush to be a strong, decisive wartime leader, voters wouldn't want to swap horses.

I also thought the campaign should be forward-looking. Incumbents who run on past achievements often get defeated. Bush's campaign needed to be about big, important things for the future—"something new plus more of what he's doing," as one planning document put it. And I knew that Bush did not want a lonely victory; his chances of getting things done in a second term largely depended on having allies in Congress and in governorships.

I knew deep in my bones that this would be a tough race. Democrats were united and, in an echo of Bush's New Year's comment, my National Security Council colleagues warned that the wars in Iraq and Afghanistan could be bloody and difficult despite the rapid removal of Saddam in April 2003. War is unpredictable, they'd caution, and we could be in for a rough haul. Unfortunately, they were right. The economy had been anemic in 2002, and while growth picked up in 2003 and was to be well over 3 percent in the first three quarters of 2004, Democrats were attacking the economy's performance and the rate of job creation.

Our biggest challenge was to find voters who would swing to our side in a country that had grown more partisan and divided since we had arrived in Washington. The problem was not just Democratic activists who had never recovered from the 2000 outcome and who had developed a pathological hatred of Bush. The country itself had retreated into two very firm camps.

Our strategist Matthew Dowd showed us that since 1988, the percentage of true independents—people who split their ballot—had shrunk to as little as 7 percent of the electorate. I had Matthew's numbers put on a card and laminated to remind me that swing voters were more important than ever because there were fewer of them. The election would not just be about mobilizing Republicans and Republican-leaning independents, but about converting the few swing voters who were out there. The most important of the swing voters were suburban women, particularly those who were married and between the ages of thirty-five to fifty with kids. And among those women, we were particularly interested in those who lived in the far-distant new suburbs called the "exurbs." People in the exurbs seemed less well anchored to a political party and more up for grabs. To make sure women knew they were high priorities for the campaign, Ken and I pushed to appoint women at all levels, including as spokesman. Nicolle Wallace got the job.

Hispanics were another group we wanted to pursue, particularly observant middle-class Catholics or those who were joining the expanding ranks of evangelical Protestants. Hispanics had grown from 3 percent of the electorate in 1984 to 7 percent in 2000 and we expected they'd be around 8 percent in 2004. We also wanted to increase our numbers among African-Americans and to get a majority of Asian-American voters.

Then there were the 4 million evangelicals who had failed to turn out in 2000, many because of the last-minute revelation of Bush's 1976 DUI. The media never understood this last group. These voters were not politically involved and not necessarily as Republican or conservative as the politically active evangelicals who did vote in 2000. There were pockets of these nonvoting evangelicals in states such as Iowa, Wisconsin, and Minnesota who were opposed to the Iraq War or at least unsettled about it. Mehlman decided we would have an easier time winning over these voters if we recruited them for our grassroots efforts in every county.

We were in a death match with Democrats on voter registration. Democrats were rolling out a massive voter-registration effort run by third-party groups such as Americans Coming Together. We had to match and exceed these registration efforts or the political landscape would be tipped away from Bush.

We decided to reprise our strategy in 2000 of building an "army of persuasion," a massive volunteer effort to register new supporters, persuade Democrats and swing voters, identify Bush supporters, and then ensure they all turned out. Democrats outsourced these activities to third-party groups who paid people to perform these tasks. We believed that direct outreach from the campaign by volunteers who honestly made the case for Bush would do a better job of winning the solid support of voters. We also had no choice. We were planning to raise $176.5 million, about $76 million more than the campaign had amassed in 2000. That was a lot of money, but much less than what Democrats and Democratic interest groups were likely to spend.

A key concept developed by Mehlman was the "Bush team leader" program. We asked volunteers to do six specific tasks: recruit five other team leaders, sign up ten friends, participate in voter registration and turnout efforts, write letters to the editor or a campaign blog, host a block party at their home, and distribute materials at public events in their community. We set goals for every county in every state for each activity. Every team leader who reached their goals received thank-yous and mementos. Mehlman even tossed elective officials out of the greeting line at Air Force One arrivals so he could put in the most outstanding local Bush team leader.

The campaign put an enormous emphasis on the Internet, creating a website and building a massive list of e-mail supporters that eventually numbered 8.5 million. The tools available for this effort were rudimentary compared to applications available today. But Ken and his team stayed on the cutting edge of Web campaign ideas. Our e-campaign manager, Chuck DeFeo, and his team created dozens of novel ways to deploy the Web (many of which Obama's campaign would copy four years later), including the first online door-to-door organizing tools; maps and driving directions to polling locations, searchable on the Web and e-mailed directly to voters; a virtual precinct to contact other potential voters; "Parties for the President," the first online tool to organize house parties for Bush; an individual leader board where supporters were recognized for their hard work; public disclosure of donors; a live debate-facts site, on which we would rebut—within seconds—the statements made during the debates; and a political extranet, which allowed our field team instant access to new volunteers who'd signed up through the Bush for President website.

Another key tool for the campaign was "microtargeting." This complex analytical effort drew upon as many as 225 pieces of information we could collect on an individual household to help identify which members were likely to support Bush and turn out to vote for him. Among the pieces of information we sought were whether they owned a gun, whether their children attended private schools, what kind of magazines they subscribed to, what kind of car they owned, even what kind of liquor they preferred. No one piece of information was a reliable indicator by itself. The complicated algorithms that made sense of the relationships among these data points were prized secrets. Ken summed up how it all worked for us by suggesting we read Michael Lewis's book *Moneyball: The Art of Winning an Unfair Game.* The book is the story of the Oakland Athletics baseball team and its general manager, Billy Beane, who used statistical analysis of baseball statistics to assemble a winning team. His players didn't hit as many home runs or put up gaudy stats that got public attention. But each team member's talents knit well with the rest of the team and made them formidable as a unit on the field.

We had spent three years and several million dollars perfecting our microtargeting tool, and it was enormously helpful in focusing volunteer efforts on persuadable voters who needed personal contact to bring them into the Bush camp.

At one point, a county campaign chairman from Ohio fought his way to me through the White House switchboard after receiving a list of unregistered voters generated by microtargeting. He'd spotted a retired Navy captain and his wife who were not registered to vote, but whom our microtargeting had identified as likely Bush voters. The former Navy officer was a golfing and drinking buddy of the chairman and had even volunteered for Bush. The chairman was sure we got it wrong—sure that his friend was registered to vote. But when he called his friend to have a laugh over our screw-up, the friend admitted that in fact he and his wife hadn't gotten around to registering. The chairman was stunned. He said to me, "I don't know how you do it, but you made a believer out of me!"

As we prepared for Bush's reelection campaign, Karen Hughes and

Dan Bartlett raised questions about our media team. They wondered if a more senior advertising person than Mark McKinnon could be brought in to run things, someone with a background like Roger Ailes. But no one else existed with Ailes's experience and savvy. Besides, what mattered was whether someone had talent and Bush's confidence—and McKinnon had both. I thought displacing McKinnon would have been nuts, but I wanted to beef up our media team. So we made McKinnon the manager, broadened his team, and, unlike 2000, moved them into the campaign HQ.

The president would be nothing but a punching bag for the duration of the Democrats' nomination battle, with voters paying little attention to his case for reelection. We had to reintroduce him—to remind voters who Bush was, what he had achieved, and, more importantly, what he planned yet to do—after the Democratic candidate was picked in early 2004.

If they were smart, Democrats would copy our strategy from 2000 and use the period between winning the nomination and the party's national convention to lay the groundwork for the general election campaign. Dowd pointed out that we couldn't count on Democrats to make the same mistake twice by sitting on their hands during this period. We would need to jam something into the gears of the Democratic campaign in the spring of 2004. We had no way of knowing that we would actually pull off a major ambush against the Democratic nominee at exactly that time.

It was hard to get Bush's attention for these campaign discussions, even to update him on what we were deciding. His focus that winter and spring was on Iraq, and he made clear there would be no politics until Saddam Hussein was toppled and his regime's military decimated. We won approval from him to launch the campaign only after he was assured that he wouldn't have to campaign actively in 2003 except to attend off-the-record fund-raisers in the summer, and after he was warned that delaying much longer would make it nearly impossible for him to build a successful reelection campaign. We filed the campaign committee with the Federal Election Commission on May 16.

By now, the number of meetings was making my head spin. Ken and I had a daily 7:00 A.M. conference call without an agenda and then found ourselves talking half a dozen times or more a day. There was the daily

White House senior staff meeting at 7:30 A.M. and, at 8:15, my meeting with the directors of the offices who reported to me. After that, there was the "daily brief" with the president, held mid-morning. The campaign held two message meetings a day—one in the morning and another late in the afternoon. I sought out Dan Bartlett as often as possible during the day to stay close on communications and message issues that impinged on the campaign.

In the meantime, we kept tabs on the Democratic presidential contest by assigning a team to track each credible opponent of Bush. I was so impressed with the quality of the analyses by the opposition research team, I had ball caps made for each squad member that said "Oppo Dude."

I worried most about Senator John Edwards. He was a fresh face, articulate and engaging, and attractive to the point of being almost too pretty. He was a product of the South, which had helped Bill Clinton a dozen years before. I also thought he was completely unprincipled—he could change his views like leaves change their colors. He came across at times as shallow and opportunistic and, like the trial lawyer he was, too slick. He was a person of considerable skills but ungrounded and without much wisdom. Edwards also seemed inordinately in love with his looks, his voice, with himself.

Joe Lieberman, however, was a man for whom I had considerable admiration. He had been an impressive vice presidential candidate in 2000 and came across in public as he is in private: a thoroughly decent, well-grounded individual. Lieberman would have been a very good candidate for Democrats to have chosen; he was the closest thing they had to a "Scoop" Jackson Democrat (Henry "Scoop" Jackson was a senator from Washington State who was a hawk on national security but liberal on domestic issues). Lieberman had a reassuring presence, was an outspoken voice against the worst and most degrading elements of our popular culture, and was one of the architects of the "New Democratic" Party that helped lay the centrist policy foundation for Bill Clinton's win in 1992. Lieberman would have considerable appeal to independents and wavering Republicans, I thought, but his virtue was his vice: he had been far too supportive of the Global War on Terror and Bush's national security policies to have a shot at the 2004 Democratic nomination. The party had moved hard left, while Lieberman had not.

Dick Gephardt had served as majority, then minority, leader of the House, remained attractive to parts of the Democratic base, and was from the Midwest—all of which were to his advantage. But he remained as colorless as he had been in his 1988 presidential bid, and this time organized labor had more attractive options than in 1988, when its leadership and membership rallied for Gephardt. I actually thought Gephardt a decent person and that the country would not have been in bad hands if he were elected. He was too liberal for my taste, and it was hard for me to get past how he had fed anti-Bush anger after the 2000 election by initially refusing to say Bush was "legitimate." But he wasn't as reckless as other Democratic hopefuls. I called him when he dropped out to tell him he would have been a worthy opponent.

General Wesley Clark was running a vanity candidacy. His bid was so poorly organized and his presentation so badly made that he ended up looking overly ambitious and slightly ridiculous. He was once thought of as a serious public figure, but many people were cured of that impression by watching him run for president.

And Senator Bob Graham of Florida was just plain weird. What else could be said of a man who cataloged his every act—including his choice of breakfast cereal and even his bathroom visits—in little notebooks? I knew we just couldn't be that lucky to get him as our opponent.

The early favorite among Democrats was Vermont's bantam governor, Howard Dean. He was also my personal favorite, but not because I liked him. I'd met him at the 1995 National Governors Association summer meeting he'd hosted in Burlington. He struck me as an insufferable know-it-all, an attitude he carried into his presidential campaign. He couldn't help patting himself vigorously on his own back. Early on, he proclaimed himself Master of the Internet. The day he announced he'd collected six hundred thousand names on his e-mail list, I called Mehlman for our latest tally. The Bush list was ten times the size of his. We just didn't brag about it.

Dean wasn't just the antiwar candidate, he came across as anti-everything. He was so off-putting that we would actually have had a chance for a big sweep—on the order of Reagan's 1980 win against Carter—if he had been our opponent. To the degree I could get the president to opine about the Democratic field, he expressed a desire to run against Dean. We knew we could beat him like a drum.

At one stage, when it looked as if Dean might actually be the front-runner, I had our first television ad put in the can, ready to show immediately if he became their nominee. It consisted of his closing remarks at the March 2003 California Democratic Convention, where he said, "I want my country back! We want our country back! I'm tired of being divided! I don't want to listen to the fundamentalist preachers anymore. I want America to look like America, where we are all included, hand in hand, walking down. We have [a] dream. We can only reach the dream if we are all together—black and white, gay and straight, man and woman. America! The Democratic Party! We are going to win in 2004!"

When I saw the tape of his appearance, I could hardly contain my glee. I thought he looked like a madman, bringing the assorted left-wingers at the convention to their feet with rhetoric and a style that would turn off most Americans. Dean's conclusion was just over thirty seconds, but with a little tweaking it could fit a thirty-second spot that needed no voiceover or explanation. It wasn't what he said, but how: he came across as nasty, mean, and unlikable. In focus group tests, virtually everyone reacted strongly, even passionately, against the footage of Dean, including voters who shared his opinions.

But Dean flamed out, as Democratic voters clued in to what most of the rest of the country would have come to know had he won the nomination: the former governor of Vermont came across as unstable and unreliable. Dean's primal "scream"—emitted by him following his third-place finish in Iowa—perfectly captured the problem.

John Kerry had the strongest campaign team in the field, was a good debater, and could be an aggressive and effective prosecutor on behalf of his views. And his record as a veteran was a big asset—though not as big of an asset as he thought it was.

Kerry was also a Massachusetts liberal, something the Bushes had experience running against. George H. W. Bush's opponent in 1988 was the state's governor, Michael Dukakis, a liberal so trapped inside his views that he couldn't see how they could make him look like he lacked compassion. During the second presidential debate that year, moderator Bernie Shaw asked Dukakis, "Governor, if [your wife] Kitty Dukakis were raped and murdered, would you favor an irrevocable death penalty for the killer?" Dukakis responded, "No, I don't, Bernard. And I think you know that I've opposed the death penalty during all of my life." His candidacy never recovered from the comment that made him look like an emotionally cold fish.

Kerry was Dukakis's lieutenant governor, and he, too, was without compassion. His liberalism made him vulnerable because he was arrogant with a condescension that was impossible to contain. To put it plainly, he was not a likable person. And his wife, Teresa Heinz Kerry—heiress of the Heinz ketchup fortune—only added to his problems. I knew her when she was married to Republican senator John Heinz of Pennsylvania. Heinz had been a client of mine before his tragic death in a plane accident. Teresa Heinz was a nightmare: I once saw her throw a water bottle at a staff assistant who had angered her over nothing. I was told that behavior was routine.

Kerry projected an image of coolness, aloofness, and barely hidden disdain for the hoi polloi—as did his wife. I assumed this would come through in a general election campaign. If it did, we had a reasonable chance at beating him at the tape. But it would not be easy.

CHAPTER 24

Drugs and Marriage

———— • ◆ • ————

One of Bush's strengths in his reelection was his brand of compassionate conservatism. In late 2003, two major domestic issues took center stage. The first—creating a Medicare prescription drug benefit— was planned. The second one—gay marriage—took us by surprise and the country by storm. The first allowed us to display compassionate conservatism's substance, the second its style. Neither was without its controversies.

Medicare was created in the 1960s, and was stuck in that era. While the medical profession developed new techniques, new treatments, and a new reliance on drugs to manage and treat disease, Medicare's model still relied heavily on surgery and long hospital stays. By 1998, private health insurers paid more than half of all prescription drug expenditures while Medicare paid thousands of dollars to operate on a stomach ulcer but not the hundreds of dollars for pills that could have prevented the ulcer. That didn't make sense.

Bush wanted to use market forces to shape a Medicare prescription drug program that would be responsive to consumers, cost less than federal entitlements typically do, and provide seniors with a wide range of choices that would evolve over time to meet changing needs. He had run on creating a market-based—not government-run—program in the 2000 campaign.

But creating one was not a universally popular thing to do among Republicans. Some GOP members of Congress opposed the drug program because they believed it enlarged the welfare state. I disagree: it modernized an archaic health-care system and relied on the free market to bring costs down. I believe it was one of the best pieces of legislation Bush signed into law, because it reflected his core values as a compassionate conservative.

Before that could happen, we needed to win over a few unusual allies. One of my tasks during this three-year effort to get the legislation passed was to hold the hand of the American Association of Retired Persons, or AARP, an organization that was predisposed to favor a drug benefit but leery of joining with a Republican president on a high-profile domestic reform. I wooed AARP's CEO, Bill Novelli. Speaker Denny Hastert and Senate majority leader Dr. Bill Frist also kept open lines to the group. AARP finally came aboard, and its decision to do so left Senate Democratic leader Tom Daschle, the unions, and *New York Times* op-ed columnists fuming mad. They all said in one way or another that the venerable organization had been enlisted to "gut" Medicare.

The vote in the House on the night of November 21 took place as Bush returned from a visit to London and a stay at Buckingham Palace. He phoned wavering and undecided congressmen from Air Force One high over the Atlantic and remained up well after midnight to make calls at home. The House finally voted between 3 A.M. and 5:55 A.M. on the morning of November 22. The tally at first stalled out at 216 to 218 against us. House leaders kept the vote open and, using the kind of horse-trading that has always been a part of politics, flipped enough members to arrive at 220 to 215 for the Medicare overhaul. When the gavel came down, only sixteen Democrats had voted to provide seniors a prescription drug benefit under Medicare. The rest wanted a more expensive government-run program. The Senate vote a few days later involved much less drama—54 to 44 with the support of eleven Democrats, or about a fifth of that party's caucus.

The passage of the bill not only left Medicare intact, it also unleashed results that should make any conservative happy. Because private companies deliver the benefit, most Medicare recipients have cut their yearly drug costs in half because of competition. Low-income seniors have received extra help with their premiums and deductibles for drug coverage (some pay no premium or deductible). Private Medicare insurance coverage options have been strengthened. And a new Health Savings Account option was created so all Americans could save more money tax-free for medical expenses. This new low-cost health-insurance product put coverage within reach for millions, especially those who work for small businesses.

The battle over this bill exposed a sharp ideological difference between the two parties, with the Republicans' faith in the markets ultimately winning the argument. Democrats on the House Ways and Means Committee had offered an amendment to have the government set the premium's price, locking it in at $37 a month the first year. Republicans, believing in competition, voted this down. The Republicans were right to do so: the average first-year premium, thanks to the relentless power of competition, was only $22 a month.

The advantage of our free enterprise system showed up in another powerful way. Because of the wide range of options available, more seniors signed up for the program than expected. But even with those extra enrollees, the program's costs today are running a third less than forecast because competition did what it always does—it drove down costs and improved the product. The Medicare prescription drug benefit is the only major government health initiative that has cost less than was originally estimated.

Medicare was a fight we had asked for, and won. Gay marriage was an ugly fight we had not asked for but could win if we handled it with care. Done right, our response to gay marriage could show it was possible to bring a courteous and caring tone to a divisive issue. The issue also revealed the nuttiness of the Left, which never saw how persistent America's traditionalism really was. Instead, the Left seemed convinced that Bush and I engineered the issue's emergence to drive Bush partisans to the polls. But, of course, it was a liberal state supreme court that brought the issue to the fore.

On November 18, 2003, a 4–3 decision of the Massachusetts Supreme Judicial Court legalized gay marriage in the state. The majority opinion, written by Chief Justice Margaret H. Marshall, the wife of the very liberal former *New York Times* columnist Anthony Lewis, was the culmination of a legal strategy pursued by gay rights advocates. The gay rights movement had turned to the courts because it wasn't able to make any headway in the state legislatures. For at least six years, they had filed a series of lawsuits in Massachusetts, New Jersey, Indiana, Arizona, and other states, hoping to hit upon a sympathetic judge who would declare that gay couples had a constitutional right to same-sex marriage.

Gay rights groups were elated by the Massachusetts decision, but public reaction was swift. Supporters of traditional marriage quickly announced that they would work to block same-sex marriage in Massachusetts and defend traditional marriage in states where citizens could place pro-marriage measures on the ballot.

The press naturally wanted to know where the president and his Democratic competitors stood. President Bush opposed the decision and immediately pledged to defend traditional marriage as the cornerstone of a strong society. Howard Dean supported the Massachusetts decision and gay marriage, while John Kerry, Dick Gephardt, and Joe Lieberman opposed gay marriage but made vaguely positive noises about the ruling. Kerry later straddled the issue during the 2004 general election campaign by defending traditional marriage and then attacking it, often in the same speech.

While Bush supported same-sex partner rights such as hospital visits and health coverage, he did call for a constitutional amendment defending the institution of marriage. His concern was that state court decisions would undermine the Defense of Marriage Act (DOMA), passed by Congress and signed by President Clinton in 1996, defining marriage as a legal union between one man and one woman and saying that states need not recognize a marriage from another state if it is between persons of the same sex. If DOMA fell, the only way left to defend traditional marriage was a constitutional amendment.

Neither Bush nor I regret his stand on gay marriage. The issue was thrust upon us and we were perfectly willing to make our case. To overturn the time-honored definition of marriage is a socially revolutionary act. To do so through the courts and against the will of the people makes the attempt even more radical. The definition of marriage should be settled through the normal channels of democratic self-government, by the will of the people, through their representatives and the people's votes on ballot initiatives.

Bush was not fully comfortable with the issue emerging during a national campaign. He thought it was likely to bring out the worst on both sides: emotional charges of prejudice would fly before anyone would be willing to consider that compassionate Americans could disagree. On top of that, I am certain that members of his family, some friends, and his vice president didn't share Bush's strong support for traditional marriage. He was determined to be very careful in the arguments he made and the tone he used.

The issue grew more intense, but Bush's rhetoric did not. Massachusetts governor Mitt Romney was forced into a battle with his legislature in an effort to overturn the decision. And in February 2004, San Francisco mayor Gavin Newsom poured gallons of gasoline on the controversy by issuing city marriage licenses to same-sex couples. This was too much for the state's governor, Arnold Schwarzenegger, who ordered the state attorney general to "take immediate steps to obtain a definitive judicial resolution of this controversy." By May 2004, Missouri had become the first of twelve states in 2004 to qualify a ballot initiative in defense of traditional marriage. All twelve measures in defense of traditional marriage passed, with support ranging from 57 percent to 86 percent.

To discourage resistance, gay marriage supporters decided those who disagreed with them had to be bigots. Representative John Lewis of Georgia, for instance, wrote, "I've heard the reasons for opposing civil marriage for same-sex couples. Cut through the distractions, and they stink of the same fear, hatred, and intolerance I have known in racism and in bigotry." This made gay marriage the kind of issue most political candidates dread—not because they don't know where they stand, but because no one likes being branded a hater.

But Bush had this advantage: what critics on the left didn't appreciate is that most voters don't believe that opposing gay marriage makes you a homophobe. The *Chicago Tribune* editorial page got it right when it said, "The point Bush's critics are missing is that 'moral issues' are no longer a mere political wedge. They're real, grown-up issues now. And after believing their culture has been under assault for decades, such voters were drawn to the polls."

In the end, whether a state had a marriage ballot measure didn't affect Bush's share of the vote: he increased his portion of the vote between 2000 and 2004 by an average of 2.7 points in the states without referenda and by an average of 2.5 points in the eleven states with defense-of-marriage initiatives on the November ballot, a statistically insignificant difference.

But the Massachusetts Supreme Judicial Court decision *did* affect the 2004 election by motivating culturally conservative Democrats and independents who might otherwise have voted Democratic to abandon Kerry over his wobbly views on marriage. We saw it in polling, where Bush did better among Catholics, evangelicals, African-American churchgoers, and older working-class voters than we had expected. We saw it in our campaign activities, with many African-American and Latino evangelical churchgoers and faithful Catholic communicants citing marriage as a major reason why, as Democrats, they crossed party lines to support Bush.

But some political commentators claimed I single-handedly injected gay marriage into the 2004 election. Cleveland's *Plain Dealer* asserted in an editorial that I "helped mastermind a wedge issue to motivate the ex-urbanites to vote—a proposed ban on gay marriage." A *Baltimore Sun* columnist said, "Karl Rove plotted to keep the enthusiasm of ultraconservative Christians by scapegoating gays and lesbians." The former theater critic of the *New York Times,* columnist Frank Rich, wrote of "the twin fears that Mr. Rove relentlessly pushed on his client's behalf: fear of terrorism and fear of gays." The writer Andrew Sullivan, a fierce advocate for gay marriage, blogged that I led a "binge of hate-filled niche campaigning, polarization and short-term expediency."

Of course, I played absolutely no role in the Massachusetts decision. I didn't file the lawsuit, argue the case, or write the opinion. But I saw up close how it benefited my candidate: gay rights activists bent on defeating George W. Bush helped reelect him by overreaching on same-sex marriage. Bush's views were shared by most Americans. All he had to do was make his position clear and keep the tone civil.

CHAPTER 25

Trapping Kerry,
Making Peace with McCain

———•◆•———

S unday, March 28, 2004, was a big day for the Breakfast Club, but not in the way we expected. As we broke up at about 4 P.M., school buses bearing the name of "Utley's Transportation" pulled up in front of my house and disgorged eight hundred protesters. Many wore black T-shirts emblazoned with the word *power*. They were from the National People's Action (NPA), an alliance of left-wing community organizations. They had a practice of choosing a government official to picket at their annual Washington meeting. That Sunday, the NPA mob chose my flower beds to stomp on as they tried to force their way into my home. Their signs protested the administration's immigration views. I thought that strange, since President Bush was a known advocate of immigration reform. Then they became ugly, screaming obscenities, surrounding the house, pounding on windows, and scaling the backyard fence.

I called the Secret Service and the D.C. police. One Secret Service Uniformed Division officer and then his sergeant showed up and moved the protesters off my lawn and into the street. The sergeant recommended a meeting with the protest spokeswoman, Emira Palacios, in exchange for the group's agreeing to depart. The people with the bullhorns leading the near riot had decided that the face of the protest should be this small, confused woman, and it irritated me. I read Ms. Palacios the riot act, brought her to tears, and told her to leave. Not my best moment.

In a campaign, you have to be equally skilled at playing offense and defense. I'd much rather be on offense. That had been very much on my mind as the Breakfast Club met two weeks earlier on Sunday, March 14. High on the agenda was an impending visit by the presumptive Democratic nominee, Senator Kerry, to Marshall University in Huntington, West Virginia. We had heard Kerry would use his stop in West Virginia to blast the president's spending on veterans while meeting with a group of people who had served in the military.

Defending against the attack would be easy. While restraining the growth rate of overall discretionary federal spending, Bush had increased the Veterans Affairs budget almost as much in four years as Clinton did in eight. But rather than playing defense, I wanted to go on offense. After all, Kerry had voted against the last funding bill for the troops in Iraq and Afghanistan. That bill had appropriated $87 billion for fiscal year 2004 with special provisions for body armor, higher combat pay, and improvements in health care for reservists and their families, as well as the essentials of fuel, ammunition, food, and logistical support. It passed the Senate by a vote of 87 to 12 on October 17, 2003. All the "no" votes came from Democrats and one independent.

On the day of the vote, Kerry said: "I cannot vote for the President's $87 billion request because his is not the most effective way to protect American soldiers and to advance our interests." Just a month earlier, Kerry had implied that voting against wartime funding bills was abandoning the troops. He said, "I don't think any United States senator is going to abandon our troops and recklessly leave Iraq to whatever follows as a result of simply cutting and running." So, I asked, why not use Kerry's vote to flip the attack back onto him?

We settled on a new television ad criticizing Kerry's vote. It would have to go up in West Virginia on Monday to greet his arrival. The ad—called "Troops"—replaced all the other ones the Bush-Cheney campaign was running in the state. It cost only $11,000 to produce, a fraction of what most campaign spots cost and less than a Madison Avenue ad agency would spend on coffee and doughnuts while shooting a perfume ad.

The ad presented several problems for Kerry. It reminded West Virginians he'd voted for the war but was now striving to be more antiwar than any other Democrat. It portrayed Kerry as a flip-flopper—someone who would vote to send troops into combat and then vote against funding them. And it undermined his attack on the president for supposedly failing veterans by pointing to Kerry's opposition to higher combat pay and better health care for reservists. It worked on all kinds of levels. Little did we know Kerry's response would do more damage to his candidacy than we could have accomplished on our own.

Early Tuesday afternoon, John Kerry appeared at Marshall University, accompanied by several of his shipmates from Vietnam. The audience consisted of about 230 invited guests, mostly veterans wearing their distinctive VFW and American Legion caps. Kerry knew about our ad. "The Republican attack machine has welcomed me to West Virginia today with another distortion," Kerry said. He then offered a confusing defense of his "no" vote, saying he would have supported the funding bill had it been coupled with a tax increase. He pointed out that he had offered an amendment to the bill to do just that, but it had failed, 42 to 57.

It was a sign of how tone-deaf Kerry was. He was arguing that raising taxes was more important than giving American troops the support they needed while in combat in Afghanistan and Iraq. And what's more, he was arguing that because he lost his bid to hike taxes he couldn't put his liberalism aside to support the troops.

Then Kerry gave us the line that perfectly encapsulated who he was and the have-it-both-ways candidacy he was building. He said, "I actually did vote for the $87 billion before I voted against it." Mehlman and I were talking on the phone when the sentence was broadcast on cable TV. Uncharacteristically for the buttoned-up Mehlman, he used a common swear word to describe what he'd just heard.

I was dumbfounded, too. Kerry had revealed that the concerns about him were entirely justified. In thirteen words, he told Americans he was an unreliable, inconsistent, weak flip-flopper unfit for the Oval Office.

By themselves, Kerry's thirteen words would not have been enough. They were powerful because they reinforced what people already suspected. He had been for and against NAFTA, for and against the Patriot Act, for and against No Child Left Behind, for and against the Iraq War, and now he was both for and against funding our troops. Voters worried that Kerry did not have the character and judgment to be president; his words sealed the argument, though we had to remind voters about it that fall.

I also suspected Kerry understood he was on weak ground. In poker (which I don't play), serious players look for what they call a "tell"—a gesture, habit, or twitch that gives away an opposing player's state of mind. With Kerry, it's the word *actually*. From January 2003 to July 2004, he used *actually* forty-six times in debates, speeches, and press conferences, almost always when he was exaggerating or trying to extract himself from difficulty.

Most in the media immediately grasped the comment's significance, but the Kerry campaign did not. Kerry's press spokeswoman explained that the senator had cast "a protest vote," as if that made voting against troops in combat more palatable. Kerry further compounded his mistake by opposing increased military spending and the deployment of a ballistic missile defense system in a speech the next day at George Washington University. He was making the argument for us: at a time when the nation was at war, he was weak on defense.

At McKinnon's direction, we took the "Troops" ad and recut it to add footage of Kerry saying the infamous words in West Virginia. The final spot went up in all target states. Focus groups told us later that it was our most powerful and persuasive TV message, and it helped close the deal with voters up for grabs.

We had made an opening, led our opponent down a path he should not have taken, and exposed a character flaw. That kind of thing is powerful in politics. But it is also distasteful to some people on the public stage. People like Colin Powell.

I admire Powell's many years of service to our country and I think he was a fine secretary of state. But I sensed he never felt comfortable around me because he looked down on me as a "politico." According to news reports, Powell was "put off" by me. My impression was that Powell was a fairly effective political infighter himself, but it was something he liked to keep hidden from view. I could tell when Powell was annoyed at me, because he would address me as "Private Rove" and order me to drop and give him twenty push-ups.

He'd say it with a smile on his face—but only when he felt I was messing where he didn't think I should be, failing to share his opinion, or raising objections to a State Department nominee whose criticism of the president or opposition to his election should, in the secretary's mind, be overlooked for Foggy Bottom's greater good.

I usually laughed off Powell's occasional sarcastic greeting, but on May 27, 2004, with Powell irritated at me over something now long forgotten, I followed orders. I dropped and gave him twenty push-ups. Right at the entrance of the Oval Office. I could tell it had unsettled him as he nervously encouraged me to stop and get up. But I finished, then jumped to attention and saluted. Powell was rattled. He had an awkward smile. Mine was real. It was the last time Powell ever asked me to drop and give him twenty.

For me, the lighthearted moment outside the Oval was a welcome, momentary diversion. We had John Kerry wobbling from his West Virginia mistake: now we needed to keep him off balance by unleashing a summer offensive. But first, I needed to heal a rift left from the 2000 primaries.

Earlier that month, media chief Mark McKinnon had called to say John Weaver, McCain's strategist, wanted to meet with me. Weaver said he wanted to bury the hatchet over what he felt was a long-running feud between us; I didn't know we had one. His real motive, I thought, was to get McCain on Bush's reelection team. McCain was thinking seriously about running for president in 2008, or at least his people were thinking about him doing it. And after rumors flew that he had discussed becoming John Kerry's running mate, McCain wanted to get back into the GOP's good graces. The president, in turn, wanted to reach out to independents. Rapprochement made sense for both. Bush also just liked McCain.

I'd meet with Weaver, but wanted Mark to come. Following the 2000 election, Weaver had left the Republican Party with a blast at the president and had become a Democrat. The McCains were said to blame me for every bad thing that had happened to them in the 2000 campaign. I wanted someone in the meeting who could act as a witness, if it became necessary.

On Wednesday, May 12, from about 8:15 to 9:00 A.M., John, Mark, and I met at a coffee shop kitty-corner from the White House. John got right to the point. He reflected on the years we'd worked together in Texas, talked about how the passage of time and a health scare had caused him to think about what was really important in life, and said he wanted to put aside any differences between us. It was not the easiest thing for John to say, and I told him I appreciated it. He then asked how McCain could help Bush get reelected, and I said any help would be welcome.

John called back in early June with dates Senator McCain could join the president. We invited McCain to join one of the swings the president would be taking through the West. One question was whether I should go on the trip. The president wisely suggested I stay at the White House. With a grin, he said I could work on any problems I had with McCain later.

In their first appearance together, President Bush and Senator McCain stood before six thousand soldiers at Fort Lewis in Washington State. The base was home to the first brigades equipped with "Strykers," new fighting vehicles designed for urban warfare that carry eleven soldiers into combat and pack a punch. Strykers run on eight tires, not treads, so they're quiet and fast: their top speed is sixty miles per hour. Iraqis took to calling them "ghosts" because they appeared silently and quickly.

President Bush prefers those who introduce him at events to do so for about a minute. McCain went on for eight—the president didn't mind a bit. McCain lauded Bush's abilities as a wartime president. Bush returned the praise, calling it "a privilege to be introduced to our men and women in uniform by a man who brought such credit to the uniform." He added, "The United States military has no better friend in the United States Senate than John McCain." Both men emphasized the importance of Iraq in the war on terrorism and praised the troops for their sacrifices, courage, and effectiveness.

Later at a Reno, Nevada, campaign stop, they appeared before ten thousand wildly enthusiastic supporters. McCain was again generous in his introduction and blunt when the press asked why he was now campaigning with Bush: "First time I was asked." The rumors that McCain was joining Kerry's ticket turned into stories that McCain was firmly in Bush's corner. As a result, Kerry looked weak again: his campaign had hyped his VP discussion with McCain before actually getting McCain on board. If you don't get what you've hyped, you hurt yourself.

That August gave us another opportunity to highlight Kerry's flip-flopping. In October 2002, he had voted for the use-of-force resolution in Iraq. Using language even tougher than the administration's, he'd said, "When I vote to give the President of the United States the authority to use force, if necessary, to disarm Saddam Hussein, it is because I believe that a deadly arsenal of weapons of mass destruction in his hands is a threat, and a grave threat, to our security and that of our allies in the Persian Gulf region." But a year later, Kerry turned antiwar. On ABC's *This Week,* Kerry proclaimed that Bush had "rushed to war." In January 2004, when MSNBC's Chris Matthews asked him directly if he was an antiwar candidate, Kerry responded, "I am, yeah—in the sense that I don't believe the President took us to war as he should have, yes, absolutely." Was he disavowing his vote, or trying to have it both ways?

The Bush-Cheney campaign prodded the press to cover the contradiction, but nothing happened. Finally, in late July, the president asked if he should raise the issue himself. I was surprised he was eager to do it, but he sensed an opportunity to cement people's views of his opponent. He was right. He inserted a new paragraph into a speech in New Hampshire the afternoon of Friday, August 6.

"Now, there are some questions that a Commander-in-Chief needs to answer with a clear 'yes' or 'no,' " the president said. "My opponent hasn't answered the question of whether, knowing what we know now, he would have supported going into Iraq. That's an important question and the American people deserve a clear 'yes' or 'no' answer. I have given my answer. We did the right thing, and the world is better off for it."

The president's instinct was that Kerry would not avoid a direct challenge. Three days later, Kerry took the plunge. He was asked if he stood by his vote to grant President Bush the authority to invade Iraq. "Yes, I would have voted for the authority. I believe it was the right authority for a president to have," he said. He went on to challenge the president to answer four questions—about having had no plan to win, rushing to war, misleading Americans, and not having enough allies.

But none of his questions mattered. What Kerry didn't realize was that having voted for the war, then having criticized going to war, and now, two years later, having reiterated his support for his vote to go to war, he painted one of two pictures for voters, and neither was pretty: either he had been willing to be misled to go to war, or he now supported a rush to war that he had earlier opposed.

John Kerry's "flip-flop" record was on full display and we were on a roll. Now it was off to a four-state swing with Senator McCain, starting in Florida. As we boarded Air Force One, the president told me that while he was getting his CIA briefing, I should go back and entertain the senator.

I didn't have any idea how to handle the situation, and the walk from the president's office at the front of the plane back to the guest cabin was painfully short. So I jumped right in and somehow maneuvered the conversation to the subject of McCain's flight training in Pensacola, the day's first stop. He quickly turned funny, warm, and self-deprecating, spinning out stories that involved a little sports car, large quantities of alcohol, and exotic women with names like "Marie, the Flame of Florida." I have rarely laughed as much. I came away thinking he must have been one wild young Navy aviator.

The first rally was at the Pensacola Civic Center, which can hold ten thousand people. The building was packed, electric, and loud. I was standing next to McCain in the tunnel under the stage when the announcer's voice boomed out, "Ladies and gentlemen, Senator John McCain!" We could feel the crowd's reaction as it rolled down the tunnel. And then the announcer yelled, "And the president of the United States!" A wall of noise slammed into us. McCain's jaw dropped at its force. The president had to motion for McCain to proceed onto the stage.

The two men joined hands and raised their arms, and the crowd cheered louder. McCain has limited movement in his shoulders because of his war injuries. The president remembered this and quickly lowered his arms as the two men continued acknowledging the enthusiastic greeting. Overcome by the crowd's reaction, McCain leaned over to say something to the president. It looked like he was burying his head in the president's shoulder. You've probably seen the photograph of this moment; Democrats used it widely in the 2008 campaign.

At this rally, Bush closed the trap he'd sprung on Kerry four days earlier. "Almost two years after he voted for the war in Iraq," Bush said, "and almost 220 days after switching positions to declare himself the antiwar candidate, my opponent has found a new nuance. He now agrees it was the right decision to go into Iraq." The crowd cheered as the president removed from the table one of the major issues of the campaign. "After months of questioning my motives and even my credibility, Senator Kerry now agrees with me that . . . knowing everything we know today, he would have voted to go into Iraq and remove Saddam Hussein from

power. I want to thank Senator Kerry for clearing that up." The crowd
went wild.

We had a midday event in Niceville and ended with a rally in Panama
City, 130 miles east of Pensacola, where twenty-five thousand people had
gathered in a driving rain that miraculously stopped as the president and
McCain arrived. This part of Florida was Bush territory, and supporters
lined almost the entire route even in the rain. They were holding homemade signs (some painted on bedsheets), flying flags, or waving from
businesses, homes, or schools. McCain was captivated and took to hitting
me on the arm and exclaiming, "Look at that! Look at that!" as we passed
displays of support. By day's end, I was bruised from shoulder to elbow
and happy to be so. That night, an ebullient McCain stayed in the guesthouse at the president's Crawford, Texas, ranch.

The next morning, while the president went for a bicycle ride with
McKinnon and others, McCain and I sat in the ranch house drinking
coffee and talking politics for what turned out to be nearly two hours.
McCain looked tense, and I suspected he was still uneasy around me. But
I couldn't find a way to clear the air. So we just talked about states, electoral votes, and the chances of other Republican candidates. As we talked
the tension dissipated. The conversation grew warmer as we discovered
our common appetite for political gossip. I found out years later that
after the bike riders returned, showered, and dressed, the president kept
them from breaking in on the senator and me for thirty minutes more. "I
want Rove and McCain to marinate a little longer," he told his peloton.

As we parted at the Phoenix hotel Wednesday night after rallies in
New Mexico and Arizona, I impulsively gave McCain my cuff links,
which he had admired earlier. They were made from commemorative
coins minted after Theodore Roosevelt's death in 1919, and Roosevelt is
McCain's hero. I think he appreciated the gesture. A relationship that had
been very strained was, at least for now, cordial. That was as much as I
could hope for.

CHAPTER 26

Suspense and Victory

————— • ◆ • —————

By the summer of 2004, I believed that President Bush would win reelection—but the contest would be hard fought and close.

The president's approval rating had topped 90 percent in the aftermath of the September 11, 2001, terrorist attacks. But now his numbers had come back down to earth and while the economy had improved, the Iraq War weighed on voters' minds. It wasn't just that stockpiles of WMD had never materialized, but that, as the war dragged on, Americans lost hope in a quick exit. And then there was the charge "Bush lied" about the reasons to go to war. Democrats congregated in Boston to nominate John Kerry for president and focused relentlessly on Bush's credibility.

Still, I knew we could prevail when I saw Kerry mount the convention stage and open his speech by saying, "I'm John Kerry and I'm reporting for duty." Kerry's snappy salute confirmed that his campaign was about the past. He bet that his Vietnam service would convince Americans he was the strong leader they wanted for a post-9/11 world. Kerry did emerge from his convention with a modest lead—50 percent versus Bush's 44 percent—but it could be overcome.

I'd settled on New York for our convention because it would symbolize what Bush had done to help rebuild the country after 9/11 and because I knew Mayor Michael Bloomberg would see to it that we raised the money we needed to pull off the event. I'd also scheduled the convention as late as possible so that we'd have the shortest span to live on the $74.62 million we would receive in federal matching funds. We had sixty-two days to spend our matching funds. Kerry—who held his convention in July—had to make his federal funds last thirty-four days longer.

Our convention goals were simple: portray Bush as a strong wartime leader, and focus on the future. On Monday night, the first of the convention, John McCain took the stage to say that Bush "has not wavered, he has not flinched from the hard choices." Former New York mayor Rudy Giuliani followed him and told voters "in times of dangers, as we are in now, Americans should put leadership at the core of their decision." The following night, California governor Arnold Schwarzenegger praised Bush's "perseverance, character and leadership" in the war on terrorism as "a leader who doesn't flinch, doesn't waver, does not back down." Somewhere deep in Madison Square Garden, our speech editors were stuck on the phrases "not flinching" and "not wavering." I wanted the subtlety of a jackhammer. Laura Bush followed the Governator with a heartfelt defense of her husband, saying "you can count on him, especially in a crisis."

To make sure Bush was focused on the future, we replaced the phrase "next term" with "new term" and packed the convention schedule with events highlighting the goals the president had set for his second four years. Bush's acceptance speech had so many forward-looking policy proposals that Jim Angle of Fox News and others said it sounded more like a State of the Union address than an acceptance speech. That was fine with me. We came out of the convention with Gallup showing the race at Bush 52, Kerry 45. But I knew Bush's lead wouldn't last.

IN AUGUST, AS WE readied for the convention, an important and potentially decisive drama was playing out as the "Swift Boat Veterans for Truth" stormed to national prominence. The group had been formed in March, after Kerry wrapped up the Democratic nomination. It drew a little attention with a May 4 news conference criticizing Kerry's antiwar campaign during the 1970s and raising questions about his military record. But by August 4, the group had raised $500,000—enough to start running an ad called "Any Questions?" in which thirteen veterans said Kerry was "not being honest" and was "lying about his record." The ad initially played in Wisconsin, Ohio, and West Virginia. Democrats and their sympathetic commentators in the media called on Bush to repudiate the ad. So did McCain, who called the spot "dishonest and deplorable" and compared it to what he claimed happened to him during the 2000 primaries. However, McCain accepted the Bush campaign's denial of any connection to the group, saying, "I can't believe the president would pull such a cheap stunt." Cheap or not, McCain was right: the Bush campaign had nothing to do with it.

On August 20, the stakes increased dramatically. The Swift Boat Veterans announced their second ad, "Sellout," which featured footage of Kerry speaking before Congress in 1971, when he accused the American military of atrocities in Vietnam. Kerry had said, "They had personally raped, cut off ears, cut off heads . . . randomly shot at civilians . . . razed villages in a fashion reminiscent of Genghis Khan. . . ." The ad interspersed his words with the voices of veterans, two of whom had been Vietnam POWs.

The next day, Kerry pressed the Federal Election Commission to order the ad's removal, and he put up his own spot accusing Bush of running a "smear" campaign. The charge was ludicrous and ineffective. "Sellout" was devastating because it featured John Kerry's long face and his own Brahmin-accent words. It was Kerry, not someone else, slandering his Vietnam comrades. It didn't matter if Kerry accused (without any evidence) the Bush campaign of being behind the ad. The ad raised disturbing questions from Kerry's character that would not go away. It also rekindled passions from the closing days of the Vietnam War and raised the question of whether the Left would force us to lose another war we could win and for which America had already made considerable sacrifices.

By now, Bush could not dodge the controversy and, on August 23, he responded to a reporter's question by calling for an end to all ads by independent groups. Democrats refused. A key element of their reelection plan was "independent expenditure" advertising and other activities run by liberal groups and unions. The "Swifties" also dismissed the president's call, saying they would keep running ads. They ran seven new ones before the end of the campaign, spending about $19 million. They were easily the most effective independent ads of 2004.

Of course, I was blamed for the Swift Boat ads, accused of helping to organize the group, orchestrating its activities, and creating its messages. I had no role in any of it, though the Swifties did a damned good job. I always thought Kerry's fury at the ad and its backers was driven mostly by the fact of his disgraceful testimony. That 1971 appearance before Congress, which helped make him a public figure, had come back to haunt him. He could not stand the rough justice now being dispensed.

Even so, I still have indigestion about how campaign finance laws have led to an explosion of independent groups like this. Their rise has reduced the role candidates and parties can play in a campaign, while groups such as the Swift Boat Veterans for Truth, which are responsible to no one over the long term, play a larger one. But in 2004, that was a moot point. Campaign finance laws were what they were—and there emerged a group of war veterans who decided not to let John Kerry get away with his insults from thirty years before.

ON WEDNESDAY, SEPTEMBER 8, a potentially dangerous new phase of the general campaign began for us. When it ended a few weeks later, so did the forty-three-year career of one of America's most prominent journalists: Dan Rather.

It started with a three-fer. First, CBS's *60 Minutes* released memos allegedly written in 1972 by Bush's squadron commander that showed George W. Bush "did not meet his performance standards and received favorable treatment." The same day, a Democratic power broker and former Texas lieutenant governor sought public forgiveness for supposedly getting Bush into the Air National Guard in 1968. And then a Democratic front group called "Texans for Truth" unveiled a TV ad attacking Bush's Guard service.

The Democratic power broker, Ben Barnes, was forced to admit he was not asked by the Bushes to call the head of the Air National Guard on young George W. Bush's behalf, but by a Houston oilman. And the television attack ad didn't stick, even where it was seen.

But CBS's documents kicked up a storm. They were four memos allegedly prepared by Lieutenant Colonel Jerry B. Killian, Bush's squadron commander, who had died in 1984. In them, Killian had allegedly written that "Bush failed to carry out a direct order . . . to undertake a medical examination that was necessary for him to remain a qualified pilot" and that Killian felt pressured by a superior, Colonel Walter B. "Buck" Staudt, to "sugar coat" Bush's officer evaluations.

Staudt immediately denied pressuring Killian or having been called by Barnes on Bush's behalf. Then Killian's family raised questions about the memos' authenticity. So did his staff sergeant, who had initially been identified by CBS as a corroborating witness. Dan Bartlett weighed in to explain the reason Bush didn't take the medical exam: After being turned down for a special program that might have seen him shipped to Vietnam, Bush had let his active flight status lapse. The Guard was phasing out Bush's aircraft, he was near the end of his term of service, and it made more sense to spend training dollars and hours on those who were staying in the Guard—not on somebody with only a short time left.

The big blows to CBS's credibility came when bloggers suggested the documents were fake. The memos used a superscript—a style of font—unavailable in typewriters of that day but commonly used later on personal computers. The CBS handwriting expert who had been hired to verify all four memos looked at only one and "had not an opinion about [their] typography." And the memo alleging Staudt was pressuring Killian was written eighteen months after Staudt retired. The memos contained wrong addresses, and their style violated military protocol about the use of names, titles, and unit designations. Killian's former commander, retired Major General Bobby W. Hodges, who CBS said was its "trump card" in backing up its claims, said the network "misled" him. He believed the documents were forgeries.

Dan Rather had received the documents (via his CBS News producer Mary Mapes) from Bill Burkett, a retired Texas Army National Guard officer with a long history of attacking the Guard's leadership and Bush. Burkett even claimed to have witnessed Joe Allbaugh and Dan Bartlett shredding documents at Guard headquarters, a charge vigorously denied by both men. How Burkett had come into possession of the documents was unclear. He refused to make himself available, relying on his lawyer, David Van Os, to speak for him. (I'd helped defeat Mr. Van Os when he ran for the Texas Supreme Court in 1998.)

Less than two weeks into the controversy, CBS began distancing itself from Rather, admitting it had "grave doubts" about the documents and that the story should not have been aired. It took two more days for CBS to apologize. Rather said he still believed the memos.

Of course, Maureen Dowd, the *New York Times* columnist, repeated Democratic "speculation about whether Karl Rove, the master of dirty tricks and surrogate sleaze, could have set up CBS in a diabolical preemptive strike to undermine damaging revelations" about Bush's National Guard service. Diabolical indeed. For this scheme to work, it required me to convince a Bush-hating source to provide falsified memos to Dan Rather through his Bush-hating producer, and then get Rather to take the bait and publish the story, despite how obviously fake the memos were. My critics were again investing me with superhuman powers.

Almost two weeks were devoted to the Bush–National Guard controversy. Within the Bush camp, we had gone from initial alarm and anger at the smear—it was clearly meant as a knockout blow against Bush—to watching with delight as bloggers, not reporters, dethroned one of America's most prominent anti-Bush journalists. The revelation that a liberal journalist used fake documents to damage the president actually energized Bush's supporters. My sense was that some voters still up for grabs moved a little our way, too. Bush had mostly stayed out of the fight and, by the time it was over, came off as the victim of a dirty trick.

But I was worried going into the debates. Bush had not participated in any during the primaries and was rusty. Kerry had honed his anti-Bush message during the nomination process and came into the debates knowing exactly the lines he wanted to use and the broad case he wanted to make. Bush would also be tempted, like all incumbents, to spend too much time defending his record rather than laying out his second-term plans. And lastly, Bush thought Kerry was a pedantic and arrogant flip-flopper and didn't like the Massachusetts senator. I was worried those feelings would show through.

Bush diligently studied his briefing books, and the prep sessions themselves were fairly relaxed. At one of them, Condi Rice asked a question while pretending she was an average citizen. She started her question by saying, "I am a single mother of two." Upon hearing that, I jumped up and said, "I knew it!" But despite the fun, Bush's performances ranged from flat to okay. He clearly didn't like debating and was going through the motions. That attitude carried through his first showdown with Kerry.

Bush did well enough on substance, but Kerry clearly won on style. Bush looked annoyed and irritated. I told Bush afterward that his dislike for Kerry was making him come across as unlikable. Others close to Bush—including Ken, Karen, Mark, and Dan—irritated him a bit by making the same point.

Of course, the debate needed a Rove Controversy to be complete. A photo showing a bulge in the back of Bush's suit coat kicked off speculation that he had strapped a wireless device to his back so staff could feed him the answers. Salon.com's Dave Lindorff asked, "Was President Bush literally channeling Karl Rove in his first debate with John Kerry?" No device was involved—just some bad tailoring. But the frenzied speculation on the Internet and in the mainstream press showed how shallow the media were and how irrational Bush's critics (and mine) had become.

In the second debate, in St. Louis, Bush stifled his annoyance with Kerry. A lot of time was spent on Iraq, with Kerry saying Bush rushed to war and went it "alone." Bush got off one of his better lines by shooting back that Kerry should tell that to the British, Italians, Poles, and twenty-seven other countries with troops in Iraq. Kerry got into trouble on taxpayer funding of abortion by giving a nuanced answer that was impossible to understand. Bush responded, "I'm trying to decipher that. My answer is, we're not going to spend taxpayers' money on abortion." The exchange played to Bush's strengths—he was straightforward, candid, and knew his own mind.

In the final debate, in Arizona, it was Kerry who let his dislike for his opponent show through. His meanness also surfaced. Kerry brought up Vice President Cheney's daughter Mary, telling the country she "is a lesbian" and then using her to support a point he was making about the Defense of Marriage Act. This was a jarring moment; the word *lesbian* had never been used before in a presidential debate. I was in a portable building nearby watching the debate with Condi Rice, Margaret Spellings, and others, and some let out gasps when they heard Kerry's remark. I knew in an instant Kerry had made a bad misstep; he looked nasty and his comment dominated the coverage in the days that followed. It helped that Lynne Cheney publicly criticized Kerry, saying he was "not a good man" and accusing him of a "cheap and tawdry political trick." Mary said nothing herself, but her sister, Liz, chided Kerry's campaign chairwoman, Mary Beth Cahill: "I think what you saw after the debate with Senator Kerry's campaign chairwoman coming out and saying that Mary Cheney was fair game confirms what seems to be pretty obvious, which is that they were trying to score some political points." Vice President Cheney also spoke out, calling Kerry "a man who will do and say anything to get elected."

The debates ended up helping our reluctant debater. Gallup showed a small but durable lead for Bush, 49 to 46.

THE CAMPAIGN ENTERED ITS final weeks and it was at this point that all the careful planning and organizing for our "Army of Persuasion" had to pay off. This army's task was to help maximize Republican turnout, draw millions of previously uninvolved voters into the election, and snatch several million Democrats from the Kerry column. On the final weekend, Secretary of Commerce Don Evans and former Reagan speechwriter Peggy Noonan were among those knocking on an estimated 5 million doors.

Last-minute tracking showed significant movement in two states that had been considered out of reach: Hawaii and New Jersey. Cheney wanted to make a surprise grab for the Aloha State. I liked his audacity and backed the idea: he flew all night for an 11 P.M. rally in Hawaii the day before the election. This was the first time since 1960 anyone on a presidential ticket campaigned in the islands. It was worth it just to see Cheney wearing a lei.

Monday, November 1, was George W. Bush's final day of his final race. I was determined to make sure it wasn't an easy one. Over the course of nineteen hours, from 6:30 A.M. Monday until 1:40 A.M. on Tuesday, he delivered seven speeches in a 2,548-mile, six-state dash for votes in the critical battlegrounds of Ohio, Pennsylvania, Wisconsin, Iowa, and New Mexico, before heading home to Texas for a last formal rally at Southern Methodist University that started at 11 P.M. on election eve.

The SMU event was by far the most emotional. I looked around the arena and saw faces of friends who a decade before had helped put a young man and his wife on their journey to the Texas Governor's Mansion. They were now congregated on a fall night, rooting for him to return to the White House. All the years, all the miles, all the labor, and all the memories came together in this moment.

As I took my seat in the staff section, people started applauding. I wondered what was going on until I realized some people were chanting my name. I appreciated the sentiment and did my best to keep my emotions in check. It was my final rally, too.

Around 1 A.M. on Election Day, I started receiving our final tracking data in the double-wide trailer where the senior staff slept at the Crawford ranch.

We were up 4 in Ohio and even in Florida. Florida felt better than that, but I didn't like our position in either state. I decided we would add two Election Day stops onto the trip back to Washington: one in the I-4 corridor of Florida and the other in Columbus, Ohio. By 1:30 A.M., Deputy Chief of Staff Joe Hagin, who was in charge of Air Force One, called to say only one stop was possible. I asked Mehlman to choose. He picked the Buckeye State. Mehlman's decision made Hagin, who's from Cincinnati, happy. Mehlman and I had the same instinct: the race in Ohio felt closer than Florida. I told the president the bad news Tuesday morning. He thought he was finished with campaigning, so he was grumpy, but he liked the prospect of losing about as much as I did.

It was an overcast morning in Crawford when the president and First Lady, along with daughters Barbara and Jenna, cast their ballots at the Volunteer Fire Department. As they voted, RNC chairman Ed Gillespie called my cell. I mugged for the press scrum standing a few feet away, pretending that Ed was giving me exciting news about turnout.

In truth, you can't possibly know anything definitive about Election Day turnout until precinct officials begin to report how many voters showed up at specific times during the day. And even when precincts report how many voters have turned out, you don't know whether that's bad for that precinct for that time of day or how many absentee votes have been cast already. Much of Election Day is taken up with rumors, wildly inaccurate reports, and a fascination with the weather you simply don't see among political people the other 364 days of the year. If you're an optimist, it always seems to be raining on Election Day where the opposition is concentrated, or if you are a pessimist, in your own strongholds.

We were on final approach to Andrews Air Force Base when Matthew Dowd's deputy, Sara Taylor, called me from headquarters with the first wave of exit polls. Of course, nobody but a few people inside the news organizations sponsoring these exit polls is supposed to see them. But in the age of the Internet and e-mail, exit polls quickly make their way into the political community's bloodstream. Campaigns begin to rejoice or brood, depending on the news. And reporters and commentators who should know better than to shape their coverage on an unreliable wave of data while Americans are still deciding, do so anyway.

I took the numbers down on a note card balanced on my knee. They were bad: We were losing Ohio. We were dead even in Florida. North Carolina was gone. Minnesota was out of play. Arizona, South Carolina, and Colorado were too close to call. Mississippi—Mississippi!—was close. State after state would fall to the Kerry campaign, according to the exit polls. The president was on his way to a crushing defeat.

Though everyone else was strapped in and Air Force One was seconds from the runway, I went forward to the president's cabin. There was no sugarcoating it. "The exit polls are dreadful," I told him, and then ran down the numbers and states. "If they're accurate, we're not going to win."

Bush looked shocked; he sucked in his breath, tightened his jaw, and said, "That doesn't sound right to me. What happened?" I told him I didn't know and I emphasized these were preliminary results. On one level, he didn't believe or accept them; but on another, he had to acknowledge this might be the outcome.

I was sick to my stomach. We didn't have time to discuss things in detail before disembarking the plane—and frankly, I didn't want to. The quicker we escaped the place where the bad news had been shared, the better I would feel. The helicopter ride of less than ten minutes from Andrews to the South Lawn of the White House seemed to take years. As Marine One touched down, the president, who had been staring out the window, turned and said, "Everyone put on your game face." We exited to a mass of clicking photographers and eager reporters. The president went upstairs to the private quarters, and I went to my office in the West Wing. I thought we'd pulled off the game-face strategy, but chief White House usher Gary Walters told Susan Ralston the next day he knew there had been bad news; we all looked grim.

When I arrived in the West Wing, a foot-tall stack of first-wave exit data greeted me. After calling Darby to share the bad news, I dove into the stack. What I found shocked and profoundly angered me. An imbecile could see these reports were trash. The exits had the Republican candidate for president losing white men in Florida, which had not happened since 1964. The exits had Bush losing Pennsylvania by 18 and New Hampshire by 17. But the previous week's state polls, on average, showed us down 2 in Pennsylvania and down 1 in New Hampshire. The exits showed women were nearly three out of every four voters in Minnesota, nearly two out of every three in North Carolina, and nearly 60 percent nationally. This was impossible: women consistently make up 52 to 54 percent of the vote. The more I dug into the state-by-state numbers, the more I was convinced they were terribly wrong.

I called the president and then briefed Andy Card. I had gone from being sick to steaming. I knew the networks and cable channels would shape their evening coverage based on erroneous numbers and, just as in 2000, what was said on the air early could have an effect on turnout in the Midwest and West.

I called Darby to tell her to forget everything I had told her earlier: the numbers were crap. We were going to win. I didn't know that for certain just yet, but the corrupted exits made me defiant. Then I got on the phone and began calling big players in the media. So did Mehlman and Dowd, who had been so depressed by the exit polls that he barricaded his office door that afternoon and refused to come out. Because Matthew's dark Irish pessimism had kicked in, we decided to substitute Sara Taylor for face-to-face briefings on the exits with the press who were set up at headquarters.

The calls were not encouraging. Every objection we raised was batted away as press contacts checked with the Edison/Mitofsky network exit poll consortium in New Jersey and reported back. The weird female-to-male ratio? We were told Kerry had changed the nature of the electorate. What about the discrepancies between the last week's public polls and the exits? After checking with the geniuses in New Jersey, one commentator told me Kerry was winning the undecideds. That galled me. The undecideds in Pennsylvania and New Hampshire made up less than 5 percent of the electorate!

Bush kept calling from the private quarters to see how we were doing. I told him I wasn't sure we were having any effect on the coverage but it made me feel good to complain. He relished the reports I gave of the responses I had received from some of the best political minds in the nation's press. His father wandered by around 5 P.M. while I was in the middle of one of my tirades with a reporter. It helped cool me down a little to explain things to President Bush 41.

The first states to be heard from finished voting at 7 P.M. As that time drew near, my staff—Susan Ralston, Israel Hernandez, B. J. (short for Barbara Jo) Goergen—and I moved over to the State floor of the White House, where we'd set up an election night war room. There were two large-screen TVs, a bank of phones, four computer terminals, and a thick notebook. Mehlman had directed the RNC's computer wizards to write a program that allowed us to monitor election returns in real time. My computer screen featured a map of the country. All I had to do was click on a state, and a map and its statewide returns would pop up. Click on a county and its returns would appear. The notebook contained the numbers of votes and percent we needed for every county in every battleground state in order to win. All I had to do was compare results for a county or state from the computer screen against the notebook figures, and I could quickly get a sense of how well we were doing. Susan, Israel, and B.J. sat to my left with terminals and phones. They tracked down anyone I needed to talk to and kept an open line to Mehlman at headquarters.

We started the night with a bang: Bush jumped to a big early lead in Kentucky and Indiana. If Americans thought Bush deserved to go to hell, we would have seen it in those early returns.

When the polls closed in Florida, I dove into the numbers, clicking on counties north of Tampa Bay. The first two I investigated were Pasco and Hernando. The president had made stops in both exurban counties, and the news was good. Bush had won Pasco by just under 1,000 votes in 2000; now he appeared to be on his way to a lead of nearly 19,000. The news was similar in Hernando. I called Jeb to compare notes; he was hearing a similar pattern. As we talked, I clicked down the counties on Florida's northeast coast: Duval, St. Johns, Volusia, Brevard, Seminole, Indian River. We were beating our targets in every county and by wide margins. Even in the big Democratic strongholds of Palm Beach, Broward, and Miami-Dade, the president was doing better than he needed to carry the state. I gave up worrying about Florida. For the rest of the evening, I returned to the Sunshine State only if I needed to feel really good.

Ohio was the next nail-biter. The rule of thumb was that if a Democrat carried Cuyahoga County, the area around Cleveland, by 150,000 votes, he won the state. Kerry was on track to a nearly 227,000-vote margin in Cleveland, but he wasn't going to win Ohio. Bush was overperforming in virtually every other county. In sparsely populated counties in the southeast of the state, such as Belmont, Gallia, Harrison, and Monroe, we beat our targets by nearly double digits. And in the Northwest and Southwest, we were burying Kerry. Democrats had boosted turnout in Cleveland and Columbus, but we had more than countered their efforts.

About 9:14 P.M., the president's father came by the war room. I told him the night would be long, but I fully expected Ohio to be in our column and, with it, the election. He seemed pleased but skeptical. Dowd called to say the exit poll models were changing and the networks were being told Florida was plus 3 for Bush and New Mexico, Iowa, and Wisconsin were now even. Bush 41 perked up at the news.

By around 9:30 P.M., I felt confident enough to suggest to Andy Card that we brief the senior staff, who were watching the returns in the Roosevelt Room. Like the rest of the political universe, they had heard the early exit polls and had concluded the evening would end badly. Some of them had even discouraged their spouses from coming to the White House. I plowed through the door on the room's north side and blurted out that I expected a big victory in Florida and a solid win in Ohio. If we added in the other states we expected in our column, Bush would have a comfortable victory in both the Electoral College and the popular vote. They were skeptical; even their crazed colleague couldn't perk up that room.

Shortly after I'd returned from the Roosevelt Room, former First Lady Barbara Bush and the Bush daughters dropped by the Family Dining Room to check in. They were politely doubtful about my predictions, which was understandable—the TV commentary was practically giving the election to Kerry. For example, Robert Novak said on CNN that he had "been on the phone to some Republicans in Ohio and they're very pessimistic," that it was "an uphill climb [for Bush] in Ohio," and that it was "going to be a very difficult thing for Bush to be elected." That was just one of the many anti-Bush verdicts we heard through the evening.

By 10:30 P.M., I talked with Mehlman and we agreed it was time for an all-out spin offense. We would call the network reporters and show Bush was outperforming his vote percentage in virtually every county

from 2000 and Kerry was running behind Gore's numbers by a significant margin. We spent the next half hour drawing the media's attention
to this trend, but it didn't do any good. The press continued to express
skepticism about a Bush victory and touted a surprisingly strong Kerry
showing.

By just after eleven, it came down to Ohio and Nevada; together, they
had enough electoral votes to push us over the top. Laura Bush dropped
by the war room around this time, and the president followed her a few
minutes later, exclaiming as he entered, "This is the election that will
never end." Ten minutes later, at 11:39 P.M., ABC called Florida for
Bush. I called Darby just before midnight and told her to bring Andrew
to the White House. We were going to win, and I wanted them to be
there when we went over the top.

The war room was now packed with the president's family and
friends, who were drifting down from the private quarters. It was fun to
have them there, but we had work to do and some of them were a little
sloshed and in the way. At one point, I told one of the president's closest
friends to pipe down and stop bothering my staff or get the hell out.

Around midnight, we had a problem in New Mexico. Counties in the
northern and western parts of the state that contained lots of Indian reservations had not turned in their boxes on time as required by state law.
We were up by 14,000 votes with nearly 95 percent of the vote in, but
these heavily Democratic counties were holding boxes out. I talked with
New Mexico senator Pete Domenici's chief of staff, Steve Bell, and we
agreed Domenici would call the counties and warn them they were violating the law. The last thing we needed was a close New Mexico election
where ballot boxes had mysteriously gone missing for hours.

As the evening wore on, I swam in a raging flood of data and found it
difficult to look at the numbers on the screen, write them on my pad,
look at the notebook, adjust my glasses, find the right column in the
notebook, and then scribble the number I found there next to the number from the screen. I looked around the room and spotted the one person I thought I could count on to help me keep track of this complicated
puzzle. "Condi," I yelled, "get over here and help me!" For the next several hours, the future secretary of state helped make sense of the flood of
data, thumbing through the notebook whenever I barked out a state and
county, and reading me the numbers she found.

At 12:38 A.M., I got off the phone from an Ohio review with the campaign headquarters and told the war room the state was "cooked" and in our column. Three minutes later, Fox called Ohio for the president. Andy Card congratulated me, setting off a spate of hugs and handshakes as the tension temporarily broke. I was standing next to Condi, and the president's close friend from Texas, Jim Francis, was standing on the other side of her. Condi leaned over to me and said, "Congratulations, after all we did to screw it up." Jim doubled over in laughter. As luck would have it, the photographer on the other side of the room chose that moment to snap a picture. So did Darby: I have the same photograph from two different angles. Even better was the photo Darby took a few moments before as Fox News put up its graphic awarding Ohio to Bush. I was on the phone with the president when it happened; I've got a phone to my ear and Andrew standing next to me giving two thumbs-up with a big grin. Take it from me, there's nothing like shepherding two winning presidential campaigns and celebrating both with your son.

With Ohio, we were at 269 in the Electoral College. Iowa, Nevada, and New Mexico were still up in the air, but any one of them would put us over the top.

At 1:20 A.M., Senator Pete Domenici called. The missing New Mexico Indian Country boxes had shown up and Pete thought we had won the state. Then minutes later, Mary Beth Cahill, Kerry's campaign manager, told the press they wanted provisional ballots in Ohio to be counted. Provisional ballots are votes that are disputed, usually for a clerical reason: Was the person registered? Has the voter already voted? I felt a shiver: Would this crowd try to do in Ohio what Gore had done in Florida? But how could they even think that was smart? There were 158,642 provisional ballots and Bush's lead was over 120,000. Kerry would have to take 88 percent of the provisional ballots to win. That simply wasn't going to happen. I talked with Mehlman and we dispatched a team of lawyers and political operatives to Columbus. They were soon airborne and ready to counter any Democratic efforts to plunge the country into a repeat of 2000.

I spent the next two hours, from 1:30 A.M. to 3:30 A.M., working the phones in Ohio, New Mexico, Iowa, and Nevada. In between my calls, the guy who lives above the war room—the president—besieged me, asking, "What's the latest?" Bush had retreated to the White House private quarters but was nervously chomping on a cigar and frantic for the latest intelligence. More than once, I had to let him wait on hold while I wrapped up a call or two from the field. Finally, he couldn't stand it and reappeared in the war room just before 2:30 A.M.

British prime minister Tony Blair had tried to reach the president. Blair had gone to bed in London with the early exit polls pointing toward the defeat of his friend and trans-Atlantic partner. Now he'd awakened to the news Bush appeared headed to victory. When they finally talked in the war room at 2:44 A.M., Bush told the prime minister, "I haven't been up this late since college."

At 3:30 A.M., the Associated Press called Nevada for Bush. Within half an hour, so did ABC and CNN. CBS did, too, but stubbornly refused to put the state's three electoral votes into Bush's column. We now had more than 270 Electoral College votes, though different networks had called different states. It was a sign of how exhausted we were that we then spent the next hour debating whether Bush should declare victory. Being the hothead, I said declare victory. But Bartlett and Hughes wanted the media to declare Bush the winner before he spoke. Speaking in the middle of the night, they argued, would look rushed and unpresidential. They were right.

By 4:30 A.M., Karen Hughes and Cheney's political confidante Mary Matalin were peacefully asleep on the floor of the White House Family Dining Room.

I started to prepare talking points: Bush had received more votes than any other president in history and was the first since 1988 to receive a popular vote majority. His margins in the still outstanding target states were so large he was destined to win.

Around 5:30 A.M., I decided I needed a few minutes of shut-eye and a shower. I'd been up for twenty-four hours and had slept perhaps four hours in the previous two days. I was running on empty. There was nothing more I could do, so I set out for home to get some sleep. As I passed by the Secret Service desk near the West Wing basement exit, the Uniformed Division officer on duty told me Bob Schieffer of CBS wanted to speak to me. The call was routed to the phone next to a nearby couch. I slumped down on it, concerned that I might not get up if the call lasted too long. Bob got right to the point: "When will the president speak?" he asked. I said something vague. Like all good journalists, Bob had a follow-up: "Was the president reluctant to speak and declare victory until the media called the election for him?" That was exactly the wrong question to ask me at that hour, after the night I had had. I told him that the president had just received more votes than had ever been cast for a candidate in history and Bush didn't need the media to validate his election, thank you very much. I hung up and walked out of the West Wing.

Don't tell me the stupid exit polls didn't color the coverage in 2004.

CHAPTER 27

The Democrats Unleashed

————•◆•————

Presidential second terms are generally unhappy. Just how unhappy was outlined in a sobering memorandum prepared after the 2004 election by the White House's Office of Strategic Initiatives. It argued that second terms were often tarnished by scandal or unpopular wars, or were lackluster because a president pursued a timid agenda or had won reelection by an appeal based on personality rather than ideas.

Right after the election, President Bush asked me to steer not only his politics but also the West Wing domestic policy process. I gained additional duties and the title of Deputy Chief of Staff for Policy and, with them, an early taste of what the memo had warned about.

One of the first decisions we faced concerned the sequencing of the president's major initiatives. What should we tackle first—reform of Social Security or immigration? Social Security reform was more challenging. No president had attempted to alter the system since 1983, because Democrats found it easy to scare seniors into thinking their safety net was about to be ripped away. But I felt the issue was less politically dangerous than in the past, in part because Bush had twice won the presidency while explicitly promising to modernize Social Security. Several senators—including Elizabeth Dole, Jim DeMint, John Sununu, and Norm Coleman—had won their seats doing the same thing. When it came to immigration reform, on the other hand, we and other Republicans had done little to lay a foundation for action. So without spending much time on the question, we picked Social Security.

For the best of reasons, and to his everlasting credit, Bush did what political leaders are constantly faulted for avoiding: taking on hard, politically risky tasks. He strove to make responsible changes now to forestall less wrenching ones later—and in the process he was mauled by Democrats and abandoned by Republicans, in a disgraceful performance by the former and a disappointing one by the latter.

Social Security needs to be reformed because it is going broke. By 2016, annual payments to Social Security recipients will exceed annual Social Security revenues. By 2037, the so-called Social Security trust fund will be exhausted and the system will be bankrupt. Social Security recipients will immediately see their monthly checks cut by a third or the country will have to enact a $350 billion-a-year tax increase, the largest in world history.

Today, fewer wage earners support more Social Security recipients than ever before. In 1950, 16 people paid into Social Security for everyone drawing on it. By 2005, there were 3.3 people paying into the system for every recipient. And by 2040, there will be an estimated 2.1 people paying in for every person taking out. The Social Security system that had improved the twilight years of tens of millions of senior Americans is badly in need of repair.

In fact, Social Security's financial problems began pinching the federal budget long before 2016. Since 1965, Social Security tax receipts had grown larger each year. But these revenues peaked in 2008, and the annual surplus declined each year thereafter. This matters because the "trust fund" is not kept in a bank or invested. Any surplus in the "trust fund" is borrowed by the rest of government and spent. The IOUs for these $2.4 trillion in loans from Social Security are kept in the most valuable file cabinet in the world at the Bureau of the Public Debt in Parkersburg, West Virginia. Budget writers and appropriators have less money to spend because the Social Security receipts available for borrowing are declining.

Bush started working on Social Security modernization in 2001. With a fifty-fifty Senate, we knew Congress wouldn't take up the issue anytime soon. To foster a bipartisan consensus, the president recruited

retired New York Democratic senator Daniel Patrick Moynihan to chair
a commission.

Moynihan was an inspired choice. His integrity and reputation made
him a trusted figure among the elderly—especially on the issue of Social
Security—and gave the bipartisan commission stature.

At a May 2, 2001, Rose Garden ceremony, Bush gave the Moynihan
Commission three charges: preserve the benefits of all current retirees and
those nearing retirement, return Social Security to sound financial footing, and allow younger workers the option of personal savings accounts.
Recommendations were due by the fall. I helped recruit commission
members, coming up with the idea of Richard Parsons, who at the time
was AOL Time Warner co–chief operating officer, to join Moynihan as
co-chair. I thought Parsons's calm, deliberative manner would help build
a consensus.

Having no senators or representatives on it insulated the commission
from election pressures, but it also meant its recommendation would
have less congressional buy-in. Moynihan and Parsons reached out to the
Hill, but Democratic leaders—with the exception of New York congressman Charlie Rangel, an old friend of Moynihan's—blew them off. Democrats even held a press conference to attack the commission's interim
report before it was finalized.

Then came 9/11. All of Congress's energy was then focused elsewhere.
For the next four years, the commission drafted a menu of options for
the day when interest in the subject could be rekindled. The president
continued making the case for reform in the 2004 campaign, which allowed him to turn the heat up in his 2005 State of the Union speech.
Calling Social Security "a great moral success of the 20th century," Bush
said, "we must honor its great purposes in this new century. The system,
however, on its current path, is headed toward bankruptcy. And so we
must join together to strengthen and save Social Security." As was his
habit, Bush placed all his chips on the table.

But the political currents were alreaady treacherous. Many Democrats
in the House chamber that night yelled "No, no!" when Bush claimed,
with complete accuracy, that Social Security "would be exhausted and
bankrupt" in forty years. In his televised response to the president's address, Senator Harry Reid called Social Security reform "dangerous" and

said it meant a "guaranteed benefit cut of 40 percent or more." The former phrase was poll-tested rhetoric; the latter was simply a lie.

The Democratic leadership sent out marching orders: Democrats were not to engage with us. I talked with Congressman Allen Boyd, ranking Democrat on the House Ways and Means Social Security subcommittee, who praised Moynihan's leadership and said he wanted to work with the administration on the commission's blueprint. But he told me he couldn't because House Democratic leaders told him not to. Every Democrat toed the party line.

If Democrats were united in opposition, Republicans were divided. Some House Republicans told us to put out a specific plan. GOP senators, on the other hand, discouraged this, saying they needed the political cover of bipartisan talks; they couldn't afford to be out there defending a specific White House proposal. The truth was that congressional Republicans were unenthusiastic about the whole enterprise. As Jim McCrery of Louisiana, a senior Republican on Ways and Means, put it, "It creates a political problem that appears to me to be very difficult to surmount."

We miscalculated: we took the initial reticence we encountered among some Republicans, especially senior leaders, as skepticism that Bush would stay engaged on the issue. But in truth, too many Republicans had lost their nerve. I missed this: I was too caught up in working on a big change, and banking too much on a newly reelected president's ability to move Congress.

Bush wasn't willing to leave the issue completely in Congress's hands, however. In his 2005 State of the Union address, he called for what would have been the most consequential change to Social Security in its seventy-year history—private accounts for individual workers.

On one level, Social Security operates like a traditional pension. Workers all pay into a pool, which the government uses to pay benefits to retirees. Workers don't have an individual account they can draw on, borrow against, or invest in a way that makes sense for them. They aren't amassing a retirement nest egg, and their benefits are only loosely tied to how much they pay in. A policy change in Washington could change their benefits.

So Bush proposed giving younger workers the option of directing some of their Social Security tax payments into a personal account that could be invested in broadly based indexed funds, much like the "Thrift Savings Plan" available to federal employees. The president believed that younger workers should be able to take part of the money they pay into the system and set it aside in their own retirement accounts, as a nest egg for their futures. Bush explained why he thought personal accounts are a better deal:

> Your money will grow, over time, at a greater rate than anything the current system can deliver—and your account will provide money for retirement over and above the check you will receive from Social Security. In addition, you'll be able to pass along the money that accumulates in your personal account, if you wish, to your children or grandchildren. And best of all, the money in the account is yours, and the government can never take it away.

I wanted to counter opposition by having the president barnstorm the country. He made sixty stops in sixty days, starting February 3, 2005. We wanted to make it possible for Democrats in Republican-leaning districts to support reform. Republicans couldn't pass Social Security modernization on a party-line vote, and the only way Democrats could vote against their leadership was if they were convinced people back home supported the change.

But the presidential barnstorming didn't do any good. Six of the seven Democratic senators in red or red-leaning states visited by Bush opposed his personal investment accounts; the seventh was tepid. Most congressional Democrats denied the problem required action despite survey after survey that showed Americans believed Social Security was going bankrupt. Democrats justified ignoring the problem by saying the crisis was a long way off. Democrats also insisted Bush take private personal accounts off the table before negotiations could begin, even though the Clinton administration had proposed forcing all workers to have some of their Social Security contributions put into stocks.

On April 28, in another effort to jump-start the debate, Bush embraced a proposal that would have protected low-wage workers and cut Social Security's projected shortfall. The idea, "progressive indexing," was proposed by commission member Robert C. Pozen, a Democrat and an investment manager. Social Security benefits are small, but they do increase over time based on a formula that takes into account both inflation and an index that averages the national increase in wages. Pozen wanted to keep that formula for the bottom 30 percent of wage earners, but for top-tier earners calculate benefit increases using inflation only. Everyone would get a Social Security check equal to or greater in purchasing power than they would receive today, but low-wage earners would receive the more generous benefit increases the country could not afford for everyone. This one change would have eliminated roughly two-thirds of the Social Security shortfall. A *New York Times* survey showed support for the idea. But it did nothing to change the situation on Capitol Hill.

Senate Finance Committee chairman Chuck Grassley tried, and failed, to broker an agreement among his committee's Republicans. He was willing to shelve private accounts to get support from the moderate Republican senators Gordon Smith of Oregon and Olympia Snowe of Maine, but they wouldn't embrace a solvency fix like progressive indexing. The ranking Democrat on Senate Finance, Max Baucus, wasn't even willing to talk. By August, we were losing airspeed and altitude. Some said it was because personal accounts would divert too much money from Social Security or would "cut" benefits too deeply (though benefits continued to grow at inflation for the wealthiest 1 percent of wage earners and faster than inflation for everyone else).

In retrospect, it was a mistake to lead the second term by pressing for Social Security reform. If we had led with immigration reform—another issue the president cared about deeply—we would almost certainly have gotten it passed because Democrats said they would work with Bush on it. That success might have produced enough bipartisan confidence to tackle Social Security. And, looking back, a grand bargain might have been possible: the Republicans could have put personal accounts aside, the Democrats could have put tax increases aside, and both sides might have embraced a form of progressive indexing and raising, over the course of decades, the age at which people can receive their full benefits from 67 to 70. That would have made the system solvent, and Republicans could have fought for personal accounts another day. I looked for the opening for such a maneuver, but we never got close. And in late August, the costliest and one of the deadliest hurricanes in American history hit southeast Louisiana and the Mississippi Gulf Coast, and that was the end of Social Security reform.

In the end, the Republican Congress never voted on a reform plan—by the fall of 2005, Speaker Hastert and House majority leader Tom DeLay told the president they were moving on. The real problem is that Congress doesn't like dealing with problems that can be postponed for another day.

SOCIAL SECURITY WAS A public failure, and we suffered another setback in 2005 as well—although this one came disguised as a victory. On July 28, the Senate Banking Committee passed a bill to regulate more closely government-sponsored enterprises (GSEs). In April 2001, the Bush administration had warned Congress of problems with them, principally with the Federal National Mortgage Association ("Fannie Mae") and the Federal Home Loan Mortgage Corporation ("Freddie Mac"). They were highly leveraged, meaning as little as a 1.3 to 2 percent decline in housing values could wipe the companies out. Failure could cause huge repercussions on financial markets, affecting not just their shareholders and the housing sector but companies and economic activity across the board.

Our bill would have subjected Fannie Mae and Freddie Mac to the kinds of federal regulation that banks, credit unions, and savings and loans have to comply with. No Democrat supported it and, most important of all, Senator Chris Dodd threatened to filibuster if Banking Committee chairman Richard Shelby, Alabama's senior senator, attempted to bring it to the floor. Dodd got his way—and thus helped pave the way to the largest financial crisis since the Great Depression.

Fannie Mae and Freddie Mac were created decades ago to help make mortgages available to poor and middle-class Americans. They both would buy mortgages from lenders, bundle them together, and sell them as securities to investors around the world. Congress chartered Fannie in 1938 and Freddie in 1970, but both were publicly traded companies and a favorite of stock pickers who assumed the U.S. Treasury would bail out the companies if they got into trouble. This helped Fannie and Freddie borrow money more cheaply than competitors. By 2000, they had accumulated $2.1 trillion in mortgage-backed paper, and regulators were becoming nervous that the two financial institutions were making increasingly risky loans in pursuit of bigger margins and larger profits.

Starting in 2001, we tried to limit this risk by raising the amount of capital they had to keep on hand, force them to get preapproval of new loan activities, and limit the size of their portfolios. It made no sense to regulate banks, savings and loans, and credit unions, but not Fannie and Freddie.

In January 2003 our concern grew when Freddie announced it had to restate its earnings for the past three years because of accounting problems. On its board during part of this period was Rahm Emanuel, who later became President Obama's chief of staff. In September, Freddie acknowledged its accounting was under investigation by the Securities and Exchange Commission and that federal regulators had uncovered billions in earning manipulations. Fourteen months later, the SEC found Fannie had overstated its earnings by $9 billion.

Fannie and Freddie combined had spent about $170 million over the previous decade on lobbying. Now, to stop our reforms they were unleashing their vast army of high-profile, high-priced Republican and Democratic lobbyists. Acting in narrow self-interest, they used this muscle to stop regulation. I had personal experience with their well-organized influence peddlers. At a congressman's invitation, I spoke to some of his constituents at a Capitol Hill meeting, and during the session, a local mortgage banker berated me for Fannie Mae's unfair borrowing advantage in the capital markets. I told him we favored regulating them like banks, credit unions, and savings and loans. He seemed satisfied, but Fannie and Freddie weren't. By the time I got back to the White House, I had messages from some of their Republican lobbyists whom I knew personally, saying they understood I had concerns about Fannie and Freddie and could they come in to talk? I refused: I'd heard and seen enough. Fannie and Freddie had hundreds of such people on their payrolls.

During the four years when the legislation to regulate them worked its way through Congress, Fannie and Freddie nearly doubled in size, purchasing another $2 trillion in mortgages. They partnered with some of the worst actors in the business—who were busy lowering standards and writing riskier mortgages.

The economic danger didn't faze Fannie and Freddie's congressional allies, who ranted at Bush officials who testified on the need for reform. The comments ranged from cautionary—"if it ain't broke, don't fix it" is how Delaware senator Thomas Carper and Ohio congresswoman

Stephanie Tubbs Jones put it—to belligerent, with New York congressman Gregory Meeks yelling he was "just pissed off" we had raised the
issue of regulating Fannie and Freddie.

Other Democrats were blissfully dismissive. California congresswoman Maxine Waters attacked Secretary of Housing and Urban Development Mel Martinez, saying, "We do not have a crisis at Freddie Mac,
and in particular Fannie Mae, under the outstanding leadership of Mr.
Frank Raines." New York senator Chuck Schumer opined, "We're using
the recent safety and soundness concerns . . . as a straw man to curtail
Fannie and Freddie's mission." He later said, "I'll lay my marker down
right now, Mr. Chairman. . . . I think Fannie and Freddie need some
changes, but I don't think they need dramatic restructuring." Rhode Island senator Jack Reed echoed Schumer, accusing reformers of "throwing
out the baby with the bathwater."

These statements were irresponsible enough, but the leading reform
opponents—this tale's true villains—were Democratic congressman Barney Frank of Massachusetts and Connecticut senator Chris Dodd. Frank
first dismissed our fiscal warnings, suggesting administration officials
would "exaggerate a threat of safety and goodness [to] conjure up the
possibility of serious financial losses to the Treasury, which I do not see"
and called Fannie and Freddie "fundamentally sound financially." Later,
Frank went so far as to argue that this "is an artificial issue created by the
administration. . . . I don't think we are in any remote danger here." Even
as Fannie and Freddie collapsed and helped drive the financial crisis of
2008, Frank labeled Bush's call for reform "inane."

Dodd was less angry than Frank—though this could be said of virtually everyone on Capitol Hill—but he was just as wrong in his diagnosis
of the problem and his opposition to reform, saying in 2004 that these
companies were "one of the great success stories of all time." As Fannie
and Freddie spiraled downward, Dodd suggested Bush "immediately reconsider his ill-advised" call for reform. Dodd had received preferential
treatment on his mortgages from one of the biggest bad actors in the
lending business, Countrywide. Despite this—and proving there is nothing as brazen as a politician with a sweetheart mortgage deal and no
conscience—Dodd went on after Fannie and Freddie were rescued with
taxpayer dollars to attack the Bush administration for not recognizing
that they were in trouble. "Why weren't we doing more . . . I have a lot

of questions about where was the administration over the last eight years." Once the problem helped spark a crisis, Frank and Dodd voted in 2008 for the Bush administration's reform bill, which they had opposed in 2005. It was perhaps the most blatant case of hypocrisy I have witnessed in Washington, where hypocrisy is common currency.

In the three years after reform stalled in the Senate, Fannie and Freddie acquired another $1.27 trillion in mortgages. Their total holdings of $5.4 billion made them owners of half the nation's mortgages. And 45 percent of all their purchases between 2005 and 2007 were subprime and other nonprime loans.

When Freddie Mac and Fannie Mae collapsed at the end of 2008, after housing values had dropped 12.8 percent since 2006, they were the accelerant that turned a minor economic downturn into a worldwide calamity. The housing collapse is largely a story of greed and irresponsibility made possible by abuse of a government-bestowed privilege. But the unwritten story of the whole affair is that if Democrats had granted the Bush administration the regulatory powers it sought, the housing crisis would not have been nearly as severe, the financial sector's collapse not nearly as damaging, the economy's slide not nearly as steep or lengthy, and global distress not nearly as widespread.

Among those Democrats who backed Dodd's filibuster and opposed reform was the freshman senator from Illinois, Barack Obama. He was the third-largest recipient of campaign gifts from Fannie and Freddie employees in 2004. Since winning the White House, he has pointed to the economic problems he "inherited," but he has never owned up to his role in creating them.

IN 2005, CONGRESS APPROVED the first major energy bill in a decade. It was a victory for the administration, though one that has long been misunderstood.

Bush's energy bill made an unprecedented commitment to conservation. There were new, higher efficiency standards for federal buildings and household products, funding for research on conservation technologies, and incentives for deploying them. The bill expanded the use of domestic energy, including clean coal, nuclear, oil, and gas. The effects on nuclear energy were particularly powerful: When Bush came into office, no nuclear plant had been built since the 1970s. When he left

Washington, there were applications at the Nuclear Regulatory Commission for twenty-two new power plants. The bill helped ensure America would have the affordable energy essential to power our economy by expanding oil and gas exploration on the outer continental shelf and public lands.

The bill diversified America's energy supply by dramatically expanding research into alternative and renewable energy from wind, solar, biomass, cellulosic ethanol, lithium-ion batteries, and hydrogen fuel cells. The research done under Bush will lead to deployment of these new technologies under Obama—except for hydrogen research: for inexplicable reasons, it was the one alternative energy program the new administration canceled in 2009. And Bush's legislation helped update and modernize the electricity grid, encourage the use of "smart grid" technologies, and make it easier to build transmission lines.

Then there was the continuing struggle over spending. Bush's victories on the budget included his never having to veto one in his first six years, because Congress stayed within the boundaries he set. But because he never vetoed a budget during that time, he was criticized as a big spender. This criticism is wrong.

President Clinton's last budget increased domestic nonsecurity discretionary spending by 16 percent. Bush cut that to 6.2 percent in his first budget, 5.5 percent in his second, 4.3 percent in his third, 2.2 percent in his fourth, and then below inflation on average for his second term, as Republicans generally backed Bush's domestic requests. Only a handful of Democrats backed the 2001 Bush budget and one did so in 2003; otherwise, Democrats refused to support his budgets.

All our hard work to reduce domestic nonsecurity spending was washed away by congressional Republicans. They insisted on earmarks that culminated in the 2005 highway bill's famous "Bridge to Nowhere"— which would have spent hundreds of millions to extend a roadway to a nearly uninhabited island in Alaska. Even though Congress repealed the "Bridge to Nowhere" after public outcry, the reputation of congressional Republicans had been badly damaged—and by extension, ours.

Democrats being Democrats, one of President Obama's first actions upon taking office was to sign a bill that resulted in a 9.7 percent increase in discretionary spending for Fiscal Year 2010, nearly four times the increase Bush had proposed. Obama had attacked Bush's deficits (which averaged roughly 2 percent of GDP) but as president proposed a budget plan for deficits to run 5.3 percent of GDP over the next decade. I suspect most Americans feel misled: when Obama criticized Bush, it wasn't for too small a deficit.

IT WAS THE DULL, cloudy afternoon of January 26, 2005, when I returned a call from Senator Harry Reid. I spent much of the next hour looking out my window into the South Lawn's trees and hedges as I listened to the Senate's top Democrat make an extraordinary offer.

Since I spent part of my childhood in Nevada and have family and mutual friends there, Reid and I had made efforts to get to know each other over the Bush White House years. He and his wife, Landra, had come to my house for dinner and we later met at a restaurant. He had given me a signed copy of his book. We tried to be cordial. Reid lost control of his rhetoric in public, once calling Bush "a loser" and accusing the president of lying. His insults were sometimes followed by contrite calls by him to the White House chief of staff apologizing for the excesses of his speechwriters or his slip of the tongue.

But this day, Reid didn't want to talk about Nevada or apologize. He wanted a deal on judges. Senate Democrats had been blocking five Bush nominees for appeals court vacancies: Priscilla Owen, Bill Pryor, Janice Rogers Brown, Henry Saad, and William Myers. Anger over the Democratic obstructionism was rising among voters and Democrats were paying a political price for it. In 2002 and 2004, they had lost Senate and House seats. It was only the second time in history that a president's party gained seats in both chambers in back-to-back elections. The other time was in 1932 and 1934 under FDR.

Reid got right to the point. The battle over judges was tying up the Senate. He wanted a way out. "Every one of these people is morally unfit to be on the bench," Reid said in a sweeping and unjustified condemnation. But if the president withdrew three of them, Reid would work to deliver Senate Democrats for the remaining two, with no filibuster. "You pick the two, we don't care," Reid said.

Such a deal would have been devastating for the president, the judiciary, and the country. It would have encouraged Democrats to be even more vicious in their assaults on the president's choices and given license to Republicans to act in a similar fashion in future Democratic administrations. Rather than paying a price for obstructionism, Democrats would have been rewarded. I was taken aback by Reid's offer.

"If all five were morally unfit for the bench, how could you allow any of them to be approved?" I asked. Didn't he have an obligation to oppose someone if they were "morally unfit" for the job? Reid mumbled something about trying to find a way around the problem.

I let loose. "Senator, do you even know who these people are you're opposing? Do you even know who they are and what they have done?" He allowed that he didn't; all he could do was to repeat standard Democratic talking points, saying they were "morally unfit." His slander angered me, so I reminded him that Judge Charles Pickering, who had just withdrawn his nomination to the 5th Circuit after two years of being pounded by Democrats, had taken on the Ku Klux Klan and worked with a former Democratic governor to encourage racial reconciliation in Mississippi. Democrats, however, were attacking him as a bigot!

"I know Priscilla Owen," I continued. She had been my client when she ran for the Texas Supreme Court. A first-class appellate specialist at one of Houston's best firms, she was apolitical and had run for the Texas Supreme Court because it was tarnished by scandal. Elected in an upset after voluntarily limiting the size of campaign donations, she was re-elected with 84 percent after being endorsed by every newspaper that opined on the contest. That wouldn't have happened if she were a right-wing nut. Yet that was what Democrats were calling her.

I suspect by now Reid was hoping I'd shut up, but I wasn't finished. There was Bill Pryor. "You are attacking him as a religious extremist," I told Reid. Pryor had been elected Alabama attorney general with strong support from fellow social conservatives. But when Alabama chief justice Roy Moore violated state law by placing the Ten Commandments in the state Supreme Court building and then defied a federal court order to remove it, Pryor prosecuted him for violating the Canons of Judicial Ethics and saw that Moore was removed from office. That wasn't popular with social conservatives, I reminded Reid, but Pryor knew his responsibility was to uphold the law.

Then there was Judge Janice Rogers Brown, a thoughtful California Supreme Court justice who if confirmed would be the first African-American woman on the U.S. Court of Appeals for the D.C. Circuit. Her life was a stirring tale of overcoming prejudice and challenge. Her father was a sharecropper and she had worked her way through college as a single mother.

"If this cycle of mindless character assassination doesn't stop, we'll look back twenty or thirty years from now and see that real damage was done to our courts," I said to Reid. I told him that respected lawyers looked at the way reputations were routinely distorted in the confirmation process and said "no thanks" to being considered for a vacancy.

Reid was unmoved. His only response was to say the president could have three rather than just two nominees. I was stunned at his cynicism and willingness to treat judicial nominees as if they were minor-league baseball prospects to be traded. I told him it was unlikely the White House would accept such an arrangement but that I would pass it on. I left unspoken that one reason the deal would be unacceptable was that Reid insisted the president publicly withdraw his nominees while Reid merely promised to do his best privately to get the remaining names through. We had frequently found Reid was an unreliable partner; I was fairly certain that he would prove to be just as untrustworthy in this situation as he had been in others.

The White House didn't accept Reid's offer and instead pressed for up-or-down votes on all the nominees. The battle tied up the Senate for four more months. Then in May, seven Republican senators and seven Democratic senators, led by John McCain and Ben Nelson, came together to agree to filibuster judge nominations only in "extraordinary circumstances." The Democrats agreed to break party ranks to allow a floor vote on nominees, while Republicans agreed to buck their party leaders if the GOP attempted to do away with the sixty-vote cloture requirement for bringing nominees to the floor.

On May 24, the Gang of 14 agreed to an up-or-down vote on Owen, Rogers Brown, and Pryor. Owen was first to be confirmed, by a vote of 55–43 the next day. Only two "Gang of 14" Democrats broke ranks to support her being seated on the 5th Circuit, but the Gang's pledge won her a floor vote and confirmation. It was an emotional moment when I called to congratulate her at the Texas Supreme Court.

Rogers Brown was approved with a 56–43 vote on June 8. Pryor was confirmed the next day, 53–45. Henry Saad later withdrew after failing to win the Gang's backing because the two Democratic senators from his home state of Michigan opposed him (Senator Levin wanted his cousin appointed) and senatorial courtesy proved too powerful a force even for the rest of the Gang. Bill Myers withdrew as well, after drawing opposition from environmental groups for his service as Interior's solicitor general.

As it turned out, the spasm of goodwill that produced a compromise over the federal judges was about to be tested further. On July 1, 2005, Associate Justice Sandra Day O'Connor announced her resignation from the U.S. Supreme Court. Bush now had the rare chance to appoint his own candidate to the Court.

The White House had been preparing for this possibility since the spring of 2001, when a small group—consisting of Vice President Cheney, Attorney General John Ashcroft, Chief of Staff Andy Card, White House Counsel Alberto Gonzales, and me—began discussing possible nominees. The vice president's chief of staff, Scooter Libby, sat in at Cheney's request, and Harriet Miers joined our deliberations after Gonzales replaced Ashcroft at Justice and Miers had become White House counsel.

We studied thick notebooks containing biographies, summaries of court opinions, articles, writings, and commentary on possible choices. Not being a lawyer, I had particular difficulty making sense of the material. Gonzales, Libby, and Miers helped me navigate it. After there was a vacancy, we also received financial statements and other documents provided by those under consideration.

I'd been primarily put in the group as a link to outside groups interested in the Supreme Court. Now I began systematically working my way through them to solicit input on potential nominees. I made it clear that while the president was interested in their opinions, no group had veto power. There were one or two oddball recommendations, but almost every serious name proposed already had a big black notebook. I was surprised how many potential nominees asked not to be considered. Some simply didn't want to go through the agony of a confirmation. They had seen what had happened to Robert Bork in 1987 and to Clarence Thomas in 1991 and wanted no part of it.

There were almost a dozen names on the list to fill the O'Connor seat, including a number of women and minorities. At the end of a round of at least one and, in some instances, two interviews by the working group, the president visited personally with several candidates before settling on Judge John Roberts of the D.C. Circuit Court of Appeals.

In his interview, Roberts was less impressive than I expected; I'm not certain why. He came across as restrained and guarded. Maybe he didn't quite know what to make of our group, or maybe we expected too much of him in an interview. After all, his answers were precise, intelligent, and concise—so much so, we got to ask Roberts more questions than any other candidate. And despite my initial reaction, he fared well by comparison: I found myself measuring other interviewees against Roberts's performance, finding some too arrogant, some too timid, others too hazy.

The lawyers asked Roberts the legal mumbo jumbo. I asked the layman's questions: When did he know he was a conservative? His answer was revealing. He had grown up in an apolitical Indiana household that talked little about politics. But when he went off to Harvard and participated in the typical late-night college bull sessions, he realized he thought differently about the world than his classmates and that he was conservative. This said to me that his philosophy was deeply ingrained, an admirable trait for a member of the Supreme Court, since, after being confirmed, only intellect and values define a justice's opinions.

I asked which former Supreme Court justice he most admired. Roberts answered Justice Robert Jackson, FDR's attorney general. Appointed by Roosevelt in 1941, he had been expected to affirm New Deal positions but instead demonstrated a fidelity to the Constitution that Roberts admired. Roberts added a second justice he admired, then-sitting Chief Justice William Rehnquist. I told him he couldn't consider a current justice, but Roberts said he was overruling me. He had clerked for Rehnquist and seen how Washington tried to change Rehnquist after he went to the Supreme Court, but how Rehnquist had stayed true to himself and his values. I shared these answers with Bush. On July 19, 2005, the president met with Roberts, whose intelligence, precision, and demeanor impressed him. Bush felt Roberts would be a consensus builder, a true leader on the Court.

Roberts did not draw unanimous support from our group. Some wanted Judge Mike Luttig of the 4th Circuit. Luttig struck me as highly intelligent, but also unlikely to be a good colleague who could win other justices over to his opinion. There was arrogance in his answers, a whiff that he was entitled to the post. A decent interval after he wasn't picked, he resigned from the appellate bench.

On July 19, Bush announced his selection at a televised announcement in the State Dining Room. The Robertses' young son, Jack, handsomely dressed in seersucker shorts and jacket, began dancing out of camera shot as the president named his father to the Supreme Court. I almost laughed out loud.

The White House was stretched thin, so we decided to bring in an outside "Sherpa" to guide Roberts through the tough confirmation process. I suggested we get Ed Gillespie for the task. He assembled a team from communications, press, legislative affairs, the White House counsel's office, and the Department of Justice. They had to introduce Roberts to the Judiciary Committee and the broader Senate while dampening a dozen fires a day, protecting his record and image from public attacks, answering hundreds of written questions from senators, and preparing the judge for what could be unpleasant hearings by staging mock ones. It was a huge task.

Senator Orrin Hatch was particularly helpful in preparing Roberts. His knowledge and relationships of nearly thirty years gave him keen insights, telling the team the buttons to push with each senator. He was, however, talkative. One weekend, Gillespie returned what he thought would be a quick call to Hatch as he drove out of the White House to join his family at the New Jersey beach. The conversation ended only after Ed had driven to Annapolis, fought his way over a jam-packed Bay Bridge, and was nearing the Delaware ferry to southern New Jersey.

Roberts had three meetings with New York senator Chuck Schumer. Roberts thought Schumer was trying to find a way to vote "yes." Being more paranoid than the judge—or perhaps more familiar with Schumer's style—I thought the chairman of the Democratic Senatorial Campaign Committee was probing for weaknesses or hoping for a remark he could use to blow up the nomination.

On September 3, 2005, while Roberts's nomination was pending before the Senate Judiciary Committee, Roberts's role model, Chief Justice William Rehnquist, died at the age of eighty. He had been diagnosed with thyroid cancer in October 2004 and aggressive radiation and chemotherapy kept him away from the Court until the following July. I had seen him backstage before the 2005 inaugural, sitting on the side of the corridor leading to the platform. Frail and weak, he had to be helped to his feet. But when his moment in the program approached and the music started, he squared up his shoulders and marched determinedly down the steps to administer the oath to George W. Bush. I thought Rehnquist looked awful and that his days were numbered. He hung on for eight months.

On September 6, Bush withdrew Roberts's nomination for the O'Connor seat and named him instead to fill the now-vacant chief justice seat. Six days later, the Senate Judiciary Committee began three days of hearings. Roberts's performance was much better than his initial interview with our vetting group. He was dazzling: fully prepared, at ease, confident without being arrogant. Democrats couldn't lay a glove on him.

Two weeks later, the Senate confirmed John Roberts as the seventeenth chief justice by a vote of 78 to 22. Senate Democrats split right down the middle.

Meanwhile, our Supreme Court nomination group had been working on names to fill the O'Connor seat. We offered Bush about a dozen possibilities, even more diverse than our earlier list. Having not named a woman first for the O'Connor seat, Bush felt he would, all things being equal, like to nominate a woman to fill the remaining vacancy. A new name happened to be on our list: Harriet Miers, Bush's White House counsel. On October 3, Bush nominated her for the O'Connor seat.

What first attracted Bush was her record. She was a legal pioneer: the first woman managing partner of a major Texas law firm, first woman president of both the Dallas Bar Association and then the Texas Bar Association, and a powerhouse in the American Bar Association. She was a first-rate litigator with a keen legal mind. She had also been elected to the Dallas City Council and later appointed by Governor Bush as chairman of the Texas Lottery Commission, where she'd cleaned up a scandal-ridden agency. She also had an enormous capacity for work. You knew you'd arrived early at the White House if Harriet's classic old red Mercedes wasn't already parked near the entrance to the West Wing basement.

Bush also knew she was a strong conservative who would strictly interpret and apply the Constitution as written. She was sixty, slightly older than many high-court nominees, but we felt she could be counted on to serve a long time. She had also impressed some people in Washington, first by her insanely competent organization as staff secretary and then in her dealings with Congress during her stint as deputy chief for policy. Senate Democratic leader Harry Reid told Bush he would support Miers and felt other Democrats would as well. Even Judge Roberts, before he was confirmed himself, told us he admired Miers's cast of mind and her legal reasoning and could see her as an excellent addition to the Court. For Bush and the rest of us, the nomination was not just a sentimental favorite, it also made a lot of sense.

But what made sense to us didn't to our usual allies. In that respect, I didn't serve the president well. My job, after all, included outreach to the groups interested in the Court. For many of them, the Supreme Court is an intellectual crown jewel, and Miers lacked the proper credentials. Harriet had not been active in the Federalist Society or other conservative legal groups. She had not served on the federal bench, where she could have built a record that would have given them confidence. She had graduated from Southern Methodist University Law School; some of our allies couldn't conceive of a justice from outside the the Ivy League. And she was virtually unknown to them, even after five years in Washington. She had stayed focused on work and had not ingratiated herself to Washington's conservative legal circles.

My antennae should have been sharper. We expected to be hit by adversaries, but it was our friends who carried the fight against Harriet, with influential columnists like Charles Krauthammer and George Will coming out strongly against her over issues of constitutional scholarship, experience, and lack of engagement.

In backing Harriet, we were asking conservatives to trust us. For some, the stakes were too high—and their history with a previous Bush made them more skittish than normal. They recalled how they had trusted the senior President Bush and his chief of staff, John Sununu, on the Supreme Court nomination of David Souter, who turned out to be a doctrinaire liberal. Conservatives would not stand for another disappointment. Rather than trust Bush, they wanted a known quantity. When Miers came under fire from conservatives, Democrats like Reid who had promised to back her disappeared. Senate Judiciary Committee chairman Arlen Specter essentially doomed her nomination when he said she "lack[ed] experience." Democrats then piled on a questionnaire she filled out for her 1989 Dallas City Council race that demonstrated she was pro-life. Apparently, Democrats think some litmus tests are appropriate.

Harriet could see she would get approved only with a tremendous expenditure of the president's political capital—and even then confirmation was unlikely. A nomination that started out with such high hopes for those of us who knew Harriet was turning into a disaster. On October 27, she withdrew her name, acting with enormous grace. That surprised no one who knew her. It was an emotional and difficult moment for Bush and the First Lady. Four days later, Bush nominated 3rd Circuit Court of Appeals judge Samuel Alito.

Judge Alito had impeccable credentials as a conservative jurist and the outside groups were as enthusiastic about Alito as they had been wary of Miers.

He had a wonderful life story as the son of an immigrant father; his parents were both teachers. But my dominant impression from his interview with the vetting group was that he was painfully shy. The poor man was shaking when he came into the dining room at the vice president's residence. There was nothing we could do to put him at ease. He just sat there twitching, sweating, and visibly distraught. But boy, was he smart. Judge Alito's answers demonstrated he had a brilliant mind and deep legal wisdom. He was so good at explaining his views that even a nonlawyer like me understood what he was saying without feeling talked down to.

Probing for weaknesses, Democrats delayed his hearing until January 9, 2006, and then hammered him for four days, one more day than Roberts had suffered. There were moments of humor: Senator Joe Biden asked Alito a question that consisted of a twenty-four-minute monologue that made even me embarrassed for the senator. Senator Ted Kennedy harangued Alito for almost as long, saying he was prejudiced against "average Americans," sexist, corrupt, and a racist. It was ugly, unfair, and despicable but seemed almost second nature to Kennedy. I kept thinking that even he must have known how wrong it was.

Alito was never in trouble, given the obvious power of his intellect. But in a key moment in response to the attacks by Kennedy and other Democrats, Republican senator Lindsey Graham exposed the brutal attacks on Alito by sympathetically asking him, "Are you really a closet bigot?" Hearing the question, Alito's wife was overcome with emotion and fled the room weeping. The Democrats' attempt to tarnish Alito backfired.

Senator John Kerry phoned in a request for a filibuster against Alito from the Swiss Alps. Gillespie said it was "the first time anyone has ever yodeled for a filibuster," and fed the line to Scott McClellan, who needed help in his daily battles with the press corps. Democrats attempted to filibuster on January 30 but fell short. Among those supporting the filibuster was Barack Obama. The next day Judge Alito was approved by a 58–42 margin, with only four Democrats supporting him. It was a capstone to a difficult but ultimately successful effort, and Roberts and Alito's ascension to the Supreme Court counts among Bush's greatest and most lasting domestic legacies.

CHAPTER 28

Anything for a Scalp

———— • ◆ • ————

B y the summer of 2005, the Wilson-Plame story had been going on
for two years. I had already made three grand jury appearances.
While I had done nothing wrong, had committed no crime, and had
done everything asked of me by the prosecutor, I remained trapped. I
kept hoping this expensive and draining episode would end—but things
were about to get far worse. Special Prosecutor Patrick Fitzgerald wanted
to harpoon a whale.

I have always tried to keep my personal life from affecting my work.
The investigation itself was nerve-racking, but the media's coverage of it
severely tested my discipline. Increasingly, I had moments where I felt I
was losing control.

One morning I turned on the television in my office while waiting
for a meeting, and on popped Don Imus. He was talking with NBC's
State Department correspondent Andrea Mitchell about how I was going
to be raped in prison and theorized how that fat little porker—me—
would squeal. It was a tasteless, disgusting, and disturbing comment that
elicited no reprimand from Mitchell. She simply laughed and a few tit-
ters later was on to the next subject. Mitchell embodied an attitude many
of her media colleagues shared: they don't just exhibit a cynical detach-
ment from the events and people they cover, they actually enjoy the misery of others.

The media camped outside my house whenever rumors bubbled up about something happening with the case. It upset Darby so much she took action. One day, she distracted a photographer by shouting at him. The poor guy was new to his job and didn't know that he was trespassing by standing in our yard while waiting to capture me driving into my driveway. She called him "paparazzi." He said he was just there to get a photo of me. Darby asked, "How many pictures do you need of him in his car?" He was so shaken, he never got a chance to remove his lens cap as I drove up behind him, pulled into the garage, and shut the door. Our home life was punctuated by such small victories.

Several newspeople apologized to Darby, particularly photographers who said they didn't like that part of their jobs. Her response was that they didn't have to do that job. I had a little, but only a little, more compassion for them.

But then, I didn't have to deal with reporters who arrived after I'd departed for the White House and then refused to leave so Darby could take Andrew to school without his being photographed. There were other ugly moments: the mother of one of Andrew's high school friends was overheard saying how much she looked forward to my going to jail. It was too much for Darby. As soon as school was out, she took Andrew to our place in Florida and did not return until classes started that fall. I couldn't blame her—she had reached her limit.

Some other people had reached their limits, too. One of them was *Time*'s Matt Cooper. In July 2005, he faced the prospect of going to jail for one of the most sacred principles of press freedom: protecting a source. Cooper had refused to tell Special Prosecutor Fitzgerald about conversations with unnamed parties about Valerie Plame and Joe Wilson and now faced jail time if he continued to refuse to name names. Matt Cooper said he would go to jail rather than give up his sources.

Only there weren't any confidential sources. I was the source he was making a fuss about, and I had long ago officially given blanket permission through my lawyer for any reporter I had spoken with to talk to investigators. I had nothing to hide. Cooper had the waiver from the moment he got his subpoena from Fitzgerald. I assume Cooper was making a scene because he wanted to milk the drama of being a journalistic martyr, and put himself on a par with the *New York Times*'s Judith Miller, who was sent to jail July 6 for refusing to reveal her contacts with Scooter Libby.

The morning of July 13, Cooper's attorney, Dick Sauber, called my attorney, Bob Luskin. If Cooper didn't talk that day in court, he would go to jail. Sauber asked Luskin if the waiver I had given in January 2004 covered Matt Cooper. Luskin, a little irritated, asked Sauber if he had read the waiver, which covered "any person" I might have been in touch with.

Sauber asked, "Would you give any additional assurances?" Now Luskin got more than a little irritated. Sauber was trying to make me the fall guy for Cooper's melodramatic, and plainly unnecessary, refusal to testify. Now that Cooper was actually facing prison time, he was desperately constructing a way out of defending High Journalistic Principles, as if there were any involved in his situation. When confronting the real moment, he ran up the white flag. Only he still wanted to look heroic when he did it, and he wanted my help to do so.

Luskin told Sauber he wasn't going to get in the middle of whatever was going on between Sauber and Fitzgerald. "If Pat Fitzgerald wants me to do something, I am willing to do it," he told Sauber, who shot back, "Will you call Fitzgerald?" Sauber helpfully had Fitzgerald's cell number handy. Luskin was unenthusiastic about being Matt Cooper's lawyer's errand boy, but he wanted to be responsive to Fitzgerald if the prosecutor was really generating all this commotion.

Luskin dialed the number and asked the prosecutor what he wanted him to do. Fitzgerald was exasperated and told Luskin it was up to him. But Luskin did not want to meddle in whatever give-and-take had already gone on between Fitzgerald and Sauber. So he replied, "I'm not a free agent. If you don't ask to do something, I'm not going to do anything." Fitzgerald allowed it would be helpful if Luskin helped remove any of Cooper's remaining excuses. The prosecutor seemed frustrated with Cooper and his lawyer.

Luskin called Sauber back and offered to send a letter reiterating that the January 2004 waiver applied to any contact any reporter had had with me. Sauber asked if I could sign the letter. Luskin recalled the problems Scooter Libby created for himself by sending a letter to Judith Miller, which raised questions about his motives. Luskin would not put me in that spot. "No, no," Luskin replied, and said he would sign it. He drafted and e-mailed the letter a few minutes later. Sauber then sent Luskin a reply that said Luskin "[had] consulted" with me and that "Mr. Rove affirms" waiving any claim of confidentiality. Luskin had never talked to me. He was merely confirming to Sauber what anyone with a basic understanding of the English language would have known from reading the blanket waiver.

Cooper, having melted under the heat, now responded by telling a bald-faced lie. In front of a bank of cameras at the federal courthouse, Cooper said that "in what can only be described as a stunning set of developments, that person agreed to give me a personal, unambiguous, uncoerced waiver that I could speak to the grand jury." Cooper looked foolish to me. His statement implied, as a Cox News Service reporter put it, that I "had reached out to Cooper to absolve him of his pledge of confidentiality." He even suggested I encouraged him to testify.

This was false: Cooper had long ago been released from any conditions imposed by our conversation being off the record, and had never before questioned the scope of the waivers I'd signed in December 2003 and January 2004. Now, he felt he needed cover for climbing down from his "principled" defense of confidential sources, and I was it.

Cooper's stunt increased press scrutiny of me by making it appear that I had been trying to hide something. Luskin's phone already rang all day with calls by reporters trying to confirm a wild rumor or pry loose a bit of information. Things died down in the afternoon and the calls started again at 10:30 at night, when stories were posted on the Internet. Luskin ordered Darby, Andrew, and me not to read anything on the Web because so much of it was unbelievably personal and hurtful, not to mention wrong.

Meanwhile, all I could do was work as long as I could each day at the White House and hunker down at home on the weekends when the deathwatch was on, leaving for errands or a movie or a meal when the press departed. It would have been a brutally lonely summer with my family in Florida were it not for the presence of a close friend, Frank Lavin. Frank had just finished as the U.S. ambassador in Singapore and was starting as undersecretary for international trade at the Commerce Department. We'd known each other since I was the executive director of the College Republicans and he was an intern from Phillips Academy, a prep school in Andover, Massachusetts. I was the best man in his wedding. His family was still in Asia for the summer, so he moved into our spare bedroom. Smart, funny, irrepressible, Frank was about as good a presence in my house that summer as I could have hoped for. Darby's encouraging phone calls and e-mails also eased the stress.

I confess that in my frustration over being holed up, I indulged in a few juvenile pranks. One Saturday, a particularly large press contingent had collected across the street from the house on rumors of an imminent indictment. They set up large umbrellas next to their cameras; many brought lounge chairs to ease their watch. Once reporters got settled, Frank and I took turns using a remote to open my garage door. The crews would bolt from their chairs, man their cameras, and get ready to film my departure. We'd then lower the door, and they would eventually return to their chairs. When they settled in, we'd raise the garage door again. That we could inflict ourselves on the press from the comfort of two stuffed chairs in my library added to our enjoyment. I eventually had Frank's preteen daughter, Elizabeth, bring out a homemade peach pie to take the edge off any hostility our childish game might have engendered.

Late in the summer and into the fall, I started seeing strange cars parked for hours in the neighborhood. There were always two people—generally men—and it seemed to me they were watching the house. They made me extremely nervous and I was at a loss as to what to do. Who were these people and what were they doing? Rashly, I walked the dog by one of the cars for a closer look at the possible threat and was startled by a vaguely familiar face in the front seat, hidden behind dark glasses and a ball cap and partially turned away from me. It was a Secret Service officer. He and his partner were keeping watch on my family. Later, the Secret Service Uniformed Division cars that patrolled the diplomatic residences in the area took to parking in front of the house, too.

October turned out to be the cruelest month. Fitzgerald had called Luskin in early October to inform him that he wanted me to make a fourth appearance before the grand jury. He told Luskin that he felt obliged to give me a "target warning." My status—and jeopardy—had dramatically increased. If I were made a "target," it would mean that, all other things being equal, the government intended to indict me.

I got the word from Luskin about the target warning while traveling with Andrew and Darby to Texas colleges Andrew was considering. The news put a damper on what should have been a happy time. Darby immediately knew something was wrong. I told her what had happened, but decided against telling Andrew. As he happily thought about what college to attend, we wanted to shield him from the news and all that might follow from it.

My next grand jury appearance was scheduled for October 14. The day before my testimony, the media mob, now larger than before, arrived well after I'd left for the White House. Darby was concerned about the press scrum rushing her and Andrew as they went to school in her car, which was parked on the street. She called and asked me if I could let the press know I had left. I did, but also suggested she open the garage door to show them my car wasn't there. Darlene Superville of the Associated Press wrote a piece about my garage's contents, accompanied by a photograph.

By now, Luskin was drowning in press calls. Dan Bartlett suggested I hire Mark Corallo, a crisis communications specialist who used to be chief spokesman at the Department of Justice under Attorney General John Ashcroft. Corallo quickly threw himself into the media wars, relieving the demands on Luskin, and providing sage advice. Guilty of nothing, I now had both a lawyer and a "crisis communicator."

My fourth sojourn with the grand jury was brutal from the first moment. The questioning was long, rapid, and wide-ranging. I soon realized Fitzgerald was not asking questions of me but speaking to the grand jury members, painting a word picture for them. His picture, when complete, was intended to make the jury conclude I hadn't told the truth under oath.

For instance, Fitzgerald dwelt at length on Novak's 1992 article about mismanagement of the Texas Victory Committee effort. Hadn't I been his source? When I said I hadn't been, and parried with Novak's on-the-record denial at the time, Fitzgerald was dismissive.

Fitzgerald also hammered on my inability to recall talking to Cooper and my fuzziness about when exactly I had talked to Card and Gonzales. "Two by Six"—the idea that two White House staffers were tasked with calling six reporters to plant the story of Wilson's wife sending him to Africa—came back up. Fitzgerald machine-gunned me, rattling off topics whose connection to the issue of Valerie Plame I simply did not understand. He said things I knew to be untrue, seemed unconcerned with my answers, and took up lines of questioning more to say something to the grand jury than to elicit information from me. I was on the receiving end of the proverbial kitchen sink, complete with pots and pans, rolling pins, dishes, and glasses. Did I know Robert Novak had put his column about Fran Townsend to bed before I returned his call? Did I know Novak did not talk to the CIA until after he talked with me? Did I, did I, did I? During every previous visit, the grand jury members seemed bored and listless. That day, they hung on Fitzgerald's every word as he built to his conclusion.

There's an old saw that with the right grand jury, a good prosecutor can indict a ham sandwich. When Fitzgerald finished with me, I felt like that ham sandwich. I left the jury room shaken. I told Luskin the special prosecutor wanted to indict me but that it wasn't clear to me what for.

That feeling was confirmed a few days later. Luskin had long before told Fitzgerald, "Before you make up your mind, let's talk." Now the time to talk had arrived. Fitzgerald called Luskin to say, after my grand jury appearance, "All things being equal, we are inclined to indict your client." Bob broke the news to me as gently as he could, leaving the impression the danger had ratcheted up but that I was still some distance from indictment. I appreciated Bob's effort but I knew the way things were heading. I didn't sleep that night and not too well for the next week. I redoubled my efforts to keep the investigation separate from the rest of my life. But it was impossible to wall off one from the other. Luskin and Fitzgerald agreed Luskin would fly to Chicago, away from the Washington, D.C., media spotlight, for what turned out to be a monumental meeting.

Before the meeting, Luskin told Fitzgerald he appreciated that there had been no leaks from Fitzgerald's operations. But he told Fitzgerald that from his experience at the Justice Department, he knew that an operation as hermetically sealed as Fitzgerald's could become divorced from reality. Would Fitzgerald consider drawing on outsiders he respected to get a reality check about what he was learning in the case? Luskin recommended David Margolis, a highly respected career Justice official whom both men knew and who had been Luskin's mentor in his early days at the department. Fitzgerald said he'd think about it, then called back to say having some outside voices was a good idea, but he wouldn't ask Margolis. Instead Fitzgerald would draw in people in his U.S. attorney's office who had been uninvolved in the investigation. It sounded to me like he was staying inside his bubble, but Bob assured me it was better than just listening to people on the special prosecutor's task force in Washington.

Early Thursday morning, October 20, Luskin flew to Chicago to meet with Fitzgerald and two deputies. Fitzgerald raised the issue of getting the Justice Department lawyers in Washington who had been assisting him on a speakerphone. Luskin objected, saying that having people on a speakerphone lobbing in questions and comments would destroy the flow and undermine the discussion. Fitzgerald agreed. They set to work on a detailed road map that Fitzgerald's office had drawn up of the case.

Their discussions went on for hours, with Fitzgerald and Luskin volleying back and forth with a growing pile of documents on the floor. The other two lawyers sat and listened. At first, Fitzgerald and Luskin covered Fitzgerald's secondary concerns. Had I been truthful about not being Novak's source for his 1992 article on mismanagement of the senior Bush's Texas campaign? When had I talked with others in the White House about my conversation with Novak? Fitzgerald and Luskin went round and round in what Luskin later said was the most intense five hours of lawyering he has ever done.

As it turned out, Fitzgerald was a big fan of Dunkin' Donuts coffee. Every so often, the group broke for coffee and Luskin and Fitzgerald walked to the Dunkin' Donuts across the street. They were not even noticed going in and out of the building. The high-profile corruption trial of Illinois governor George Ryan was going on at the time, but Luskin and Fitzgerald passed the press scrum as if under an invisibility cloak. It was Luskin's elvish powers at work.

Luskin was unruffled and in complete command of the material. He got the sense they were dealing with side issues, none of them worthy of an indictment. Novak's 1992 piece quoting unnamed politicos critical of Rob Mosbacher's stewardship of the Texas effort for Bush 41 was small potatoes, Luskin thought.

Sure enough, Fitzgerald turned to what was really bothering him: my conversation with Matt Cooper. Was I lying about not being able to recall my phone conversation with him the morning of July 11, 2003? If I was telling the truth, they were inclined to accept my explanations on the 1992 article and everything else. But if I was lying about Cooper, then they assumed I was lying about a lot more. The Cooper conversation was the loose thread Fitzgerald was pulling on.

Luskin pushed back. Why would I tell the truth about my conversation with Novak five minutes into my first interview with the FBI in October 2003 and then intentionally try to hide my contact with Cooper—which was a much less meaningful conversation? If there was no legal exposure from talking with Novak, why would I lie about Cooper? It didn't make sense. Moreover, by the time I had talked with Cooper on the morning of July 11, I knew from a mutual friend that Novak's column would barbecue Wilson. And if I were really trying to "out" Plame, why would I discourage Cooper from writing a piece? If I were seeking to dissuade Cooper from writing, what motive was there to conceal the phone conversation? Luskin also pointed to the fact that I had brought to Fitzgerald's attention my e-mail to Steve Hadley, typed quickly after my still-unremembered call with Cooper. I wouldn't have done that if I were trying to conceal the Cooper conversation, and I certainly would have mentioned the Hadley e-mail in my February 2004 testimony if I had seen it by then. Why would I have intentionally lied about something that was confirmed by my own e-mail—which I put into their hands?

Fitzgerald allowed these were persuasive arguments and was inclined to accept them, but there was one thing he couldn't get his head around. If I didn't remember I'd talked with Cooper, then why in December 2003 or January 2004 did I ask my aides Susan Ralston, Israel Hernandez, and B. J. Goergen to find any evidence of contact with Matt Cooper—any phone records, notes, memo, or scrap of paper that would link Cooper and me? At best, my request was convincing evidence I did remember talking to Cooper. Otherwise, how would I have known even to look for evidence of a call I later claimed not to have remembered? At worst, Fitzgerald suspected, I was looking to find evidence of a contact so I could destroy it.

So after all these years—after all the grueling testimony and fear of indictment and huge legal expenditures by me—this is what it came down to. Not a violation of any law about disclosing the identity of an intelligence officer. Not breaking the 1982 Intelligence Identities Protection Act or the 1917 Espionage Act. Special Prosecutor Patrick Fitzgerald was preparing an indictment because I had told my staff to find any evidence I had contact with Matt Cooper. My request established—in Fitzgerald's mind—that my later failure to recall the conversation was a lie.

Then came the surprising answer from my lawyer's lips. "Pat, that was because of me," Luskin told Fitzgerald. In early November 2003 Bob had drinks one evening with Viveca Novak, a *Time* reporter and friend, at Cafe Deluxe. Over wine (her) and vodka (him), Novak told Luskin that her colleague Matt Cooper had insisted around *Time*'s Washington bureau that he had talked to me. Luskin was shocked—there was no evidence of a call on my logs, and in all our conversations, I had mentioned only the conversation with Bob Novak. Luskin told Viveca that Cooper must be wrong. Immediately after having that drink, Luskin called me at home to share the news. It didn't jar any recollection; I was still drawing a blank. So Luskin told me it was important to get Ralston, Hernandez, and Goergen to scour the office records to see if they might confirm the contact. I did so first thing the next morning: they ransacked the office for several days and found only an earlier phone message from Cooper, which I'd apparently not returned when Cooper called again on July 11.

Luskin's revelation stunned Fitzgerald. "You rocked my world," Fitzgerald told Luskin. The special prosecutor's intention going into the meeting had been to indict me. Now he didn't know what he would do. But nothing would happen in the immediate future as he contemplated this case-shattering revelation.

Bob called me at the White House with the news. I closed my office door when I was told who was on the line, and sat down at my desk. My legs were unable to hold me up. Bob quickly told me there would be no indictment, at least for now, and then described in detail the meeting and Fitzgerald's central concern. He was confident we could reassure the special prosecutor on the point and remove any chance of indictment. As I sat there trying to absorb all he was saying, I felt a jumble of emotions. The first was relief that the threat of being indicted, booked, arraigned, and tried was now remote.

At the same time, anger jostled with my sense of liberation. I had made four grand jury appearances, seen my wife and son subjected to countless hours of abuse and fear, depleted my family's savings to pay hundreds of thousands of dollars in legal fees, and worried endlessly about what might happen. It wasn't just me: many junior White House aides—with smaller salaries and even smaller savings—also incurred hefty legal fees. And all of this not because I'd broken any law by saying "I've heard that, too" to Bob Novak. That was ruled out very early in this drama: there was no law broken when Novak's original (and then still mysterious) source told him about Valerie Plame. No, I had faced the prospect of indictment because Patrick Fitzgerald wondered why I'd asked my staff to comb my records to see if I'd talked to Matt Cooper. Why on earth hadn't Fitzgerald simply asked me why I had done that in one of my four grand jury appearances? It could have cleared everything up then. If Fitzgerald ever broached the subject, it was in such an elliptical fashion that I didn't catch it.

Luskin had told me many times that Patrick Fitzgerald was simply doing his job. But the news of what he had been focused on simply confirmed my view that the special prosecutor was looking for a trophy. It looked like Fitzgerald had long ago concluded there had been no underlying crime. But because I'd tried to pin down if I had talked to Matt Cooper, Patrick Fitzgerald had been ready to indict me for lying to federal investigators.

In any event, I thanked Luskin profusely, barely keeping my emotions in check, and listened without comprehending as he explained what was likely to happen next. After I hung up, I dialed Darby and told her. She was both astonished at Fitzgerald's focus and relieved that Luskin had cleared up a misunderstanding. When our conversation ended, I placed the receiver in its cradle and wept. But not for long. As hard as I'd labored for three years to hide from my West Wing colleagues my fear and anguish and to shove it down into a dark hole under a heavy lid, I wasn't going to let them see me overcome with relief, either. Besides, I didn't want to jinx anything. What if Fitzgerald came up with another side issue to slap a nice big pelt on his wall? It was not going to be over until it was finally over.

Aware Luskin had had a meeting with Fitzgerald, one of Libby's lawyers, Joe Tate, called Luskin and asked, "How did it go?" Luskin allowed the conversation had been constructive. "How long?" Tate asked. When Luskin replied, "Five hours," there was silence from Tate. "We got twenty minutes," he said.

I felt it was time to take Susan Ralston and another aide who sat outside my office, Taylor Hughes, to lunch in the White House mess and apologize for being stressed the previous months. I didn't know exactly how to say it and fumbled around for a few minutes, but I could see they appreciated the effort. I couldn't tell them it was over, though I thought it was, but I owed them much for their professionalism and loyalty. Taylor was surprised by my mentioning that Scooter's kids were being teased at school about the possibility that their father would go to jail. She thought it an odd concern for me. After all, Andrew was facing the same comments about me.

A few days later, Fitzgerald called Luskin. He wanted to come by Luskin's office with the FBI's Jack Eckenrode on Tuesday, October 25, to interview him. The FBI led the questioning, putting on the record all that Bob had told Fitzgerald in Chicago. In the meantime, Luskin had called Viveca Novak to give her a heads-up that he'd given Fitzgerald her name and she would be called about their meeting.

By Thursday, October 27, Fitzgerald had let Scooter Libby's lawyers know he was going to be indicted the following day. Fitzgerald had confirmed to Luskin on the 25th that nothing would happen to me that week, at a minimum. I was nervous. It was clear Fitzgerald had originally intended to indict Libby and me on the same day. Although Luskin had been told nothing would happen for a while, I had become paranoid and didn't feel safe from the prosecutor's reach. In case the day brought bad news for me, my fellow deputy chief of staff, Joe Hagin, had my car moved to a place that would allow me to get out of the White House complex by a side gate. I would still have to face cameras at home.

But Fitzgerald didn't mention me at his news conference after indicting Libby. Instead he gave a dramatic rundown of what had happened to Ms. Plame, spoke about how an investigation works, and outlined his case for indicting Libby on five felony counts of lying to investigators and misleading the grand jury.

Before the announcement, Scooter came by my office while I was away in a meeting. Fond of mountain biking and touch football games, he was on crutches after breaking his foot. Told I was out, he said to let me know he'd stopped by. Taylor Hughes was struck by how hard and emotionless he seemed, though he tried to smile. He was gone by the time I returned from my meeting.

I still remained the object of frequent protests, mostly by young left-wingers and sometimes at my home. For example, on Saturday, October

15, three young men with huge Bush, Cheney, and Rice masks that covered their heads and torsos appeared, armed with a bullhorn. I saw them as I left to drive a houseguest to the airport. When Andrew appeared at his bedroom window, their leader spotted him and began yelling through his bullhorn, "Your father is guilty for the deaths of thousands of Iraqis! He is going to prison! I repeat, your father is going to prison!" Darby bolted out of the house and confronted him, asking him to stop. The man with the bullhorn said that he was within his rights. Darby said, "Yes, you are within your rights, and I am asking that you have some compassion." The other two masked figures started to leave and tried to get him to go. The buffoon stood there with his bullhorn and shouted his insult a few more times before heading off.

The three showed up again on Halloween, confronting Darby, me, and our neighbors at the table we had all set up on our street so we could hand out candy more easily. I might have punched one of the protesters were it not for our equally irritated neighbors, who formed a picket line and calmly walked the three idiots down the street and back to their car. It was fun for the Lefties when they had a free shot with their masks and bullhorn, but when a voluble academic, a towering investment banker, and their wives quietly expressed displeasure at their antics, they slunk away. Halloween brought out the protesters: In a previous year, we were hassled by a person wearing a Richard Nixon mask and carrying a pastel-colored submachine gun. Lucky for him, the Secret Service Uniformed Division officer nearby was good at telling the difference between fake and real weapons.

After Libby's indictment, Fitzgerald called Luskin to say he needed to record Luskin's testimony. On December 2, 2005, the special prosecutor took Luskin's deposition at the law firm of Patton Boggs. Fitzgerald had also gotten Viveca Novak's recollection of the meeting on the record and was satisfied.

On a lighter note, the *Onion* tabloid published a parody on December 21, 2005, accusing me of leaking that Santa Claus didn't exist. Fitzgerald saw it and sent an e-mail to Luskin saying he was now expanding his investigation to look into the charges. Fitzgerald had made my life hell, but I finally got to see his sense of humor.

After an inexplicable delay of almost half a year, I was summoned for a fifth appearance before the grand jury, on April 26, 2006. There had been a brief contretemps in the weeks before. Luskin had told Fitzgerald I would come but needed to be able to review my prior testimony to avoid an inadvertent contradiction. After all, my first grand jury visit had been three years before. The prosecutor refused. Luskin filed a request with the court; the motion was argued in a private hearing and Chief Judge Thomas F. Hogan quickly ruled for us. The FBI brought the transcripts over to the Patton Boggs law office for us to review.

On the way into the courthouse for my appearance, I asked Bob what the record was for grand jury appearances by a client of his. Had any of his clients done more than five? His answer brought me up short. He'd never had a client appear more than once.

I spent only a short time in the grand jury room, but it was long enough to bring my total time spent testifying to close to thirty hours—more than a full day of being grilled. Fitzgerald asked if Luskin had told me about his conversation with Viveca Novak and had I then asked my staff to search my office records? He had, and I did. When I finished, he thanked me for my answers and asked the grand jury if any of them had questions. They seemed bored: I can't remember if they asked anything. I was relieved to have faced what I hoped was my last interrogation by Patrick Fitzgerald. We never spoke again.

Luskin and I rode down in a courthouse elevator crowded with reporters who'd been assigned to the story that day. They didn't know what Luskin and I knew about the purpose of my visit, that it was to answer the prosecutor's last remaining concern. They assumed my indictment was likely and imminent. I wanted to grab them, shake them hard, and tell them I was out, free, in the clear—that they weren't going to get a story under their byline on page one, above the fold, in large type, about a White House aide's indictment and fall from grace.

But instead I joked with them while trying to project calm and good cheer as the elevator took me farther away from the nondescript grand jury room that I had come to loathe.

At just the moment in spring 2006 that all danger was dissipating, some in the press acted as if it were ramping up. Chris Matthews was the worst, predicting on air that I would soon be indicted, telling Don Imus on May 12 an indictment could come as early as that day or the next week. Matthews's MSNBC colleagues Dan Abrams and David Shuster also kept predicting my indictment, with Shuster saying on May 9, "If you are betting, do not bet on Karl Rove getting out of this." There was a certain glee in his reporting. MSNBC seemed to have made a management decision that predicting my indictment was good for ratings.

Those in the press eager for an indictment paid an inordinate amount of attention to Truthout.org, a website where blogger Jason Leopold reported on Saturday, May 13, that I had already been indicted and had been informed of it the day before at a thirteen-hour meeting with Fitzgerald in Luskin's office at Patton Boggs. Leopold said the special prosecutor had "instructed one of the attorneys to tell Rove that he has 24 business hours to get his affairs in order, high level sources with direct knowledge of the meeting said." Leopold's article was a complete fabrication by "a journalist who has battled drug addiction and mental illness and been convicted of grand larceny," as the *Washington Post*'s Howard Kurtz helpfully pointed out nine days later. Fitzgerald got a kick out of the fictitious account and e-mailed Luskin to see how he felt after such a long day.

Still, Luskin's phone lit up with reporters who took their cue from a nut with Internet access. Thirty-five reporters called Luskin or Corallo to ask about the Truthout report. As luck would have it, Luskin had taken his cat, Charlotte, to the veterinarian for her annual physical and hadn't been in his office the day of the alleged meeting. An enterprising reporter tracked down Luskin's vet and called the clinic. But it turns out that there is kitty-doctor confidentiality and the vet would neither confirm nor deny Charlotte's visit. Luskin had fun with any reporter stupid enough to call him about the blog by passing on the news that Charlotte's "stools were free of harmful parasites, which is more than I can say for this case."

Finally, on Monday, June 12, 2006—just shy of three years after Bob Novak's column appeared—Patrick Fitzgerald called Bob Luskin to say no action would be taken against me. He would send a letter confirming this and authorizing Bob to make the news public the next day.

Luskin reached me on the phone as I sat on the runway at Reagan National Airport, waiting to fly to New Hampshire. The plane was full, but I felt completely alone, with every last bit of energy used up. I was limp. I knew I would not be coherent if I called Darby, and besides, the cabin doors were closing. I asked Bob to call her: it would mean a lot if Darby heard the news from him. He got ahold of her as she was driving her aunt, Bea McRae, and her cousin, Janet Lovitt, to the airport to return home to Mississippi after attending Andrew's high school graduation. My sister-in-law, Perla Hickson, was in the car. That was one emotional automobile. The women said a collective prayer of gratitude. Darby and Perla stopped at the National Cathedral on the way home from the airport to give thanks. When I arrived home that night, I still felt numb. The threat was gone, but so were all my emotions.

The next day, Luskin released a written statement saying, "In deference to the pending case, we will not make any further public statements about the subject matter of the investigation. We believe the special counsel's decision should put an end to the baseless speculation about Mr. Rove's conduct." Characteristically, Fitzgerald's spokesman refused all comment.

While neither I nor the White House communications shop wanted any dancing with the ball in the end zone, Mark Corallo urged me to be seen by press cameras and to, for God's sake, be smiling. I enlisted Taylor Hughes to walk with me to a meeting in the Eisenhower Executive Office Building, and tipped off the press. The *New York Times*'s cutline called Taylor "an unidentified aide." Her photo sparked an Internet contest on the hottest White House aide. She won.

My ordeal was at long last over. But I was not elated or joyously relieved. I was still in shock, perhaps the result of steeling myself for bad news and walling off the investigation from the rest of my existence. Darby and I had been freezing our faces into masks for so long, we were now subdued in our reaction. We feared upsetting things, creating some new situation that might lead to further anguish and danger. It was difficult to celebrate, even when the neighbors brought over a special cake from Watergate Pastry with "Congratulations" written on top in blue frosting, surrounded by six strawberries. It tasted like ashes; everything had lost its flavor.

In July, the Wilsons filed a civil suit seeking damages from the vice president, Scooter, and me. They were unsuccessful in cashing in. The good news was that the federal government paid the legal tab on that case.

Only one public mystery remained: Who was Novak's original source? On August 29, 2006, the mysterious leaker was revealed to the world: it was Richard L. Armitage, Colin Powell's deputy at State and a consummate Washington insider. The manner in which Armitage's involvement became known was classic Armitage: former colleagues of his leaked it to the *Washington Post,* and, I suspect, at his direction. The media did not stake out his home as they had previously done mine. No footage materialized on the network news that night of him entering his home or leaving in his car. No angry *New York Times* editorial erupted the next day. And Andrea Mitchell certainly didn't go on Imus to chortle at prison rape jokes involving the stocky weightlifter-diplomat. Armitage was one of Washington's privileged insiders and part of the ruling class. The *Washington Post* did, however, reward Armitage with an exculpatory editorial that said he "was not out to punish" Joe Wilson. The *Post* also noted that had Armitage's role been known earlier, the investigation and all that followed it might have been avoided. I agree.

So why wasn't it known earlier? I had gone to Chief of Staff Andy Card and White House Counsel Alberto Gonzales in the fall of 2003 and told them about my conversation with Bob Novak. Armitage didn't come forward to tell anyone at the White House. Instead, General Counsel William H. Taft IV of the State Department told Gonzales in the fall of 2003 that the Department had information about the incident pertinent to the investigation but would share it with Justice only, not the White House. Powell, Armitage, and Taft hid from the White House the fact that Armitage had been Novak's source even as I coughed up what I'd said, to whom, and when. Powell even went on television at the end of September 2003 and denied any knowledge of the incident. Had Armitage not told even his boss by then?

Powell had an odd reaction to the whole affair. I ran into him at a formal Washington dinner in 2007. He was blocking the aisle and grandly grabbed my hand and boomed out that he had someone he wanted me to say hello to. With that, he turned aside to reveal his guest, Rich Armitage, standing behind him. Powell laughed and grinned broadly as Armitage and I awkwardly shook hands and said hello. The former secretary enjoyed the spectacle.

I ran into Armitage two years later in a security line at Dulles Airport. Darby was with me. I told Armitage I was delighted to see him because my wife had always wanted to meet him. He blanched, mumbled a "pleased to meet you" to Darby, and fled as quickly as he could. It was petty on my part but I felt better for it.

Luskin, who says he never stepped as close to the edge with a client as he did with me, has a charitable view of Patrick Fitzgerald. The prosecutor never leaked, and he treated Luskin with respect and was forthcoming about his evidence and his concerns. Not every prosecutor would have acted that way. Most would have held on to their evidence until I was on the stand and then sprung it on me Perry Mason–style to pin me "to a wall like a butterfly," Luskin says. All fair points, and I accept them. But there is another side to the ledger. How many prosecutors, having found no underlying offense, would have kept at it as Patrick Fitzgerald did?

On November 4, 2005, I cut from the newspaper a photo of Scooter Libby and his wife in the backseat of a car on the way to his arraignment. I put it in my home office desk drawer. I have looked at it frequently in the years since so as not to forget that moment. But for the work of a brilliant lawyer in unraveling and ending the quixotic obsession of a special prosecutor, there went I.

CHAPTER 29

Katrina

———— •◆• ————

I know y'all are trying as hard as you can, but it ain't cuttin' it," the president said. "I wanna know why. We gotta do better."

The president was speaking in a Situation Room videoconference on Friday, September 2, 2005, four days after Hurricane Katrina hit the Gulf Coast and hours before Bush himself would visit the region. Also participating were Secretaries Rice and Rumsfeld; Secretary of Homeland Security Michael Chertoff; Secretary of Housing and Urban Development Alphonso Jackson; the chairman of the Joint Chiefs of Staff, General Richard Myers; FEMA director Michael Brown; Army Lieutenant General Russel Honoré; Andy Card, Steve Hadley, me, and others. Bush was annoyed at conflicting reports about the number of refugees at the Superdome and New Orleans Convention Center and whether food and water were being delivered. It was a frustrating moment at the end of the terrible week of the most devastating storms to hit the United States in a century.

When she finally dissipated, Katrina had killed more than 1,700 people, made 450,000 refugees, destroyed more than 300,000 homes, and caused an estimated $125 billion in damage.

The entire Gulf Coast had been vulnerable to Katrina's immense power—but no place more than New Orleans, which sits mostly below sea level and is surrounded by water. Computer models had long anticipated a horrific disaster if a Katrina-like storm ever hit the city.

. That is why National Hurricane Center director Max Mayfield urged New Orleans mayor Ray Nagin to issue a mandatory evacuation the previous Saturday. The city's own emergency plan, required under federal law, specified for Nagin to order one seventy-two hours in advance of any hurricane's landfall. But when Mayfield called Nagin, no evacuation had been ordered and only thirty-four hours remained before Katrina's expected landfall on Monday morning. "This was only the second time I called a politician in my life," Mayfield told *Time* magazine. "I wanted to be able to go to sleep knowing I had done everything I could do."

And Mayfield had. Unfortunately, Mayor Nagin and Louisiana governor Kathleen Blanco had not. According to a bipartisan congressional report, "Neither Blanco nor Nagin . . . ordered a mandatory evacuation until Sunday morning. . . . This extraordinary storm required extraordinary measures, which the Governor and Mayor did not take." Nagin delayed the evacuation order while his legal staff researched whether the city would be liable for the costs of closing hotels and other businesses if it turned out to be a false alarm. Sunday morning at 9:14 Central, in a move that has gained little attention, President Bush called Blanco to plead that she and Nagin carry out the evacuation plan. The mayor finally issued the order moments later at 9:30 A.M. on Sunday—only twenty-one hours before landfall. Had Nagin issued the order on Friday, most of the estimated seventy thousand people stranded in New Orleans would have been out of harm's way—perhaps on school buses that were later photographed parked underwater, or on the special Amtrak train that left the city Sunday night virtually empty.

In an August 28 Sunday morning videoconference between the president, FEMA director Brown, and disaster emergency officials from throughout the region, federal preparations drew strong praise from Louisiana officials. Colonel Jeff Smith, deputy director of the Louisiana Office of Homeland Security and Emergency Preparedness, said Governor Blanco "is very appreciative of the federal resources that have come into the state and the willingness to give us everything you've got," later telling the president that "our coordination is as good as it can be." Smith's deputy talked of the evacuations then under way, saying "we're way ahead of the game there," while Smith claimed "the evacuation process is going much better than it did during Hurricane Ivan" in 2004. When Brown asked Smith, "Do you have any unmet needs?" the Louisianan quickly answered, "No."

On Monday, August 29, the president was in Arizona when Katrina came ashore south of Buras, Louisiana, at 6:10 A.M. With winds of 150 miles per hour and storm surges of thirty-four feet, the hurricane then moved northeast over the Gulf and hit land again near Pearlington, Mississippi. Bush flew later that day to San Diego. The early reports we received on the road were that the storm damage was contained, the levees were holding, and that New Orleans would be spared. But that hope gave way when the Lower Ninth Ward's levee breached. By 2:00 P.M., 20 percent of the city was flooded. Eighty percent of New Orleans would soon be underwater.

In a sign of a fundamental problem, however, Secretary of Homeland Security Michael Chertoff was not receiving accurate information. At 10 A.M., officials in the Louisiana disaster emergency center in Baton Rouge told him the levees were holding. White House Deputy Chief of Staff Joe Hagin asked Blanco about the levees and the Superdome and was assured they were both okay. At 1 P.M., Chertoff talked with Brown, who was in Baton Rouge with Louisiana officials. Brown reiterated that the levees were holding. He was hearing the same reports the Louisianans were. This led Chertoff and the White House to believe the storm damage was not as bad as it actually was. It wasn't until late Monday night that word that the levees had been breached began to make its way up the chain of command. It was early Tuesday morning before Chertoff was told. False reports plagued us every step of the way.

Bush spent Monday night in San Diego monitoring the situation and speaking with Cabinet and White House officials. He awoke before dawn on Tuesday to learn that the Seventeenth Street Canal levee had been overwhelmed. Lake Pontchartrain, Louisiana's largest lake, would soon flood the city. By the time we arrived back in Crawford, Texas, Tuesday night, Bush had decided we would fly to Washington Wednesday morning. This would allow Cabinet members and key staffers, many spread across the country on vacation, to convene.

As Bush returned to Washington on Wednesday, Air Force One was diverted to fly low over New Orleans and the devastated Mississippi Gulf Coast to allow the president to see for himself some of the damage. This drew waves of criticism of Bush for not landing to personally inspect the damage, a topic to which I will return. After arriving at the White House and being briefed, the president gave a Rose Garden update on the relief effort. His remarks were heavy on statistics—the number of meals being transported, the liters of water and pounds of ice on the way. But the public was seeing gripping television images of thousands of stranded people, many without food or water, pleading for help.

In a sign of how bad things were, thousands upon thousands of people had taken shelter in the Convention Center. This was unplanned, so state officials had not stockpiled food and water. After Chertoff was asked about the situation on Thursday on National Public Radio, he called General Russel Honoré, who had been designated commander of the joint federal task force responsible for coordinating military relief efforts. The report came back that people were in the Convention Center parking lot, barbecuing. A total of fifteen hundred people were stranded, Chertoff was told. Chertoff insisted the building be searched. When it was, ten to fifteen thousand hungry, thirsty, dirty refugees were discovered in dark squalor. Inexplicably, National Guardsmen were also in the facility but did not interact with the refugees. Food and water were immediately dispatched and arrangements made to move them as quickly as possible.

Behind the scenes, White House staff engaged in a complicated, high-stakes legal and constitutional battle with Louisiana's governor—which had huge ramifications for New Orleans and the administration.

As events unfolded, it became clear that Ray Nagin was no Rudy Giuliani and Kathleen Blanco was no Haley Barbour, the governor of neighboring Mississippi who responded with enormous skill and alacrity when Katrina smashed his state. Nagin and Blanco were, by almost every account, overwhelmed and overmatched by events. And their respective staffs were extremely critical of each other, which made cooperation even more problematic. To be fair to the governor and the mayor, they faced a unique situation; no American city of the size of New Orleans had ever been submerged before. Nevertheless, they were simply not up to the challenge.

For example, when Blanco called the White House early Wednesday morning to speak to the president, he was then airborne. She was connected with Homeland Security advisor Fran Townsend. Blanco told her,

"Send everything you've got!" Townsend asked the governor what she needed. Blanco simply repeated she needed Washington to "send everything you've got!" Townsend told the governor she wasn't able to guess what the governor was requesting and could Townsend speak to her National Guard adjutant general or her disaster emergency director to find out what specifically the state needed? Townsend was finally put in touch with someone in Louisiana who provided a list.

Later that day Blanco reached the president. "I just asked him for help," she later said. But this time she had a specific request—forty thousand federal troops. "I just pulled a number out of the sky," she later admitted. But what Blanco couldn't say was what she needed them for, which would dictate the kind of units we would dispatch. Did she need engineering, medical, or other specialized support? If she just needed bodies to hand out water and deliver MREs, she had thousands of Louisiana National Guard and agreements with every other governor to dispatch available National Guard units upon request.

It seemed her big concern was public safety: she wanted the U.S. military to restore order. But that was illegal. Since the Posse Comitatus Act of 1878, the military cannot be used for law enforcement and only the president can command the U.S. military, not state or local officials. Blanco didn't seem to get this.

From our perspective, we needed a unity of command. Because we weren't getting clear information or specific requests from Blanco, our strong preference was to "federalize" the event. That would have placed the National Guard and all other state and local entities involved under federal direction, namely, under General Honoré. A native Louisianan known in the military as "the Ragin' Cajun," he was the right man.

But there are only two ways the federal government can take over. The first is for the governor to request it. California governor Pete Wilson had done just that after the Northridge earthquake in 1994, knowing the response was beyond the state's capacity. The other way is for the president to declare a region in a "state of insurrection" under the 1807 Insurrection Act and send in troops to put down the "revolt."

FEMA director Mike Brown asked Governor Blanco to request that the administration federalize the effort on Tuesday, the day after Katrina hit. She declined. The issue went back and forth for two more days, with Townsend getting information via back channels that the governor's adjutant general was insisting the governor not surrender control. Whether this was true and, if so, whether it was because he feared her being shunted aside or simply did believe there were enough National Guard from Louisiana and surrounding states available is not clear.

There was resistance within the administration to sending in the U.S. military, both because it was believed plenty of National Guard troops would get to New Orleans sooner and because the Department of Defense was understandably concerned about having the U.S. military arresting looters, shooting snipers, and policing the Superdome. The better solution was to federalize the National Guard with the blessing of the governor and let Honoré coordinate the local police, the state and federal disaster management, the National Guard, and any U.S. military units he might request. But since Blanco wasn't going to agree to this action, we had to decide if the president should strip a sitting governor of her authority over disaster efforts—an act almost unprecedented in American history.

This is where things stood on Friday morning as the president flew to the region. By now he was extremely (and understandably) unhappy with the response of every level of government—state, local, and federal. "The results are not acceptable," he said grim-faced as he left the White House around 9:00 A.M. Eastern. As we were heading to the Gulf Coast region, Governor Blanco dispatched 6,500 National Guard troops to help restore order to New Orleans.

We flew into Mobile at 10:30 A.M. to meet Mississippi governor Barbour and Alabama governor Bob Riley, began viewing Katrina's damage along the Mississippi coast about 12:30 P.M., and then choppered into New Orleans.

"I don't think anybody can be prepared for the vastness of the destruction," Bush said after walking through Biloxi, Mississippi. The president comforted two weeping sisters whose house had collapsed. Another woman told Bush how she and her family and neighbors, including two children, ages two and five, had ridden out the storm for five hours on a small flat boat named the S.S. *Minnow* (after the boat in the 1960s television series *Gilligan's Island*). "The only one not crying," the woman said, "was the 5-year-old girl." This story caused Bush to tear up.

I wandered the streets as the president toured neighborhoods and came upon a man dressed in a New Orleans Saints T-shirt, shorts, and flip-flops. He was a native Mississippian who had gone east to work in Atlantic City casinos as a young man. But when his home state began allowing casinos along the Gulf Coast, he and his wife returned to the region they loved and bought a lovely home overlooking the water. Now, he told me, all that remained was a slab of concrete and the clothes on his back. He and his wife rode out the storm in the vault at the bank where she worked. They were sleeping there still. It was heart wrenching, yet through his tears, he said they'd stay, rebuild, and never leave. We soon boarded choppers for an aerial survey.

From the air, it looked like the hand of God had wiped off the map the entire fifty-mile Mississippi coastline. I could see a wavy pattern back off the beach along the entire coast. It was the wall of debris created where the hurricane surge had crested and dropped the pieces of homes, buildings, trees, and cars in its grip.

It was on this trip that Bush made his infamous "Brownie, you're doing a heck of a job!" comment about FEMA director Mike Brown. Bush's comment about Brown is well-known. What is almost never aired are Riley's and Barbour's remarks immediately preceding Bush's. Both governors complimented Brown, with Riley saying, "I want to thank Mike Brown and his staff. FEMA has absolutely been great." Barbour followed by saying, "I want to join with Bob. The federal government is great—FEMA and all of your people who are on the ground." Bush was responding to compliments others had offered to Brown and attempting to buck up the spirits of a man who was under siege. That, rather than piling on, is a Bush instinct. Brown was soon relieved of his duties—but the president was not going to denounce him in public.

I identified with the president's instinct, but I had opposed Brown's being named FEMA director following Joe Allbaugh's resignation in March 2003, because I didn't think he had the background for the job: he had been the judges and stewards commissioner for the International Arabian Horse Association before serving as FEMA general counsel.

Bush knew I hadn't been for Brown, so when I traveled with the president to Florida to survey hurricane damage in 2004 and heard compliments of Brown, the president jokingly suggested I owed the FEMA director an apology. I sought Brown out to tell him about the praise being thrown his way. Governor Jeb Bush was within hearing distance and told me afterward I was mistaken: state and local officials, not the feds, always did the important work. I didn't realize then just how right he was.

In Brown's defense, FEMA did right by Alabama and Mississippi. Both had well-organized state emergency efforts that worked seamlessly with the agency, other federal departments, and local governments. That was not the case with Louisiana; the state was dysfunctional, as every after-action analysis of Katrina has shown. FEMA's structures and procedures simply could not make up for the inability of local and state governments to execute basic functions.

In a natural disaster, the affected area's state government is in charge, not FEMA. The 1988 Stafford Act is the federal law governing disaster relief. It says that before Washington can provide assistance "the Governor shall take appropriate response action under State law and direct execution of the State's emergency plan." After a presidential declaration, the federal government can provide resources "in support of State and local assistance efforts . . . coordinate all disaster relief assistance . . . provide technical and advisory assistance to affected State and local governments" and "assist State and local governments in the distribution" of medicine, food, and other emergency supplies. But nowhere does the Stafford Act say the federal government is in charge; FEMA provides assistance in response to state requests and picks up most of the tab.

Our helicopters arrived at the last stop of the trip, the New Orleans International Airport, where Governor Blanco met us. Also waiting were Senators Mary Landrieu and David Vitter, as well as Congressmen Bobby Jindal and William Jefferson. New Orleans mayor Ray Nagin was already aboard Air Force One, which was good, since we had been worried over the past few days about even finding him.

The emergency command center in City Hall had been abandoned at some point Tuesday, and it was unclear how much Nagin had been there before it was shut down. We had to count on rare moments when he was in a truck or car with his cell phone recharging. I'd dial his cell again and again until he answered. On Thursday I let him know we were coming the next day, and then connected again that morning to confirm we'd meet at Air Force One, which would fly into the New Orleans airport while we choppered over the Mississippi coast. Nagin said he hadn't bathed or had a hot meal since before the hurricane, so I arranged for him to use the president's shower on Air Force One and the crew to feed him. Though the mayor was prone to extreme public statements, he and the president developed a friendly relationship, which didn't stop Nagin from springing unpleasant surprises.

We met with the president in Air Force One's conference room. Bush sat at the head of the table with Homeland Security secretary Michael Chertoff at the opposite end. Nagin sat immediately to Bush's left with the senators next to him. Blanco sat to the president's right with the congressmen next to her. I was immediately behind her, seated on the couch. The mayor and governor both seemed shell-shocked, scattered, and without a clue as to what they needed.

The president tried to get a situation report from the governor and the mayor, but they had little useful information. As they tried to share what little they had, Senator Landrieu broke in with a wild, emotional outburst about how children were dying on rooftops and in attics all over New Orleans. She calmed down and the conversation between the president, governor, and mayor resumed. A few minutes later, Landrieu did it again. She established a pattern early on of making outlandish, totally unsubstantiated charges and ridiculous requests. I understood how upsetting the situation was, but now was not the time to break down. Everything that could be done to pluck people off rooftops was being done.

It became clear that four days into the crisis, the governor and the mayor were simply not communicating with each other. At one point, Nagin suggested that Honoré be put in charge of the whole effort. That was our position. But Blanco was against it. The conversation took an astonishing turn when it sounded as if Nagin and Blanco were each saying the other was responsible for public safety in New Orleans. To clarify it, the president asked Nagin who was responsible for public safety in his city. Nagin allowed that it was the governor. Bush then asked the same question of Blanco. After a few moments, she blurted out, "I think it's the mayor." That captured, in a nutshell, our problem.

The president then asked the governor to join him in the forward cabin and reviewed with her the issues we had been grappling with for days. He reminded her that federal law prohibited the military from being turned over to a governor in order to provide law enforcement. The president reminded her of the two ways to "federalize" the disaster: she could request it, or Bush could declare southeast Louisiana in a "state of insurrection." Bush was willing to do the latter: units of the 82nd Airborne were standing by and could be on the ground within hours. But the message would be that Louisiana's officials were incompetent and unable to keep the peace.

The president was even willing to share a command structure if Blanco requested federalization: Honoré would report to her as commander of the National Guard units and to Bush as commander of the U.S. military. She left Bush thinking she might accept that arrangement, but she wanted twenty-four hours to mull it over. Bush didn't think New Orleans could afford the delay.

We tried to speed the process up upon our return to Washington later that day. Shortly before midnight, Chief of Staff Andy Card faxed a proposed "Memorandum of Agreement Concerning Authorization, Consent and Use of Dual Status Commander for JTF [Joint Task Force] Katrina"—making Honoré a member of the Louisiana National Guard. National Guard troops would not have to be put under federal control, since Honoré would be under the governor's command. Honoré would report to Blanco in his role as a Louisiana National Guard officer and to Washington in his role as a regular Army officer. We would get the coordination and a capable leader while Blanco's fears about ceding authority over the National Guard would be allayed. But even before the memo was sent to Baton Rouge, Townsend heard it would be turned down. Blanco rejected it the next morning. Meanwhile, tens of thousands of National Guard moved to New Orleans or to staging areas around Baton Rouge.

Experts were not certain the reports of looting, gunfire, and disturbances in New Orleans would meet the legal test of an insurrection, but the collapse of the city's police department and the inability of the state police to get control of the situation worried us. At Townsend's suggestion, Attorney General Alberto Gonzales and FBI director Robert Mueller had been given the job of rounding up federal law enforcement agents from Immigrations and Customs, DEA, FBI, and any other agency that had "Section 1812" powers. That's the part of the federal code that spells out who can carry a badge, make an arrest, and perform other law enforcement duties. The first of what became four hundred federal law enforcement agents moved toward New Orleans on Thursday.

By Saturday morning, September 3, the president had decided he wasn't going to let the muddle on the ground keep him from acting. He authorized the dispatch of 7,200 active-duty U.S. military to the area, the first major commitment of regular ground forces in the crisis. The Pentagon also announced an additional 10,000 National Guard troops would be sent to Louisiana and Mississippi, raising the total Guard contingent to about 40,000.

The U.S. military could not perform law enforcement duties, but National Guardsmen—paired with federal, state, and local law enforcement officials—could. We felt that if we sent the military, they could relieve law enforcement officials, who could resume their policing duties. If arrests needed to be made, we hoped there would be local or state police officers nearby who could be called upon. We were skirting the law, but conditions demanded it. In the end, Honoré effectively federalized the situation through the sheer force of personality, if not formally. Nagin was a big fan of Honoré and the state adjutant was terrified of crossing him, as was most everyone else.

Even then, we were fearful of an incident. The military is trained to attack and kill. Police are trained to contain, disarm, and arrest. Skills important in Iraq were not the same ones needed to restore order in New Orleans. Fortunately, the city turned out to be far less lawless than the media projected, so no incidents occurred.

Seventeen days after Katrina's landfall, President Bush stood in a deserted Jackson Square in New Orleans's French Quarter to deliver a prime-time address to the nation. He commended the rescue efforts and turned the nation's attention to the task of rebuilding. "The federal government will be fully engaged," he promised, "but Governor Barbour, Governor Blanco, Mayor Nagin, and other state and local leaders will have the primary role in planning for their own future."

Bush announced that an unprecedented $60 billion in disaster relief had been appropriated. Washington eventually would commit twice that amount to rescue, recovery, and rebuilding efforts. Bush also named Donald E. Powell, the head of the Federal Deposit Insurance Corporation and a former Texas banker, as coordinator of Gulf Coast Rebuilding to cut red tape and speed Washington's aid. One of Blanco's early requests was to spend half a billion dollars of housing assistance money on a tourism advertising campaign. We turned that idea down.

No amount of federal aid could get around Louisiana's dysfunctional political habits. When Katrina hit, Louisiana Office of Homeland Security and Emergency Preparedness officials were already under federal investigation for waste, mismanagement, and missing funds—and one was later convicted. There was a striking disparity between the pace of recovery efforts in Mississippi and Louisiana, and it can be explained by their different political cultures. I saw this firsthand on every one of the thirteen event-packed trips we made to the Gulf Coast—but never clearer than on March 1, 2007.

We flew into Mississippi and were met by Governor and Mrs. Barbour, two mayors, and the Mississippi National Guard adjutant general. The group toured Long Beach, meeting with families getting back on their feet with help from FEMA and the Mississippi recovery effort. Then it was on to Biloxi City Hall to meet with about fifty local elected officials and community leaders. It was remarkable how focused everyone was on practical, step-by-step actions to bring their communities back. There were no demands for billions more in federal dollars. We were asked to encourage Louisiana mosquito-abatement district officials to return calls from their Mississippi counterparts about joint eradication efforts. Could something be done about modifying a U.S. Fish and Wildlife ruling on wetlands that was hampering the recovery? These people were under a lot of pressure but were focused on timetables, action, and results. We choppered on to New Orleans.

We had a late lunch with state and local elected officials and leaders of the state's recovery efforts at Lil' Dizzy's, a classic French Quarter dive locals don't mention to tourists for fear it will become too crowded. The place looked like it was falling down. Inside were bowed walls, warped wooden floors, battered tables and chairs. But this being New Orleans, the food was good beyond description. We appreciated the Louisiana custom of arranging meetings around meals.

That turned out to be the only good part of the lunch. Unlike the Mississippi meeting, there was no agenda, organization, or sense of progress. The president tried to bring order by suggesting that Mayor Nagin and each of the parish presidents report on the recovery in their areas. Nagin offered a largely incoherent, rambling comment, and pointed a finger at state officials for every problem. Then each parish president had his say. There were plenty of complaints about the slow pace of the state in getting checks of up to $150,000 to eligible homeowners whose homes were destroyed or severely damaged by Katrina. Mississippi had already settled almost all the claims for housing assistance. In eight months, Louisiana had fully processed just 2,780 out of 111,887 applications. No one in the room—not even the Louisianans in charge of the program—knew how to speed things up.

I was sandwiched between the best and the worst of the parish presidents near one corner of the table. To my right was Jefferson Parish president Aaron Broussard, who crisply reported on rebuilding in the suburbs west of New Orleans. He had concerns about the state housing program, but the parish had plenty of sales tax revenues and FEMA and state funds. His report was professional. To my left was then–St. Bernard Parish president "Junior" Rodriguez.

Junior offered a different tone. Officials in Rodriguez's parish were under scrutiny for authorizing extensive overtime pay to parish employees in the recovery efforts. He started by pointing toward Nagin and complaining about "chocolate man there," making reference to an unfortunate moment when the mayor had expressed his hope New Orleans would remain a majority African-American, or "chocolate," city. Then Junior jammed his thumb toward Congressman William Jefferson, sitting to his left. "Now old Jeff here, he done put da' money in da' refrigerator. That's real cool hard cash," Junior proclaimed. Everyone in the room tightened at this reference to Jefferson, in whose freezer FBI agents had discovered $90,000 in marked bills back in August 2005. (He would eventually be convicted of eleven counts of bribery, racketeering, and money laundering.) Rodriguez was just getting warmed up. "Now I'm telling people I done put da' money I stole in my septic tank because da' septic man told me he'd give me half off if I'd dig up my tank myself, and I want those FBI boys who are investigating me to do it for me!" His show was entertaining but not very helpful.

We worked our way around the room to each parish president. One asked the president to revise upward a debris-removal contract a friend had won immediately after Katrina by undercutting other bidders; Bush demurred. Then Archbishop Alfred Hughes was asked about the Catholic Church's extraordinary efforts in helping restart New Orleans schools. The church, Teach For America, community leaders, and New Orleans expatriates such as Walter Isaacson, the bestselling author and chairman of the Aspen Institute, vowed to use Katrina to turn around the city's failed school system. As the archbishop described the heroic strides to get schools back open, Junior started whispering in my ear that the archbishop was "a goddamn liar." The problem was Junior's whisper could be heard around the room. The more the archbishop talked, the louder and more agitated Junior got. I could not figure out how the archbishop was provoking Junior's wrath. "If he says dat again, I'm going to call him a liar!" he said to no one in particular. "I may go to hell for it, but he's a goddamn liar!"

After the lunch finally drew to a close, City Council president Oliver Thomas had a few words with the president. The New Orleans council president has almost as much power as the mayor, and Thomas made it clear he wanted to work with Don Powell and felt reasonable agreements could be made on any remaining issues. Afterward, Bush remarked it was good that at least one New Orleans official had his head on straight and his focus right. We toured an impressive charter school, a new housing development, and then returned to Air Force One.

Just before we got airborne, Nagin announced he was filing a $77 billion lawsuit against the Army Corps of Engineers. He had failed to mention it at lunch. The suit was dismissed the following January. Then, on August 13, 2007, City Council president and mayoral hopeful Oliver Thomas was indicted for solicitation of a bribe and, uncharacteristically for a New Orleans politician, soon resigned from office and pled guilty. Nagin was later reelected mayor, defeating Louisiana lieutenant governor Mitch Landrieu, the senator's brother.

JOURNALISTS AND THE FEDERAL government itself took opportunities to enumerate the mistakes we made around Katrina. I have my own list. First, we did not have the ability to get real-time information and so did not realize the initial reports we were getting were wrong. The most important of 125 recommendations contained in the assessment of the federal response was to develop a system to provide FEMA directly with real-time information—what emergency management people call "situational awareness."

Our second big mistake was flying over the region in Air Force One on Wednesday, rather than landing. We shouldn't have dropped into New

Orleans, because it would have been disruptive, but we should have gone to Baton Rouge, the site of Louisiana's disaster command center.

I'm one of the people responsible for this mistake. From observing 9/11 and disaster recovery efforts after other hurricanes and tornadoes, I knew time is precious in the hours immediately after a disaster. A presidential visit can interfere with those efforts. A president can't pull people off roofs in flooded neighborhoods or get bottled water and MREs to dehydrated, hungry, displaced individuals—but his presence can delay the rescue workers who do. So I argued the president should not drop into New Orleans Wednesday but rather come back two days later. Governor Barbour called Joe Hagin twice to plead that the president not come Wednesday. Hagin asked Governor Blanco and she agreed, as did her very political staff.

Our decision was right for the relief effort but wrong for President Bush's public standing. In disasters like Katrina, a president can come across as unengaged if he is not seen in a crowded command center, moving through flooded neighborhoods on an airboat, or surveying damage close up from a chopper.

But our worst mistake was that we did not seize control of the situation in Louisiana sooner. As the Air Force One meeting showed, Nagin and Blanco couldn't even agree on who was responsible for public safety in New Orleans. The president should have ordered a federal takeover and taken the heat for pushing Louisiana officials aside. Honoré was up to the task of cutting through the disinformation, making critical decisions, understanding what was needed, and pushing everyone into action. And we should have sent the U.S. military troops in right away, regardless of Pentagon objections. We were too passive for too long. Louisiana's failures became our failures anyway.

Early press reports—of ten thousand dead, of rapes and murders and gunshots in the Superdome—added to the sense of chaos and horror and turned out to be largely false. However, they shaped people's early and ultimately permanent impressions and some may have even cost some people their lives (cable news reports of a sniper on the Superdome caused rescue bus drivers and medical workers to refuse to approach it for several hours, fearing for their own safety).

Yet tens of thousands of people came together to pull off one of history's largest rescue operations, moving about a quarter of a million residents out of a flooded city in a week. The Department of Defense's response was the largest military deployment inside the United States since the Civil War. And some efforts, especially by the Coast Guard and faith-based institutions, were heroic.

In the end, Katrina led to dozens of critical reforms in how the federal government responds to emergencies and how states and communities plan for natural disasters. The administration followed through on Bush's Jackson Square pledges, providing $120.7 billion for recovery, disaster response, levee repair, flood protection, health care, housing, education, and relocation assistance. Other cities looked at New Orleans's delay in ordering a mandatory evacuation and learned its high cost.

It galled me that Bush was blamed for the failures of Blanco and Nagin, but he was more interested in getting the Gulf Coast back on its feet. To reduce the blame game, he deliberately took more on his own shoulders than he should have, saying, "When the Federal Government fails to meet such an obligation, I, as President, am responsible for the problem, and for the solution."

Mississippians recognized the help Washington provided. Led by Governor Barbour and local leaders, the recovery effort there was a model. In Louisiana, the people of New Orleans stepped up when their public servants let them down. Thousands of ordinary people with no history of activism but with a deep love for their city cleaned up debris, opened up schools, rebuilt homes, replanted trees, restored neighborhoods, and showed that the Crescent City would not be destroyed by even the mightiest of winds.

They voted out a corrupt congressman and voted in a tough district attorney, their first inspector general, and the most reform-oriented City Council in memory. Dedicated educators, the Catholic Church, and business leaders reversed a decades-old decline in the schools. The city's world-famous artists, musicians, and chefs charged back into New Orleans, providing the energy to revitalize decimated neighborhoods and reinvigorate the local economy. Today, there are more restaurants open in New Orleans than before Katrina, joining new museums, art galleries, and music clubs. The city will host the NCAA basketball Final Four in 2012 and the Super Bowl in 2013. Unemployment is low and the city's prospects as a center for exports, trade, and tourism are bright.

But Louisiana remains Louisiana. So in 2017, when New Orleans revels in its unique heritage and becomes one of America's few large cities to celebrate its tercentennial, some local politicians will still likely be using Katrina as a political billy club. And you know who their target will be.

CHAPTER 30

Republicans on the Run

———— • ◆ • ————

Two thousand and six started with a bang, literally. On February 11, 2006, just before 6 P.M. Central, Vice President Dick Cheney accidentally shot my lawyer during a weekend quail hunt in South Texas.

My ties to the incident could have set off every conspiracy nut in America. The accident happened at the ranch of my old friends, Anne and Tobin Armstrong. And the victim was Harry M. Whittington, Jr., my lawyer; his name appears on the organization papers for Rove + Company. Harry is also my good friend. I also played a pivotal but ineffectual role in making the public aware of the incident.

The Secret Service immediately notified the Kenedy County sheriff and the White House Situation Room. I told Bush the news about an hour after the shooting. His immediate concern was for Whittington, who was also the president's friend. Then I talked to Katharine Armstrong (my longtime friend and Tobin and Anne's daughter) about Harry's condition. He had been taken to a Kingsville hospital and then airlifted to Corpus Christi.

I thought the vice president's office was handling press notification but I awoke the next morning to find out nothing had been said. That was a problem. I called Katharine. At dinner at the ranch the night before, other members of the hunting party were worried that Cheney was crushed by the accident. Cheney had asked the Armstrongs how they wanted news of the incident to be made public. Anne decided she wanted the *Corpus Christi Caller-Times* to be notified first. I tried to tell the vice president Sunday morning that we needed to let everyone know, but he tersely refused, wanting to respect the Armstrongs' wishes. Cheney's staff couldn't change their boss's mind. On Sunday around 9 A.M. Central, Katharine began calling every name and number she had for the *Caller-Times*. It was close to midday before a reporter called her back. The *Caller-Times* put out the word online, and by mid-afternoon, the rest of the press had pounced on the story.

Cheney later took full responsibility during an interview, saying, "I'm the guy who pulled the trigger and shot my friend, and that's something I'll never forget." Harry went home Friday from the hospital, with most of the pellets removed from his face, neck, and chest, and after having suffered a mild heart attack from a pellet that lodged near his heart. He described his ordeal as "a cloud of misfortune and sadness that is not easy to explain."

We had a PR disaster on our hands and sitting on it for a night and morning and dribbling news out through the local paper created unnecessary ill will among reporters. Late-night talk show hosts yukked it up. "Good news, ladies and gentlemen; we have finally located weapons of mass destruction. . . . It's Dick Cheney," David Letterman exclaimed.

The incident taught me the VP could be stubborn and unmovable; I admired him for being loyal to his friends, but in this case, following their wishes was damaging to the administration. It reinforced the impression that Cheney always operated in secret and distrusted the press.

But the shooting incident, as bad as it was, was a political pothole compared to the real disaster we were facing that year: the Congress going from Republican to Democratic control. As the White House prepared for this possibility, my role shifted. In April, Andy Card left as chief of staff and was replaced by Josh Bolten, the director of the Office of Management and Budget. Bolten wanted to name his longtime deputy, Joel Kaplan, as deputy chief for policy. The change was a relief. Reading every single piece of domestic policy paper that went to the president—often several times as they went through drafts—made my days very long, and forced me to hold my opinion in check, at least at the beginning of the process. If I didn't, it tended to bend in my direction, which short-circuited robust discussion. Now I could again range freely across the issues.

Part of my job was also to help return as many Republicans to the House and Senate as possible, and that task would be very unpleasant. Second-term midterm elections are always that way for the White House. Only once in history has the White House party gained seats in either house in a second-term midterm.

Not only did we have history against us, but there was the economy and the war. In a late October Gallup poll, a record high 58 percent of Americans thought the Iraq War was a mistake, and 64 percent thought the war was going badly. In the same poll, 55 percent said the economy was in "fair" or "poor" shape. Articulate and courageous candidates could defend the war, but the economy was a big deadweight. However, neither turned out to be the issue on which the elections, especially for the House, turned.

We knew the president and his party would both be unpopular, so we cautioned candidates—incumbents and nonincumbents alike—to avoid attacking either one: if they did, the tactic would backfire by validating Democratic efforts to say the election was about Bush and the GOP. Given a choice between two candidates arguing over who is more anti-Bush, voters will go for the Democrat every time. The way for our candidates to survive was for them to talk about what they were for.

Our Democratic opponents were smart. Both New York senator Chuck Schumer, who led the Democratic Senatorial Campaign Committee, and Chicago congressman Rahm Emanuel, who ran the Democratic Congressional Campaign Committee, understood Democrats couldn't get Congress back by running big-city liberals on a left-wing platform. Schumer recruited veterans, farmers, and pro-life Democrats like Pennsylvania state treasurer Robert Casey to run for the Senate. Emanuel enlisted moderate and conservative Democrats—even pro-life, pro-gun, and pro-God evangelicals—and settled on the powerful theme of a Republican "culture of corruption" in the House.

The conventional wisdom is that Iraq and an unpopular president cost us seats. But the "culture of corruption" charge was the one that really hurt, especially since Republicans outdid themselves that year with scandals. Americans, especially swing voters, distrust Washington and are convinced most congressmen are crooks, even in good times. By

2006 they had been handed plenty of evidence. California representative Randy "Duke" Cunningham announced in July 2005 he would not seek reelection after being accused of taking $2.4 million in bribes, including a home, cars, a yacht, antiques, and a condo in return for earmarks and government contracts. He pled guilty and resigned in November 2005. Shortly after his sentencing, his octogenarian mother, who lived in Texas, began sending me plaintive requests for a presidential pardon. We barely held his Republican district in a special election after spending $5 million.

Then House majority leader Tom DeLay was indicted on September 28, 2005, for allegedly violating Texas state campaign finance laws. If they had been the only two House Republicans in trouble, we would have survived. But they weren't. We had too many congressmen tied to jailed lobbyist Jack Abramoff, including one—Bob Ney of Ohio—I had known since my days in the College Republicans. Abramoff had given Ney $170,000 in gifts and travel, including a golf trip to Scotland, that Ney failed to report. He pled guilty and was sentenced to thirty months in prison. GOP leaders replaced Ney on the 2006 ballot with a state senator who had recently declared personal bankruptcy. She lost.

Other Republican members were accused of having done favors for Abramoff, mostly to benefit his Indian gaming clients. Among them was Congressman Richard Pombo of California, who also had to fend off accusations that he had charged the family's RV vacations to the government. I knew he was in real trouble when I found myself working the crowd at his presidential fund-raiser in Stockton while he hung out backstage. Even congressmen who survived their association with Abramoff cost us a lot of time and money. I had to tell Congressman John Doolittle he could not use the proceeds from his presidential fund-raiser to pay legal bills nor his wife a percentage of the money raised (she doubled as his fund-raiser); he had to throw everything instead at winning reelection. He did, and scraped by.

But 2006 brought out all kinds of crazy behavior among Republican members. New York congressman John Sweeney was defeated after the release of a tape of his wife calling 911 and saying he was "knocking her around the house." This was after pictures surfaced of the four-term congressman seeming to be drunk at a fraternity party. Congressman Charlie Taylor of North Carolina lost after the *Wall Street Journal* broke a story about his ties to suspect Russian bankers. Arizona congressman Rick Renzi won reelection, but only after a hugely expensive campaign during which he had to fend off rumors that he was under investigation by the FBI for suspect land deals. He was later indicted for corruption.

Then there was Congressman Don Sherwood, an affable sixty-five-year-old Republican congressman from northeast Pennsylvania whose predicament forced me to have one of the most difficult conversations I ever had with the president. Sherwood's problem was a twenty-nine-year-old Peruvian mistress. He admitted the affair but denied he choked her, which she had claimed in her $5.5 million lawsuit. Sherwood's wife stood by his side and even wrote a letter to voters that said basically, "I've forgiven him and so can you." But no ad had been put up to broadcast her message more widely. So I was forced to explain to the president why the Republican House majority depended on his going to Pennsylvania not only to campaign for Sherwood, but to ask Sherwood's wife to appear in a television ad repeating her letter's message. Bush made the trip and the request, but no such spot ever appeared. Sherwood lost in a district Bush carried with 60 percent.

Despite all these challenges, Republicans had recaptured some momentum in September; some candidates didn't seem so doomed two months before the election. But those advances evaporated on September 28. That day, ABC News revealed that Florida Republican Mark Foley had sent inappropriate e-mails to an underage, male former House page. The network had thirty-six pages of instant messages from Foley—many messages explicit and all disturbing—to two other male former House pages. I talked to Congressman Tom Reynolds shortly after he'd met with GOP leaders as the news broke. Reynolds convinced his colleagues to demand Foley immediately resign, though this would turn the seat over to the Democrats because it was too late to replace Foley on the ballot. Reynolds was sickened by Foley's behavior, and I didn't blame him.

House Democratic campaign chief Rahm Emanuel reportedly knew about the Foley e-mails since late 2005. A Democratic Hill staffer had given them to Emanuel's communications director, Bill Burton, according to one report. But Congressman Emanuel did not report Foley to the Ethics Commission, perhaps preferring to keep the e-mails for use as a campaign issue. If true, apparently Emanuel didn't feel any moral requirement to keep his Republican colleague from preying on other underage pages in the meantime. I believe Emanuel had a responsibility to report what he knew of Foley's behavior immediately.

We suffered more blows in October. The FBI raided the lobbying offices of Pennsylvania congressman Curt Weldon's daughter, investigating her dealings with a suspect Russian trading company. He lost. Veteran congressman Jim Leach of Iowa told GOP chairman Ken Mehlman that if the RNC did another mailing or ad in his district, he would caucus with the Democrats in January. Mehlman stopped helping Leach. He lost. Pennsylvania Republican congresswoman Melissa Hart refused to run any ads attacking her Democratic opponent, who was happy to abuse her voting record in spot after spot. I was recruited to call her and beg her to defend herself. Her response was to run an ad in which she charged the Democrat was being mean. She lost.

On election night, Democrats took control of both the Senate and the House of Representatives, picking up six seats in the upper chamber (one more than the historic average) and twenty-nine in the lower (one more than the historic average). Underneath the surface, it was a lot closer than those numbers portrayed. Control of the Senate came down to 2,847 votes out of 61.2 million cast in Senate races—that was Democrat Jon Tester's margin over Montana senator Conrad Burns, who'd been tainted by an association with Abramoff. The fourteen closest races that settled control of the House of Representatives were decided by a margin of 27,022 votes out of 81 million cast in all House races. At least ten House Republicans were directly involved in or somehow tainted by allegations of wrongdoing.

Some analysts blamed the election on Iraq. But if the war was the deciding issue, how is it that Joe Lieberman, the Connecticut senatorial candidate running as an Independent, got more votes than his Democratic and Republican opponents combined? Congressman Chris Shays of Connecticut, who was up against a strong antiwar Democratic opponent, made victory in Iraq the central issue in his race, traveled to the Middle East fourteen times, lost the *New York Times* editorial endorsement for the first time in his career, but was reelected. Congresswoman Heather Wilson of New Mexico, a member of both the Armed Services and Intelligence committees, prevailed in a district John Kerry carried even though she was challenged by the incumbent state attorney general, who outspent her. Six-term Indiana congressman John Hostettler raised a third of what his Democratic opponent did and spent much of it on an ad bragging he'd voted against the Iraq War. He lost in a district Bush had carried with 62 percent in 2004.

Others said Bush's majority could have survived if he had fired Secretary of Defense Donald Rumsfeld before the election. I disagree. First, it would have looked like politics was influencing decisions about the war and would have damaged the military's faith in Bush as commander in chief. But secondly, Bush couldn't remove Rumsfeld and leave the post vacant for weeks or months. It had to be a seamless move from the old secretary of defense to the new, and we couldn't make that happen. That summer, I looked into whether FedEx CEO Fred Smith, Bush's original choice for the post in 1999, was now available. He wasn't. Robert Gates was uninterested when first approached; it wasn't until October when National Security Advisor Steve Hadley talked to him again that we thought he might take it.

Third, Democrats would have used the confirmation hearings of a new secretary of defense to make the war the centerpiece of the fall campaign. Democrats had already effectively deployed their party's few remaining high-profile pro-defense faces, such as Congressmen Ike Skelton and Jack Murtha, to question whether the United States could ever prevail militarily. In the face of this, the spinelessness of some Republicans would have meant that an almost completely unified antiwar Democratic Party would have been duking it out in Congress with a demoralized and split GOP. Hardly helpful to Republican chances.

A few blame our congressional losses on Bush's push for comprehensive immigration reform that year. Then how come so many immigration restrictionists were soundly defeated? For example, in Arizona, an incumbent Republican congressman and a former state senator running in an open race in a seat previously held by the GOP lost in districts George W. Bush carried easily. Both Republican candidates were opponents of immigration reform.

Other critics, especially Democrats, laid the blame for the GOP's defeat entirely at Bush's feet. It is true presidents are almost always liabilities in the second midterm. But Bush did more events for his party's candidates and raised more money for them than he had two years before. And if Bush was such a drag, why were Republican losses in 2006 about average for second-term midterms?

I was still moping when President Bush called Sunday night, November 12, to gossip. He had just talked with President Clinton. My view of conversations between two presidents is that they are among the most privileged of exchanges. I wouldn't break that seal of secrecy if not for the fact that Clinton repeated his thoughts to me the next day, after a groundbreaking ceremony for the Martin Luther King, Jr., Memorial.

Clinton told me that before the election, he and Democratic strategist James Carville had been keeping track of the generic ballot, which measures the relative strength of the two parties. The Democrats had a 13-point advantage just before Election Day. By comparison, Republicans had a 6-point advantage on the generic ballot going into the 1994 House elections and had picked up 54 seats. Clinton and Carville thought the Democratic 13-point lead would translate into a loss of at least 60 House seats for Republicans. Instead, Republicans lost 29. Clinton told me, "no one's ever going to give you credit, but it was sheer genius what you and Mehlman did with the seventy-two-hour task force. We should have won twice as many seats, but we didn't because of what you all did to get out your vote. No one will give you credit, but I know what you did."

I appreciated President Clinton's kind words but they were cold comfort: a Democratic Congress meant playing a lot more defense. But we never gave up on our offense and, perhaps foolhardily, took a second run at immigration reform.

Bush had begun to work on reform early in 2001 because he believed America had a border that wasn't protected, the nation had an urgent need for temporary workers, and he could forge a compromise between those who wanted to punish lawbreakers and those who recognized their value as workers in a very broken system. But 9/11 derailed the effort. Instead, the administration focused on ensuring that terrorists could not enter or remain in the United States.

Over the next seven years, he doubled the size of the Border Patrol and tripled its budget. When Bush arrived in Washington, there were 11 miles of pedestrian fencing and vehicle barriers *total*—and 37 miles of all-weather road—along the southern border. When he left office, there were 296 miles of pedestrian fencing (and 74 more in development), 282 miles of vehicle barriers (and 18 more in development), 80 miles of all-weather road, and lots of technology from cameras to infrared systems to side-looking radar to sophisticated observation posts, all aimed to make our border more secure. It worked: In the early 1990s, hiring a human smuggler—a "coyote"—cost around $500 a person. By 2008, the price had risen to between $1,500 and $2,500, a sign it was getting harder to cross the border illegally.

Bush also ended "catch and release," the practice of picking up illegal aliens from countries other than Mexico and then releasing them on their own recognizance until their deportation hearing, for which most never showed. Bush thought it encouraged contempt for law. So he expanded the facilities to hold these illegals until deportation hearings. In 2000, it took nearly a hundred days on average to process someone out of the country. When Bush left office, it took less than twenty. His administration also organized a system so employers could check the eligibility of job applicants.

But these weren't enough. There needed to be a comprehensive new law that addressed each facet of the problem: border security, guest workers, and the status of the illegal aliens already here. After the midterms, Arizona senator Jon Kyl called me to say he was willing to reengage and Senators Lamar Alexander of Tennessee and John Cornyn of Texas told me on a bird hunting trip that they had been thinking about ways around the impasses that held the effort up. The president restarted his efforts in the 2007 State of the Union address.

But I saw how difficult the battle would be when the president attended the Democratic House retreat in February 2007 in Williamsburg, Virginia. It was a triumphant moment for Democrats, having recaptured the House majority they lost in 1994. After the president spoke, Congressman Luis Gutierrez made an impassioned plea for moving forward on immigration. He received spotty applause. I was sitting off to the side: between Gutierrez and me was a table of senior African-American members, including the new Judiciary chairman, John Conyers, and the new Ways and Means chairman, Charlie Rangel. Few at this table applauded and some shook their heads "no" as Gutierrez talked.

But prodded by Senator Ted Kennedy and energized by key Republicans such as Kyl, the Senate took up the issue again. Republicans were worried about amnesty and wanted to require that illegal aliens return to their country of origin to apply to remain in the United States. Some Democrats were prodded by their union supporters about a guest worker program. Other Democrats opposed making it harder for extended family members to immigrate while making it easier for those with education and skills to apply to work and become citizens, as Bush desired.

Senators began lining up with amendments. That was a good sign: giving more senators a chance to amend the bill provides them a way to say yes to the final one. The White House legislative folks called it a "vote-arama." It would take weeks for the Senate to make its way through the 150 proposed amendments, but it was necessary. Unfortunately, we had not taken into consideration Majority Leader Harry Reid's quirkiness. He decided the long battle would rile up emotions in the Senate and pulled the bill down on June 7 as the Senate readied for the vote-arama. He did so without discussing it with the White House or the bill's sponsors.

The Senate had been on the edge of passing comprehensive immigration reform that addressed all three elements of immigration: enforcement, guest workers, and the status of those already here. But Reid blew that opportunity with his rash decision. All hell broke loose. The bill's powerful sponsors hammered him. He caved. But the only way Senate rules allowed the majority leader to bring the bill up again was to limit its amendments to a handful. This greatly reduced the chance for members to improve the bill. On June 28, 2007, immigration reform failed on a vote of 53 to 46.

Neither Republicans nor Democrats rose to the moment. Some Republicans suggested illegal immigrants needed to pay for their original offense of crossing the border by being rounded up and deported. I was worried about all the costs of doing this: it would cost tens of billions of dollars, hurt our economy by depriving it of vital workers, and damage the GOP's standing among the nation's fastest-growing population. I was also worried about the moral cost of such a move: we'd be chasing down people, most of whom, while they'd broken the law by coming here, had since contributed to our economy, raised their families, and come to love America. All our families were immigrants once.

Many Democrats refused to deny welfare benefits to illegal aliens. They also opposed any guest worker program—but rather than kill it outright, they wanted to make it impossible to operate. So organized labor got Reid to allow votes on amendments that would limit the size of any guest worker program (rather than making the size depend on the number of available jobs) and end it in five years (which meant few companies would participate). Some senators who claimed to support comprehensive immigration sided with labor in gutting the bill. Most prominent among them was the son of an immigrant, Illinois freshman senator Barack Obama. It was an early sign of his audacious hypocrisy.

CHAPTER 31

The Surge

———— •◆• ————

In December 2006, George W. Bush made the second-most consequential decision of his presidency. His most consequential decision
was going to war in Iraq. Three years later, as America faced almost certain defeat there, Bush bucked conventional wisdom in Washington and
ordered a major shift in U.S. strategy. He did this despite the opposition
of congressional leaders of both parties and much of the foreign policy
establishment and existing military leadership. At the time, only 30 percent of Americans approved of his performance as president.

How Bush came to order what later became known as "the surge" can
be traced to events in 2005. That year, Iraq held three democratic elections: a January legislative election to draft a constitution; an October
countrywide referendum on a national constitution; and December elections for a national assembly. Each produced moving images of Iraqis
waving purple fingers, stained to show they had voted. Each election was
marred by violence and terrorist threats. But the overall thrust of them
was positive and indicated that perhaps Iraq was on a good path. Turnout
was high, with even disaffected Sunnis voting more heavily in each suc-
cessive election.

The result was that even critics of the Bush administration talked
about an "Arab Spring"—a flowering of freedom in a region untouched
by the tide of liberty that had swept much of the world in the previous

quarter century. The *New York Times* columnist Thomas Friedman spoke about having reached a democratic "tipping point" in the Arab Middle East, declaring, "We're seeing the equivalent of the fall of the Berlin Wall there."

That optimism was bolstered by events in Lebanon. Nearly destroyed by a bitter civil war, Lebanon had spent three decades occupied by Syria and seemed destined to remain under its thumb. But two years after we removed Saddam Hussein and following the assassination of former prime minister Rafik Hariri, a prominent anti-Syrian politician, the Lebanese people forced the withdrawal of Syrian troops from their country. In what some called the Cedar Revolution, elections produced a new government that was much more independent than anything Lebanon had seen in a long time. A key leader of the Lebanese democratic movement argued that his small nation might not have seen change had it not been for Bush's actions in Iraq. "I was cynical about Iraq," said Walid Jumblatt, the head of the Lebanese Druze population. "But when I saw the Iraqi people voting [in January 2005], eight million of them, it was the start of a new Arab world. The Syrian people, the Egyptian people, all say that something is changing. The Berlin Wall has fallen. We can see it."

Our optimism about the promise of Iraqi democracy led us to believe political progress would produce progress on security. The more Iraqis participated in shaping their future, the more of a stake they would have in a free Iraq. We knew it was especially important to include the minority Sunnis who had been in control during Saddam's brutal reign and were bitter about losing power.

But political progress wasn't producing security. Instead, Iraqis were being brutalized by the bitter-enders of Saddam's regime, terrorists led by al-Qaeda, Islamic extremists from Syria, and Iranian meddlers. These groups terrorized Iraqis who cooperated with the United States or the new Iraqi democratic government. These thugs knew that if the Iraqis lost their fear, the terrorists' days were numbered. Our strategy depended on training and equipping Iraqi forces. As Iraqi forces stood up, American and coalition forces could stand down, and the U.S. presence in Iraq could be reduced.

Our theory wasn't working, because we weren't the only actors influencing the course of events. Al-Qaeda had come to realize that Iraq was the central front in the war on terror. "The most important and serious issue today for the whole world is this Third World War, which the Crusader-Zionist coalition began against the Islamic nation," Osama bin Laden declared in an audio message to Muslims in Iraq posted on jihadist websites. "It is raging in the land of the two rivers [Iraq]. The world's millstone and pillar is in Baghdad, the capital of the caliphate." Bin Laden knew the stakes of this struggle: "It is either victory and glory or misery and humiliation." The American soldier was, he once told a reporter, "a paper tiger." He felt America could be driven from the battlefield as it had been in Vietnam. So Iraq had become a struggle between democracy and radical Islam. For that reason, al-Qaeda was behind many of the most spectacular attacks there.

The organization and its allies desperately feared democracy's powerful antidote to its extremist ideology. So it would quickly move to kick the legs out from any civil society Iraqis themselves were building. Abu Musab al-Zarqawi, al-Qaeda's leader in Iraq, warned Osama bin Laden in a letter that "democracy is coming" and "with the deployment of [Iraqi] soldiers and police, the future has become frightening."

The Iraqi army and police were too often not well enough prepared, too corrupt, or not sufficiently loyal to the central government to maintain order against these fanatics. American forces would secure an area and turn it over to Iraqi forces only to see terrorist thugs move in and destabilize the area again. As a consequence, the United States suffered the pain of warfare without seeing a net positive result. Iraqis themselves saw that, too. What's more, al-Qaeda wasn't simply carrying out random attacks. Its goal was to spark a religious civil war that would set Shiites and Sunnis at each other's throats. If such a war were started, democracy would never have a chance.

"The key to change," Zarqawi wrote, was "targeting and hitting" the Shiites, which "will provoke them to show the Sunnis their rabies . . . and bare the teeth of the hidden rancor." He continued, "I come back and again say that the only solution is for us to strike the religious, military, and other cadres among the Shi'a with blow after blow until they bend to the Sunnis."

On February 22, 2006, al-Qaeda made its boldest attempt to spark a civil war by bombing the "Golden Mosque" in Samarra, sixty-five miles north of Baghdad. The mosque, formally known as the Askariya shrine,

held two ninth-century tombs of revered Shiite imams. No one was killed
when two powerful bombs were detonated at dawn, but the gilded dome
of one of Shiite Islam's holiest sites was shattered. This attack triggered a
wave of retaliation by the Shiites, many of whom had been brutalized by
the Sunnis during Saddam's years of tyranny.

We held our breath for six weeks as Iraq simmered with violence. Our
hope was that the Shiite violence would remain contained and then end.
But by April, Shiite militias and death squads were stepping up attacks
on Sunni neighborhoods. Sunnis responded. AK-47s, bombs, and rocket-
propelled grenades (RPGs) were killing hundreds each week. Eighty percent of the violence was concentrated within one hundred miles of
Baghdad. The peaceful provinces were beginning to fear the whole country would unravel.

It seemed likely that it might. After all, Iraq had no real government
at that moment. Since the December parliamentary election, its leaders
had dawdled, feuded, and delayed instead of agreeing on a prime minister. Finally, in late May 2006, the dominant Shiite parliamentary groups
settled on Nouri al-Maliki, picking him because he was thought to be so
weak no faction feared his installation. A few weeks later, we received our
first piece of unequivocal good news: Zarqawi was dead. The ruthless
al-Qaeda leader had been tracked down by American forces and killed
when F-16 jets pounded the house he was hiding in with two five-
hundred-pound bombs. Seventeen raids on al-Qaeda safe houses and
other terrorist centers in the Baghdad area followed the air strike. But
even with al-Maliki's selection and the death of the top al-Qaeda operative in Iraq, the violence spread.

American and Iraqi forces attempted to reestablish control of the capital during the summer with "Operation Together Forward." When it
failed, "Operation Together Forward II" was launched. Its results were
also disheartening: violence in Baghdad had increased more than 40 percent by the fall of 2006. These two efforts were to be the last major operations premised on our initial strategy of training Iraqis and withdrawing
American forces from the areas they had secured. Once American forces
left the cities to return to their bases, the terrorists and militias simply
came back.

In a way, the American strategy was replicating General William

Westmoreland's "search and destroy" strategy of the Vietnam war, with a similarly unsatisfactory outcome. We needed an updated version of General Creighton Abrams's "ink blot" strategy, which called for concentrating forces on key areas, securing them, and spreading out to secure ever larger sections of the country. Eventually the ink blots overlap and you control the entire country. Abrams's approach met with far more success than did Westmoreland's—but by the time it was carried out in Vietnam, starting in 1968, American public opinion and the political class were turning against the war. The Nixon administration was eventually forced to withdraw despite Abrams's success.

As Iraq was coming unhinged, an important political shift was taking place back home. The efforts to say Bush had lied about the war and the failure to find WMD led some congressional Democrats who had initially supported the Iraq War to turn hard against it. Representative John Murtha, a defense hawk, declared in November 2005 that the American military had done its job and should come home within six months. This gave cover for Democrats to go into full-throated, all-out opposition to the war. They sought to make Iraq "Bush's War" rather than America's war. They wanted Iraq to do to Bush what Vietnam had done to Lyndon Johnson: break his presidency.

Republicans weren't driven by the same motivation as Democrats, nor did they turn against the war as early or in nearly the same numbers. Still, by 2006, some congressional Republicans began to lose their nerve and to break with the president. Oregon senator Gordon Smith joined Nebraska senator Chuck Hagel, a longtime skeptic. Nervous Republican members of Congress asked me if the president would consider a troop withdrawal to save the 2006 elections. The Republican leader in the Senate, Mitch McConnell, went so far as to ask the president directly, and then went public with his nervousness about his party's midterm prospects. The president found this offensive. He wasn't going to make a decision about war based on election considerations. But wobbly Republicans were a clear sign that time was running out.

As the violence in Iraq intensified, it became clear to me that Bush wanted to change our military efforts on the ground. He told me that what we were doing was not working and that it was unlikely to work, even though we now had a willing partner in the Maliki government.

Bush ordered a complete review of our strategy and reiterated that he was not interested in surrender. He insisted on what almost everyone else said was a pipe dream: a plan that would lead to victory.

The Iraq strategy review would be conducted by National Security Advisor Stephen J. Hadley, not by Rumsfeld's Department of Defense or Rice's Department of State. Hadley, who had been Condi's deputy for the first term, is a trim, quiet gentleman lawyer with long experience in foreign affairs, great knowledge of the world, and tremendous judgment. He is also one of the nicest people in Washington; he avoided the spotlight as much as some people longed for it.

Hadley's review was way out of my lane, but Bush and I did talk often about how to sustain political support for the war. I told him that as long as Americans were convinced the administration was committed to victory and our soldiers were not set up as targets on street corners for creative bomb makers, we would find enough support to sustain the effort. But we had to show progress. What was often lost in the analysis of public opinion and the war is that many of those who disapproved of Bush's handling of the war were not antiwar. Rather, many wanted to win and didn't think we were serious about it.

I also got the sense from talking with President Bush that he agreed with General David H. Petraeus that soldiers must integrate with local people to win their trust and confidence and to make political progress. Our current strategy had it the other way around. Petraeus, who wrote his dissertation at Princeton on the military lessons of the Vietnam War, had served several tours of duty in Iraq and distinguished himself in, among other places, Mosul, where his "hearts-and-minds" approach had largely succeeded. Bush made a point of telling me I should read Petraeus's new counterinsurgency manual as soon as it was ready. This was a sign of where the president's thinking was.

I was drawn into the Iraq strategy review not in a central role but rather on its edges as someone who could give advice on sustaining political support for the president's decisions. Those edges were important because if we lost public support for the war, it would be very difficult to do the heavy lifting necessary to win it. Already, the policy advice coming from the Joint Chiefs of Staff (JCS) and the State Department rested, in part, on assumptions that Congress and the American people had little stomach for anything except a drawdown and withdrawal. These assumptions seemed dodgy to some of those involved in the review, such as Dr. Peter Feaver, a Duke political scientist then at the NSC as a special advisor for strategic planning. Feaver believed that drawdown and withdrawal were not our only options. I agreed and defended his arguments in conversations with colleagues involved in the review.

My White House team was also a conduit for outside information and counsel, which sometimes took the form of attention to substantive critiques by administration allies such as retired General Jack Keane and American Enterprise Institute scholar Fred Kagan. Both were prescient voices on Iraq and were important architects in what turned out to be the surge. I got them in to brief Bolten, and later they briefed Bush. Voices saying we could still win the war were extremely rare in 2006; I wanted them heard in the White House inner sanctum.

I also helped manage the tempo and pacing of the president's public appearances and his outreach to other influential leaders. We needed a large outreach operation as the president considered making a fundamental change in strategy. The polls run by the Republican National Committee were particularly helpful in identifying where we were failing to explain our policy and which messages were persuasive.

Bush's strategy was not driven by polling—it was strengthened by it. If we were to be successful, we needed an accurate reading of where people really stood on the war. How many voters wanted to throw in the towel? And how many were upset with the progress of the war because we weren't winning? This and other information was critical for Republicans running for reelection. We needed to show them that they could survive Iraq and we also needed to make the case to the American people that leaving Iraq would have profound consequences for our country, our military's morale, and our national security. What we needed to do was rally public support by demonstrating that we had a plan with a high chance of success. "Public sentiment is everything," Lincoln once said. "With public sentiment, nothing can fail. Without it, nothing can succeed."

I didn't pretend to be Carl von Clausewitz or Henry Kissinger, but I knew the Iraq War wasn't going well, that the Bush presidency was in peril, and that unless we made changes, public support would crater. If that happened, we would lose not only Iraq but our ability to prevail against terrorism. I expressed these views to the president.

Neither of us realized that parts of the military itself would fiercely resist any plans to overhaul strategy in an attempt to win the war. Some Pentagon leaders thought that putting soldiers alongside Iraqis, as Petraeus's counterinsurgency approach called for, would put too much strain on the military. Their worry was that to carry out the strategy we would have to extend combat tours, and, because the military had already extended combat tours in Iraq, that keeping troops in Iraq longer or cutting short the period in which they rested and reset back in the United States before being redeployed would "break" the Army and Marines.

Bush countered that there were two ways to break the military. One was to overstretch it. The other was to allow it to be defeated. And he argued that the latter would be far worse. But Bush accepted the concerns as legitimate and struck a compromise. He would support increasing the size of the Army and Marines. This wouldn't prevent troops from serving longer combat tours, but it would signal that extended tours were a temporary solution, not a permanent policy.

The "surge" was a bad name for the new strategy. It made it sound as if the president was simply adding troops to fight the fires of Iraq. But his strategy was much more than that. He was also deploying these new troops to protect civilians by moving U.S. forces out of bases and into hotspots in Baghdad and the massive Anbar province that had seen brutal terrorist attacks. Anbar is largely Sunni and therefore had been a key recruiting ground for the enemy. But the province's tribal leaders had begun turning against al-Qaeda in the summer of 2006—the terrorists' brutality was simply too much for them. By providing security to civilians in Anbar and defeating the terrorists there we could strike at the heart of the insurgency. And that's largely what happened. As the Marines applied our counterinsurgency strategy, Iraqis felt safer and more of them were willing to cooperate with coalition forces in confronting al-Qaeda, especially its foreign fighters.

During the strategy review, General Peter Pace, chairman of the Joint Chiefs, also argued that to be successful, any military "surge" had to be matched by two other "surges." First, the Iraqis needed to commit their own army and police and not turn a blind eye to private militias that had sprung up around the country. Second, there needed to be greater efforts to rebuild the economy, create a civil society, and establish functioning government on the local and national level. To do this, we needed a "civilian surge," including "provincial reconstruction teams" made up of civilians—retired U.S. government officials or industry experts.

On December 6, 2006, just as we were putting the final touches on our strategy review, the Iraq Study Group (ISG) issued its report. Washington has many blue-ribbon panels that issue reports no one reads. This was not one of them. Chartered by Congress and led by former secretary of state James A. Baker III, a Republican, and former Indiana congressman Lee Hamilton, a Democrat, ISG could provide the substance that many leaders in Washington were desperately hoping would justify turning against the war.

And that's nearly what happened. The report said, "The primary mission of U.S. forces in Iraq should evolve to one of supporting the Iraqi army. . . . By the first quarter of 2008, subject to unexpected developments in the security situation on the ground, all combat brigades not necessary for force protection could be out of Iraq." There it was, a timetable and a call for withdrawal. One of ISG's seventy-nine recommendations also read in part, "We could . . . support a short-term redeployment or surge of American combat forces to stabilize Baghdad, or to speed up the training and equipping mission, if the U.S. commander in Iraq determines that such steps would be effective." The report tried to have it both ways by justifying both deploying a new strategy and pulling out. It was like a Rorschach inkblot test—everyone read what they wanted into it. The danger for us was that opinion makers might quickly conclude that the bipartisan, objective study group had just recommended that we withdraw from Iraq.

To counter this, we emphasized the recommendations supporting the surge and the president then did several things. He pushed for a new counterinsurgency strategy to secure and win over the civilian population; sent what would ultimately be thirty thousand additional troops to Iraq; and installed a new ground commander in Iraq, David Petraeus. American combat troops were going to live, sleep, and eat with Iraqis to provide them the security they desperately needed and wanted.

We wanted to announce our plan in December but decided to wait until January so the new secretary of defense, Robert Gates, who replaced Rumsfeld after he resigned in November, could review it, offer his thoughts, and bless the final plan.

The new strategy was announced January 10, 2007, in a twenty-minute nationally televised speech by the president delivered from the White House Library. The speech was not well received, which is what I anticipated. At this point, people were not interested in words. They wanted results. On Iraq, we had little credibility left with the public: 71 percent of Americans thought the Iraq War was going badly and only 11 percent supported escalating the war by adding additional U.S. forces, which is exactly what Bush was proposing to do. It would be June before all the "surge" troops arrived in Iraq and full operations began—and months before we could begin to see the new policy's full impact.

Democrats, emboldened by the 2006 elections, immediately pounced. Senator Ted Kennedy proclaimed the surge "an immense new mistake." Then-senator Barack Obama declared he was "not persuaded that 20,000 additional troops in Iraq are going to solve the sectarian violence. . . . I think it will do the reverse." Senators Joe Biden and Hillary Clinton both called it "a tragic mistake." So did Senator John Kerry, who forecast, "It won't end the violence; it won't provide security . . . it won't turn back the clock and avoid the civil war that is already under way; it won't deter terrorists . . . it won't rein in the militias." John Kerry had been wrong on Vietnam and would be proven wrong here on every count.

More worrisome for us, some Republicans spoke against the plan. Minnesota senator Norm Coleman said, "[I don't believe] an expansion [of the surge] of 20,000 troops in Iraq will solve the problems." Kansas senator Sam Brownback joined him. Maine Republican Olympia Snowe signaled "concerns," while GOP Senate whip Trent Lott suggested he might oppose the surge. "We've got to say to the Iraqis, 'Congratulations. Saddam is dead. We've given you an opportunity for peace and freedom. It's yours,' " he said.

The president did have a few crucial allies. Senators John McCain and Joe Lieberman were key to keeping aboard those members of Congress, Democrat and Republican, who wanted victory but were under intense pressure to abandon the fight. It was a courageous stand for McCain. Some Republicans were cautioning him to keep his distance from the "surge" if he wanted to win the GOP nomination for president in 2008.

Pete Wehner, director of the Office of Strategic Initiatives and one of my deputies, sent me and others an e-mail two days after the president's speech. The tone of Pete's note was panicked, which was unusual for him.

He was worried that a few influential Republicans such as Senators John Warner and Richard Lugar would travel down Pennsylvania Avenue from the Capitol to meet with the president and say it was time to draw the curtain on Iraq. To keep that from happening, we all agreed we had to come up with a way to give Petraeus time. There was no point in thinking much beyond the summer; if things weren't moving in our direction by then, there was little we could do to stop Congress from shutting down the war.

Still, I thought it would be difficult for Democrats to vote against funding the troops, especially after Kerry had suffered a sustained pounding over the issue in his 2004 presidential campaign. Senator Warner, a Republican, signaled he expected Congress to have the right to approve the president's shift in strategy, saying, "Congress is entitled to an opportunity to independently look at the situation." In response, Bush made clear he believed he had "the authority as commander in chief to move ahead with the deployment, regardless of what the Democratic-controlled Congress does."

But Warner was really signaling that he was prepared to put a time limit on using funds for combat operations. And that was a real threat. The president could veto legislation that specifically cut off war funding, but Congress appropriated every dime spent by the federal government. To keep money flowing, we needed congressional support. So the White House stepped up its outreach to members of Congress, frequently shuttling Rice, Gates, Hadley, and others to the Hill. We also increased efforts to keep Republicans on the reservation so they would vote to keep funding the war.

Democrats edged dangerously close to rooting for defeat. Majority Leader Harry Reid, for example, declared in April that the Iraq War was "lost, and this surge is not accomplishing anything." Even some people in the administration were defeatists. Some leaked from late May through July to the *New York Times* and the *Washington Post* that "growing political pressure" was forcing us to work on "Plan B," which "would, in many ways, track the recommendations of the Baker-Hamilton report." These officials were "eager for significant withdrawals before the president leaves office in January 2009" and suggested we could cut our troop levels in Iraq in half in 2008. "The issue now is when do we start withdrawing troops and at what pace," said one anonymous official, who apparently assumed the new strategy would fail. Some aides suggested, "It would be wiser to announce plans for a far more narrowly defined mission for American troops that would allow for a staged pullback." All of this ignored the president's desire to win the war and his understanding that the Petraeus strategy would take time.

The final batch of extra troops arrived in June, but unnamed administration officials were greasing the skids for retreat even before the soldiers had a chance to go to work. I thought their acts were disloyal to the president and a terrible disservice to the country. They made me furious. Fortunately, we never had to turn to "Plan B." When General Petraeus and Ambassador Ryan C. Crocker came back to Washington in September to testify about their efforts before a joint hearing of the Foreign Affairs and Armed Services committees, they had some good news.

The left-wing group MoveOn.org, however, was determined to smear Petraeus before he had a chance to share it. It ran a full-page ad in the *New York Times* accusing him of treason and of lying to Congress. The ad's headline read: "General Petraeus or General Betray Us? Cooking the Books for the White House." Accusing a decorated military leader of treason was an incendiary charge. MoveOn went on to attack Petraeus as "a military man constantly at war with the facts" and argued "the surge strategy has failed."

MoveOn's leaders defended the ad as "successful in what it was intended to do: call the credibility of Petraeus' testimony into question." The ad itself—for which the *New York Times* had charged MoveOn a discounted rate of $65,000 rather than the normal $142,000 for a full page—may have been prompted by congressional Democrats. *Politico* reported that one unnamed Democratic senator complained "no one [in the Senate] was willing to call Petraeus 'a liar on national TV,' " and so they were "hoping instead that 'outside groups will do it for us.' " Congressman Rahm Emanuel echoed MoveOn's attack by saying Petraeus's written report to Congress deserved "the Nobel Prize for creative statistics or the Pulitzer for fiction."

But Petraeus and Crocker, while careful not to paint a "rosy scenario," documented significant, and in some cases stunning, political and military progress in Iraq. They cited new legislation spelling out powers and responsibilities of local and provincial governments, the reintegration of Baathists into Iraqi society, an increase in oil revenue and foreign investment, and a drop in civilian deaths and overall violence due to the killing and capturing of al-Qaeda leaders and the strengthening of the Iraqi security forces and the police.

While acknowledging that major challenges remained, and noting that no one could guarantee success in Iraq, Crocker was able to declare, "A secure, stable, democratic Iraq at peace with its neighbors is attainable."

This pronouncement—careful, measured, empirical, and true, delivered by a widely respected career diplomat who had opposed the war in the first place—was enormously important. General Petraeus was able to say the improved security situation made it possible for the additional troops Bush ordered to Iraq in January 2007 to return home by July 2008. But Petraeus also warned against a more rapid withdrawal because it could "result in the further release of the strong centrifugal forces in Iraq and produce . . . dangerous results." Petraeus, having showed beyond any doubt that the surge was working, was telling Congress it would be responsible for the bad outcome if it pulled out prematurely.

By the end of 2007, things were improving even beyond our best hopes. In December, Major General Joseph Fil, commanding general of the Multinational Division Baghdad and 1st Cavalry Division, reported that since November 2006, attacks against citizens in Baghdad had dropped almost 80 percent and vehicle-borne improvised explosive device (IED) incidents had declined approximately 70 percent. Hundreds of shops were opening in southern Baghdad, compared to less than a handful in January 2007. In addition, refugees were returning and more foreign jihadists were staying away. And Sunnis in Iraq, as well as across most of the Islamic world, were turning against al-Qaeda, both its ideology and its tactics. Every measure had shown enormous improvement.

The success of the surge led more Americans to support the war. In May, the *New York Times* and CBS found 35 percent of Americans said taking military action against Iraq was the right thing to do and 61 percent said the United States should have stayed out. By July, it was 42 percent to 54 percent. The numbers baffled the *Times,* but I knew they were due to the success of the surge.

By March 2008, Prime Minister Nouri al-Maliki—himself a Shiite—felt confident enough to confront the largest Shiite militia, the Mahdi Army, in Basra and in the militia's northeast Baghdad stronghold. Maliki personally directed the Iraqi security forces as they killed, captured, disarmed, and dismantled the sectarian forces. This would have been unthinkable two years before.

For months, even as the surge began to show success, leading Democrats were determined to deny it. When Speaker Pelosi was asked by CNN's Wolf Blitzer about it, she said, "There haven't been gains, Wolf. The gains have not produced the desired effect, which is the reconciliation of Iraq. This is a failure. This is a failure." But by 2008, progress was clearly beyond dispute. An increasing number of Democrats began to concede the fact. Some ceased trying to undermine it. Most simply stopped talking about it. A few even recognized their errors.

In June 2003, I had traveled with Bush to the Middle East. One of the stops was Sharm el Sheik in Egypt, where the president and five regional leaders met. While cooling my heels waiting for them to finish a private session, I was introduced by a White House colleague to a top aide to Abu Mazen (known to many as Mahmoud Abbas), the leader of the Palestinian Authority. The aide jokingly introduced himself as "Abu Mazen's Karl Rove." After polite chatter, the conversation turned serious. "Does America know the entire world changed when Baghdad fell?" he asked. He talked about how the emergence of democracy in the Middle East could end old conflicts and bring peace with Israel. So much was possible with Saddam gone and the possibility of freedom flourishing throughout the region. He wanted to know if Americans had the stomach and resolution to finish the job by stabilizing Iraq and confronting terrorism. In the days that followed, I often thought about his question. Did America have the resolve to win this new and dangerous conflict? Yes, America did—because its president did.

CHAPTER 32

Yes, It Was Fun

———•◆•———

I approached my time at the White House in this spirit: take the work seriously, but not yourself. So I developed a reputation as a prankster. Humor helped relieve the pressure that sometimes came from having a front-row seat on history.

National Economic Council director Al Hubbard habitually left his keys in the very nice BMW he drove to the White House, and one day I moved it without his knowing. Later, others saw him standing where his car had been, yelling, "My car is gone! They've stolen my car!" into his cell phone. That was impossible; he had parked inside the most heavily guarded complex in the world. I enlisted a co-conspirator in the prank so I could keep a straight face when I told Hubbard I saw someone get out of his car earlier that day.

But sometimes I didn't have to instigate anything to be reminded that life in the service of George W. Bush could be fun. For instance, there was the affair of the missing sock at Buckingham Palace. I joined the president on his visit to London in November 2003 and thoroughly enjoyed my regal accommodations in the palace's East Wing, right next to the Centre Room, on whose balcony the royal family stands to wave to adoring crowds below.

My suite came with antique furniture, gorgeous paintings, beautiful carpets, and a valet named Philippus Steenkamp. He offered to draw my bath each morning (I declined) and laid out my clothes every morning.

The morning of the final day, I unrolled what I thought was a pair of socks to discover that somewhere between washing machine and suitcase, one sock had made its escape. I had spare pairs in my suitcase, but my luggage was being loaded onto Air Force One, having been dispatched to the plane the night before.

No one else in the traveling party had extra socks. I panicked, my mind filling with images of me in the formal departure line, thanking the queen and Prince Philip with one sockless foot. I made my way down to the president's suite to borrow a pair. Unfortunately, the president's baggage had just left for the plane. Fretting that I might create a diplomatic incident, I made my way to the Centre Room. There I commiserated with the British military officers assigned as our liaisons, commanded by the queen's equerry-in-waiting, who had the impeccably British name of James Duckworth-Chad.

At that moment, the Centre Room doors opened. All the valets trooped in like a squad of commandos in livery, led by one cheeky lad bearing a giant silver platter with an ornate cover. In a loud voice, he proclaimed, "In the name of her Majesty, Elizabeth the Second, by the Grace of God of the United Kingdom of Great Britain and Northern Ireland, and of Her other Realms and Territories, Queen, Head of the Commonwealth, Defender of the Faith, it is our honor to present to you . . . a pair of the Royal Socks!" With a flourish, he removed the cover to reveal—to my enormous relief—a pair of plain black socks. I put them on and a few minutes later found myself in the departure line, thanking the queen and her consort for their hospitality. I still have the pair but refuse to wear my one real connection to royalty.

There were moments in the White House when I badly needed to find humor in an incident because malice, not socks, was involved—such as when I was accused of taking part in an exorcism. In the spring of 2001, I was visited by Deal Hudson, a leader of the 2000 Bush campaign's Catholic outreach; Father John C. Cregan of Blessed Sacrament Catholic Church in Alexandria, Virginia; and Carl Anderson, head of the Knights of Columbus.

Our pleasant visit focused on engaging more Catholics in our agenda. As our meeting ended, Father Cregan spontaneously offered to close with prayer. I was struck by his quiet sincerity as we bowed our heads and he blessed the work to be done in the office. It was touching and I was grateful.

That innocuous visit was turned five years later into something sinister. In their 2006 biography of me, *The Architect,* Wayne Slater and James Moore described the impromptu blessing as a "deeply spiritual ceremony" and implied it was an exorcism. They said I joked that Hillary Clinton's former occupancy was "a reason the place needed to be purged of evil spirits." Moore and Slater also characterized me as "the administration's premier agnostic" (which would be a surprise to my rector), "who'd been raised in a completely irreligious home" (which would be a surprise to my parents and grandparents).

The passage from *The Architect* roused bloggers into a frenzy about a West Wing exorcism of the former First Lady's office. A *Newsday* reporter squeezed two days of coverage out of it. By the time the story died, I had been described as a dark magician, and my guests had been turned into "three high-ranking Catholic priests." Fortunately, early in my White House days, I learned that the best way to survive Washington is to keep a sense of absurdity about it.

That's how I handled the annual press dinners that Washington's press corps ritualistically throws every year. The White House Correspondents' Association Dinner has the highest profile and frothiest mix of journalists, politicos, and celebrities. Every sitting president since Calvin Coolidge has attended at least one and is expected to make gracious comments—and then sit an arm's length from the podium as he is insulted, belittled, and scorched. It is great sport to watch, but lousy to participate in. White House senior staff are expected to attend with the president.

The dinners are usually held in the Washington Hilton ballroom, which is reminiscent of George Jetson's living room, only larger. In my experience, most White House staff would rather be home getting a good night's sleep. Not so for celebrities. To them, these are hot tickets. It seemed that each year, more and more stars, recording artists, celebrities, and weirdos scammed invitations. At one dinner, the now-junior senator from Minnesota (but then a comic) came up to me and said, "I'm Al Franken. I hate you. You hate me." I thought it a strange greeting, considering I'd never even met him. I replied, "I don't know you, so how could I hate you?" When Franken realized his line didn't inflame me, he scampered off to use it on former deputy secretary of defense Paul Wolfowitz—who told the obnoxious comedian to go f*** himself.

Just about anything can happen on nights when Hollywood meets Washington and entertainment competes with politics, as it did one evening in the spring of 2007. I was a guest of the *New York Times* at the White House Correspondents' Dinner. *Times* columnist Maureen Dowd sat at the next table, talking with a thin, severe woman. They would both look at me, Maureen would jerk her thumb toward me, and then they'd turn back and talk to each other energetically. I sensed trouble.

The thin, severe woman at the next table was Laurie David, the producer of Al Gore's *An Inconvenient Truth* and soon-to-be-former wife of Hollywood director and *Seinfeld* co-creator Larry David. Sheryl Crow, country rock star and former fiancée of my fellow Austinite, Lance Armstrong, sat nearby. Ms. David and Ms. Crow had formed an environmental group under the banner of "The Stop Global Warming College Tour." Ms. David came to my table.

After a member of the media introduced us, Ms. David began with an urgent plea for the president to do something—anything—about global warming. I explained the United States was underwriting more global climate science than the rest of the world combined. Ms. David said it didn't matter, because all the scientific questions had been answered. She asked if I'd seen the recent issue of *Sports Illustrated* that suggested Miami's Dolphin Stadium was going to be flooded as a result of global warming and rising sea levels. I became unduly flip, asking her if the stadium was more than seventeen inches above sea level. She looked quizzical. I said the Intergovernmental Panel on Climate Change consensus opinion was that if greenhouse gas emissions were left unchecked, sea levels were likely to rise between seven and twenty-three inches over the next hundred years, with a midrange projection of seventeen inches. With the stadium sixty inches above sea level, professional sports could continue to be played in Miami.

Unfazed, Ms. David launched a harangue about how the president didn't have anyone around him who knew anything about science. I countered that he did, starting with his science advisor, Dr. John Marburger. At that moment, Sheryl Crow appeared at my elbow and snapped, "Which oil companies and corporations paid for his research?" I suggested before she maligned somebody she should know a bit about him. I pointed out Marburger's distinguished career. He'd been director of the respected Brookhaven National Laboratory, president of the State University of New York at Stony Brook, and chairman of the physics department at the University of Southern California, where he was a renowned expert in nonlinear optics. Crow had not heard the name and was unimpressed.

Then the conversation got loopy. Ms. David said the United States needed to follow China's lead on global warming. Crow seconded the motion. I countered that China had an economy one-fifth the size of America's yet it was projected to pump out more greenhouse gases than the United States by year's end. Our country was far more efficient in its energy use. It was China that should be emulating the United States on energy efficiency and emission reduction!

Ms. David now began a slow retreat, edging away as Crow pinched and poked me with a bony index finger. Like most healthy, red-blooded American men, I have always harbored a fantasy of being touched in an inappropriate way by an attractive female celebrity. But this wasn't exactly what I had in mind, and I asked her to stop. Crow rattled on, gave me one last emphatic jab, and said, "You can't speak to me like that. You work for me!" I told her I did not work for her, but for the American people. She spat out "I am the American people" and the conversation came to a close. No one had covered themselves in glory.

The purpose of the needless confrontation became clear the next day when David and Crow blogged on the Huffington Post that they'd wanted a confrontation in the most public way possible. Ms. David told the Associated Press, "I honestly thought that I was going to change his mind, like, right then and there." Anytime someone uses the word *honestly* in a sentence, it is a dead giveaway the opposite is true.

I learned later that despite her sanctimony, Ms. David may not practice the environmentalism she preaches. In 2009, a local newspaper reported that she and a neighbor had been cited for environmental violations at their multimillion-dollar properties on Martha's Vineyard, including illegally cutting off the tops of trees and constructing without a permit on protected wetlands. I would compare carbon footprints with her any day.

Unfortunately, this wasn't my only uncomfortable black-tie moment.

In March 2007, at the Radio and Television Correspondents' Association Dinner, I accompanied the president to a private reception before the dinner began. The night's entertainment was two comedians, Brad Sherwood and Colin Mochrie from ABC's improvisational comedy show, *Whose Line Is It Anyway?* After chatting with me, Sherwood blurted out, "You're actually not a bad guy; not like the devil they paint you to be." Great, I thought to myself. I've won acceptance from Hollywood.

I was a guest of CNN, seated for the dinner about three rows back, near the left-hand side of the head table. Sherwood was one table to my right and in the front row. I should have started to worry when he kept looking at me and waving.

As the official entertainment, Sherwood and Mochrie first plucked NBC News anchor Brian Williams and NBC senior vice president Cheryl Gould out of the audience to provide sound effects for a goofy skit about a lawyer and a hunter (a jab at Cheney's 2006 hunting accident). The skit ended with the two distinguished media figures burping "The Battle Hymn of the Republic."

When the skit ended, Sherwood announced he would need fresh volunteers for the finale. He jumped off the stage and strode straight toward me. I panicked and broke eye contact, hoping that if I didn't see him, he wouldn't pick me. I could sense him brushing by the side of my table. Then a huge hand came to rest on my shoulder, as he boomed into his handheld microphone. There was nothing I could do but allow him to propel me to the stage as more than three thousand people cheered. As I walked past the head table, I glanced at the president, who was clearly amused at my predicament, and at Speaker Nancy Pelosi, who seemed almost as ill at ease as I was.

Mochrie and Sherwood broke the news: "Karl, the reason we brought you up here is—we're very excited—the three of us are going to debut a rap song together." I didn't know what to think; I focused on remaining calm. Sherwood began bantering, asking what I liked to do for fun. I stood there stiff and uncomfortable, wondering why the heck I was allowing myself to be mocked, and answering his questions with more than a little irritation. Then it hit me: There were several dozen television cameras at the back of the ballroom trained on me and a couple of thousand journalists hooting and hollering. I could remain annoyed and aggravated, or I could make the best of an awkward situation and be a good sport.

Before I knew it, Sherwood yelled, "I think we're ready—so *kick it!*" and began singing a clever rap song he improvised from the information he'd just pried from me, dubbing me "M.C. Rove." Mochrie played the "beat box" and chimed in with sound effects.

So there I was, flailing around and living up to the saying about Norwegians: they don't dance, they twitch. That night, I twitched as hard as I could. Sherwood and Mochrie had recruited David Gregory and Ken Strickland, both of NBC News, as backup dancers. Gregory is a worse dancer than even I am but had evident enthusiasm for his role. Sherwood was quite creative, rattling on for over two minutes with his rap song, saying, for example: "That's right, he can't be beat / Because he's so white from his head to his feet / But he will rap it when you give him a chance / Look at him move doin' a rappin' dance / That's true, he's a dancing resident / He is the sidekick to the president / He's going way above / Tell me what is your name," to which I shouted "M.C. Rove!"

At one point, I took out my cell phone and pretended to make calls while Sherwood continued rapping, and I continued twitching and shouting "M.C. Rove" at the end of each verse. Finally, the music ended and the ballroom applauded. The dancers and rappers shook hands and I fled the stage. Speaker Pelosi's face conveyed abject horror, as if she had just seen a favorite family pet slaughtered. As I passed the president, I could see he was enjoying my discomfort. "You're fired," he spat at me. I made my way to my seat while still in a daze.

When the president's party left the ballroom for the motorcade, my first instinct was to call Darby. I wanted to warn her that her husband, who barely danced at his own wedding, had now rapped and swayed in front of people who ordered ink by the barrel and videotape by the mile. The Washington Hilton is notorious for blocking any cell phone signal, so I couldn't dial her until I emerged from the building and stumbled into the support van. She recognized my caller ID and before I could say anything, she blurted out, "Oh, my God!" The entire dinner had aired live on C-SPAN. She had witnessed every horrifying moment. We agreed I needed to let Andrew know his father would soon be a nationally ridiculed figure. I dialed his cell phone at college. He, too, recognized the caller ID and answered, "Dad, that was awesome!" His roommates screamed in the background, "Way to go, Mr. Rove!" and then broke into raucous laughter. My mortification was complete.

Talk show hosts had a field day with M.C. Rove. When David Letterman aired part of the clip on his late-night program, he called the segment "Why the World Hates Us" and called my performance "unconstitutional." But some commentators said I'd been a good sport, which is all I could hope for. Even so, I decided to be gracious to my tormentors, and the next morning I called Sherwood and Mochrie to ask if they had time before leaving for the West Coast to stop by the White House for coffee. They agreed and swung by on their way to the airport. I gave them a quick tour of the West Wing and then, without warning, the president's aide opened the hallway door into the Oval and Bush called them in for a visit. Brad Sherwood's wife, who came with him, was so overwhelmed at finding herself in the Oval Office that she began crying. The two comedians seemed uncharacteristically at a loss for words.

The next day, I boarded a commercial flight and two very large guys sitting across the aisle inquired if I was "M.C. Rove" and asked for autographs. Then they laughed. And when I got an iPhone, Andrew programmed it so if I opened YouTube, a video of my performance would boot up. There was no escaping it: the moniker and my mortification stick to me to this day.

CHAPTER 33

Leaving the White House

————— ·◆· —————

Ifirst started thinking about leaving the White House when Special Prosecutor Patrick Fitzgerald told my lawyer the investigation into the Plame affair was over. I was in the clear—but there were rumors that some in the West Wing thought my usefulness had come to an end.

I needed to know if those rumors reflected Bush's thinking. So at the end of one day in the summer of 2006, I asked the president if it was time for me to go. He rejected my question by laughing, waving his hand dismissively, and saying we would walk out together on January 20, 2009, and there was no need to talk about it again.

I was relieved and grateful for his support, and I thought the matter was settled. But a shift in circumstances the next spring caused my own thinking and feelings to change.

Two events during spring 2007 freed me to seriously consider departing. First, Chief of Staff Josh Bolten told all the commissioned officers that they should either leave shortly or be prepared to stay through to the end of the term. The president was intent on "sprinting to the finish" and Josh wanted an energetic team in place to help him do so. In a way, this gave me permission to think about leaving. The other event was the arrival in the West Wing in late June of former RNC chairman Ed Gillespie to lead the communications shop. With Gillespie in place, I could leave with confidence that an experienced hand would be on board to handle anything that came up.

I had spent almost a decade going all out for George W. Bush. Now felt like time to go. The Plame investigation had exhausted more than my physical reserves. It had also burned through a significant portion of my family's finances. I'd made sure that no one really knew just how big of a bite my legal tab had taken out of my savings, but I had juggled as long as I could without putting my family's financial security at risk.

More important than money, however, was the toll that my life had taken on my wife and son. I could see more clearly how the press attention, the protesters surrounding our house, the ugly anonymous letters, and the snarky Internet postings had weighed on them, even if I'd been able to block most of it out.

There are downsides to having 70 percent of the American people recognize your name and face, especially when some of them hate your guts and consider you the epitome of evil or Beelzebub himself. Andrew had taken to positioning himself ahead of me as we moved through airports as if he were my Secret Service agent. I joked about it with Darby, who replied grimly, "Don't you understand he's worried about your safety?"

I knew I would miss the work and my colleagues. It is true that after that many years, relations with some had frayed. Still, many had become close personal friends. I also felt I would be deserting the president at a moment when he needed every stalwart around him. The polls were lousy and the criticism of him unrelenting. But I knew in my heart that no one is indispensable, and I had started to question whether I was doing the best thing for him by staying.

I was changing, too, and I knew it. I wondered if I was becoming small-minded, taking offense too easily, and adopting a viewpoint simply because it was the opposite of someone else's, not because I had concluded it was the correct opinion. That kind of thing is generally a sign to step off the playing field.

There never seemed to be a right moment to raise the issue, but I finally arranged to have lunch with the president to let him know of my decision. We ate in his private dining room, just off the Oval Office, the giant portrait of John Q. Adams looming over us, and Ferdy, the mess steward, bustling around. We had our standard fare—he a low-fat hot dog, me a peanut butter and honey sandwich, with vanilla yogurt for dessert, his with chocolate sauce, mine with caramel. I told him I thought it was time for me to go. I explained the condition of my family's finances, my feeling that I wasn't giving him everything he deserved, and that I was ready for a break. The first reason he understood and accepted; the other two he immediately discarded—one as wrong and the other as a reason for a long August vacation. He said he didn't want to see me go but understood about the family.

The lunch created crosscurrents of feelings in me. I was relieved to have had a conversation I was dreading. I felt angry that financial circumstances were forcing me to leave. But I felt grateful the president had supported my complicated decision. Bush hugged me as our lunch broke and gave me a pat on the cheek, as he had at other moments on our journey together when he didn't want to say more. That was enough. I didn't need or want to say any more, either.

I stuck my head in Josh's office as the day wound down and told him of my decision. He later told me he was shocked but not surprised. At the time, he said I could stay as long as I felt comfortable, so I told him I would leave during the August break.

In the meantime, I focused even more on my job, not wanting to give a single hint I was slowing up, slacking off, or turning my attention elsewhere. Besides, I still had White House commitments to fulfill. One of them was appearing at the Aspen Ideas Festival in July, as I had in years past. Nothing like spending a few days in the cool mountain air with rich liberals to remind me how nutty they can be. I flew to Denver, and rather than wait for the short connecting flight to Aspen, I drove. It would take only an hour or two longer, the road was pretty, and it would give me a chance to stop and take pictures for Darby of what used to be Kokomo, Colorado, the little town where I'd lived as an infant. To reach Kokomo, I'd have to drive back roads, not the interstate.

The last big pass before coming into Aspen on State Highway 82 from the southeast is Independence Pass, elevation 12,095 feet. It's stunningly beautiful but packed with hairpin curves. I decided to take a break at the little town nestled at the base of the pass.

There's not much to Twin Lakes, population 219, except an old schoolhouse, some ramshackle buildings, and a couple of charming but beaten-up hotels and diners, including the Nordic Lodge—which, given my family's Norwegian roots, caught my eye. I stopped and went in. The reception area was empty except for a vaguely familiar man who seemed in charge. He looked at me with a surprised expression, as though he recognized me but was shocked I'd walked in his door.

He asked if I was Karl Rove. When I said I was, he introduced himself. "I'm Charles Gandy. I was the last Democratic state representative from East Dallas when you defeated me in 1984." The first thing I thought was, Uh-oh. And my second thought was, At least he said it with a smile on his face. Gandy went on to explain that after his defeat, he'd left Dallas but stuck around Texas and ended up raising money for Jim Hightower's 1990 reelection as Texas agriculture commissioner. "You beat me there, too," he said.

Gandy continued smiling as we talked about his transportation consulting work, how he'd ended up buying the Nordic Lodge, and how much we both enjoyed Austin. He said he'd read in the local paper I was speaking at the Aspen Institute, but he was surprised I'd stopped at his lodge, especially without an entourage.

He then reminded me he was close to Mike Moeller and Pete McRae, Jim Hightower's aides who had been found guilty of bribery and conspiracy. I told him he probably shouldn't mention to them that we'd met, as they blamed me for their troubles. Gandy told me he was aware of that. The conversation started to peter out and he asked what he could do for me. I told him I'd love a cup of decaf and use of his restroom.

When I returned from the restroom, there was a big, tall guy with his back to me, talking to Gandy. The man was so large, I couldn't see Gandy, but I could hear my fellow Texan saying, "You won't believe who just came in here—Karl Rove!" he said, drawing out the syllables with a flourish.

That massive mountain of a man, whom I'd never seen before and did not know, quickly spat out, "I'd like to hit that son of a bitch." Gandy responded, "Well, there he is," and pointed to me. I expected a right to the jaw, but as my potential assailant flung himself around and looked down at me, his glower changed to an expression of total surprise.

That was the moment I needed. I brushed past him exuding a false sense of confidence, stepped up to the counter to pick up my decaf, and then continued the drive to Aspen. After my encounter at the Nordic Lodge, the Aspen Institute crowd of caustic critics was almost a letdown.

On the day my retirement was announced, I was overwhelmed with relief. I managed to listen to the president's tender parting words on the South Lawn, and to deliver mine and not break down in tears. But I was also anxious; I'd seen colleagues leave the White House, only to suffer months of depression. I wondered if I would feel the same way. Darby dismissed that concern, saying I was too much of a type A personality to sit around, and besides, there were plenty of other wonderful chapters ahead in life. She was right: I was determined not to be like a neighbor whose conversations were dominated by the things he claimed he had done decades before to save the Reagan presidency.

To my surprise, I received one of the most powerful lessons of my time in the White House in my last week there. President Bush was going to Reno, Nevada, to address the American Legion National Convention on Tuesday, August 28, 2007. The president had been in Reno for brief campaign stops over the years, but this was the first time since hostilities began against the Taliban in October 2001 that his schedule allowed him to meet with the local families of men from northern Nevada who had died in Afghanistan or Iraq.

After the president's speech to eight thousand American Legion members and their spouses in the Reno-Sparks Convention Center ballroom, we went to a nearby set of meeting rooms to greet the families of twelve dead soldiers. My job was to stand in the corner and take notes on any issues that might come up, such as parents not getting a flag, benefit checks going to the wrong address, or a still-missing gravestone.

Handling these meetings was among the toughest and most important of all my White House duties. They were moving, gut-wrenching, and draining. Here, after all, were people who'd lost a loved one, yet almost every one of them believed in the mission, accepted that their loved one had died in a noble cause, and were coping with a devastating loss in a way that was both touching and inspiring. Here also was George W. Bush as both commander in chief and counselor in chief, comforting those who had lost a loved one because he had ordered them into harm's way. A president is never lonelier than he is in bearing this burden. And it was my job to help make certain that anything he could do to ease the family's pain was done. This particular meeting was harder than most. I had spent part of my childhood near Reno, and while I didn't know these men personally, I knew the neighborhoods they had grown up in and the communities that nurtured them.

We walked into one of the meetings to be greeted by a mom, a dad, and their second son, a ramrod-straight Marine second lieutenant. Their oldest son—Marine First Lieutenant Nathan Krissoff—had been killed by an IED in the dangerous Anbar province on December 9, 2006. Nathan was a counterintelligence officer with the 3rd Recon Battalion when he was killed. He was just twenty-five. I later read the articles from local papers after his death. He was remembered as an athletic young man with a great sense of humor and even greater promise. You could see his joy for life in the pictures that accompanied the articles. He loved poetry and was captain of his college swim team, an accomplished alpine skier, and a world-class kayaker who had qualified with his younger brother for the U.S. Junior National Kayak Team. He'd joined the Marines after graduating from Williams College because the events of 9/11 made him want to serve his country. His younger brother, Austin, had been so inspired by Nathan's decision that he, too, enlisted in the Marines. After Nathan's death, it had fallen to Austin to take charge of communicating details of the memorial services and funeral to family, friends, classmates, and fellow Marines.

Nathan's mother, Christine, began to talk. I've been around a lot of powerful people, including leaders of nations, two popes, members of Congress, Supreme Court justices, and captains of industry. But I have rarely been in the presence of someone with such quiet power and dignity.

Christine spoke of her pride in her sons. She talked about the letters, phone calls, and e-mails she received from Nathan while he was in Iraq. She discussed the consequences of victory and defeat in the Global War on Terror and her hopes for the world she wanted her remaining son, and perhaps grandchildren, to live in. And she told the president how proud Nathan was that Bush was his commander in chief. Mrs. Krissoff spoke with clarity, precision, and enormous poise, and I could see that the president was deeply moved. I lowered my head and tried to wipe my eyes without being noticed.

The entire time she was speaking, her husband said nothing; he simply fidgeted in his chair. I have been to enough of these meetings to know that there can be deeply conflicting emotions in one family and that when someone's not talking, it tends to be a sign they are mad. Generally, they're not mad at anyone in particular, but at life itself. This family clustered in the small room had lost a son and brother, and now their younger son would follow his brother's path into combat with a deployment to Iraq in March 2008.

The conversation came to an end and President Bush asked if there was anything he could do for the Krissoffs. At this, the dad—Dr. Bill Krissoff—spoke up. "Yes," he said. "I'm a pretty good orthopedic surgeon. When my younger son is deployed to Iraq next March, I would like to be working as a Navy medical officer, but they won't let me, because I am sixty-one years old. Will you give me an age waiver, Mr. President?"

I was startled. It was the last thing I expected him to say. This man, stricken with grief, wanted to honor the death of a son and the service of another by joining the military at an age when most people are thinking about retirement. The president, who always wanted to fulfill every request but knew this one might be a bit more difficult, nodded in my direction and said, "Talk to Karl." That snapped me back to action and Bill and I exchanged business cards. That was Tuesday.

On the way back to Washington, the Air Force One crew treated me to Tex-Mex food and a farewell cake. We ate it while watching an eight-minute slide show that White House photographer Eric Draper had prepared. The first part, set to the music from the movie *Air Force One,* consisted of serious photographs, some from important days including 9/11 and the night of the 2004 election. The second section was a sendup: shots of me wearing Elvis dark glasses on the trip with Japanese prime minister Koizumi to Graceland, offering doughnuts to a bemused vice president, wearing a giant corncob hat on a campaign trip to Iowa, playing cards with the president while wearing a surgical mask and him wearing surgical gloves (don't ask), and performing as "M.C. Rove." The final segment of Eric's show drew from pictures of me with my close friends from the White House and with famous people I'd met along the way, such as Pope John Paul II and the queen of England. While I was flying back to Washington, I later learned, National Economic Council director Al Hubbard and his deputy, Keith Hennessey, were wrapping my car in cellophane after covering the windows with Post-it notes. Their prank got splashed onto national television. In response, I lured Hubbard outside to admire his handiwork and arranged for Uniformed Division officers to handcuff him with a White House photographer nearby to memorialize the moment. The picture remains a treasured memento, autographed by its handcuffed victim. I got a group of children visiting the White House complex to unwrap the car and strip the Post-it notes off the windows. I rewarded them with the stuffed animals Hennessey had used to decorate the car.

On Wednesday, I got back to serious work in Washington. I checked out Dr. Krissoff with friends in Reno. He had been trained at the University of Colorado School of Medicine, practiced at several Reno area hospitals, and was a really good surgeon. He was also in great physical shape, perhaps because he'd been a lifelong runner and outdoorsman who enjoyed kayaking with his boys on the boisterous Truckee River. He faxed me his file and application for the Navy Medical Corps. There are no doctors in the Marines; Navy docs care for them. That's why Marines never speak unkindly about Navy medical personnel. I made a clean copy of Bill's application and put it in a file folder.

Early Thursday morning, the file was on the president's desk before his regular session with General Peter Pace, chairman of the Joint Chiefs of Staff and a Marine himself. After Pace went into the Oval Office, I parked myself in the anteroom with a lap full of paperwork and waited for them to finish. When Pace came out, I made certain he had the file. I asked him if the president had said something to him about it. He said the president had and that he would look into it and get back to me soon. I told him he would have to call someone else; I was leaving the next day.

Friday, August 31, was my last day at the White House. I gave senior staff colleagues and my own deputies and assistants paperweights—a plaster cast of an elaborate Eisenhower Executive Office Building doorknob mounted on a wooden base. The wood had been retrieved from an elm tree on the North Lawn of the White House that had toppled in a storm the year before.

I signed the last of several hundred thank-you letters to people who had been helpful to me at the White House. I was feted by the mess personnel at their staff meeting and given a handsome chef smock, which

Darby would frame and display in our kitchen. My staff had also arranged for cakes to be delivered to the mess staff, ushers, Medical Unit, Secret Service, Counter Assault Team, Uniformed Division officers, military office, and White House telephone operators, each with a thank-you letter. The Counter Assault Team guys sent me a signed picture of us taken months before.

One of the final things I did was sit down and handwrite a letter to Bill Krissoff telling him how inspiring he had been.

As the time to depart for the airport approached, I noticed that Laura Jenkins, my assistant, continued to find excuses to keep me from leaving: a piece of paper I needed to make a decision about, a file folder I needed to classify, a task left undone I needed to assign. Finally, she received a phone call, and her requests stopped. Laura and I said our good-byes, and Darby, our friend Rod Richburg, and I left the office, walked down the West Wing stairs, and began making our way to the car waiting on West Executive Drive. I was stopped near the basement exit by friends in the Secret Service Uniformed Division and by some of the crew from the mess who wanted to say good-bye. It was nearly three o'clock, but there seemed to be more than the normal number of staff milling around the basement door that led to West Executive. In a moment, I found out why.

I walked out of the West Wing to find the street lined on both sides by White House staff, who began applauding as Darby, Rod, and I emerged. Many of my senior colleagues were lined up along the roadway. Other staffers stood on the Navy Steps leading down from the Eisenhower Executive Office Building overlooking the road. I felt overwhelmed and almost paralyzed. I looked to my right and saw my West Wing co-workers clapping, some of them with tears. It hit me that this would be the last time I would leave the White House as an aide to the president. This was the end of a great chapter. I felt like sitting down and bawling.

I grabbed Darby's arm and said to her, "Let's get going," as I waved to the crowds on both sides of the street and pulled her and Rod to the car. In a moment, we were at its doors. I gave one last wave before throwing myself into the front seat and telling our driver and friend, Shakeel Urrehman, to get us the heck out of there. We pulled out of the North

Gate while several Uniformed Division officers saluted; we turned left onto Pennsylvania Avenue, made our way past the checkpoint at Seventeenth, and pointed south to Reagan National Airport.

We made it in time to catch our flight to Texas. Darby and I then picked up Andrew at college, and did what any right-thinking Texans do on the first day of dove season: we drove to the Big Bend to go bird hunting.

As I stood under a clear Texas sky the next morning with friends and family, enjoying the outdoors, I reflected on the extraordinary events of my last week at the White House—and I was surprised how much my thoughts kept turning to the Krissoff family.

Then I realized I'd made a mistake. I'd written the wrong person in my final moments of the White House. I had written Bill Krissoff, but I hadn't written his wife, Christine. She was the woman who had lost her oldest son, knew her only other child was going into combat, and when her husband said to her, "I want to join the Navy at the age of sixty-one," she had replied, "Honey, that sounds like a great idea." That night, I sat down at a desk at the Gage Hotel in Marathon, Texas, and wrote her a letter.

Several weeks later, I got a note from Bill and Christine. He had received his waiver and had been ordered to report for basic training in San Diego. Nothing was certain, but Bill was on his way. He and Christine shuttered up their nice home in Reno and moved into a small apartment in San Diego while they waited to see if he could pass basic training. I never had a doubt. I could see his spirit and hers.

Bill Krissoff was commissioned November 17, 2007, as a lieutenant commander in the Navy Medical Corps. His son Austin told him, "Welcome to the fight." I later found out that Bill had passed in months a training regimen that takes most new naval officers years. In his spare time, he would work out with a Navy captain and go kayaking with younger officer candidates, many of whom he would leave far in his wake. He is an orthopedist in a Forward Resuscitative Surgical System, a combat medical unit that saves lives and limbs of injured Marines near the front lines. And while his son Austin was on his second tour in Iraq, Bill was deployed there as well. I exchanged e-mails with him the summer of 2009 while he was on duty in Baghdad. He had received good news that day: the Navy had offered, and he had accepted, a thirty-six-month extension of his active-duty status. He would be providing health care to Marines when he turned sixty-five. He was hoping to get an assignment to Afghanistan, especially if Austin drew a tour of duty there.

I have tried to keep up with Bill and Christine as best I can. I exchange letters and e-mails with them, introduce them to friends living in their new hometown, send flowers on holidays, and pray for their safety and comfort and that of their son. I came to understand, more powerfully and clearly than ever before, what the president meant when he said that in these visits with the loved ones of the fallen "the comforter becomes comforted by the spirit and pride of these families." And like so many others who have met people like the Krissoff family over the years, I marveled at how our nation produces people like Nathan, Austin, Bill, and Christine. To see bravery, sacrifice, and love of country in such personal terms leaves a mark on your soul. It also deepened, in ways I could never imagine, my love for our country and for Americans who rise in times of consequence and challenge. As long as this nation produces people like the Krissoff family, America will remain not only the greatest nation on the planet, but the most noble in history's long sweep.

CHAPTER 34

Rove: the Myth

———— • ◆ • ————

I may have left the White House stage, but my legend remained and, weirdly, grew. Even after my departure, I continued to be an obsession for conspiracists on the left. Their most preposterous charge—and the one that killed my already tenuous faith in the press—was that I arranged to have the Democratic governor of Alabama prosecuted.

I wouldn't normally dignify the charge by raising it again, except that it was aired repeatedly, in seventeen editorials in the *New York Times,* on *60 Minutes,* and in nearly fifty segments on MSNBC, despite my repeated denials that I had anything to do with the prosecution. Here is the real story.

Don Siegelman spent twenty years working his way up from Alabama's secretary of state to attorney general to lieutenant governor before winning the Yellowhammer State's governorship in 1998. He was the subject of a criminal investigation begun in 1999, a fact known when he ran for reelection in 2002. He was narrowly defeated by Republican congressman Bob Riley but planned to run again in 2006.

However, in October 2005, federal prosecutors indicted Siegelman on charges he had solicited a $500,000 bribe, conspired to hide it, and obstructed justice. He lost the Democratic primary and, in October 2006, was found guilty on seven counts and sentenced to seven years in prison.

Then in June 2007, *Time* reported that an Alabama lawyer named Dana Jill Simpson had given an affidavit on May 21 claiming that she had been on a conference call following the 2002 election with Riley campaign advisor Bill Canary, who allegedly said, "Karl has spoken with the Department of Justice and the Department of Justice was pursuing Don Siegelman." This mysterious "affidavit" appeared out of the blue in a leak to a *Time* reporter. Simpson said she took "Karl" to mean me. Canary and everyone else on the supposed call denied publicly that any such call took place or that my name had ever been discussed in any such context. Canary's wife was the U.S. attorney whose office had indicted Siegelman, though she had later recused herself from the case.

That didn't matter to the *New York Times*. One of its editorials breathlessly declared, "There is reason to believe" that Siegelman's "prosecution may have been a political hit"—and of course called for congressional testimony by me. Then the *Times,* which until then had been merely obsessive, became hysterical. In August 2007, the paper cited Simpson's May 21 affidavit as "growing evidence that the Justice Department may have singled out people for criminal prosecutions to help Republicans win elections." In September, the newspaper called for congressional hearings.

But I had nothing—zip, zero, nada—to do with the Siegelman prosecution. Like other Americans, I learned about it by reading the morning paper, which might even have been the *New York Times*. And the career prosecutor who brought the case backed me up, saying in response to *Time's* June 1 story that "Karl Rove had no role whatsoever in bringing about the investigation or prosecution of former Governor Don Siegelman. . . . That decision was made by me, Louis V. Franklin, Sr., as the Acting U.S. Attorney in the case, in conjunction with the Department of Justice's Public Integrity Section and the Alabama Attorney General's Office. . . . Our decision was based solely upon evidence in the case, evidence that unequivocally established that former Governor Siegelman committed bribery, conspiracy, mail fraud, obstruction of justice, and other serious federal crimes."

One of the nation's least reliable papers was relying on two unreliable sources—Dana Jill Simpson and Don Siegelman. Siegelman was trying to avoid prison. And Simpson, well, because I never met the woman, or had any of the dealings with her that she claims, I could only conclude that she must be a nut looking for a television camera and brief celebrity-hood. That became clear after Simpson spoke to the House Judiciary Committee staff in September 2007.

Simpson repeated her story about the conference call that never took place and offered this fresh piece of information: Judge Mark Fuller, who presided over Siegelman's trial, was in on the conspiracy to prosecute Siegelman. Her proof? She claimed Fuller owned stock in an aviation company (he did) that had government contracts—to provide fuel, air-craft maintenance, and flight suits to the Air Force. That was it. Pure goofiness.

CBS gave the story its next big bump on February 24, 2008, when Scott Pelley interviewed Simpson on *60 Minutes*. She claimed she and I knew each other and worked together on Alabama campaigns. Over those years, she alleged, I had asked her to undertake tasks for me, including opposition research. She said I had tasked her in 2001 with shadowing Siegelman to get pictures of him "in a compromising sexual position."

I was flabbergasted that Pelley had bought her story. His producers had called me about Simpson the previous October. I told them I had never met the woman or worked with her in any campaign or capacity. It sounded to me like they were fishing, and I had no interest in elevating Simpson's claim by going on camera. After the producers' call, I phoned colleagues and clients from my Alabama campaigns to see if I'd met the woman and simply forgotten. Everyone said she had never been involved in any GOP campaigns and had become known only because of her "affidavit."

It struck me as odd that five months later, Pelley did not call to say that *60 Minutes* was going with the story and that he wanted to give me a chance to tell my version. Instead I heard the story would run Sunday when CBS started promoting it the previous Thursday. I watched the February 24 broadcast and then stewed about it for several weeks before calling Pelley on March 31 to list all the ways I thought he had failed to exercise due diligence. While cordial, Pelley was unresponsive. So I followed up with a letter on April 2, summarizing my concerns.

For example, I had been involved in Alabama campaigns from 1994 to 2000. Did Pelley ask Simpson in which of those campaigns she worked as "an operative" with me? And if so, did Pelley check out her claims by calling the candidates or managers or reviewing campaign· expenditure reports to see if there was evidence she was really an "operative"? Did Pelley ask when and where we met in 2001, when she was supposedly asked to follow Siegelman and photograph him? Why did Pelley think it made sense to ask someone with no particular detective experience to go on a mission with such potential to blow up? And why had Simpson left this exploit out of her 2007 House Judiciary Committee interview? Wasn't it odd that in the 143 pages of her interview, she said nothing about having met me, having worked with me in campaigns, or being asked by me to undertake an undercover assignment? Did Pelley uncover any evidence Simpson had shadowed Siegelman? Did he ask for travel records, itineraries, or expense reports that showed Simpson's travel matched up with the governor's schedule? In our phone call, he said she told people at the time she was shadowing Siegelman. I was astounded: If she'd told others at the time that she was a CIA agent, would he have accepted it as the truth?

In a letter two weeks later, Pelley answered virtually none of my questions. Despite its flimsiness, the story stayed alive for nearly two years. MSNBC devoted parts of at least forty-five shows to the controversy, with anchor Dan Abrams interviewing Siegelman on his April 7, 2008, show. Like Pelley, Abrams had not looked into Simpson's background and uncritically repeated her and Siegelman's claims, so I wrote him a letter similar to the one I had written Pelley, raising many of the same questions.

I also asked Abrams if he really believed such a scheme could be operated so effectively that it would manipulate the career prosecutor who brought the cases and the FBI agents who conducted the investigation. "It seems," I wrote him, "you believe that the absence of any concrete evidence is itself evidence of the conspiracy. If you don't have any proof Karl Rove did it, that absence is proof enough. I am that good."

When I went on ABC's *This Week* on May 25, 2008, George Stephanopoulos asked me near the end of the show whether I "directly or indirectly discussed the possibility of prosecuting Don Siegelman with either the Justice Department or Alabama Republicans." I replied, "I found out about Don Siegelman's investigation and indictment by reading about it in the newspaper." Stephanopoulos thought that wasn't good enough, saying, "but that's not a denial," though it clearly was. So I went further:

"I heard about it, read about it, learned about it for the first time by reading about it in the newspaper." Even that didn't satisfy the insatiable *New York Times,* which editorialized a week later that I "did not directly deny being involved." But of course I had.

There have now been two reviews of the issue by the Department of Justice's Office of Professional Responsibility (OPR). The first was triggered by complaints from a fired employee in the U.S. attorney's office. It centered on the question of misconduct by the U.S. attorney and concluded she'd acted entirely appropriately. The second review, prompted by Siegelman's claims about me, has yet to be released. But I was interviewed by OPR lawyers, who seemed amused by Ms. Simpson's wild charges. Apparently, Ms. Simpson refused to participate in their review. Repeating her charges to OPR investigators under oath would have opened her up to prosecution for false statements. When I had finished my deposition, the lawyers turned off their taping equipment and asked if I knew Simpson's current whereabouts. She had disappeared. I suggested they contact her former lawyer—the legal counsel for the Democratic National Committee.

While this was going on, I had become in March 2007 the target of another bunch of conspiracy buffs. Democrats accused me of having ordered the firings of seven U.S. attorneys in December 2006 because they had refused to prosecute Democrats. In reality, Attorney General Alberto Gonzales and top aides removed the attorneys after a two-year review of all U.S. attorneys that began after the 2004 election. They made the decision because the attorneys were not performing well or were going to leave anyway, not because they were disloyal to the Republican Party. No one in the White House compiled a list of U.S. attorneys to be removed or ordered the Justice Department to add a name to the list.

I did pass on three complaints about one of the names on the list: David Iglesias, the U.S. attorney for New Mexico. First, that he failed to do anything about voter fraud in the 2004 election that was so egregious that the Bernalillo County (Albuquerque) clerk, a Democrat, and the sheriff, a Republican, had both called for a federal investigation. I also passed on the complaint that Iglesias, in order to get publicity in preparation for a future political campaign, had personally bungled a high-profile corruption case involving the past and current state treasurers by interfering with the career prosecutors who were handling the trial. I also forwarded claims that Iglesias had sat for months on an indictment involving charges of corruption by prominent Democrats in the construction of the Bernalillo County Courthouse, refusing to file it until after the 2006 election for fear he would offend prominent Democrats he might need if he ran for the U.S. Senate. I could understand not issuing a politically charged indictment a few days before the election. The timing of Judge Walsh's indictment of former Reagan defense secretary Caspar Weinberger just days before the 1992 presidential election was egregious. But sitting on an indictment for nine to twelve months, allegedly because of political considerations, seemed inappropriate.

I did not know if these complaints were correct, but it was up to Justice Department officials, specifically those in the Executive Office for U.S. Attorneys, to determine if they were. My responsibility was to pass on such complaints to appropriate officials. Even so, the Bush White House was not like the Clinton White House, where political director Rahm Emanuel was in weekly contact with Justice. We showed deference to the Justice Department's special position: communications flowed through the White House Counsel's office to the designated officials at Justice. So I passed the complaints on to the Counsel's office, which decided whether to send them on to Justice, and raised to Attorney General Gonzales the question of the department's policy on prosecuting voter fraud.

Democrats went crazy when they discovered, as part of the U.S. attorneys controversy, that I had supported my former staffer Tim Griffin, the genius opposition researcher in the 2000 campaign, for an appointment as U.S. attorney for the Eastern District of Arkansas. Why not? He was well qualified, having graduated from Tulane Law, practiced with an outstanding New Orleans firm, had been a special assistant to then–assistant attorney general Michael Chertoff (head of Justice's criminal division), had been detailed as a special assistant U.S. attorney in the Eastern District of Arkansas, and was an Army reserve officer in the Judge Advocate General's Corps (he was to do a tour of duty in Iraq). Griffin had previously been interviewed by a Justice Department panel of career and noncareer officials and unanimously recommended for another U.S. attorney's post.

The real problem with Griffin was that Arkansas Democrats worried this would credential him as a future candidate for elective office. But so what? Many U.S. attorneys have gone on to careers in elective politics, both Republicans (New York mayor Rudy Giuliani) and Democrats (Rhode Island senator Sheldon Whitehouse).

Justice had a reason for each one of its December 2006 removals: the U.S. attorney for Southern California, Carol Lam, failed to give sufficient priority to prosecuting immigration cases (and Democratic senator Dianne Feinstein complained about it in a letter to the attorney general); the U.S. attorney for Arizona, Paul Charlton, failed to follow department guidelines of the application of the death penalty; the U.S. attorney for Nevada, Daniel Bogden, failed to prosecute immigration or Internet child pornography cases unless given a bigger budget; another—the U.S. attorney for the Northern District of California, Kevin Ryan—was a superb lawyer but a terrible manager; and so forth.

It's worth pointing out that there had been no outrage when Bill Clinton fired the Arkansas U.S. attorney investigating the Rose Law Firm and Hillary's missing records or told the U.S. attorney in Chicago investigating a powerful Democrat, Ways and Means Committee chairman Dan Rostenkowski, to clear out his desk.

Under the Constitution, the president's power over the U.S. attorneys is absolute. He could remove them if he thought they parted their hair on the wrong side—and Congress couldn't stop him. However, Bush was weakened after the 2006 elections and the issue's political value was irresistible to the hyperpartisans and ultraliberals on the House Judiciary Committee. The committee had already subpoenaed White House Chief of Staff Josh Bolten and former White House counsel Harriet Miers over the 2006 removals and the White House refused to allow them to appear. Democrats wrapped the issue of the U.S. attorneys' removal and Siegelman's claims of selective prosecution together and began braying for me. On May 22, 2008, the House Judiciary Committee subpoenaed me. As *Politico* reported, Chairman John Conyers was overheard just off the House floor saying, "We're closing in on Rove. Someone's got to kick his ass." Later that day, he admitted, "We want him for so many things, it's hard to keep track." There the issue stayed as lawyers wrangled over the question of executive privilege.

The Bush administration and I were willing to provide the information the Judiciary Committee wanted, but in a way that protected any president's executive privilege not to have aides routinely summoned to Congress to testify. Presidents need to protect their ability to get candid advice. My lawyer, Bob Luskin, offered for me to visit with staff or members informally about Siegelman and Simpson's claims or provide written answers to their questions, so Congress got its information while the president's prerogatives were protected. But Judiciary Democrats wouldn't hear of it, and President Bush's lawyers forbade me from cooperating. So the issue stayed bottled up in the courts, and Judiciary Democrats hoped for a court victory or a Democratic White House. And the legal bills—paid out of my own pocket—continued coming. I think that was part of the Democrats' plan: bleed me, punish me by running up my tab.

On March 4, 2009, the Obama White House announced it had brokered a deal. In essence, it told the Judiciary Committee to accept our offer of providing information while protecting presidential privilege. Harriet and I would voluntarily appear to answer the committee's questions behind closed doors, under oath, in a transcribed interview. I did so in two marathon sessions on July 7 and July 30, 2009.

I almost felt sorry for my chief interrogator, California congressman Adam Schiff. He was clearly not prepared. The committee staff drew up questions, many of them duplicative, and Schiff appeared to be seeing them for the first time when he sat down. There were long pauses as he silently read the questions before repeating them to me. At times, the questioning veered close to lunacy. Focusing on the issue of "selective prosecutions," one Democratic staff interrogator wanted to know who had suggested the U.S. attorney for the Southern District of Mississippi, and how he had come to be appointed. I told him he had been strongly recommended by Senator Trent Lott. The guy didn't seem to know that the same U.S. attorney later prosecuted Lott's own brother-in-law, famed trial lawyer Dickie Scruggs. Talk about impartial application of the law!

There were virtually no questions about Siegelman, and finally, Democratic committee staffers admitted during one of our breaks that they considered Dana Jill Simpson an unreliable witness they had no intention of calling back.

DESPITE THESE CONTROVERSIES, I enjoyed a new experience: being a spectator at a presidential campaign rather than a participant. Among other things, I learned that it is much easier to pontificate on campaigns than it is to run them. You get to comment on mistakes instead of being forced to clean them up.

I especially enjoyed watching a formidable new political talent enter the scene. Barack Obama reminded me of John Lindsay's unofficial slogan for his 1965 New York mayoral race: "He is fresh and everyone else is tired." He was not only the first African-American candidate with a serious chance, he was young and charismatic, and positioned himself as both trans-partisan and the embodiment of a new kind of politics.

I also believe, quite immodestly, that Obama borrowed smartly from the Bush-Cheney playbook of 2000 and 2004. Like Bush in 2000, he worked relentlessly to diminish the opposition's hostility. Just as Bush had done with Gore in 2000, Obama created the sense he was comfortable with his life outside the Oval Office, in contrast to the Clintons, whose lifelong ambitions for the White House made people uncomfortable. Obama also emphasized centrist views, making it difficult to attack him as a traditional Democratic liberal. For example, he didn't talk about raising taxes on the top 5 percent; he talked about cutting taxes for the 95 percent of Americans making under $250,000 a year. And between June 1 and Election Day, for every four words he uttered about cutting taxes, he mentioned only one word about raising them—and then generally only to say he felt the top rate should be what it was in the Clinton era. He also talked incessantly about cutting deficits and "ending government programs that do not work." This came across to most people as reassuring—or at least not threatening.

Obama was clever strategically, but he also made sure to have important tactical advantages, starting with money. Between May 31 and Election Day, Obama and the Democratic National Committee raised and spent $850 million. McCain and the Republican National Committee raised and spent $550 million. Obama also discarded the Democratic Party's previous reliance on paid workers and duplicated the Bush-Cheney volunteer "army of persuasion." He also understood how valuable the Internet was to organizing and communicating. And he worked hard to pull away small but significant slices of the Republican electorate, including evangelicals, veterans, and military families.

These strategic and tactical moves were crucial because, as intensely as voters were looking for change, they also had serious reservations about Obama's experience for the job: the final ABC/*Washington Post* poll found 42 percent of Americans said he was unqualified to be president.

It turns out that 42 percent were on to something. Obama took office in the glow of a historic election, with an enormous amount of goodwill and a rapturous press in his corner. He needed to be only average for some people to place him on Mount Rushmore. But his first year in office, his job approval in the Gallup poll fell to 50 percent faster than all but two presidents since FDR. Only Ford (by pardoning Nixon) and Clinton (by raising the issue of "Don't ask, don't tell") got there quicker.

There are many reasons for his sharp decline in popularity, starting with the fact that President Obama has governed in a manner far different than he advertised in his campaign. He has governed from the left rather than the center, unleashing a massive flood of spending; offering a budget blueprint that doubles the national debt in five years and nearly triples it in ten; pressing for a massive federal takeover of health care after running campaign ads calling "government-run health care . . . extreme"; and pushing a huge energy tax that would punish not just the wealthy but anyone who flips a light switch, drives a car, or buys anything manufactured or shipped in the United States.

Another thing that has badly hurt President Obama is that his claims—especially on health care—are simply at odds with reality. He said ObamaCare would not add to the deficit, would bend the cost curve down, and would reduce premiums, while the evidence shows just the opposite. Obama said that under his plan people could keep the insurance they had. Independent groups have shown this claim is simply false. At one point, President Obama was even so brash as to claim his plan would not cut Medicare benefits—even though the White House's own fact sheets said at the time that two-thirds of health-care reform would be paid for by $622 billion in Medicare and Medicaid cuts. The deceptions have badly injured his credibility.

These developments about Obama surprised many people—but not me. I had met Obama and watched him up close ever since he came to Washington as a freshman senator in early 2005. Over the next three years, I saw him accomplish little but position himself brilliantly for a presidential run. I also found out that while he liked to project the image of a judicious, disciplined, and fair-minded man, he was not so behind the scenes. In private, he plays fast and loose with the facts and his accusations.

Shortly after the publication of Obama's *The Audacity of Hope,* my deputy Barry Jackson asked, "Did you know you're in his book?" I didn't, but there I was on page 33, accused of saying something I'd never said:

> For a younger generation of conservative operatives who would soon rise to power, for Newt Gingrich and Karl Rove and Grover Norquist and Ralph Reed, the fiery rhetoric was more than a matter of campaign strategy. They were true believers who meant what they said, whether it was "No new taxes" or "We are a Christian nation."

While I readily admit to believing and saying the part about taxes, I certainly don't believe and have never said, "We are a Christian nation." It's one thing to say that America is a nation of faith, that our country draws on the Judeo-Christian ethic, and that we celebrate the First Amendment's protection of the "free exercise" of religion. It's entirely something else to say, "We are a Christian nation." What happened to the Jews? The Muslims? The Hindus? The Buddhists? The skeptics and nonbelievers? In America, you can have any faith—or not believe at all— and still be just as good an American as anyone else. I put the offending page in my pocket and went about my business. I had forgotten Senator Obama was due at the White House later that day for a meeting.

That afternoon, I walked down to the West Wing basement to get a cup of coffee from the mess before the meeting. The West Wing is surprisingly small, with only two stairways connecting the three floors. I was clambering down one of them to get my coffee when I ran into Obama, who had arrived early. We chatted, starting as we almost always did with the latest antics of our mutual friend, Ken Mehlman, Obama's Harvard Law School classmate.

My feistiness, however, got the best of me. After a few moments, I said to the senator, "I understand I'm in your book." He appeared to draw a blank and said that he didn't think that was the case. I said, "Oh no, you've got me in there saying 'We are a Christian nation.' Can you tell me where I said that?" He demurred, saying he didn't attribute that to me. I replied, "No, you've got my name and the word 'said' and quote marks. People will think I said that. So where did I?"

At this point, Obama appeared to recall that my name was mentioned in his book, but protested I had incorrectly described the text. I couldn't resist. I pulled the copy from my jacket. He looked surprised and began insisting he really wasn't saying what he had quoted me as saying. After a few moments, the conversation drew to an awkward and unsatisfactory conclusion; he was unwilling to acknowledge the mistake or apologize. It seemed to me he didn't much care that he had attributed to me something I had never said and found offensive.

But Obama remembered the moment. On April 26, 2008, I attended the White House Correspondents' Dinner as a guest of *Newsweek* editor Jon Meacham. At the dinner, Jon sat between me and Valerie Jarrett, one of Michelle and Barack Obama's closest friends, who advised the campaign and joined them in the White House. During the dinner, Jarrett e-mailed Obama on her BlackBerry to let him know she was breaking bread with Satan himself. He e-mailed her back and Jarrett made the mistake of showing Jon and me his reply, which was "Rove hates me." I knew Senator Obama was alluding to our run-in over the passage in his book. I asked Jarrett to tell him I wasn't in the habit of hating people.

Barack Obama has held himself up as the truest, purest proponent of a fresh new style of politics. He said he decided to run for president because he believed that Americans "were hungry for a new kind of politics, a politics that focused not just on how to win but why we should, a politics that focused on those values and ideals that we held in common as Americans; a politics that favored common sense over ideology, straight talk over spin." So it was notable that in his book he *was* practicing old-style politics. I am the first to concede this wasn't an earth-shattering event. But these kind of small, seemingly unimportant acts can reveal a great deal about a person.

Though we didn't discuss it in our West Wing encounter, Obama also went on in his book to describe me and other conservatives as "eerily reminiscent of some of the New Left's leaders during the sixties," who "viewed politics as a contest not just between competing policy visions, but between good and evil." Now, that is rich, isn't it? The last time I checked, I hadn't bombed any government building (like, say, Obama's great friend William Ayers); or asked that God "damn" America (like, say, Obama's former pastor and close friend Jeremiah Wright); or declared that I was proud of my country for the first time in my life only when I was in my forties (like, say, Obama's wife, Michelle).

Nor had I ever seen political opponents as pure evil and my political allies as all good. It is one thing to paint your political opponents in such nasty and condescending terms; it is worse to do that while hailing yourself as the incarnation of civility and high-minded discourse. Then again, this is the same man who, on the campaign trail, paraphrased Sean Connery from *The Untouchables:* "If they bring a knife to the fight, we bring a gun," and who in a public speech warned a Democratic congressman who had dissented on Obama's stimulus bill, "Don't think we're not keeping score, brother." I couldn't help but take away the lesson that Chicago politicians will always be Chicago politicians, no matter what they proclaim themselves to be. And from his actions in office, I take it that liberal politicians will always be liberal politicians, no matter what they campaigned as.

EPILOGUE

By providence or fate, I have been part of some of the most controversial elections and presidential decisions in recent American history. Politics is a profession that evokes mixed feelings. Most mothers may still want their children to grow up to be president but don't want them to become politicians on their way there. Many people view politics as grubby, shallow, and dirty, built on distasteful compromises and promises meant to be discarded.

That is not the full story. At its heart and in its results, politics is the great, moving expression of our democracy. There are knaves and fools in politics, but the arena is also filled with people motivated by high ideals and great causes who work with skill, integrity, and honor.

And politics needs to be judged by its history and results. The American political system is the envy of the world, the greatest governing achievement in human history. But it did not appear easily or overnight. It came from fractious debates and fallible men. The Founders expected politics to be unruly—after all, that was the politics of their time. So despite missteps and tense moments, large egos and short tempers, they labored to create our founding documents, which are the greatest ever struck off at any time by the mind and purpose of man, to paraphrase British prime minister William Gladstone.

At its best, politics is about advancing human dignity and prosperity. And so I say with the author John Buchan that "Politics is still the greatest and most honorable adventure." For me, it has been a joy.

That adventure has taken me down many interesting paths and brought me into the company of many worthy, admirable people, most especially George W. Bush. But I never really expected to walk through the gates of 1600 Pennsylvania Avenue, as I did on January 20, 2001. That afternoon, I thought I knew more than I actually did. In the thousands of days that followed, I was to learn essential truths about the importance of courage and moral clarity to the presidency and therefore our country.

Presidents who leave a large mark on history share certain traits. One is their ability to rise to the clear and present challenges that face the country. Lincoln, for example, tackled a pressing moral issue that fifteen presidents before him had avoided—slavery. FDR came into office three years after the stock market crashed. And Ronald Reagan had to deal with a flagging economy and an ascendant Soviet Union. Each man came into office with a plan, however imperfect, to deal with the crisis.

But others find themselves forced to face the unknowable. Eight presidents—from John Tyler to Gerald Ford—gained the Oval Office as a result of the assassination or resignation of their predecessor. These men quickly came to understand that the presidency they were handed was not necessarily the one they wished to have.

Consequential presidents have another thing in common: They focus on big purposes and great goals that will serve the country well for decades. While being tugged at from all directions, they maneuver every day, often raggedly, to achieve vital ambitions. Sometimes they are forced to improvise, because history hurls extraordinary challenges their way.

Bush both rose to the moment he was handed and pursued ambitious policies. He won an extremely close and controversial election on a domestic platform, but on September 11, 2001, he found himself and the nation facing a new enemy on a new kind of battlefield.

It was not simply that terrorists had struck mighty buildings in New York and Washington and plowed a deep hole in a tranquil Pennsylvania field. The attacks were part of an assault on the Western idea of a free society, the latest in a string of attacks against the U.S. embassies in Kenya and Tanzania in 1998, the Khobar Towers in 1996, the USS *Cole* off the coast of Yemen in 2000, and, of course, the World Trade Center in 1993.

The 9/11 attacks were part of a broader offensive by radical Islamists to rip apart civil society and grab power from Indonesia and the Philippines to Afghanistan to Iran to Lebanon and into North Africa. These radical Islamists were driven by a well-constructed and enduring ideology that in the age of weapons of mass destruction posed an intolerable threat to American security and interests.

Atop a crushed fire truck, amidst the rubble of shattered towers, Bush showed moral clarity and courage that were to prove vital to confronting this enemy. Bush realized that we were in a new struggle against a global totalitarianism that, while different in important respects, was as aggressive as Communism in its Cold War heyday.

His critical insight was that Western ideas of freedom, democracy, and open markets provided a bulwark against this new tyranny. So in addition to routing the Taliban and destroying al-Qaeda, he sought to plant democracy firmly in Afghanistan and Iraq, the historic center of the Middle East. He saw that by promoting freedom, the United States could give millions of Muslims a compelling reason to stand with us in this struggle. Such conviction is too rare in leaders: I am confident his actions will be judged by history as brave and right.

He placed the same simple idea—that the most effective way to strengthen a society is to drive toward greater human liberty—at the center of his domestic work. But instead of confining his ambitions to long-standing Republican issues such as tax cuts (he won two significant rounds there), he went deep into Democratic territory to show how government can use the tools of capitalism to soften its rough justice.

He showed how competition and transparency could improve and modernize education, retirement systems, and health care. On education, he sought reforms that would remove false claims of success so parents could know the real results and demand better of their local schools— a policy that would lead to greater opportunities for children of all backgrounds.

He also fought to create health savings accounts, to help workers save more for their own retirement, and to launch private accounts in Social Security that would enable individuals to control some of the money they paid into the system. He made more prescription drugs available to seniors with a new program that used market forces to drive down costs.

To augment private charitable efforts, he stripped away biases in federal policies against faith-based organizations. And he brought to Washington many of the ideas conservatives had talked about for generations— giving more power to individuals, bolstering ownership, and removing arbitrary government restraints on the economy—but applied them to areas of American life that his party had often neglected.

There is a natural tension in politics between those who push for big ideas and those who concentrate on the practical realities of governing. Bush provided a bridge between those two groups; he saw horizons, but he also delivered in the here and now. His focus on a bold conservative agenda, offered with confidence and without apology, was the basis of two presidential victories and eight years in the White House.

I have long admired America's leaders who thought big and acted on their convictions. George W. Bush was that kind of leader. His presidency was not without errors; none is. But taken in their totality, his achievements over eight years were impressive, durable, and significant.

History will render its verdict on his presidency in the fullness of time, and I have little doubt that verdict will be kind. I am proud to have been part of the long journey of a man of courage and consequence who sought to provide conservative reform of great institutions in need of repair and kept America safe in its hour of peril.

NOTES

CHAPTER 1: A BROKEN FAMILY ON THE WESTERN FRONT

19 *"informed his wife"*: James Moore, "The Closets of Karl and Ken," Huffington Post, September 4, 2006.

19 *"suffered emotional damage"*: Paul Alexander, *Machiavelli's Shadow: The Rise and Fall of Karl Rove* (New York: Modern Times, 2008), p. 33.

19 *"a man of almost"*: James Moore and Wayne Slater, *The Architect: Karl Rove and the Dream of Absolute Power* (New York: Three Rivers, 2006), p. 135.

19 *"I am sorry I caused you"*: Letter from Reba Rove to Louis C. Rove, Jr., February 4, 1971. The letter also thanks my father, saying, "You went beyond the call financially."

19 *She wrote again to deny:* Undated 1971 letter from Reba Rove to Louis C. Rove, Jr.

20 *"passed away quietly at home"*: James Moore and Wayne Slater, *The Architect: Karl Rove and the Dream of Absolute Power* (New York: Three Rivers, 2006), p. 135.

20 *"The seventy-six-year-old Rove"*: Ibid.

CHAPTER 2: KING OF THE COLLEGE REPUBLICANS

24 *"derelicts and hippies"*: George Tagge, "Dixon Blames G.O.P. in Hippie Gate Crashing," *Chicago Tribune*, July 17, 1970.

24 *On average:* Turnout as percent of VEP, document by Prof. Michael McDonald, George Mason University.

29 *inducted during the Vietnam War:* Selective Service System, http://www.sss.gov/induct.htm. *Statistical Abstract of the United States*, http://www.census.gov/compendia/statab/.

29 *"who went out of their way"*: Dan Balz, "Citing His Vietnam Service, Kerry Assails Cheney, Rove," *Washington Post*, April 17, 2004.

29 *"I'm just not going to be accused"*: Ibid.

29 *including former senator Max Cleland:* Scott Shepard, "Kerry Kick-Starting Campaign with News Ads, Faces and Harsher Critique of Iraq War," Cox News Service, September 1, 2004.

30 *who received student deferments:* There were 15.97 million men granted student deferments (classified 1-S or 2-S) from 1964 to 1973, according to the *Statistical Abstract of the United States*, 1965–74 eds., http://www.census.gov/prod/www/abs/statab1951-1994.htm.

30 *"You can't get a thirty-five-year-old"*: Karl Rove, interview by Dan Rather, *CBS Evening News*, CBS, January 18, 1972. You can watch the interview at: http://www.youtube.com/watch?v=9HPnW4EBed4.

31 *50 percent for McGovern:* 1972 CBS News Exit Poll, available online through the Roper Center: http://www.ropercenter.uconn.edu/cgi-bin/hsrun.exe/Roperweb/Catalog40/Catalog40.htx:start=TopSummary_Link?Archno=USCBS1972-NATELEC.

32 *"I don't know anyone"*: Jeff Dufour, "Omigod! A Republican in NYC!," *The Hill*, August 30, 2004.

37 *"the Post ran a story"*: John Saar, "GOP Probes Official as Teacher of 'Tricks,' " *Washington Post*, August 10, 1973.

41 *the GOP lost four Senate seats:* Statistics of the Congressional Election of November 4, 1974, p. 22, http://clerk.house.gov/member_info/electionInfo/1974election.pdf.

CHAPTER 3: PLANTING ROOTS IN TEXAS

47 *Democrats lost a vital advantage: White v. Regester,* 41 U.S. 755 (1973).

51 *Jennifer Fitzgerald:* Yes, the same woman who tabloid journalists suggested had an affair with George H. W. Bush, a charge I found completely improbable, given what I knew of him and saw of her. Rumors of an affair first appeared in the *New York Post* in 1992, and Kitty Kelley babbles at length about it in her unauthorized 2004 biography, *The Family: The Real Story of the Bush Dynasty.* Both stories strike me as trash.

59 *"ended Ms. Guerrero's political career":* Wayne Slater, "Rivals Again Fault Bush Over Rumors," *Dallas Morning News,* December 2, 1999, reprinted in *Bush's Brain,* p. 27.

59 *We had sketchy information:* One trio of journalists says I had been given Lena's transcript and passed it on to the press (Carl M. Cannon, Lou Dubose, and Jan Reid, *Boy Genius: Karl Rove, the Architect of George W. Bush's Remarkable Political Triumphs,* New York: PublicAffairs, 2003, pp. 62–63). I did not. A transcript would have made it all the easier to prove Lena had lied.

60 *My detractors say:* James Moore and Wayne Slater, *Bush's Brain: How Karl Rove Made George W. Bush Presidential* (Hoboken, N.J.: Wiley, 2003), pp. 43–59. The charge is more subtly made in *Boy Genius,* pp. 31–36.

61 *"There is no doubt":* Guillermo X. Garcia and John C. Henry, "Bug Found in Office of Clements Aide," *Austin American-Statesman,* October 7, 1986.

61 *removed the bug: Bush's Brain,* pp. 33 and 46.

61 *refused to take a polygraph: Bush's Brain,* p. 45.

61 *bugging my own office: Bush's Brain,* pp. 54–56; *Boy Genius,* pp. 35–36; Melinda Henneberger, "Driving W.," *New York Times Magazine,* May 14, 2000.

62 *Yet another myth: Bush's Brain,* pp. 72–73; Paul Alexander, *Machiavelli's Shadow,* pp. 34, 37–38.

62 *discovered enough to indict:* Christy Hoppe, "Ex-Hightower Aide, 4 Others Indicted; Ex-Agriculture Officials Face Fraud Charges," *Dallas Morning News,* January 9, 1991. Jerry White and Scott W. Wright, "Ex-Agricultural Officials Sentenced to Jail, Fines; Prosecution, Defense Criticize Judge for Punishments," *Austin American-Statesman,* November 20, 1993.

63 *death sentence for my nomination:* Texas Senate Staff Services, pas08-22-91, Senate Nominations Committee, Excerption: Karl C. Rove, East Texas State Board of Regents, March 26, 1991, tape 1.

CHAPTER 4: WHAT IS A ROVIAN CAMPAIGN?

64 *"mainly of throwing mud":* Anna Quindlen, "Obama the Unruffled," *Newsweek,* October 27, 2008.

64 *"electoral legerdemain":* James Moore and Wayne Slater, *Bush's Brain: How Karl Rove Made George W. Bush Presidential* (Hoboken, N.J.: Wiley, 2003), p. 15. James Moore and Wayne Slater, *The Architect: Karl Rove and the Dream of Absolute Power* (New York: Three Rivers, 2006), p. 6.

64 *"fear-based, smear-based":* Arianna Huffington, "The Internet and the Death of Rovian Politics," Huffington Post, October 20, 2008, http://www.huffingtonpost.com/arianna-huffington/the -internet-and-the-deat_b_136400.html.

64 *"Even the most hardened cynics":* Matt Taibbi, "The Return of Rove," RollingStone.com, October 16, 2008, http://www.rollingstone.com/politics/story/23482821/the_return_of_rove.

65 *Past races can help:* A trait recognized by Mark Halperin and John F. Harris, who write on page 266 of their book, *The Way to Win: Taking the White House in 2008,* that it is my practice to "study the past—with actual studies" (New York: Random House, 2006).

66 *cheating at golf:* Evan Thomas et al., *Back from the Dead: How Clinton Survived the Republican Revolution* (New York: Atlantic Monthly Press, 1997), p. 190.

66 *"Ozone Man":* Ann Devroy, "Bush, Clinton Begin Finish Line Sprint; Upbeat President, Charged by Polls, Steps Up Rhetoric," *Washington Post,* October 30, 1992.

66 *"most advanced gizmos":* Mark Halperin and John F. Harris, *The Way to Win,* p. 227.

66 *"We are the change"*: Barack Obama, Super Tuesday Speech, Barack Obama Headquarters, Chicago, February 5, 2008.

66 *"Together we can have"*: Ronald Reagan, televised campaign address, "A Vital Economy: Jobs, Growth, and Progress for Americans," October 24, 1980.

67 *focus groups had told Dole:* Alison Mitchell, "Politics: Political Memo; In an Era When the Polls Are King, Cookie-Cutter Campaigns," *New York Times*, November 4, 1996. Senator Bob Dole, interview by Bob Schieffer, *Face the Nation*, CBS News, April 21, 1996.

68 *Tony Schwartz:* Margalit Fox, "Tony Schwartz, Father of 'Daisy Ad' for the Johnson Campaign, Dies at 84," *New York Times*, June 17, 2008.

68 *famous 1964 "Daisy" ad:* Tony Schwartz, *The Responsive Chord: How Radio and TV Manipulate You, Who You Vote for, What You Buy, and How You Think* (Garden City, N.Y.: Anchor, 1973), pp. 93–94.

68 *"We are not concerned":* Ibid., p. 96.

69 *"came across as too negative":* Memo to Governor William P. Clements, Jr., from Karl Rove, September 4, 1985.

70 *"sharpen the differences":* The Architect, p. 288.

70 *average presidential election:* Center for the Study of the American Electorate, 2006 and 2008 Reports, http://www.american.edu/ia/cdem/csae/pdfs/2008pdfoffinaledited.pdf and http://www.american.edu/ia/cdem/csae/pdfs/csae061109.pdf.

70 *number of true swing voters:* VNS data and 2002 postelection surveys.

72 *results of his 2004 reelection:* Analysis of official county election returns from all fifty states' election authorities, compiled by the RNC Political Analysis Department.

72 *He even increased:* Edison/Mitofsky and VNS Exit Polls, 2000 and 2004. Readers should be cautioned that smaller exit poll subsamples for minority groups in battleground states carry higher margins of error.

72 *"Karl Rove did not leave":* Donna Brazile, "In Rebuilding Party, Democrats Need to Start From Scratch," *Roll Call*, November 4, 2004.

72 *"They were smart":* Adam Nagourney, "Democratic Leader Analyzes Bush Victory," *New York Times*, December 11, 2004.

72 *At any given time:* Center for the Study of the American Electorate, 2008 Report, http://www.american.edu/ia/cdem/csae/pdfs/2008pdfoffinaledited.pdf.

72 *They are less interested:* Among the more interesting studies on this question is: "Who Votes, Who Doesn't, and Why," Pew Research Center for the People & the Press, October 18, 2006, http://people-press.org/report/292/who-votes-who-doesnt-and-why.

74 *"destroy the opponent":* Paul Alexander, *Machiavelli's Shadow: The Rise and Fall of Karl Rove* (New York: Modern Times, 2008), pp. 15–16.

75 *"We are witnessing":* Arianna Huffington, "The Internet and the Death of Rovian Politics," Huffington Post, October 20, 2008, http://www.huffingtonpost.com/arianna-huffington/the-internet-and-the-deat_b_136400.html.

75 *embarrassing, but often highly relevant:* Chico Marx, dressed up as Groucho Marx, uttered these words: "Who you gonna believe, me or your own eyes?"

76 *the spot featured a woman:* Coalition for Family Values, ad transcript, from the files of Harold See.

76 *"honest and kind man":* Bill Poovey, "See Blasts New Ads," *Mobile Register*, November 1, 1996.

77 *"through a friend":* "Statement by Judi See," *Mobile Register*, November 2, 1996.

77 *One gullible magazine:* Joshua Green, "Karl Rove in a Corner," *The Atlantic*, November 2004, http://www.theatlantic.com/doc/200411/green.

78 *persistent Rove myths:* Wayne Slater interview, "Karl Rove—The Architect," PBS *Frontline*, April 12, 2005, http://www.pbs.org/wgbh/pages/frontline/shows/architect/interviews/slater.html.

78 *"I don't attack people":* James Moore, "Smear Artist," Salon.com, August 28, 2004, http://dir.salon.com/story/news/feature/2004/08/28/moore_rove_swift_boat/index.html.

79 *more than $4 million:* Texas A&M University Poll, April 15–23, 1994. Wayne Slater, "Richards, Bush Disclose Fundraising Totals," *Dallas Morning News*, February 9, 1994.

CHAPTER 5: CONQUERING TEXAS

81 *summoning them to testify:* Debbie Graves, "Proposition 1 Backers Turn Tables, Seek Finance Plans from Opponents," *Austin American-Statesman*, May 6, 1993.

82 *"My job gave me a glimpse":* George W. Bush, *A Charge to Keep* (New York: William Morrow, 1999), p. 58.

83 *I loaded him up with books:* Michael Novak, *Character and Crime: An Inquiry into the Causes of the Virtue of Nations* (Lanham, Md.: University Press of America, 1987); Michael Novak, *The Spirit of Democratic Capitalism* (Lanham, Md.: Rowman & Littlefield, 1991); Myron Magnet, *The Dream and the Nightmare: The Sixties' Legacy to the Underclass* (New York: William Morrow, 1993); Marvin Olasky, *The Tragedy of American Compassion* (Washington, D.C.: Regnery, 1992).

84 *"saps the soul":* Bush, *A Charge to Keep*, p. 25.

84 *"head her and hoof her":* At a joint appearance at the Greater Dallas Crime Commission, Williams called Richards a liar and refused to shake her hand after she'd suggested, just a few days earlier, that his Midland bank had profited from its business ties to a suspected drug money launderer. Mark Ward, "Political Barbs Draw Blood; Williams Refuses Richards' Handshake After Latest Accusation," *Austin American-Statesman*, October 12, 1990. Roberto Suro, "In Texas, Governor's Race Becomes a Horse Race," *New York Times*, October 29, 1990.

85 *"If you want":* Paula Dittrick, "Bush's Eldest Son to Run for Texas Governor," United Press International, November 8, 1993.

85 *"Our leaders should be judged":* Alan Bernstein and R. G. Ratcliffe, "Governor Hopeful Bush: Look Past Personalities," *Houston Chronicle*, November 9, 1993.

86 *"1,100 member multiagency task force":* Christy Hoppe, "Candidates Offer Crime Plans; Voter Issue is Hot Despite Decrease in Violent Offenses," *Dallas Morning News*, January 6, 1994.

86 *state's twenty-two media markets:* This means there are twenty-two areas around Texas where people watch the same local television stations, giving each area a sense of regional cohesion.

86 *education reform program:* James E. Garcia, "Bush Backs Home-Rule Plan for Schools," *Austin American-Statesman*, February 22, 1994.

87 *voters were concentrated in the six biggest:* Census Bureau data: http://www.census.gov/popest/archives/1990s/MA-99-03a.txt.

88 *"shrub":* Molly Ivins, "1994 Holds Bag of Political Treats," *Austin American-Statesman*, January 5, 1994; Thaddeus Herrick, "Campaign '94: It's Nasty Out There; Texans Fed Up with Politics in General," *Houston Chronicle*, November 7, 1994; R. G. Ratcliffe, "Bush Says Richards Ad Tries to 'Demean' Him," *Houston Chronicle*, August 31, 1994.

89 *"no to amateur gunslingers":* Terrence Stutz, "Republicans to Vote on Handgun Referendum," *Dallas Morning News*, March 6, 1994.

90 *Richards flip-flopped:* David Elliot, "Richards Backs Off Waterway Defense," *Austin American-Statesman*, July 26, 1994.

90 *"Prince Charming":* David Elliot, "Richards' Speech Sets Off Debate on Values with GOP," *Austin American-Statesman*, June 22, 1994.

90 *"pro-family":* Ibid.

92 *"some jerk":* R. G. Ratcliffe, "Richards Touts Teachers at Rally in Texarkana; Governor Calls Opponent a 'Jerk,' " *Houston Chronicle*, August 17, 1994.

92 *"The last time":* Sam Howe Verhovek, "Texas Challenger Uses Thick Skin and a Smile," *New York Times*, August 22, 1994.

92 *"I simply don't agree":* "Head of Bush's E. Texas Campaign Faults 'Homosexual Activists,' " Associated Press, August 26, 1994.

92 *"has never asked anyone applying":* R. G. Ratcliffe, "Campaign '94: Bush Clarifies His Policies on Gays," *Houston Chronicle*, August 27, 1994.

93 *"Bush [could] step forward":* James Moore, "Smear Artist," Salon.com, August 28, 2004, http://dir.salon.com/story/news/feature/2004/08/28/moore_rove_swift_boat/index.html. Moore's frequent writing partner, Wayne Slater, called Senator Ratliff several times years later to ask him if I'd put

the senator up to the attack. Ratliff told him absolutely not. (Interview with Senator Bill Ratliff, March 20, 2009.) Slater must not have shared this information with his coauthor.

93 *The sole proof:* Carl M. Cannon, Lou Dubose, and Jan Reid, *Boy Genius: Karl Rove, the Architect of George W. Bush's Remarkable Political Triumphs* (New York: PublicAffairs, 2003), pp. 73–74.

93 *"known for his principle":* Ibid.

93 *"Man, after that":* Stuart Eskenazi, "It's a Texas Ritual: Candidates Tote Guns, Hunt Votes," *Austin American-Statesman,* September 1, 1994.

94 *" 'Nice shot?' ":* Michael Graczyk, "Gubernatorial Candidate Bush Misfires; Faces Fine for Shooting Wrong Bird," Associated Press, September 2, 1994.

95 *the race deadlocked:* "Governor's Race a Dead Heat, According to Poll," *Austin American-Statesman,* October 2, 1994. The *Houston Post* and KHOU-TV sponsored the survey.

95 *the opening we needed:* Dave McNeely, "Claims of Mudslinging Can Be Misleading," *Austin American-Statesman,* October 16, 1994.

96 *"the steel magnolia of Texas":* Lori Stahl and Sam Attlesey, "Perot Endorses Richards; Bush Plays Down Impact," *Dallas Morning News,* November 2, 1994.

97 *"Texas is big business":* Ibid

97 *He recaptured the suburbs:* Calculations based on Texas county-by-county election results: http://www.uselectionatlas.org/RESULTS/datagraph.php?fips=48&year=1990&off=5&elect=0&f=0; 1994: http://elections.sos.state.tx.us/elchist.exe.

97 *Suburban women . . . Hispanics:* R. G. Ratcliffe, "Election Reshapes Texas Political Arena," *Houston Chronicle,* November 13, 1994.

97 *up from 33 percent:* "In-Depth Coverage on Election Night," CBS News Transcripts, November 6, 1990.

CHAPTER 6: A NEW KIND OF GOVERNOR

101 *"I just spent more time":* Elizabeth Mitchell, *W: Revenge of the Bush Dynasty* (New York: Hyperion, 2000), p. 314.

102 *canned oysters:* Dave McNeely and Jim Henderson, *Bob Bullock: God Bless Texas* (Austin: University of Texas Press, 2008), p. 137.

102 *sleep off a bender:* McNeely and Henderson, p. 69.

102 *two Thanksgiving dinners:* McNeely and Henderson, pp. 116–17.

102 *favorite Bob Bullock story:* Renae Merle, "Bush Delivers Eulogy at Bullock's Burial," Associated Press, June 20, 1999.

105 *"If you're gonna f*** me":* McNeely and Henderson, pp. 262–63.

105 *"You're a cocky little":* McNeely and Henderson, p. 259.

106 *"The governor passed":* Paul Burka and Patricia Kilday Hart, "The Best and the Worst Legislators 1995," *Texas Monthly,* July 1995.

106 *education package:* It passed the Texas Senate on Friday, May 26, by a vote of 30–1 and was approved by the House the next day by a margin of 116–20.

CHAPTER 7: GLIMMERS OF THE WHITE HOUSE

116 *"stiffly delivered":* Richard L. Berke, "Governor Bush Becoming One to Watch in G.O.P.," *New York Times,* August 25, 1997.

117 *"I respect and admire":* A. Phillips Brooks and Ken Herman, "Bullock Endorses Bush, Not Mauro; Rejection Shakes Up Former," *Austin American-Statesman,* November 21, 1997.

118 *$13 million:* Ken Herman, "It's Official: Bush in Governor's Race," *Austin American-Statesman,* December 4, 1997; Jay Root, "Bush Launches Bid for a Second Term," *Fort Worth Star-Telegram,* December 4, 1997.

118 *"Juntos Podemos":* If we had copyrighted it, perhaps we could have claimed royalties from the 2008 Obama campaign.

118   *Mark McKinnon would handle:* Ken Herman, "Ex-Democratic Adviser Joins Bush Campaign," *Austin American-Statesman*, April 10, 1998.

119   *"I hope you haven't forgot":* Dave McNeely and Jim Henderson, *Bob Bullock: God Bless Texas* (Austin: University of Texas Press, 2008), p. 247.

120   *a giant among that crowd:* C. David Kotok, "Hagel Touts George Bush Jr. for President in 2000," *Omaha World Herald*, August 10, 1998.

121   *one debate in mid-October:* R. G. Ratcliffe, "Bush Agrees to Debate; Mauro Criticizes Time," *Houston Chronicle*, October 1, 1998.

121   *race tied at 37 percent:* Wayne Slater and Sam Attlesey, "Latest Poll Finds Bush Headed for a Landslide; Sharp, Perry Appear Tied for Texas' No. 2 Job," *Dallas Morning News*, October 22, 1998.

122   *first Republican . . . to carry El Paso:* Bush won just over 50 percent of El Paso voters, up 6 points from his performance there four years before.

122   *"haven't made up my mind":* John Moritz, Mede Nix, "Bush Calls for GOP to Validate Landslide," *Fort Worth Star-Telegram*, November 5, 1998.

CHAPTER 8: THE GRAND PLAN

123   *"this far out in front":* Ken Herman, "GOP Looks to Bush as the Life of the Party," *Austin American-Statesman*, November 5, 1998.

134   *"A good leader":* Juan B. Elizondo Jr., "Bush Team Covers GOP Bases; Exploratory Committee Draws on Congress, Varied Views and Experience," *Austin American-Statesman*, March 8, 1999.

134   *"please stow your expectations":* Ron Hutcheson, "Bush Starts Campaign, Says He'll Be 'Next President,' " *Fort Worth Star-Telegram*, June 13, 1999.

134   *"I'm running for the president":* NBC Nightly News, June 12, 1999.

134   *"the responsibility era":* "A New Era of Responsibility," excerpts from Governor Bush's announcement, *New York Post*, June 15, 1999.

135   *"He doesn't need":* Clay Robison, "Ex-President Bush Says Son Doesn't Need His 'Voice From Past,' " *Houston Chronicle*, June 14, 1999.

135   *with 45 percent of the vote:* "New Polls Show Bush Holding Lead," Associated Press, June 15, 1999.

135   *"litmus test":* John DiStaso, "Exuberant Bush Sweeps Through NH; Foes Quick to Hit Bush Abortion Comment," *Union Leader* (Manchester, N.H.), June 15, 1999.

136   *"wonderful personality":* Ron Fournier, "Bush Raises $35.5 Million in First Half of Year, Trouncing Rivals," Associated Press, June 30, 1999.

136   *"staggering":* Peter Jennings, *World News Tonight*, ABC, June 30, 1999; Brian Williams, *The News with Brian Williams*, MSNBC, June 30, 1999.

136   *"dropped a bomb":* Dick Polman, "Bush Reports a Record Haul, $36 Million, in Just 6 Months," *Philadelphia Inquirer*, July 1, 1999.

136   *"opponents slack-jawed":* Phil Kuntz and Glenn R. Simpson, "Bush Campaign Is Likely to Reject Federal Matching-Fund System," *Wall Street Journal*, July 1, 1999.

CHAPTER 9: STUNG BY NEW HAMPSHIRE, RESCUED BY SOUTH CAROLINA

137   *"political community gave it meaning":* David Yepsen, "Straw Poll Proves It Has Meaning," *Des Moines Register*, August 23, 1999. Yepsen is now the director of the Paul Simon Public Policy Institute at Southern Illinois University.

139   *"Get-the-Governor":* Kevin Merida, "Hitting A Man While He's Up; In New Hampshire, an Evening of Get-the-Governor," *Washington Post*, December 3, 1999.

139   *"didn't dominate":* Dan Balz, "In Debate, Bush Kept His Balance But Didn't Dominate," *Washington Post*, December 3, 1999.

139 *"often retreated":* Richard L. Berke, "Confident Bush Takes No Risks in First Debate," *New York Times*, December 3, 1999.

141 *"too big, too tilted":* Richard W. Stevenson, "Tuesday's Big Test: How Deep in the Heart of Taxes," *New York Times*, January 30, 2000.

141 *"aura of willful levity":* Frank Bruni, "As the Hours Melt Away, the Hard Edges Soften," *New York Times*, February 1, 2000.

142 *media fell for it:* Deborah Orin, "Now to See Who Wins Real GOP," *New York Post*, February 24, 2000.

143 *trailed by 8 points:* Bush campaign tracking polls in South Carolina conducted by Voter/Consumer Research, January 12 and 13, 2000, and February 6, 7, and 8, 2000.

143 *Our national lead cratered:* Gallup polls, January 25–26, 2000 and February 4–6, 2000.

144 *"drive up McCain's negatives":* Nancy Gibbs, with James Carney, John F. Dickerson, and Michael Duffy, "McCain's Moment," *Time*, February 14, 2000.

145 *"I'm going to win here":* Rachel Graves and Schuyler Kropf, "Campaign Hits S.C.," *Post and Courier* (Charleston, S.C.), February 3, 2000.

145 *McCain decried Washington influence peddlers:* John M. Broder, "McCain Finds Support From Odd Corner: Lobbyists," *New York Times*, February 11, 2000.

145 *statements condemning Bush's visit:* "Bush Opponents Describe Campaign Stop at College as 'Racist,' " Cox News Service, February 3, 2000.

145 *editorial writers chimed in:* "An Ugly Nod to Racism," *Palm Beach Post* (Florida), February 10, 2000.

146 *leaked his concerns to the press:* Ibid.

146 *Burch delivered a blistering:* Terry M. Neal and Thomas B. Edsall, "Polls Show McCain Is Surging in S. Carolina," *Washington Post*, February 4, 2000.

146 *"some whacko":* Jay Root and John Moritz, "Bush Returns to Austin to 'Recharge,' " Knight Ridder, February 5, 2000.

146 *"dismay at the misinformed accusations":* Marc Lacey, "Five Senators Rebuke Bush for Criticism of McCain," *New York Times*, February 5, 2000.

147 *"The spot went too far":* Eric Pooley, with reporting by James Carney with Bush, John F. Dickerson with McCain, and Maggie Sieger/Detroit, "Read My Knuckles," *Time*, February 28, 2000.

150 *"hatchet job du jour":* Peter Marks, "Bush and McCain in Ad War, to the Delight of Democrats," *New York Times*, February 12, 2000.

150 *"run no attack or response":* Dan Balz and Terry M. Neal, "McCain Pulls Negative Ads; Bush Refuses to Go Along With 'Old Washington Trick,' " *Washington Post*, February 12, 2000.

150 *"unleashed the dogs of war":* Pooley, "Read My Knuckles."

150 *"I'm going to make sure":* Frank Bruni, "Amid Attacks, a Battle to Claim High Ground," *New York Times*, February 12, 2000.

150 *Bush had moved back:* Bush campaign tracking polls in South Carolina conducted by Voter/Consumer Research, February 6, 7, 8, 9, 10, 11, and 13, 2000.

151 *"my good friend George Bush":* Doyle McManus and Judy Pasternak, "Campaign 2000: No Clear Signs Back Up McCain's Claims of Bush 'Push Poll,' " *Los Angeles Times*, February 16, 2000.

151 *his involvement in the Keating Five:* The Keating Five scandal erupted in 1989 and involve allegations that five senators—Democrats Alan Cranston of California, Dennis DeConcini of Arizona, John Glenn of Ohio, and Donald W. Riegle of Michigan, along with John McCain—had improperly intervened on behalf of Charles W. Keating, Jr., chairman of the Lincoln Savings and Loan Association.

151 *"three described questions":* McManus and Pasternak, "Campaign 2000: No Clear Signs." Interestingly, Ms. Duren's name was not on the McCain list of complainers, and she refused to talk to the media after her town hall appearance.

152 *"fairly common":* Jim Yardley, "Calls to Voters at Center Stage in G.O.P. Race," *New York Times*, February 14, 2000.

152 *"purview of legitimate polling":* Frank Newport, editor in chief of the Gallup poll, interview by Linda Wertheimer, *All Things Considered*, National Public Radio, February 14, 2000.

152 *"Rove invented"*: Ann Banks, "Dirty Tricks, South Carolina and John McCain," *The Nation*, January 14, 2008.

152 *"created the push poll"*: "The anatomy of a smear campaign—Rove's Push Polls" by lawnorder, posted August 26, 2004, Daily Kos, http://www.dailykos.com/story/2004/8/26/31853/5881.

152 *"Bush loyalists . . . claimed"*: Ron Suskind, "Why Are These Men Laughing?," *Esquire*, January 2003.

153 *"partying, playing, drinking"*: Inside Politics, CNN, February 14, 2000.

153 *"Rove-orchestrated whispering campaign"*: Banks, "Dirty Tricks, South Carolina and John McCain."

154 *"his letter was not coordinated"*: Richard Hand, interview by Jonathan Karl, *Inside Politics*, CNN, February 14, 2000.

154 *some reporters peddled:* Jackie Kucinich and Bob Cusack, "Eight Years After S.C., Karl Rove Works with Sen. McCain's Camp," *The Hill*, September 8, 2008.

154 *"charges and countercharges"*: All debate quotes are from the CNN.com transcript, *Larry King Live: South Carolina Republican Debate*, February 15, 2000, http://transcripts.cnn.com/TRANSCRIPTS/0002/15/lkl.00.html.

155 *voted for Bush:* Pooley, "Read My Knuckles."

156 *"broke into tears"*: Ibid.

156 *"unforgiving concession speech"*: Ibid.

156 *"negative message of fear"*: Remarks Following the South Carolina Primary, Project Vote Smart, http://votesmart.org/speech_detail.php?sc_id=72173&keyword=&phrase=&contain=.

CHAPTER 10: THE BIG MO'

158 *"compassionate conservative"*: David E. Rosenbaum, "The 1998 Elections: The States—Governors; Middle of the Road Led to Victory in Races for Governors," *New York Times*, November 5, 1998.

158 *in their own communities:* Arthur C. Brooks, *Who Really Cares: The Surprising Truth About Compassionate Conservatism; America's Charity Divide; Who Gives, Who Doesn't, and Why It Matters* (New York: Basic Books, 2006).

159 *education the number-one issue:* Presidential Election Exit Poll Results—Part 1, http://www.cnn.com/ALLPOLITICS/1996/elections/natl.exit.poll/index2.html.

160 *"There is a good reason"*: David Gergen, "A Bigger Nest Egg," *U.S. News & World Report*, June 5, 2000.

161 *created the Internet:* Al Gore, interview with Wolf Blitzer, *Late Edition with Wolf Blitzer*, CNN, March 9, 1999; "The Best of Al Gore's Lies and Exaggerations," RNC Research Briefing, October 9, 2000.

161 *model for* Love Story: Eric Pooley and Karen Tumulty, "Can Al Bare His Soul?," *Time*, December 15, 1997; "The Best of Al Gore's Lies and Exaggerations," RNC Research Briefing, October 9, 2000.

161 *crusade against tobacco:* Al Gore, in a speech at the Democratic National Convention, August 28, 1996; "The Best of Al Gore's Lies and Exaggerations," RNC Research Briefing, October 9, 2000.

161 *discovered the Love Canal chemical disaster:* Katharine Q. Seelye, "Gore Borrows Clinton's Shadow Back to Share a Bow," *New York Times*, December 1, 1999; "The Best of Al Gore's Lies and Exaggerations," RNC Research Briefing, October 9, 2000.

161 *lived on a farm:* ABCNews.com, December 23, 1999; "The Best of Al Gore's Lies and Exaggerations," RNC Research Briefing, October 9, 2000.

161 *never grew tobacco:* "Al Gore, Q&A," *San Jose Mercury News*, February 15, 2000; "The Best of Al Gore's Lies and Exaggerations," RNC Research Briefing, October 9, 2000.

161 *didn't know that his visit:* Al Gore, interview by Katie Couric, *Today*, NBC News, January 24, 1997; "The Best of Al Gore's Lies and Exaggerations," RNC Research Briefing, October 9, 2000.

162 *faced enemy fire:* Myra MacPherson, "Al Gore and the Window of Certainty," *Washington Post*, February 3, 1988. Richard A. Serrano, "Struggle with Conscience Was Gore's Biggest Vietnam Battle," *Los Angeles Times*, October 15, 1999; "The Best of Al Gore's Lies and Exaggerations," RNC Research Briefing, October 9, 2000.

162 *sent people to jail: The Tennessean*, October 4, 1987; "The Best of Al Gore's Lies and Exaggerations," RNC Research Briefing, October 9, 2000.

162 *led the fight for a Nuclear Test Ban Treaty:* Gore 2000 website, October 14, 1999; "The Best of Al Gore's Lies and Exaggerations," RNC Research Briefing, October 9, 2000.

162 *always been pro-choice:* Al Gore, Remarks at Women for Gore Event, June, 1, 1999; "The Best of Al Gore's Lies and Exaggerations," RNC Research Briefing, October 9, 2000.

162 *co-sponsored McCain-Feingold: The New York Times*, November 24, 1999; "The Best of Al Gore's Lies and Exaggerations," RNC Research Briefing, October 9, 2000.

162 *supported the death penalty: The Associated Press*, November 19, 1999; "The Best of Al Gore's Lies and Exaggerations," RNC Research Briefing, October 9, 2000.

162 *wrote the Superfund:* Al Gore, The League of Women Voters Democrat Debate, April 16, 1988; "The Best of Al Gore's Lies and Exaggerations," RNC Research Briefing, October 9, 2000.

162 *supported welfare reform: New York Times*, January 27, 2000; "The Best of Al Gore's Lies and Exaggerations," RNC Research Briefing, October 9, 2000.

162 *"Your main pitfall":* CBSNews.com, January 30, 2000; "The Best of Al Gore's Lies and Exaggerations," RNC Research Briefing, October 9, 2000.

162 *"who's no stranger to exaggeration":* Frank Bruni, "Bush Questions Gore's Fitness for Commander in Chief," *New York Times*, May 31, 2000.

162 *"an exaggeration that may have been":* Melinda Henneberger, "The 2000 Campaign: Off to War; For Gore, Army Years Mixed Vietnam and Family Politics," *New York Times*, July 11, 2000.

CHAPTER 11: THE CHENEY CHOICE

166 *credentials the Arkansas governor lacked:* Peter Goldman, Thomas M. DeFrank, Mark Miller, Andrew Murr, and Tom Mathews, *Quest for the Presidency 1992* (College Station: Texas A&M University Press, 1994), p. 277. Also Jack W. Germond and Jules Witcover, *Mad as Hell: Revolt at the Ballot Box, 1992* (New York: Warner, 1993), p. 331.

168 *Cheney was a likely pick:* "Ex-Defense Chief to Head Search for Bush VP," *Houston Chronicle*, April 26, 2000; Mike Allen, "For Gore, Commemorative Pins and Needles," *Washington Post*, April 28, 2000.

169 *person of deep faith:* Danforth later wrote a book, *Faith and Politics*, bitterly attacking social conservatives and decrying their influence in the GOP specifically and politics generally. It could have made for a challenging period at the White House if Governor Bush had taken my advice.

172 *volume on past House Speakers:* Richard Cheney and Lynne V. Cheney, *Kings of the Hill: Power and Personality in the House of Representatives* (New York: Continuum, 1983).

173 *Pete Williams had a source:* "Cheney Changes Voter Registration, Boosts Bush Running Mate Chances," Associated Press, July 21, 2000.

174 *Vargas saying "a new name":* Elizabeth Vargas, *World News Tonight*, ABC News, July 22, 2000; Russ Mitchell, *CBS Evening News*, July 22, 2000.

174 *didn't take long for the attacks:* Ceci Connolly and Thomas B. Edsall, "Cheney May Help Gore Clear Two Key Hurdles," *Washington Post*, July 27, 2000; Rowland Nethaway, ". . . But Where's the Excitement?," *Ventura County Star* (California), July 28, 2000; Linda Seebach, "Is Dick Cheney Really a Texan?," Scripps Howard News Service, July 28, 2000.

175 *"acceptance speech of exceptional elegance":* David S. Broder, "Gov. Bush, Powering Ahead," *Washington Post*, August 6, 2000.

176 *"proved he has first-class wordsmiths":* Mary McGrory, "Loved It, Dubya," *Washington Post*, August 6, 2000.

CHAPTER 12: DERAILED BY A DUI

177 *Down by 17 points: USA Today*–CNN–Gallup poll cited in Frank Bruni, "The 2000 Campaign: The Debates; Campaign Aides Set Tone for Next Big Test in Race," *New York Times*, August 21, 2000.

178   *"more reinventions than Madonna":* Mike Allen, "Bradley Engenders a Cult of Personality; For Many Supporters, 'Integrity' Is More Important Than His Stands on Issues," *Washington Post*, December 19, 1999.

178   *equal partner:* Ceci Connolly, "Gore Makes It Official: He'll Run in 2000," *Washington Post*, January 1, 1999.

178   *"disappointed":* Ceci Connolly, "Gore, Clinton Face Toughest Loyalty Test; Vice President Sets Out to Blaze Own Trail," *Washington Post*, June 16, 1999.

178   *"attack dog":* "Al Gore's Reinvention Tour," RNC Research Briefing, August 9, 2000.

178   *optimist and intellectual:* Ceci Connolly, "Gore Aides Seek Huge Party TV Ad Buy," *Washington Post*, May 23, 2000; Brian Blomquist, "Gore Is Deaf to Stop Attack Advice," *New York Post*, May 28, 2000; "Al Gore's Reinvention Tour."

178   *new Democrat:* Ellen Nakashima and David Maraniss, "13 Ways of Looking at Al Gore and Race," *Washington Post*, April 23, 2000.

178   *angry populist:* Robert Kuttner, "Al Gore, the Populist," *American Prospect*, July 24, 2000, http://www.prospect.org/cs/articles?article=al_gore_the_populist; Dan Balz, "Gore's Balancing Act: Centrist Agenda, Populist Pitch," *Washington Post*, August 14, 2000; Marie Cocco, "Convention 2000/The Democrats/Bam! Gore Packs a Populist Punch," *Newsday*, August 18, 2000; Mark Weisbrot, "Populism Sells: Now How About the Real Thing?," *Times Union* (Albany, N.Y.), August 29, 2000; Thomas B. Edsall, "Populism 'Working' for Gore; Themes Securing Base, Analysts Say," *Washington Post*, September 15, 2000.

178   *"Alpha Male":* Maureen Dowd, "The Alpha-Beta Macarena," *New York Times*, November 3, 1999; "Al Gore's Reinvention Tour."

178   *conference in late August:* Robert G. Kaiser, "Academics Say It's Elementary: Gore Wins," *Washington Post*, August 31, 2000; Adam Clymer, "And the Winner Is Gore, If They Got the Math Right," *New York Times*, September 4, 2000; Ronald Brownstein, "Gore Outflanks Bush in Pursuit of Swing Votes," *Los Angeles Times*, September 12, 2000; "Gallup Poll: Majority of Americans Expect Gore to Win," CNN *Early Edition*, September 19, 2000.

179   *political scientists were assuming:* Ibid.

179   *"He is, big time":* Mike Allen, "Bush Appeals for 'Plain-Spoken Folks' in Office," *Washington Post*, September 5, 2000.

179   *turnabout is not fair play:* Richard L. Berke and Rick Lyman, "Training for a Presidential Race," *New York Times*, March 15, 1999; Adam Clymer, "Correspondence/My Media Moment; a Bush-League Aside Vaults an Onlooker into the Campaign's Glare," *New York Times*, September 10, 2000.

180   *"using expletives":* Jake Tapper, "Major League Asshole," Salon.com, September 4, 2000.

180   *"facing sniper fire":* CBS Morning News, CBS News, September 8, 2000.

180   *least helpful was Senator Arlen Specter:* Richard Berke and Frank Bruni, "G.O.P. Leaders Fret at Lapses in Bush's Race," *New York Times*, September 7, 2000.

180   *"Well, that's Washington":* World News Tonight, ABC News, September 7, 2000.

180   *"big government plan":* You can view the "RATS" ad at: http://www.youtube.com/watch?v=2NPKxhFQMs.

180   *"bureaucrats":* Richard L. Berke, "Democrats See, and Smell, Rats in G.O.P. Ad," *New York Times*, September 12, 2000.

181   *"That's all I want to say":* Ibid.

181   *Snow had actually broken the story:* Special Report Roundtable (Tony Snow with Bill Sammon, Jeff Birnbaum, Juan Williams), *Special Report with Brit Hume*, Fox News, August 28, 2000.

181   *unscripted town hall meetings:* Governor George W. Bush, "Maintaining Prosperity" speech, Green Bay, Wisconsin, September 28, 2000.

182   *earned us some good press:* Jena Heath, "Bush Gets Good TV Reviews; Gore Campaign Plays Defense," *Chattanooga Times Free Press*, September 24, 2000.

182   *"Shilohgate":* Walter V. Robinson, "Gore Misstates Facts in Drug-Cost Pitch," *Boston Globe*, September 18, 2000; "Bush's 'Message Make-Over'; Gore Flub & Made Up Costs Skipped; Lynne Just

Like Hillary; NY Times Found a Biased Network Media Research Center," Media Research Center, September 19, 2000, http://www.mediaresearch.org/cyberalerts/2000/cyb20000919.asp#2; NRO Staff, "The Gore Lies," National Review Online, October 4, 2000, http://article.nationalreview .com/?q=ZmExMjFlNzFmNWM5YWYwYzBiNWFmOTMzNmExOTkzZDU=. In June 1999 the American Veterinary Medical Association had discredited the report the Gore campaign cited as backup. ("His Lips Are Moving," *New York Post*, September 20, 2000.)

182   Globe *reported that wasn't true:* Walter V. Robinson, "Gore Misstates Facts in Drug-Cost Pitch," *Boston Globe*, September 18, 2000.

182   *Gore was twenty-seven:* Walter Shapiro, " 'Untruthful' Label Could Dog Al Gore," *USA Today*, September 20, 2000.

182   *meant just 62¢ a day:* Gore 2000 press release, "Gore 2000: Who Benefits from the Bush-Cheney Tax Plan?," September 20, 2000. He was recycling an earlier attack: see "Gore Talks Tax Cut as Riverboat Tour Ends," United Press International, August 21, 2000.

182   *"a stretch I wouldn't make":* Calvin Woodward, "Tax Group Questions the Way Gore Is Using Its Numbers to Attack Bush," Associated Press, September 20, 2000.

183   *"All they . . . would have to do":* Cal Thomas, "The Smell of Gore's Oily Politics," *Washington Times*, September 27, 2000.

183   *Summers, had similarly trashed:* CNN News Day, CNN, September 21, 2000.

183   *"short-term political gain":* Alison Mitchell, "The 2000 Campaign: The Texas Governor; Bush Criticizes Gore for Wanting to Use Petroleum Supply," *New York Times*, September 22, 2000.

183   *before Gore entered Congress:* "Gore: Union Song Was a Joke," AP Online, September 22, 2000.

183   *The story broke:* Dan Balz, "FBI Assessing Delivery to Gore Adviser; Apparent Bush Debate Prep Materials Sent to Former House Member Downey," *Washington Post*, September 14, 2000.

184   *a young Gore aide had bragged:* George Lardner, Jr., "Staffer Suspended by Gore's Campaign; Aide Boasted of Bush Camp 'Mole,' " *Washington Post*, September 24, 2000.

184   *" 'Karl Rove's fingerprints' ":* Jake Tapper, "Spy vs. Spy" Salon.com, September 26, 2000, http:// archive.salon.com/politics/feature/2000/09/26/tricks/index.html.

184   *FBI was focused on Yvette Lozano:* James Dao, "The 2000 Campaign: The Debates; Bush Aides Question Inquiry into Stolen Debate Material," *New York Times*, September 27, 2000.

184   *pleaded guilty in May 2001:* Christopher Marquis, "Ex-Aide to Media Firm Is Charged in Theft of Bush Debate Tape," *New York Times*, March 7, 2001. "Aide Linked to Bush Camp to Admit Fraud in Tape Case," Associated Press, May 26, 2001. Ross E. Milloy, "Woman Sentenced to Year in Prison for Stealing Debate Tape," *New York Times*, September 1, 2001.

186   *"has to stand during class":* The First Gore-Bush Presidential Debate, University of Massachusetts, Boston, October 3, 2000, Debate Transcript, Commission on Presidential Debates.

186   *"more than enough desks":* Bill Nichols, "Bush Battles 'The Man,' and Gore's Student Gets a Desk," *USA Today*, October 5, 2000.

187   *"I'll help you do that, Joe":* The Lieberman-Cheney Vice Presidential Debate, Centre College, Danville, Kentucky, October 5, 2000, Debate Transcript, Commission on Presidential Debates.

188   *Bush ahead of Gore:* CNN/*USA Today*/Gallup poll taken October 17–19, 2000; Keating Holland, "Tracking Poll: Bush May Be Expanding Lead Over Gore," CNN, October 20, 2000.

188   *"He just told me no":* Melanie Eversley, "NAACP Ad Blitz to Feature Bush Hate-Crime Reference," *Atlanta Journal-Constitution*, October 14, 2000.

188   *"I'm Renee Mullins":* Special Report with Brit Hume, Fox News Channel, October 24, 2000.

189   *"unclear what hate crimes":* Morton Kondracke, Mara Liasson, interview by Brit Hume, *Special Report with Brit Hume*, Fox News Channel, October 24, 2000.

189   *At a Spokane rally:* Joel Connelly, "Al Gore on the Attack in Spokane; Bush the Target as Vice President Tells Crowd That Every Vote Counts," *Seattle Post-Intelligencer*, October 24, 2000.

189   *"incendiary":* Mara Liasson, interview by Brit Hume, *Special Report with Brit Hume*, Fox News Channel, October 24, 2000.

190   *"a picture of integrity":* Alison Mitchell, "Bush Acknowledges an Arrest for Drunken Driving in 1976," *New York Times*, November 3, 2000.

190 *"It's an accurate story"*: Dan Balz, "Bush Acknowledges 1976 DUI Arrest," *Washington Post*, November 3, 2000. Most of the *Washington Post* coverage was on page A1 while the *New York Times* buried its coverage inside the first section.

190 *"not to drink and drive"*: Balz, "Bush Acknowledges 1976 DUI Arrest."

191 *"flogging a dead horse"*: Alicia C. Shepard, "A Late-Breaking Campaign Skeleton," *American Journalism Review*, December 2000.

191 *went with the story*: Shepard, "A Late-Breaking Campaign Skeleton"; Carey Goldberg, "Maine Lawyer Delights in Leaking Bush's Arrest," *New York Times*, November 4, 2000.

191 *"You wiener"*: Goldberg, "Maine Lawyer Delights in Leaking Bush Arrest."

191 *"acted out with Monica"*: Jerry Harkavy, "Dem Activist DUI source; Lawyer Connolly Unrepentant," Associated Press, appearing in the *Bangor Daily News* (Maine), November 4, 2000.

191 *"may help people evaluate"*: "Bush Campaign Fends Off Truthfulness Questions After DUI Disclosure," CNN.com, November 3, 2000, http://archives.cnn.com/2000/ALLPOLITICS/stories/11/03/bush.dui/.

191 *"our dysfunctional alcoholic society"*: Bill Nemitz, "Conspiracy? He Doesn't Have the Time," *Portland Press Herald* (Maine), November 5, 2000.

192 *Childs who called:* Dieter Bradbury, "Mystery DUI Query Surfaces," *Portland Press Herald* (Maine), November 5, 2000.

192 *that part sounded fishy:* Stephan A. Kurkjian and David Armstrong, "Bush Downplayed Drinking; '78 Comments Got License Back," *Boston Globe*, November 4, 2000; Bradbury, "Mystery DUI Query Surfaces."

192 *"dirty politics"*: "Bush Campaign Fends Off Truthfulness Questions After DUI Disclosure," CNN.com.

192 *"We're not commenting"*: Tom Raum, "Bush 'Not Proud Of,' but Admits Maine DUI Conviction 25 Years Ago," Associated Press, appearing in the *Bangor Daily News*, November 3, 2000.

192 *"not something we would engage in"*: Balz, "Bush Acknowledges 1976 DUI Arrest."

193 *Consider the national impact:* Survey by Pew Research Center for the People & the Press, conducted by Princeton Survey Research Associates, November 2–5, 2000, and based on telephone interviews with a national adult sample of 2,254. Pew says the DUI issue had no effect, with those concerned about the DUI offset by those who blamed the Democrats for the last-minute attack, but that's not what my gut, anecdotal evidence, and the Maine tracking indicate.

193 *28 percent said Bush's DUI:* Confidential Memo from John McLaughlin (of John McLaughlin & Associates) to Tom Cole, Chris Henick, Clint Key, and Boyd Marcus, "Gore's Drunk-Driving Smear; Post-Election Analysis," November 9, 2000.

193 *Bush did drop 2 percent:* Bush lost New Mexico by 366 votes, or 0.06 points; Wisconsin by 5,708 votes, or 0.22 points; Iowa by 4,144 votes, or 0.31 points; and Oregon by 6,765 votes, or 0.44 points.

193 *a margin of 305 to 232:* There were 105,405,100 votes cast in the 2000 presidential contest. (Federal Election Commission, "2000 Official Presidential General Election Results," December 2001, http://www.fec.gov/pubrec/2000presgeresults.htm.)

194 *dead even at noon:* 2000 Exit Polls by the Hour, Bush Campaign Document provided by Adrian Gray.

195 *Florida was the big prize:* CNN Election Night Coverage, transcript, November 7, 2000.

195 *we'd win big:* We did: even though turnout was less than expected, Bush carried the 10 counties with 67 percent of the vote.

195 *"7 P.M. in the East"*: CNN Election Night Coverage, transcript, November 7, 2000.

195 *Bush went on to win Ohio:* That works out to be a Bush lead of 165,109 votes in Ohio and 40,978 in West Virginia. (2000 Election Results, Ohio secretary of state and West Virginia secretary of state.)

196 *had projected Gore the winner:* Joan Konner, James Risser, and Ben Wattenberg, "Television's Performance on Election Night 2000, A Report for CNN," January 29, 2001.

197 *a sign of gross bias:* Judy Woodruff: "CNN says that the state of New Mexico goes into the corner of

Al Gore. Vice President Gore picks up the five electoral votes in the state of New Mexico." CNN Election Coverage, transcript, November 7, 2000.

198   *I used the occasion:* Ibid.

CHAPTER 13: THIRTY-SIX DAYS IN HELL

203   *"harvesting":* David Boies, *Courting Justice: From NY Yankees v. Major League Baseball to Bush v. Gore, 1997–2000.* (New York: Hyperion, 2004), p. 428.

203   *"trolling for votes":* Ibid., p. 429.

203   *Ron Klain ignited:* David S. Broder and Ceci Connolly, "Democrats Urge Gore Not to Push It Too Far; Line Drawn Between Recounts, Lawsuits," *Washington Post,* November 11, 2000.

203   *24 votes were left uncounted:* Charles Lane, "Gore Could Win if Fla. Race is Unresolved by Dec. 18," *Washington Post,* November 11, 2000.

203   *"AFTER VOTING, CHECK":* U.S. Supreme Court Per Curiam opinion, *Bush v. Gore,* December 12, 2000.

204   *"Our democratic process":* "Bush Campaign Holds Press Conference," CNN transcript, November 9, 2000; Ken Herman, "War of Words Is Steering This Election Toward Crisis," *Austin American-Statesman,* November 10, 2000.

204   *Democrats supervised the machines:* Bush Campaign Holds Press Conference, CNN transcript, November 9, 2000.

205   *bribing derelicts with cigarettes:* Mike Johnson, "GOP Urges McCann to Investigate Vote; Party Alleges Hundreds of Accounts of Potential Voter Fraud in Milwaukee," *Milwaukee Journal Sentinel,* November 11, 2000.

205   *Gore's lead fell to 6,825:* Loie Fecteau, "Turmoil in Overtime," *Albuquerque Journal,* November 10, 2000.

207   *29 percent of military:* Richard Perez-Pena, "Counting the Vote: The Absentee Ballots; G.O.P. and Democrats Trading Accusations on Military Votes," *New York Times,* November 19, 2000.

207   *"take another look":* Senator Joseph Lieberman, interview by Tim Russert, *Meet the Press,* NBC News, November 19, 2000.

209   *"substantial margins":* David Boies, *Courting Justice,* p. 429.

209   *"expressed doubt":* Ibid., p. 376.

213   *"I think that's right":* Oral argument of Theodore Olson, lawyer for Texas governor George W. Bush, and response of Supreme Court justice Kennedy, Oral Argument Before the U.S. Supreme Court, December 11, 2000, *NewsHour with Jim Lehrer* transcript, p. 2.

214   *Justice Kennedy, who was concerned:* Supreme Court Justice Kennedy, during oral arguments by David Boies, lawyer for Vice President Gore, Oral Argument Before the U.S. Supreme Court, December 11, 2000, *NewsHour with Jim Lehrer* transcript.

214   *"I did not find really a response":* Supreme Court Justice O'Connor, Oral Argument Before the U.S. Supreme Court, December 11, 2000, *NewsHour with Jim Lehrer* transcript, p. 28.

214   *take a hike:* Boies makes no mention of the refusal of the Florida Supreme Court to respond to the clear direction of the U.S. Supreme Court's December 4th order in his *Courting Justice: From NY Yankees v. Major League Baseball to Bush v. Gore,* pp. 443–46.

214   *after being told not to:* Supreme Court Justice Scalia, Oral Argument Before the U.S. Supreme Court, December 11, 2000, *NewsHour with Jim Lehrer* transcript, p. 29.

214   *"You say it can vary":* Supreme Court Justice Kennedy, Oral Argument Before the U.S. Supreme Court, December 11, 2000, *NewsHour with Jim Lehrer* transcript, p. 32.

CHAPTER 14: THE REAL WEST WING

217   *"We want Bush to understand":* William Raspberry, "Some Questions for Jesse Jackson," *Washington Post,* December 22, 2000.

219   *Bush did win praise:* Howard Kurtz, "For the Transition, Old Whine in a New Bottle," *Washington Post,* January 8, 2001.

219   *The Dow Jones was down 9 percent:* "Nasdaq Sets Record (again)," CNN Money, March 10, 2000,
      http://money.cnn.com/2000/03/10/markets/markets_newyork/; "Nasdaq Trades More than Three
      Billion Shares for the First Time; Composite Index Also Posts Record Point and Percentage,"
      Nasdaq.com, January 3, 2001, http://www.nasdaq.com/newsroom/news/pr2001/ne_section01
      _001.html; Mark Trumbull, "Dow Nudges Peak of Six Years Ago," *Christian Science Monitor*, Sep-
      tember 18, 2006, http://www.csmonitor.com/2006/0918/p01s02-usec.html; http://www.nyse.tv/
      dow-jones-industrial-average-history-djia.htm.

220   *Rumsfeld gave an impressive interview:* Thomas Ricks, "Pentagon Nomination Delay 'Becoming an
      Issue,' " *Washington Post*, December 27, 2000.

223   *one by* USA Today*:* Dennis Cauchon, "Newspapers' Recount Shows Bush Prevailed," *USA Today*,
      May 15, 2001, http://www.usatoday.com/news/washington/2001-04-03-floridamain.htm.

223   *another by a large:* Dan Keating, *Democracy Counts: The Media Consortium Florida Ballot Project*,
      Washington Post, Paper prepared for presentation at the annual meeting of the American Political
      Science Association, Boston, August 2002; Dan Keating and Dan Balz, "Florida Recounts Would
      Have Favored Bush," *Washington Post*, November 12, 2001.

223   *Both ballot studies revealed:* The *USA Today/Miami Herald/*Knight Ridder study used four standards.
      By three of the standards, Bush held the lead. The fourth standard (the "clean punch" standard)
      gave Gore a "razor-thin" win, by counting fully removed chads as legal votes. Gore would have won
      Florida by 3 votes if this standard had been applied to undervotes. The media consortium study
      found that when uncounted ballots (for example, dimpled ballots) in Florida were examined, voter
      intent was clear enough to give Gore the narrowest of margins.

223   *"the legitimate 43rd president":* Congressman Dick Gephardt, interview by Tim Russert, *Meet the
      Press*, NBC News, December 17, 2000.

225   *Clinton staff had trashed offices:* Robert Pear, "White House Vandalized in Transition, G.A.O.
      Finds," *New York Times*, June 12, 2002; "The White House: Allegations of Damage During the
      2001 Presidential Transition," U.S. General Accounting Office (GAO-02-360), June 2002.

227   *"formidable adversary":* Ron Suskind, "Mrs. Hughes Takes Her Leave," *Esquire*, July 1, 2002.

228   *"Strategery":* Dana Milbank, "Serious 'Strategy'; As Rove Launches Elaborate Political Effort, Some
      See a Nascent Clintonian 'War Room,' " *Washington Post*, April 22, 2001.

229   *poll found that only 51 percent:* R. W. Apple, Jr., "The Inauguration: News Analysis; Tradition and
      Legitimacy," *New York Times*, January 20, 2001.

229   *Bush's disapproval rating:* "Historical Insights: The First 180 Days in Presidential Job Approval," Of-
      fice of Strategic Initiatives, April 30, 2001.

229   *he had a mandate:* Kenneth T. Walsh, "The Morning After the Ball," *U.S. News & World Report*,
      January 29, 2001.

230   *clear 180-day plan:* Richard W. Stevenson, "The Inauguration: The Agenda; To Do: 1. Undo Most
      Recent Actions of My Predecessor," *New York Times*, January 21, 2001.

230   *special education money:* Senator James M. Jeffords, *My Declaration of Independence* (New York:
      Simon & Schuster, 2001), p. 66.

230   *already on autopilot:* In 2001, $1.0 trillion—or roughly 53 percent—of government's annual outlay
      of $1.9 trillion was considered mandatory spending. If you add in net interest, it rises to $1.2 tril-
      lion, or 63 percent, of federal spending. Historical Tables, Budget of the United States Govern-
      ment, Fiscal Year 2009, Table 8.1, http://www.whitehouse.gov/omb/budget/fy2009/pdf/hist.pdf.

230   *focus on results:* The administration did include in its budget a $1 billion increase for special educa-
      tion funding. Analytical Perspectives, Budget of the United States Government, Fiscal Year 2002,
      p. 197.

231   *His targets were Jeffords:* Senator Tom Daschle with Michael D'Orso, *Like No Other Time: The 107th
      Congress and the Two Years that Changed America Forever* (New York: Crown, 2003), pp. 61–72.

231   *"cows, committees, and co-workers":* Daschle with D'Orso, *Like No Other Time*, p. 69.

231   *"Jim was blown away":* Ibid.

231   *"suggesting that [his] motivation":* Senator James M. Jeffords, *An Independent Man: Adventures of a
      Public Servant* (New York: Simon & Schuster, 2003), p. 282.

231   *"we shook hands":* Daschle with D'Orso, *Like No Other Time*, p. 70.

232   *"thinking of switching"*: Ibid., p. 94.

232   *"disagree with the president"*: Jeffords, *My Declaration of Independence,* p. 116.

CHAPTER 15: THINKING BIG

235   *"Enough is enough"*: Remarks by the President to the U.S. Chamber of Commerce, Washington, D.C., April 16, 2001.

235   *It reduced federal income tax:* Tax rates went from 15, 28, 31, 36, and 39.6 percent to 10, 15, 25, 28, 33, and 35 percent. "Summary of the Economic Growth and Tax Relief Reconciliation Act of 2001," Committee of Ways and Means, 6/6/01, http://www.house.gov/ryan/hottopicarchive/2001Tax_Chart.pdf. Also see Frank Pellegrini, "Dissecting Bush's Tax-Cut Plan," *Time,* February 27, 2001.

235   *"Robin Hood in reverse"*: Senator Paul Wellstone of Minnesota, quoted in "Daschle Joins Criticism of Bush Tax Cut Plan," *Aberdeen American News,* February 9, 2001.

235   *"skewed to the wealthiest"*: Senator Mark Dayton of Minnesota, quoted in ibid.

235   *In fact, 31.2 percent:* Urban Institute–Brookings Institution Tax Policy Center Analysis, "EGTRRA: Distribution of Income Tax Change by AGI Class, 2002," November 19, 2002, http://www.tax policycenter.org/numbers/displayatab.cfm?DocID=324.

235   *Families earning $40,000:* Scott A. Hodge, "How the Bush Tax Cuts Affect Families with Children at Different Income Levels," Tax Foundation *Fiscal Facts,* January 7, 2003, http://www.taxfounda tion.org/publications/show/211.html.

236   *The bottom 20 percent:* Scott Moody and Scott A. Hodge, "Bush Tax Cuts Erased Income Tax Burden for 7.8 Million Families," Tax Foundation *Fiscal Facts,* August 17, 2004.

236   *Bush years witnessed:* On June 1, 2007, "the Bureau Of Labor Statistics Released New Jobs Figures—157,000 Jobs Created In May," from "Job Creation Continues—More Than 8 Million Jobs Created Since August 2003," *Business Wire,* June 1, 2007.

236   *From 2000 to 2008:* According to the Bureau of Economic Analysis, real GDP grew from $11.2 trillion in 2000 to $13.3 trillion in 2008. See http://www.bea.gov/national/Index.htm.

236   *American economy grew:* Bureau of Economic Analysis Historic Data: GDP 1969–2008.

236   *$4.5 trillion in growth:* Japan's GDP (purchasing power parity) in 2008 was $4.329 trillion (*CIA World Factbook*).

236   *returned us to "deficit spending"*: Gore senior advisor Ron Klain, quoted in "Bush Preserving His Tax Cut Even at the Expense of Deficit Spending, Says Gore Campaign," US Newswire, September 19, 2000.

237   *proposed fiscal 2002 alternative:* FY2002 Budget Resolution: Senate Democratic Alternative Budget; Senate Budget Committee Democratic Staff, April 5, 2001; Brief Analysis of President Bush's Budget Submission of April 9, 2001, Senate Budget Committee Democratic Staff, April 12, 2001.

237   *Because of NCLB:* Math: http://www.nationsreportcard.gov/ltt_2008/ltt0002.asp; reading: http://www.nationsreportcard.gov/ltt_2008/ltt0003.asp.

238   *Improvements were greatest:* http://www.nationsreportcard.gov/ltt_2008/ltt0003.asp.

238   *test scores have risen:* Tom Loveless and Michael J. Petrilli, "Smart Child Left Behind," *New York Times,* August 28, 2009; Fact Sheet: No Child Left Behind Has Raised Expectations and Improved Results, http://georgewbush-whitehouse.archives.gov/infocus/bushrecord/factsheets/No-Child-Left-Behind.html.

238   *Other critics say NCLB:* "Katherine Shaver," Coloring Outside Curriculum Lines to Depict the Drop in Arts Education," *Washington Post,* March 6, 2008.

238   *"desperately underfunded"*: "A Conversation with Arne Duncan, Education Secretary," *Minneapolis Star Tribune,* March 25, 2009.

238   *Bush increased federal outlays:* No Child Left Behind funding has increased 34 percent since 2001. Department of Education Fact Sheet, http://74.125.93.132/search?q=cache:dORY3WfY3_IJ: origin.www.gpoaccess. gov/usbudget/fy08/pdf/budget/education.pdf+no+child+left+behind+bush+ increa sed+federal+funding+outlays+%25&cd=3&hl=en&ct=clnk&gl=us&client=firefox-a.

238 *In 1996, only 16 percent:* Karlyn Bowman, "Election Results from A to Z," American Enterprise Institute, January 1, 2001, http://www.aei.org/issue/12234.

239 *talked about education endlessly:* Ibid.

239 *"The days of discriminating":* Remarks by the President at National Prayer Breakfast, Washington Hilton Hotel, Washington, D.C., February 1, 2001, http://georgewbush-whitehouse.archives.gov/news/releases/20010201.thml.

239 *set up a White House office:* The departments of Education, Health and Human Services, Housing and Urban Development, Justice, and Labor. Executive Order 13279 of December 12, 2002: Equal Protection of the Laws for Faith-Based and Community Organizations.

239 *roughly 10.8 percent:* Federal Competitive Funding to Faith-Based and Secular Non-Profits for Fiscal Year 2007 (Based on a Review of 138 Programs and 35 Program Areas at 11 Federal Agencies), http://georgewbush-whitehouse.archives.gov/government/fbci/data-collection- 2007.html; "Innovations in Compassion, The Faith-Based and Community Initiative: A Final Report to the Armies of Compassion," White House, December 2008.

239 *Faith-Based Office:* Seattle Hebrew Academy.

239 *historic preservation funds:* For example, the historic Old North Church in Boston received a "Save America's Treasure" grant.

239 *housing aid jeopardized:* St. Francis House, in Sioux Falls, South Dakota (see http://www.hud.gov/news/release.cfm?CONTENT=pr02-029.cfm) and the Salvation Army in Janesville, Wisconsin.

239 *"patronage for its friends":* Paul Krugman, "Gotta Have Faith," *New York Times,* December 17, 2002; *Reverend Paul Martin, Macedonia Baptist Church, quoted in Virginia Culver, "Faith-Based Initiative Gets Mixed Reviews," Denver Post,* January 31, 2001; Marc Stern, lawyer with the American Jewish Congress, "Not All Say Amen to Bush's Crusade; Religious Agenda Raises Concerns," *Houston Chronicle,* February 2, 2001.

239 *"one of the largest patronage programs":* Representative Chet Edwards, Democrat of Texas.

240 *Associated Press investigated:* Laura Meckler, "AP Exclusive: Records Show $1 Billion Given to Faith-based Groups in 2003," Associated Press, January 2, 2005.

240 *"punched a dangerous hole":* "Using Tax Dollars for Churches," New York Times, December 30, 2002; Marianne Means, "President Should Just Leave Religious Charities Alone," *San Diego Union-Tribune,* July 15, 2001; Reverend Barry W. Lynn, executive director of Americans United for Separation of Church and State, quoted in Bill Sammon, "Bush Rolls Back 'Secular' Rules on Faith Groups; Order Opens Charities to Funds," *Washington Times,* December 13, 2002.

240 *the courts disagreed:* The Freedom from Religion Foundation took its suit against the White House Conferences to the Supreme Court and lost. *Hein v. Freedom From Religion Foundation,* 551 U.S. 587, 127 S. Ct. 2562 (2007). The U.S. Supreme Court sided in 2006 with the administration in a 5–4 decision. While the decision went down on "standing" grounds, the justices did not cite any evidence of religious favoritism at the conferences. The American Jewish Congress sued Notre Dame for sending AmeriCorps participants to teach at Catholic schools in poor communities (*American Jewish Congress v. Corporation for National and Community Service University of Notre Dame,* 399 F3d 351) and lost at the U.S. Court of Appeals.

240 *"religious organizations . . . to discriminate":* Laura Murphy, director, ACLU National Office, "The Bush Presidency: Initiatives to Federally Fund Faith-Based Charities," CNN, January 29, 2001.

240 *protected by Title VII: Corp. of Presiding Bishop of Church of Jesus Christ of Latter-Day Saints v. Amos,* 483 U.S. 327, 332 n.9 (1987).

240 *Obama chose to preserve:* From then-presidential candidate Barack Obama, "Remarks, Council for Faith-Based and Neighborhood Partnerships," Zanesville, Ohio, July 1, 2008; President Barack Obama, "This Is My Hope. This Is My Prayer," Address to National Prayer Breakfast, February 5, 2009.

241 *emission reduction targets:* The latest available data show that sixteen of the countries that ratified Kyoto are on track to meet their targets, while Germany, Japan, and eighteen other countries that ratified the treaty are not. Alex Morales, "Greenhouse-Gas Emissions Drop 0.1% in Developed World," Bloomberg.com, November 17, 2008, http://www.bloomberg.com/apps/news?pid=20601 082&sid=~a5aiwQLstMgU&refer=canada.

241 *China got off scot-free:* July 2002 testimony of James Connaughton, Chairman of the Council on Environmental Quality.

241 *"radical"... "politically untenable":* William Drozdiak, "Global Warming Talks Collapse," *Washington Post*, November 26, 2000.

241 *unanimously passed a resolution:* Vote on Senate Resolution 98, July 25, 1997, Yeas: 95; Nays: 0; Not Voting: 5; http://www.senate.gov/legislative/LIS/roll_call_lists/roll_call_vote_cfm.cfm?congress=105&session=1&vote=00205.

241 *Kyoto did both:* H. Sterling Burnett, "Regulating Greenhouse Gas Emissions," Brief Analysis, No. 494, National Center for Policy Analysis, November 18, 2004.

241 *group heard from scientists:* President Bush Discusses Global Climate Change, June 11, 2001. White House news release, http://georgewbush-whitehouse.archives.gov/news/releases/2001/06/20010611-2.html.

241 *"if the world doesn't like it—tough":* Thomas L. Friedman, "Foreign Affairs; 95 to 5," *New York Times*, May 29, 2001.

242 *"it must not stand":* "Dubya's Global Warming Rollback," CBSNews.com, March 28, 2001.

242 *Here are facts:* Energy Security, Energy Poverty, and Greenhouse Gas Emission Reductions: Hearing Before the H. Comm. on Foreign Affairs, Subcommittee on Asia, the Pacific, and the Global Environment, 109th Cong. (2007, statement of Dr. Margo Thorning, managing director, International Council for Capital Formation. In addition, in 2007, America's greenhouse gas intensity had declined by nearly 10 percent from 2002 levels and the nation was on track to reduce greenhouse gas intensity 18 percent by 2012.

242 *Bush committed $22 billion:* John J. Fialka, "Warm Words for Climate Report," Washington Wire (*Wall Street Journal* blog), February 2, 2007.

242 *"affordable, new, more advanced":* Declaration of Leaders Meeting of Major Economies on Energy Security and Climate Change, G-8 Summit, July 9, 2008.

242 *Bush's persistent leadership:* Editorial, "Kyoto's Long Goodbye," *Wall Street Journal*, July 11, 2008.

242 *air, water, and land:* Air: See the EPA's Air Trends reports: http://epa.gov/air/airtrends/ozone.html; http://epa.gov/air/airtrends/nitrogen.html; http://epa.gov/air/airtrends/carbon.html; and http://epa.gov/air/airtrends/sulfur.html. Water: See *Drinking Water and Ground Water Statistics for 2008*, page 8, http://www.epa.gov/safewater/databases/pdfs/data_factoids_2008.pdf; *National Summary of State Information Reporting Year 2008*, http://iaspub.epa.gov/waters10/attains_index.control, and *Water Quality Conditions in the United States: A Profile from the 2000 National Water Quality Inventory*, http://www.epa.gov/305b/2000report/factsheet.pdf. Land: See Dina Cappiello, *Obama, Bush Share Similar Cleanup Statistics*, Associated Press, Aug. 9, 2009; White House Fact Sheet, *President Signs Legislation to Clean Environment & Create Jobs*, Jan. 11, 2002, http://georgewbush-whitehouse.archives.gov/news/releases/2002/01/20020111-4.html.

242 *moved at a faster pace:* See previous note for Clinton/Bush air quality comparisons. For a comparison of Bush administration results on sulfur dioxide compared to the Clinton administration, see page 70 of *Air Quality in America: A Dose of Reality on Air Pollution Levels, Trends, and Health Risks* by Joel M. Schwartz and Steven F. Hayward, http://www.aei.org/docLib/20080317_AirQuality.pdf.

243 *in just two years:* In the first two years after the brownfields legislation was passed, the EPA awarded 272 grants to clean up brownfields (an average of 136 per year), while only 437 had been awarded from 1995 to 2002 (an average of 62 per year). The number of brownfield grants more than doubled after the 2002 Act. See Table 1 on page 9 of http://www.gao.gov/new.items/d0594.pdf.

246 *to Kass's surprise and ours:* Jay Lefkowitz, "Stem Cells and the President: An Inside Account," *Commentary*, January 2008.

246 *Bush twice vetoed:* Bush vetoed both the Stem Cell Research Act of 2005 on July 19, 2006, and the Stem Cell Research Act of 2007 on June 20, 2007.

246 *articles in* Cell *and* Science: Kazutoshi Takahashi, et al., "Induction of Pluripotent Stem Cells from Adult Human Fibroblasts by Defined Factors," *Cell* 131 (November 30, 2007), pp. 861–72, and Junying Yu et al., "Induced Pluripotent Stem Cell Lines Derived from Human Somatic Cells," *Science* 318, no. 5858 (December 2007), pp. 1917–20. Link to abstract: http://www.sciencemag.org/cgi/content/abstract/318/5858/1917.

247 *these cells could be obtained:* The researchers did not necessarily endorse Bush's position. The leader of the American team, Dr. James A. Thomson, co-wrote an op-ed opposing the administration's policy. Alan I. Leshner and James A. Thomson, "Standing in the Way of Stem Cell Research," *Washington Post*, December 3, 2007.

CHAPTER 16: 9/11

251 *"a national tragedy":* Remarks by the President After Two Planes Crash Into World Trade Center, Emma Booker Elementary School, Sarasota, Florida, September 11, 2001, http://www.whitehouse .gov/news/releases/2001/09/20010911.html.

252 *after the president has boarded:* On September 11, 2001, there were fifty-one passengers on Air Force One, including the president, aides, guests, Secret Service, the press, and crew.

257 *"defining moment":* President George W. Bush, interview by Scott Pelley, *60 Minutes II*, CBS, September 10, 2003, http://www.cbsnews.com/stories/2002/09/11/60II/main521718.shtml.

257 *without violating the Hatch Act:* The Hatch Act, passed in 1939, prohibits federal employees from using government equipment for political purposes.

259 *media herd was slimmed:* Ann Compton, ABC; Doug Mills, Associated Press photographer; Sonya Ross, Associated Press; George Christian, CBS cameraman; and Erik Washington, CBS soundman, remained aboard Air Force One.

260 *"We will do whatever":* "Remarks by the President Upon Arrival at Barksdale Air Force Base," Barksdale Air Force Base, Louisiana, September 11, 2001, htp://www.whitehouse.gov/news/releases/ 2001/09/20010911-1.html.

260 *Just before 1:30 P.M.:* An excellent summary of the events of the president and his traveling party on September 11 up to this point in the day can be found in the pool report filed by Judy Keen of *USA Today* and Jay Carney of *Time* at http://www.usatoday.com/educate/vpp-keen-poolrpt.htm.

261 *"at war against terror":* Karen Hughes, *Ten Minutes from Normal* (New York: Viking, 2004), p. 242.

261 *Tenet raised the possibility:* Condi Rice recalls President Bush asking CIA director George Tenet during the videoconference, "Who do you think did this to us?" She recalls Tenet replying, "Sir, I believe its al Qaeda. We're doing the assessment but it looks like, it feels like, it smells like al Qaeda." *60 Minutes II*, CBS, September 10, 2003, http://www.cbsnews.com/stories/2002/09/11/60II/ main521718.shtml.

263 *"the face of war in the twenty-first century":* Ari Fleischer recalls the moment a little differently, reporting that Bush said, "That's the twenty-first-century war you just witnessed." Ari Fleischer, *Taking Heat: The President, the Press, and My Years in the White House* (New York: William Morrow, 2005), p. 150.

CHAPTER 17: GROUND ZERO

271 *"There is still an army":* Ari Fleischer, Karen Hughes, and I all scribbled notes, but I trust Karen's stenographic abilities more than mine. Karen Hughes, *Ten Minutes from Normal* (New York: Viking, 2004), p. 247.

273 *"I don't think about myself":* "Remarks by the President in Telephone Conversation with New York Mayor Giuliani and New York Governor Pataki, September 13, 2001, 11:00 A.M.," http://george wbush-whitehouse.archives.gov/news/releases/2001/09/20010913-4.html.

275 *"passengers who defied":* The president's speech can be seen at http://www.youtube.com/watch? v=GchISQIuVlg.

275 *"most dramatic":* President George W. Bush, Bush-Cheney Alumni Association Event, January 7, 2009. Bush also said at the event that his speechwriter Mike Gerson called it Bush's "best speech."

278 *easy mark for an end run:* Memorandum by Nina Bishop, 2007.

279 *Beckwith, who suddenly realized:* Nina and I didn't know it at the time, but a microphone stood in a small enclose only a few yards from us. Our view of it was blocked by debris and the crowd. It was a less dramatic venue than the one I stumbled on moments earlier. Bob Beckwith later told me he

could see the nearby command center tent from his perch on the pumper and thought the president was likely to speak from the battery of microphones there.

279 *"no, you stay right here":* "Then & Now: Bob Beckwith," CNN.com, September 7, 2005, http://www.cnn.com/2005/US/09/07/cnn25.beckwith.tan/index.html.

279 *"I want you all to know":* Bush's bullhorn speech can be seen at http://www.youtube.com/watch?v=MiSwqaQ4VbA&feature=related.

279 *handed the bullhorn off:* The bullhorn was briefly lost to public sight. New York State Police Colonel Daniel Wiese, head of Governor Pataki's security detail, ended up with it. Pataki, Wiese, and Bob Beckwith later presented the bullhorn to the president in the Oval Office on February 25, 2002.

279 *"We can't just judge him":* Douglas Brinkley, interview by John Gibson, *Special Report: America United,* Fox News Channel, September 15, 2001.

281 *not likely to be answered:* The last person found alive at Ground Zero—Genelle Guzman-McMillan—was rescued around 12:30 P.M. on September 12, more than two days before the president arrived at the Javits Center. Only five people were pulled alive from the rubble after the first day. John Cloud, "11 Lives: The Survivor—A Miracle's Cost," Time.com, September 1, 2002, http://www.time.com/time/covers/1101020909/asurvivor.html.

283 *"They were saluting":* Richard Keil, "With the President: A Reporter's Story of 9-11," *Rochester Review* 67, no. 1 (Fall 2004), http://www.rochester.edu/pr/Review/V67N1/feature1.html.

284 *"Beck, do you know":* "Then & Now: Bob Beckwith." Since 9/11, Bob has traveled the world speaking and raising money for the New York Firefighters Burn Center Foundation.

CHAPTER 18: STRIKING BACK

287 *what the American people expected of us:* As I stated in my June 22, 2005, speech to the Conservative Party of New York, "In the wake of 9/11, conservatives believed it was time to unleash the might and power of the United States military against the Taliban; in the wake of 9/11, liberals believed it was time to . . . submit a petition. I am not joking. Submitting a petition is precisely what Moveon.org did. It was a petition imploring the powers that be to 'use moderation and restraint in responding to the terrorist attacks against the United States.' "

291 *Some critics used Bush's call:* Thomas L. Friedman, "9/11 and 4/11," *New York Times,* July 20, 2008; Thomas L. Friedman, "Let's Talk About Iraq," *New York Times,* June 15, 2005; Paul Krugman, "King of Pain," *New York Times,* September 18, 2006; Editorial, "A Day On," *New York Times,* September 5, 2005.

291 *urging Americans to "go shopping":* Ben Feller, "Bush Challenges Country to Volunteer," Associated Press, September 8, 2008; Barack Obama in Second Presidential Debate, Belmont University, Nashville, Tenn., October 7, 2008, transcript: http://www.cnn.com/2008/POLITICS/10/07/presidential.debate.transcript/.

291 *Stengel, repeated the charge:* Richard Stengel, "A Time to Serve," *Time,* August 30, 2007.

291 *it was not Bush but Frank Pellegrini:* Frank Pellegrini, "The Bush Speech: How to Rally a Nation," *Time,* September 21, 2001.

292 *He started on September 18:* "President Launches Online American Relief and Response Effort, Remarks by the President, Rose Garden, September 18, 2001," White House Press Releases, http://georgewbush-whitehouse.archives.gov/news/releases/2001/09/20010918-1.html.

292 *He reiterated this call:* "Address to a Joint Session of Congress and the American People, United States Capitol, Washington, D.C., September 20, 2001," White House Press Releases, http://georgewbush-whitehouse.archives.gov/news/releases/2001/09/20010920-8.html.

292 *Bush announced:* President Announces "America's Fund for Afghan Children," East Room, October 11, 2001, White House Press Releases, http://georgewbush-whitehouse.archives.gov/news/releases/2001/10/20011011-8.html.

292 *students across the globe:* http://www.friendshipthrougheducation.org/.

293 *The results are there:* By the end of 2008, the Freedom Corps website had received more than 23 million visitors and listed more than 4 million opportunities for volunteers, according to Free-

dom Corps staff members. And the number of Americans volunteering each year grew from 59.8 million Americans in 2002 to 65.4 million in 2005, before leveling off at 61 million in 2007. (Source from U.S. Bureau of Labor Statistics, 2002–2007, in collaboration with the U.S. Census Bureau and Corporation for National and Community Service.)

293 *"Our response must be sweeping"*: Presidential radio address to the nation, September 15, 2001.

294 *The Patriot Act:* H.R. 3162 (Uniting and Strengthening America by Providing Appropriate Tools Required to Intercept and Obstruct Terrorism—USA Patriot Act of 2001): 98 yeas; 1 nay; 1 not voting (Mary Landrieu, D-La.). All forty-nine Republicans voted Yea. Forty-eight Democrats voted yea and only one voted nay (Russ Feingold, D-Wis.). Independent Jim Jeffords (Vt.) also voted yea.

294 *"Money is the lifeblood"*: President Freezes Terrorists' Assets, Remarks by the President, Secretary of the Treasury O'Neill and Secretary of State Powell on Executive Order, Rose Garden, September 24, 2001.

296 *"When the Bush administration decided"*: Jack Goldsmith, *The Terror Presidency: Law and Judgment Inside the Bush Administration* (New York: Norton, 2007), p. 113.

296 *Pelosi was in attendance:* Siobhan Gorman, "CIA Says It Briefed Congressional Leaders," *Wall Street Journal*, May 8, 2009; the CIA document chronicling congressional briefings on interrogations can be viewed by accessing the May 8 *WSJ* column online at http://online.wsj.com/article/ SB124174688873899443.html. Senator Jay Rockefeller of West Virginia, Chairman of the Senate Select Committee on Intelligence, also deserves to be singled out. On the matter of enhanced interrogation techniques, he said, "[W]e now know that essential information was withheld from the Congress on many matters[,] and decisions were made in secret by senior Bush administration officials to obscure the complete picture" (*Congressional Record:* April 22, 2009 (Senate), Page S4 561-S4566). But Rockefeller had been repeatedly briefed on the CIA's covert antiterror interrogation programs beginning as early as February 2003; how could he possibly say vital information was withheld from him? More than thirty congressional sessions had been devoted to the interrogation program, and Sen. Rockefeller was present at eighteen of them according to the CIA document chronicling congressional briefings on interrogations ("What Congress Knew About 'Torture,'" *Wall Street Journal*, January 6, 2009; Siobhan Gorman, "CIA Says It Briefed Congressional Leaders," *Wall Street Journal*, May 8, 2009).

298 *"I'll talk to you guys"*: "Miranda Rights for Terrorists," The Blog (*Weekly Standard*'s blog), posted by Stephen F. Hayes on June 10, 2009, http://www.weeklystandard.com/weblogs/TWSFP/2009/06/ miranda_rights_for_terrorists.asp.

298 *"I know that this program saved lives"*: George Tenet, *60 Minutes* interview, CBS, April 29, 2007, interview transcript, http://www.cbsnews.com/stories/2007/04/25/60minutes/main2728375 .shtml. For more information on EITs, see Marc Thiessen's book, *Courting Disaster: How the CIA Kept America Safe and How Barack Obama Is Inviting the Next Attack.*

299 *"As late as 2006"*: Michael Hayden and Michael B. Mukasey, "The President Ties His Own Hands on Terror," *Wall Street Journal*, April 17, 2009.

299 *"We have people walking around"*: Stuart Taylor, Jr., "Did Torture Save Lives?," *National Journal*, April 25, 2009.

299 *killing three hundred thousand:* Iraq Foundation website, www.iraqfoundation.org.

300 *There was a bipartisan consensus:* A regime-change policy, the Iraq Liberation Act, was endorsed by Congress and signed into law on October 31, 1998. And in mid-November 1998, the Clinton administration publicly stated that the United States would go beyond containment to promoting a change of regime in Iraq. Kenneth Katzman, *Iraq: U.S. Regime Change Efforts and Post-Saddam Governance*, Congressional Research Service (CRS) Report for Congress, updated January 7, 2004.

300 *congressional Democrats peppered the president:* Among these Democrats were Senator Robert Byrd (Neil A. Lewis and David Sanger, "Bush May Request Congress's Backing on Iraq, Aides Say," *New York Times*, August 29, 2002); Representative Ellen O. Tauscher (James Dao, "Call in Congress for Full Airing of Iraq Policy," *New York Times*, July 18, 2002); Senator Russ Feingold (David Enrich, "Lawmakers Demand Consultation Prior to US Attack on Iraq," States News Service, August 6, 2002); and Representative John Conyers ("Conyers Warns Bush," *Grand Rapids Press*, August 26, 2002).

300 *"they expected President Bush"*: Lewis and Sanger, "Bush May Request Congress's Backing on Iraq, Aides Say."

300   *"Simply put"*: Actual letter or Niels C. Sorrells, "Iraq Hearing Leaves Members Wanting More Information," *Congressional Quarterly Daily Monitor*, September 10, 2002.

301   *"We just want to know"*: Emily Pierce, "Democrats Cite 1990 Precedent for Scheduling a Vote on Iraq," *Congressional Quarterly*, September 10, 2002.

301   *"The conduct of the Iraqi regime"*: President George W. Bush's Remarks to the U.N. General Assembly, September 12, 2002.

302   *"I think there will be a vote"*: Dave Boyer, "Democrats Drop Delay On Iraq Vote; But Hold Off On Advocating Use of Force Resolution," *Washington Times*, September 18, 2002.

302   *Daschle would dispute:* Peter Baker, "Rove's Version of 2002 War Vote Is Disputed," *Washington Post*, December 1, 2007.

302   *I can't find a shred of evidence:* It should be noted that Daschle's assertion in 2007 that Bush was responsible for the pre-election vote drew support from an unusual corner—Bush White House press secretary Ari Fleischer, who said that the administration "determined the timing, not the Congress. I think Karl in this instance just has his facts wrong." (Baker, "Rove's Version of 2002 War Vote Is Disputed.") But with all due respect to my former White House colleague and friend, Ari is the one who got this wrong.

303   *The margin was much larger:* The 1991 Persian Gulf War Resolution passed the House 250–183 and the Senate 52–47.

303   *The leaders of eight European countries:* Jose María Aznar, Jose-Manuel Durão Barroso, Silvio Berlusconi, Tony Blair, Vaclav Havel, Peter Medgyessy, Leszek Miller, and Anders Fogh Rasmussen, "United We Stand; Eight European Leaders Are as One with President Bush," *Wall Street Journal*, January 30, 2003. All told, more than thirty-five countries ended up providing support for the Iraq War, from deploying combat units to help with intelligence and logistics to the use of naval and air bases.

303   *He had enormous credibility:* We later learned that Powell, despite having spent four days and nights at the CIA in advance of his testimony in order to fact-check his claims, made statements that turned out to be wrong. It was a devastating thing to happen—but further evidence that there was no effort to lie. Powell knew how important this testimony was, not only to his credibility but to the credibility of the country. He did all he thought necessary to ensure his claims were accurate. But he, like virtually all the rest of the world, was misled by faulty intelligence.

304   *"My fellow citizens"*: President Bush Addresses the Nation, Oval Office, March 19, 2003, http://georgewbush-whitehouse.archives.gov/news/releases/2003/03/20030319-17.html.

CHAPTER 19: WHAT BIPARTISANSHIP?

306   *"the jury is still out"*: House Minority Leader Richard Gephardt's Regular Press Briefing, Location: H-206, U.S. Capitol, Washington, D.C., September 20, 2001 (Federal News Service).

307   *"swiftly rejected"*: Glenn Kessler and Juliet Eilperin, "Democrats Resist Bush's Push for Stimulus Heavy on Tax Cuts," *Washington Post*, October 5, 2001.

307   *"failures of bipartisanship"*: Glenn Kessler and Juliet Eilperin, "GOP Forced Bush Change on Stimulus, Democrats Say; Gephardt Cites 'Failures of Bipartisanship,'" *Washington Post*, October 12, 2001.

308   *passed by a single vote:* The bill passed by a vote of 215 to 214 on December 6, 2001. Voting yes were 21 Democrats and 194 Republicans. Voting no were 189 Democrats, 23 Republicans, and two independents. "Roll-Call Vote in the House on the Trade Authority Bill," *New York Times*, December 7, 2001.

308   *Hayes voted on principle:* Smith and Tauscher did vote for TPA when it came back up for a vote the following July on a conference committee report that reconciled the differing versions approved by the House and Senate. There were no substantive differences from the House version they'd voted against in December. A net of four additional Democrats shifted from no to yes. We let Hayes vote against the conference report because we would still have a three-vote margin. Mike Allen and Juliet Eilperin, "House Backs Trade Power for President; Narrow Vote Ends 8 Years of Battle Over Authority," *Washington Post*, July 28, 2002.

309   *Pickering had taken on:* Neil A. Lewis, "President Renominating Federal Judge Lott Backed," *New York Times*, January 8, 2003.

309   *"I'd urge Karl Rove":* Byron York, "Democrats Kill Again," National Review Online, September 5, 2002.

310   *rated him "well-qualified":* American Bar Association, "Ratings of Article III Judicial Nominees: 108th Congress," updated 1/10/08. League of United Latin American Citizens, February 11, 2003, http://www.lulac.org/advocacy/press/2003/estrada.html.

310   *"fidelity to his own insistence":* Editorial, "Judicial Nominations Scorecard," *Washington Post*, August 9, 2002.

311   *a surprise when the president announced:* "Remarks by the President in Address to the Nation, Cross Hall, June 6, 2002," http://georgewbush-whitehouse.archives.gov/news/releases/2002/06/20020606-8.html.

311   *in 1962:* Joseph Slater, *Homeland Security vs. Workers' Rights? What the Federal Government Should Learn from History and Experience, and Why*, 6 U. Pa. J. Lab. & Emp. L. 295, 302 (2003–2004).

312   *Some observers said I did the ad:* Stephen Holden, "Postulating a Dark Side to a Bush Operative's Work," *New York Times*, August 27, 2004; Anita Gates, "Movies: Critics Choice," *New York Times*, October 31, 2004.

312   *"Karl Rove and his minions":* Cynthia Tucker, "Our Opinion: Cleland's Pain Is Kerry's Gain," *Atlanta Journal-Constitution*, August 1, 2004.

312   *"the Rove machine":* Wayne Madsen, "Forgive Rather for Falling Prey to Dirty Trick," *Augusta Chronicle* (Georgia), October 1, 2004. Mr. Madsen frequently drinks swamp water and suffers fevers accordingly.

312   *"surrogates, led by Rove":* The ubiquitous James Moore in his ironically titled "Smear Artist," Salon.com, August 28, 2004.

312   *running comics devoted to: Doonesbury*, Sunday edition, September 23, 2007; Jim Galloway and Bob Kemper, "The Chambliss comics," Political Insider, *Atlanta Journal-Constitution* blog, September 24, 2007.

312   *"character assassination":* Bob Kemper, "Loyalty to Bush Helps Georgian Rise," *Atlanta Journal-Constitution*, February 6, 2005.

312   *I did not conceive:* Chambliss himself says I wasn't to blame, stating, "Karl was not involved in my campaign. That was my ad." Bob Kemper, "Attack Ad on Cleland Blamed on Rove," *Atlanta Journal-Constitution*, August 14, 2007.

312   *Chambliss consultant Tom Perdue drafted:* Link to the Chambliss ad: http://www.youtube.com/watch?v=tKFYpd0q9nE.

312   *"As America faces terrorists":* Rich Lowry, "Max Cleland, Liberal Victim," National Review Online, July 29, 2004, http://www.nationalreview.com/flashback/lowry200407291758.asp. Article first appeared on NRO on February 20, 2004.

312   *"not questioning his patriotism":* Kemper, "Loyalty to Bush Helps Georgian Rise."

312   *" 'how-dare-you-attack-my-patriotism' ":* Jim Wooten, "Senate Race Not About Patriotism," *Atlanta Journal-Constitution*, June 18, 2002; Lowry, "Max Cleland, Liberal Victim."

313   *his voting record was more liberal:* Among those he cast were ones against keeping the Boy Scouts from being kicked out of public schools, against a ban on partial-birth abortion, and for gun control. Cleland had a 62 percent Liberal Composite Score from the nonpartisan *National Journal*, a "D" from the National Rifle Association, a 0 percent from National Right to Life from 1999 to 2002, a 16 percent lifetime rating from the American Conservative Union, and anemic ratings from the National Federation of Independent Business. Sources: "Senators' Ratings," *National Journal*, February 1, 2003; email from Andrew Arulanadam of the National Rifle Association; National Right to Life Committee, http://capwiz.com/nrlc/home; American Conservative Union, http://www.acuratings.org/ratingsarchive/2002/2002Senate.htm. In his first two years in the Senate, Cleland received a 44 percent rating from NFIB, a 16 percent rating for the middle two years of his term, and then, in his final two years as he ran for reelection, a 63 percent score. Phone call to National Federation of Independent Business. Who says reelections don't affect the voting records of nimble liberal politicians?

313   *he did poorly in the debates:* Kemper, "Loyalty to Bush Helps Georgian Rise."

313 *"wanted to take me out":* Paul Alexander, *Machiavelli's Shadow* (New York: Modern Times, 2008), p. 136.

314 *slots are highly coveted:* Description of Directors' Compensation, taken from Sallie Mae's April 2002 Proxy Report, http://www.salliemae.com/NR/rdonlyres/A0450B59-A4A0-4586-9B4C -253FF335008B/544/2002proxy.pdf.

314 *Devolites represented:* Peter Baker, "Tom Davis Gives Up," *New York Times*, October 5, 2008.

314 *He and Devolites were married:* Devolites and her husband, John, filed for divorce in September 2000. Davis and his wife, Peggy, divorced in the fall of 2003. Devolites and Davis married in June 2004; Lisa Rein, "Va. Republicans Devolites, Davis to Marry," *Washington Post*, March 26, 2004. Amy Gardner, "Can Va.'s Davis Team Divorce Themselves From Politics?," *Washington Post*, November 10, 2007.

315 *"A poor choice of words":* John Mercurio, "Lott Apologizes for Thurmond Comment," CNN.com, December 10, 2002, http://archives.cnn.com/2002/ALLPOLITICS/12/09/lott.comment/.

315 *Lott's fellow conservatives:* Conservative writers and editors who spoke out against Lott include David Frum, "Speak Up, Trent," David Frum's Diary, National Review Online, December 9, 2002, http://frum.nationalreview.com; Jonah Goldberg ("Trent Lott's Blunder," National Review Online's "The Corner," December 9, 2002, http://www.nationalreview.com/thecorner/02_12_08_corner _archive.asp#001595); Tony Blankley (interview by Chris Matthews, *Hardball*, MSNBC, December 9, 2002); Lisa Schiffren and Deroy Murdock (interview by Arthel Neville, *Talkback Live*, CNN, December 9, 2002); and Fred Barnes (panel segment of *Special Report with Brit Hume*, Fox News Channel, December 9, 2002).

315 *"there are a lot of times":* Tom Daschle, Press Conference on the New Democratic Senate Campaign Committee Leadership, DNC Headquarters, Washington, D.C., December 9, 2002 (Federal News Service).

316 *"thirty years ago":* Thomas B. Edsall and Brian Faler, "Lott Remarks on Thurmond Echoed 1980 Words," *Washington Post*, December 11, 2002. These remarks had originally appeared in a Jackson *Clarion-Ledger*, November 3, 1980, report.

316 *"you put your foot in your mouth":* Senator Trent Lott, interview by Larry King, *Larry King Live*, CNN, December 11, 2002.

316 *inserted into a speech:* President Bush's speech, "President Bush Implements Key Elements of his Faith-Based Initiative," Downtown Marriott Hotel, Philadelphia, December 12, 2002.

316 *"for opening old wounds":* "Lott Apologizes Anew for Comments," CNN.com, December 14, 2002, http://archives.cnn.com/2002/ALLPOLITICS/12/13/lott.comment/index.html.

316 *"took Trent's call just minutes":* Senator Tom Daschle with Michael D'Orso, *Like No Other Time: The 107th Congress and the Two Years That Changed America Forever* (New York: Crown, 2003), p. 36.

317 *"blunt" and "angry":* Senator Trent Lott, *Herding Cats: A Life in Politics* (New York: ReganBooks, 2005), p. 259.

317 *"powerful White House staffers":* Ibid., p. 263.

317 *"good for American politics":* Senator Trent Lott, interview by Chris Matthews, *Hardball*, MSNBC, November 1, 2005.

CHAPTER 20: JOE WILSON'S ATTACK

318 *someone I'd never heard of:* In one of life's ironies, Wilson and I attended the same Episcopal church in Washington, he the 9 A.M. service and me the 11 A.M. I may have met him once; the rector asked me to speak to a men's group after 9/11, and I vaguely remember being introduced to a strutting former ambassador who may have been Wilson.

319 *"eight days drinking sweet mint tea":* Joseph C. Wilson IV, "What I Didn't Find in Africa," *New York Times*, July 6, 2003.

319 *"very senior officials":* Joseph C. Wilson IV, interview by Bill Hemmer, *American Morning*, CNN, July 7, 2003. No reporter ever asked Wilson to name the "very senior officials in the vice president's office" that he claimed to have talked to.

320 *"somebody from [the president's] own staff"*: Ben Ehrenreich, "Unfair Game: Joseph Wilson on the Cost of Telling the Truth in Washington," interview with Joseph C. Wilson IV, *L.A. Weekly*, November 6, 2003, http://www.laweekly.com/2003-11-06/news/unfair-game/; Joseph C. Wilson IV, interview by Larry King, *Larry King Live*, CNN, May 3, 2004.

320 *"hothouse environment of Air Force One"*: George Tenet with Bill Harlow, *At the Center of the Storm: My Years at the CIA* (New York: HarperCollins, 2007), p. 457.

321 *Tenet later told me:* Conversation with George Tenet, December 8, 2009.

321 *"We see nothing that would dissuade us"*: "Press Gaggle by Ari Fleischer, July 7, 2003," http://georgewbush-whitehouse.archives.gov/news/releases/2003/07/20030707-5.html.

321 *"Knowing all that we know now"*: Walter Pincus, "White House Backs Off Claim on Iraqi Buy," *Washington Post*, July 8, 2003; David E. Sanger, "Bush Claim on Iraq Had Flawed Origin, White House Says," *New York Times*, July 8, 2003.

322 *"sniping" at him:* Tenet, *At the Center of the Storm*, p. 463.

322 *"incoming flak"*: Ibid., p. 461.

322 *"accounts from 'senior administration' "*: Ibid., p. 463.

322 *"a technique usually reserved"*: Ibid., p. 465.

322 *"CIA's counter-proliferation experts"*: Statement by George J. Tenet, Director of Central Intelligence, July 11, 2003, https://www.cia.gov/news-information/press-releases-statements/press-release-archive-2003/pr07112003.html.

323 *"expanding commercial relations"*: Ibid.; Susan Schmidt, "Plame's Input Is Cited on Niger Mission; Report Disputes Wilson's Claims on Trip, Wife's Role," *Washington Post*, July 10, 2004; Peter Grier, "Yellowcake to 'Plamegate,' " *Christian Science Monitor*, November 15, 2005.

323 *"We conclude that"*: Review of Intelligence on Weapons of Mass Destruction, Report of a Committee of Privy Counselors, Chairman: The Rt. Hon. The Lord Butler of Brockwell KG, GCB, CVO (better known as the *Butler Report*), July 14, 2004, p. 123.

323 *little coverage of these findings:* ABC was the only one of the three major news networks to report on the Butler Report's finding: assessments that Iraq sought uranium from Africa were "well-founded" (*World News Tonight with Peter Jennings*, July 19, 2004, ABC News transcript). The *New York Times* published one news story, buried in the "Washington Memo" section on page 14 (Richard W. Stevenson and David Johnston, "New Reports Reopen Debate Over Whether Iraq Sought Uranium in Niger," *New York Times*, July 18, 2004). The *Washington Post* didn't publish a single news story on the British reaffirmation.

323 *"former Nigerien officials knew"*: Tenet statement, July 11, 2003.

324 *"delivered orally"*: Joseph C. Wilson 4th, "What I Didn't Find in Africa," *New York Times*, July 6, 2003.

324 *"the standard operating procedure"*: Joseph C. Wilson IV, interview by Bill Hemmer, *American Morning*, CNN, July 7, 2003.

324 *"we did not brief it to the President"*: Tenet statement, July 11, 2003.

324 *"the dates were wrong"*: Schmidt, "Plame's Input Is Cited on Niger Mission."

324 *"When I came back from Niger"*: Joseph C. Wilson IV, interview by Andrea Mitchell, *Meet the Press*, NBC, July 6, 2003.

324 *"there was no mention"*: Tenet statement, July 11, 2003.

325 *"In an interview with Committee staff"*: Report on the U.S. Intelligence Community's Prewar Intelligence Assessments on Iraq, Select Committee on Intelligence, United States Senate, July 7, 2004, Additional Views of Chairman Pat Roberts, joined by Senator Christopher S. Bond, Senator Orrin G. Hatch, pp. 444–45.

325 *Italian forgeries:* Schmidt, "Plame's Input Is Cited on Niger Mission."

325 *"has good relations"*: Valerie Plame Wilson, *Fair Game: My Life as a Spy, My Betrayal by the White House* (New York: Simon & Schuster, 2007), pp. 185–86.

325 *"Joe abruptly got up"*: Ibid.

325 *"These 16 words should never"*: Tenet statement, July 11, 2003.

326 *He took "comfort"*: Tenet, *At the Center of the Storm*, p. 469.

326 *"had quite another view":* Ibid.

326 *What I found interesting:* Tenet writes that after his phone call to Hadley, he had his executive assistant follow up with a memo to Gerson and Hadley. The White House removed the language, Tenet explains. But just to be sure the White House understood, a senior analyst from the CIA sent yet another memo over to the White House (p. 450).

327 *"I should have recalled":* Randall Mikkelsen, "Bush Aide Takes Rap on Data," *Globe & Mail* (Canada), July 23, 2003.

327 *"relationship with the administration":* Tenet, *At the Center of the Storm,* p. 475.

328 *"you know his wife works at CIA":* Robert D. Novak, *The Prince of Darkness: 50 Years Reporting in Washington* (New York: Crown Forum, 2007), pp. 3–5.

328 *Not a single argument I made:* Robert Novak, "Bush Sets Himself Up for Another Embarrassment," *Chicago Sun Times,* July 10, 2003.

328 *"an asshole":* Novak, *The Prince of Darkness,* p. 1.

329 *"Oh, you know that, too":* Ibid., p. 7.

329 *Novak said he received the confirmation:* Ibid., p. 9.

329 *Ari Fleischer pulled aside:* Scott Shane, "Former Press Secretary Dispels Many Illusions," *New York Times,* January 30, 2007.

330 *we talked briefly about welfare:* Cooper then wrote about welfare. Matthew Cooper, "The Welfare Merry-Go-Round: Part 2," *Time,* September 22, 2003.

331 *"mentioned in passing that a [1999]":* Bob Novak's column actually said "1988" here, but it appears to be a typo. According to the official CIA statement, Wilson said that "in June 1999 a businessman approached [a former Nigerien official] and insisted that the former official meet with an Iraqi delegation to discuss 'expanding commercial relations' between Iraq and Niger." https://www.cia .gov/news-information/press-releases-statements/press-release-archive-2003/pr07112003.html.

331 *"Two senior administration officials":* Robert D. Novak, "Mission to Niger," *Washington Post,* July 14, 2003.

CHAPTER 21: BUSH WAS RIGHT ON IRAQ

332 *"to be forthcoming":* Jim VandeHei and Helen Dewar, "Democrats Sharpen Attack on Bush Over Iraq; Political Assault Focuses on Current Instability and Intelligence Used to Justify War," *Washington Post,* July 16, 2003.

332 *"presidential sanction":* Nicholas Thompson, "John Kerry Turns the Fire Hose on Bush," *Salon,* July 16, 2003.

333 *"The fact that Zarqawi certainly":* Senator Jay Rockefeller, interview with Wolf Blitzer, *Wolf Blitzer Reports,* CNN, February 5, 2003; Stephen F. Hayes, "Rolling Rockefeller," *Weekly Standard,* June 30, 2005, http://www.weeklystandard.com/Content/Public/Articles/000/000/005/781bpfho .asp?pg=1; Stephen F. Hayes, "Jay Rockefeller's Amnesia and the White House's Weakness," *Weekly Standard,* June 5, 2008, http://www.weeklystandard.com/Content/Public/Articles/000/000/015/ 181kczhv.asp.

333 *"tentative conclusion":* VandeHei and Dewar, "Democrats Sharpen Attack on Bush Over Iraq."

333 *"Hussein's belligerent intentions":* "US Opponents of Iraq War Resolution Say CIA Report Bolsters Their Position," VOA News, October 9, 2002, http://www.voanews.com/english/archive/.

334 *"There is no doubt that":* Letter to President Bush, signed by senators Bob Graham, Joe Lieberman, Jesse Helms, John McCain, Trent Lott, Sam Brownback, and Richard Shelby and congressmen Harold Ford, Tom Lantos, and Henry Hyde, December 5, 2001.

334 *"We are in possession":* Senator Bob Graham, interview by Bob Schieffer, *Face the Nation,* CBS News, December 8, 2002.

334 *"intentionally misleading the American people":* Former Vice President Al Gore, in a speech at Georgetown University Law School, June 24, 2004. "Gore Rips Bush on al Qaeda-Saddam Link," CNN.com, June 25, 2004; speech transcript, MoveOn.Org, June 24, 2004.

334 *"He betrayed this country":* Katharine Q. Seelye, "Gore Says Bush Betrayed the U.S. by Using 9/11 as a Reason for War in Iraq," *New York Times,* February 9, 2004.

334 *"Iraq's search for weapons":* Former Vice President Al Gore, in remarks made at the Commonwealth Club in San Francisco, September 23, 2002, http://www.commonwealthclub.org/archive/02/02-09gore-speech.html.

335 *Hillary Clinton:* Senator Hillary Rodham Clinton, in a statement delivered on the Senate floor, explaining her decision and vote on the joint congressional resolution on Iraq—"S.J. Res. 45, A Resolution to Authorize the Use of United States Armed Forces Against Iraq," October 10, 2002, full statement at http://clinton.senate.gov/speeches/iraq_101002.html; video at http://www.freedomagenda.com/iraq/wmd_quotes.html.

335 *John Kerry:* Senator John Kerry, in an argument delivered in the Senate chamber, supporting President Bush's request for the authority to disarm Saddam Hussein, October 9, 2002, Congressional Record.

335 *Harry Reid:* Senator Harry Reid, interview by Judy Woodruff, *Inside Politics*, CNN, September 18, 2002; Reid, in a statement on his website, as of November 7, 2005, http://www.weeklystandard.com/weblogs/TWSFP/2005/11/finally_some_offense_senator_j.asp.

335 *Ted Kennedy:* Senator Ted Kennedy, remarks at the Johns Hopkins School of Advanced International Studies, September 27, 2002, Federal News Service transcript.

335 *Carl Levin:* Senator Carl Levin, in a statement delivered on the Senate floor, October 4, 2002, http://levin.senate.gov/newsroom/release.cfm?id=211525.

335 *Robert Byrd:* Senator Robert C. Byrd, in a statement delivered on the Senate floor, October 3, 2002. "Threats and Responses; Excerpts of Speeches Made on Senate Floor Regarding Resolution on Iraq," *New York Times*, October 4, 2002.

335 *Barbara Boxer:* Senator Barbara Boxer, in remarks delivered on the Senate floor, October 3, 2002. http://web.archive.org/web/20021017220016/http://boxer.senate.gov/newroom/200210/20021003_frelat.html.

335 *Dick Gephardt:* Representative Dick Gephardt, on Capitol Hill, September 19, 2002, "Congressional Reaction to Iraq Resolution Is Mixed," CNN.com, http://archives.cnn.com/2002/ALLPOLITICS/09/19/bush.congress.iraq/.

335 *Henry Waxman:* Representative Henry Waxman, "Statement Regarding the Possible War with Iraq," October 10, 2002, http://www.house.gov/waxman/news_files/news_statements_res_iraq_10_10_02.htm.

335 *Madeleine Albright:* Secretary of State Madeleine Albright, Remarks before the Chicago Council on Foreign Relations, Chicago, November 12, 1999, Department of State Dispatch, November 1999.

335 *William Cohen:* Secretary of Defense William Cohen, interview by Wolf Blitzer, *Late Edition with Wolf Blitzer*, CNN, April 20, 2003.

335 *"to threaten his neighbors":* Transcript: President Clinton Explains Iraq Strike, CNN.com, December 16, 1998, http://www.cnn.com/ALLPOLITICS/stories/1998/12/16/transcripts/clinton.html.

335 *"Congress had nothing close":* Editorial, "Decoding Mr. Bush's Denials," *New York Times*, November 15, 2005.

335 *not "markedly different":* The Commission on the Intelligence Capabilities of the United States Regarding Weapons of Mass Destruction, Report to the President of the United States (better known as the *Silberman-Robb Report*), March 31, 2005, p. 14.

335 *The vote in the House:* http://www.govtrack.us/congress/billxpd?bill=hj107-114. Interestingly, during the vote on Iraq in 1991, there was far more disagreement and debate about the nature of the threat than there was in 2002.

335 *Of the 110 Democrats:* Internal research document.

336 *"an extensive nuclear program":* George Gedda, "Iraq Admits Having Nuclear Program," Associated Press, July 8, 1991; Paul Lewis, "No Hint of Arms Found in Iraqi Ministry," *New York Times*, July 30, 1992.

336 *first led by a Swede:* Ambassador Rolf Ekéus is a Swedish diplomat and disarmament expert who was executive chairman of UNSCOM from 1991 to 1997.

336 *then by an Australian:* Following Ekéus, Ambassador Richard Butler was executive chairman of UNSCOM from 1997 to 1999. Prior to that, he was the Australian ambassador and permanent representative to the United Nations.

336 *"no convincing evidence"*: Chief U.N. Weapons Inspector Hans Blix's report to the U.N. on Iraq, January 27, 2003, transcript of Blix's remarks: http://www.washingtonpost.com/wp-srv/world/transcripts/blix_012703.html.

336 *"foolish in the extreme"*: Richard Butler, *The Greatest Threat: Iraq, Weapons of Mass Destruction, and the Crisis of Global Security* (New York: PublicAffairs, 2000), p. xvii.

336 *He had used chemical weapons*: *Report on the U.S. Intelligence Community's Prewar Intelligence Assessments on Iraq*, Select Committee on Intelligence, U.S. Senate, July 7, 2004, "Section XVII. Saddam Hussein's Human Rights Record," pp. 394–403. And as Duelfer pointed out, "WMD had even played a role in crushing the Shi'a revolt in the south following the 1991 cease-fire."

337 *the head of German intelligence warned*: August Hanning, Chief of the BND, the German intelligence agency located in Berlin. Jeffrey Goldberg, "The Great Terror," *New Yorker*, March 25, 2002. Center for Defense Information, March 2001, http://www.cdi.org/dm/2001/issue3/emd.html.

337 *Saddam also took active steps*: Douglas J. Feith, *War and Decision: Inside the Pentagon at the Dawn of the War on Terrorism* (New York: HarperCollins, 2008), p. 329; *Silberman-Robb Report*, p. 156.

337 *"In Saddam's view"*: Charles Duelfer, *Comprehensive Report of the Special Advisor to the DCI on Iraq's WMD (The Duelfer Report)*, September 30, 2004, Vol. I of III, "Key Findings," p. 1.

337 *David Kay*: Kay was a former weapons inspector for UNSCOM; he served as the ISG's first supervisor, from June to December 2003. ISG was in existence from April 2003 to September 2004.

337 *"explained that he purposely gave"*: *Duelfer Report*, Transmittal Message, p. 9.

337 *"Saddam believed WMD had deterred"*: *Duelfer Report*, Vol. I, "Key Findings," p. 1, September 30, 2004.

337 *"had not given up his aspirations"*: Statement by David Kay on the Interim Progress Report on the Activities of the Iraq Survey Group (ISG) Before the House Permanent Select Committee on Intelligence, the House Committee on Appropriations, Subcommittee on Defense, and the Senate Select Committee on Intelligence, October 2, 2003. Feith, *War and Decision*, p. 472.

337 *"Saddam wanted to re-create"*: *Duelfer Report*, Vol. I, "Key Findings," p. 1; Feith, *War and Decision*, p. 326.

338 *"intent to retain the intellectual capital"*: Duelfer, *Report*, Vol. II, "Key Findings," p. 1; Feith, *War and Decision*, p. 327.

338 *"Saddam directed a large budget increase"*: *Duelfer Report*, Vol. I, "Realizing Saddam's Veiled WMD Intent," p. 59; Feith, *War and Decision*, p. 328.

338 *"We have discovered dozens"*: *Duelfer Report*, Vol. III, "Key Findings," p. 3; Feith, *War and Decision*, p. 327.

338 *"key turning point"*: *Duelfer Report*, Volume I, "Key Findings," p. 1; Feith, *War and Decision*, p. 193.

338 *"to re-create Iraq's WMD capability"*: *Duelfer Report*, Volume I, "Key Findings," p. 1.

338 *Inspectors disputed that figure*: "The Current Crisis and Buildup; The U.S. Military: Cutting-Edge Weaponry Eclipses Even That Used in the Gulf War," *Seattle Times*, January 26, 2003.

339 *This was more weapons*: Former Assistant Secretary of Defense Philip E. Coyle, "Finding Saddam Hussein's Weapons of Mass Destruction," Center for Defense Information, http://www.cdi.org/nuclear/iraq-wmd.cfm (first published in the *San Diego Union-Tribune*, April 23, 2003).

339 *"As we all know"*: Secretary of State Colin L. Powell's Remarks to the U.N. Security Council, New York, March 7, 2003.

339 *"Iraq retained some BW-related"*: *Duelfer Report*, Vol. III, "Key Findings," p. 2; Feith, *War and Decision*, p. 330.

339 *"I think people below"*: Douglas Jehl, "The Struggle for Iraq: Weapons Search; Iraqis Removed Arms Material, U.S. Aide Says," *New York Times*, October 29, 2003.

339 *Moshe Yaalon, Israel's top general*: Jack Kelly, "A Syrian Sidestep? About Those Iraqi WMDs: More Signs Are Pointing to a Neighborly Transfer," *Pittsburgh Post-Gazette*, February 5, 2006.

340 *"[a threat] to the well-being"*: President Clinton addressing the nation from the Oval Office, after ordering a strike on military and security targets in Iraq, December 16, 1998. Transcript of speech: http://www.cnn.com/ALLPOLITICS/stories/1998/12/16/transcripts/clinton.html. Video of

speech: http://www.youtube.com/watch?v=ENAV_Uolfgc&eurl=http://brianakira.wordpress
.com/2008/02/03/clinton-kerry-gore-call-for-war-against-saddams-iraq/.

340   *"The dictator of Iraq":* President George W. Bush, March 16, 2003.

340   *"From the end of one of the couches":* Bob Woodward, *Plan of Attack* (New York: Simon & Schuster, 2004), pp. 249–50.

341   *a lengthy* Washington Post Magazine*:* Karen DeYoung, "Falling on His Sword; Colin Powell's Most Significant Moment Turned Out to be His Lowest," *Washington Post Magazine*, October 1, 2006.

341   *"It is safe to say":* Michael R. Gordon and General Bernard E. Trainor, *COBRA II: The Inside Story of the Invasion and Occupation of Iraq* (New York: Pantheon, 2006), pp. 132–33.

341   *"were substantiated":* Rockefeller Report*,* June 5, 2008.

342   *a majority of Americans:* Lydia Saad, "No Evidence of Declining Support for Iraq War," Gallup, July 28, 2005, www.gallup.com/poll/17572/Evidence-Declining-Support-Iraq-War.aspx.

CHAPTER 22: THE SPECIAL PROSECUTOR AND ME

344   *"appear to lack nerve endings":* Lisa de Moraes, "Fox to Comedy Writers: Let's Try This at Home," *Washington Post*, July 15, 2008.

345   *hadn't noticed the CIA's July 11 statement:* Statement by George J. Tenet, Director of Central Intelligence, July 11, 2003.

345   *Iraq had attempted to acquire:* Ibid.

345   *CIA had concerns:* Ibid.

345   *"Matthews was blunt":* Joseph Wilson describes Chris Matthews's phone call to him on page one of his book *The Politics of Truth: Inside the Lies That Led to War and Betrayed My Wife's CIA Identity* (New York: Carroll & Graf, 2004).

346   *"Is it a feeding frenzy":* MSNBC's *Hardball with Chris Matthews*, July 16, 2003, transcript.

346   *their friend Chris Matthews:* Wilson, *The Politics of Truth*, pp. 1, 4–5.

346   *even used it as the title:* Valerie Plame Wilson, *Fair Game: My Life as a Spy, My Betrayal by the White House* (New York: Simon & Schuster, 2007).

346   *"a good place" to begin:* Wilson, *The Politics of Truth*, pp. 372–73.

346   *House Democrats were promising:* Anne Q. Hoy, "Probes Expected in ID of CIA Officer," *Newsday*, July 23, 2003.

346   *"look at the issue":* Anne Q. Hoy, "Schumer Seeks CIA Leak Probe," *Newsday*, July 25, 2003.

346   *"not ready, yet":* David Ballingrud, "Blown Cover," *St. Petersburg Times*, August 10, 2003.

346   *"At the end of the day":* Mike Allen and Dana Milbank, "Bush Vows Action if Aides Had Role in Leak; Democrats' Demand for Special Counsel Rejected," *Washington Post*, September 30, 2003.

347   *my name was a metonym:* Timothy Noah, "Did Rove Blow a Spook's Cover?," *Slate*, September 16, 2003, http://slate.msn.com/id/2088471/.

347   *"Justice Department is looking into":* Mike Allen and Dana Priest, "Bush Administration Is Focus of Inquiry; CIA Agent's Identity Was Leaked to Media," *Washington Post*, September 28, 2003.

347   *quotes from an unnamed:* Ibid.

347   *"purely and simply for revenge":* Ibid.

348   *"the CIA has an obligation":* Secretary of State Colin Powell, interview by George Stephanopoulos, *This Week*, ABC News, September 28, 2003; Mike Allen "Bush Aides Say They'll Cooperate With Probe Into Intelligence Leak," *Washington Post*, September 29, 2003.

348   *"no evidence Rove was":* Allen and Milbank, "Bush Vows Action if Aides Had Role in Leak."

350   *focused on a September 29 call:* The FBI apparently was concerned this call was an effort by Novak (or Novak and me) to cook a story.

352   *"Ashcroft disqualified himself":* Eric Lichtblau, "Special Counsel Is Named to Head Inquiry on Leak," *New York Times*, December 31, 2003.

352   *"money, chairs or sticky pads":* Rebecca Carr, "Leak Probe Shifts Gears; Attorney General Turns

Search for Who Revealed CIA Agent's Identity Over to Special Prosecutor," *Atlanta Journal-Constitution*, December 31, 2003.

352 *"Eliot Ness with a Harvard":* Ibid.

355 *Mosbacher had the wrong guy:* Stefanie Scott, "GOP Adviser Fired After Leak About Bush Campaign Shakeup." *San Antonio Express-News*, September 19, 1992.

356 *inexplicably agreed to an article:* Vicky Ward, "Double Exposure," *Vanity Fair*, January 2004.

357 *"a limited number of questions":* Susan Schmidt and Carol Leonnig, "Reporter Held in Contempt in CIA Leak Case," *Washington Post*, August 10, 2004.

357 *citation against Cooper was dropped:* Carol D. Leonnig, "Journalist Testifies in CIA Case; Contempt Charges Against Time Reporter Are Dropped," *Washington Post*, August 25, 2004.

358 *article on welfare reform:* Matthew Cooper, "The Welfare Merry-Go-Round: Part 2," *Time*, September 22, 2003, http://www.time.com/time/magazine/article/0.9171.1005746.00.html.

359 *put his Townsend column to bed:* Robert Novak, "Bush Sets Himself Up for Another Embarrassment," *Chicago Sun-Times*, July 10, 2003.

CHAPTER 23: GETTING READY FOR KERRY

363 *"swap horses when crossing streams":* Abraham Lincoln, "Reply to Delegation from the National Union League," June 9, 1864. Lincoln's remarks were published in the June 10, 1864, issue of the *New York Times*—and can be viewed at http://www.thelincolnlog.org.

363 *economy had been anemic in 2002:* Source: U.S. Bureau of Economic Analysis Historic GDP Table, "Gross Domestic Product: Percent change from preceding period," Updated June 25, 2009.

364 *Hispanics had grown from 3 percent:* Roper Center, Public Opinion Archives, "How Groups Voted" for years 1984, 2000, 2004, http://www.ropercenter.uconn.edu/.

369 *in little notebooks:* Ann Blackman, "Take Note of Bob Graham; Could Florida's Popular Senator Be Al Gore's Veep?," *Time*, July 17, 2000.

370 *"I want my country back":* Governor Howard Dean, M.D., "Address to California State Democratic Convention," Sacramento, Calif., March 15, 2003.

371 *"opposed the death penalty":* The Second Bush-Dukakis Presidential Debate, October 13, 1988, Debate Transcript, Commission on Presidential Debates.

CHAPTER 24: DRUGS AND MARRIAGE

372 *By 1998, private health insurers:* "Prescription Drug Benefits: Applying Private Sector Management Methods to Medicare," Statement of William J. Scanlon, Director, Health Financing and Public Health Issues, Health, Education, and Human Services Division, Testimony Before the Committee on Science, U.S. Senate, March 22, 2000.

374 *voted this down:* The amendment didn't pass. There were 175 ayes and 255 nos. (Final Vote Results on H.AMDT.197 for Roll Call 330, June 27, 2003, http://clerk.house.gov/evs/2003/roll330.xml.)

374 *less than was originally estimated:* "Lower Medicare Part D Costs Than Expected in 2009," Centers for Medicare and Medicaid Services, August 14, 2008; Morton M. Kondrake, "Medicare Drug Plan Ought to Be Model for Health Reform," *Roll Call*, June 11, 2009.

374 *legalized gay marriage in the state: Goodridge v. Department of Public Health*, 440 Mass. 344 (Mass. 2003).

374 *wasn't able to make any headway:* The movement failed two key legislative tests in 1998 in Hawaii and Alaska (John Cloud, "For Better or Worse," *Time*, October 26, 1998). On November 3, 1998, voters in Hawaii would pass a constitutional amendment to allow the state legislature to ban same-sex marriages ("Hawaii Gives Legislature Power to Ban Same-Sex Marriage," CNN.com, All-Politics, November 3, 1998). That same year, 68 percent of Alaska voters also approved a constitutional amendment defining marriage as the union between a man and a woman (Elaine Herscher, "Same-Sex Marriage Suffers Setback," *San Francisco Chronicle*, November 5, 1998).

375 *a series of lawsuits:* Massachusetts: lawsuit filed April 11, 2001: *Goodridge v. Department of Public*

Health (Yvonne Abraham, "Gays Seek Right to Marry; Mass. Lawsuit Goes Beyond Civil Unions," *Boston Globe*, April 12, 2001). New Jersey: lawsuit filed June 26, 2002: *Lewis v. Harris* (Kate Coscarelli, "Same-Sex Couples Sue for Right to Marry in N.J.," *Star-Ledger* [Newark], June 27, 2002). Indiana: lawsuit filed August 22, 2002: *Morrison v. Sadler* (Matthew Tully, "Same-Sex Marriage Heading to Court," *Indianapolis Star*, August 22, 2002). Arizona: lawsuit filed July 7, 2003: *Standhardt v. Superior Court ex rel. County of Maricopa* (Paul Davenport, "Gay Couple Sues to Overturn Marriage Ban," Associated Press, July 14, 2003). Vermont lawsuit (*Baker v. State*) filed before Alaska/Hawaii on July 22, 1997: ("Vt. Gays Sue for Right to Marry," *Boston Globe*, July 22, 1997). The Vermont Supreme Court ruled on December 20, 1999, that homosexual couples must receive the same benefits and protections afforded heterosexual couples who marry, but stopped short of allowing them to legally wed. (Cheryl Wetzstein, "Vermont Supreme Court OKs Same-Sex 'Protections,' " *Washington Times*, December 21, 1999.)

375   *Howard Dean supported:* Dean boasted that he was "proud [as Vermont governor] to sign the nation's first law establishing civil unions for same-sex couples." Kerry said, "While I continue to oppose gay marriage, I believe that today's decision calls on the Massachusetts state legislature to take action to ensure equal protection for gay couples." Gephardt said, "I do not support gay marriage, but I hope the Massachusetts legislature will act in a manner that is consistent with today's . . . ruling." Lieberman said, "Although I am opposed to gay marriage, I have also long believed that states have the right to adopt for themselves laws that allow same-sex unions." Dennis Kucinich explicitly endorsed the ruling, saying, "The right to marry is a civil right that should not be denied." Susan Page, "Gay Marriage Looms Large for '04," *USA Today*, November 19, 2003; David Guarino and Andrew Miga, "Landmark Ruling; Dem Candidates Embrace Spirit But Keep Distance," *Boston Herald*, November 19, 2003.

375   *often in the same speech:* David M. Halbfinger, "Kerry Is Grilled on Gay Marriage and Attacks Bush on Sept. 11 Commission," *New York Times*, March 8, 2004; Paul Farhi, "Kerry Again Opposes Same-Sex Marriage," *Washington Post*, May 15, 2004.

375   *he did call for a constitutional amendment:* President Bush said, "Marriage is a sacred institution between a man and a woman. Today's decision of the Massachusetts Supreme Judicial Court violates this important principle. I will work with congressional leaders and others to do what is legally necessary to defend the sanctity of marriage." Statement by the president, November 18, 2003, http://georgewbush-whitehouse.archives.gov/news/releases/200/11/20031118-4.html.

376   *San Francisco mayor Gavin Newsom:* Rachel Gordon, "The Battle Over Same-Sex Marriage: Uncharted Territory," *San Francisco Chronicle*, February 15, 2004.

376   *"take immediate steps":* Governor Schwarzenegger's Letter to Attorney General Lockyer Regarding Same-Sex Marriage," February 20, 2004, http://gov.ca.gov/press-release/3209/.

376   *Missouri had become the first:* Missouri passed its constitutional amendment with 71 percent of the vote in August 2004, three months before the other eleven states would pass their amendments on the November ballot. Jon Sawyer and Mary DeLach Leonard, "Voters Speak and Pundits Are Listening," *St. Louis Post-Dispatch*, August 8, 2004.

376   *support ranging from 57 percent:* Arkansas, 75 percent; Georgia, 76 percent; Kentucky, 75 percent; Michigan, 59 percent; Mississippi, 86 percent; Missouri, 71 percent; Montana, 67 percent; North Dakota, 73 percent; Ohio, 62 percent; Oklahoma, 76 percent; Oregon, 57 percent; Utah, 66 percent. Election Results From CNN.com "2004 Election Results," http://www.cnn.com/ELECTION/2004/pages/results/ballotmeasures/.

376   *"I've heard the reasons":* John Lewis, "At a Crossroads on Gay Unions," *Boston Globe*, October 25, 2003.

376   *"The point Bush's critics":* John Kass, "Moral of This Election: Don't Dismiss Values," *Chicago Tribune*, November 7, 2004.

377   *statistically insignificant difference:* Analysis of turnout data from Dr. Michael McDonald, George Mason University, http://elections.gmu.edu/voter_turnout.htm.

377   *"helped mastermind a wedge issue":* "Exit Karl Rove," *Plain Dealer* (Cleveland), August 14, 2007.

377   *"Karl Rove plotted":* Cynthia Tucker, "Don't Let Theocrat Get a Heartbeat Away from Presidency," *Baltimore Sun*, February 18, 2008.

377   *"the twin fears":* Frank Rich, "If Terrorists Rock the Vote in 2008," *New York Times*, June 29, 2008.

377   *"binge of hate-filled":* Andrew Sullivan, "Rove Exits," The Daily Dish (Sullivan's blog at andrew sullivan.theatlantic.com), August 13, 2007.

CHAPTER 25: TRAPPING KERRY, MAKING PEACE WITH MCCAIN

378   *disgorged eight hundred protesters:* Ed Henry, "Heard on the Hill" column, *Roll Call*, March 30, 2004.

378   *National People's Action (NPA):* Steve Ginsberg, "Demonstrators Swarm Around Rove's Home," *Washington Post*, March 29, 2004.

379   *Bush had increased:* Christine Scott, "Table 1: Historical Budget Authority for the Department of Veterans Affairs (VA) in Current and Constant (2007) Dollars, FY1940–FY2007," Veterans Affairs: Historical Budget Authority, Fiscal Years 1940 through 2007, CRS Report for Congress, June 13, 2008; Daniel H. Else, Christine Scott, Sidath Viranga Panangala, "Military Construction, Veterans Affairs, and Related Agencies: FY2008 Appropriations," CRS Report for Congress, updated August 2, 2007; U.S. Department of Veterans Affairs website, Fiscal Year 2009 Budget Submission, http://www.va.gov/budget/summary/2009/index.htm.

379   *That bill had appropriated:* David Firestone, "Lawmakers Back Request by Bush on Funds for Iraq," *New York Times*, October 18, 2003; Jonathan Weisman, "House and Senate Back Iraq Aid Plan; Cost and Duration Among Deep Misgivings," *Washington Post*, October 18, 2003.

379   *All the "no" votes:* Source: U.S. Senate Roll Call Votes 108th Congress—1st Session, http://www .senate.gov/legislative/LIS/roll_call_lists/roll_call_vote_cfm.cfm?congress=108&session=1&vote= 00400#position); Final Vote Results for Roll Call 562, http://clerk.house.gov/evs/2003/roll562 .xml.

379   *"I cannot vote for":* Kerry participating in prevote debate on Senate floor, as recorded in "Emergency Supplemental Appropriations for Iraq and Afghanistan Security and Reconstruction Act, 2004," Congressional Record, October 17, 2003, Pages S12816–S12817, from Congressional Record Online via GPO Access, wais.access.gpo.gov.

379   *"simply cutting and running":* David Paul Kuhn, "Kerry's Top Ten Flip-Flops, Part II," CBSNews .com, September 29, 2004.

379   *The ad—called "Troops":* Bush-Cheney '04 Ad: "Troops," created by Ashley O'Connor, Matthew Taylor, and Sara Taylor.

380   *The audience consisted of:* Scott Finn: "Visit Portends Close Political Battle," *Charleston Gazette* (West Virginia), March 16, 2004.

380   *"The Republican attack machine":* Ken Fireman, "Things Getting Rough Already," *Newsday*, March 17, 2004.

380   *confusing defense of his "no" vote:* News release: "Kerry Calls for Shared Sacrifice by Wealthiest 1% of Americans to Pay for $87 billion Iraq Supplemental," October 2, 2003, http://kerry.senate.gov/ low/record.cfm?id=212683; U.S. Senate Roll Call Vote: http://www.senate.gov/legislative/LIS/ roll_call_lists/roll_call_vote_cfm.cfm?congress=108&session=1&vote=00373; Glen Johnson, "Kerry Criticizes Bush for Failing to Protect Troops in Iraq," *Boston Globe*, March 17, 2004.

381   *"a protest vote":* Howard Kurtz, "Ad Attacks Kerry Vote on Iraq Funds," *Washington Post*, March 17, 2004.

381   *further compounded his mistake:* Nick Madigan and Katharine Q. Seelye, "Cheney Attacks Kerry's Record on the Military," *New York Times*, March 18, 2004.

381   *"put off" by me:* Richard L. Berke and David E. Sanger, "Some in Administration Grumble as Aide's Role Seems to Expand," *New York Times*, May 13, 2002.

382   *rumors flew:* Howard Kurtz, "The Running Story of John McCain," *Washington Post*, April 12, 2004; Adam Nagourney, "A Quick and Quiet Search to Fill the Democratic Ticket," *New York Times*, April 4, 2004; "Poll Finds Hypothetical Kerry-McCain Ticket with Advantage Over Bush-Cheney," Associated Press, May 27, 2004; *Lou Dobbs Tonight*, CNN, April 6, 2004; *The Chris Matthews Show*, NBC News, April 11, 2004.

383   *any help would be welcome:* One news account of the Weaver meeting had me saying, "We didn't know he [McCain] would help" (James Carney, "Frenemies: The McCain-Bush Dance," *Time*, July 16, 2008). That's not accurate. It was clear to us in the White House what McCain wanted.

383 *"a privilege to be introduced"*: Mike Allen, "Bush, McCain Look Beyond Differences: In Appearance at Washington Army Base, Republicans Rally Veterans' Support," *Washington Post*, June 19, 2004.

383 *"First time I was asked"*: Elisabeth Bumiller, "Bush and McCain, Together, Call Iraq War a Conflict Between Good and Evil," *New York Times*, June 19, 2004.

383 *rumors that McCain was joining*: Face the Nation transcript, June 20, 2004.

383 *"When I vote to give"*: "Senator Kerry Speech on Iraq War Resolution," C-SPAN.org, October 9, 2002.

384 *"rushed to war"*: Interview with Senator Kerry, ABC's *This Week*, October 12, 2003.

384 *"I am, yeah"*: Interview with Senator Kerry, MSNBC's *Hardball*, January 6, 2004.

384 *"Now, there are some questions"*: "President's Remarks at Stratham, New Hampshire, Picnic," White House Press Release, August 6, 2004.

384 *"Yes,. I would have voted"*: Patrick Healy, "Kerry Says He'd Still Vote to Authorize Iraq War," *Boston Globe*, August 10, 2004.

385 *"Marie, the Flame of Florida"*: "Marie, the Flame of Florida" was the nickname of an exotic dancer McCain dated while in flight school in Pensacola. John McCain with Mark Salter, *Faith of My Fathers: A Family Memoir* (New York: Random House, 1999), p. 154.

385 *"Almost two years after"*: "President's Remarks at Pensacola, Florida, Rally, Pensacola Civic Center," White House Press Release, August 10, 2004.

CHAPTER 26: SUSPENSE AND VICTORY

387 *a modest lead*: Richard Morin and Dan Balz, "Convention Gives Kerry Slight Lead Over Bush," *Washington Post*, August 3, 2004.

388 *our matching funds*: "FEC Certifies Public Funds for Bush-Cheney Ticket," Federal Election Commission, released September 2, 2004, http://www.fec.gov/press/press2004/20040902fund.html; "FEC Certifies Public Funds for Kerry-Edwards Ticket," Federal Election Commission, released July 30, 2004, corrected August 20, 2004, http://www.fec.gov/press/press2004/20040730funds.html.

388 *"has not wavered"*: Jarrett Murphy, "Speakers to Laud Bush as Strong Leader in Treacherous Times," CBS/Associated Press, August 20, 2004.

388 *"a leader who doesn't flinch"*: Kathy Kiely, "Schwarzenegger Says 'Country Is in Good Hands,' " *USA Today*, August 31, 2004.

388 *"you can count on him"*: Jeff Zeleny, "Women, Moderates Hear Call to Unite Behind 'Steady Hand,' " *Chicago Tribune*, September 1, 2004.

388 *Jim Angle of Fox News*: On the Record with Greta van Susteren, Fox News transcript, September 3, 2004; Mark Sandalow, "Bush's Vision for U.S.—Idealistic and Strong; Analysis: President Returns to Softer Tone of 2000 Campaign," *San Francisco Chronicle*, September 3, 2004; David Gergen, interview by Ted Koppel, *Nightline*, ABC News, September 2, 2004.

388 *Bush 52, Kerry 45*: "Poll: Bush Apparently Gets Modest Bounce," CNN.com, September 6, 2004.

388 *"not being honest"*: Maria L. La Ganga and Stephen Braun, "The Race to the White House; Veterans Attack Kerry on Medals, War Record," *Los Angeles Times*, August 5, 2004.

389 *"dishonest and deplorable"*: Scott Shepard, "McCain Denounces Ad Accusing Kerry of Lying About Vietnam Combat Record," Cox News Service, August 5, 2004.

389 *"I can't believe"*: Ibid.

389 *"smear" campaign*: Jay Newton-Small, "Kerry Challenges Bush to Halt 'Smear Campaign' by Vietnam Vets," Bloomberg, August 22, 2004.

389 *They ran seven new ones*: A Chronology of Swift Boat Veterans for Truth (SBVT) ads in 2004:

   August 26: SBVT release the ad "Gunner."

   August 31: SBVT release the ad "Medals."

   September 17: SBVT release the ad "Dazed and Confused."

   September 21: SBVT release the ad "Friends."

   September 30: SBVT release the ad "Never Forget."

October 13: SBVT launch their final, all-out push with two new TV ads ("Why?" and "They Served") charging that Kerry betrayed his comrades and "can't be trusted."

John J. Miller, "What the Swifties Wrought," *National Review*, November 29, 2004.

390   *attacking Bush's Guard service:* Katharine Q. Seelye and Ralph Blumenthal, "Documents Suggest Guard Gave Bush Special Treatment," *New York Times*, September 9, 2004.

390   *The Democratic power broker:* Barnes told Dan Rather it was Houston oilman Sid Adger who asked him to recommend George W. Bush for the Air National Guard (Ben Barnes, interview by Dan Rather, *60 Minutes II*, CBS News, September 8, 2004, http://www.cbsnews.com/stories/2004/09/08/60II/main642060.shtml). But Adger died in the mid-1990s, so there was no way of confirming with Adger that he asked Barnes to make the call. This only fueled claims that Barnes's charge was dubious. Barnes prided himself on being called "the fifty-first Democratic senator" and had a special reason to dislike Bush: during Bush's gubernatorial years, an investigation of problems at the Texas lottery revealed that as a lobbyist, Barnes was receiving $3 million a year from two lucrative contracts with the private operator of the lottery, GTECH. Although there was never any allegation of illegality, Barnes's deal was criticized as overly generous and was stopped when then–Lottery Commission chair Harriet Miers asked GTECH to end his contract. GTECH paid Barnes a $23 million severance. R. G. Ratcliffe, "Barnes Again Moves into Spotlight," *Houston Chronicle*, March 9, 2009; John Fund, "Lotto Trouble," *Wall Street Journal*, October 21, 2005.

391   *"sugar coat" Bush's officer evaluations:* Michael Dobbs and Thomas B. Edsall, "Records Say Bush Balked at Order," *Washington Post*, September 9, 2004.

391   *"had not an opinion":* William Safire, "Those Discredited Memos," *New York Times*, September 13, 2004.

391   *the memo alleging Staudt:* Ibid.

391   *memos contained wrong addresses:* Michael Dobbs and Howard Kurtz, "Expert Cited by CBS Says He Didn't Authenticate Paper," *Washington Post*, September 14, 2004.

391   *the network "misled" him:* Editorial, "Stop the Stonewall, Dan," *New York Post*, September 14, 2004; Michael Dobbs, "Gaps in Service Continue to Dog Bush," *Washington Post*, September 12, 2004.

391   *his lawyer, David Van Os:* Ralph Blumenthal, "Ex-Guardsman Is Said to Be a CBS Source," *New York Times*, September 16, 2004.

391   *should not have been aired:* Jim Rutenberg, "CBS News Concludes It Was Misled on National Guard Memos, Network Officials Say," *New York Times*, September 20, 2004.

391   *CBS to apologize:* Jim Rutenberg and Kate Zernike, "CBS Apologies for Report on Bush Guard Service," *New York Times*, September 21, 2004.

392   *"speculation about whether Karl Rove":* Maureen Dowd, "Pre-emptive Paranoia," *New York Times*, September 16, 2004.

393   *"Was President Bush literally":* Dave Lindorff, "Bush's Mystery Bulge," Salon.com, October 8, 2004; Mike Allen, "Bulge Under President's Coat in First Debate Stirs Speculation," *Washington Post*, October 9, 2004.

393   *"I'm trying to decipher that":* Dan Balz and Mike Allen, "A Debate on Iraq and the Home Front; Bush and Kerry Clash Sharply Over Economy, Stem Cells, Health Care and the War," *Washington Post*, October 9, 2004.

393   *"cheap and tawdry political trick":* Richard Simon, "Lynne Cheney Pulls Grandchild into the Fray," *Los Angeles Times*, November 1, 2004.

393   *"I think what you saw":* Liz Cheney, interview by Bill O'Reilly, *O'Reilly Factor*, Fox News Channel, October 20, 2004.

394   *"a man who will do":* Simon, "Lynne Cheney Pulls Grandchild into the Fray."

394   *small but durable lead:* The Early Show, CBS News transcript, October 18, 2004.

394   *estimated 5 million doors:* "Landscape: Playing to Stereotype," *Hotline*, November 19, 2004.

394   *the first time since 1960:* Lyndsey Layton, "Cheney Hopes Aloha Stop Sways Hawaiians; All-Night Flight Aimed at Chance to Capture Four Usually Democratic Electoral Votes," *Washington Post*, November 2, 2004.

394   *Cheney wearing a lei:* New Jersey and Hawaii showed the most improvement in 2004 for Bush out

of all the states. He received 6 percent more of the vote in New Jersey and 8 percent more of the vote in Hawaii in 2004 compared to his percentage in 2000. Source: www.uselectionatlas.org.

394 *votes in the critical battlegrounds:* Elisabeth Bumiller (David E. Sanger and Richard W. Stevenson contributed reporting), "The 2004 Campaign: The President; From Bush, a Late Call for Support Across Party Lines," *New York Times*, November 2, 2004.

398 *finished voting at 7 P.M.:* The Eastern Time Zone portions of Indiana and Kentucky closed at 6 P.M.; both states have counties in Central time, so the networks didn't call them in 2004 until 7 P.M.

CHAPTER 27: THE DEMOCRATS UNLEASHED

405 *exceed annual Social Security:* A Summary of the 2009 Annual Social Security and Medicare Trust Fund Reports, http://www.ssa.gov/OACT/TRSUM/tr09summary.pdf.

405 *By 2037:* Ibid.

405 *largest in world history:* http://www.ssa.gov/history/pdf/tr04summary.pdf; http://www.ssa.gov/OACT/TR/TR04/lr6F8-2.html.

405 *And by 2040:* Centrists.org: Issue Summary: Social Security Reform, January 20, 2005; http://www.centrists.org/issue_summaries/wealth_socialsecurity.html.

405 *Since 1965, Social Security:* D. Mark Wilson, "Removing Social Security's Tax Cap on Wages Would Do More Harm Than Good," Heritage Foundation, October 17, 2001.

405 *peaked in 2008*: This has in fact happened (http://www.ssa.gov/OACT/TR/2009/lr4b1.html). The recession caused 2009 to produce a much smaller Social Security surplus than 2008.

405 *The IOUs for these:* Trust Fund Data at the end of 2008, Social Security Online, August 13, 2009, http://www.ssa.gov/OACT/TR/2009/III_cyoper.html#156168.

406 *Bush gave the Moynihan Commission:* "Remarks by the President and Social Security Announcement, President's Commission to Strengthen Social Security," May 2, 2001.

406 *"dangerous":* "Senator Harry Reid's Response to the State of the Union Address, February 2, 2005," https://democrats.senate.gov/newsroom/record.cfm?id=231454&.

407 *"creates a political problem":* Sheryl Gay Stolberg and Carl Hulse, "Cool Reception on Capitol Hill to Social Security Plan," *New York Times*, February 4, 2005.

408 *"Your money will grow":* President George W. Bush, State of the Union Address, February 2, 2005.

409 *support for the idea:* Fifty-nine percent favored the idea. CBS News/*New York Times* poll, June 10–15, 2005.

410 *meaning as little as a 1.3 to 2 percent:* Even today, it is difficult to get a precise figure of how leveraged Fannie and Freddie were when they collapsed. Columnist Robert Samuelson suggested their leverage exceeded 60:1 when they collapsed. Robert J. Samuelson, "Wall Street's Unraveling," *Washington Post*, September 17, 2008. Less than three months before Fannie collapsed, mutual fund manager John Hussman estimated Fannie was leveraged 40:1. John P. Hussman, "The 2% Solution," Hussman Funds website, July 14, 2008, http://hussman.net/wmc/wmc080714.htm. Chicago bank and finance professional Joe Specht wrote in his analysis before Fannie collapsed that it was leveraged 78:1. Joe Specht, "Fannie Mae—Or May Not," Seeking Alpha website, July 11, 2008, http://seekingalpha.com/article/84545-fannie-mae-or-may-not.

410 *This helped Fannie and Freddie:* Lawrence J. White, *Focusing on Fannie and Freddie: The Dilemmas of Reforming Housing Finance, Journal of Financial Services Research* 23:1, pp. 43–58, 2003 (see page 44).

411 *vast army of high-profile:* Lisa Lerer, "Fannie, Freddie Spent $200M to Buy Influence," *Politico*, July 16, 2008.

411 *writing riskier mortgages:* Peter J. Wallison and Charles W. Calomiris, "The Last Trillion-Dollar Commitment: The Destruction of Fannie Mae and Freddie Mac," AEI's *Financial Services Outlook*, September 2008, available at www.aei.org/outlook/28704.

411 *Thomas Carper:* "Amid Scandals, Lawmakers Mull Regulatory Reform for GSEs," *National Journal*'s CongressDaily, October 17, 2003.

412 *Stephanie Tubbs Jones*: Sandra Fleishman, "Fannie Mae, Freddie Mac Say They're Sound," *Washington Post*, March 28, 2001.

412 *"just pissed off"*: Representative Gregory Meeks, House Financial Services Committee Hearing, September 25, 2003.

412 *"We do not have a crisis"*: Representative Maxine Waters, House Financial Services Committee Hearing, September 25, 2003.

412 *"We're using the recent"*: Senator Charles Schumer, Senate Banking Committee Hearing, October 16, 2003.

412 *"I'll lay my marker down"*: Senator Charles Schumer, Senate Banking Committee Hearing, April 6, 2005.

412 *"throwing out the baby"*: Senator Jack Reed, Senate Banking Committee Hearing, June 15, 2006.

412 *"exaggerate a threat"*: Representative Barney Frank, House Financial Services Committee Hearing, September 10, 2003.

412 *"fundamentally sound financially"*: Representative Barney Frank, House Financial Services Committee Hearing, September 11, 2003.

412 *"an artificial issue"*: Representative Barney Frank, "Frank: GSE Failure a Phony Issue," *American Banker*, April 21, 2004.

412 *"inane"*: Eric Dash, "Fannie Mae's Offer to Help Ease Credit Squeeze Is Rejected, as Critics Complain of Opportunism," *New York Times*, August 11, 2007.

412 *"one of the great successes"*: Senator Chris Dodd, Senate Banking Committee Hearing, February 2004.

412 *"immediately reconsider"*: Dash, "Fannie Mae's Offer to Help Ease Credit Squeeze Is Rejected."

412 *"Why weren't we doing more"*: Dawn Kopecki, "Fannie Mae, Freddie 'House of Cards' Prompts Takeover," *Bloomberg News*, September 9, 2008.

413 *another $1.27 trillion in mortgages:* Fannie Mae accounted for $753 billion of that figure; Freddie Mac accounted for $522 billion. Fannie Mae and Freddie Mac SEC reports for 2008, Form 10-K.

413 *half the nation's mortgages:* Zachary A. Goldfarb, "Paulson Urges New Structure for Fannie and Freddie," *Washington Post*, January 8, 2009.

413 *And 45 percent:* Peter J. Wallison and Charles W. Calomiris, "The Last Trillion-Dollar Commitment: The Destruction of Fannie Mae and Freddie Mac," AEI's *Financial Services Outlook*, September 2008, www.aei.org/outlook/28704.

413 *third-largest recipient:* http://www.opensecrets.org/news/2008/07/top-senate-recipients-of-fanni.html.

414 *Bush cut that to 6.2 percent:* unpublished data from the Office of Management and Budget.

415 *"a loser"*: Erin Neff, "Del Sol High School Appearance: Reid Calls Bush 'A Loser,' " *Las Vegas Review-Journal*, May 7, 2005.

415 *In 2002 and 2004:* Preelection and postelection polling in both 2002 and 2004 suggests the judge issue played a role in Democratic losses. Survey by New Models. Methodology: Conducted by Winston Group on November 2, 2004 and based on telephone interviews with national registered voters who voted in the 2004 presidential election sample of 1,000.

416 *That wouldn't have happened:* Senator Rick Santorum, "Majority Vote Should Trump Minority Rule," *Washington Post*, April 17, 2005.

416 *removed from office:* Ten Commandments Judge Removed from Office," CNN.com, November 14, 2003, http://www.cnn.com/2003/LAW/11/13/moore.tencommandments/.

420 *He assembled a team:* Joining Gillespie were Steve Schmidt from the communication shop, Dana Perino from press, Jamie Brown from legislative affairs, and Bill Kelly from the counsel's office. Rachel Brand and Kristi Remington led the DOJ contingent.

423 *"lack[ed] experience"*: Kimberly Hefling, "Specter Decries Bush 'Pummeling' on Miers," Associated Press, *Seattle Post-Intelligencer*, October 11, 2005.

423 *"average Americans"*: U.S. Senate Judiciary Committee Hearing on Judge Samuel Alito's Nomination to the Supreme Court, Part I of III, Transcript Courtesy of FDCH e-Media, *Washington Post*, January 9, 2006.

423 *"really a closet bigot?"*: U.S. Senate Judiciary Committee Hearing on Judge Samuel Alito's Nomination to the Supreme Court, Part III of III, Transcript Courtesy of CQ Transcriptions, *Washington Post*, January 11, 2006.

424 *"yodeled for a filibuster"*: Charles Babington, "Kerry Defends Senate Filibuster on Alito as 'a Vote of History,' " *Washington Post*, January 28, 2006.

CHAPTER 28: ANYTHING FOR A SCALP

426 *would go to jail*: "Reporter Went from Protecting to Talking," Associated Press, July 13, 2005.

427 *a letter to Judith Miller*: Scooter Libby wrote to the imprisoned Judith Miller on September 15, 2005, reminding her that "the public report of every other reporter's testimony makes clear that they did not discuss Ms. Plame's name or identity with me." Many observers, including Judge Reggie Walton and Special Counsel Patrick Fitzgerald, thought the letter contained cryptic references and could have been an attempt to sway Miller's testimony before the grand jury.

428 *"[had] consulted"*: Rebecca Carr, "Time Magazine Reporter Testifies in CIA Leak Investigation," Cox News Service, July 13, 2005.

428 *"what can only be described"*: Schmitt, "Journalist Jailed for Not Revealing Source to Court," *Los Angeles Times*, July 7, 2005.

428 *"had reached out to Cooper"*: Carr, "Time Magazine Reporter Testifies in CIA Leak Investigation."

428 *He even suggested*: Schmitt, "Journalist Jailed for Not Revealing Source to Court."

430 *my garage's contents*: Darlene Superville, "An American Garage: Like a Lot of Folks, Rove Has Stuff Piled Up," Associated Press, October 17, 2005.

434 *"that was because of me"*: And no relation to Robert Novak.

436 *Luskin had called Viveca Novak*: Viveca Novak left *Time* magazine after a dispute over her role in the case, taking a buyout package in March 2006. Anne E. Kornblut, "Grand Jury Gets Rove Testimony Over C.I.A. Leak," *New York Times*, April 27, 2006.

436 *gave a dramatic rundown*: Text of Patrick Fitzgerald's Statement at Press Conference, *Editor & Publisher*, http://www.editorandpublisher.com/eandp/news/article_display.jsp?vnu_content_id=10013 92240.

437 *On a lighter note*: "Rove Implicated in Santa Identity Leak," *The Onion*, December 21, 2005, http://www.theonion.com/content/node/43691.

438 *an indictment could come*: "Matthews on Rove Indictment: 'It Could Be Today,' " ThinkProgress, May 12, 2006, http://thinkprogress.org/2006/05/12/matthews-on-rove-indictment-it-could-be -today/.

438 *"If you are betting"*: David Shuster, *Abrams Report*, MSNBC, May 9, 2006. Even after Fitzgerald said no action would be taken, Shuster wouldn't back off. He seemed to suggest his sources were wrong, not him. *Countdown*, MSNBC, June 13, 2006.

439 *Truthout.org*: Jason Leopold, "Karl Rove Indicted on Charges of Perjury, Lying to Investigators," Truthout, May 13, 2006, http://www.truthout.org/article/karl-rove-indicted-charges-perjury-lying -investigators.

439 *"instructed one of the attorneys"*: Ibid.

439 *"a journalist who has battled"*: Howard Kurtz, "Rove Lawyer Has a Pet Peeve," *Washington Post*, May 22, 2006.

439 *"stools were free"*: Ibid.

440 *"In deference to"*: "Rove Will Not Be Charged in Plame Affair," White House Bulletin, June 13, 2006.

440 *Richard L. Armitage*: R. Jeffrey Smith, "Ex-Colleague Says Armitage Was Source of CIA Leak," *Washington Post*, August 29, 2006.

441 *"was not out to punish"*: "End of an Affair," *Washington Post*, September 1, 2006.

441 *denied any knowledge*: Secretary of State Colin Powell, interview by George Stephanopoulos, *This Week*, ABC News, September 28, 2003; Mike Allen, "Bush Aides Say They'll Cooperate With Probe Into Intelligence Leak," *Washington Post*, September 29, 2003.

CHAPTER 29: KATRINA

443 *"I know y'all are trying":* James Carney, "Living Too Much in the Bubble?," *Time*, September 11, 2005.

443 *When she finally dissipated:* All times in this chapter are Central Daylight Time (CDT) unless otherwise noted. "Hurricane Katrina: Timeline of Key Events," *Hurricane Katrina: A Nation Still Unprepared* (S. Rpt. 109–322, Special Report of the Committee on Homeland Security and Governmental Affairs, United States Senate Together with Additional Views), 2006; FEMA Report, *Hurricane Katrina in the Gulf Coast: Mitigation Assessment Team Report, Building Performance Observations, Recommendations, and Technical Guidance,* last updated October 25, 2006.

444 *"I wanted to be able":* Max Mayfield, testimony before a hearing on "The Lifesaving Role of Accurate Hurricane Prediction," Disaster Prevention and Prediction Hearing, U.S. Senate Committee on Commerce, Science, and Transportation, September 20, 2005, 109th Congress, 1st session, 11; "4 Places Where the System Broke Down," *Time*, September 11, 2005; Lise Olsen, "City Had Evacuation Plan but Strayed from Strategy," *Houston Chronicle*, September 8, 2005; Keith O'Brien and Bryan Bender, "Chronology of Errors: How a Disaster Spread," *Boston Globe*, September 11, 2005.

444 *"Neither Blanco nor Nagin": A Failure of Initiative: Final Report of the Select Bipartisan Committee to Investigate the Preparation for and Response to Hurricane Katrina,* U.S. House of Representatives, February 15, 2006, p. 109.

444 *delayed the evacuation order:* Bruce Nolan, "Katrina Takes Aim," *Times-Picayune*, August 28, 2005.

444 *9:30 A.M. on Sunday:* "Hurricane Katrina: Timeline of Key Events," *Hurricane Katrina: A Nation Still Unprepared.*

444 *seventy thousand people stranded: A Failure of Initiative*, p. 111.

444 *Blanco "is very appreciative":* Mississippi, Alabama, and Florida officials expressed similar satisfaction with FEMA's preparations.

445 *"any unmet needs?":* FEMA videoconference transcript, August 28, 2005.

445 *hit land again:* "Hurricane Katrina in the Gulf Coast: Mitigation Assessment Team Report; Building Performance Observations, Recommendations, and Technical Guidance," FEMA 549/July 2006.

445 *hearing the same reports:* Evan Thomas, "After Katrina: Michael Chertoff: 'What the Hell Is Going On?'; In Washington, a Struggle to Find Answers to Terrible Questions," *Newsweek*, December 26, 2005.

445 *Lake Pontchartrain:* There was no barrier where the canal emptied into Lake Pontchartrain, and as lake water surged south into the canal, the force was too much for the levee. Chertoff reported there was no possibility of plugging the gaps and that Pontchartrain would soon overwhelm the city.

447 *"I just pulled a number":* Evan Thomas, "Katrina: How Bush Blew It," *Newsweek*, September 19, 2005.

447 *after the Northridge earthquake:* "A $6.6-Billion Plea After a 6.6 Quake; Administration's Request Merits Quick Approval," *Los Angeles Times*, January 26, 1994; Peter Wenner, "L.A. Takes the Quake," *Orange County Business Journal*, May 30, 1994.

447 *She declined:* Eric Lipton, Eric Schmitt, and Thom Shanker, "Political Issues Snarled Plans for Troop Aid," *New York Times*, September 9, 2005.

448 *an act almost unprecedented:* Ibid.

448 *We flew into Mobile:* Presidential schedule for Friday, September 2, 2005: 10:35 A.M. CDT: President Arrives in Alabama, Briefed on Hurricane Katrina, Mobile Regional Airport, Mobile, Alabama; 12:15 P.M. CDT: President Tours Biloxi, Mississippi Hurricane Damaged Neighborhoods, Biloxi, Mississippi; 5:01 P.M. CDT: President Remarks on Hurricane Recovery Efforts, Louis Armstrong New Orleans International Airport, Kenner, Louisiana.

448 *"The only one not crying":* Elisabeth Bumiller, "Promises by Bush Amid the Tears," *New York Times*, September 3, 2005.

449 *"Brownie, you're doing":* Presidential Briefing, Mobile, Alabama, September 2, 2005.

449 *when I traveled:* I traveled with President Bush to Florida on September 29–30, 2004. We surveyed the damage done by Hurricane Jeanne in the towns of Lake Wales and Stuart.

450 *picks up most of the tab:* Robert T. Stafford Disaster Relief and Emergency Assistance Act, PL 100-707, signed into law November 23, 1988; amended the Disaster Relief Act of 1974, PL 93-288.

450 *unclear how much Nagin:* Mayor Ray Nagin's testimony before the U.S. Senate Homeland Security and Governmental Affairs Committee, February 1, 2006; Douglas Brinkley, *The Great Deluge: Hurricane Katrina, New Orleans, and the Mississippi Gulf Coast* (New York: Harper Perennial, 2007).

452 *under the governor's command: A Failure of Initiative,* p. 206.

452 *four hundred federal law enforcement agents:* "Update: United States Government Response to the Aftermath of Hurricane Katrina," Department of Homeland Security Documents, September 2, 2005.

453 *total Guard contingent:* Manuel Roig-Franzia and Spencer Hsu, "Many Evacuated, but Thousands Still Waiting," *Washington Post*, September 4, 2005. Those 7,200 troops came from the 82nd Airborne Division at Fort Bragg, North Carolina; the 1st Calvary Division at Fort Hood, Texas; the 1st Marine Expeditionary Force at Camp Pendleton, California; and the 2nd Marine Expeditionary Force at Camp Lejeune, North Carolina.

453 *"The federal government":* "President Discusses Hurricane Relief in Address to the Nation," Jackson Square, New Orleans, Louisiana, September 15, 2005, http://georgewbush-whitehouse.archives.gov/news/releases/2005/09/20050915-8.html.

454 *one was later convicted:* Ken Silverstein and Josh Meyer, "Katrina's Aftermath; Louisiana Officials Indicted Before Katrina Hit; Federal Audits Found Dubious Expenditures by the State's Emergency Preparedness Agency, Which Will Administer FEMA Hurricane Aid," *Los Angeles Times*, September 17, 2005; "No Prison for Former Top State Homeland Security Officials," Associated Press State & Local Wire, January 11, 2007.

454 *I saw this firsthand:* "Say what you will about former President George W. Bush and his administration's handling of Hurricane Katrina and its aftermath—the man knew how to put together a post-Katrina White House visit to New Orleans and the Gulf Coast." Nine months passed before President Obama made his first presidential visit to the region—and he only stayed four hours. Jonathan Tilove, "Obama Has Failed to Match Bush's Multiple Visits," *Times-Picayune*, October 10, 2009.

455 *Louisiana had fully processed:* The Road Home, Weekly Situation & Pipeline Report, Week 35, February 23-March 1, 2007, http://www.road2la.org/newsroom/pipeline.htm. "Program Misses Goal, Gains Momentum," Associated Press, March 1, 2007.

455 *Officials in Rodriguez's parish:* Karen Turni Bazile, "Parish's Overtime Raises Eyebrows; St. Bernard Spends Millions in Extra Pay," *Times-Picayune*, April 30, 2006.

455 *"chocolate man there":* During a January 16, 2006, parade honoring Martin Luther King, Jr., Mayor Nagin said displaced African-American residents of New Orleans would soon return to the city and that it would "be chocolate at the end of the day." John Pope, "Evoking King, Nagin Calls N.O. 'Chocolate' City," *Times-Picayune*, January 17, 2006.

455 *eventually be convicted:* Dionne Searcey, "Jefferson Guilty in Bribery Trial," *Wall Street Journal*, August 6, 2009.

456 *$77 billion lawsuit:* "New Orleans Files $77 Billion Claim Against Corps," CNN.com, March 2, 2007, http://www.cnn.com/2007/US/03/01/katrina.claim/index.html.

456 *suit was dismissed:* Susan Finch and Mark Schleifstein, "Corps Off Hook for N.O. Canal Lapses," *Times-Picayune*, January 30, 2008.

456 *lieutenant governor Mitch Landrieu:* Frank Donze, "Contrite Councilman Resigns; Admits Taking Bribe," *Times-Picayune*, August 13, 2007.

457 *fearing for their own safety:* New Orleans police chief Eddie Compass, as quoted by Robert Mendick, "Gang Rule and Rape in Hurricane Dome," *Evening Standard* (London, England), September 2, 2005; Scott Benjamin, "Mayor Predicts Thousands Dead," CBS News, September 6, 2005, http://www.cbsnews.com/stories/2005/09/04/katrina/main814703.shtml; Susannah Rosenblatt and James Rainey, "Katrina Takes a Toll on Truth, News Accuracy," *Los Angeles Times*, September 27, 2005. A good truth vs. fiction account of Superdome anarchy is Brian Thevenot and Gordon

Russell, "Reports of Anarchy at Superdome Overstated," *Seattle Times*, September 26, 2005, http://seattletimes.nwsource.com/html/nationworld/2002520986_katmyth26.html.

458 *largest military deployment:* Hearing on Hurricane Katrina: Preparedness and Response by the Department of Defense, the Coast Guard, and the National Guard of Louisiana, Mississippi, and Alabama Before Select Comm., 109th Cong., October 27, 2005, written statement of Paul McHale, Assistant Secretary of Defense for Homeland Defense.

458 *"When the Federal Government": A Charge Kept: The Record of the Bush Presidency, 2001–2009*, p. 115.

CHAPTER 30: REPUBLICANS ON THE RUN

461 *"I'm the guy":* Ralph Blumenthal, "From Arrival to Errant Shot, a Timeline of Cheney's Hunting Accident," *New York Times*, February 16, 2006.

461 *"a cloud of misfortune":* John Pomfret, "Cheney Hunting Companion Is Released from Hospital," *Washington Post*, February 18, 2006.

462 *Only once in history:* That was 1998, when backlash to impeachment gave Democrats a five-seat gain in the House. "Democrats Enjoy a Big Night After a Hard-to-Read Election," CNN, November 3, 1998, http://www.cnn.com/ALLPOLITICS/stories/1998/11/03/election/overview/overview/.

462 *"fair" or "poor":* http://www.gallup.com/poll/1633/Iraq.aspx; http://www.gallup.com/poll/1609/Consumer-Views-Economy.aspx#2.

463 *after being accused:* "Crooked Congressman Going to Prison," CNN, March 3, 2006, http://www.cnn.com/2006/LAW/03/03/cunningham.sentenced/.

463 *resigned in November 2005:* "Congressman Resigns After Bribery Pleas," CNN, November 28, 2005.

463 *$170,000 in gifts and travel:* Susan Schmidt and James V. Grimaldi, "Ney Sentenced to 30 Months in Prison for Abramoff Deals," *Washington Post*, January 20, 2007.

463 *sentenced to thirty months:* Ibid.

463 *Congressman Richard Pombo:* Jonathan Weisman, "Ethics Issue May Not Rouse 11th District," *Washington Post*, June 4, 2006. Rep. Pombo lost to a little-known Democrat, Jerry McNerney, in the 2006 congressional elections, but was never charged with a crime.

463 *Even congressmen who survived:* For instance, President Bush flew to California in early October 2006 to campaign for Representative John Doolittle. Ina Jaffe, "Abramoff Ties Stick to California Rep. Doolittle," NPR News, October 5, 2006, http://www.npr.org/templates/story/story.php?storyId=6200978. Doolittle's wife, Julie, headed a fund-raising firm that was retained by Abramoff. Joel Seidman, "FBI Raids Abramoff-Linked Congressman's Home," NBC News, April 19, 2007, http://www.msnbc.msn.com/id/18183698/. Doolittle won reelection by a 49–46 percent margin in 2006, but announced his retirement from the House in early 2008. Samantha Young and Erica Werner, "California Rep. Doolittle Announces Retirement from Congress," *San Francisco Chronicle*, January 10, 2008. Ultimately, neither Doolittle nor his wife was ever charged in the Abramoff affair. Steve Wiegand, "Doolittle, Wife Named as Unindicted Co-conspirators in Corruption Case," *Sacramento Bee*, September 29, 2009.

463 *"knocking her around the house":* Brendan J. Lyons, "Congressman's Wife Called Police: Sweeney Campaign Says the Document Concerning a Domestic Incident Is False and Concocted," *Albany Times Union*, October 31, 2006.

463 *drunk at a fraternity party:* Sweeney attended a party on April 21, 2006, at the Alpha Delta Phi house at Union College in Schenectady, N.Y. Photos of the party surfaced a week later. Raymond Hernandez, "Party Photographs Put a Congressman on the Defensive," *New York Times*, April 29, 2006.

464 *suspect Russian bankers:* John R. Wilke, "Seat in Congress Helps Mr. Taylor Help His Business," *Wall Street Journal*, October 11, 2006.

464 *indicted for corruption:* "Rep. Rick Renzi Indicted on Federal Fraud Charges," Fox News, February 22, 2008. The Justice Department had added five new corruption charges against Rep. Renzi. (Susan Crabtree, "Feds Expand Case Against Renzi," *The Hill*, October 5, 2009.)

464 *He admitted the affair:* Richard Leiby, "The Reliable Source," *Washington Post*, May 4, 2005.

464 *A Democratic Hill staffer:* Naftali Bendavid, *The Thumpin': How Rahm Emanuel and the Democrats Learned to Be Ruthless and Ended the Republican Revolution* (New York: Doubleday Broadway, 2007), p. 174.

465 *Curt Weldon's daughter:* Michael Forsythe and Robert Schmidt, "Home of Representative Weldon's Daughter Raided by FBI Agents," Bloomberg, October 17, 2006. Karen Weldon was never charged in the case. Thomas Fitzgerald, "Ex-U.S. Attorney Meehan Announces Run for Congress," *Philadelphia Inquirer*, September 15, 2009.

465 *At least ten:* The historical average numbers are for all second midterms in the twentieth century (1906, 1918, 1938, 1950, 1958, 1986, and 1998). These numbers are compiled from the clerk of the House and the clerk of the Senate's Web pages, http://clerk.house.gov/member_info/election info/index.html and http://www.senate.gov/reference/common/generic/Elections.htm. The list of seats where wrongdoing had been alleged is AZ-05, CA-11, FL-16, KS-02, NC-11, NY-20, OH-18, PA-07, PA-10, and TX-22, which comes from a November 2006 internal document.

466 *Democrats had already effectively:* Shailagh Murray, "The About-Face of a Hawkish Democrat," *Washington Post*, November 25, 2005.

467 *13-point advantage:* Democrats held a 49–36 percent lead on the generic ballot. Fox News Poll, November 4–5, 2006, among likely voters.

468 *make our border more secure:* U.S. Department of Homeland Security News Release: Remarks by Homeland Security Secretary Michael Chertoff at the 2008 End of the Year Address, Georgetown University, Washington, D.C., December 18, 2008; Chad C. Haddal, Yule Kim, and Michael John Garcia, *Border Security: Barriers Along the U.S. International Border*, Congressional Research Service (CRS) Report for Congress, March 16, 2009; Fact Sheet: "United States Takes Steps to Improve Border Security, Immigration," January 28, 2008. Data on all-weather roads from U.S. Department of Homeland Security, White House Dashboard, November 2008.

468 *the price had risen:* Wayne Cornelius, "Controlling Unauthorized Immigration from Mexico: The Failure of 'Prevention through Deterrence' and the Need for Comprehensive Reform," http://www.immigrationpolicy.org/images/File/misc/CCISpresentation061008.pdf.

469 *tens of billions:* The average cost of a felony arrest through arraignment is roughly $2,500. If there are 12 million illegals, that's $30 billion right there. The average cost of incarceration of an illegal alien for their deportation hearing is $97 a day for thirty-six days. For 12 million illegal aliens, that's $52 billion. The cost of moving them out of the country is roughly $1,000. Add another $12 billion, for a total of $94 billion so far.

CHAPTER 31: THE SURGE

471 *"the surge":* More detail on the surge decision can be found in Fred Barnes's *Weekly Standard* articles: "The Roads Not Taken; How We Narrowly Avoided Defeat in Iraq," October 29, 2007; "They Can't Handle the Truth; The Democrats and the Surge," January 6, 2008; "The Surge Effect; The Gamble Is Paying Off for Bush and McCain," January 21, 2008; "How Bush Decided on the Surge; A Year Ago, We Were Losing in Iraq. Then the President Made the Most Momentous Decision of His Presidency," February 4, 2008; "Remember Those Benchmarks?; Unheralded Political Advances in Iraq," February 25, 2008.

472 *a democratic "tipping point":* Thomas Friedman, interview by Ted Koppel, *Nightline*, ABC News, February 22, 2005.

472 *"I was cynical":* Walid Jumblatt, quoted by David Ignatius, "Beirut's Berlin Wall," *Washington Post*, February 23, 2005.

473 *"a paper tiger":* Osama bin Laden, interview by John Miller, ABC News, May 1998, available at http://www.pbs.org/wgbh/pages/frontline/shows/binladen/who/interview.html.

473 *"democracy is coming":* Letter purportedly from Abu Musab al-Zarqawi to Osama bin Laden, intercepted February 2004, Coalition Provisional Authority, http://www.cpa-iraq.org/transcripts/20040212_zarqawi_full.html.

473 *"The key to change":* Ibid.

474 *attacks on Sunni neighborhoods:* Thomas E. Ricks, "Shrine Bombing as War's Turning Point De-

bated: Administration Says Event Increased Violence, but Many Iraq Experts Disagree," *Washington Post*, March 13, 2007.

474   *killing hundreds each week:* In the few days following the shrine bombing, 1,300 people were killed. Patrick Cockburn, "Bombing of Samarra Shrine Sparks Fears of Reprisals," *Independent*, June 14, 2007.

474   *killed when F-16 jets pounded:* Ellen Knickmeyer and Jonathan Finer, "Insurgent Leader Al-Zarqawi Killed in Iraq," *Washington Post*, June 8, 2006.

474   *violence in Baghdad had increased:* James A. Baker, III, and Lee H. Hamilton, *The Iraq Study Group Report: They Way Forward—A New Approach* (New York: Vintage, 2006), p. 11.

475   *turning against the war:* Guenter Lewy, *America in Vietnam* (New York: Oxford University Press, 1978), pp. 133–139.

475   *Murtha, a defense hawk:* Charles Babington, "Hawkish Democrat Joins Call For Pullout," *Washington Post*, November 18, 2005.

477   *Dr. Peter Feaver:* Peter Feaver provides an inside view of the Iraq Strategy Review in his "Anatomy of the Surge," *Commentary*, April 2008.

479   *Chartered by Congress:* Baker and Hamilton, *The Iraq Study Group Report*.

479   *"The primary mission":* Ibid., p. 73.

480   *little credibility left:* Tim Grieve, "Unhappy Campers," Salon.com, January 10, 2007.

480   *only 11 percent supported:* CNN Poll, December 15–17, 2006.

480   *"an immense new mistake":* Jim Rutenberg, "Democrats Rush to Frame Political Debate Over Troops," *New York Times*, January 10, 2007.

480   *"not persuaded that 20,000":* Peter Wehner, "Liberals and the Surge: Wrong from the Beginning," *Commentary*, November 2008. A week later, Obama argued Bush's change in strategy would "not prove to be one that changes the dynamics significantly" (Peter Wehner, "Obama, Democrats, and the Surge," *Weekly Standard*, July 28, 2008). This was a change from Obama's position during his 2004 Senate campaign, when he backed a surge, saying he "would be willing to send more soldiers to Iraq if it is part of a strategy that the President and military leaders believe will stabilize the country and eventually allow America to withdraw" (Peter Wehner, "Obama's War," *Commentary*, April 2008).

480   *"a tragic mistake":* Wehner, "Liberals and the Surge."

480   *"won't end the violence":* Wehner, "Obama, Democrats, and the Surge."

480   *"[I don't believe]":* Dana Milbank, "For GOP Senators, Bush's Next Step in Iraq Means a Delicate Dance," *Washington Post*, January 10, 2007.

480   *Kansas senator Sam Brownback:* Michael Abramowitz and Robin Wright, "Bush to Add 21,500 Troops in an Effort to Stabilize Iraq," *Washington Post*, January 11, 2007.

480   *"We've got to say":* Peter Baker and Robin Wright, "Pelosi, Reid to Urge Bush to Begin Iraq Pullout; President Considering Three 'Surge' Options," *Washington Post*, January 6, 2007.

481   *"Congress is entitled":* David E. Sanger and Jeff Zeleny, "Bush Facing a Deep Divide with Democrats Over Talk of Increasing Troops in Iraq," *New York Times*, January 6, 2007.

481   *had "the authority as commander":* Michael A. Fletcher, "Bush: 'We're Going Forward'; More Troops Called the Only Iraq Option," *Washington Post*, January 15, 2007.

481   *"lost, and this surge":* Jed Babbin, "Harry Reid, Loser," *Human Events*, April 20, 2007.

482   *"It would be wiser":* David E. Sanger and David S. Cloud, "White House Said to Debate '08 Cut in Troops by 50%," *New York Times*, May 26, 2007; David E. Sanger and Thom Shanker, "General's Report on Iraq Progress Has Competition," *New York Times*, June 24, 2007; David E. Sanger, "In White House, Debate Is Rising on Iraq Pullback," *New York Times*, July 9, 2007; David E. Sanger and Thom Shanker, "Fending Off a Deadline: Bush Seeks Time on Iraq," *New York Times*, July 13, 2007; David Ignatius, "After the Surge; the Administration Floats Ideas for a New Approach in Iraq," *Washington Post*, May 22, 2007; David Ignatius, "Damage Control in the Mideast," *Washington Post*, July 22, 2007.

482   *"a military man constantly":* "General Petraeus or General Betray Us," political action committee ad, released by MoveOn.org, September 10, 2007, http://pol.moveon.org/petraeus.html.

482   *"successful in what"*: "Our Ad on General Petraeus," Move.On.org, http://pol.moveon.org/petraeus_ad.html.

482   *discounted rate of $65,000:* Howard Kurtz, "New York Times Says It Violated Policies Over MoveOn Ad," *Washington Post*, September 24, 2007.

482   *"Nobel Prize for creative statistics":* Wehner, "Liberals and the Surge."

483   *"A secure, stable, democratic Iraq":* "Statement of Ambassador Ryan C. Crocker, United States Ambassador to the Republic of Iraq, Before a Joint Hearing of the Committee on Foreign Affairs and the Committee on Armed Services," September 10, 2007.

483   *"result in the further release":* General David Petraeus, "Report to Congress on the Situation in Iraq," September 10–11, 2007.

483   *jihadists were staying away:* Michael Howard, interview with General David Petraeus, "U.S. Says the Flow of Jihadists into Iraq Has Been Staunched: Country's Neighbours Have Taken Action, Petraeus Says; Insurgent Attacks at 2005 Levels Since October," *Guardian*, December 7, 2007.

483   *baffled the* Times: Janet Elder, "Same Old Question, Different Answer. Hmmm.," *New York Times*, July 29, 2007.

484   *"There haven't been gains":* Representative Nancy Pelosi, interview by Wolf Blitzer, *Late Edition with Wolf Blitzer*, CNN, February 10, 2008.

CHAPTER 32: YES, IT WAS FUN

487   *"deeply spiritual ceremony":* James Moore and Wayne Slater, *The Architect: Karl Rove and the Dream of Absolute Power* (New York: Three Rivers, 2006), pp. 95–96.

487   *a West Wing exorcism:* "Rove's Exorcists 'Cleansed' Hillary's Office," Wonkette.com, September 6, 2006, http://wonkette.com/198828/roves-exorcists-cleansed-hillarys-office; Glenn Thrush, "Rove Denies 'Demon' Rumors," *Newsday*, September 7, 2006.

487   *A Newsday reporter:* Glenn Thrush, "Blessed Debate Over Rove Rite," *Newsday*, September 8, 2006. The *Dallas Morning News* and Associated Press also picked up the story on September 7.

487   *"three high-ranking Catholic priests":* "The Hillorist," in the "Up Front" section, *American Prospect*, September 17, 2006.

488   *White House Correspondents' Dinner:* A few days after the 2007 WHCA Dinner, *New York Times* spokeswoman Catherine Mathis confirmed that the newspaper had decided to no longer participate in the event, but gave no reason for the decision.

488   *more global climate science:* John J. Fialka, "Warm Words for Climate Report," Washington Wire (a *Wall Street Journal* blog), February 2, 2007, http://blogs.wsj.com/washwire/2007/02/02/warm-words-for-climate-report/.

488   *projection of seventeen inches:* The Intergovernmental Panel on Climate Change Fourth Assessment Report, *Climate Change 2007*; Working Group I Report: "The Physical Science Basis." http://www.ipcc.ch/ipccreports/ar4-wg1.htm.

488   *stadium sixty inches above:* You can find the altitude of various buildings by typing their addresses into a U.S. Geological Survey viewer and performing an elevation query, here: http://nmviewogc.cr.usgs.gov/viewer.htm.

489   *I countered that China:* Brad Knickerbocker, "China Now World's Biggest Greenhouse Gas Emitter," *Christian Science Monitor*, June 28, 2007.

489   *David and Crow blogged:* http://www.huffingtonpost.com/laurie-david-and-sheryl-crow/karl-rove-gets-thrown-und_b_46501.html.

489   *"I honestly thought":* John Heilprin, "Rove Debates Warming With Crow, David," Associated Press, April 22, 2007.

489   *environmental violations:* Sam Bungey, "Shattered Peace on North Road: Noted Environmental Activist Cited for Chilmark Wetlands Violations; Neighborhood Is Caught in Turmoil," *Vineyard Gazette*, June 12, 2009, http://www.mvgazette.com/article.php?21380.

490   *"debut a rap song":* You can view my rap debut at http://www.youtube.com/watch?v=pWRSgjDEQy0.

CHAPTER 33: LEAVING THE WHITE HOUSE

494 *70 percent of the American people:* Gallup Poll, August 13–16, 2007. Sample of 1,019 adults nationwide; margin of error: plus or minus three percent.

496 *"I'm Charles Gandy":* I actually didn't run the campaign against Gandy, and I suspect his defeat had more to do with his being a very liberal legislator in an increasingly conservative area, but I guess when you lose it's always better to blame it on the most convenient bogeyman you can find—and for Gandy, I was it. In 2000, Gandy ran for the Democratic nomination for the U.S. Senate, hoping to oppose Senator Kay Bailey Hutchison in the general election. He lost, however, to a Democratic candidate named Gene Kelly who could charitably be characterized as a nut when it came to his perennial but quixotic political campaigns.

496 *the moment I needed:* Mary Ann Akers, "Best Regards, From Karl Rove, Budding Author," Akers's WashingtonPost.com blog, The Sleuth, July 24, 2007, http://voices.washingtonpost.com/sleuth/2007/07/best_regards_from_karl_rove_bu_1.html.

CHAPTER 34: ROVE: THE MYTH

504 *subject of a criminal investigation:* "U.S. Attorney Steps Aside in Siegelman Probe; Canary Says No Conflict Found; Move Voluntary," *Birmingham News*, May 17, 2002; "Racketeer or Political Dear? Fed Indictment Must Distinguish Bribes from Contributions," *Birmingham Weekly*, November 3–10, 2005.

504 *sentenced to seven years:* "Siegelman Gets 7-plus Years," *Mobile Register*, June 29, 2007; Editorial, "Freed Alabama Ex-Governor Sees Politics in His Case," *New York Times*, March 29, 2008. A good summary of what Siegelman allegedly did can be found at http://www.foxnews.com/story/0.2933.287275.00.html. The 11th Circuit Court of Appeals went into more detail on Siegelman's actions in its opinion on the former governor's appeal of his conviction. It can be found at http://www.ca11.uscourts.gov/opinions/ops/200713163.pdf.

505 *"Karl has spoken":* Adam Zagorin, "Rove Named in Alabama Controversy," *Time*, June 1, 2007.

505 *denied pubicly that any such call:* 60 *Minutes* transcript, CBS News, February 24, 2008.

505 *"There is reason to believe":* Editorial, "Questions About a Governor's Fall," *New York Times*, June 30, 2007.

505 *"growing evidence":* Editorial, "Selective Prosecution," *New York Times*, August 6, 2007.

505 *newspaper called for congressional hearings:* Editorial, "The Strange Case of an Imprisoned Alabama Governor," *New York Times*, September 10, 2007.

505 *"Karl Rove had no role whatsoever":* "Statement of Louis V. Franklin, Sr., Acting U.S. Attorney in the Siegelman/Scrushy Prosecution," U.S. Department of Justice, June 6, 2007, http://www.usdoj.gov/usao/alm/Press/scrushy_statement.html; "Affidavit Doesn't Prove Politics Sparked Probe of Siegelman, Davis Says," *Birmingham News*, June 21, 2007.

506 *Simpson repeated her story:* Interview of Dana Jill Simpson, U.S. House of Representatives, Committee on the Judiciary, Washington, D.C., September 14, 2007, pp. 52–56.

506 *"compromising sexual position":* 60 *Minutes* transcript, CBS, February 24, 2008.

506 *I followed up with a letter:* The text of my letter can be found at www.rove.com/notes/132.

507 *she said nothing:* Interview of Dana Jill Simpson, U.S. House of Representatives, Committee on the Judiciary, Washington, D.C., September 14, 2007.

507 *I wrote him a letter similar:* My April 13, 2008, letter to Abrams can be found at http://corner.nationalreview.com/post/?q=YmY4YTBmMDg3NDljYWY0NTViNmMxNzgwOGUzZTk1NGI. Full text of Abrams's April 21, 2008, letter to me can be found at http://www.msnbc.msn.com/id/24244611.

508 *"did not directly deny":* Editorial, "Karl Rove Talks, but Doesn't Answer," *New York Times*, June 2, 2008.

508 *target of another bunch:* Dan Eggen, "Justice Official 'Horrified' Phone Call Was Seen as Threat," *Washington Post*, March 12, 2007.

509 *Bush White House was not like: An Investigation of the Immigration and Naturalization Service's Citi-*

zenship USA Initiative, Department of Justice/Office of the Inspector General Report, Section VII: "White House/NPR Involvement in the CUSA Program," July 2000, 4–5; Daniel Klaidman, "Independent's Day," *Newsweek*, July 20, 2009.

510   *complained about it in a letter:* Senator Dianne Feinstein wrote a letter to Attorney General Gonzales on June 15, 2006, asking whether Carol Lam was prosecuting enough illegal immigrants. Full text of letter can be read here: http://www.huffingtonpost.com/chris-weigant/more-leahy-and-less-feins_b_43962.html.

510   *had already subpoenaed:* William Branigin, "House Panel Sues to Force Bush Aides to Table," *Washington Post*, March 11, 2008.

510   *"We're closing in":* "Conyers: 'We're closing in on Rove,'" posted by Ryan Grim, The Crypt *(Politico* blog), May 15, 2008.

510   *willing to provide the information:* The exchange of letters between my lawyer, Bob Luskin, and Representative Conyers can be found at http://judiciary.house.gov/newscenter.aspx?A=979.

512   *raised and spent $550 million:* Karl Rove, "McCain Couldn't Compete with Obama's Money," *Wall Street Journal*, December 4, 2008. While President Obama dramatically beat the McCain campaign in fund-raising, it is interesting to note that President Bush was able to defeat Senator John Kerry in 2004 despite being outspent by $121 million. Karl Rove, "Obama Hasn't Closed the Sale," *Wall Street Journal*, October 16, 2008.

513   *poll found 42 percent:* ABC/*Washington Post* Poll, October 22, 2008, http://www.washingtonpost.com/wp-srv/politics/documents/postpoll_102308.html.

513   *He said ObamaCare:* Congressional Budget Office Letter to the Honorable Charles Rangel, July 17, 2009, and Congressional Budget Office Letter to the Honorable Steny Hoyer, July 25, 2009.

513   *White House's own fact sheets:* Paying for Health Care Reform: $313 Billion in Additional Savings to Create a Deficit Neutral Plan," http://www.whitehouse.gov/MedicareFactSheetFinal/.

514   The Audacity of Hope: Barack Obama, *The Audacity of Hope* (New York: Crown, 2006), p. 33.

515   *"hungry for a new kind of politics":* Barack Obama, "Our Moment Is Now," Remarks, Des Moines, Iowa, December 27, 2007.

515   *"eerily reminiscent":* Barack Obama, *The Audacity of Hope*, pp. 33–34.

516   *"If they bring a knife":* "Obama: 'We Bring a Gun,'" The Caucus (*New York Times* politics blog), June 14, 2008, http://thecaucus.blogs.nytimes.com/2008/06/14/obama-we-bring-a-gun/.

516   *"Don't think we're not":* "At House Democratic Meeting, Obama Rallies His Allies," 44: The Obama Presidency (a *Washington Post* blog), posted by Paul Kane, March 30, 2009, http://voices.washingtonpost.com/44/2009/03/30/at_house_democratic_meeting_ob.html.

ACKNOWLEDGMENTS

Many thanks to my agent, Robert B. Barnett. He and his associate at Williams & Connolly, Michael O'Connor, guided me through the publishing world and convinced skeptical minds to be open to this book and author.

In a project such as this, there is always an indispensable person. In this instance, she is my editor, Priscilla Painton. She flew in from Paris to meet me over chicken potpies at my dining room table and off we went. Her former *Time* colleagues told me she would be fun, tough, brilliant, and decisive. I was not disappointed and constantly surprised.

Pete Wehner is not only a close friend and trusted former colleague, but also helped craft every chapter and episode. I have come to rely on his judgment, and my respect for his intellect, already enormous, has only grown through this project.

Then there's Brendan Miniter, who amazed Priscilla, Pete, and me with his skillful line edits. He is both gifted and self-effacing: humility and real talent are rarely seen together.

I am grateful for the monumental efforts of my researcher, Erin Montgomery. Through the recommendation of our mutual friend Fred Barnes, she was first on this project and demonstrated great skill throughout. She organized a mountain of paper, almost wore out the Internet in research and fact checking, and remembers all and recalls all.

Many thanks for the research assistance of Michael Ellis, Kristin Davison, Andrew Rove, Kevin Patrick Hickson, Peter Rough, Caleb Weatherl, and Elizabeth Lavin. They all spent hours in dusty archives or collecting and organizing material on the Web. They were often acting under Sheena Tahilramani's expert guidance. As my chief of staff, Sheena has organized my life of punditry, writing, and speaking, ably assisted by Kristin Davison.

I benefited enormously from the invaluable comments of those who read the entire book in one of its many variations and commented on the manuscript: Dana Perino, Ed Gillespie, Chris Michel, Mary Matalin, Darby Rove, and Michael Szczerban.

Josh Bolten, John Bridgeland, President George W. Bush, Steve Hadley, Israel Hernandez, Taylor Hughes, Jay Lefkowitz, Yuval Levin, I. Lewis "Scooter" Libby, Bob Luskin, Ken Mehlman, Susan Ralston, Dr. Daron Shaw, Secretary Margaret Spellings, Fran Townsend, and Dr. Paul Wolfowitz not only made themselves available for interviews but also read important parts of the manuscript. I am grateful for all their insights.

Chuck Blahous, James Connaughton, Dr. Peter Feaver, Keith Hennessey, Barry Jackson, Karen Johnson, Holly Kuzmich, Steve McMillin, Marc Thiessen, and Jim Towey devoured and improved major swatches of the manuscript.

Others who made themselves available for interviews or provided material include Joe Allbaugh, Secretary James A. Baker III, Mickey Barnett, Dan Bartlett, Becky Beach, Steve Bell, Bob Bennett, Judge Bascom Bentley, Representative Elton Bomer, President George H. W. Bush, Reverend Kirbyjon Caldwell, Secretary Andy Card, Senator Saxby Chambliss, Kathryn Biber Chen, Vice President Dick Cheney, Liz Cheney, Secretary Michael Chertoff, Maria Cino, Jamie Clements, Delegate Barbara Comstock, Senator John Cornyn, Father John C. Cregan, Mark Dangerfield, Chuck DeFeo, Amanda Downes, Eric Draper, Randy Enwright, Pete Ernaut, Tucker Eskew, Secretary Don Evans, Sarina de Feijter, Justine Fox-Young, James B. Francis, Jr., Tony Fratto, Brad Freeman, Michael Gerson, Ben Ginsberg, Tim Goeglein, Barbara Jo Goergen, Attorney General Alberto Gonzales, Blake Gottesman, Maggie Grant, Adrian Gray, Reverend and Mrs. Charles C. Griffin, Tim Griffin, Rayne Guilford, Mark Gustavson, Joe Hagin, Chris Henick, General Russel Honoré, Al Hubbard, Karen Hughes, Cathy and Walter Isaacson, Laura Jenkins, Cliff Johnson, Tom Josefiak, Joel Kaplan, Jeremy Katz, Karen Keller, Rusty Kelly, Dr. Ed Lazear, Dr. Larry Lindsey, Colleen Litkenhaus, Joel Maiola, Eddie Marinzel, Jack Martin, Mark McKinnon, T. Vance McMahan, Dave McNeely, Manning McPhillips, Harriet Miers, Dan

Mintz, Sig Muessig, Caroline Nugent, Ashley O'Connor, Jack Oliver, Todd Olsen, Justice Priscilla Owen, Pat Oxford, Gerald Parsky, Tom Perdue, Bill Phillips, Don Powell, Jack Roberts, Kelley McCullough Robertson, Patrick Rogers, Alma Rove, Eric Rove, Olaf Rove, Reba Rove, Ludmilla Savelieff, Matt Schlapp, Justice Harold See, Secretary George Shultz, Senator David Sibley, Matt Smith, Stuart Stevens, Beth Ramp Sturgeon, Marc Sumerlin, Chris Tanner, Sara Taylor, Heath Thompson, Warren Tompkins, Jan van Lohuizen, Peter Wallison, Logan Walters, and Jared Weinstein.

All the forenamed are responsible for correcting and forestalling mistakes. I am accountable for the errors that remain, and I apologize for anyone whose name is missing from this list.

I am grateful for the friendship of Mary Matalin, the faith of Threshold publisher Louise Burke, and the quiet professionalism of Anthony Ziccardi, Jean Anne Rose, and Jen Robinson, as well as all the unnamed editors, lawyers, and staff of Simon & Schuster. Thanks also to Don Walker and Kim Nisbet of the Harry Walker Agency, my speaking agents.

There are good friends who helped not just by supplying information, reading drafts, and making suggestions, but also by their encouragement and heartfelt support—especially Frank Lavin, Katharine Armstrong and Ben Love, H. David Herndon, C. Patrick Oles, Jr., and Ben Stein.

Finally, Darby and Andrew Rove not only lived through the days described here, but also suffered through the research and writing of this book. For that, I am eternally grateful.

INDEX